ELEVENTH EDITION

Elements of
ARGUMENT

A Text and Reader

Annette T. Rottenberg

Donna Haisty Winchell

Clemson University

Bedford/St. Martin's

Boston ▪ New York

For Bedford/St. Martin's

Publisher for Composition: Leasa Burton
Executive Editor: John E. Sullivan III
Developmental Editor: Michelle McSweeney
Senior Production Editor: Gregory Erb
Senior Production Supervisor: Dennis Conroy
Marketing Manager: Emily Rowin
Editorial Assistant: Rachel Childs
Copyeditor: Alice Vigliani
Indexer: Steve Csipke
Photo Researcher: Christine End/Creative Compliance
Senior Art Director: Anna Palchik
Text Design: Lisa Buckley
Cover Design: Donna Lee Dennison
Cover Photo: © Oliver Eltinger/Corbis
Composition: Achorn International, Inc.
Printing and Binding: RR Donnelley and Sons

For information, write: Bedford/St. Martin's, 75 Arlington Street, Boston, MA 02116
  (617-399-4000)

ISBN   978-1-4576-6236-2

Acknowledgments

Acknowledgments and copyrights for text appear at the back of the book on pages 615–21, which constitute an extension of the copyright page. It is a violation of the law to reproduce these selections by any means whatsoever without the written permission of the copyright holder.

Acknowledgments and copyrights for images appear on the same page as the text and art selections they cover; these acknowledgments and copyrights constitute an extension of the copyright page. It is a violation of the law to reproduce these selections by any means whatsoever without the written permission of the copyright holder.

Preface

Purpose

Where do our students — some of our youngest voters and our future leaders — get their take on current events? Where do they get their news? Probably not from sitting down and watching network broadcasts or listening to the radio like their parents and grandparents did. Probably not from reading a newspaper regularly either. More likely they get it from Facebook or Twitter, which means they get it in bits and pieces, and on the run. Where do they read or hear arguments? Again, probably in short digital bursts. Their idea of debate may come from the most recent presidential debates. More likely, it comes from comments made online in response to YouTube videos or blog postings. They may get today's political news from Jon Stewart or Glenn Beck, from the cover of *Time*, from cnn.com, or from skits on *Saturday Night Live*. Their most consistent source of headlines may be cnn.com, fox.com, or Yahoo! News.

In order to get our students really thinking and writing about argument, we have to get them to slow down and practice the art of critical reading — and listening. We have to get them to analyze sustained argumentative discourse, and we have to give them a vocabulary to be able to talk about it. The vocabulary we use in this text incorporates Aristotle's ancient rhetoric, Carl Rogers's notion of common ground, and Stephen Toulmin's three principal elements of argument: claim, support, and warrant. In addition, we present the concepts of definition, language, and logic as critical tools for understanding and responding to arguments.

We also have to get our students to write sustained argumentative discourse. They have to learn to apply their knowledge of claim, support, and warrant. They have to understand that successful arguments require a blend of *logos*, *pathos*, and *ethos*. They have to appreciate the significance of audience as a practical matter. In the rhetorical or audience-centered approach to argument, to which we subscribe in this text, success is defined as acceptance of the claim by an audience. Arguers in the real world recognize intuitively that their primary goal is not to demonstrate the purity of their logic, but to win the adherence of their audiences.

To do so, students must read critically and reflect on what others have to say. The Internet has redefined what research means to our students. A large part of the challenge is not to find sources but to eliminate the thousands of questionable ones. Faced with the temptation to cut and paste instead of read and understand, students need more help than ever with accurate and fair use of sources. We provide that help in the context of an increasingly digital world.

Organization

Part One of *Elements of Argument* begins with an introduction to Aristotelian, Rogerian, and Toulmin approaches to argumentation. Next it addresses the critical reading of written as well as visual and multimodal arguments, and it then provides instruction on writing responses to arguments. Part One is rich in selections that both illustrate various arguments and offer practice for student analysis.

Part Two devotes one chapter apiece to the chief elements of argument — claim, support, and warrant. Straightforward explanations simplify these concepts for students, and examples are drawn from everyday print and online sources — essays, articles, graphics, reviews, editorials, and advertisements — by both student and professional writers.

Part Three details important matters of reading and writing effective argument: definition, language, and logic. Chapter 8 teaches students the importance of defining key terms as well as the nature of the extended definition essay. Chapter 9 deals with the power of word choice, and Chapter 10 covers the various logical fallacies as well as how to identify and avoid logical errors in arguments.

The first three parts of the book — comprising Chapters 1 through 10 — include four unique feature boxes to enhance and reinforce the text. "Writer's Guide" boxes give practical advice on how to write effective arguments and response essays; "Strategies" boxes provide more in-depth information on important skills such as prereading and annotating texts. New "Essentials" boxes summarize and reinforce basic argument concepts, and the new "Research Skills" boxes explain a variety of academic research tasks. (These two new boxes are explained further under "New to This Edition.")

Part Four takes up the process of researching, writing, and documenting arguments. Chapter 11 focuses on planning and research, including how to narrow a topic as well as how to find and evaluate sources. Chapter 12 addresses drafting and revising written arguments as well as oral presentations. Chapter 13 covers documentation and provides two sample research papers, one employing the Modern Language Association (MLA) documentation system and the other employing the American Psychological Association (APA) documentation style.

Part Five, "Debating the Issues," includes a pair of readings related to each of five current debatable topics: derogatory use of the word *retard*, business ethics, human stem cell research, princess culture, and paying college athletes. Each pair illustrates contrasting opinions on the same issue and is followed up with discussion questions and writing suggestions.

Part Six, "Multiple Viewpoints," expands the concept of debate to present multiple arguers in action. Each of the six chapters in this part includes five to six text readings plus a visual argument on a single controversial issue, presenting that issue from a range of perspectives. The topics are ones now in the news and on engaged citizens' minds: social networking, keeping schools safe from violence, ethical costs of food, the risks of competitive sports, freedom of speech, and medical ethics.

Part Seven, "Classic Arguments," includes such class-tested arguments as Jonathan Swift's "A Modest Proposal," Henry David Thoreau's "Civil Disobedience," and Sojourner Truth's "Ain't I a Woman?"

New to This Edition

As is the case with each edition of *Elements of Argument*, we have updated readings throughout to keep information current and subjects interesting. In this eleventh edition, over three-quarters of the readings are new. In the newly configured Debating the Issues section (now Part Five), new issues include the pros and cons of princess culture and of paying college athletes. In Part Six, two of the Multiple Viewpoints topics are also new; they explore the matter of keeping schools safe from violence and the price of competitive sports in our society. In the Classic Arguments section, we have added four essays not included in the previous edition: the Declaration of Independence, an excerpt from Rachel Carson's *Silent Spring*, Thurgood Marshall's "Reflections on the Bicentennial of the United States Constitution," and Sojourner Truth's "Ain't I a Woman?"

This eleventh edition of *Elements of Argument* has been revised to work more effectively for students working in a variety of environments. A new Chapter 3, "Examining Multimodal Arguments," shows students how to apply concepts of rhetoric and logic to spoken, visual, online, and other multimedia arguments. Throughout the text, an abundance of new visual arguments — including ads, photographs, screen shots, and graphics — provide visual examples and opportunities for analysis. To help extend what students read and learn in *Elements of Argument* to the kinds of media they are most familiar with and excited by, we have integrated compelling multimodal selections throughout: Dedicated e-readings in LaunchPad Solo (packaged for free) at **macmillanhighered.com /rottenberg** extend the book beyond the printed page, offering instruction and practice on multimedia arguments such as speeches, blogs, slide shows, and videos. For a complete list of e-readings, online tutorials, and exercises, see the last page or the table of contents. Instructors can log in for free; they can also use the free LaunchPad Solo tools to upload a syllabus, readings, and assignments to share with the class. Students can purchase access at **macmillanhighered.com /rottenberg**.

To further enhance the multimodal aspect of the text, and for instructors who want to apply current events to their argument course, see our new blog, "Argument in the Headlines." In our regularly updated posts, we use argument concepts to frame issues in the news, helping students relate the text and the course to their everyday lives. Students are encouraged to visit the blog at the end of each chapter. You can find the blog at **blogs.bedfordstmartins.com /bits**.

Expanded coverage of traditional rhetorical issues such as audience and purpose spans all chapters, helping students grasp the importance of clear communication in a variety of situations. And more student essays, with documented sources, serve as models for effective writing and proper formatting.

Our fresh new page design, which highlights important information and improves navigation, is both inviting and functional. The new design also allows readings to be more clearly grouped and distinguished from the text, and it provides a better interaction of annotated sample selections with readings for practice and analysis. The wider trim size better accommodates marginal annotations and visuals, and showcases our new text boxes: "Essentials" and "Research Skills."

Essentials boxes — 23 total — briefly summarize and reinforce important argument concepts. Research Skills boxes enhance the first ten chapters of the book by teaching valuable research topics. A related practice exercise on each research skill is included at the end of each chapter.

Finally, the research chapters have been reorganized so that coverage of documenting in-text sources and works cited entries are now in the same chapter (13), accompanied by sample student papers that demonstrate MLA and APA formatting.

Also Available

A briefer edition, *The Structure of Argument*, Eighth Edition, is available for instructors who prefer a shorter text with fewer readings. It includes Chapters 1 through 18, excluding the Multiple Viewpoints and Classic Arguments. See **macmillanhighered.com/structure/catalog** for details.

Acknowledgments

This book has profited by the critiques and suggestions of instructors who responded to a questionnaire: Andrea Alden, Arizona State University; Marty Ambrose, Edison State College; Jacqueline Beamen, Camden County College; Charles Bevis, University of Massachusetts Lowell; Andrew Bourelle, University of New Mexico; Harry Costigan, Camden County College; Ruthellen Cunnally, Des Moines Area Community College; Sarah Setnes Dale, Des Moines Area Community College; Allison Dieppa, Florida Gulf Coast University; Cindy Drummond, Des Moines Area Community College; Gwyn Enright, San Diego City College; Hedda Fish, San Diego State University; Christine Gillette, Arizona State University; Bruce Glenn, Arizona State University; Catherine Hayter, Auburn University; Robert Hiatt, Florida Gulf Coast University; Carrolle Kamperman, Baylor University; JoAnn Lopez, Chaffey College; Elizabeth McNeil, Arizona State University; Patrick Muana, Lone Star College–CyFair; Carolina Ruiz, Lone Star College–CyFair; Guy Shebat, Youngstown State University; Lupco Spasovski, Arizona State University; and Will Zhang, Des Moines Area Community College. We also thank those reviewers who chose to remain anonymous.

We are grateful to those at Bedford/St. Martin's who have helped in numerous ways large and small: Karen Henry, Leasa Burton, John Sullivan, Rachel Childs, Kalina Ingham, Martha Friedman, Sue Brown, Anna Palchik, Greg Erb, Karen Baart, and, most especially, Michelle McSweeney.

Get the Most out of Your Course
with *Elements of Argument*

Bedford/St. Martin's offers resources and format choices that help you and your students get even more out of your book and course. To learn more about or to order any of the following products, contact your Bedford/St. Martin's sales representative, e-mail sales support (sales_support@bfwpub.com), or visit the Web site at **macmillanhighered.com/elements/catalog**.

LaunchPad Solo for Elements of Argument: Where Students Learn

LaunchPad Solo for Elements of Argument provides engaging content and new ways to get the most out of your course. Get unique, book-specific materials in a fully customizable course space; then adapt, assign, and mix our resources with yours. *LaunchPad Solo for Elements of Argument* includes multimodal readings, such as video, audio, images, and Web texts; interactive exercises and tutorials for reading, writing, and research; and LearningCurve, adaptive, game-like practice that helps students focus on the topics where they need the most help.

Student access is **free** when packaged with *Elements of Argument*. Order ISBN 978-1-4576-9130-0 to ensure your students can take full advantage. Students who rent a book or buy a used book can purchase access to online materials at **macmillanhighered.com/rottenberg**.

Instructors receive access with an evaluation or desk copy. Visit **macmillanhighered.com/rottenberg** and register as an instructor. For technical support, visit **macmillanhighered.com/getsupport**.

Choose from Alternative Formats of *Elements of Argument*

Bedford/St. Martin's offers a range of affordable formats, allowing students to choose the one that works best for them. For details, visit **macmillanhighered.com/elements/formats**. A Bedford e-Book to Go, a portable, downloadable e-book, is available at about half the price of the print book. To order the Bedford e-Book to Go for *Elements of Argument*, use ISBN 978-1-4576-9134-8. For details about other popular e-book formats, visit **macmillanhighered.com/ebooks**.

Select Value Packages

Add value to your text by packaging one of the following resources with *Elements of Argument*. To learn more about package options for any of the following products, contact your Bedford/St. Martin's sales representative or visit **macmillanhighered.com/elements/catalog**.

LearningCurve for Readers and Writers, Bedford/St. Martin's adaptive quizzing program, quickly learns what students already know and helps them practice what they don't yet understand. Game-like quizzing motivates students to engage with their course, and reporting tools help teachers discern their students' needs. *LearningCurve for Readers and Writers* can be packaged with *Elements of Argument* at a significant discount. An activation code is required.

To order *LearningCurve* packaged with the print book, use ISBN 978-1-4576-9450-9. For details, visit **macmillanhighered.com/englishlearningcurve**.

i-series   This popular series presents multimedia tutorials in a flexible format — because there are things you can't do in a book.

- **ix visualizing composition 2.0** helps students put into practice key rhetorical and visual concepts. To order *ix visualizing composition* packaged with the print book, use ISBN 978-1-319-00987-8.
- **i-claim: visualizing argument** offers a new way to see argument — with six multimedia tutorials, an illustrated glossary, and a wide array of multimedia arguments. To order *i-claim: visualizing argument* packaged with the print book, use ISBN 978-1-319-00988-5.

Portfolio Keeping, **Third Edition, by Nedra Reynolds and Elizabeth Davis** provides all the information students need to use the portfolio method successfully in a writing course. *Portfolio Teaching*, a companion guide for instructors, provides the practical information instructors and writing program administrators need to use the portfolio method successfully in a writing course. To order *Portfolio Keeping* packaged with the print book, use ISBN 978-1-4576-9448-6.

Make Learning Fun with *ReWriting 3*

bedfordstmartins.com/rewriting
New open online resources with videos and interactive elements engage students in new ways of writing. You'll find tutorials about using common digital writing tools, an interactive peer review game, Extreme Paragraph Makeover, and more — all for free and for fun. Visit **bedfordstmartins.com/rewriting**.

Instructor Resources

macmillanhighered.com/elements/catalog
You have a lot to do in your course. Bedford/St. Martin's wants to make it easy for you to find the support you need — and to get it quickly.

The Instructor's Manual for *Elements of Argument* is available as a PDF that can be downloaded from the Bedford/St. Martin's online catalog at the URL above. In addition to chapter overviews and teaching tips, the instructor's manual includes strategies for teaching argumentation, sample syllabi, and classroom activities.

Teaching Central offers the entire list of Bedford/St. Martin's print and online professional resources in one place. You'll find landmark reference works, sourcebooks on pedagogical issues, award-winning collections, and practical advice for the classroom — all free for instructors.

Bits collects creative ideas for teaching a range of composition topics in an easily searchable blog format. A community of teachers — leading scholars, authors, and editors — discuss revision, research, grammar and style, technology, peer review, and much more. Take, use, adapt, and pass the ideas around. Then, come back to the site to comment or share your own suggestion.

Brief Contents

Contents

2 Examining Written Arguments   34

3   Examining Multimodal Arguments 61

PART TWO Analyzing the Elements   147

6 Support: Backing Up a Claim 174

PART THREE   Using the Elements   237

9 Language: Using Words with Care   262

10 Logic: Understanding Reasoning 296

PART FOUR Researching and Crafting Arguments

11 Planning and Research

12 Drafting, Revising, and Presenting Arguments   372

13 Documenting Sources 400

PART FIVE   Debating the Issues   441

20   Violence on Campus   500

How Far Will We Go to Keep Our Schools Safe?

23 Freedom of Speech   546

Are Limitations on Our Rights Ever Justified?

PART SEVEN Classic Arguments   577

Understanding ARGUMENT

Approaches to Argument

Social networking sites have changed the nature of human discourse. They provide an easy means of staying in touch with people all over the world, a means of sharing the most trivial or the most exciting news. You can tell your friends you are headed to the gym, or you can tell them you are headed for a breakup. You can debate in real time about your politics or your sports teams. You can reestablish old relationships and establish new ones. You can share pictures of your family or your cat's most recent antics.

Through social networking, we have the means of presenting a public persona like never before. Some of you may not want to "friend" your parents because of the public persona you project online. You may not want prospective employers to see some of the comments or pictures you post on Facebook. Some college students use LinkedIn for their professional contacts and Facebook or another social networking site for their personal contacts.

The very language of social networking captures its public nature. If someone writes on a wall, the message is intentionally made public. Facebook users can control who their "friends" are, but in practice a "friend" is anyone to whom you are willing to give access to your page. These are the people who can see the writing on your wall, for good or ill.

HANGE CHANGE WE CAN BELIEVE IN

Hey Hil, Whatchu doing?

Running the world.

FIGURE 1.1 Texts from Hillary. Meme juxtaposes a *New York Times* image of President Barack Obama with the Reuters photograph of Clinton. The meme, posted on the *Texts from Hillary* Tumblr in 2012, satirically suggests that Obama and Clinton were texting. textsfromhillaryclinton .tumblr.com.

In writing online, as in other writing that you do, you have to be aware of your audience. You also have to be aware of the context, or rhetorical situation, of what you write and what you read. Consider the Internet meme, one of our newest forms of communication, and how it depends on context for its humor. An Internet meme is a bit of culture in the form of an idea, image, or behavior spread electronically through the culture with the speed of a virus. One of the most familiar memes in 2012 showed Secretary of State Hillary Clinton, in sunglasses, aboard a military plane en route to Libya, looking at her Blackberry while her entourage milled about in the background. The original photo was snapped by Reuters photographer Kevin Lamarque. Two friends, Stacy Lambe and Adam Smith, decided to have some fun with it, and thus Texts from Hillary was born.

Reading and Discussion Questions

1. Look at Figure 1.1. What is significant about where President Obama and Secretary of State Clinton are and what each is doing?

2. At the time, what was demanding a good deal of Obama's attention? (Signs in the background reading "Change we can believe in" are a clue.)

3. Why might meme authors Lambe and Smith have had Obama use such informal language?

4. Lambe and Smith posted 32 Hillary memes. When they froze their site, they had received 83,000 shares on Facebook, 8,400 Twitter followers, and over 45,000 Tumblr followers — and a post from Clinton herself. What does this response suggest about memes?

Two pictures and a few words can be good for a laugh. However, they can go further to make a serious statement. Even a simple visual can present an argument. For example, consider Figure 1.2. The sign, marketed to store owners, uses the traditional symbol for "no" to make the point that those wearing hoodies are not welcome.

Reading and Discussion Questions

1. Look at Figure 1.2. Why would store or restaurant owners put a sign like this in their window?

2. Why do you think some people have a problem with hoodies?

3. What specific event took place in February 2012 that made the hoodie symbolic? (Try searching the terms "hoodie" and "symbol of injustice.") How did something as simple as a hoodie factor into the events of that night?

Electronic media have added a whole new dimension to the study of rhetorical situations, but the theoretical study of rhetoric has been around since the time of the Greek philosopher Aristotle, who defined rhetoric as all available means of persuasion. The means of persuasion available have expanded from the oral argument of the law court of ancient Greece to include documents transmitted electronically, e-mail, Twitter, pictures, audio, video, and mixed media. This textbook will explore the forms that argument takes in the twenty-first century and, as the title suggests, its elements.

What Is Argument?

In this book, we use the term **argument** to represent forms of discourse that attempt to persuade readers or listeners to accept a position on a controversial issue. In argument, as in all forms of communication, a person (the writer or speaker) presents a text *about* something (the subject) and *for* someone (the audience). These three main components can be viewed as a triangle:

FIGURE 1.2 No Hoodies sign. SmartSign.

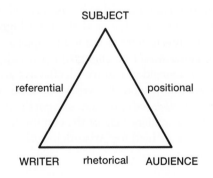

The legs that connect each of the components represent the three main relationships that we study in argument. The relationship between writer and subject is the **referential relationship**. That between writer and audience is the

rhetorical relationship.[5] The third leg of the triangle, that connecting subject and audience, considers the reader's notions about an issue, or his or her position on an issue. Thus we have labeled that leg of the triangle the **positional relationship**.

Dating back to 400 B.C.E., with the work of Aristotle and other Greek philosophers, the study of argument has evolved over the centuries as scholars continually examine what makes an argument most effective. Although they may use different words and emphasize different ideas, the approaches to argument given in this book — those of Aristotle as well as those of American psychologist Carl Rogers and British philosopher Stephen Toulmin — share important similarities and overlapping concepts, and the basic relationships in the communication triangle are evident in all three. However, even though the basic relationships among writer, audience, and subject remain in place, today's world presents both arguers and audiences with new challenges and new opportunities in creating and understanding argument texts.

Most of the argumentative writing presented in this book will deal with matters of public controversy, an area traditionally associated with the study of argument. As the word *public* suggests, these matters concern us as members of a community. In the arguments you will examine, human beings are engaged in explaining and defending their own actions and beliefs and opposing or compromising with those of others. They do this for at least two reasons:

1. to justify what they do and think, both to themselves and to their audiences
2. to solve problems and make decisions.

In the arguments you will write in this course, you will be doing the same.

Aristotelian Rhetoric

Aristotle wrote a treatise on argument that has influenced its study and practice for well over two thousand years. He used the term **logos** to refer to logical appeals and the term **pathos** to refer to emotional appeals. He believed that in an ideal world, logic alone would be enough to persuade. He acknowledged, however, that in the less-than-ideal real world, effective arguments depend not only on *logos* and *pathos* but also on the writer's or speaker's credibility, which he called **ethos**. Together, *ethos*, *logos*, and *pathos* were the primary focus of Aristotle's *Rhetoric*. The writer-audience leg of the communications triangle — the **rhetorical** component — is named for Aristotle's work.

---

[5] The terms *rhetorical* and *referential* come from James Moffett, *Teaching the Universe of Discourse* (Boston: Houghton Mifflin, 1968), p. 18. He illustrates the two with a grid crossing *rhetorical* and *referential*.

Ethos

Aristotle considered *ethos* to be the most important element in the arguer's ability to persuade the audience to accept a claim. He named intelligence, character, and goodwill as the attributes that produce credibility. Today we might describe these qualities somewhat differently, but the criteria for judging a writer's credibility remain essentially the same:

- Writers must convince their audience that they are knowledgeable and as well informed as possible about the subject.
- Writers must persuade their audience that they are not only truthful in the presentation of evidence but also morally upright and dependable.
- Writers must show that as arguers with good intentions, they have considered the interests and needs of others as well as their own.

A reputation for intelligence, character, and goodwill is not often earned overnight. And it can be lost more quickly than it is gained. Once writers or speakers have betrayed an audience's belief in their character or judgment, they may find it difficult to persuade that audience to accept subsequent claims, no matter how sound the data and reasoning are. Witness the fall from grace of those like Lance Armstrong and Oscar Pistorius, athletes who were formerly held in high esteem. Former president Bill Clinton is unusual in that he has regained much of the esteem he lost when he lied to the American people about his sex life.

Logos

Logos refers to the logic of an argument: the evidence or proof that supports a writer's claim. Aristotle taught that there are two types of proof to offer in support of an argument: the example and the enthymeme. In simplest terms, this meant induction and deduction. **Induction** is the process of generalizing from specifics (examples). Aristotle was less concerned with providing a large number of examples than with providing one particularly apt one. **Deduction** is the process of applying a generalization to a specific instance.

An **enthymeme** is a variation on the syllogism, the foundation of deductive reasoning. In a **syllogism**, a major premise and a minor premise lead to a logical conclusion.

Syllogism:

Major premise: All mammals are warm blooded.

Minor premise: Dolphins are mammals.

Conclusion: Dolphins are warm blooded.

Because premises in a syllogism are generally certain, the conclusions are rarely disputable. Aristotle defined an enthymeme as a syllogism in which the conclusion is probable, but not certain, because it deals with human affairs, not scientific fact.

Aristotle's Enthymeme:

Major premise: Mass murderers are narcissists.

Minor premise: Seung-Hui Cho was a mass murderer.

Conclusion: Seung-Hui Cho was a narcissist.

Today we use the term **enthymeme** to refer to a syllogism in which one of the premises is *implied* rather than stated outright.

Modern Enthymeme:

Major premise (implied): Bombs that detonate are lethal.

Minor premise: The bomb is going to detonate in one minute!

Conclusion: Let's get out of here!

Pathos

Pathos is appeal to the emotions. An audience can be moved by the logic of an argument alone, but more often emotional appeal combines with logic and ethical appeal to sway the audience. Appeals to the emotions and values of an audience are an appropriate form of persuasion unless (1) they are irrelevant to the argument or draw attention from the issues being argued or (2) they are used to conceal another purpose. The most popular emotional appeals are to pity and to fear. A picture of a starving child in Africa is a legitimate emotional appeal unless the picture leads donors to send money that goes largely to administrative costs and not to the children who need help. It is legitimate to arouse fear of the consequences of texting while driving if the descriptions are accurate. It is not legitimate to scare a family into buying an insurance policy they cannot afford by appealing to their fear of ruinous medical bills if the insurance would not provide the promised relief.

An argument becomes personal when it hits close to home. We can sometimes look objectively at society's problems until our own children are threat-

> ### RESEARCH SKILL ▸ Using Databases
>
> What is the first step you should take when you need to do some research?
>
> If your response is to go to *Google*, the answer is yes and no. In your daily life, if you need to look up some factual information, you can find it quickly on *Google* or another similar search engine. For most assignments for your classes, the answer is no.
>
> For one thing, remember that *Google* finds *any* reference to your search term and doesn't discriminate based on quality. Anyone can post on the Internet, so there is no control over accuracy. You will also be inundated with far more sources than you could ever look at.
>
> If you had checked *Google* for information about Aristotle when this book went to press, you would have found these numbers:
>
> "Aristotle" — 20,100,000 results
> "Aristotle" and "argument" — 5,390,000 results
> "Aristotle's argument" — 7,640,000 results
> "Aristotle" and "rhetoric" — 2,550,000 results
> "Aristotle's rhetoric" — 538,000 results
>
> *Wikipedia* will be near the top of the list for many subjects, but you shouldn't plan to use *Wikipedia* as a source for college work. It lacks the authority your professors will expect.
>
> Where, then, should you start? At the library, by prowling the shelves? Don't rule out electronic sources. Instead, find out what databases your school has access to and which of those databases are most appropriate for your research.
>
> For example, a good general database for academic subjects is Academic OneFile. There, a search for information about Aristotle yields these results:
>
> "Aristotle" — subject search 1,212 results
> keyword search 10,000 results
> "Aristotle" and "argument" — 4 results (subject)
> 310 results (keyword)
> "Aristotle" and "rhetoric" — 55 results (subject)
> 217 results (keyword)
>
> As you can see, by the end of this search you are reaching a manageable number of sources to explore. Even with 55 results, a quick look at the titles will eliminate some and let you know which ones are worth investigating.
>
> The numbers refer to articles in academic journals, generally the ones most widely accepted by college faculty.
>
> You will learn more about finding sources in Chapter 11.

ened or our own livelihood is in jeopardy. Then emotion enters the picture and often outweighs logic.

Some individuals and groups are quick to take advantage of human willingness to show compassion to others. Our emotional response to an event like the Boston Marathon bombings is to contribute to those who have suffered loss or injury. In our emotional vulnerability, though, unfortunately, we have to guard against those who are only out for personal gain and may collect gifts that will never reach the victims.

Ancient Rhetoric Today

How can we apply the teachings of Aristotle in the digital age? We can use the same vocabulary and study the same writer-subject-audience relationships, but we must also take into account the many cultural and technological changes that have occurred in the past two thousand years.

Writers — but more commonly speakers — in Aristotle's world of the fourth century B.C.E. were very limited in audience and in subject matter. As far as the rhetorical relationship is concerned, inventions like the printing press, and later the telegraph, gave writers access to a wider and wider range of audiences; more recent developments such as blogs, Facebook, and Twitter have increased exponentially the audiences a writer can reach. Moreover, today's audiences have more access to background information about authors, enabling readers to consider a writer's *ethos* for themselves. In addition, readers are more active participants in today's rhetorical relationships: They are encouraged to think critically about and respond to the arguments they encounter, and they can do so instantly and publicly in online forums.

The amount of information available at the click of a mouse has also exploded. That means that the relationship between writer and subject — the referential relationship — has also changed with the times. Technological advances have raised expectations about what an arguer should know about a subject. Living in the information age as we do, writers must be able to find, understand, evaluate, and manage information from a seemingly endless range of sources — and then synthesize that information into a coherent argument.

Technology has also greatly influenced the audience-subject relationship. In the limited world of ancient Greece, it was relatively easy to predict what an audience would know about a subject. There was more of a shared worldview than has existed in more recent times. In ancient Greece, rigid rules dictated the organization of a speech, and the examples were drawn from well-known narratives, true or fictional. Today it is much more difficult for a writer to place himself or herself in someone else's position and try to see a subject from that person's point of view. And, just as writers do, readers also have more access to information than ever before. Readers, therefore, can — and do — form opinions based on their own chosen sources, which may contradict the evidence presented by the writer.

ARGUMENT ESSENTIALS
Aristotelian Rhetoric

Three means of appealing to an audience:

- *Ethos* — appeal based on the writer's or speaker's credibility
- *Logos* — logical appeal
- *Pathos* — emotional appeal

Two types of proof:

- Inductive reasoning — drawing a conclusion based on examples
- Deductive reasoning — drawing a conclusion based on probability

READING ARGUMENT

Seeing Aristotelian Rhetoric

The essay that follows was written a few weeks after the death of twenty students and six adults in the school shooting at Sandy Hook Elementary School in Newtown, Connecticut. It has been annotated to show key features of Aristotelian rhetoric used by the author.

In Gun Control Debate, Logic Goes out the Window
RICHARD J. DAVIS

President Obama has decided to move ahead with a variety of gun control measures, and Sen. Dianne Feinstein has proposed a new assault weapons ban. While Washington debates new proposals on gun control, attention also needs to focus on obstacles to effective enforcement of existing gun laws, including the ban imposed by Congress on the Bureau of Alcohol, Tobacco, Firearms and Explosives creating a federal database of firearms transactions.

> Davis will focus on one obstacle to enforcement of existing gun laws, the ban on creating a federal database.

A discussion of the origin of that ban, which was initially enacted in response to a proposal made when I served as the assistant Treasury secretary overseeing the bureau, is useful to a better understanding of the dynamics of the debate over specific gun control proposals. Sadly, both then and now, logic often loses out.

> *Ethos:* Davis establishes his credibility.
>
> Thesis: Logic lost out in the past, and it is losing out now.

Early in 1978, the proposal we developed was relatively simple: Manufacturers, wholesalers, and retailers would file reports of sales of firearms with the bureau, but to avoid the argument that the bureau was impermissibly creating a national registry of gun owners, retailers would not be required to list the name of the retail purchaser.

The rationale for creating a centralized firearms transaction database was twofold. First, it would speed up the ability to trace guns found at crime scenes, since even with the less sophisticated technology then available, such traces would still be able to be done virtually instantaneously.

> *Logos:* Major premise: Speeding up the tracing of guns would be beneficial to society. Minor premise: A federal database would speed up the tracing of guns. Conclusion: A federal database would be beneficial.

5   Second, and even more significant, it would allow the bureau to analyze the flow of firearms to identify potential diversions to the illegal gun market. For example, if a hundred handguns a week were going to one dealer in a small town in Virginia, that would suggest the possibility that guns were being sold illegally by that dealer to individuals smuggling them to New York or other

> Major premise: Allowing the bureau to analyze the flow of firearms would be beneficial. Minor premise: A federal database would enable the

Richard J. Davis was the Assistant Secretary of the Treasury for Enforcement and Operations during the Carter administration (1977–1981). He is now a lawyer in New York. The article appeared on cnn.com on January 25, 2013.

bureau to analyze the flow of firearms. Conclusion: A federal database would be beneficial.

Ethos: He admits his naiveté and his mistake.

Faulty logic used by opposition (see page 313).

Either/or fallacy: Either we stop it all, or we do nothing (see page 312).

Response to faulty logic uses induction: Examples of laws that work, although not 100% of the time, lead to the conclusion that gun laws would also save lives and be worth enacting.

Deduction based on induction from examples.

states. By allowing this kind of analysis, the bureau could target investigative resources on dealers mostly likely to be violating the law.

Proceeding with what can only be described as youthful naiveté, the day the proposed regulations were published, I convened a briefing for interested parties, including the NRA and other anti-gun control groups. After all, none of these proposals would in any way alter the rules relating to gun ownership.

The hope was that understanding the limited nature of the proposal would mute their opposition. I was very wrong. We had to withdraw the proposals, and Congress punitively reduced the bureau's budget and ultimately banned it from creating such firearms transaction databases.

The opposition to the proposed regulations was intense, with opponents writing hundreds of thousands of often angry letters, both to Treasury and to members of Congress. Little of the opposition, however, focused on the actual proposals themselves.

One common thread to the opposition was the "slippery slope argument," which argued that the regulation would create a centralized list of all gun owners' names — which it would not have done — or would lead to the creation of such a list, which would then enable the government to seize everyone's weapons and put us on a path to dictatorship.

After all, it was argued, this is what the Nazis had done.   10

Another often-used argument was that what we were proposing would not stop all criminals from securing or using firearms, and therefore it was not something worth doing.

Arguments like these prevent an honest discussion of any proposal to address the problem of gun violence in America. The assumption that any regulation of firearms sets us on the path to confiscation of weapons is not only ludicrous on its face, it ignores all political reality. And, if the test for any proposal is whether it totally solves the problem being addressed, then no action would be taken addressing so many of society's important issues.

Why require the use of seat belts if wearing a seat belt does not always save a life in an accident? Why prohibit people from carrying guns onto planes if it doesn't eliminate all risk of hijacking? Why prohibit providing assistance to terrorists if it doesn't stop all terrorist acts? Why require tests for the issuance of driver's licenses if it doesn't stop all accidents?

We require these regulations because they address problems that need to be addressed and because if these regulations can save some lives, they are steps worth taking. So it should be with the gun debate.

No proposal, or set of proposals, will ever stop all gun crime. But the 1978   15
proposals could have stopped some illegal sales of guns by renegade dealers.

And things like forced waiting periods for gun purchases, requiring back-ground checks for firearms buyers at gun shows, and a ban on assault weapons would certainly save some lives.

Maybe it is thousands of lives over time; maybe it is hundreds. But isn't every life saved worth it? Would it not have been worth it if even some of the lives lost at Sandy Hook could have been saved because the shooter did not have an assault weapon?

Gun control is not the total answer to the problem of mass shootings, but it plainly needs to be part of any meaningful response. Let's hope that this time the debate on gun control will be a more sensible one.

Examples

Pathos: emotional appeal

Returns to his thesis idea that logic should not lose out

Practice: Aristotelian Rhetoric

Examine the print advertisement shown on page 14, and answer the questions below.

Reading and Discussion Questions

1. How did the creators of this ad use an unusual point of view to achieve humor?
2. Look carefully at all of the visual elements of the ad. How are they used in subtle and not-so-subtle ways to advance the ad's theme? What is that theme?
3. Look closely at all of the text and consider how it too advances theme.
4. Does the ad make use of *logos, ethos, pathos,* or a combination of these types of appeal? Explain.
5. How do similar ads that you have seen related to animals in need of a home use *pathos* differently?

A Person Is the Best Thing to Happen to a Shelter Pet
THE SHELTER PET PROJECT

The Humane Society of the United States, Maddie's Fund®, and the Ad Council.

Practice: Aristotelian Rhetoric

Applying the comments on the Richard J. Davis essay on pages 11–13 as a model, analyze the following blog post using Aristotle's terminology. Then answer the questions at the end of the essay.

I Am Adam Lanza's Mother

LIZA LONG

Three days before 20-year-old Adam Lanza killed his mother, then opened fire on a class-room full of Connecticut kindergartners, my 13-year-old son Michael (name changed) missed his bus because he was wearing the wrong color pants.

"I can wear these pants," he said, his tone increasingly belligerent, the black-hole pupils of his eyes swallowing the blue irises.

"They are navy blue," I told him. "Your school's dress code says black or khaki pants only."

"They told me I could wear these," he insisted. "You're a stupid bitch. I can wear whatever pants I want to. This is America. I have rights!"

5   "You can't wear whatever pants you want to," I said, my tone affable, reasonable. "And you definitely cannot call me a stupid bitch. You're grounded from electronics for the rest of the day. Now get in the car, and I will take you to school."

I live with a son who is mentally ill. I love my son. But he terrifies me.

A few weeks ago, Michael pulled a knife and threatened to kill me and then himself after I asked him to return his overdue library books. His 7- and 9-year-old siblings knew the safety plan — they ran to the car and locked the doors before I even asked them to. I managed to get the knife from Michael, then methodically col-lected all the sharp objects in the house into a single Tupperware container that now travels with me. Through it all, he continued to scream insults at me and threaten to kill or hurt me.

That conflict ended with three burly police officers and a paramedic wrestling my son onto a gurney for an expensive ambulance ride to the local emergency room. The mental hospital didn't have any beds that day, and Michael calmed down nicely in the ER, so they sent us home with a prescription for Zyprexa and a follow-up visit with a local pediatric psychiatrist.

We still don't know what's wrong with Michael. Autism spectrum, ADHD, Oppositional Defiant or Intermittent Explosive Disorder have all been tossed around at various meetings with probation officers and social workers and coun-selors and teachers and school administrators. He's been on a slew of antipsychotic and mood altering pharmaceuticals, a Russian novel of be-havioral plans. Nothing seems to work.

At the start of seventh grade, Michael was   10 accepted to an accelerated program for highly

Liza Long, from Boise, Idaho, is an author, musician, and mother of four who blogs under the name Anarchist Soc-cer Mom. This particular post, which appeared originally on her blog and then on December 16, 2012, on thebluereview.com, quickly went viral in the wake of the Newtown school shooting.

gifted math and science students. His IQ is off the charts. When he's in a good mood, he will gladly bend your ear on subjects ranging from Greek mythology to the differences between Einsteinian and Newtonian physics to Doctor Who. He's in a good mood most of the time. But when he's not, watch out. And it's impossible to predict what will set him off.

Several weeks into his new junior high school, Michael began exhibiting increasingly odd and threatening behaviors at school. We decided to transfer him to the district's most restrictive behavioral program, a contained school environment where children who can't function in normal classrooms can access their right to free public babysitting from 7:30–1:50 Monday through Friday until they turn 18.

The morning of the pants incident, Michael continued to argue with me on the drive. He would occasionally apologize and seem remorseful. Right before we turned into his school parking lot, he said, "Look, Mom, I'm really sorry. Can I have video games back today?"

"No way," I told him. "You cannot act the way you acted this morning and think you can get your electronic privileges back that quickly."

His face turned cold, and his eyes were full of calculated rage. "Then I'm going to kill myself," he said. "I'm going to jump out of this car right now and kill myself."

15 That was it. After the knife incident, I told him that if he ever said those words again, I would take him straight to the mental hospital, no ifs, ands, or buts. I did not respond, except to pull the car into the opposite lane, turning left instead of right.

"Where are you taking me?" he said, suddenly worried. "Where are we going?"

"You know where we are going," I replied.

"No! You can't do that to me! You're sending me to hell! You're sending me straight to hell!"

I pulled up in front of the hospital, frantically waving for one of the clinicians who happened to be standing outside. "Call the police," I said. "Hurry."

Michael was in a full-blown fit by then, 20 screaming and hitting. I hugged him close so he couldn't escape from the car. He bit me several times and repeatedly jabbed his elbows into my rib cage. I'm still stronger than he is, but I won't be for much longer.

The police came quickly and carried my son screaming and kicking into the bowels of the hospital. I started to shake, and tears filled my eyes as I filled out the paperwork — "Were there any difficulties with . . . at what age did your child . . . were there any problems with . . . has your child ever experienced . . . does your child have . . ."

At least we have health insurance now. I recently accepted a position with a local college, giving up my freelance career because when you have a kid like this, you need benefits. You'll do anything for benefits. No individual insurance plan will cover this kind of thing.

For days, my son insisted that I was lying — that I made the whole thing up so that I could get rid of him. The first day, when I called to check up on him, he said, "I hate you. And I'm going to get my revenge as soon as I get out of here."

By day three, he was my calm, sweet boy again, all apologies and promises to get better. I've heard those promises for years. I don't believe them anymore.

On the intake form, under the question, 25 "What are your expectations for treatment?" I wrote, "I need help."

And I do. This problem is too big for me to handle on my own. Sometimes there are no good options. So you just pray for grace and trust that in hindsight, it will all make sense.

I am sharing this story because I am Adam Lanza's mother. I am Dylan Klebold's and Eric Harris's mother. I am James Holmes's mother. I am Jared Loughner's mother. I am Seung-Hui Cho's mother. And these boys — and their mothers — need help. In the wake of another horrific national tragedy, it's easy to talk about guns. But it's time to talk about mental illness.

According to *Mother Jones*, since 1982, 61 mass murders involving firearms have occurred throughout the country. Of these, 43 of the killers were white males, and only one was a woman. *Mother Jones* focused on whether the killers obtained their guns legally (most did). But this highly visible sign of mental illness should lead us to consider how many people in the U.S. live in fear, like I do.

When I asked my son's social worker about my options, he said that the only thing I could do was to get Michael charged with a crime. "If he's back in the system, they'll create a paper trail," he said. "That's the only way you're ever going to get anything done. No one will pay attention to you unless you've got charges."

30   I don't believe my son belongs in jail. The chaotic environment exacerbates Michael's sen-sitivity to sensory stimuli and doesn't deal with the underlying pathology. But it seems like the United States is using prison as the solution of choice for mentally ill people. According to Human Rights Watch, the number of mentally ill inmates in U.S. prisons quadrupled from 2000 to 2006, and it continues to rise — in fact, the rate of inmate mental illness is five times greater (56 percent) than in the non-incarcerated population.

With state-run treatment centers and hos-pitals shuttered, prison is now the last resort for the mentally ill — Rikers Island, the LA County Jail, and Cook County Jail in Illinois housed the nation's largest treatment centers in 2011.

No one wants to send a 13-year-old genius who loves Harry Potter and his snuggle animal collection to jail. But our society, with its stigma on mental illness and its broken healthcare sys-tem, does not provide us with other options. Then another tortured soul shoots up a fast food restaurant. A mall. A kindergarten class-room. And we wring our hands and say, "Some-thing must be done."

I agree that something must be done. It's time for a meaningful, nation-wide conversation about mental health. That's the only way our nation can ever truly heal.

God help me. God help Michael. God help us all.

Reading and Discussion Questions

1. Why is the essay called "I Am Adam Lanza's Mother"? (After all, she isn't.) What is her purpose in telling her story?

2. Where in the essay does Long most clearly state her thesis?

3. What type of appeal is Long using when she recounts the details of Michael's violence and threats of violence?

4. Where does she make use of logical appeal?

5. Does Long come across as a credible person? In other words, what sort of *ethos* does the essay convey?

6. Research the online responses to Long's blog post, and formulate your own response.

Rogerian Argument

Carl Rogers was a twentieth-century humanistic psychologist who translated his ideas about therapy into communication theory. As a therapist, he believed that the experience of two people meeting and speaking honestly to each other would have a healing effect. In later years he became convinced that the same principles of nondirective, nonconfrontational therapy that emphasized attentive listening could work not only for couples and small groups but also for large groups, even nations, to create more harmonious relationships.

Such nonconfrontational communication between individuals or among groups is hampered, Rogers believed, by the fact that there is no longer anything approaching a shared worldview. In the past, those like Copernicus and Galileo who saw reality differently were often condemned or even killed. Rogers wrote, "Although society has often come around eventually to agree with its dissidents ... there is no doubt that this insistence upon a known and certain universe has been part of the cement that holds a culture together."[6] In the Rogerian approach to argumentation, effective communication requires both understanding another's reality and respecting it.

Rogers's approach to communication is based on the idea of mutual elements or **common ground**. A writer or speaker and an audience who have very different opinions on a highly charged emotional issue need a common ground on which to meet if any productive communication is going to take place. In the midst of all of their differences, they have to find a starting point on which they agree. In 1977 Maxine Hairston summed up five steps for using Rogerian argumentation that incorporate the two essentials of the approach — being able to (1) summarize another's position with understanding and clarity and (2) locate common ground between two different positions:

1. Give a brief, objective statement of the issue under discussion.

2. Summarize in impartial language what you perceive the case for the opposition to be; the summary should demonstrate that you understand their interests and concerns and should avoid any hint of hostility.

3. Make an objective statement of your own side of the issue, listing your concerns and interests but avoiding loaded language or any hint of moral superiority.

---

[6] "Do We Need 'a' Reality?" *A Way of Being* (New York: Houghton Mifflin 1980), p. 103.

4. Outline what common ground or mutual concerns you and the other person or group seem to share; if you see irreconcilable interests, specify what they are.

5. Outline the solution you propose, pointing out what both sides may gain from it.[7]

Rogerian argument places more emphasis on the relationship between audience and subject than other rhetorical theories do. It emphasizes the audience's view of the subject and places it in juxtaposition to the writer's. Understanding another's ideas with the clarity and lack of a judgmental attitude that Rogers proposed requires taking on, temporarily, that other's point of view—walking a mile in his shoes—and seeing the subject with his eyes.

As shown on the communications triangle below, the Rogerian approach seeks to find common ground between the writer's and audience's relationship to the subject.

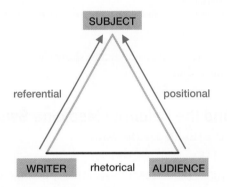

In an essay written using the Rogerian approach to argumentation, the thesis or claim will be one that reconciles opposing positions—at least as far as that is possible with the sorts of emotionally charged subjects that call for a non-confrontational approach in the first place.

Consider the example of management and striking union members. The situation can quickly degenerate into shouting matches and violence with little progress toward resolution. The union can make demands, which the management turns down, and the shouting matches begin again. Rogers would advocate the seemingly simple method of the two sides listening to each other with understanding. Management has to be able to explain the union's position in a way that the union members feel is fair before it can present its own. And then the reverse. This approach is time consuming, but it can keep the discussion from dissolving into anger and impasse. The resolution—parallel to the

---

[7] Maxine Hairston, "Carl Rogers's Alternative to Traditional Rhetoric," *College Composition and Communication*, December 1976, pp. 375–76.

ARGUMENT ESSENTIALS
Rogerian Argument

- Presents opponent's views accurately and objectively.
- Presents writer's views fairly and objectively.
- Explains what common ground exists between the two positions.
- Thesis statement presents a compromise between the two positions.

---

thesis of an essay employing the Rogerian method — will most likely be a compromise between the two positions.

In writing an essay using the Rogerian method, the test of the writer's *ethos*, or ethics, is how fairly she sums up her opponent's views. A common tactic for unethical writers is to attack an opponent for something he never said. This puts the opponent in the position of trying to defend a position that he does not believe and sidetracks the whole argument — which is exactly what the unscrupulous writer is trying to do.

READING ARGUMENT

Seeing Rogerian Argument

The essay that follows has been annotated to show the key features of Rogerian argument used by the authors.

Katie Couric and the Celebrity Medicine Syndrome
JULIA BELLUZ AND STEVEN J. HOFFMAN

An email with the subject line "OMG" recently came from one of our mothers, and it contained chilling information about the HPV vaccine. "200 people have died from it," Mom claimed, "and it does not even last long enough to prevent cervical cancer."

> First three paragraphs show dangers of celebrities as medical spokespeople.

Her source was not her doctor, a new study or the Food and Drug Administration. Her information came from a recent episode of Katie Couric's ABC talk show about "all sides" of the "HPV controversy."[4] Since then, most of the alarmist vaccine claims made in the episode have been debunked. But Mom

---

Julia Belluz is a health journalist and a journalism fellow at MIT. Steven J. Hoffman is an assistant professor of clinical epidemiology and biostatistics at McMaster University and a visiting assistant professor at the Harvard School of Public Health. Their article appeared in the December 18, 2013, edition of the *Los Angeles Times*.

---

[4] In a "For the Record" box accompanying this article, the *LA Times* notes, "[Couric's] show reported that there have been more than 200 claims filed, including 11 from families who believe the vaccine caused their children's deaths." —EDS.

remains a victim of celebrity medicine: She heard a warning from someone famous, believed it and spread the misinformation.

Unfortunately, Mom is not alone. Celebrities have crept into our medicine cabinets and kitchens, influencing what pills we pop, tests we order, and foods we fear. More often than not, their advice and products are dubious. "Then why do so many people believe them?" Mom asked.

This time, we have an answer. One of us — Hoffman — just published a review of research on celebrity in the December 18 issue of the *British Medical Journal*. It addresses this question.

5   The review draws on studies from a range of disciplines and synthesizes key narratives on celebrity followership. The conclusion? Our brains, psyches, and societies appear to be hardwired to trust celebrities, whether on anti-vaccine antics or miracle medicines.

Economics tells us that we use celebrity endorsements as signals or short-cuts for judging qualities such as validity or relevance. So when Bill Clinton recommends veganism, his approval elevates animal-free eating even though his expertise lies more with foreign policy than nutrition.

The halo theory from marketing studies explains how celebrities' success in one area — say, acting — makes people presume they are competent in unrelated areas — say, medicine. This influences how we interpret their health messages no matter how nonsensical, and may explain why Gwyneth Paltrow has become a credible advisor on vitamin D deficiency, even though she didn't go to medical school nor is she a health expert.

Classical conditioning suggests that we learn to psychologically associate unrelated stimuli in a way that exposure to them achieves similar responses. This means warm feelings toward celebrities are stirred up in us by the things they pitch. It's no surprise, then, that PepsiCo paid Beyoncé $50 million to promote its products.

Neuroscience studies also help explain why these endorsements work on us. Brain scans have demonstrated that images of celebrities increase activity in our medial orbitofrontal cortices, the region responsible for forming positive associations. So if you're an Angelina Jolie fan, seeing her image lights up this part of the brain, making you more likely to think highly about whatever she is promoting, even when it's something extreme like a double mastectomy to prevent breast cancer.

10   Reason should help us overcome an illogical addiction to celebrity health advice. Questioning prescriptions from prominent people and asking about the evidence behind them could save us time, money, and harm. But, as the science shows, celebrity influence is not rational.

The first step to addressing celebrity medicine is recognizing that it is a human vulnerability and a serious public health challenge. Doing that can empower us to think twice before we take advice from the stars.

Second solution: Listen to the celebrities. But learn from them what they are good at — attracting attention.

We should also use these new insights to rethink how we promote healthy living and evidence-based decision-making. Actress and anti-vaccine activist Jenny McCarthy may be their arch-nemesis, but doctors and public health practitioners can learn from her. Making vaccines, exercise, and oral hygiene as attractive as celebrities would be more valuable than any million-dollar endorsement deal and more effective than any detox diet. It might also save Mom from putting her most sacred asset — her health — into the well-manicured hands of famous people.

Compromise: Learn from celebrities not about health but about how to promote health.

Practice: Rogerian Argument

Use a Rogerian approach to analyze the following essay. Use the comments on the preceding essay as a model. Then answer the questions that appear at the end of the essay.

The "Unnatural" Ashley Treatment Can Be Right for Profoundly Disabled Children
PETER SINGER

Five years ago, the parents of a profoundly intellectually disabled girl born in 1997, known only as Ashley, told the world about a controversial treatment they were using on their child. It included giving her hormones so that she would remain below normal height and weight, as well as surgery, which included a hysterectomy to remove her uterus and a bilateral breast-bud removal to prevent her breasts from developing. Ashley's mental age was that of a three-month-old. She was unable to walk, talk, hold a toy, or change her position in bed. Her parents were not sure she recognized them. There was no prospect of her mental condition ever improving.

The treatment was approved by the ethics committee at Seattle children's hospital, where it was carried out. It began when Ashley was six,

and was made public when she was nine. The aim of the surgery was to keep Ashley small and light, so that her parents could continue to move her around frequently and take her with them when going out with their two other children. The uterus removal was intended to spare her the discomfort of menstrual cramps; the surgery to prevent the development of breasts aimed to make her more comfortable when she was

Peter Singer is a professor of bioethics at Princeton University and Laureate Professor in the Centre for Applied Philosophy and Public Ethics at the University of Melbourne. His books include his 1975 *Animal Liberation*, which helped inspire the animal rights movement; *Practical Ethics* (3rd ed., 2011); *Rethinking Life and Death* (1996); and *The Ethics of What We Eat* (2006). This article was posted on guardian.co.uk on March 16, 2012.

lying down or had a strap across her chest in her wheelchair. Nevertheless, when it became public, many objected to it. Some said it was "unnatural," others that it violated Ashley's dignity, that it was not in her best interests, and that it could lead down a slippery slope of parents "modifying" their children for their own convenience.

Today, Ashley is fourteen. Her mental condition has not changed, but her size and weight have remained that of a nine-year-old. Her father remains convinced that he and his wife made the right decision for Ashley, and that the treatment made her more likely to be comfortable, healthy, and happy. He describes her as "completely loved" and her life "as good as we can possibly make it." There seem to be no grounds for holding the opinion that the treatment was not in Ashley's best interests.

As for the claim that it was unnatural, well, in one sense all medical treatment is unnatural; it enables us to live longer, and in better health, than we naturally would. Perhaps the most "natural" thing for Ashley's parents to do with their severely disabled daughter would have been to abandon her to the wolves and vultures, as parents have done with such children for most of human existence. Fortunately, we have evolved beyond such "natural" practices, which are abhorrent to civilized people. The issue of treating Ashley with dignity was never, in my view, a genuine one. Infants are adorable, but not dignified, and the same is true of older and larger human beings who remain at the mental level of an infant. You don't acquire dignity just by being born a member of the species Homo sapiens.

5   What of the slippery slope argument? The *Guardian* has found twelve families that have used the "Ashley treatment" and believes more than one hundred children may have been administered with hormones to keep them small. The fact that a few other families are using the treatment, however, does not show there has been any descent down a slope. Take the cases of "Tom" and "Erica," two other severely intellectually disabled children who have been given similar treatment to Ashley. Their mothers are convinced that the treatment has enabled their children to live happier lives, and are grateful to Ashley's father for being open about how they are coping with Ashley's disability.

Curt Decker, director of the U.S. National Disability Rights Network, has been quoted as saying that the treatment could lead to "the idea that people with disabilities don't have to be kept alive or integrated in society." There is no reason to believe those children's interests are better understood by disability rights activists without cognitive impairments than they are understood by the children's parents. The best that can be done for profoundly disabled children with caring families is to keep them with their families, and that is more likely to happen if the families are able to lift them and move them, so that they can care for them at home.

Decker and some other disability rights activists have been calling for the Ashley treatment to be banned. A more reasonable approach would be to require hospital ethics committee approval for such treatments, to ensure they are used only on the most profoundly intellectually disabled patients, where there is no prospect of improvement. The ethics committee should permit the treatment only when it is convinced it is in the best interests of those children. It is hard to see why a procedure that, on the available evidence, is beneficial to them, should be banned.

Reading and Discussion Questions

1. Why did Ashley's parents decide to have the multiple medical procedures performed on their daughter?
2. What four objections to the parents' decision are mentioned in paragraph 2?
3. What is Singer's response to each of these objections?
4. Does Singer ever cross the line and fail to treat objectively and fairly those who disagree with him?
5. In what sense is Singer's proposal a compromise?

The Toulmin Model

Although Aristotle and Rogers, centuries and worlds apart, have both made significant contributions to rhetorical theory, we made the decision to organize this text around an argumentative model that we believe is more helpful in reading and writing arguments in a systematic manner: the Toulmin Model. The late Stephen Toulmin provided the vocabulary about argumentation that gives this book its structure.[5]

Toulmin's model, proposed in 1958 in *The Uses of Argument*, was designed to analyze courtroom arguments. Only after his model had been introduced to rhetoricians by Wayne Brockriede and Douglas Ehninger did he discuss its rhetorical implications in *Introduction to Reasoning* (1979). Of the six key terms in Toulmin's model, we draw heavily on three: claim, support, and warrant.

The Toulmin model addresses all three legs of the communication triangle, connecting writer, subject, and audience.

---

[5] Stephen Toulmin, *The Uses of Argument* (Cambridge: Cambridge University Press, 1958).

The Claim

The **claim** (also called a proposition) answers the question "What are you trying to prove?" It will generally appear as the thesis statement of an essay, although in some arguments it may not be stated directly. There are three principal kinds of claim (discussed more fully in Chapter 5): claims of fact, of value, and of policy. **Claims of fact** assert that a condition has existed, exists, or will exist and are based on facts or data that the audience will accept as being objectively verifiable.

- The diagnosis of autism is now far more common than it was twenty years ago.
- Fast foods are contributing significantly to today's epidemic of childhood obesity.
- Climate change will affect the coastlines of all continents.

All these claims must be supported by data. Although the last example is an inference or an educated guess about the future, a reader will probably find the prediction credible if the data seem authoritative.

Claims of value attempt to prove that some things are more or less desirable than others. They express approval or disapproval of standards of taste and morality. Advertisements and reviews of cultural events are one common source of value claims, but such claims emerge whenever people argue about what is good or bad, beautiful or ugly.

- *Silver Linings Playbook* does an excellent job of depicting bipolar disorder.
- Abortion is wrong under any circumstances.
- The right to privacy is more important than the need to increase security at airports.

Claims of policy assert that specific policies should be instituted as solutions to problems. The expression *should*, *must*, or *ought to* usually appears in the statement.

- The electoral college should be replaced by popular vote as the means of electing a president.
- Attempts at making air travel more secure must not put in jeopardy the passengers' right to privacy.
- Existing laws governing gun ownership should be more stringently enforced.

Policy claims call for analysis of both fact and value.

Practice

1. Classify each of the following as a claim of fact, value, or policy.
   a. Solar power could supply 20 percent of the energy needs now satisfied by fossil fuel and nuclear power.

    b. Violence on television produces violent behavior in children who watch more than four hours a day.

    c. Both intelligent design and evolutionary theory should be taught in the public schools.

    d. Some forms of cancer are caused by viruses.

    e. Dogs are smarter than cats.

    f. The money that our government spends on foreign aid would be better spent solving domestic problems like unemployment and homelessness.

    g. Wherever the number of illegal aliens increases, the crime rate also increases.

    h. Movie sequels are generally inferior to their originals.

    i. Tom Hanks is a more versatile actor than Tom Cruise.

    j. Adopted children who are of a different ethnic background than their adoptive parents should be raised with an understanding of the culture of their biological parents.

    k. Average yearly temperatures in North America are already being affected by climate change.

    l. Human activity is the primary cause of climate change.

2. Which claims listed above would be most difficult to support?

3. What type or types of evidence would it take to build a convincing case for each claim?

The Support

Support consists of the materials that the arguer uses to convince an audience that his or her claim is sound. These materials include evidence and motivational appeals to needs and values. The **evidence** or data consists of facts, statistics, and testimony from experts. The **appeals to needs and values** are the ones that the arguer makes to the values and attitudes of the audience to win support for the claim. These appeals (also known as *emotional* or *motivational* appeals) are the reasons that move an audience to accept a belief or adopt a course of action. (See Chapter 6 for a detailed discussion of support.)

The Warrant

Certain assumptions underlie all the claims we make. In the Toulmin model, the term **warrant** is used for such an assumption, a belief or principle that is taken for granted. It may be stated or unstated. If the arguer believes that the audience shares the assumption, there may be no need to express it. But if the audience seems doubtful or hostile, the arguer may decide to state the assumption to emphasize its importance or argue for its validity. The warrant, stated or not, enables the reader to make the same connection between the support and the claim that the author does. In other words, you have to accept the warrant in order to accept the author's claim based on the evidence provided.

Claim: The popular vote should replace the electoral college as the means of electing the president.
Support: The popular vote gives each voter one vote for president.
Warrant: The president should be elected by a system that gives each voter one vote.

Claim: A picture ID should be required for eligibility to vote.
Support: Picture ID's would cut down on voter fraud.
Warrant: A requirement that cuts down on voter fraud should be implemented.

Claim: In the United States, 1 in 68 children has an autism spectrum disorder.
Support: That number is based on the latest report from the Centers for Disease Control.
Warrant: The latest report from the Centers for Disease Control is a reliable source of information on the incidence of autism spectrum disorders in the United States.

Claim: The 2013 movie *Evil Dead* is a much better movie than the original 1981 *The Evil Dead*.
Support: The new movie is much more realistic.
Warrant: A more realistic movie is better than one that is less realistic.

One more important characteristic of the warrant deserves mention. In most cases, the warrant is a more general statement of belief than the claim. It can, therefore, support many claims, not only the one in a particular argument. For example, the warrant that being safe is worth a small loss of privacy expresses a broad assumption or belief that we take for granted and that can underlie claims about many other practices in American society. (For more on warrants, see Chapter 7.)

Toulmin and the Syllogism

You will see some similarities between Toulmin's three-part structure of claim, support, and warrant and the classical deductive syllogism articulated by Aristotle. In fact, a comparison of the two may help in understanding the warrant.

The syllogism is useful for laying out the basic elements of an argument, and it lends itself more readily to simple arguments. It is a formula that consists of three elements: (1) the major premise, (2) the minor premise, and (3) the conclusion, which follows logically from the two premises. The following syllogism summarizes a familiar argument.

Major premise: Advertising of things harmful to our health should be legally banned.

Minor premise: Cigarettes are harmful to our health.

Conclusion: Therefore, advertising of cigarettes should be legally banned.

Cast in the form of the Toulmin model, the argument looks like this:

Claim: Advertising of cigarettes should be legally banned.

Support (Evidence): Cigarettes are harmful to our health.

Warrant: Advertising of things harmful to our health should be legally banned.

Or in diagram form:

SUPPORT ⎯⎯⎯⎯⎯⎯⟶ CLAIM

Cigarettes are harmful   Advertising of cigarettes
to our health.   should be legally banned.

WARRANT

Advertising of things harmful
to our health should be
legally banned.

ARGUMENT ESSENTIALS

The Toulmin Model

Claim — the proposition that the author is trying to prove. The claim may appear as the thesis statement of an essay but may be implied rather than stated directly.

- *Claims of fact* assert that a condition has existed, exists, or will exist and are based on facts or data that the audience will accept as being objectively verifiable.

- *Claims of value* attempt to prove that some things are more or less desirable than others; they express approval or disapproval of standards of taste and morality.

- *Claims of policy* assert that specific plans or courses of action should be instituted as solutions to problems.

Support — the materials used by the arguer to convince an audience that his or her claim is sound; those materials include evidence and motivational appeals.

Warrant — an inference or assumption; a belief or principle that is taken for granted in an argument.

In both the syllogism and the Toulmin model, the principal elements of the argument are expressed in three statements. You can see that the claim in the Toulmin model is the conclusion in the syllogism — that is, the proposition that you are trying to prove. The evidence (support) in the Toulmin model corresponds to the minor premise in the syllogism. And the warrant in the Toulmin model resembles the major premise of the syllogism.

While the syllogism is essentially static, with all three parts logically locked into place, the Toulmin model suggests that an argument is a *movement* from support to claim by way of the warrant, which acts as a bridge. Toulmin introduced the concept of warrant by asking, "How do you get there?" (His first two questions, introducing the claim and support, were "What are you trying to prove?" and "What have you got to go on?")

READING ARGUMENT

Seeing the Toulmin Model

The following essay has been annotated to show the key features of the Toulmin model used by the author.

In Health, We're Not No. 1
ROBERT J. SAMUELSON

It turns out that being American is bad for your health, relatively speaking.

Claim of value

Anyone interested in health care ought to digest the findings of a massive new report from the National Research Council and the Institute of Medicine, which compared Americans' health with that of people in other advanced countries. After spending 18 months examining statistics and studies, the panel reached a damning conclusion: The United States ranks below most advanced countries.

Support: testimony from experts

Consider. Life expectancy at birth is 78.2 years in the United States, lower than the 79.5-year average for the wealthy countries belonging to the Organization for Economic Cooperation and Development (OECD); Japan's life expectancy is 83. Among 17 advanced countries, the United States has the highest level of diabetes. For 21 diseases, U.S. death rates were higher in 15 (including heart and lung diseases) than the average for these same countries.

Support: statistics

Here, in somewhat clunky language, is the report's sobering summary:

5   "The U.S. health disadvantage is more pronounced among socioeconomically disadvantaged groups, but even advantaged Americans [described as "white, insured, college-educated"] appear to fare worse than their counterparts in England and some other countries."

What to make of this?

The report's most important contribution is to show that much of the U.S. "health disadvantage" doesn't reflect an inadequate health-care system but lifestyle choices, personal behaviors, and social pathologies. The gap in life expectancy is concentrated in Americans under 50. Among men, nearly 60 percent of the gap results from more homicides (often gun-related), car accidents (often alcohol-related), and other accidents (often drug-related) than in comparable nations. For children under 5, car accidents, drowning, and fire are the largest causes of death.

Support: statistics and motivational appeal

Robert J. Samuelson, a contributing editor at *Newsweek*, has written a column for the *Washington Post* since 1977. This essay was posted on washingtonpost.com on January 16, 2013.

Support: statistics and
motivational appeal

Teen pregnancy is another big problem. Among girls 15 to 19, the pregnancy rate is about 3.5 times the average of other advanced societies. "Adolescent motherhood affects two generations, children and mothers," the report notes. Adolescent mothers often don't finish high school. "Their children face a greater risk of poor child care, weak maternal attachments, [and] poverty." Similarly, the incidence of AIDS in America is nearly nine times the OECD average.

The health-care system can't cure these ills, which are social problems with health consequences. Those who expect the introduction of the main elements of the Affordable Care Act ("Obamacare") in 2014 to improve Americans' health dramatically are likely to be disappointed. The lack of insurance is a problem, but it is not the main health problem, in part because the uninsured already receive much uncompensated care.

Support: statistics

To be fair: Some of these social problems show progress. America's slippage is mostly relative to better outcomes elsewhere. Since 1980, the U.S. murder rate has dropped by roughly half (but remains higher than in many peer countries); traffic deaths per miles traveled have fallen by more than half since 1975 (though decreases abroad are greater); teen birth rates have fallen to a seven-decade low (but are higher than in most wealthy nations); and U.S. life expectancy is rising (but more slowly than elsewhere).

10

Support: fact

Nor does the new report exonerate the U.S. health-care system from blame for the "health disadvantage." Despite enormous spending, the system is "deeply fragmented across thousands of health systems and payers . . . creating inefficiencies and coordination problems."

Support: facts and statistics

Much specialized care is of high quality; recovery rates for hospitalized U.S. stroke and heart attack victims are higher than in many wealthy nations. Cancer treatment is superior. But primary care is weak. Only 12 percent of U.S. doctors are general practitioners compared with 18 percent in Germany, 30 percent in Britain, and 49 percent in France. In 2009, Americans visited doctor's offices an average of 3.9 times; the OECD average is 6.5 times. Patients may not get needed care; one study found that Americans "receive only 50 percent of recommended" treatments.

Support: motivational appeal

The report's authors searched in vain for an overarching explanation for the peculiar determinants of Americans' health. But it missed the most obvious possibility: This is America. The late sociologist Seymour Martin Lipset argued that American "exceptionalism" is a double-edged sword. Values we admire also inspire behaviors we deplore. The emphasis on individual autonomy and achievement may aid a dynamic economy — and also feed crime and drug use.

Similar tendencies affect health care. The love of freedom and disdain for authority may encourage teen pregnancy and bad diets. The competitive nature of society may spawn stress that hurts the health of even the well-to-do. The suspicion of concentrated power may foster a fragmented delivery system. Commendable ambitiousness may push doctors toward specialization with its higher income and status.

Warrant: Americans' health is bad because of American values.

15   Ever optimistic, Americans deny conflicts and choices. We excel at self-delusion. Asked by pollsters to rate their own health, Americans say — despite much contrary evidence — that they're in better shape than almost anyone. We think we're No. 1 even if we aren't.

Practice: The Toulmin Model

Analyze the following article using Toulmin's three key terms: claim, support, and warrant. Use the above Robert J. Samuelson essay as a model. Then answer the questions that appear at the end.

Latest 3-D Films Add Dimension, Not Appeal
JONATHAN WINCHELL

An epidemic of lazy filmmaking has swept over Hollywood in the last few years post-*Avatar*.

James Cameron shot his epic 2009 film in 3-D and showed the world what was possible with the medium. The film ended up being the highest-grossing film of all time.

In an attempt to cash in on the success of *Avatar*, Hollywood has been releasing more 3-D films. The major problem is that many of these films are shot in the standard 2-D format but digitally transfigured into 3-D. I refuse to pay three dollars more to see a film retrofitted in 3-D when the filmmakers couldn't spend the time and money to actually shoot it that way.

A film will often hog two or more screens at a multiplex because it is being projected in both 2-D and 3-D. If a director shoots a film in 3-D — such as Ang Lee with *Life of Pi* or Martin Scorsese with *Hugo* — I am more than willing to experience the film the way the filmmakers intended it to be seen.

3-D, like computer generated imagery, or CGI, is being used far too often and sloppily, but it is just a tool. Used sparingly and artistically, it can result in glorious visions.

Hollywood has become more and more like a factory, churning out corporate-manufactured products for mass consumption. 3-D is a surcharge that isn't worth the money unless the product is genuine.

Retrofitting a film in the present is bad enough, but Hollywood has sunk even lower. This Friday, the 1939 classic *The Wizard of Oz* is being rereleased in theaters, only this time

5

When he published this article on September 17, 2013, in the student newspaper at the University of South Carolina, the *Daily Gamecock*, Winchell was the paper's movie reviewer.

in IMAX 3-D. A whole new generation will be exposed to a bastardization of this timeless masterpiece.

Victor Fleming's original film was carefully crafted by many artists — the director, cinematographer, set designers, lighting technicians — to look a certain way in 2-D. To alter the work is to disregard and disrespect the original intent of the artists. It is a form of artistic vandalism.

While retrofitting a film in 3-D is not as egregious as colorizing a film — adding color to black-and-white films — it is still inexcusable.

10   When James Cameron released a retrofitted 3-D version of his film *Titanic*, the second highest grossing film of all time, he absolutely had the right. Unless the original director gives permission, no changes should ever be made to a film.

An exception is if a director is deeply involved with and oversees the 3-D retrofitting of the film. Then, the conversion is fair game.

I cannot wait to see Alfonso Cuarón's sci-fi film *Gravity*, especially in IMAX. That means I have to see it in retrofitted 3-D, though.

The film uses state-of-the art special effects, and Cuarón said that "because of the technology . . . it was practically impossible" to shoot in 3-D. He said the conversion started "three and a half years ago, to go through pains to make sure that it was the closest thing to native 3-D."

If filmmakers like Cuarón have an artistic reason for retrofitting a film in post production, I say the decision is valid. I always prefer that a film be actually shot in 3-D, but I want to see it the way the filmmaker intends it to be seen.

Most post-production conversions are nothing more than shameless cash grabs and are not done for artistic reasons. I want 3-D to mean what it stands for: 3 dimensions.   15

It can transport the spectator visually into a new world through technology. I don't want it to only stand for "three dollars."

Reading and Discussion Questions

1. What claim is Winchell supporting in the essay? What type of claim is it?
2. What is Winchell's primary type of support?
3. If you wrote an enthymeme based on Winchell's argument, what would it look like?
4. Do you find his argument convincing? Why, or why not?

Assignments for Understanding Approaches to Argument

Reading and Discussion Questions

1. How are the traditional (Aristotelian) and the Toulmin approaches to argumentation different? How are they similar?

2. Do you believe that presidential debates are good examples of argumentation? Explain.

3. What are some of the controversial issues in the field of your major or a major that you are considering? Analyze one or more of them using Toulmin's terms: claim, support, and warrant.

4. When you write essays and reports for your classes, how do you establish your credibility? In contrast, how do students lose their credibility with the instructors who read their work?

5. What are some situations you have been in — or have read or heard about — in which people's opinions were so far apart that the best you could hope for was compromise rather than total victory for one side or the other?

Writing Suggestions

1. Write an essay in which you support your opinion about whether a federal registry of firearms transactions should be created.

2. Write an essay in which you discuss how technological advances have changed an audience's ability to evaluate a speaker's *ethos*.

3. Write an essay in which you discuss how both Aristotelian and Rogerian argument are useful in contemporary politics.

4. Write an essay in which you identify some of the issues about which it is most difficult to achieve common ground, and explain why.

5. Write an essay in which you explain why different warrants or underlying assumptions make it so difficult to reach a compromise on the issue of gun control.

RESEARCH ASSIGNMENT

1. Every library will have access to different databases for student use. Find a list of the databases available to you, and do a search for articles about how Carl Rogers's theories about therapy relate to argument. You will have to try different combinations of search terms to find the best information. Write down what you discover about sources available to you.

2. What are two specialized databases that might be a starting point for information related to your major or a major that you might choose?

---

bits

To see what you are learning about argumentation applied to the latest world and national news, read our *Bits* blog, "Argument and the Headlines," at **blogs.bedfordstmartins.com/bits**.

Examining
Written Arguments

Consider the cardboard sign shown in Figure 2.1. It is a brief message — "Jesus had two dads" — but the point is clear. These four words make a statement in favor of same-sex marriage. They also suggest that there is nothing immoral about it because it was Jesus's heritage. This brief statement carries a lot of meaning because of the context within which it is understood.

An argument can be summed up on a sign, in a tweet, in an ad, or on a bumper sticker. Think of the contexts that give meaning to these statements from bumper stickers. Some are funny; all have a point to make.

Against abortion? Then don't have one.

If the environment were a bank, we would already have saved it.

Gun nuts are keeping us from controlling nuts with guns.

From Seneca Falls to Selma to Stonewall WE TRANSFORM AMERICA

A full response to any argument means more than understanding the message. It also means evaluating, deciding whether the message is successful, and then determining *how* it succeeds or fails in persuading us. In making these judgments about the arguments of others, we learn how to deliver our own. We try to avoid what we perceive to be flaws in another's arguments, and we adapt the strategies that produce clear, honest, forceful arguments.

Critical reading is essential for mastery of most college subjects, but its importance for reading and writing about argument, where meaning is often complex and multilayered, cannot be overestimated. The ability to read arguments critically is essential to advanced academic work — even in science and math — since it requires the debate of multifaceted issues rather than the memorization of facts. Just as important, learning to read arguments critically helps you develop the ability to *write* effective arguments — a process valued at the university, in the professional world, and in public life.

Prereading

You will frequently confront texts dealing with subjects unfamiliar to you, and you should have a plan of action for prereading them; that is, for getting an overview of a piece before you read. As the Strategies box demonstrates, the most important things to understand about a text before you read it include the title, purpose, author, and target audience.

Following the Strategies box are two essays. The first includes annotations demonstrating the prereading steps. The second is part of a Practice exercise in which you can employ the prereading strategies yourself.

FIGURE 2.1 Signs can contain brief arguments.
Elias Kass

Strategies for Prereading

1. **Pay attention to the title.** The title may state the purpose of the argument in specific terms. It may also use a particular style of language — such as humorous, inflammatory, or somber — to set the tone for the argument.

2. **Understand the kind of text you are reading.** Where and when was it published? Is it a response to another text, or perhaps to an event? Certainly if it is argumentative writing, it is at least a response to a perceived problem. Was there something specific that led an author to write about this subject in this way at this particular time? What background about the subject are you familiar with?

3. **Learn about the author.** As a rule, the more information you know about an author, the easier and more productive your reading will be. You should learn to read in a way that enables you to discover not just meaning in the text itself but information about the author's point of view, background, motives, and ideology. Such understanding comes not only from close analysis of a text but also from (a) background reading on the author and/or the subject and (b) discussion with your classmates and instructors on the material.

4. **Imagine the context in which the author was writing and the target audience.** Was it a specific or general audience? Does the text come from a journal that publishes primarily conservative or liberal writers? What values and ideals are shared by the author and the audience most likely to agree with the argument? How might these values help make sense of the context? What sort of audience might be most strongly opposed to the argument, and why?

READING ARGUMENT

Seeing Prereading

The following is a screenshot of a blog post. It has been annotated to show the key strategies for prereading in a written text.

On Pins and Needles Defending Artistic Expression
CAROL ROSE

Context and audience: The article was posted on Boston.com, the free portion of an electronic component of the *Boston Globe*. The site probably has a wide and diverse readership, although the nature of this blog probably draws a segment of the readership interested in politics.

Kind of text: The article appears to be part of a regular blog on privacy, freedom, and legal issues.

Title: The words *pins* and *needles* imply discomfort. The word *defending* signals that the author will take the side of artistic expression. The date of the article is given below the title.

Author: As the executive director of the Massachusetts ACLU, Rose probably leans toward a liberal point of view. (See "About the author" overlay at top right.)

About the author
Carol Rose is executive director of the American Civil Liberties Union of Massachusetts. A lawyer and journalist, Carol has spent her career working for and writing about human rights and civil liberties, both in the United States and abroad. More »

http://boston.com/community/blogs/on_liberty/2010/04/on_r

boston.com

Search

HOME   TODAY'S GLOBE   NEWS   YO

On Liberty
Carol Rose analyzes privacy, freedoms, and the law

« Back to front page   Text size

On pins and needles defending artistic expression
Posted by Carol Rose, On Liberty April 8, 2010 03:48 PM   Print | Comments (10)

f Share 11   Tweet 0   in Share 0   +1 0   ShareThis 174   E-mail

Stroll down any Massachusetts street on a sunny day and you are will see a lot of bare skin adorned with some nifty (and some not-so-nice) tattoos.

Once the emblem of American GI's and Japanese yakuzas, tattoos have become ubiquitous among the under-30 crowd. It's the rare person who hasn't fallen under the spell of the needle and dye. Even the trend-setting Institute for Contemporary Art in Boston is opening an exhibit next week featuring Mexican tattoo artist, Dr. Lakra.

Carol Rose is a lawyer and journalist and serves as executive director of the American Civil Liberties Union of Massachusetts. She posted this article on the On Liberty column of boston.com on April 8, 2010.

But did you know that tattooing was recently illegal in Massachusetts and many other states? It's true. It took a lawsuit by the ACLU in 2000 to strike down restrictions on tattoo artists in Massachusetts, thus ensuring that this ancient form of self-expression is no longer criminalized in our Commonwealth.

On April 15 at 7 p.m., the ICA will feature a conversation about the case with ACLU attorney Sarah Wunsch, who was co-counsel with Harvey Schwartz in litigating the challenge to the Massachusetts law banning tattooing.

To some people, such legal victories seem only skin deep. But on closer examination, the right to tattoo is part and parcel of our right to artistic expression.
The art of "body art" goes back literally thousands of years. Tattooed mummies have been found in all parts of the world, including Egypt, Libya, Asia and South America. A five thousand year old man, nick-named "otzi the ice man" by the people who dug him up, reportedly bore 57 tattoos -- although they may have simply been scars from arthritis (apparently it can be hard to tell the difference after 5,000 years).

The first tattoo shop in New York was set up in 1846 and came to Boston soon thereafter. Soldiers from both sides in the civil war revived the ancient tradition of wearing tattoos as a sign of military prowess. Today, surveys show that more than one-third of Americans under age 30 have tattoos, and the numbers are growing.

Despite the historical persistence of tattooing, however, the law on tattooing as free expression isn't a slam-dunk. States have some right to ensure the sanitary operation of tattoo parlors and courts are still sorting out the hard cases, such as whether employers can require employees to cover tattoos. But our nation nonetheless has made progress in defense of tattooing as a fundamental form of artistic expression. Even South Carolina and Oklahoma -- two hold-out states -- recently passed laws legalizing tattooing as skin art.

Personally, I am content to let the Mother Nature etch her motif into my tender hide without additional help from dye and needles. But even I can't resist the fascination with tattooing as an ancient and compelling form of human expression. As the ICA enticement for its upcoming show attests: "From cave walls to touch screens, no surface is off limits to the creativity of artists and designers. What about the most accessible surface of all, our own bodies?"

This blog is not written or edited by Boston.com or the Boston Globe.
The author is solely responsible for the content.

Context and audience:
Although posted on Boston.com, the Web site clarifies that it is independent from the site's content.

Practice: Prereading

Before you read the article on page 38, consider these questions:

1. Think about the title. Skim the first paragraph. Where is the piece set?
2. When and where was the piece published? How is the publication's purpose described?
3. What do you learn from the biographical information that provides background for the episode in the airport?
4. Does the article seem targeted to a specific or a general audience?

I Belong Here

AMIN AHMAD

Cure Ignorance

ENVIRONMENT   **MIND & BODY**   **POLITICS**   **ARTS**   **MEDIA**   **SCIENCE & TECH**   **FOOD**

I am living in Boston with my American fiancée when we decide to take a vacation in the UK. Standing in the customs queue at a London airport, we compare passports. Hers is sleek and clean, whereas my Indian passport resembles a small, tattered Bible. My photograph is pasted in, and spelling mistakes are corrected in Wite-Out.

My passport tells the story of my immigrant life: my student and work visas; all the entry and exit stamps as I traveled between India and the United States. Soon my fiancée and I will be married, and I'll have a brand-new U.S. passport in which to write the next chapter of my life.

RELATED CONTENT

Off With Her Gene! Dethroning a Termite Queen

Research shows disabling Neofem2, a recently discovered termite "queen gene," causes her subjects to...

What Happens in the Sweat Lodge Stays in the Sweat Lodge

What does the American Indian community have to say about the deaths of three spiritual seekers at a...

Indiana Jones and the Movie of the Fake Skulls

When Indiana Jones and the Kingdom of the Crystal Skull hits theaters next month, viewers will marve...

Fact-Checking the Gasbags of TV and Talk Radio

The fact-checking website PolitiFact.com is taking on the truth-distorting pundits of TV and talk ra...

When we reach the British immigration official, she gives my fiancée's passport a quick look and is done. Then she fingers the worn cardboard cover of mine, sighs, and says, "Would you please step this way for an immigration check."

The official gestures to a wooden bench where an old Sikh man in a saffron turban and a huddled Bangladeshi family sit.

I'm not like them, I want to say to the official. *I live in Boston*. But all the official sees is a brown face and an Indian passport. My fiancée says she will sit with me. The official shrugs.

Sitting on the hard wooden bench, I watch each white person clear immigration in seconds and am filled with hopelessness; the British, who ruled my country for decades and taught me the English that I speak, have always had the power to keep me out of their country.

Next to me the old Sikh man is crying silently. He smells of wood smoke and tobacco and reminds me of an uncle. The Bangladeshi family looks like an obscure branch of my own. A wave of solidarity washes through me, and I go from hopelessness to calm resignation. It feels right somehow to be sitting with these people. I belong here.

My fiancée tugs at my sleeve. The official is waving my passport at me. "I knew everything would be OK," my fiancée says, smiling a big, confident, American smile.

But I am angry. I don't want to enter the UK anymore. Let them keep their damn country. My place is here, with *my* people. I could sit on this bench all day with them.

But of course I don't. My fiancée is already walking away. I follow her and collect my passport, with its red entry stamp. At the exit doors I glance back at the bench and see the Bangladeshi family, glassy-eyed with fear, and the old Sikh man, still crying.

From the *Sun*, January 2010. Reprinted by the permission of the author.

From *The Sun*, January 2010. Reprinted by permission of the author.

Amin Ahmad was born in Calcutta, India; lived for a time in Boston; and now lives in Washington, DC. His work has appeared in *The Harvard Review*, *The New England Review*, *Narrative*, *The Sun*, and *Utne Reader*. As A. X. Ahmad, he published his first novel, *The Caretaker*, in 2013. This essay appeared in *The Sun* magazine (January 2010), which, according to its editors, "for more than 30 years has used personal essays, short stories, interviews, poetry, and photographs 'to invoke the splendor and heartache of being human.'" It was reprinted in *Utne Reader* (May–June 2010).

Reading and Discussion Questions

1. How and why are Ahmad and his fiancée treated differently at the airport?
2. With whom does he identify rather than with his fiancée?
3. Where does he mean he belongs when he says, "I belong here"?
4. What is ironic about the fiancée's statement "I knew everything would be okay"? Why does he specifically refer to her *American* smile?
5. What is Ahmad's argument?

Reading for Content and Structure

The next step in the critical reading process is comprehension — understanding what an author is trying to prove. Comprehending academic arguments can be difficult because they are often complex and often challenge accepted notions. Academic writing also sometimes assumes that readers already have a great deal of knowledge about a subject and therefore can require further research for comprehension.

Readers sometimes fail to comprehend a text they disagree with or that is new to them, especially in dealing with essays or books making controversial, value-laden arguments. Some research even shows that readers will sometimes remember only those parts of texts that match their points of view.[1] The study of argument does not require you to accept points of view you find morally or otherwise reprehensible, but to engage with these views, no matter how strange or repugnant they might seem, on your own terms.

Reading arguments critically requires you to at least temporarily suspend notions of absolute "right" and "wrong" and to intellectually inhabit gray areas that do not allow for simple "yes" and "no" answers. Of course, even in these areas, significant decisions about such things as ethics, values, politics, and the law must be made, and in studying argument you shouldn't fall into the trap of simple relativism: the idea that all answers to a given problem are equally correct at all times. We must make decisions about arguments with the understanding that reasonable people can disagree on the validity of ideas. Read others' arguments carefully, and consider how their ideas can contribute to or complicate your own. Remember Carl Rogers's approach (see Chapter 1) and look for common ground between your beliefs and those of the author. Also recognize that what appears to be a final solution will always be open to further

---

[1] See, for example, Patrick J. Slattery, "The Argumentative, Multiple-Source Paper: College Students Reading, Thinking, and Writing about Multiple Points of View," *Journal of Teaching Writing* 10, Fall/Winter 1991, pp. 181–99.

negotiation as new participants, new historical circumstances, and new ideologies become involved in the debate.

Working with the Text

Here are some suggestions about how to approach reading an argument. Remember: Your instructors will have considerations like these in mind when reading your written arguments, so they can help you with writing as well as reading an argument.

1. **Skim the reading for the main idea and overall structure.**
   - Are there subheadings or other divisions?
   - If it is a book, how are the chapters organized?
   - What is the claim or thesis statement that the piece is supporting? It will usually be in the first or second paragraph of an essay or in the introduction or first chapter of a book, but it may come at the end of the reading.

2. **Pay attention to topic sentences.** The topic sentence is usually the first sentence in a paragraph, but not always. It is the general statement that controls the details and examples in the paragraph.

3. **Don't overlook language signposts, usually transitional words and phrases:** *but, however, yet, nevertheless, moreover, for example, at first glance, more important, the first reason, next,* and so on.

4. **Consider any visuals** that are included with the text. Do they provide evidence to support the written argument? Do they set a mood or enhance the argument in other ways? (For help examining visuals, see Chapter 3.)

The best way to read a difficult text is with pen, pencil, and highlighter in hand. If it is an online text, it is worth printing a copy to hold the text in hand and mark it up. Scrolling from page to page on the computer screen does not let you see the structure of a piece as well as spreading the pages out in front of you does.

Strategies for Marking Up a Text

One purpose of annotating a text is to comprehend it more fully. Another is to prepare to write about it.

1. **If you use a highlighter as you read a text, use it sparingly.** You might consider a more targeted approach to highlighting, focusing only on thesis statements and topic sentences, for example.

2. **More useful: Make marginal notes,** perhaps underlining the portion of the text that each note refers to. Some of the most useful marginal notes will be those that summarize key ideas in your own words. Such paraphrases force you to understand the text well enough to reword its ideas, and reading the marginal notes is a quick way to review the text when you do not have time to reread all of it.

3. **Make notes on both what a piece of writing says and how it says it.** Notations about how a piece is written can focus on structural devices such as topic sentences, transitional words or phrases, and the repetition of ideas or sentence structure.

4. **Interrogate the text as you read.** Make note of surprising or interesting points, and don't be afraid to question or disagree with a point made by the author.

5. **Note similarities** that you see between the text you are reading and others you have read or between the text and your own experience.

READING ARGUMENT

Seeing Content and Structure

The following article has been annotated by a student reader to show its content and structure. After reading the article, answer the questions at the end.

A Tale of Two Airlines

CHRISTOPHER ELLIOTT

In travel, as in life, there are heroes and villains. There's good and evil. And there's Southwest Airlines and Spirit Airlines.

Sets up a clear comparison/contrast structure.

Both are no-frills discount carriers, and both are success stories in the economic sense. But that's where the similarities end.

Similarities exist, but he will focus on differences.

Spirit is known for its preponderance of fees, the risqué tone of some of its ads (as in the naughty "MILF" acronym for its "Many Islands, Low Fares" sale), and a take-it-or-leave-it attitude toward customer service. Southwest has a reputation for inclusive fares (one of the few airlines left that don't charge extra for a checked bag), a Texas-style hospitality (concerts on planes), and its famous customer-focused way.

A brief contrast sets up Spirit as the villain and Southwest as the hero.

A look at these airlines offers a window into the relationship between air carriers and their customers, revealing why the modern flying experience can be so infuriating.

Christopher Elliott is a consumer advocate for *National Geographic Traveler*, MSNBC, Tribune Media Services, and the *Washington Post*. He advocates for travelers through a weekly syndicated column, Travel Troubleshooter, and his column in *National Geographic Traveler*, The Insider. More recently he has begun applying his knowledge of customer-service disputes to a broader range of business-to-consumer transactions, not just travel-related ones. This article is from his Insider column in the December 2012/January 2013 issue of *National Geographic Traveler*.

Southwest:
Examples of
excellent customer
service

For Southwest — the Dallas carrier founded in 1971 — customer service   5
is part of its corporate DNA. Consider what happened to Robert Siegel. The
retired engineer and his wife, Ruth, were scheduled to fly from West Palm
Beach to Philadelphia when Ruth was diagnosed with lung cancer; her doctor
ordered her to cancel the trip. Even though the tickets were nonrefundable,
Siegel requested an exception. "Within one week, a complete credit had been
posted to my credit card," he says.

What's wrong
with that?

Southwest routinely waives its requirements in the interests of "Customer Service." (It also has an annoying habit of uppercasing key words, like
"People.") Several years ago, one of its pilots even held the plane for a passenger so that he could make his grandson's funeral. It doesn't punish customers
with ticket change fees or price its less restricted tickets so that only business
travelers on an expense account can afford them. It's not perfect, of course.
Southwest's prices can sometimes be significantly higher than the competition's. And its one-class service is too egalitarian for many business travelers.

Spirit: Customers
treated like cargo

Spirit Airlines styles itself as the anti-Southwest. The airline, based in the
suburbs of Fort Lauderdale, has its roots in the trucking business, which may
explain a lot: Its customers often complain that they are treated like cargo.
Seems Spirit wouldn't have it any other way.

Spirit often does the exact opposite of what Southwest would. When
Vietnam vet Jerry Meekins was told his esophageal cancer was terminal and
advised by his doctor to cancel his flight from Florida to Atlantic City, the
airline refused a refund request. Only after veterans groups intervened did the
carrier cave, and only reluctantly. In an effort to not set a precedent, CEO Ben
Baldanza said he personally would pay for the refund, not his airline.

Spirit has
many fees . . .

And Spirit does love fees. Fully one-third of its ticket revenue comes from
fees (compared with 7.5 percent for Southwest). Spirit argues that its passengers just crave low fares, and that all of the extras are optional. But some
passengers complain that the fees aren't adequately disclosed and that some
are ridiculous (a $100 charge to carry — that's right, carry — a bag on a plane
if you didn't prepay a lower fee online). Where Southwest's employees have a
reputation for being sociable, Spirit's can be on the surly side. Baldanza once

Wow!

inadvertently replied directly by e-mail to a passenger this way: "Let him tell
the world how bad we are. He's never flown us before anyway and will be back
when we save him a penny."

. . . but the fares are
low.

Baldanza has a point, and it's one that drives consumers (and consumer   10
advocates) crazy: If you can navigate the maze of fees, restrictions, and Spirit's
$9 Fare Club ($60 per year, with automatic reenrollment whether you fly or
not), you can travel for impressively low fares. And stockholders love their

shares of SAVE (Spirit's ticker symbol) about as much as they do Southwest's (aptly, LUV).

    I'd say Spirit enjoys playing the villain as much as Southwest likes being the hero. Spirit certainly hasn't suffered for it financially. These two airlines represent one of travel's most enduring paradoxes: that companies offering poor customer service can succeed as well as those offering good customer service. Spirit's success defies an easy explanation, unless you have a degree in psychology. Spirit taps into the very human need to snag a deal. But understanding what makes us tick and the way we can be manipulated points to a better future for every traveler. See, Southwest and Spirit are not the only examples of travel's curious yin and yang. Whether you're staying at a hotel, renting a car, or taking a cruise, you've faced the same kinds of choices between companies. At the beginning of 2013, many of these companies find themselves at a crossroads, wondering which path to take: the embrace of a LUV or the thriftiness of a SAVE. Both clearly work in the short term. But Southwest operates on the principle that, eventually, customers will catch on.

Each airline likes its role.

    Then again, maybe not. If people continue to fall for the ultralow, lots-of-strings-attached rates, then the treatment of passengers like cargo might continue indefinitely. Travelers must consider more than the price when they book their ticket or make arrangements to take a cruise or rent a car. They have to take a company's service reputation into account, too. <u>Reward the heroes of the travel industry with your business. Otherwise, the villains win.</u>

Customers have a choice.

Thesis statement

Reading and Discussion Questions

1. The essay is a contrast between the two airlines. What specific aspects of the two does Elliott contrast?
2. What thesis or claim is Elliott supporting? What point does he make beyond the ways in which the two airlines differ? Is his essay based on a claim of fact, value, or policy?
3. What types of support does Elliott offer?

Summarizing

One skill required by the Rogerian approach to communication is the ability to summarize another's ideas fairly and objectively, just as in more confrontational forms of argumentation a writer or speaker cannot build a successful case on a misunderstanding or misinterpretation of an opponent's position. At least, such a case will not hold up under careful scrutiny. The ability to summarize is also a basic research skill used in writing research papers, as discussed in Chapter 11. Summarizing is the cornerstone on which all other critical reading and writing tasks are built.

RESEARCH SKILL ▶ Summarizing

When summarizing long or difficult texts, try some of the following strategies to help you comprehend the essential points of the text.

1. **Reread the introduction and conclusion after you have read the text once or twice.** These two sections should complement each other and offer clues to the most significant issues of the text.

2. **For a difficult text, you may want to list all the subheadings (if they are used) or the topic sentence of each paragraph.** These significant guideposts will map the piece as a whole: What do they tell you about the central ideas and the main argument the author is making?

3. **Remember that when you summarize, you must put another's words into your own (and cite the original text as well),** so do not simply let a list of the subheadings or chapter titles stand as your summary. They likely won't make sense when put together in paragraph form, but they will provide you with valuable ideas regarding the central points of the text.

4. **Remember that summarizing also requires attention to overall meanings and not only to specific details.** Therefore, avoid including many specific examples or concrete details from the text you are summarizing, and try to let your reader know what these examples and details add up to. As you write the summary, remember that it should
   - be shorter than the original
   - be objective instead of stating opinions
   - identify the author and the work
   - use present tense
   - summarize the main points of the whole work or passage, not just part of it.

A summary can be either referential or rhetorical. A **referential summary** focuses on an author's ideas about the subject. A **rhetorical summary** summarizes the text in terms of rhetorical or structural choices the author made. (See Chapter 1 for a full discussion of the rhetorical approach.) The following examples are summaries of the article on page 41.

Referential (Content) Summary

According to Christopher Elliott in his article "A Tale of Two Airlines," both Southwest Airlines and Spirit Airlines are successful discount carriers, but where Spirit is a "villain," Southwest is a "hero." Where Spirit has lots of fees, risqué ads, and poor customer service, Southwest does not charge extra for checked bags, is welcoming, and takes pride in its famous customer service, even waiving its own regulations in special circumstances to help a customer. Spirit originated as a trucking line and still treats customers "like cargo." Each airline seems to like the role it plays. A customer can save money flying Spirit because of its low fares, but as long as fliers are willing to be treated like cargo to save money, they will be rewarding the villains instead of the heroes of the travel industry.

Strategies for Writing Rhetorical Summaries

These approaches are not mutually exclusive, so you may get some repetition in the answers to questions like the following; but overall, the questions provide a means of discovering what to say about an author's rhetorical strategies. Not every question will apply to every reading.

Aristotelian Rhetoric

- Does the author make use of examples?
- Does he make use of deductive reasoning, showing how a generalization applies to a specific case?
- Does he make use of logical appeal? emotional appeal? appeal based on his own credibility? a combination of these types of appeal?

Rogerian Argument

- Does the author sum up an opposing point of view fairly and accurately?
- Does she attempt to establish common ground between conflicting positions?
- Does she present a compromise between the competing positions?

The Toulmin Model

- Does the author support a claim of fact? a claim of value? a claim of policy?
- Does he support his claim with facts? with statistics?
- Does he support his claim with appeals to the needs and values of his audience?
- Does he support his claim with expert opinion?

Rhetorical (Structure) Summary

In his article "A Tale of Two Airlines," Christopher Elliott *contrasts* two airlines: Southwest and Spirit. He *points out* that both are successful airlines, but then *focuses* on how the two differ in fees, tone, and customer service. Elliott *provides examples* of how Southwest goes out of its way to provide excellent customer service, even waiving its own regulations in exceptional circumstances while Spirit refuses to make exceptions. Elliott *explains* that Spirit's treatment of its customers reflects its origins as a trucking business. He *warns* that as long as customers reward Spirit by choosing its low fares in spite of its bad customer service, the villains in the world of commercial airlines will win.

READING ARGUMENT

Practice: Summarizing

The following article has been annotated to show major rhetorical approaches the author employed. Read it, and then answer the questions that appear at the end of the article.

Gun Debate: Where Is the Middle Ground?

MALLORY SIMON

Opening example

Amardeep Kaleka will never forget the moment when his father laid on the ground and prayed.

Satwant Singh Kaleka had been shot five times while wrestling a gunman in a Sikh temple in Oak Creek, Wisconsin. His turban was knocked off, and two kids and a priest crawled up beside him. Together, they prayed.

Amardeep Kaleka went to the temple and stared at that spot.

His father did not survive. He died along with five others.

"It felt like he was praying and putting something into the zeitgeist and imprinting it," he told CNN. His son hoped it would lead to a changing tide on gun violence.   5

Emotional appeal

As he began his meditation that day, Amardeep made a vow: He would do whatever he could to ensure nobody ever went through what his family had.

"It just came over me that you can't stay silent," he said. "You can't continue to allow violence like this to happen haphazardly at a church, at a school, any place."

That was August 2012.

Related example

Four months later, 20 children and six adults were gunned down in Newtown, Connecticut.

That school massacre has led many people, including Kaleka, 33, to question where we go from here as a country. Or if we will ever get there at all.   10

It led him to stand up at a gathering here on Thursday, CNN's *Guns Under Fire: An AC360° Town Hall Special*, and ask a panel of advocates with polar opposite views if they could agree on anything. If there was actually any middle ground.

Looking for common ground

"After meeting with so many senators, so many gun proponents and gun control advocates, it seems like they're recycling the same jargon all the time," he said, explaining his reason for the question. "So I was just hoping, let's get to the common ground."

The panel included National Rifle Association board members, the president of the Brady Campaign to End Gun Violence, law enforcement representatives, and other participants voicing viewpoints across the spectrum.

Was there a consensus?

Mallory Simon is a writer and senior producer of online presentations for CNN. This piece appeared on cnn.com on January 31, 2013.

15   Sort of.

      "There's a lot of common ground," Sandra Froman, a member of the NRA board of directors and a former president of the group, said at the town hall. "We don't want people who are insane to have guns, we don't want terrorists to have guns. Part of this national dialogue is coming together." Expert representing
one position: There
is common ground.

      So everyone agreed: Something has to happen. The devil is in the details. Common ground

      "I think the common ground clearly exists from a policy standpoint when talking about background checks," said Dan Gross, president of the Brady Campaign to End Gun Violence. Expert representing
another position: There
is common ground.

      But it isn't that simple. It never is when it comes to gun control.

20   "The NRA is not against background checks," Froman said. "We support making sure they are enforced. We're not supporting more background checks of law-abiding citizens."

      Her remarks signaled a slight change in the NRA's stance.

      In a heated back and forth, the two debated whether it was truly harmful to force everyone who wants to purchase a gun — whether at a gun store, a gun show, or in a private sale — to go through a background check.

      Froman talked about how the current background check system was broken, noting that an "instant check" in Colorado can actually take about 10 days. Example

      "We have to get it working before we add any more checks," she said, noting that requiring everyone to undergo a check would take a lot of resources and money. Logical appeal

25   Philadelphia Police Commissioner Charles Ramsey spoke from his experience, saying whatever it took, whatever the price tag, it would be worth it to stem the violence. Expert opinion

      "Please, don't worry about the cost. I'll spend the money," he said, a line that drew massive applause from the crowd at George Washington University. "It's a much greater cost than human lives. We have to do something. The status quo is not acceptable." Appeal to the need for security

      When Kaleka, the son of one of the Sikh shooting victims, rose to ask his question about finding a middle ground, he wasn't just talking about policy. He also meant in our collective way of thinking. A filmmaker, Kaleka has made a documentary about violence in America. There are too many facets to the problem, he says.

      "It's a culture of violence. And that has to do with guns, that has to do with mental illness, it has to do with stigmatizing people, it has to do with the media, everything about our culture." Deductive reasoning

      Many appeared to think he was right.

"Everybody's got to step up on this," Ramsey said. "That's prosecutors, the   30
courts, everyone. If we're serious about this it can't just be a series of laws that
are passed."

Much of the discussion inside the town hall went beyond politics and
legislation. One heated debate focused on whether armed guards should be
posted at schools.

That's a proposal that's been discussed by former congressman Asa
Hutchinson.

Emotional appeal/appeal to needs and values

"What is more important than the education and the safety of those children?" he asked, noting that if malls have armed security, so should schools. "I
believe an armed security presence is very important."

It's an idea that Veronique Pozner thinks about. Her son Noah was killed
in the shooting at Sandy Hook Elementary in Newtown.

Example

"I think there might be a certain power in deterrence," she said. "In the   35
case of Newtown, it's clear that the perpetrator did choose the path of least
resistance, the most vulnerable defenseless victims. He didn't head for the high
school where he could have been tackled."

Appeal to need for security

While she said she wasn't sure an armed guard would have saved her son, she
did say it made her feel more comfortable dropping off her other children at the
new school for Sandy Hook children, a building that does have armed guards.

Colin Goddard, who survived the Virginia Tech shooting, said he understood the desire to protect children, but he didn't understand why arming
guards is the go-to solution.

Logical appeal

"I just don't understand why the first idea put forth is something that
might help at the last second," he said, to massive applause from the audience.
"We can do things in advance to keep a dangerous person and a gun from
coming together in the first place."

Deductive reasoning

That's the conversation that usually leads to a debate about mental health.
It is an area President Barack Obama has pledged resources to; he and many
others hope to keep guns out of the hands of the mentally ill.

The difficulty comes in figuring out who poses a threat.   40

Expert opinion

"We look at behavior and what's going on in the person's life, the social
dynamics and what are the personality issues that make that person think
acting out dangerously is a way to handle their problems," said Mary Ellen
O'Toole, a former FBI special agent and criminal profiler.

A possible compromise

Froman, the NRA board member, said she'd like to see more sharing of
resources to ensure a database of the mentally ill would prevent them from
having access to guns.

But Liza Long, whose blog post *I Am Adam Lanza's Mom* went viral after the Newtown shooting, said perhaps we were thinking about this all wrong. What if it wasn't just about identifying threats, but actually making a change.

"We spend a lot of time talking about keeping guns out of the wrong hands," she said. "What if we could put those resources to making people less dangerous."

45   For Kaleka, at the end of the day, progress on enforcing background checks would be a step in the right direction.

> A positive move that different sides might agree on

He recognizes that no solution will make everyone happy. But he wishes every advocate, no matter their point of view, would think about the issue as if they were in his shoes.

"When you are a survivor or a victim or someone close to you dies, it's everyday you think about it," he said. "Gun advocates or scholars or people making money about it, they probably think about it 10 percent of how much we think about it. We go to the bathroom and think about it. We take a cold shower one day, and we start to cry. We wake up in the middle of the night with night sweats, and we have to live with it. Every breath is taken with some thought of violence and safety."

> Emotional appeal, *pathos* (appeal based on Kaleka's credibility)

He thinks it is time the country does the same: that its citizens think about the issue with every breath.

"I can never go another moment in my life without thinking about it. My wife, my brother, my mother, the people of Newtown, they will not go a moment for the rest of their life without thinking about it," he said. "Personally I think the tide is changing, the zeitgeist is moving towards justice. Hopefully, once we stop the fear mongering on both sides we can finally get to the point of what makes sense."

> Need to work toward common ground

50   His greatest hope: That the will to do something about the violence does not die along with those who never had to.

> Emotional appeal

Reading and Discussion Questions

1. Which of the three approaches to argument — Aristotelian rhetoric, Rogerian argument, or the Toulmin Model — seems the one best suited to use in discussing this particular essay? Why?

2. Is there information about the essay that you got from the other two approaches that complements what you learned through that primary approach? that contradicts it?

Writing Assignments

1. Use what you learned from the annotations on "Gun Debate: Where Is the Middle Ground?" to write a one-paragraph rhetorical summary of the essay. Remember that a rhetorical summary focuses on choices that the author made, not just on the ideas.

2. Write a one-paragraph referential summary of the essay, focusing on content rather than rhetorical choice.

Practice: Summarizing

Read and annotate the following article, using the Christopher Elliot article on pages 41–43 and the Mallory Simon article on pages 46–49 as models. Then answer the questions that appear at the end of the article.

The Gay Option
STEPHANIE FAIRYINGTON

I came out to my mother in a letter. I was 28. "I was born this way," I wrote, following with the most shattering high note of self-loathing I can think of: "If there were a straight pill," I lamented, "I'd swallow it faster than you can say the word *gay*."

I didn't mean either of these things. I said them because I knew they would elicit pity and absolve my mother of the belief that her parenting was to blame for my same-sex attractions. It worked. Five years later, my mother continues to talk about my lesbianism as if it were a genetic defect like Down syndrome — a parallel she's actually drawn — because clearly, in her mind, no one would choose such a detestable and challenging state of being.

This is not a message I'm proud to have sent. Contrary to how I actually feel about my sexuality, it suggests that I'm drowning in a sea of self-disgust, desperately grasping for a heterosexual lifeboat to sail my way out of it. But would my mother have been as sympathetic and tolerant if she thought I had a choice in the matter?

Would conservative allies support us if they believed we could help it?

If the answer is no, and I believe it is, what does it say about our self-worth and status in society if we, as gay people, must practice a politics of pity to secure our place in the world? It says, for one, that we don't have a place at the table. It says that we are tolerated, but not accepted. It says, ultimately, that it's time to change our rhetoric.

Until homosexuality is cast and understood as a valid choice, rather than a biological affliction, we will never rise above our current status. We will remain Mother Nature's mistake, tolerable (to some) because our condition is her fault, not ours.

By choice, I don't mean that one can choose one's sexual propensities any more than one can

5

Stephanie Fairyington is the cofounder and editor of *The Slant* and a freelance journalist in New York. A version of this article appeared in the Winter 2010 issue of *Dissent* as "Choice as Strategy: Homosexuality and the Politics of Pity"; the excerpt here appeared in *Utne Reader*, May–June 2010.

choose one's personality. What I mean is that it's a choice to act on every desire we have, and that acting on our same-sex attractions is just as valid as pursuing a passion for the Christian faith or Judaism or any other spiritual, intellectual, emotional, or physical craving that does not infringe on the rights of others. And it should be respected as such.

As a firm Kinsey 6 — with 6 being the gayest ranking on sexologist Alfred Kinsey's 1-to-6 scale of sexual orientation — I understand the resistance to putting *choice* and *homosexuality* in the same sentence. My same-sex attractions were awakened in me at such a young age that they felt as much a part of me as my limbs. In the late 1990s, when I was coming out, had someone told me that I had chosen my deepest, most tender and passionate affections, it would have been like telling me that I had chosen the arms and legs I have.

But I have plenty of desires, like throwing my fists in the faces of conservative Republicans, which for one reason or another, I don't act on; my desire for women is not one of them. Biology is not destiny, and I am the architect of my own life, as is everyone. My point is not to challenge or even enter the debate about whether or not some combination of nature and nurture contributes to the formation of an inclination toward one's own sex. My point is that most inquiries into the origins of homosexuality are suspect, and their service to us is limited, if not perilous.

A politics of *choice* would be one that regards same-sex desire enough to announce it as a conscious decision rather than a predetermined abnormality. No matter how bumpy the ride or long the journey, *choice* as a political strategy is the only ride out of Freaksville.

Forty years ago, gay activists had a similar view, taking their cues from radical lesbian feminists who believed that heterosexuality and homosexuality were products of culture, not nature. "In the absence of oppression and social control," writes historian John D'Emilio, gay liberationists believed that "sexuality would be polymorphous"— fluid, in other words. Back then they talked about "sexual preference," which implies choice, as opposed to "sexual orientation," which does not.

It wasn't until the 1970s that the mental health establishment and its gay allies put forth the view that homosexuality is a permanent psychological condition and debunked the notion that it was a mental illness in need of a cure. Then came the 1980s and 1990s and a slew of shoddy and inconclusive scientific research on the biological origins of gayness, reinforcing the belief that sexuality is predestined. Both psychological and medical discourses formed today's dominant paradigm, which insists that sexuality is inborn and immutable.

The LGBT activists who have helped construct this sexual framework are neither lazy nor naive in their thinking, as D'Emilio points out in his essay "Born Gay?," a crisp case against the politics of biological determinism. As a political strategy, it has helped reap enormous benefits, from antidiscrimination legislation to adoption rights in some states and civil unions in others. The reasons this model of sexuality is politically expedient and effective are threefold.

First, if sexuality is understood as predestined and therefore fixed, it poses less of a challenge to the hetero monolith than does a shifting spectrum of desire. It protects straight people, in other words, from the threat of homosexuality. Second, by presenting homosexuality as a biological fact as firm and absolute as race or sex, gay activists have formed an identity the law can recognize and can follow in the footsteps of civil rights legislation. Third, it's conceptually easier to understand sexuality as a permanent trait rather than the complex, ever-morphing mess that it often is.

But for all the success this politics has had, in the end, it's not only shortsighted but rife with limitations—and dangers. As lesbian activist Joan Nestle told me, it's not good politics to cling to the "born gay" edict because "the use of biological 'abnormalities' was used by the Nazis when they measured the nostril thickness of imprisoned Jews to prove they were an inferior race; and when colonizers measured the brains of Africans to make a case for their enslavement; and when doctors at the turn of the century used the argument that the light weight of women's brains proved their inferiority to men. I do not want to enter into this sad history of biological dehumanization as the basis for gay rights."

15   All the studies that gay sympathizers and activists invoke to justify our right to same-sex love cast homosexuality as a loud hiccup at the dinner table of normality. As such, we're put on par with other undesirable deviations from nature's norm, taunting eugenics with the keys to eliminating us. This is the ugly underbelly of our biology-centered claims to human rights.

The typical conservative assault on homosexuality casts it as a sinful choice that can be unchosen through a commitment to God and reparative therapy. And the left usually slams into this simplistic polemic by taking up the opposite stance: Homosexuality is not a choice, and because we can't help it, it's not sinful.

By affirming that homosexual practice and identity *are* a choice, we can attach an addendum—it's a good choice—and open the possibility of a more nuanced argument, one that dismantles the logic of the very premise that whom we choose to love marks us as sinful and immoral and interrogates the assumption that heterosexuality is somehow better for the individual and society as a whole.

In my conservative Republican family, signs already point to a kind of readiness to engage homosexuality as a legitimate decision. Recently, I called my mother in California to throw out my "born-gay-pity-me" garbage. She didn't swallow my pill of choice with ease, but managed to cough up an exasperated, "Well, whatever makes you happy." That's one down and a nation to go.

Reading and Discussion Questions

1. At the beginning of paragraph 2, Fairyington says, "I didn't mean either of these things." To what two things is she referring? How does that relate to her title?

2. Five years later, how does she feel about the way she came out to her mother?

3. What does she mean when she says that homosexuality should be "cast and understood as a valid choice" (para. 5)? Isn't current thought that homosexuality is not a choice?

4. What two views of homosexuality is Fairyington contrasting? Where does she best sum up the contrast? Is the essay primarily a comparison and contrast essay?

5. Analyze the places in the essay where Fairyington discusses sexuality in political terms. What point is she trying to make?

Writing Assignments

1. Write a one-paragraph rhetorical summary of "The Gay Option."
2. Write a one-paragraph referential summary of the essay.

Evaluation

An **evaluation** builds on a summary by incorporating not only the argument's main point but also the reader's reaction to it. In Chapter 4 we will look more closely at how to build an effective response to an argument; in this section we will briefly consider how to read not just with an ear for comprehension but also with a critical eye. Your overall goal is to make a careful judgment of the extent to which an argument has succeeded in making a point.

When you set out to evaluate a work, keep two points in mind:

- An argument that you disagree with is not necessarily wrong.
- An argument written by a published author or so-called expert is not necessarily right.

Critically evaluating an argument means not simply reading a text and agreeing or disagreeing with it, but doing serious analytical work that addresses multiple viewpoints before deciding on the argument's effectiveness.

Strategies for Evaluating Arguments

1. **Disagree with the author if you feel confident of the support for your view,** but first read the whole argument to see if your questions have been answered. Be cautious about concluding that the author hasn't proved his or her point.

2. **Talk about the material with classmates or others** who have read it, especially those who have responded to the text differently than you did. Consider their points of view. Defending or modifying your evaluation may mean going back to the text and finding clues that you may have overlooked.

3. **Consider the strengths of the argument,** and examine the useful methods of argumentation, the points that are successfully made (and those which help the reader to better understand the argument), and what makes sense about the author's argument.

continued

4. **Consider the weaknesses of the argument,** and locate instances of faulty reasoning, unsupported statements, and the limitations of the author's assumptions about the world (the warrants that underlie the argument).

5. **Consider how effective the title of the reading is** and whether it accurately sums up a critical point of the essay. Come up with an alternative title that would suit the reading better, and be prepared to defend this alternative title.

6. **Evaluate the organizational structure of the essay.** The author should lead you from idea to idea in a logical progression, and each section should relate to the ones before and after it and to the central argument in significant ways. Determine whether the writer could have organized things more clearly, logically, or efficiently.

7. **Notice how the author follows through on the main claim, or thesis, of the argument.** The author should stick with this thesis and not waver throughout the text. If the thesis does waver, there could be a reason for the shift in the argument, or perhaps the author is being inconsistent. The conclusion should drive home the central argument.

8. **Evaluate the vocabulary and style the author uses.** Is it too simple or complicated? Are key terms and concepts defined? When considering style and vocabulary, keep in mind the audience the author was initially writing for.

ARGUMENT ESSENTIALS
Examining Written Arguments

The following steps will help you understand any written argument.

1. **Preread the article** to gain background information on the title, author, purpose, and audience.

2. **Read the article for content and structure.**
   - Pay attention to the organization and how the argument is shaped.
   - Read actively: Mark up the text and ask questions as you read.
   - Look for visuals that may enhance the argument.
   - Summarize the main point of the argument in your own words.
   - Referential summaries focus on content.
   - Rhetorical summaries focus on strategy.

3. **Evaluate the argument's effectiveness.**
   - Keep an open mind to opposing views.
   - Objectively consider the argument's strengths and weaknesses.
   - Consider the appropriateness of the title.
   - Determine how effective the argument's organization is.
   - Decide how well the argument supports its main claim or thesis.
   - Evaluate the use of language and the definitions of key terms.

READING ARGUMENT

Seeing Evaluation

The following article has been annotated by a student reader to demonstrate
reading for content and structure as well as critical evaluation. The article is followed by a student response essay.

The Internet Is a Surveillance State
BRUCE SCHNEIER

I'm going to start with three data points.

One: Some of the Chinese military hackers who were implicated in a
broad set of attacks against the U.S. government and corporations were identified because they accessed Facebook from the same network infrastructure
they used to carry out their attacks.

Two: Hector Monsegur, one of the leaders of the LulzSac hacker movement, was identified and arrested last year by the FBI. Although he practiced
good computer security and used an anonymous relay service to protect his
identity, he slipped up.

> Examples: All 3 got caught because of the Internet. But isn't this a good thing?

And three: Paula Broadwell, who had an affair with CIA director David
Petraeus, similarly took extensive precautions to hide her identity. She never
logged in to her anonymous e-mail service from her home network. Instead,
she used hotel and other public networks when she e-mailed him. The FBI
correlated hotel registration data from several different hotels — and hers was
the common name.

5   The Internet is a surveillance state. Whether we admit it to ourselves or
not, and whether we like it or not, we're being tracked all the time. Google
tracks us, both on its pages and on other pages it has access to. Facebook does
the same; it even tracks non-Facebook users. Apple tracks us on our iPhones
and iPads. One reporter used a tool called Collusion to track who was tracking
him; 105 companies tracked his Internet use during one 36-hour period.

> Thesis *
>
> Examples

Increasingly, what we do on the Internet is being combined with other
data about us. Unmasking Broadwell's identity involved correlating her Internet activity with her hotel stays. Everything we do now involves computers,
and computers produce data as a natural by-product. Everything is now being

> Topic sentence
>
> Internet activity is combined with other sources.

Bruce Schneier is a security technologist and author of *Liars and Outliers: Enabling the Trust Society Needs to Survive* (2012). This article appeared on cnn.com on March 16, 2013.

saved and correlated, and many big-data companies make money by building up intimate profiles of our lives from a variety of sources.

Facebook, for example, correlates your online behavior with your purchasing habits offline. And there's more. There's location data from your cell phone, there's a record of your movements from closed-circuit TVs.

This is ubiquitous surveillance: All of us being watched, all the time, and that data being stored forever. This is what a surveillance state looks like, and it's efficient beyond the wildest dreams of George Orwell.

Sure, we can take measures to prevent this. We can limit what we search on Google from our iPhones, and instead use computer web browsers that allow us to delete cookies. We can use an alias on Facebook. We can turn our cell phones off and spend cash. But increasingly, none of it matters.

There are simply too many ways to be tracked. The Internet, e-mail, cell phones, web browsers, social networking sites, search engines: these have become necessities, and it's fanciful to expect people to simply refuse to use them just because they don't like the spying, especially since the full extent of such spying is deliberately hidden from us and there are few alternatives being marketed by companies that don't spy.

This isn't something the free market can fix. We consumers have no choice in the matter. All the major companies that provide us with Internet services are interested in tracking us. Visit a website and it will almost certainly know who you are; there are lots of ways to be tracked without cookies. Cellphone companies routinely undo the web's privacy protection. One experiment at Carnegie Mellon took real-time videos of students on campus and was able to identify one-third of them by comparing their photos with publicly available tagged Facebook photos.

Maintaining privacy on the Internet is nearly impossible. If you forget even once to enable your protections, or click on the wrong link, or type the wrong thing, you've permanently attached your name to whatever anonymous service you're using. Monsegur slipped up once, and the FBI got him. If the director of the CIA can't maintain his privacy on the Internet, we've got no hope.

In today's world, governments and corporations are working together to keep things that way. Governments are happy to use the data corporations collect — occasionally demanding that they collect more and save it longer — to spy on us. And corporations are happy to buy data from governments. Together the powerful spy on the powerless, and they're not going to give up their positions of power, despite what the people want.

10

(margin annotations)

Repeats thesis
Reference to *1984*
Topic sentence:
Counter measures

But (transition):
They don't work.

Topic sentence

Examples

Topic sentence

Example

Topic sentence

What *do* the people want?

Fixing this requires strong government will, but they're just as <u>punch-drunk</u> on data as the corporations. <u>Slap-on-the-wrist</u> fines notwithstanding, no one is agitating for better privacy laws.

Language a bit over-the-top? Exaggeration?

15   <u>So, we're done.</u> Welcome to a world where Google knows exactly what sort of porn you all like, and more about your interests than your spouse does. Welcome to a world where your cell phone company knows exactly where you are all the time. Welcome to the end of private conversations, because increasingly your conversations are conducted by e-mail, text, or social networking sites.

And welcome to a world where all of this, and everything else that you do or is done on a computer, is saved, correlated, studied, passed around from company to company without your knowledge or consent; and where the government accesses it at will without a warrant.

Argument assumes that data mining is a bad thing — is it? And we have hardly fought against it.

Welcome to an Internet without privacy, and we've ended up here with hardly a fight.

Giving Up Our Privacy: Is It Worth It?
WHITNEY CRAMER

Whitney Cramer
ENGL 203-017
Dr. Winchell
September 17, 2012

Giving Up Our Privacy: Is It Worth It?

The Internet is many things to many people. It provides a quick way to find information, an easy way to shop from the comfort of home or dorm room, and a way to stay in touch with friends and family. Most of us would probably not think of the Internet as a means of surveillance — that is, until we read Bruce Schneier's essay "The Internet Is a Surveillance State," posted to cnn.com on March 16, 2013. Primarily through his use of examples, Schneier builds a convincing case that by using the Internet, we have given up our privacy without even a fight, but he fails to acknowledge what some of his other examples reveal: that there are times when we *want* the Internet to be a surveillance state.

Schneier opens his essay with examples of three people who have been caught in indiscretions at least and in crimes at most by means of the Internet. Chinese hackers who targeted the American government and corporations were caught because they accessed Facebook on the same network. Hector Monsegur, another hacker, was caught by the FBI when he made one mistake and revealed his identity. Paula Broadwell's affair with the director of the CIA was discovered because she emailed him using public networks. But aren't these exactly the types of crimes and indiscretions that we should want revealed? Schneier writes, "If the director of the CIA can't maintain his privacy on the Internet, we've got no hope" (56). But do we want the director of the CIA to use his Internet privacy to hide his wrongdoing?

Part of the reason we have no hope is that governments and corporations have joined forces to track us. Schneier cites Google, Apple, and Facebook as examples of companies that track users. Facebook, for example, combines what it knows about your online activity with information about your offline buying habits. Governments use what corporations collect, and corporations use what the government collects, for a price. Perhaps most unsettling, cell phones and closed-circuit TV's can be used to track your movements. Big Brother knows where you are and what you are doing (Schneier 56).

Schneier gives examples of things we can do to protect our privacy, but he admits that none of them matter. We could turn off our cell phones and our computers, but we have become so used to them that we would rather give up our privacy than give up our electronics. We could limit what we search, use aliases, and use cash rather than credit, but since the spying is not obvious, it is easy to ignore. And there is the other side of the issue — the good that Internet surveillance does. In spite of his opening examples, Schneier fails to acknowledge that for those who are doing no wrong, Internet surveillance may be annoying, but it may be worth the loss of privacy to protect the innocent against those who use the Internet to commit crimes.

Work Cited

Schneier, Bruce. "The Internet Is a Surveillance State." *cnn.com*. Cable News Network, 16 Mar. 2013. Rpt. in *Elements of Argument: A Text and Reader*. 11th ed. Annette T. Rottenberg and Donna Haisty Winchell. Boston: Bedford, 2014. 55–57. Print.

Assignments for Examining Written Arguments

Reading and Discussion Questions

1. The chapter opens with some examples of bumper stickers as argument. What are some bumper stickers that you have seen, and what points were they making?

2. Protest signs also make arguments in just a few words. What examples have you seen? You can find numerous examples on *Google* or *Flickr*.

3. Where an essay or an image is published can, in itself, make a statement. Are you aware of certain publications that have a political bias? Consider how even advertisements are geared for the target audience of any given magazine. Locate two ads for the same product or type of product but published in different magazines. How are the ads targeted to the different target audiences?

4. Where do you in your daily life read written arguments? Where in newspapers, for example, are arguments published? Where do you find them online?

5. Locate a print or online editorial. Use what you have learned in this chapter to examine it for content, structure, and rhetorical strategies.

Writing Suggestions

1. Choose a print or online editorial, and write an essay analyzing the author's rhetorical strategies.

2. Choose two editorials or argumentative essays on different sides of the same issue and write an essay comparing the authors' rhetorical strategies.

RESEARCH ASSIGNMENT ▶ **Summarizing**

Do a database search to find a long magazine or journal article (at least 1,200 words) on a topic that interests you: sports, politics, the environment, entertainment, education, or the like.

1. Use the advice in this chapter to preread and then read the article. If possible, print it out and mark up the text.

2. On a separate sheet of paper, list each of the article's subheadings or main ideas, and then summarize each section's point in your own words.

3. Follow the Research Skill box on page 44 and the Strategy box on page 45 to write a paragraph that briefly and objectively summarizes the article. Your paragraph may be either referential (p. 44) or rhetorical (p. 45) — you should be able to identify which type of summary you are writing and explain what makes it so.

bits

To see what you are learning about argumentation applied to the latest world and national news, read our *Bits* blog, "Argument and the Headlines," at **blogs.bedfordstmartins.com/bits**.

Examining Multimodal Arguments

Of course, not all public arguments are written. In addition to the critical reading skills discussed in Chapter 2, special scrutiny is needed when listening to and viewing arguments in other media. We use the term **multimodal** in the title of this chapter because now we turn to arguments that use words in combination with another medium or that use a mode other than the printed word to get a message across — pictures, audio, video, and digital media.

Visual Rhetoric

In examining written arguments, we used three steps to help uncover the essential elements of claim, support, and warrant:

- Prereading
- Reading for content and structure
- Evaluation

The same general principles apply in looking at visual rhetoric, but we will change them a bit. With the visual, structure is more closely related to rhetorical strategy than to content, so we have broken that one step into two.

- **Prereading.** With a visual, prereading includes noticing who took or otherwise created the picture or graphic, but often more important are the context and purpose. It may also be relevant where the visual was published, if it was, and when. Print ads, especially, are targeted for a particular audience. The same ad, in different versions, often appears in different publications. With a political cartoon, the political context is critical to understanding the humor. Graphics are meant to convey information about a particular issue.

- **Reading for content.** To "read" a visual means to see what is there — pictures and text. Published images are usually carefully planned to convey a message by means of who or what is shown.
- **Reading for rhetorical strategies.** As a viewer, consider the composition of the visual. Why did the photographer place things where he or she did? Why are some objects in sharp focus and others not? Why, in an ad, is the text a certain size and placed in a certain location? How does the eye move about the ad? Why is the logo where it is? the product? In a cartoon, what does the physical appearance suggest about the characters? In a graphic, what data are being highlighted?
- **Evaluation.** Consider how effective the visual is in achieving its purpose. How does a photograph make you feel? Does an ad make you want to purchase a product? Does the cartoon make you consider a new perspective? Does a graphic aid your understanding of a complex issue?

Not every visual image makes a statement or presents an argument. Some, however, do so in a way that the printed word alone cannot. If an image arouses emotion in you or brings to mind a controversial issue, it is making some kind of statement to you. What statement, for example, does Figure 3.1 make to you?

The reading strategies given above are general guidelines for all visuals. The following pages discuss additional considerations for specific types of visuals: photographs, print advertisements, political cartoons, and graphics.

Photographs

You've probably seen powerful still images in photographic journalism: soldiers in battle, destruction by weather disasters, beautiful natural landscapes, inhumane living conditions, the great mushroom clouds of early atomic explosions. These photographs and thousands of others encapsulate arguments of fact, value, and policy: *The tornado devastated the town. The Grand Canyon is our most stupendous national monument. We must not allow human beings to live like this.* Sometimes captions are used to help get the photograph's message across.

FIGURE 3.1 Homeless Family. Bruce Ayres/Getty Images

READING ARGUMENT

Examining Photographs

The next two pictures gained wide circulation in the aftermath of Hurricane Katrina in 2005. They seemed innocuous enough when seen without commentary, except to show the extent of the flooding. The text accompanying the pictures, however, shows the bias of those who described the pictures. The wording produced such a response that *Yahoo!* offered this statement:

> Yahoo! News regrets that these photos and captions, viewed together, may have suggested a racial bias on our part. We remain committed to bringing our readers the full collection of photos as transmitted by our wire service partners.[1]

Looting
DAVE MARTIN

A young man walks through chest-deep water after looting a grocery store in New Orleans on Tuesday, August 30, 2005. AP Photo/Dave Martin

[1] The Yahoo! News statement can be found at http://news.yahoo.com/page/photostatement.

Finding
CHRIS GRAYTHEN

Two residents wade through chest-deep flood water after finding bread and soda from a local grocery store after Hurricane Katrina came through New Orleans, Louisiana. Chris Graythen/Getty Images

Practice: Examining Photographs

Look at the images that follow on pages 65–68, and then answer the questions on pages 68–70.

Milvertha Hendricks, 84, Waiting in the Rain outside the New Orleans Convention Center on September 1, 2005

ERIC GAY

AP Photo/Eric Gay

At the Time of the Louisville Flood (1937)
MARGARET BOURKE-WHITE

Time Life Pictures/Getty Images

Edgar Hollingsworth Rescued from His Home after Hurricane Katrina (2005)

BRUCE CHAMBERS

© Bruce Chambers

Texting and Driving
MICHAEL KRASOWITZ

Michael Krasowitz/Getty Images

Reading and Discussion Questions

1. Look closely at the photograph of a flag-draped woman taken following Hurricane Katrina (p. 65). Who is pictured? What sort of expression does she have on her face? Then consider why the elderly woman might have a blanket that looks like an American flag draped over her. What do you know about the rescue of Katrina victims that might be relevant to the way you "read" the picture as an argument? Under the circumstances, how might the flag blanket be seen as symbolic? What claim might you infer from the picture?

2. Now compare the picture to the next photo, "At the Time of the Louisville Flood," taken in 1937 by Margaret Bourke-White (p. 66). Do you see any similarity in the messages being conveyed by each? Explain.

3. Look at the photograph of Edgar Hollingsworth, the seventy-four-year-old man being rescued (p. 67). Hollingsworth survived the hurricane but was found near death in his home fourteen days after the storm. He died four days later in the hospital. The reactions this picture has elicited provide an excellent illustration of varied responses to the same visual image. Consider how the responses below may have been shaped by each viewer's own perspective. What is your interpretation of the photograph?

- A typical headline accompanying the photo called the discovery of Hollingsworth a "miracle rescue." According to a report from Post-Gazette.com, "The rescue was a bright spot on a day in which the owners of a nursing home were charged in the deaths of dozens of patients killed by hurricane floodwaters, the death toll in Louisiana jumped to 423 and the New Orleans mayor warned that the city is broke."[2] And according to Keith Sharon of the *Orange County Register*, "The rescue pumped up the spirits of [California] Task Force 5, which has been mostly marking the locations of dead bodies for the last week."[3]

- *USA Today* termed the photo "iconic."[4] Marcia Prouse, director of photography at the *Orange County Register*, had a similar view: "This man's story needs to be told. He's an important symbol of the hurricane.... It's anybody's father or grandfather."[5]

- The photo has become known throughout the Internet as the *Katrina Pietà*. The *Pietà* alluded to is Michelangelo's famous sculpture of Mary holding the body of Christ after his crucifixion. The way that the National Guardsman is holding Hollingsworth is reminiscent of Mary's pose, and the link to the loving mother of Jesus leads to a positive interpretation of the scene.

- For some, the sight of two white aid workers and one Hispanic one aiding a black man provides a sharp contrast to other images that stress the racial tension that grew out of Katrina's aftermath.

- Others were enraged by rules that could have kept the rescue team from entering Hollingsworth's home to rescue him. Keith Sharon wrote, "In the past few days, the Federal Emergency Management Agency has ordered searchers not to break into homes. They are supposed to look in through a window and knock on the door. If no one cries out for help, they are supposed to move on. If they see a body, they are supposed to log the address and move on." The rescue team went against orders in breaking down the door to reach Hollingsworth. Sharon added that earlier "they had been frustrated when FEMA delayed their deployment for four days, housing them in the Hyatt Regency in Dallas."[6] The Sharon quotes are referenced on DailyKOS.com, under the title "American Shame: The Edgar Hollingsworth Story."[7]

---

[2] See www.post-gazette.com/news/nation/2005/09/14/A-miracle-rescue-and-rising-death-toll-in-New-Orleans.html.

[3] See www.ocregister.com/news/force-192709-hollingsworth-task.html.

[4] See http://usatoday30.usatoday.com/news/nation/2005-11-10-hollingsworth-katrina_x.htm.

[5] See www.filmjournal.com/pdn/esearch/article_display.jsp?vnu_content_id=1001137235.

[6] Keith Sharon, "Survivor Rescued 16 Days after the Hurricane," *Orange County Register*, September 14, 2005.

[7] See www.dailykos.com/story/2005/9/14/12516/3649.

4. Look at the picture titled "Texting and Driving" on page 68. The photographer's intent seems fairly clear in this photo. What is in focus? What isn't? Why?

5. What argument is this photo making?

Print Advertisements

In 1947, one analyst summed up the goals of the advertiser, which are still very relevant today:

1. attract attention
2. arouse interest
3. stimulate desire
4. create conviction
5. get action[8]

Alluring photographs from advertisers — car companies, animal-rights groups, restaurants, sporting goods manufacturers, clothiers, jewelers, movie studios — promise to fulfill our dreams of pleasure. On a very different scale, animal-rights groups show photographs of brutally mistreated dogs and cats; children's rights advocates publish pictures of sick and starving children in desolate refugee camps.

But photographs are not the only visual images used by advertisers. Other kinds of illustrations — as well as signs and symbols, which over the years have acquired connotations, or suggestive significance — are also used as instruments of persuasion. The flag or bald eagle, the shamrock, the crown, the cross, the hammer and sickle, the rainbow, and the swastika can all rouse strong feelings for or against the ideas they represent. These symbols may be

---

ARGUMENT ESSENTIALS
Visual Rhetoric

Use these four steps as basic guidelines for analyzing visual rhetoric:

- **Preread.** Consider who created the visual, what the context was, and whether and where it was published.

- **Read for content.** With visual rhetoric, this means "reading" both the pictures and the text.

- **Read for rhetorical strategies.** Consider the placement and focus of text and visuals. In general, what draws your eye?

- **Evaluate.** How does the image make you feel? What mood does it create? Is it effective in achieving its goal?

---

[8] J. V. Lund, *Newspaper Advertising* (New York: Prentice Hall, 1947), p. 83.

defined as abbreviated claims of value. They summarize the moral, religious, and political principles by which groups of people live and often die. In commercial advertisements we recognize symbols that aren't likely to enlist our deepest loyalties but, nevertheless, have impact on our daily lives: the apple with a bite in it, the golden arches, the Prudential rock, the Nike swoosh, and a thousand others.

In fact, a closer look at commercial and political advertising, which is heavily dependent on visual argument and is something we are all familiar with, provides a useful introduction to this complex subject. We know that advertisements, with or without pictures, are short arguments, often lacking fully developed support, whose claims of policy urge us to take an action: Buy this product or service; vote for this candidate or issue. The claim may not be directly expressed, but it will be clearly implicit. In print, on television, or on the Internet, the visual representation of objects, carefully chosen to appeal to a particular audience, can be as important as, if not more important than, any verbal text.

Consider these questions as you analyze print advertisements:

1. Who is the sponsor?
2. What does the sponsor want me to do or believe?
3. Is there sufficient text to answer questions I may have about the claim?
4. Are the visual elements more prominent than the text? If so, why?
5. Does the arrangement of elements in the message tell me what the sponsor considers most important? If so, what is the significance of this choice?
6. Does the visual image lead me to entertain unrealistic expectations? (Can using this shampoo make my hair look like that shining cascade on the model? Does the picture of the candidate for governor, shown answering questions in a classroom of eager, smiling youngsters, mean that he has a viable plan for educational reform?)

READING ARGUMENT

Examining Print Advertisements

The print advertisement on page 72 has been annotated with careful attention paid to the questions listed above. The ad is followed by a brief analysis that shows prereading, reading for content, reading for rhetorical strategies, and evaluation.

Stop Climate Change before It Changes You
WORLD WILDLIFE FUND

STOP CLIMATE CHANGE
BEFORE IT CHANGES YOU.

WWF   for a living planet

World Wildlife Fund

Frightening visual more prominent than text; intended to show that humans are threatened by climate change

No evidence to support claim

Claim (that humans will turn into fish if we don't stop climate change) is exaggerated.

Message is clear: Stop Climate Change.

Sponsor is WWF: World Wildlife Fund.

Analysis

The advertisement is for the WWF, or World Wildlife Fund, a nonprofit environmental organization. The ad appeared in Belgium in 2008.

The creepy-looking visual is more prominent than the text. The front and top of the person's head are well lit, to show that a human face has turned into a fish face. The message here is that we could all be living under water if the sea level rises. The text is brief and direct: "Stop Climate Change before It Changes You." The text is located at the bottom of the ad, and it reinforces the image's message: that humans are threatened by climate change. The friendly-looking panda and WWF logo are small and are placed at the very bottom of the ad.

The ad is certainly attention-getting, and you really need to look at it for a minute to figure out what is going on. However, the human with a fish face is quite unrealistic, and the scare tactic used in the ad seems too heavy-handed. This ad may work for readers who already believe that climate change must be stopped. In that case, the ad is simply reinforcing readers' existing worldview as a way to generate support for the WWF. But the ad would probably be less effective in convincing more conservative readers because it lacks any evidence to support the claim that climate change is threatening the human species.

Practice: Examining Print Advertisements

Practice your analytical skills by applying the four steps — prereading, reading for content, reading for rhetorical strategies, and evaluation — to the following ad. Be sure to keep in mind the questions on page 71.

Takeout Can Eat Up Your Savings
AMERICAN INSTITUTE OF CPAs

American Institute of CPAs and the Ad Council

Political Cartoons

Knowing the context of a political cartoon is essential to both understanding it and appreciating its humor. These cartoons age quickly. You can go back to historical cartoons and appreciate them only if you know the context in which they were created. If today's political cartoons are not created and published quickly, they will have lost their currency and their humor. Remember that if the cartoon is an argument, it has a claim. Consider what the claim is and how the artist used both drawing and text to articulate that claim. Often the picture will provide the support. Since political cartoons are generally judgmental, there will be a warrant on which that judgment is based; puzzling out that warrant may help you understand the cartoon.

READING ARGUMENT

Examining Political Cartoons

The success of this cartoon depends on the audience's knowledge of Obamacare, or the Patient Protection and Affordable Care Act of 2010, and the difficulties encountered in getting its Web site up and running in late 2013. In the cartoon, Obama is clearly recognizable — and clearly unhappy. The elephant, a long-time symbol of the Republican Party, stands back and lets Obama bear the weight of the patient on the stretcher — the beleaguered Affordable Care Act, which we know by virtue of the letters ACA on his arm. One of the cleverest features of the cartoon is the broken computer monitor in place of the patient's head. Had the program's Web site worked efficiently from the beginning, the process of signing up would have received far less attention and Obama would have received far less criticism.

Obamacare EMT
MARTIN KOZLOWSKI

Martin Kozlowski

Practice: Examining Cartoons

Analyze this cartoon with a different focus from the previous one. It will help if you think what warrant is behind it. The context of this cartoon was the aftermath of Typhoon Haiyan in the Philippines in November 2013.

Did You Feel That?

PAT BAGLEY

"DID YOU FEEL THAT? FOR A MINUTE IT FELT LIKE WE WERE TRENDING RIGHT UP THERE WITH MILEY CYRUS."

PoliticalCartoons.com/Pat Bagley

 Go to **macmillanhighered.com/rottenberg** for another cartoon to analyze.

Graphics

Graphics are charts, graphs, diagrams, and other visuals that provide an alternative to presenting information as text. They can offer a concise, efficient way of getting information across easily and quickly. A bar graph can show at a glance if sales are higher or lower in the fourth quarter than in the third. A pie chart can make clear how much of the national budget is spent on defense. A map can show emerging centers of population growth.

Different types of graphics serve different purposes. It's important to read accurately the type of graphic you are examining. Always look at the title of the graphic, which should be descriptive, and for labels and keys that will help you understand the information being presented. Color will often serve to make contrasts more striking and simply to make the graphic more visually appealing. Of course, you should always take note of who created or sponsored the graphic as you consider what argument it is making.

READING ARGUMENT

Examining Graphics

The following graphic on tobacco has been annotated for you.

Tobacco's Shifting Burden
theworld.org

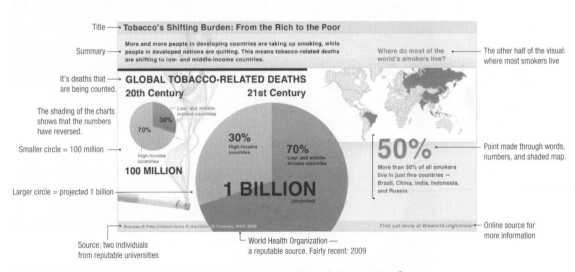

Kim Ducharme, Sonia Narang, and David Baron. Reproduced courtesy of Public Radio International® and PRI'S THE WORLD® from radio series "Cancer's New Battleground: The Developing World." http://www.pri.org/cancer.

Practice: Examining Graphics

Analyze this graphic sponsored by the Union of Concerned Scientists (ucsusa .org), and answer the questions that follow.

Where Your Gas Money Goes
UNION OF CONCERNED SCIENTISTS

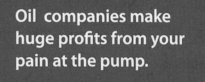

Where Your Gas Money Goes

$50.00 fill-up

Oil companies make huge profits from your pain at the pump.

Keep the profits in your pocket by investing in fuel efficiency.

$19.61 Private and Publicly Traded Oil Companies

$13.63 Government-Owned Oil Companies

$7.00 Taxes

$4.87 Refining

$4.08 Distribution and Marketing

$0.81 Gas Stations

© Union of Concerned Scientists 2013
Source: UCS Report, Where Your Gas Money Goes
For more information, visit www.ucsusa.org/gasmoney

Courtesy of Union of Concerned Scientists

Reading and Discussion Questions

1. "Read" the graphic. What is it saying?
2. The ad was sponsored by the Union of Concerned Scientists. What might you speculate about that group? What does your research reveal about it?
3. Does the group have a purpose in the ad beyond explaining where your gas money goes? If so, what is it?
4. What are some conclusions you can draw from the ad?

Audiovisual Rhetoric

Where in our daily lives do we see examples of argumentation that go beyond print? We see it on the television news and on talk shows that deal with politics. We hear news and opinions on the radio, and we hear political speeches and debates.

Audiovisual rhetoric includes all that the human voice adds, from a regional dialect to a tinge of nervousness; television includes all that the visual dimension adds, from body language to hair style. And, of course, in television commercials we see most of the features of print ads with the addition of sound and motion.

- **Prereading.** Prereading an argumentative speech or a debate that you are going to hear delivered orally means knowing the affiliation of the speaker or debaters and what biases you might expect from each. It also means knowing as much as possible about the topic or topics to be discussed. Prereading broadcast news or talk shows means noticing the network or station and acknowledging any known biases that suggests. With some news organizations, it won't take long for a liberal or conservative bias to become obvious. The sponsors of a show may be relevant. For talk shows, a practical part of prereading is finding out who the guests will be. That information is often available online in advance. What are the affiliations of the various guests and of the host? For commercials, prereading means determining what company's or organization's ad it is—and sometimes that's hard to tell.
- **Watching or listening for content.** Aside from the regional dialect or the tinge of nervousness, the body language or the hairstyle, what is being said? Televised news will incorporate photographs, video, and graphics along with the script. By way of all that, what are viewers being told? As you hear different speakers on a talk show or in a debate, can you start to recognize their positions on the issues? With commercials, what is being sold?
- **Watching or listening for rhetorical strategies.** How are you being "told" or "sold"? As you listen to a speaker or a debater, are you aware of any errors in logic? Does the speaker or debater support his or her claims? Are there unspoken warrants that you do not agree with? If news is not the objective reporting of facts that it should be, how is bias revealed? Is the news slanted

for a particular audience? In analyzing commercials for rhetorical strategies, consider (1) all of the questions you considered in analyzing print ads and (2) any others that will reveal how an ad with speech, music, and special effects might appeal to a viewer logically, emotionally, and ethically.

- **Evaluation.** How effective is a speaker or debater in building a convincing case for the intended audience? How effective is "the news" in delivering the news? How effective is the talk show in presenting a legitimate exchange of opinions and not a shouting match? How effective is the commercial in selling a product or service?

Television Commercials

Television commercials have come of age since their first appearance in 1941 with an ad for Bulova watches. The cost of that ad? Nine dollars. Of course, we all know what a big business commercials are today. The cost of a thirty-second commercial during the Super Bowl hit four million dollars in 2013.

Television commercials can be analyzed much like print ads.

- **Prereading.** Preview a commercial, or watch it to get the general idea before breaking it down into component parts for analysis. Consider the context, including the intended audience, at what time of day the ad airs, and during what shows or types of shows it airs.
- **Reading for content.** Consider text and visuals, as you did with print ads, but also consider the action in the commercial and to what extent sound adds to its overall appeal.
- **Reading for rhetorical strategies.** Consider what audience the commercial targets and how it appeals to that audience.
- **Evaluating.** How effective is the commercial at achieving its purpose?

READING ARGUMENT

Examining Television Commercials

In 2012, Toyota changed its slogan to "Let's Go Places," replacing "Moving Forward," which had been its slogan since 2004, and did a series of commercials around the new theme. The new tagline was introduced on December 31, 2012, in launching the redesigned 2013 Avalon sedan. The stills presented here show the approach the company took in one of them. Look at the images and read the analysis that accompanies each one to understand how Toyota employed audiovisual rhetoric in its commercial.

Let's Go Places

TOYOTA

Voiceover: *Let's go places.*

Toyota

This is one of numerous shots that show Toyotas moving through different types of landscape — mountains, residential neighborhoods, snowy woods, and so on. These are some of the physical places we can go to. The varied landscape suggests that wherever you go, you can do it in a Toyota. Different locales appeal to different viewers, depending on where they live or where they would like to travel. The first series of rapid shots shows the landscape but not the car. A second shows the landscape as seen from behind the car. The movement of the camera from in front of the car to behind it gives the impression of the car outracing the camera in the rush to go places.

Voiceover: *Not just the ones you can find on a map. But the ones you can find in your heart!*

Toyota

The ad goes for emotional appeals, including shots of familiar points in the lives of everyday people. Some of them are common events like a trip out for ice cream with the family or a camping trip to the lake, and some are major events like going to the prom, bringing a new baby home, or being in a wedding.

Voiceover: *Let's go beyond everything we know and embrace everything we don't. And once we have reached our destination, let's keep going, because inspiration does not favor those that sit still. It dances with the daring and rewards the courageous with ideas that excite, challenge, and even inspire.*

Toyota

With these words the focus shifts to Toyota's tough four-wheel drive vehicles to show how they can function in rough terrain. Toyotas are even shown painted like race cars. One vehicle "dances with the daring" by launching off a ramp into the air. The whole ad campaign stresses moving instead of sitting still. The text tells us that our destination is beyond everything we know and suggests new, tougher challenges, like making the car fly through the air. The music, "It's My Life" by Tim Myers, builds from soft piano notes at the beginning to a crescendo as the car takes to the air. This portion of the ad goes beyond the comfort of earlier familiar scenes to appeal to the daredevil in most of us.

Voiceover: *Ideas that take you to a place that you never imagined. Ideas big enough and powerful enough to make the heart skip a beat and in some cases even two. Toyota. Let's go places.*

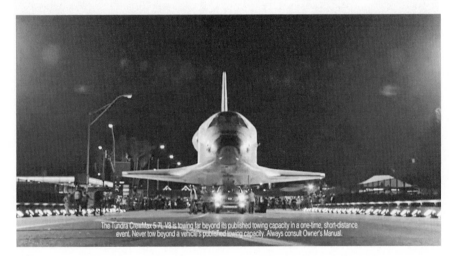

The Tundra CrewMax 5.7L V8 is towing far beyond its published towing capacity in a one-time, short-distance event. Never tow beyond a vehicle's published towing capacity. Always consult Owner's Manual.

Toyota

By the end of the ad, Toyota is appealing to viewers' pride in America. One place that you probably would not have imagined a Toyota going is the "parade route" along which the retired space shuttle *Endeavour* was pulled from Los Angeles International Airport to a downtown museum. The words "Born in America" across the front of the Toyota Tundra stress that although Toyota is a Japanese automaker, the Tundra is made in San Antonio. And the places that the shuttle has been advance the idea of humankind's ultimate journeys. The shuttle dwarfs all around it, just as its destinations dwarf most of our dreams of places we would like to go. However, the ad encourages its viewers not to place limits on themselves when they dream. A final shot of a globe reinforces the notion that there is no place, on this planet at least, that one cannot go in a Toyota.

e-Practice: Examining Television Commercials

Neon Signs (Buzzed Driving)
NATIONAL HIGHWAY TRAFFIC SAFETY
ADMINISTRATION

NHTSA

 Go to **macmillanhighered.com/rottenberg** and analyze the commercial aimed at preventing drinking and driving sponsored by the National Highway Traffic Safety Administration.

Speeches and Debates

Good speeches on controversial issues are some of the best examples of argument. Unlike the brief sound bites that we hear on the evening news or in response to a microphone thrust in a politician's face as she leaves a building, a carefully prepared speech is the closest we come in the twenty-first century to the rhetoric that Aristotle taught. Of course, those in the highest offices have speechwriters, but whoever writes public addresses for candidates or governmental officials must be skilled at blending *logos*, *ethos*, and *pathos* to move an audience to act or at least to change an opinion.

Candidates also prepare carefully for debates, but the success of the debate depends largely on the moderator. A weak moderator might allow each candidate to deliver set speeches no matter what the question or allow the whole event to become a verbal sparring match, which can be entertaining but may not clarify the candidates' positions on a wide range of issues. A strong moderator can hold the candidates to a clear response and rebuttal format that covers a lot of ground in a short time.

Listening to a speech — or reading one — requires focus on the ideas to the exclusion of the distraction of physical appearance. It requires listening for claim and support. It requires keeping in mind the audience for whom the speech is or was intended. You will learn more in Chapter 9 about making language serve the needs of argument. For now, consider how well the speeches fit the contexts in which they were delivered and how convincing you find their arguments to be.

READING ARGUMENT

Examining Speeches

The following is John F. Kennedy's Inaugural Address, January 20, 1961. It has been annotated for you.

Inaugural Address, January 20, 1961
JOHN F. KENNEDY

We observe today not a victory of party but a celebration of freedom — symbolizing an end as well as a beginning — signifying renewal as well as change. For I have sworn before you and Almighty God the same solemn oath our forebears prescribed nearly a century and three quarters ago.

Puts his inauguration in the context of American history . . .

The world is very different now. For man holds in his mortal hands the power to abolish all forms of human poverty and all forms of human life. And yet the same revolutionary beliefs for which our forebears fought are still at issue around the globe — the belief that the rights of man come not from the generosity of the state but from the hand of God.

but immediately contrasts past and present

We dare not forget today that we are the heirs of that first revolution. Let the word go forth from this time and place, to friend and foe alike, that the torch has been passed to a new generation of Americans — born in this century, tempered by war, disciplined by a hard and bitter peace, proud of our ancient heritage — and unwilling to witness or permit the slow undoing of those human rights to which this nation has always been committed, and to which we are committed today at home and around the world.

He again emphasizes the contrast — a new generation.

Let every nation know, whether it wishes us well or ill, that we shall pay any price, bear any burden, meet any hardship, support any friend, oppose any foe to assure the survival and the success of liberty.

Pledges to support liberty wherever necessary

He includes his listeners with the "we."

The parallel structure sets up a list of pledges to different countries.

His first direct reference to the Cold War and communism, a key part of the context in 1961.

Addresses South and Central America, but indirectly is threatening those "hostile powers" that threaten the Western Hemisphere

This much we pledge — and more.   5

To those old allies whose cultural and spiritual origins we share, we pledge the loyalty of faithful friends. United, there is little we cannot do in a host of cooperative ventures. Divided, there is little we can do — for we dare not meet a powerful challenge at odds and split asunder.

To those new states whom we welcome to the ranks of the free, we pledge our word that one form of colonial control shall not have passed away merely to be replaced by a far more iron tyranny. We shall not always expect to find them supporting our view. But we shall always hope to find them strongly supporting their own freedom — and to remember that, in the past, those who foolishly sought power by riding the back of the tiger ended up inside.

To those peoples in the huts and villages of half the globe struggling to break the bonds of mass misery, we pledge our best efforts to help them help themselves, for whatever period is required — not because the communists may be doing it, not because we seek their votes, but because it is right. If a free society cannot help the many who are poor, it cannot save the few who are rich.

To our sister republics south of our border, we offer a special pledge — to convert our good words into good deeds — in a new alliance for progress — to assist free men and free governments in casting off the chains of poverty. But this peaceful revolution of hope cannot become the prey of hostile powers. Let all our neighbors know that we shall join with them to oppose aggression or subversion anywhere in the Americas. And let every other power know that this Hemisphere intends to remain the master of its own house.

To that world assembly of sovereign states, the United Nations, our last   10
best hope in an age where the instruments of war have far outpaced the instruments of peace, we renew our pledge of support — to prevent it from becoming merely a forum for invective — to strengthen its shield of the new and the weak — and to enlarge the area in which its writ may run.

A request for reconciliation, but a threat of nuclear annihilation

Two different audiences are being addressed again — he is justifying nuclear buildup to both his countrymen and the communists.

Neither side in the Cold War wants the "final war" that nuclear weapons could bring.

Finally, to those nations who would make themselves our adversary, we offer not a pledge but a request: that both sides begin anew the quest for peace, before the dark powers of destruction unleashed by science engulf all humanity in planned or accidental self-destruction.

We dare not tempt them with weakness. For only when our arms are sufficient beyond doubt can we be certain beyond doubt that they will never be employed.

But neither can two great and powerful groups of nations take comfort from our present course — both sides overburdened by the cost of modern weapons, both rightly alarmed by the steady spread of the deadly atom, yet both racing to alter that uncertain balance of terror that stays the hand of mankind's final war.

So let us begin anew — remembering on both sides that civility is not a sign of weakness, and sincerity is always subject to proof. Let us never negotiate out of fear. But let us never fear to negotiate.

15   Let both sides explore what problems unite us instead of belaboring those problems which divide us.

Let both sides, for the first time, formulate serious and precise proposals for the inspection and control of arms — and bring the absolute power to destroy other nations under the absolute control of all nations.

Let both sides seek to invoke the wonders of science instead of its terrors. Together let us explore the stars, conquer the deserts, eradicate disease, tap the ocean depths, and encourage the arts and commerce.

Let both sides unite to heed in all corners of the earth the command of Isaiah — to "undo the heavy burdens . . . (and) let the oppressed go free."

And if a beach-head of cooperation may push back the jungle of suspicion, let both sides join in creating a new endeavor, not a new balance of power, but a new world of law, where the strong are just and the weak secure and the peace preserved.

20   All this will not be finished in the first one hundred days. Nor will it be finished in the first one thousand days, nor in the life of this Administration, nor even perhaps in our lifetime on this planet. But let us begin.

In your hands, my fellow citizens, more than mine, will rest the final success or failure of our course. Since this country was founded, each generation of Americans has been summoned to give testimony to its national loyalty. The graves of young Americans who answered the call to service surround the globe.

Now the trumpet summons us again — not as a call to bear arms, though arms we need — not as a call to battle, though embattled we are — but a call to bear the burden of a long twilight struggle, year in and year out, "rejoicing in hope, patient in tribulation" — a struggle against the common enemies of man: tyranny, poverty, disease, and war itself.

Can we forge against these enemies a grand and global alliance, North and South, East and West, that can assure a more fruitful life for all mankind? Will you join in that historic effort?

In the long history of the world, only a few generations have been granted the role of defending freedom in its hour of maximum danger. I do not shrink from this responsibility — I welcome it. I do not believe that any of us would exchange places with any other people or any other generation. The energy,

Still addressing Russia, which he includes in the "both sides" of the next five paragraphs

He starts here a plea for common ground.

A biblical injunction for Russia to stop oppressing other nations

Speaks directly to Americans, makes himself one of them with "my fellow citizens," calls on them to give testimony to their national loyalty

They are not being asked to go to war but to fight "tyranny, poverty, disease, and war itself."
He warns them that it will be a long, hard struggle — not very optimistic.

It is a dangerous time, but also a time of opportunity.

The most famous lines

the faith, the devotion which we bring to this endeavor will light our country and all who serve it — and the glow from that fire can truly light the world.

And so, my fellow Americans: ask not what your country can do for   25
you — ask what you can do for your country.

My fellow citizens of the world: ask not what America will do for you, but what together we can do for the freedom of man.

Here the "we" seems to be Kennedy.

Finally, whether you are citizens of America or citizens of the world, ask of us here the same high standards of strength and sacrifice which we ask of you. With a good conscience our only sure reward, with history the final judge of our deeds, let us go forth to lead the land we love, asking His blessing and His help, but knowing that here on earth God's work must truly be our own.

e-Practice: Examining Speeches

Democratic National Convention Speech
ELIZABETH WARREN

Democratic National Committee

 Go to **macmillanhighered.com/rottenberg** and analyze the speech that Elizabeth Warren gave at the Democratic National Convention in 2012.

Broadcast News

News shows were originally designed to present, in brief, the facts of what was happening around the country and around the world. The advent of twenty-four-hour news channels, however, has increasingly led to a need to fill time by talking about rather than presenting the news. Analysis of the news is crucial to understanding the events that shape our world, and hearing different perspectives can help enlighten the listening and reading public. Any subject, however, can become the subject of debate if at least two people have different opinions on it, and television networks seem never to be at a loss to find at least one advocate for any position.

From news shows that go well beyond reporting the news to expressing opinions about it, it is only a small step to political commentary shows that from their inception were meant to be a sounding board for different opinions on contemporary politics. Some of these shows have been around for decades. *Meet the Press* is the longest-running television series in the history of American broadcasting; it has been on the air for more than sixty years. The most intelligent and responsible programs usually consist of a panel of experts — politicians, journalists, scholars — led by a neutral moderator (or one who, at least, allows guests to express their views). Other examples of these programs are *Face the Nation* with Bob Schieffer, *This Week* with George Stephanopoulos, *Fox News Sunday* with Chris Wallace, and *State of the Union* with Candy Crowley.

More clearly biased news shows include the conservative *The O'Reilly Factor* and the liberal *The Rachel Maddow Show*. A variation on these are some very popular political comedy shows like *The Daily Show* with Jon Stewart and the satirical *The Colbert Report* with Stephen Colbert. Radio also has its share of news and call-in hosts who are known for their political bias, such as conservative Rush Limbaugh and liberal Stephanie Miller.

Whatever the merits or shortcomings of individual programs, significant general differences exist between arguments on radio and television and arguments in the print media. These differences include the degree of organization and development and the risk of personal attacks.

First, contributions to a panel discussion must be delivered in fragments, usually no longer than a single paragraph, weakened by time constraints, interruptions, overlapping speech, memory gaps, and real or feigned displays of derision, impatience, and disbelief by critical panelists. Even on the best programs, the result is a lack of both coherence — or connections between ideas — and solid evidence that requires development. Too often we are treated to conclusions with little indication of how they were arrived at.

Second, listeners and viewers of all spoken arguments are in danger of evaluating them according to criteria that are largely absent from evaluation of written texts. It is true that writers may adopt a persona or a literary disguise, which the tone of the essay will reflect. But many readers will not be able to identify it or recognize their own response to it. Listeners and viewers, however, can hardly avoid being affected by characteristics that are clearly definable: a speaker's voice, delivery, bodily mannerisms, dress, and physical appearance. In addition, listeners may be adversely influenced by clumsy speech containing more slang, colloquialisms, and grammar and usage errors than written texts that have had the benefit of revision.

But if listeners allow consideration of physical attributes to influence their judgment of what the speaker is trying to prove, they are guilty of evaluating the speaker rather than the argument. This is true whether the evaluation is favorable or unfavorable. (See p. 311 for a discussion of this fallacy.)

Strategies for Critical Listening

Listening is hearing with attention. It is a skill that can be learned and improved. Here are some of the characteristics of critical listening most appropriate to understanding and responding to arguments.

1. **Concentrate.** If you are distracted, you cannot go back as you do with the written word to clarify a point or recover a connection. As you listen, try to avoid being distracted by facts alone. Look for the overall patterns of the speech. Take notes using an outline of the material being covered.

2. **Pay attention to the claim and support.** Avoid focusing on the speaker's appearance and delivery. Research shows that listeners are likely to give greater attention to the dramatic elements of speeches than to the logical ones. But you can enjoy the sound, the appearance, and the drama of a spoken argument without allowing these elements to overwhelm what is essential to the development of a claim.

3. **Avoid premature judgments about what is actually said.** Good listeners try not to allow their prejudices to prevent careful evaluation of the argument. This doesn't mean accepting everything or even most of what you hear. This precaution is especially relevant when the speakers and their views are well known and the listener has already formed an opinion about them, favorable or unfavorable.

READING ARGUMENT

Examining Broadcast News

One way to detect bias in the news is to see how different networks report on the same news story. The transcript on pages 91–93 is a response from CNN to President Obama's decision to support same-sex marriage. It has been annotated to show bias in the comments.

Coverage of Obama's Announcement in Support of Gay Marriage
CNN CORRESPONDENTS

Brooke Baldwin: We're talking about this news here with a number of folks in Washington, D.C.

I want to bring in John King, because, John King, as we listen to this and we sort of let that statement reverberate, this is an election year. Talk to me about the timing of this. Obviously, this is great news for folks who support gay marriage. But certainly you talk about those independent voters who are so, so key come November, and obviously folks on Mitt Romney's team, how does this play with them?

John King, CNN Chief National Correspondent: Well, it's a gamble for the president. And we should say up front it's a bold, personal choice for the president to decide to do this publicly.

You used the word as you brought me into the conversation — *historic*. If you go back and show those pictures from ABC News just a moment ago, not only is this a political leader making this statement, Brooke. It's the president of the United States. It's the first president of the United States — he's sitting in the White House, those two flags over his shoulder, the seal of the United States of America and the American flag — this is the first American president sitting in the White House to say, I think same-sex couples should be able to marry, not just have legal unions, but able to marry.

5   And the president acknowledged the use of the term marriage. That's one of the reasons he's been hung up on this. You hear him talking about his daughters. You hear him talking about young Americans when he goes to college campuses. The president knows pretty well that young Americans are with him on this issue.

They're ahead of him on this issue even. They have pressured him. Gay Americans have supported him, the gay and lesbian community which is supporting him financially and otherwise, politically supports him. The question is, how does it play out in what we know is a very, very close, competitive election?

And even the president's own political team will tell you, there are risks here. Number one, this will energize evangelical Christians who might have some doubts about Mitt Romney. They have just seen the president of the United States sitting in the White House endorsing something they very, very much oppose on moral and religious grounds.

Marginal notes:

Emphasizes the positive, but also questions the effect on the election

Favorable slant

Appeal to patriotism. Obama is seen against a backdrop of national symbols.

Focuses on those who support Obama, emphasizing the positive

What Obama has to lose

Objective look at election math

So this will help Mitt Romney energize his base. The question is, does it cost the president? If you get addition from young voters, addition from gay and lesbians who might have been disappointed and stayed home if the president didn't go this far, if you get that addition on the Democratic side, do you also get subtraction?

Are there conservative Democrats who say, sorry, Mr. President, I'm not with you on this one? Critically to me, Brooke, in this calculation, African-Americans and Latinos. Many Latinos who are Catholics. They go to Catholic Church, where their priest tells them every Sunday homosexuality isn't just wrong, it's evil. That's what their priest tells them. It's evil.

A lot of African-American preachers in the Southern Baptist — Southern churches across this country, but particularly in Virginia, North Carolina, states the president carried last time, say the same thing.

Baldwin: Right.

Presents the risk in a positive light

King: And this is a — this is a big risk by this president. And give him credit for taking the risk. Many politicians duck from risks, but what we will watch play out now in the weeks and months ahead is how it works on turnout and the addition and subtraction, which politics in the end is about math.

Baldwin: I want to get back to you, John King, because I have more questions.

But I do want to go straight to the White House to Jessica Yellin, because, Jessica, I'm just curious, what kind of backstory do we have on this particular interview? I was mentioning to Wolf I read that this thing was put together, what, yesterday, yesterday afternoon, that they flew Robin Roberts up to Washington and then back to New York — or they will be. Tell me what you know about how this whole thing came together.

Jessica Yellin, CNN Chief White House Correspondent: Well, I know that this   15
wasn't the White House's plan to roll that — this out this week.

The president's campaign was planning to unveil their first positive ad campaign this week and start making their case for reelection. He was unveiling the congressional to-do list, which was supposed to be focused on pressing Congress on some of their major initiatives that the campaign wanted to focus on.

And then because of the vice president's comments, because of Arne Duncan, the education secretary's comment, it sort of forced the president's hand. And as you say, they put together an interview with Robin Roberts, as we understand it from sources, yesterday.

And she came up to do that interview quickly today. I understand that on ABC, while we have been on, Robin Roberts reported that she pressed the

10

president on whether he was angry with the vice president and with Arne Duncan because of their comments. And the president laughed it off, saying no.

You know, from a number of people I have spoken with outside the White House, activists on this issue, Brooke, it was their sense that they believed the president, the White House was going to come to this position before the election. I don't know if that is true, but it was their view that he was.

20   This simply forced it to happen sooner and not on a time frame of their own choosing.

His hand was forced, but he was going to take a stand before the elections anyway.

Practice: Examining Broadcast News

Locate online a broadcast response to Obama's announcement in support of same-sex marriage that has a negative bias. Annotate a transcript of it, using the previous transcript and its annotations as a model.

ARGUMENT ESSENTIALS
Audiovisual Rhetoric

Use these four steps as basic guidelines for analyzing audio-visual rhetoric:

- **Preread.** Notice a television or radio show's network or station and its sponsors, and consider any possible bias. Consider the organization or company behind a commercial and the affiliations of a speaker.

- **Watch or listen for content.** Consider what you are being told when you listen to the news. Consider what product, service, candidate, or idea a speaker or a commercial is encouraging you to accept.

- **Watch or listen for rhetorical strategies.** Consider if and how any bias is being revealed. With speeches or debates, consider how the speaker is trying to appeal to a specific audience. With commercials, consider the questions used in analyzing visual rhetoric plus any added by sound, motion, and special effects.

- **Evaluate.** Consider how effective a news show is in delivering the news in a fair manner or how effective a talk show is in allowing varied opinions to be heard. Consider whether a speaker's content and strategies are appropriate for his or her audience. Consider how effective a commercial is in selling its product, service, candidate, or idea.

Online Environments

Many of us spend a good part of our lives online. What role does argumentation play in our digital lives? Any of us can get into an argument online, but can argument in online environments be studied as a rhetorical act? How does our study of writer, subject, and audience apply when our audience can range from our best friend to someone we may never meet face-to-face? How do claim, support, and warrant apply to a Web site or a blog? How do *logos*, *ethos*, and *pathos* apply when we can communicate online behind a mask of anonymity? The prose may be informal — at times, it is the digital world's own unique shorthand — but an online argument is still grounded in the theories of Aristotle, Rogers, and Toulmin that are the focus of this book.

What the online world can also offer us that books, newspapers, and even television and radio can't — except for an occasional call-in show — is interactivity, and hyperlinks literally let us decide what direction our reading of a text will take.

- **Prereading.** In the context of electronic environments, prereading can be seen as familiarizing yourself with a new way of interacting. If you have never used Tumblr or Twitter, prereading is the step where you learn what exactly Tumblr or Twitter *is* and how to use it. You might sample a few blog posts to see if the blog covers topics of interest to you. You might explore a Web site to see who sponsors it and what it has to offer.

- **Reading for content.** This step is most relevant to blogs, forums, visual lectures, and Web sites — all of which you read or watch because you need the information or simply have an interest in the subject, and all of which are more fully developed than most Facebook posts. With social networking sites, the content is about as free of structure as a stream-of-consciousness novel. Facebook asks, "What's on Your Mind?" and millions of people type an answer. Social networking sites are your window into the lives of others; therefore, much of the content is the content of their lives, plus their views on what is happening in the world around them.

- **Online interaction.** Online environments let readers participate in ways that a static text cannot. On a social network, you can post a question, or you can tell all of your friends what your day has been like. You can comment on a blog or start your own. You can click from link to link to link in an endless chain of connections, controlling the twists and turns of your search. *Interactivity* is one of the two features that have helped the Internet revolutionize communication. The other is *hypertextuality*, or the ability to read different levels of a text by means of hyperlinks. There is no single linear way to read a Web site.

- **Evaluation.** Evaluation of online communication has to take place in the context of its purpose. Much of it is informal and certainly not polished prose. At the other extreme are Web sites that businesses depend on for their success, which must be professional in their design and content.

Networking Sites

In educational settings, closed networks are a means of linking students within one class or across several for the purpose of managing learning and providing a place to exchange ideas. Your school may use Blackboard, Angel, or Moodle as a convenient place to make announcements, explain assignments, and get students communicating with one another. Such systems allow the teacher or students to post to a class listserv and respond to one another.

On a much larger scale, the term *World Wide Web* is apt in that it is like a spider web. At any given juncture, there are multiple ways to branch off, and the strands of the web form a structure that is unbelievably complex and intricate. Online social networks are like that too. You may have Facebook friends whom you came to know — or at least to share some part of your life with — because you had a single friend in common or because of a common interest. They may be people that you might never have even struck up a conversation with in person, but your web branches in many directions for many different reasons. Sometimes that social web brings you together online with people with political and social views very different from your own. (They could be some of your best friends.) And since people like to share online the latest meme or the latest attack on President Obama or the latest dig at the NRA, you may find yourself on opposite sides of a computer screen from people whose views are diametrically opposed to your own. And then the debate begins.

ARGUMENT ESSENTIALS
Online Environments

Prereading. Familiarize yourself with the particular online environment that is new to you. Explore what it has to offer in content and in function.

Reading for content. Social networking sites provide primarily a source of information about your "friends" and their responses to the world around them. Blogs, forums, visual lectures, and Web sites may be worth exploring for information you might need or simply have an interest in.

Online interaction. Online environments let readers participate in ways that a static text cannot. Interactivity is one of the two features that have helped the Internet revolutionize communication. The other is hypertextuality, or the ability to read different levels of a text by means of hyperlinks.

Evaluation. Evaluation of online communication has to take place in the context of its purpose.

READING ARGUMENT

Examining Networking Sites

The social media exchange on pages 96–97 shows how even friends can find themselves at odds over a controversial issue. Read the text and analysis, and answer the questions that follow.

"Peaceful" Act of Compassion

WILLIAM WHARTON

William Wharton

William Wharton
June 21, 2013

Another "peaceful" act of compassion from the religion of "peace"!

Reuters

Taliban behead boy aged 10 over "spying":
Two children killed after taking food from police.
June 21, 2013
www.dailymail.co.uk
- Killed as a warning to villagers not to cooperate with Afghan government
- The boys named Khan and Hameedullah were killed on Sunday
- Their bodies and severed heads were left in their village

Sam Lane

Sam Lane
June 21, 2013

Unfortunately, Bill, stories like this just foster hate.

William Wharton
June 21, 2013

I don't hate Muslims. My son's best friend is a Muslim and I love that child like my own. But her religion teaches things that facilitate such actions as these.

Sam Lane
June 21, 2013

Kinda like the Old Testament?

William Wharton
June 21, 2013

Sam, you know as well as I that such a comparison is utterly false.

Sam Lane
June 21, 2013

I really don't. Crazy stuff in Old Testament that we are told to do.
But we know not to. Most Muslims don't kill people.
And even if Muslims are the enemy . . .
Matthew 4:44 and Romans 12:17-21.

Sam Lane

Analysis

William's sarcasm reveals his actual opinion:

Claim: Islam is not a religion of peace.
Support: The Muslims who killed these children had no compassion.
Warrant: A religion of peace does not kill children with no compassion.

Or

Major premise: A religion of peace does not kill children with no compassion.
Minor premise: These Muslims killed these children with no compassion.
Conclusion: Islam is not a religion of peace.

William's claim in the first example and conclusion in the second example are valid only if the particular Muslims who killed the children were acting in a way representative of the teachings of their religion. To prove that this is the case, William offers the example of his son's best friend, whose religion "teaches things that facilitate such actions as these." Whether or not you accept William's judgment of Islam depends largely on whether your own experience plus your knowledge of Islam convinces you that what these individuals did was in keeping with the dictates of their religion.

Sam's reasoning could be put into a syllogism in this way:

Major premise: There is crazy stuff in the Old Testament that we are told to do.
Minor premise: We know not to do crazy stuff.
Conclusion: We do not do crazy stuff that the Old Testament tells us to do.

Reading and Discussion Questions

1. Is Sam's conclusion valid?
2. How different is Sam's reasoning about Christianity from William's reasoning about Islam?
3. Is there any validity to Sam's comparing the actions of Taliban members to the teachings of the Old Testament?

Online News and Blogs

Online news sites and their less formal cousins—blogs—serve a different purpose than social networking sites do. News sites and blogs are primarily informational, although the major sites contain advertisements, and some blogs come closer to serving the function of a diary for their authors. As with their print and broadcast counterparts, news sites and especially blogs can be politically or socially biased. Many blogs have specific agendas that can be easily uncovered in the "About Us" section.

What blogs and news sites share with social networking sites is the ability for audience members to join the conversation by responding to content. Whether you are reading or writing comments in public forums such as these, remember that the most useful and worthwhile posts are both brief and reasonable. Avoid writing (and be wary of reading) posts that are inflammatory, divisive, absolute, or otherwise unreasonable.

READING ARGUMENT

Examining Online News and Blogs

The following article (and subsequent reader comments) appeared on ChristandPopCulture.com. Analyze both the article and the comments, and then answer the questions that follow.

Valedictorian Prays but Should Christians Rejoice?
ALAN NOBLE

When the State announced that it would no longer include prayer during the graduation ceremony at Liberty High School in Pickens County, South Carolina, Roy Costner IV, a valedictorian, took matters into his own hands. The local school district had received complaints from the Freedom From Religion Foundation about school sponsored prayer in the district and was concerned that the FFRF and the ACLU might cause problems if they continued to allow prayer at graduation, so they banned it.

According to the Christian News Network, however, "Costner IV wasn't going to let activist groups kick God out of his graduation. After taking the podium, Costner took his approved

Alan Noble, PhD, is a part-time lecturer at Baylor University. He is also cofounder, editor, and columnist at Christ and Pop Culture, a Web site that facilitates a global dialogue about religion and spirituality. Noble writes a weekly column, Citizenship Confusion, for the *Christ and Pop Culture* blog in the Evangelical section of patheos.com. This column appeared in June 2013.

speech and ripped it in half for all to see." To great applause, Costner IV said the Lord's Prayer in an act of defiance against the forces of secularism.

Costner IV's story has become an evangelical Internet sensation, and the video of his speech has received over 200,000 views in three days. He and his father will be interviewed on CNN in the coming days. In a society that seems increasingly antagonistic to the Christian faith, and under a government which some see as systematically oppressing Christianity, Costner IV has been hailed as a hero of the faith.

But is he? Was his act of defiance a bold stand against secular intolerance, or could it have been an instance of blindness toward Christian privilege?

5   When the Pickens County School District chose to end graduation prayers in response to threats from "activist groups," it ended school sponsored prayers, which is commonly seen as a violation of the establishment clause. Allowing the State to use Christian prayer in an official capacity can be easily interpreted by citizens as the endorsement of a particular religion, and indeed, the Supreme Court has strongly decided against school sponsored prayer based on this interpretation of the establishment clause.

However, it does seem that the school district also chose to forbid any prayers, even unofficial, unscheduled, unsponsored ones, a policy which debatably infringed upon Costner IV's rights. According to him, he was explicitly told by his principal not to mention any God in his speech: "She informed us that we could not have anything about religion or talk about God or Allah or whoever we choose to worship."

Had Costner IV prayed in defiance of the prohibition against any religious references in the graduation speeches, then it would be right for us to support him and his actions. However, according to a CNN report and Christian News Network, his prayer was a protest against the removal of prayer from school in general, including the official, school sponsored prayers:

> He . . . believes that organizations such as the Freedom From Religion Foundation . . . should stop meddling in the affairs of the Pickens County School District. The foundation, over this past school year, has leaned on the district to keep Jesus and student-led prayers out of school board meetings. . . .
>
> Costner said he set out to make a statement, one he hopes will inspire others to stand up, too, for what he sees as the good of this country.
>
> "Taking prayer out of schools is the worst thing we could do," he said.[1]

Costner IV's protest, then, was not just about his right to share his love for The Lord in his speech, but about allowing public schools to lead official Christian prayers. And it is there where I believe his complaint becomes flawed.

Should Christians Support Public Prayers?

Last year, Drew Dixon wrote a wonderful [Christ and Pop Culture] feature on a similar controversy over a school district that was forced to end prayers at football games. They also were pressured by the FFRF. In that piece, Drew rightly pointed out the uncharitable assumption which drives the idea that Christian prayers should have an official role in State functions:

> The Bible envisions public prayers being offered in the context of local churches

because prayer is a theological activity. When we pray to God out loud in church we are expressing what we believe about Him, about His kingdom, and about our place in it. Our corporate prayers teach doctrine and the New Testament is clear that Christians must teach sound doctrine (1 Timothy 1:10, 6:3; Titus 1:9). Thus the local church is an appropriate place for corporate prayer because those who pray are held accountable by the church. . . .

Nowhere does the Bible call Christians to pray at government sponsored events. The Bible calls us to proclaim the gospel on street corners and in the center of towns and everywhere we go, but it never requires that we force the government or anyone else to publicly honor our religion.[2]

10   Drew's piece . . . very thoughtfully explores the issue of civic prayers at school functions and shows how misguided it can be for us to fight for them.

Then there is the separate issue of our assumption that it is normal and appropriate for the government to use Christian prayers. Let's be honest, if a school district in Michigan had officially led Islamic prayers as a part of their graduation, we evangelicals would be citing this as an example of creeping shariah law and would demand an end to the prayers. And it would be reasonable for us to oppose such prayers, just as it is reasonable for the FFRF to ask that the public school not open their ceremonies with a Christian prayer.

There is a blindness here to Christian privilege, an assumption that Christians, and really only Christians, ought to be able to receive State sponsorship. Since Christianity has received privileged status in our government and society from its inception, we assume that we deserve to have continued dominance. So, when a group like FFRF calls for the end of school sponsored Christian prayer, we arrogantly view ourselves as persecuted.

But there is a deeper concern here: Once you allow the secular State to use the Christian faith in their machinations, it is inevitable that the manifestation of that faith will be stripped of its prophetic power, turning it into blasphemy. I have written about this phenomenon in the past, looking at how the outrage over Obama's failure to thank God during his Thanksgiving speech was misguided:

> Most manifestations of Christianity within American politics amounts to little more than [philosopher Charles] Taylor's [idea of] "vestigial ritual or prayer"—empty religious gestures meant to appeal to certain patriotic images of a Christian Nation. But what is ironic is that it is precisely these empty symbols that Christians often defend vigorously.[3]

Knowing that the State does not share the same King as we do, should we truly fight for State sponsored prayer? I am reminded of a comment Stanley Fish made in the *New York Times* regarding the effects of defending crosses on public land, a related issue of civic displays of Christianity:

> It is one of the ironies of the sequence of cases dealing with religious symbols on public land that those who argue for

their lawful presence must first deny them the significance that provokes the desire to put them there in the first place.[4]

15   Aside from these more political concerns about sponsored graduation prayers, I have some theological objections. Costner IV's prayer made little sense in the context of graduation except as an act of protest, a statement that activists should not "meddle . . . in the affairs of the Pickens County School District." From the cheers and Costner IV's tone, I worry that he was not really praying, but politically protesting. When prayer is reduced to a political protest in order to defend our right to pray to God in public, is it truly worth fighting for?

To the extent that he was protesting the principal's restriction upon his freedom of speech, I sympathize with his action, although I would argue that using prayer primarily as a political tool is inappropriate. But since he was also objecting to the ban on school sponsored prayers, Costner IV was also protesting a relatively trivial restriction upon Christianity's long history of political privilege and co-opting by the State.

As secularism continues to gain prominence in our government, it will be critical for Christians to think carefully about what battles are appropriate, what stands are worth taking, what actions are heroic. Not all restrictions on our ability to pray and speak about God in public are wrong. In this instance, I believe it was wrong for the school to forbid Costner IV from mentioning God during his speech, but insofar as it was political protest against a ban on school sponsored prayer, I believe it was misguided and blind to Christian privilege.

Comments[5]

Gayle Jordan
8 months ago

Well thought-out and articulated, Alan. I expect you sometimes feel like a lone voice of reason in the Christian community. From one on the atheism/secular side of the spectrum (and former 40-year Southern Baptist) — keep writing, keep thinking, keep calling your fellow Christians when they cross this church/state line.

Adam Winters
8 months ago

I guess I'd have two major complaints about the specific event.

On the one hand, I don't think it's a respectable practice for a student to go through the process for having a speech approved and then make a show of publicly ripping it up and doing something else. If everybody did that, graduations could get really weird and out of control.

But on the other hand, if it is indeed true that the student was explicitly told by his principal not to mention any God in his speech, then that is absolutely unacceptable to a free society. That sort of thing goes beyond the realm of state-sponsored religion. Telling students they can't acknowledge the role of their faith commitments in public speeches borders on thought-policing. I don't see why a school would get into trouble for approving a speech in which a student makes reference and application of their personal religious faith, be they Christian, Muslim, Buddhist, or whatever. In that case, I can't help but applaud such "protest" where a student takes an opportunity to give the figurative raspberry to an educational system that tries to exert too much control over its student body (for further example, see that story of the school that withheld a diploma because a girl wanted to wear a Native American feather with her graduation regalia).

Craig Dumas
8 months ago

I can understand the logic behind not having a state sponsored religion, but this sounds more like an attempt at suppression than anything else. Because me praying may offend non-Christians, I can't pray at my graduation?

I find it concerning that we're forced into something akin to a spiritual schizophrenia in this country — you can believe what you want, just don't express it in public. If it's really our worldview, how can we not bring it with us when we go out into the world?

Besides, long as there are tests in school, there will be prayer.

Scott Uselman
8 months ago

I think the problem is that we are making assumptions about Costner's motives. There are only two who know what his motive was, God and Costner. . . . What is more, if someone's motive is impure, then that person will not receive a reward except that he or she was seen by others. This is where only God can sort out that person's motives to decide what blessing that person will receive. And, we may not know what the reward was. I'm not comfortable calling someone selfish because I don't know what occurred in his heart at the time. I agree that I do

not want to open the door to other faiths being allowed to pray, but if you are a believer, then I feel like we should rejoice since God's Word was spoken, like Paul said, no matter the motive the Gospel was preached (Philippians 1:15-18). I applaud the untamed way that Costner shared his belief. Paul was a fool for the Gospel in the 1st Century; and thank God he was. . . . Politically, I think this comes down to the federal government minimizing state's rights again. Sometimes it is needed, but as far as a group from another state telling a county in another state what is acceptable and unacceptable, there seems to be something wrong in that. . . . The bottom line is we are limited to speculation. Yet, if you are a believer, then at least God is in the spotlight again.

Notes

1. Jessica Ravitz, "With His Speech, Valedictorian Brings God to Graduation," *cnn.com*, 6 Jun. 2013.
2. Drew Dixon, "Football without a Prayer: Why Pre-Football Piety Is a Bad Idea," *christandpopculture.com*, 3 Dec. 2012.
3. Alan Noble, "Defending the Empty Form of Public Faith," *christandpopculture.com*, 28 Nov. 2011.
4. Stanley Fish, "When Is a Cross a Cross?" *New York Times*, 3 May 2010.
5. Due to space constraints, we have included a few representative comments here rather than all eighty that appeared with the article. To view all comments, visit http://christandpopculture.com/citizenship-confusion-valedictorian-prays-but-should-christians-rejoice/. –Eds.

Reading and Discussion Questions

1. As a Christian columnist, why can Noble not support Costner's reciting of the Lord's Prayer?
2. Explain how the warrant underlying Costner's reason for what he did differs from the warrant underlying Noble's argument.
3. There was widespread vocal support for Costner at the graduation. Given the setting and the context, why do you think audience members cheered?
4. What assumptions underlie the readers' comments? Do any of the responders seem to have misunderstood Noble's point?

e-Practice: Examining Online News and Blogs

Global Warming Continues with No Slowdown
JEFF MASTERS

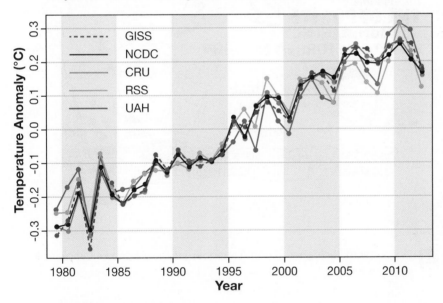

Adjusted Global Average Annual Temperature, 1979–2012

Dr. Jeff Masters, wunderground.com

 Go to **macmillanhighered.com/rottenberg** and analyze Jeff Masters's blog post about global warming.

Visual Lectures

Another source of online information comprises visual lectures, lectures delivered by means of Web technology. As with most of the resources available on the Internet, the quality can vary, but the idea is for a person or a group with expertise in a specific area to share it with anyone interested. The most common source of visual lectures is YouTube.

READING ARGUMENT

e-Practice: Examining Visual Lectures

Montessori Madness
TREVOR EISSLER

Trevor Eissler

 Go to **macmillanhighered.com/rottenberg** to view a good example of a visual lecture.

RESEARCH SKILL Evaluating Online Sources

In your search for reliable online information, you may not always find it easy to determine who is responsible for a source. A good first step is to check the domain name. Next, ask yourself some questions about the domain as well as the author of the material. Be aware that nonprofit sites are not necessarily free of bias, commercial sites may offer plenty of useful information, and sites with an *.edu* extension are not always approved by the institution.

- **.com:** A commercial site, including corporate-sponsored sites such as nike.com, as well as news sites, such as cnn.com, and personal sites. Do you recognize the name as a brand, news source, or other corporate entity? If not, do a search on the site's name to see if you can find any information about it (keeping in mind, of course, that those sites must also be evaluated). If the site is personal, what can you find out about the author?

- **.gov:** A government-sponsored site, maintained by one of the many government agencies, such as whitehouse.gov, supremecourt.gov, and dol.gov (Department of Labor). Although most government agencies should provide unbiased

information, elected officials — from the White House to your local town government — may be selective or biased in the information they provide. What do you know about the party affiliation or political agenda of the source of your information?

- **.edu:** A site sponsored by an educational institution, such as clemson.edu. Although an educational institution may be hosting the Web site, schools often allow professors and students to put up personal pages that may or may not be scholarly or trustworthy. Who is the author of the information, and what do you know about this person?

- **.org:** A site sponsored by a nonprofit group, such as heart.org (American Heart Association) or sierraclub.org. Nonprofit organizations often have a particular focus to promote: consumer protection, civil liberties, health, environment, and the like. In addition, they may be sponsored or supported by groups that have particular agendas (check the "About Us" section). Is it possible that the information provided on the site is biased in favor of the sponsor's goals?

Interactive Web Sites

One of the most useful features of the Internet is the ability to find information about almost any subject in a matter of minutes — if not seconds. We'll discuss more fully in Chapter 11 how to evaluate Web sites; for now, we will focus only on how the interactive feature of Web sites plays into their attempt to make an argument.

READING ARGUMENT

Examining Interactive Web Sites

In the following example, we have applied our usual categories to a print ad — Prereading, Reading for content, and Evaluation — but we have replaced the category Reading for Rhetorical Strategies with the category Online Interaction to explore the interactive features of an ad.

makehellcool.com

FASTRACK

Additional Web content

Reference to alleged Mayan prediction of the end of the world

Dead girl in apocalyptic scene is still chic and sexy

Company that sponsored the ad

Agency: Fisheye Solutions (Fisheye Creative Solutions Pvt. Ltd.)

Analysis

- **Prereading.** This is an ad for which context is critical. The date December 21, 2012, was significant because the end of the Mayan calendar seemed to predict that the world would end on that day. Fastrack, an Indian company that makes accessories for young people, built a whole ad campaign around the prediction. This is one of a series of ads that showed teenagers apparently dead in the aftermath of some type of destruction, but still accessorized in style.
- **Reading for content and structure.** There is the image of the young girl, of course, dead but still pretty. Her hair falls smoothly down, and her position emphasizes her thin, fit body clad in shorts and a midriff-baring tank top. She looks quite graceful, even in death. Her Fastrack sunglasses are still in place, and her Fastrack bag, watch, and shoes are still intact. She seems to be stretched across a safe that has survived whatever blast destroyed every-

thing else in sight. The background is gray and desolate. The smoke still seems to be clearing in the background and in the bottom left of the shot.

Once your attention moves away from the girl, text contributes significantly to the ad's effect. The connection to December 21, 2012, is explicit in the top right-hand corner — and the accessories really are called End of the World Gear. Fastrack's logo is in the bottom right-hand corner, with the words "move on," ironic in this context since the girl will not be moving on, nor will the rest of the world if the predictions are true. The name Fastrack suggests life on the fast track.

- **Online interaction.** The phrase "make hell cool" is designed to appeal to the teenaged audience, or Generation Next, that Fastrack products are aimed at. The Web site mentioned in the top left-hand corner, makehell cool.com, is a site where Indian teenagers could post their last words or their obituaries — or their celebratory words after December 21 passed without event — for the chance to win a trip to Thailand. These were some of the winners.

> "Hey, wait up, the party in hell doesn't start without me!"
> "Resting in peace. In hell, perhaps, but when not resting she'll be partying. Then again, that's what she loved anyway."
> "The world is coming to an end and I have nothing to wear!!"

The Web site also offers the opportunity to download a ringtone, "Stairway to Hell."

These features of the Web site — the contest, the posting of winners, and the free ringtone — are all designed to draw young people and make them active participants in the attempt to sell them Fastrack products, attempting to turn a static ad into an interactive experience.

- **Evaluation.** The response from Indian teenagers suggests that the ad was successful with at least some who took the time to explore the Web site and enter the contest. The company put enough faith in the idea to produce a series of similar ads, some featuring a male model and others, like this one, a female. Featuring an attractive young girl is a common rhetorical ploy in ads. The hope is that other girls will think that buying the products will make them like the girl, and that guys will think they can attract a girl like her. The opposite is true when the ad features a boy or a man. The fact that the girl is unmarred even in death plays on the common idea that youth are indestructible, but with a twist, since this one is dead.

The ad, of course, had a short life span because it was so closely linked to the specific date of the Mayan prediction. Still, it was very clever in its use of the prediction and innovative in using the prospect of the end of the world to sell some very successful products.

Assignments for Examining Multimodal Arguments

Reading and Discussion Questions

1. Analyze the photograph on page 62. There is no caption other than a title. What caption would you write for it?

2. Find a picture that you believe makes a statement without words. Be prepared to explain your reading of it.

3. Locate a political cartoon, and be prepared to explain to your classmates the warrant or warrants behind it.

4. Choose a television commercial, and analyze it like we analyzed the Toyota commercial.

5. Watch (and *listen to*) one of the afternoon television talk shows in which guests discuss a controversial social problem. (The *TV Guide*, daily newspapers, and online listings often list the subject. Past topics include when parents abduct their children, when children kill children, and when surgery changes patients' lives.) Analyze the discussion, considering the major claims, the most important evidence, and the declared or hidden warrants. How much did the oral format contribute to the success or failure of the arguments?

6. Watch an episode of either *The Daily Show* with Jon Stewart or *The Colbert Report*, and discuss how the show, successfully or not, tries to use humor to make serious points about political and/or social issues.

7. Locate an advertisement that you find visually and verbally interesting. Using as a model the analysis of the ad for Fastrack (pp. 106–107), what sorts of observations can you make about your ad? Exchange ads with a classmate, and discuss whether the two of you respond in the same way to each ad.

Writing Suggestions

1. Choose a photograph, and write an essay explaining how content and structure work together to make an argument.

2. Choose a print ad to analyze, and present your observations in an essay. Be sure to organize your specific observations about the ad around a clear thesis statement.

3. Write an essay analyzing a television commercial.

4. Write a paragraph explaining any bias you see in a news report by CNN or Fox News.

5. Watch one of the television talk shows that features experts on social and political issues, such as *The O'Reilly Factor*. Write a review, telling how much you learned about the subject(s) of discussion. Be specific about the features of the show that were either helpful or not helpful to your understanding.

RESEARCH ASSIGNMENT ▸ **Evaluating Online Sources**

Conduct an online search to answer the question "Is soda the leading cause of obesity?" Find one source each with domain extensions *.com, .gov, .edu,* and *.org,* for a total of four sources. For each source, answer the following questions:

1. Who is the sponsor of the Web site? What does the "About Us" section of the site reveal about the sponsor's mission? What else can you find out about the sponsor?

2. Who is the author of the material? Research this person to find any political or corporate affiliations he or she may have.

3. What is the main purpose of the site? Is the group looking for support or donations? Is it attempting to drive advertising? Is it trying to sell a product? Is it scholarly? Does it seem purely informational? How might its purpose affect its content?

Write a paragraph explaining which site you found to be the most reliable and which you determined to be the least reliable, based on the answers to your questions above.

---

bits

To see what you are learning about argumentation applied to the latest world and national news, read our *Bits* blog, "Argument and the Headlines," at **blogs.bedfordstmartins.com/bits**.

Responding to Arguments

Anytime the press covers a major speech, whether by the president, the chairman of the Federal Reserve, or the accused party in the most recent sex scandal, their next step is an analysis of every detail of the speaker's words and manner. Not only do people like to listen to arguments, but they also like to argue about them. Political pundit Bill O'Reilly has even had an analyst come in to critique the body language of political and media headliners.

An understanding of the elements of argument provides you not only with the ability to write your own arguments but also with the vocabulary to write about those of others. When you write an essay about an argument that you have read, listened to, or seen, you have two major options. You may choose to make a factual, nonjudgmental statement about the argument, or you may choose to evaluate it.

READING ARGUMENT

Seeing a Visual Argument

Remember that not every argument takes the form of an essay. You know from Chapter 3 that some arguments are multimodal — sometimes nonverbal and sometimes combining the verbal and the nonverbal. The "gun heart" photograph and accompanying text on page 111 were posted on Facebook. Although the photographer is unidentified, the words were posted by William Wharton. Student Karina Namaye wrote the response that follows the post.

Gun Heart
ANONYMOUS

Nothing says "I Love You" like giving that special someone a well-built, fully functioning and loaded firearm!
Ask my wife!

Hans Berggren/Getty Images

Killing with Kindness
KARINA NAMAYE

Karina Namaye
English 402
Dr. MacNamee
January 29, 2014

Killing with Kindness

Although the first phrase that popped into my head when I saw this picture was "killing with kindness," I don't think that is what the man who added the caption had in mind. To me, the heart, which represents love, doesn't fit with the assortment of ammunition used to form it, but to him, it does. He gave a gun to his wife as an act of love. Obviously he agrees with those who argue that people are safer in their own homes if they have guns to protect themselves and their loved ones. Since the gun is loaded, I would hope there are no children in the home. The other side of the debate is that too often a criminal will overpower a homeowner and use his own gun against him — or in this case, against her. People who hold that belief would not see giving her a gun as an act of love but as an act which endangers her. His statement "Ask my wife!" suggests that she agrees with her husband and accepted the gun as the act of love that he intended it to be. Without the caption, the picture would suggest to me the love that some gun owners have for their guns.

Writing the Claim

If you examined the most recent McDonald's commercial and wrote an essay explaining what tactics were used to try to persuade consumers to eat at McDonald's or to try McDonald's newest sandwich, you would be supporting a factual claim, or a **claim of fact**. In contrast, if you evaluated the ad's effectiveness in attracting adult consumers, you would be supporting an evaluative claim, or a **claim of value**. It's the difference between *explaining* Geico's use of a talking gecko in its ads and *praising* that marketing decision. What this means, of course, is that what you write about a commercial or any other type of argument that you see or read will itself have a claim of fact or a claim of value as its thesis.

What about a **claim of policy**, the third type of claim introduced in Chapter 1? In analyzing an argument, it would be rare to have a thesis that expressed what should or should not be done. Claims of policy are future oriented. They do not look back and express what should have been done in the past, but instead look forward to what should be done in the future. You might write an essay about what McDonald's should do in its future ads, but you would not really be writing an analysis.

> **ARGUMENT ESSENTIALS** Writing the Claim
>
> | | CLAIM OF FACT | CLAIM OF VALUE |
> |---|---|---|
> | **Responding to one argument** | Analyze it objectively. | Evaluate it. |
> | **Responding to two or more arguments** | Compare and contrast objectively. | Evaluate them in relation to each other. |

Think how claims of fact and claims of value might serve as thesis statements for essays *about* arguments. For our examples, we have drawn on two famous historical arguments. Abraham Lincoln's Gettysburg Address is the subject of Charles Adams's essay "Lincoln's Logic," which supports a claim of value:

> Lincoln's address did not fit the world of his day. It reflected his logic, which was based on a number of errors and falsehoods.

An objective analysis of the speech, based on a claim of fact, might explain the oration in the context of its time or Lincoln's use of poetic language.

Consider how your thesis looks different when you are making a *statement* about a document than when you are making a *judgment*:

Claims of fact: (statement)	The Declaration of Independence bases its claim on two kinds of support: factual evidence and appeals to the values of its audience.
	As a logical pattern of argument, the Declaration of Independence is largely deductive.
Claims of value: (judgment)	Jefferson's clear, elegant, formal prose remains a masterpiece of English prose and persuades us that we are reading an important document.
	The document's impact is lessened for modern readers because several significant terms are not defined.

In these examples based on the Gettysburg Address and the Declaration of Independence, we have been looking at one document at a time and thus at a single argument. At times you will want to compare two (or more) arguments, synthesizing their ideas. Again, there are two basic types of thesis that you might choose to support: those that *objectively analyze* the points of comparison or contrast between the two, and those that *evaluate* the two in relationship to each other. If you wrote claims about how the two pieces compare, they might look like these:

Claims of fact: Where Jefferson based his argument primarily on logical appeal, Lincoln depended primarily on emotional appeal.

Because Lincoln's purpose was to dedicate a cemetery, he left implicit most of his references to the political situation that was on the minds of his listeners. Because Jefferson knew he was justifying rebellion for King George III but also for the future, he spelled out explicitly why the colonies were breaking with England.

Claims of value: Lincoln's address is a period piece that recalls a dark chapter in American history, but Jefferson's Declaration has had a much greater impact as an inspiration for other reform movements worldwide.

Different as the two historical documents are, both the Gettysburg Address and the Declaration of Independence were effective in achieving their respective purposes.

Planning the Structure

When your purpose in writing about an argument is to support a factual claim, you will most likely use a very simple and direct form of organization called *defending the main idea.* In all forms of organization, you need to defend your main idea, or claim, with support; in this case, the support will come from the argument or arguments you are writing about.

At times, your claim may set up the organization of your essay, as was the case with the first example about the Declaration of Independence:

The Declaration of Independence bases its claim on two kinds of support: factual evidence and appeals to the values of its audience.

The body of an essay with this thesis would most likely have two main divisions: one about factual evidence, providing examples, and the other about appeals to values, also providing examples. The other thesis about the Declaration of Independence does not suggest such an obvious structure. An essay based on that thesis would need to explain how the Declaration is an example of deductive reasoning, most likely by first establishing what generalization the document is based on and then what specifics Jefferson uses to prove that the colonists' situation fits that generalization.

Remember that when you compare or contrast two arguments, there will be two basic patterns to choose from for structuring the essay. One, often called **point-by-point comparison**, discusses each point about Subject A and Subject B together before moving on to the second point, where again both subjects are discussed:

I. Introduction
II. Context
   A. Jefferson
   B. Lincoln
III. Implicitness/explicitness
   A. Jefferson
   B. Lincoln
IV. Language
   A. Jefferson
   B. Lincoln
V. Conclusion

The second, often called **parallel order comparison**, focuses roughly half the essay on Subject A and then the other half on Subject B. The points made in each half should be parallel and should be presented in the same order.

I. Introduction
II. Jefferson
   A. Context
   B. Implicitness/explicitness
   C. Language
III. Lincoln
   A. Context
   B. Implicitness/explicitness
   C. Language
IV. Conclusion

ARGUMENT ESSENTIALS Planning the Structure

- **Responding to one argument:** Organize essay according to supporting points. Responding to two or more arguments:
- **Responding to two or more arguments:** Organize essay according to a point-by-point comparison pattern or by a parallel order comparison pattern.

Using Sentence Forms to Write about Arguments

Writing in college means taking part in an ongoing conversation. You need to be respectful of what others say and write, and you need to account for their positions accurately. You'll want to be sure to clearly summarize the author's presentation. We have more to say about summary shortly, but, briefly put, in responding to an argument you must show that you understand the author's point before you either analyze it objectively or evaluate it. You'll need to be able to sum up in a neutral, fair way what the writer says.

When you present a negative evaluation of an argument, it is important to clearly explain how the previous writer approached the topic, and then explain how your view differs. There's no point in quoting or paraphrasing an author and ending with "and I agree." Sometimes the points of difference are large, sometimes small. But in writing for college, it is crucial that you explain your own understanding of a situation *and* that you express your own point of view.

It is easier to think about how you might summarize the argument of others and present your own if you have a model from which to work. This kind of model is called a *sentence form*, and it can help you to organize the presentation of others' views and your own responses to them. Here are some basic sentence forms for this kind of work.

Presenting Another's View

In _____, X claims that _____.

X's conclusion is that _____.

On the topic of _____, X attempts to make the case that _____.

These sentence forms are useful for presenting a brief summary of another's views on an issue. Note that the final sentence form implies that the writer has failed to make a convincing argument. (You would then go on to explain X's failure.)

Presenting Another's View Using Direct Quotations

In _____, X writes, "_____."

After discussing the topic of _____, X's conclusion is that "_____."

X attempts to make the case that "_____."

Quotations are a powerful way to present another's views when the language is particularly striking, clear, and succinct. (For more on using quotations, including a list of alternatives to the verb "writes," see Research Skill: "Incorporating Quotations into Your Text" on p. 121.) These templates help you to employ a key skill in making an argument: showing the work others have done on the issue. The next step is to introduce your own voice.

Presenting Another's View and Responding to It

She claims _____. It is actually true that _____.

In his essay _____, X writes that _____. However,

_____.

X attempts to make the case that "_____."

In her essay, X implies _____. However, careful consideration shows that _____.

The formula for this kind of template introduces what the author has to say and then has you take your turn with your own view of the matter.

When you agree with some of what a writer says, but not all of it, you must distinguish between the parts you think are correct and those parts that are not. Sentence forms for this kind of response include the following.

Agreeing in Part

Although most of what X writes about _____ is true, it is not true that _____.

X is correct that _____. But because of _____ it is actually true that _____.

X argues that _____. While it is true that _____ and _____ are valid points, _____ is not. Instead, _____.

These sentence templates ask you to identify those parts of the argument that are valid. Keep in mind that it is rare to disagree totally with every view expressed in an essay. A careful arguer will separate out what is correct and what is not. The writer can then focus energy on showing why these parts are not correct.

At times, you'll need to correct a distortion or misstatement of fact. Statistics, for instance, can be and often are manipulated to present the arguer's viewpoint in the best light. You may wish to propose an alternative interpretation or set the statistics in a different context, one more accurate and favorable to your own point of view. Of course, you'll want to be certain that you do not distort statistics. (For more on the importance of using statistics fairly, see the full discussion on pp. 177–78.) Here's a sentence form for correcting factual information in an argument.

> **Correcting a Factual Mistake**
>
> While X claims _____, it is actually true that _____.
>
> Although X states _____, a careful examination of _____ and _____ indicates that _____.

These templates allow you to identify a mistaken claim of fact in an argument and present evidence opposing it.

More often, rather than correcting clear mistakes of fact, you'll need to refine the argument of a writer. You may find that much of the argument makes sense to you, but that the writer does not sufficiently anticipate important objections. In those cases, a sentence form such as one of the following can help you refine the argument to make a stronger conclusion.

> **Refining Another's Argument**
>
> Although it is true, as X shows, that _____, the actual result is closer to _____ because _____.
>
> While X claims _____ and _____, he fails to consider the important point _____. Therefore, a more accurate conclusion is _____.

Such sentence forms enable you to clarify and amplify an argument.

At times, you'll need to distinguish between the views of two different writers and then weigh in with your own assessment of the situation. When two authors write on the same topic, they will most likely share similar views on some of the points. They will, however, disagree on other points. Similarly, you may find that you agree with some of what each writer has to say, but disagree with some other parts. Your job is to identify the points of contrast between the two authors and then explain how your own position differs from one or both. In those cases, you may find the following sentence forms helpful.

> **Explaining Contrasting Views and Adding Your Position**
>
> X says _____. Y says _____. However, _____.
>
> On the topic of _____, X claims that _____. In contrast, Y argues that _____. However, _____.

A careful writer makes sure the reader understands fine distinctions. The forms above help make those distinctions clear.

While sentence forms may be rather simple—perhaps even simplistic—good writers use them all the time. Once you have tried them out a few times, you'll begin to use them automatically, perhaps without even realizing it. They are powerful tools for incorporating others' views into your own work and then helping you to make careful distinctions about various parts of arguments.

Providing Support

In writing about any argument, you will need to understand the argument and to make it clear to your readers that you do. You cannot write a clear explanation or a fair evaluation if you do not have a clear understanding of your subject. You will need to look closely at the piece to recall what specific words or ideas led you to the thesis statement that you have chosen to support.

Your support for your thesis will come from the text or texts you are writing about in the form of summary, paraphrase, or quotations. The ability to summarize, paraphrase, and quote material from your source is necessary in writing about arguments, but it is also essential in writing your own arguments, especially those that require research.

ARGUMENT ESSENTIALS Using Sentence Forms

Before you analyze or evaluate another's argument, you must first be sure that you understand it. Then you can use some of the sentence forms in this section to show where it is weak and how your view is different.

- Presenting another's view
- Presenting another's view using direct quotations
- Presenting another's view and responding to it
- Agreeing in part
- Correcting a factual mistake
- Refining another's argument
- Explaining contrasting views and adding your position

Summarizing

A summary involves shortening the original passage as well as putting it into your own words. It gives the gist of the passage, including the important points, while leaving out details. What makes summarizing difficult is that it requires you to capture often long and complex texts in just a few lines or a short paragraph. To summarize well, you need to imagine yourself as the author of the piece you are summarizing and be true to the ideas the author is expressing, even when those ideas conflict with your personal point of view. You must then move smoothly from being a careful reader to being a writer who, in your own words, re-creates another's thoughts.

We summarize for many reasons: to let our boss know the basics of what we have been doing or to tell a friend why she should or should not see a movie. In your classes you are often asked to summarize articles or books, and even when this is not an explicit part of an assignment, the ability to summarize is usually expected. That is, when you are instructed to analyze an essay or to compare and contrast two novels, central to this work is the ability to carefully comprehend and re-create authors' ideas. See pages 43–45 in Chapter 2 for a more detailed treatment of summarizing.

Paraphrasing

Paraphrasing involves restating the content of an original source in your own words. It differs from summarizing in that a paraphrase is roughly the same length as the passage it paraphrases instead of a condensation of a longer passage. You will use paraphrasing when you want to capture the idea but there is nothing about the wording that makes repeating it necessary. You may also use it when the idea can be made clearer by rephrasing it or when the style is markedly different from your own. Here is an example drawn from a student paper:

> Randolph Warren, a victim of the thalidomide disaster himself and founder and executive director of the Thalidomide Victims Association of Canada, reports that it is estimated 10,000 to 12,000 deformed babies were born to mothers who took thalidomide. (40)

There is no single sentence on page 40 of the Warren article that both provides the estimate of number of affected babies and identifies Warren as one of them. Both the ideas were important, but neither of them was worded in such a unique way that a direct quote was needed. Therefore, a paraphrase was the logical choice. In this case, the writer correctly documents the paraphrase using Modern Language Association (MLA) style.

Quoting

You may want to quote passages or phrases from your sources if they express an idea in words more effective than your own. In reading a source, you may come across a statement that provides succinct, irrefutable evidence for an issue you wish to support. If the author of this statement is a professional in his or her field, someone with a great deal of authority on the subject, it would be appropriate to quote that author. Consider the student research paper in Chapter 13 by Angela Mathers about women in combat. Suppose, during the course of Angela's research for her paper, she found several sources that agree that women in the military who are denied combat experience are, as a result, essentially being denied a chance at promotion to the highest

---

ARGUMENT ESSENTIALS Providing Support

Support your claim with information from your source(s) in the form of

- **Summary** — a shortened version of the original, in your own words
- **Paraphrase** — a version of the original in your own words that is about the same length as the original
- **Quotation** — exact words from the original, placed in quotation marks

Provide documentation, usually the author and page number, whenever you use someone else's words or ideas.

ranks. Others argue that such considerations should not be a deciding factor in assigning women to combat. To represent the latter of these two positions, Angela chose to use a quotation from an authority in the field, using APA style:

> Elaine Donnelly, president of the Center for Military Readiness, says, "Equal opportunity is important, but the armed forces exist to defend the country. If there is a conflict between career opportunities and military necessity, the needs of the military must come first" (as qtd. in "Women in the Military," 2000).

It is especially important in argumentative writing to establish a source's authority on the subject under discussion. The most common way of doing this is to use that person's name and position of authority to introduce the quotation, as in the previous example. It is correct in both MLA and APA styles to provide the author's name in parentheses at the end of the quoted material, but that type of documentation precludes lending to the quote the weight of its having come from an authority. It is likely that those readers not in the military—and even some who are—will not know who Donnelly is just by seeing her name in parentheses. Your writing will always have more power if you establish the authority of each author from whose work you quote, paraphrase, or summarize. To establish authority, you may refer to the person's position, institutional affiliation, publications, or some other similar "claim to fame."

RESEARCH SKILL ▶ Incorporating Quotations into Your Text

There are three primary means of linking a supporting quotation to your own text. Remember that in each case, the full citation for the source will be listed alphabetically by the author's name in the list of works cited at the end of the paper, or by title if no author is given. The number in parentheses is the page of that source on which the quotation appears. The details of what appears in parentheses are covered in Chapter 13 in the discussion of APA (American Psychological Association) and MLA (Modern Language Association) documentation styles.

- You may choose to make a brief quotation a grammatical part of your own sentence. In that case, you do not separate the quotation from your sentence with a comma, unless there is another reason for the comma, and you do not capitalize the first word of the quotation, unless

there is another reason for doing so. In this sort of situation, there may be times when you have to change the tense of a verb, in brackets, to make the quotation fit smoothly into your text or when you need to make other small changes, always in brackets.

Examples:

APA style

James Rachels (1976), University Professor of Philosophy at the University of Alabama at Birmingham and author of several books on moral philosophy, explains that animals' right to liberty derives from "a more basic right not to have one's interests needlessly harmed" (p. 210).

MLA style

James Rachels, University Professor of Philosophy at the University of Alabama at Birmingham and author of several books on moral philosophy,

continued

explains that animals' right to liberty derives from "a more basic right not to have one's interests needlessly harmed" (210).

- You may use a traditional speech tag such as "he says" or "she writes." This is the most common way of introducing a quotation. Be sure to put a comma after the tag and to begin the quotation with a capital letter. At the end of the quotation, close the quotation, add the page number and any other necessary information in parentheses, and then add the period.

Examples:
APA style
James Rachels (1976), University Professor of Philosophy at the University of Alabama at Birmingham and author of several books on moral philosophy, writes, "The right to liberty — the right to be free of external constraints on one's actions — may then be seen as derived from a more basic right not to have one's interests needlessly harmed" (p. 210).

MLA style
James Rachels, University Professor of Philosophy at the University of Alabama at Birmingham and author of several books on moral philosophy, writes, "The right to liberty — the right to be free of external constraints on one's actions — may then be seen as derived from a more basic right not to have one's interests needlessly harmed" (210).

Students are sometimes at a loss as to what sorts of verbs to use in these tag statements. Try using different terms from this list or others like them. Remember that in writing about a printed or electronic text, it is customary to write in present tense unless there is a compelling reason to use past tense.

argues	implores
asks	insists
asserts	proclaims
concludes	questions
continues	replies
counters	responds
declares	states
explains	suggests

- You may vary the way you introduce quotations by at times using a colon to separate the quotation from a *complete sentence* that introduces it.

Examples:
APA style
For example, the Zurich Zoo's Dr. Heini Hediger (1985) protests that it is absurd to attribute human qualities to animals at all, but he nevertheless resorts to a human analogy: "Wild animals in the zoo rather resemble estate owners. Far from desiring to escape and regain their freedom, they are only bent on defending the space they inhabit and keeping it safe from invasion" (p. 9).

MLA style
The late Ulysses S. Seal III, founder of the Conservation Breeding Specialist Group and of a "computer dating service" for mateless animals, acknowledges the subordinate position species preservation plays in budgeting decisions: "Zoos have been established primarily as recreational institutions and are only secondarily developing programs in conservation, education, and research" (74).

Here is another example, also using APA style:

According to the late Ulysses S. Seal III (1982), founder of the Conservation Breeding Specialist Group and of a "computer dating service" for mateless animals, "None of these [zoo] budgets is allocated specifically for species preservation. Zoos have been established primarily as recreational institutions and are only secondarily programs in conservation, education, and research" (p. 74).

Notice that once the name of the author being cited has been mentioned in the writer's own text, it does not have to be repeated in the parentheses.

Documenting Your Sources

Chapter 13 will provide additional information about documenting sources, but you should start now documenting your use of others' work, even when the only sources you use are essays from this textbook. The single most important thing to remember is why you need to inform your reader about your use of sources. Once it is clear from your writing that an idea or some language came from a source and thus is not your own original thought or language, full documentation provides the reader with a means of identifying and, if necessary, locating your source. If you do not indicate your source, your reader will naturally assume that the ideas and the language are yours. It is careless to forget to give credit to your sources. It is dishonest to intentionally take credit for what is not your own intellectual property. Note, though, that the convention is for authors of magazine articles not to provide page numbers for their sources in the way that you will be expected to do.

The following Writer's Guide provides the general guidelines for documenting your use of sources.

WRITER'S GUIDE
Documenting Use of Summary, Paraphrase, and Quotation

---

1. **Give credit for *any ideas* you get from others**, not only for wording you get from them.
2. **Identify the author and the location of ideas that you summarize.** A *summary* is the condensing of a longer passage into a shorter one, using your own words.
3. **Identify the author and the location of ideas that you paraphrase.** A *paraphrase* is a rewording of another author's idea into your own words. A paraphrased passage is roughly the same length as the original.
4. **Identify the author and the location of language that you quote.** A *quotation* is the copying of the exact wording of your source and is placed in quotation

marks. You cannot change anything inside quotation marks, with these exceptions: (a) If there is a portion of the quotation that is not relevant to the point that you are making and *that can be omitted without distorting the author's meaning*, you may indicate an omission of a portion of the quotation with an ellipsis (. . .). If there is a sentence break within the portion you are omitting, add a fourth period to the ellipsis to so indicate. (b) If you need to make a very slight change in the quote to make the quote fit grammatically into your own text or to avoid confusion and if the change does not distort the author's meaning, you may make that slight change and place the changed portion in square brackets ([ ]). This method is used primarily to change the tense of a quoted passage to match that of your text or to identify a person identified in the quotation only by a pronoun.

5. **Make use of in-text or parenthetical documentation.** While a complete bibliographical listing for each work summarized, paraphrased, or quoted in your text is included in a Works Cited or References list at the end of your paper, each is also identified exactly at the point in the text where you use the source. If you are using the MLA system of documentation, the system most commonly used in the humanities, immediately following the sentence in which you use material from a source, you need to add in parentheses the author's name and the page number on which the material you are using appeared in the original source. However, since the credibility of your sources is critical in argumentative writing, it is even better to name the source in your own sentence and to identify the position or experience that makes that person a reliable source for the subject being discussed. In that case, you do not need to repeat the author's name in the parentheses. In fact, anytime the author's name is clear from the context, you do not need to repeat it in the parentheses.

Acceptable: The mall has been called "a common experience for the majority of American youth" (Kowinski 3).

Better: According to William Severini Kowinski, author of *The Malling of America*, "The mall is a common experience for the majority of American youth" (3).

In the APA system, the system most commonly used in the social sciences, in-text or parenthetical documentation is handled a bit differently because the citation includes the year of publication. The most basic forms are these:

The mall has been called "a common experience for the majority of American youth" (Kowinski, 1985, p. 3).

Kowinski (1985) writes, "The mall is a common experience for the majority of American youth" (p. 3).

6. **These examples show only the most basic forms for documenting your sources.** Some works will have more than one author. Sometimes you will be using more than one work by the same author. Usually Web sites do not have page numbers. Long quotations need to be handled differently than short ones. For all questions about documenting your use of sources not covered here, see Chapter 13.

Note: Unless your instructor indicates otherwise, use the page numbers on which your source appears **in this textbook** when summarizing, paraphrasing, or quoting from it instead of going back to the page numbers of the original. Also, unless your instructor indicates otherwise, use this model for listing in your Works Cited page a work reprinted here:

Isikoff, Michael. "The Snitch in Your Pocket." *Newsweek* 18 Feb. 2010: 40–41. Rpt. in *Elements of Argument: A Text and Reader*. 11th ed. Annette T. Rottenberg and Donna Haisty Winchell. Boston: Bedford, 2015. 130–33. Print.

Avoiding Plagiarism

Plagiarism is the use of someone else's words or ideas without adequate acknowledgment — that is, presenting such words or ideas as your own. Putting something into your own words is not in itself a defense against plagiarism; the source of the ideas must be identified as well. Giving credit to the sources you use serves three important purposes:

1. It reflects your own honesty and seriousness as a researcher.
2. It enables the reader to find the source of the reference and read further, sometimes to verify that the source has been correctly used.
3. It adds the authority of experts to your argument.

Plagiarism is nothing less than cheating, and it is an offense that deserves serious punishment. You can avoid accidentally slipping into plagiarism if you are careful in researching and writing your papers.

Taking care to document sources is an obvious way to avoid plagiarism. You should also be careful in taking notes and, when writing your paper, indicating where your ideas end and someone else's begin. When taking notes, make sure either to quote word for word or to paraphrase — one or the other, not both. If you quote, enclose any language that you borrow from other sources in quotation marks. That way, when you look back at your notes days or weeks later, you won't mistakenly assume that the language is your own. If you know that you aren't going to use a particular writer's exact words, then take the time to summarize that person's ideas right away. That will save you time and trouble later.

When using someone else's ideas in your paper, always let the reader know where that person's ideas begin and end. Here is an example from a student paper that uses APA style:

When zoo animals do mate successfully, the offspring is often weakened by inbreeding. According to geneticists, this is because a population of 150 breeder animals is necessary in order to "assure the more or less permanent survival of a species in captivity" (Ehrlich & Ehrlich, 1981, p. 211).

<table>
<tr><td>

ARGUMENT
ESSENTIALS Avoiding Plagiarism

- Take notes with care.
- Be clear in your writing where another person's words and ideas begin and end.
- Either quote word for word or paraphrase, not a mixture of both.
- Document your use of sources, whether you are quoting, paraphrasing, or summarizing.

</td></tr>
</table>

The phrase "according to geneticists" indicates that the material to follow comes from another source, cited parenthetically at the end of the borrowed material. If the student had not included the phrase "according to geneticists," it might look as if she only borrowed the passage in quotation marks, and not the information that precedes that passage.

READING ARGUMENT

Seeing a Claim of Value Response

Sadhbh Walshe's article "Online Gambling Is Anything but Pretty" is followed by a student response that supports a claim of value.

Title reveals her claim is going to be a claim of value.

Online Gambling Is Anything but Pretty
SADHBH WALSHE

Language shows she is judging gamblers.

Gambling is the new black in America. There was a time when a person would have to fly to Las Vegas or take a bus to Atlantic City to indulge any desire they may have to throw their money down the proverbial toilet. These days, with all but two states having some form of legalized gambling and new casinos popping up everywhere, there's no shortage of opportunities for gambling enthusiasts to enrich the casino magnates who are only too happy to facilitate them. As laws and attitudes around gambling get even more relaxed, pretty soon anyone who feels the need to burn a hole in their pocket won't even have to make the trek to the nearest casino or slot machine, they will be able to do so from the comfort of their own home.

Internet gambling (or "gaming" as its profiteers prefer to call it) is the latest way to help gamblers part with their money, and its rise is being promoted

---

Sadhbh Walshe writes commentary for the *Guardian*. This essay is from a series on society and justice, and it was published on November 20, 2013.

by cash-strapped states who are growing increasingly addicted to gambling revenue. Nevada and Delaware have already legalized online gambling, New Jersey is poised to go live with its casino-affiliated system this week and at least twelve other states are expected to follow suit next year. The burning question, however, is whether any state can really afford to rely on a morally bankrupt revenue stream, especially when they will also be required to pick up the tab for the social ills that generate it?

Good specifics

Why "morally bankrupt"? Does she mean the social ills that it generates?

Until 2011, online gambling was banned by the federal government, and it may not have been such a bad thing. There are approximately 6 to 8 million Americans who are considered to be "problem gamblers"—the kind who would be at risk of burning through their life savings to feed their addiction the way an alcoholic will corrode his own liver with excessive boozing. Obviously not everyone who gambles has a problem, but the indications are that the greater the access a person has to gambling opportunities the greater the likelihood is that they will develop a problem.

Is this her warrant?

A study that was published in 2005 by John W. Welte of the University of Buffalo's Research Institute on Addictions found that a person living within ten miles of a casino has a 50 percent greater chance of becoming a problem gambler than a person living ten or more miles away. In an interview with Chicago's *Daily Herald* about a follow up study, Welte told the newspaper that all the new gambling opportunities springing up around the country are making gambling more convenient. He said: "And if it's more convenient, more people are going to be getting into trouble."

Good detailed support

5   No one knows yet just how many more people will get into trouble when they don't even have to travel beyond their own bedroom to indulge their gambling habit, but many experts in the field are understandably worried.

At the moment, all eyes are on New Jersey to see how things pan out once Internet betting takes off. According to the Council for Compulsive Gambling of New Jersey (CCGNJ), there are already a whopping 350,000 problem gamblers in the state, and that number is expected to rise. To the state's credit, it has put some mechanisms in place to deal with the anticipated upsurge in problem gambling—every new casino that offers online betting will have to pay an annual fee of $250,000 to help fund treatment and prevention programs. Jeffrey Beck, CCGNJ's Assistant Director for Clinical Services, Treatment and Research says:

More good support for idea that addiction will increase

> This is a welcome move. Insurance programs don't cover gambling addictions and gamblers who need help usually have no money left, so we need to be able to offer free treatment.

It may seem a little cynical for a state to be creating new funds to pay for damages arising from behavior it is both encouraging and making money off of, but the real problem is that the damage control efforts are not nearly expansive enough.

We all know gambling, like other potentially harmful behaviors, is here to stay. As states make gambling more accessible, they really need to be putting adequate safeguards in place to mitigate the negative effects. So far, according to Keith Whyte, Executive Director of the National Council on Problem Gambling (NCPG), states have failed miserably to do this:

> Our biggest criticism to date is that as states decide to go into the gambling business, either through lotteries, casinos, and now the Internet, they have absolutely failed to adequately address the current social costs of gambling addiction or to expand funding for education or prevention programs before more problems arise.

Many states actually slashed funding for treatment and prevention programs even as they were opening their doors to more gambling generated revenue. As of 2010, the total amount of public funding allocated for problem gambling services was $58.4 million. That's a rather tiny share of the estimated $95 billion (and rising) in revenue generated last year. The NCPG recommends allocating at least one percent of gambling revenue for treatment and prevention services. At the moment only a tiny percentage of problem or at-risk gamblers get treatment, even as their exposure to risk is increasing.

It's interesting to note that the most vocal (and powerful) opponent of online gambling is billionaire casino magnate Sheldon Adelson, owner of several upscale resorts on the Las Vegas strip and elsewhere. Adelson has denounced online gaming as a danger to society that provides new opportunities to exploit children, the poor, and other vulnerable groups. While his motives may be questionable (considering how he has earned his billions), he may not be entirely wrong on this issue. For now, however, we should expect to see states fall like dominos due to the allure of the virtual casino and the riches it promises. Whether this easy money will be enough to cover the social costs it will inevitably engender remains to be seen.

Support is all for the claim that number of problem gamblers will increase.

Is this why it is morally bankrupt? Are these the social ills?

An Analysis of Sadhbh Walshe's Commentary on Online Gambling
CARSON KENNEDY

Carson Kennedy
English 103-003
Dr. Jones
April 3, 2014

An Analysis of Sadhbh Walshe's
Commentary on Online Gambling

In her essay "Online Gambling Is Anything but Pretty," Sadhbh Walshe focuses on how more states are legalizing online gambling, or gaming, because it brings in sorely needed revenue. She writes, "The burning question, however, is whether any state can really afford to rely on a morally bankrupt revenue stream, especially when they will also be required to pick up the tab for the social ills that generate it" (127). Walshe does a good job of explaining why she feels there will be an increase in the number of problem gamblers when gaming is widely available. However, she does not support her claim that gaming is a morally bankrupt revenue stream except by attempting to show that it will increase the number of problem gamblers. She ignores other social ills that generate gaming, or, more correctly, that gaming generates.

Claim of value

Walshe cites a study that found that there was a 50 percent greater chance that a person would become a problem gambler if he lived within ten miles of a casino than if he lived ten or more miles from one. She points out that there are already six to eight million problem gamblers in America, and she defines the term "problem gamblers" as "the kind who would be at risk of burning through their life savings to feed their addiction the way an alcoholic will corrode his own liver with excessive boozing" (127). The spread of online gambling to at least fifteen states by next year could make gambling even more accessible — for many, as accessible as their desktop or laptop computers, or iPhones.

First supporting example, summarized

Quote with page number in parentheses

Walshe focuses almost exclusively on the problem gambler. She points out that some states have wisely provided for a portion of the income from gambling to go to help those with gambling addictions (127). It may be difficult for the problem gamblers to be identified or to be reached if they are gaming in the privacy of their own homes. Gambling addiction is not the only social ill that grows out of

Second supporting example

Page number in parentheses indicates borrowed ideas.

gaming. Walshe touches on some other problems caused by gambling only in her last paragraph when she is explaining that casino magnate Sheldon Adelson says he is opposed to online gambling because it is "a danger to society that provides new opportunities to exploit children, the poor, and other vulnerable groups" (128). Walshe questions Adelson's motives in resisting online gaming, but his concerns raise issues that she does not otherwise delve into.

In her discussion of the potential effects of online gambling on the problem gambler, Walshe sounds an alarm, but she never explains fully why she considers the money from gaming to be a "morally bankrupt revenue stream" or what other social ills will become more widespread once more states make online gambling legal.

Work Cited

Walshe, Sadhbh, "Online Gambling Is Anything but Pretty." *The Guardian.com*. Guardian News and Media Ltd. 20 Nov. 2013. Rpt. in *Elements of Argument: A Text and Reader*. 11th ed. Annette T. Rottenberg and Donna Haisty Winchell. Boston: Bedford, 2015. 126–28. Print.

Seeing a Claim of Fact Response

Michael Isikoff's *Newsweek* article "The Snitch in Your Pocket" is followed by a response by student Ray Chong. Chong's argument supports a claim of fact, using a variety of examples to show how Isikoff appeals to his readers' need for security.

The Snitch in Your Pocket
MICHAEL ISIKOFF

Amid all the furor over the Bush administration's warrantless wiretapping program a few years ago, a mini-revolt was brewing over another type of federal snooping that was getting no public attention at all. Federal prosecutors were seeking what seemed to be unusually sensitive records: internal data from telecommunications companies that showed the locations

Michael Isikoff is a national investigative correspondent for NBC News, formerly with *Newsweek*. This essay was published in *Newsweek* on March 1, 2010.

of their customers' cell phones — sometimes in real time, sometimes after the fact. The prosecutors said they needed the records to trace the movements of suspected drug traffickers, human smugglers, even corrupt public officials. But many federal magistrates — whose job is to sign off on search warrants and handle other routine court duties — were spooked by the requests. Some in New York, Pennsylvania, and Texas balked. Prosecutors "were using the cell phone as a surreptitious tracking device," said Stephen W. Smith, a federal magistrate in Houston. "And I started asking the U.S. Attorney's Office, 'What is the legal authority for this? What is the legal standard for getting this information?'"

Those questions are now at the core of a constitutional clash between President Obama's Justice Department and civil libertarians alarmed by what they see as the government's relentless intrusion into the private lives of citizens. There are numerous other fronts in the privacy wars — about the content of e-mails, for instance, and access to bank records and credit-card transactions. The Feds now can quietly get all that information. But cell-phone tracking is among the more unsettling forms of government surveillance, conjuring up Orwellian images of Big Brother secretly following your movements through the small device in your pocket.

How many of the owners of the country's 277 million cell phones even know that companies like AT&T, Verizon, and Sprint can track their devices in real time? Most "don't have a clue," says privacy advocate James X. Dempsey. The tracking is possible because either the phones have tiny GPS units inside or each phone call is routed through towers that can be used to pinpoint a phone's location to areas as small as a city block. This capability to trace ever more precise cell-phone locations has been spurred by a Federal Communications Commission rule designed to help police and other emergency officers during 911 calls. But the FBI and other law-enforcement outfits have been obtaining more and more records of cell-phone locations — without notifying the targets or getting judicial warrants establishing "probable cause," according to law-enforcement officials, court records, and telecommunication executives. (The Justice Department draws a distinction between cell-tower data and GPS information, according to a spokeswoman, and will often get warrants for the latter.)

The Justice Department doesn't keep statistics on requests for cell-phone data, according to the spokeswoman. So it's hard to gauge just how often these records are retrieved. But Al Gidari, a telecommunications lawyer who represents several wireless providers, tells *Newsweek* that the companies are now getting "thousands of these requests per month," and the amount has grown "exponentially" over the past few years. Sprint Nextel has even set up a dedicated Web site so that law-enforcement agents can access the records from their desks — a fact divulged by the company's "manager of electronic surveillance" at a private Washington security conference last October. "The tool has just really caught on fire with law enforcement," said the Sprint executive, according to a tape made by a privacy activist who sneaked into the event. (A Sprint spokesman acknowledged the company has created the Web "portal" but says that law-enforcement agents must be "authenticated" before they are given passwords to log on, and even then still must provide valid court orders for all nonemergency requests.)

5   There is little doubt that such records can be a powerful weapon for law enforcement. Jack Killorin, who directs a federal task force in Atlanta combating the drug trade, says cell-phone records have helped his agents crack many cases, such as the brutal slaying of a DeKalb County sheriff: agents got the cell-phone records of key suspects — and then showed that they were all within a one-mile area of the murder at the time it occurred, he said. In the fall of 2008, Killorin says, his agents were able to follow a Mexican drug-cartel truck carrying 2,200 kilograms of cocaine by watching in real time as the driver's cell phone "shook hands" with each cell-phone tower it passed on the highway. "It's a tremendous investigative tool," says Killorin. And not that unusual: "This is pretty workaday stuff for us."

But there is also plenty of reason to worry. Some abuse has already occurred at the local level, according to telecom lawyer Gidari. One of his clients, he says, was aghast a few years ago when an agitated Alabama sheriff called the company's employees. After shouting that his daughter had been kidnapped, the sheriff demanded they ping her cell phone every few minutes to identify her location. In fact, there was no kidnapping: the daughter had been out on the town all night. A potentially more sinister request came from some Michigan cops who, purportedly concerned about a possible "riot," pressed another telecom for information on all the cell phones that were congregating in an area where a labor-union protest was expected. "We haven't even begun to scratch the surface of abuse on this," says Gidari.

That was precisely what Smith and his fellow magistrates were worried about when they started refusing requests for cell-phone tracking data. (Smith balked only at requests for real-time information, while other magistrates have also objected to requests for historical data on cell-phone locations.) The grounds for such requests, says Smith, were often flimsy: almost all were being submitted as "2703(d)" orders — a reference to an obscure provision of a 1986 law called the Stored Communications Act, in which prosecutors only need to assert that records are "relevant" to an ongoing criminal investigation. That's the lowest possible standard in federal criminal law, and one that, as a practical matter, magistrates can't really verify. But when Smith started turning down government requests, prosecutors went around him (or "judge shopping," in the jargon of lawyers), finding other magistrates in Texas who signed off with no questions asked, he told *Newsweek*. Still, his stand — and that of another magistrate on Long Island — started getting noticed in the legal community. Facing a request for historical cell-phone tracking records in a drug-smuggling case, U.S. magistrate Lisa Pupo Lenihan in Pittsburgh wrote a 56-page opinion two years ago that turned prosecutors down, noting that the data they were seeking could easily be misused to collect information about sexual liaisons and other matters of an "extremely personal" nature. In an unusual show of solidarity — and to prevent judge shopping — Lenihan's opinion was signed by every other magistrate in western Pennsylvania.

The issue came to a head this month in a federal courtroom in Philadelphia. A Justice Department lawyer, Mark Eckenwiler, asked a panel of appeals-court judges to overturn Lenihan's ruling, arguing that the Feds were only asking for what amounted to "routine business records." But he faced stiff questioning from one of the judges, Dolores Sloviter, who noted that there are some governments, like Iran's, that would like to use such records to identify political protesters. "Now, can the government assure us," she pressed Eckenwiler, that Justice would never use the provisions in the communications law to collect cell-phone data for such a purpose in the United States? Eckenwiler tried to deflect the question, saying he couldn't speak to "future hypotheticals," but finally acknowledged, "Yes, your honor. It can be used constitutionally for that purpose." For those concerned about what the government might do with the data in your pocket, that was not a comforting answer.

Misuse of Cell-Phone Tracking
RAY CHONG

Ray Chong
English 103
A. Pollard
October 12, 2012

Misuse of Cell-Phone Tracking

If you have watched many action films or police dramas at the theater or on television recently, you have probably seen law enforcement officials and others save the day by tracing the location of a cell phone as it "pings" off of towers it passes. Thousands held their breath as Halle Berry in *The Call*, for example, tried to save the life of a kidnap victim locked in the trunk of a serial killer's car by keeping in touch with her via cell phone. In "The Snitch in Your Pocket," Michael Isikoff acknowledges that the ability to track cell phones has helped law enforcement crack cases and respond to emergencies, but that the FBI and other law enforcement agencies are using cell phones more and more to track their owners, often without the benefit of a search warrant. Isikoff warns that "cell-phone tracking is among the more unsettling forms of government surveillance, conjuring up Orwellian images of Big Brother secretly following your movements through the small device in your pocket" (131).

Isikoff cites instances in which cell-phone tracking has helped crack cases. In one case, cell-phone records put the suspects in the vicinity of the murder of a county sheriff at the time it occurred. In another, officers were able to track a truckload of cocaine because the driver's cell phone was tracked in real time (132).

There are, however, instances of abuse as well. In one case, an Alabama sheriff claimed his daughter had been kidnapped in order to locate her cell phone when the truth was that she had

Opening draws in reader with familiar example.

Claim of fact

MLA-style quotation introduced with author's name and followed by page number in parentheses

Supporting detail paraphrased and identified by page number

Supporting detail

simply stayed out all night. In Michigan, police asked for information on cell phones at a certain location, claiming that they feared a
riot, when what they really wanted was information on labor-union
protesters (132).

The growing number of requests for cell-phone records is getting
attention because a few magistrates have finally started saying no.
Federal magistrates in New York, Pennsylvania, and Texas have
questioned the legality of using such information. Stephen W. Smith
in Texas and some colleagues are among those who have refused
requests for cell-phone information (132). U.S. magistrate Lisa Pupo
Lenihan wrote a fifty-six-page opinion explaining why she turned
down a request for cell-phone records in a drug-smuggling case,
and all of the other magistrates in western Pennsylvania joined her
in signing it. When the Justice Department asked a federal court
to overturn Lenihan's ruling, one judge "noted that there are some
governments, like Iran's, that would like to use such records to identify political protesters." It was not very reassuring that the Justice
Department lawyer could not deny that there is nothing in our Constitution that prevents our government's doing exactly that (133).

*Supporting detail
shows the reaction of
some magistrates.*

*An evaluative
statement, but the
main purpose of the
essay is to present
facts.*

WORK CITED

Isikoff, Michael. "The Snitch in Your Pocket." *Newsweek* 18 Feb.
2010: 40–41. Rpt. in *Elements of Argument: A Text and Reader.*
11th ed. Annette T. Rottenberg and Donna Haisty Winchell. Boston: Bedford, 2015. 130–33. Print.

Seeing a Claim of Fact Response to Two Related Arguments

Isikoff's "The Snitch in Your Pocket" (p. 130) and Bruce Schneier's "The Internet Is a Surveillance State" (p. 55) both address the loss of privacy we suffer as
a result of the technological devices that have become a part of our daily lives.
This student essay, written by Clemson University student DeRon Williamson,
compares the two. It supports a claim of fact.

How Our Technology Is Used against Us
DᴇRON WILLIAMSON

DeRon Williamson

English 103

Mrs. Brantley

September 23, 2011

How Our Technology Is Used against Us

In today's world, cell phones and computers are not just nice to have. They are necessities, or at least we have come to feel that they are. Cell phones and the Internet have replaced land lines and letters as ways of keeping in touch with family and friends. We want to be in touch instantly. However, two authors, Michael Isikoff and Bruce Schneier, explain how we are giving up our privacy in order to have that instantaneous communication and convenience.

Claim of fact

In his article "The Snitch in Your Pocket," Isikoff explains how law enforcement agencies at all levels are increasingly using cell phones to track their owners in real time and cell-phone records to track where they were at a particular time in the past. Most cell-phone owners don't even realize that their phone either has a tiny GPS or can be located as its calls are routed through specific towers. It is good that these tracking systems can be used to locate the owner in an emergency, but they can also be used to locate an owner who doesn't want his or her location to be known. More and more, law enforcement officers are tracking cell phones or attaining cell-phone records without a warrant. Only recently have a few magistrates decided to say no to requests for phone records and real time tracking (Isikoff 131–32).

Objective analysis of one argument

Parenthetical citation at end of paragraph indicates paraphrased ideas.

In his article "The Internet Is a Surveillance State," from cnn.com, Bruce Schneier uses a variety of examples to explain how Internet users are tracked. Users are tracked by Facebook, by Google, and, via their iPads and iPhones, by Apple. Data about their online activity is even correlated with their offline activity, such as purchases, to get more detail about their lives. Schneier explains how even CIA director David Petraeus could not keep his private life private. His affair with Paula Broadwell became public because she used hotel and other public networks to e-mail him, and when the hotel records were correlated, the common name was hers. The government works with corporations, corporations work with the government,

Objective analysis of second argument

Because the author's name is in the sentence, it does not have to be repeated in the parentheses.

Conclusion mentions both authors again.

and as Schneier concludes, "So, we're done. . . . Welcome to an Internet without privacy, and we've ended up here with hardly a fight" (57).

Schneier ends on this pessimistic note. Although Isikoff finds it far from comforting that it is constitutional to use cell-phone locations and cell-phone records to track users' whereabouts, at least some magistrates are starting to look a bit more closely at the numerous requests for cell-phone information and to sometimes just say no (132). Until we can say no to our cell phones and the Internet, we will just to have accept the lack of privacy.

Works Cited

Isikoff, Michael. "The Snitch in Your Pocket." *Newsweek* 18 Feb. 2010: 40–41. Rpt. in *Elements of Argument: A Text and Reader*. 11th ed. Annette T. Rottenberg and Donna Haisty Winchell. Boston: Bedford, 2015. 130–33. Print.

Schneier, Bruce. "The Internet Is a Surveillance State." *cnn.com*. Cable News Network, 16 Mar. 2013. Rpt. in *Elements of Argument: A Text and Reader*. 11th ed. Annette T. Rottenberg and Donna Haisty Winchell. Boston: Bedford, 2015. 55–57. Print.

Practice: Responding to Arguments

Read the article that begins on the next page, and answer the questions that follow.

Social Media: Establishing Criteria for Law Enforcement Use

ROBERT D. STUART

Over the past decade, social media has become a widespread presence that touches the lives of countless people, including law enforcement officers. Certain risks and rewards face officers, as well as their departments, who use social media. Missteps in its use can endanger the safety of officers and compromise criminal cases, resulting not only in embarrassment to departments but exposure to civil and criminal liability. To combat these risks, law enforcement agencies must adapt to the social media outlets that affect the lives of officers every day. To do so departments must understand the forms of social media that exist, their benefits to law enforcement, the problems they may pose, and the need to establish criteria governing their use by law enforcement officers.

Understanding Social Media

Media is a means of communication with the intent to influence a wide audience.[1] Historically, this referred to newspapers and television, but it now includes electronic forms, such as the Internet. The term *social* implies two-way communication in which the user interacts with a media source.

One form of social media is social networking, which allows multiple people to share information with one another. Facebook, MySpace, YouTube, and Twitter serve as examples of social networking Web sites. Users on a site, like Facebook, first must establish a profile containing personal data, such as their name, interests, employment, and geographic area. Other informa-

tion, such as pictures, video, and texts, also can be shared. Users can form online relationships with other people, sharing the information they have uploaded. As a security precaution, most social networking sites have settings enabling users to control what information is shared and who can see it.

Social media has crafted its own language with common words and unique definitions. For instance, a "tweet" is commonly known as the text-based sharing of information on Twitter. Likewise, a "wall" is the public or semipublic area of Facebook users' profiles in which information is shared in the social media world.[2]

Year after year social media sites continue to grow exponentially. For example, Twitter grew from 75 million registered users in 2010 to 175 million in 2011.[3] Facebook experienced similar growth, rising from approximately 350 million active users worldwide in 2010 to near 640 million a year later.[4] Additionally, the rate at which people access these sites is significant. For example, YouTube, the popular video-sharing site, receives more than 24 hours of video every minute.[5] Similarly, photo-sharing site Flickr receives more than 3,000 image uploads every minute.[6]

A 2011 survey conducted by the Institute for Criminal Justice Education (ICJE) found that

5

Robert D. Stuart, a retired major with the Montgomery, Alabama, Police Department, is the assistant chief agent at the Alabama Criminal Justice Information Center. This article appeared in the *FBI Law Enforcement Bulletin* on the fbi.gov Web site in February 2013.

over 78 percent of law enforcement respondents had a social media account.[7] Of those, over 38 percent identified themselves on their profile as policing professionals.[8] This finding illustrates the interest law enforcement officers have in social media, in addition to how they choose to identify themselves to others through social media.[9]

Applying Social Media to Law Enforcement

To their benefit law enforcement agencies can use social media for public relations, crime prevention, and criminal investigation. Departments that create a presence on social media sites open a new door of communication with the general public. By doing so citizens can receive real-time information, as well as an electronic method of asking questions, making suggestions, and providing tips that help solve crimes. For example, in 2011 Kentucky State Police investigators posted photos of jewelry, a tattoo, and a facial composite relating to an unknown body found 10 years earlier. The additional evidence provided in response to the post enabled investigators to identify the deceased person.[10]

Social media can provide an invaluable source of information for investigators. Criminals will use social media to share information about their whereabouts and those of their associates.[11] They also have been known to share photos and videos of their criminal acts.[12] Such electronic information can help apprehend fugitives, single out associate suspects, link individuals to street gangs, and provide evidence of criminal activity.

Encountering Problems

Law enforcement agencies must understand the problems that can arise when work and personal life converge in social media. Officers establish what they intend to be a personal presence in the social media world while identifying themselves as members of law enforcement. Mixing their personal and social lives with their professional ones can bring discredit to them and their departments.

Officers posting information about how sleepy they are on duty can call into question their fitness for duty in the event of a deadly force situation or a serious traffic accident. Additionally, posting photos of themselves with seized drug evidence can be harmful to the ongoing prosecution of a case because prosecutors should be consulted before evidence is shared with the public. Though officers may face disciplinary proceedings if their actions are discovered, departments may rely on a "conduct unbecoming" regulation and not a specific policy regarding social media.

When exposed, inappropriate information may lead to undesirable attention from the media and other parties. In one such instance, a defense attorney in Texas found the MySpace page of his client's arresting officer. The page listed the officer's occupation as "super hero/ serial killer" and included expressions of interest in intense violence and graphic pictures of women with carvings in their skin. The defense attorney claimed this was evidence of the officer's excessive force against his client.[13]

Criminals also can capitalize on private information publicly shared by law enforcement officers. For example, a 2011 arrest in Arizona led to the discovery of a CD containing information on over 30 officers and law enforcement support employees, all obtained through Facebook.[14]

Developing Solutions

Officers cannot be expected to refrain from maintaining a social presence on the Internet.

10

Therefore, law enforcement agencies must establish criteria for social media usage that balance the constitutional rights of officers while protecting the integrity of departments and investigations. The 2011 ICJE survey found that less than 40 percent of responding agencies had policies regarding social media use, and less than 15 percent provided training on what is appropriate to post.[15] These findings point to the development and implementation of a comprehensive agency-wide policy on social media use as a logical first step. This policy should be sufficiently broad to address the use of social media today and in the future. Consideration must be given to protect the free speech rights of off-duty officers using their own computers. However, personnel who choose to provide information about their work on social media sites will be open to scrutiny from their departments.[16]

Government entities can restrict the speech of their employees under certain circumstances, such as if the expression interferes with or compromises the mission of the department or brings into question the professionalism of the officers or the agency.[17] Social media policy should clearly delineate between protected free expression and the speech that could impact departments or officers. Agencies generally are permitted to regulate officers' conduct on social media sites if the individuals list law enforcement as their occupation or post law enforcement-related content. Administrators must decide the conduct and information to regulate.

- Photos or videos of officers, suspects, evidence, police facilities, equipment, uniforms, or weapons
- Employment, job assignment, work hours, or other related information
- Public or nonpublic information regarding police reports, criminal history, arrests, or calls for police service
- Profanity or unprofessional language and harmful images
- Derogatory comments or images about superiors or coworkers
- Work-related matters or other named officers in posts, blogs, or microblogs
- Personal social media activities while on duty and with agency resources
- Allowance by officers of the content of their social networking sites to be viewed by administrators during the course of an internal investigation

An agency's social media policy also should address the official purpose for use and the desired objectives. It should define the person or group authorized to create and maintain the social media presence on behalf of the agency. The policy also must provide guidance on what officers can share and when.

Training officers on social media guidance can be done in two steps. The first should address general computer, Internet, and social media security and privacy issues, while the second should look at the practical application of social media policy as related to officers. The training curriculum should be frequently updated and repeated to keep up with evolving technology and ensure the information remains fresh in officers' minds. Once educated, officers can take the initiative to properly protect themselves and their departments. Compliance can occur when officers understand the problem and buy into the solution.

Conclusion

Law enforcement administrators must establish appropriate controls over the use of social media

15

to increase its benefits for their departments and reduce incidents of misuse by officers. This can be accomplished by setting criteria for social media use and training personnel on these policies. In doing so, the potential of social media as a law enforcement tool that can help departments better serve the public may fully be realized.

Notes

1. Random House Webster's College Dictionary, 11th ed., s.v. "Media."
2. Martha S. Stonebrook and Richard A. Stubbs, "Social Media Glossary of Terms," in Social Networking in Law Enforcement — Legal Issues (paper presented at the IACP Conference, Orlando, FL, October 24, 2010).
3. Jake Hird, "20+ Mindblowing Social Media Statistics: One Year Later," Econsultancy, entry posted March 25, 2011, http:// econsultancy.com/us/blog/7334-social -media-statistics-one-year-later (accessed September 19, 2012).
4. Ibid.
5. Ibid.
6. Ibid.
7. Institute for Criminal Justice Education, "Social Networking Survey," http://www.icje .org/articles/SocialMediaSurvey.pdf (accessed September 18, 2012).
8. Ibid.
9. Ibid.
10. Deborah Highland, "KSP Turns to Facebook as Investigative Tool," *Bowling Green Daily News*, April 3, 2011, http://www.bg dailynews.com/news/ksp-turns-to-facebook -as-investigative-tool/article_00d04894 -3a41-59b5-96f5-631ac03ed070.html (accessed September 19, 2012).
11. Highland, "KSP Turns to Facebook as Investigative Tool."
12. Ibid.
13. "Grisly MySpace Page Gets Cop Suspended," CBS News, February 11, 2009, http://www.cbsnews.com/2100-201_162 -2088362.html (accessed September 19, 2012).
14. "Arizona Fusion Center Warning: Police Officers Targeted on Facebook," Public Intelligence, entry posted February 23, 2011, http://publicintelligence.net/ules-arizona -fusion-center-warning-police-officers -targeted-on-facebook/ (accessed September 19, 2012).
15. Institute for Criminal Justice Education, "Social Networking Survey."
16. United States v. Treasury Employees, 513 U.S. 454 (1995).
17. Connick v. Myers, 461 U.S. 138 (1983); City of San Diego v. Roe, 125 S. Ct. 521 (2004).

Reading and Discussion Questions

1. A large part of Stuart's article provides factual information about social media. It goes further, however. What was Stuart's purpose in writing the article?
2. What are some of the dangers of social media use by police officers?
3. Do you find Stuart's support convincing? Why, or why not?
4. Who was Stuart's audience? Given that audience, does his explanation of social media seem overly basic, or does it seem appropriate? Explain.

Writing Assignments

1. Write a claim of fact response, objectively analyzing Stuart's article.
2. Write a claim of value response, evaluating the effectiveness of Stuart's argument.

Practice: Responding to Arguments

Read the captioned graphics on pages 142–43, and answer the questions that appear at the end.

The Facebook Effect
RACHEL SWABY

THE FACEBOOK EFFECT  1.2 BILLION PEOPLE LIKE THIS

In 2007, social networking grabbed the attention of just 56 percent of the world's Internet users. Five years later, global engagement has jumped to 82 percent and continues to climb. We now post status updates and track down our high school sweethearts instead of emailing or, you know, actually talking to people. Here's what's trending.

HOW FACEBOOK TOOK OVER THE WORLD
Facebook hasn't always been the dominant social network everywhere. In some countries, it faced competition from other networks. The bar chart shows Facebook's global growth. The icons indicate when Facebook eclipsed another network to become No. 1 in a particular country (below).

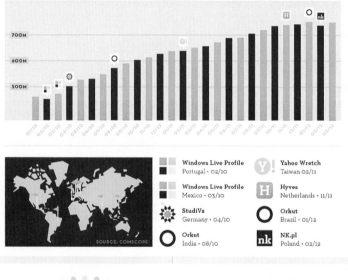

Windows Live Profile Portugal · 02/10		Yahoo Wretch Taiwan 02/11	
Windows Live Profile Mexico · 03/10		Hyves Netherlands · 11/11	
StudiVz Germany · 04/10		Orkut Brazil · 01/12	
Orkut India · 08/10		NK.pl Poland · 02/12	

SOURCE: COMSCORE

229
The average number of friends a U.S. Facebook user has
SOURCE: PEW RESEARCH CENTER

WHAT'S ON YOUR MIND?

SOCIAL SENIORS
Between July 2010 and October 2011, the age 55-and-up community embraced social networking with more enthusiasm than any other demographic. That population of users jumped 9.4 percent.

¡HOLA!

¡OLÁ!

CÓMO SE DICE "RETWEET"?
By one measure, Latin Americans use social networks the most: Almost 100 percent of the Internet population participates in at least one. Facebook, Twitter, and Orkut are the most popular.

GLOBAL MEETUP
How big is Facebook? Last year, 1 of every 7 online minutes and 3 of every 4 social networking minutes worldwide were spent on the site.
SOURCE: COMSCORE

Illustrated by Jen Adrion and Omar Noory for *AFAR*

Rachel Swaby is a freelance writer in San Francisco and a frequent contributor to *Wired*, *Gizmodo*, and *AFAR*. This infographic appeared in the May/June 2013 issue of *AFAR*.

TOP 10 MOST ENGAGED COUNTRIES

Israelis spend more time on social networks than any other country's citizens, an average of about 11 hours per month. Americans spend 6.9 hours a month. Here are the countries that spend the most time on social networks. SOURCE: COMSCORE

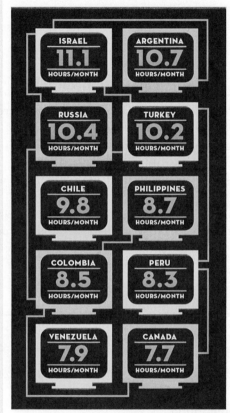

ISRAEL
11.1
HOURS/MONTH

ARGENTINA
10.7
HOURS/MONTH

RUSSIA
10.4
HOURS/MONTH

TURKEY
10.2
HOURS/MONTH

CHILE
9.8
HOURS/MONTH

PHILIPPINES
8.7
HOURS/MONTH

COLOMBIA
8.5
HOURS/MONTH

PERU
8.3
HOURS/MONTH

VENEZUELA
7.9
HOURS/MONTH

CANADA
7.7
HOURS/MONTH

THE FASTEST-GROWING SOCIAL NETWORKS

Facebook is not the only social network growing. Here are five more on the rise around the globe, with their percentage growth from October 2010 to October 2011. SOURCE: COMSCORE

TWITTER ▲ 59%

At last count, Twitter had upwards of 140 million users. International users far outweigh those stateside. When Bollywood stars started tweeting in 2010, the number of Indian users jumped 100 percent in just three months.

LINKEDIN ▲ 55%

Although LinkedIn started in the United States, 62 percent of current members reside abroad. The United States still leads with 67 million members. India is second, with 16 million.

SINA WEIBO ▲ 181%

The world's 10th-largest social network, a microblogging site, is No. 1 in China, where Twitter and Facebook are blocked.

TUMBLR ▲ 172%

In June 2012, multimedia blogging tool Tumblr pulled in some 25 million unique visitors from the United States alone.

BADOO ▲ 64%

As of September 2012, Badoo, a dating-oriented network, had 161 million users and was gaining 150,000 signups a day.

SOCIAL NETWORK GRAVEYARD

A good idea doesn't always guarantee success. In fact, the models that kicked off our socializing online are, for the most part, long gone. Before the globe caught on to social networking, there was the Globe, an early network built by two students at Cornell University. Here's the tale of social networks past. VARIOUS SOURCES

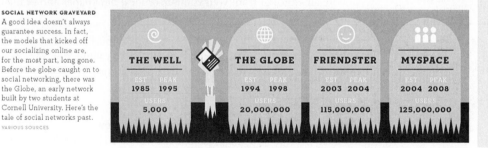

	THE WELL	THE GLOBE	FRIENDSTER	MYSPACE
EST	1985	1994	2003	2004
PEAK	1995	1998	2004	2008
USERS	5,000	20,000,000	115,000,000	125,000,000

Reading and Discussion Questions

1. What specific information about the rise of Facebook and other social networking sites does Rachel Swaby provide in this graphic?
2. How would you summarize the data that Swaby provides in this infographic?
3. What are some specific conclusions you can draw about how social media use in the United States compares to social media use elsewhere?
4. What conclusions can you draw about how your own personal use of social media compares with others'?

Writing Assignments

1. Write a claim of fact paragraph summarizing what Swaby's graphic reveals about the growth and decline of social networking sites.
2. Write a claim of value paragraph responding to Swaby's graphic and evaluating its effectiveness.
3. How is Swaby's tone in presenting her information different from the tone Stuart uses in his article? Cite examples of how her tone is revealed.
4. Swaby had a different purpose in her infographic than Stuart had in his article. Which writer do you think was more successful in achieving his or her purpose? Explain.

Assignments for Responding to Arguments

Reading and Discussion Questions

1. Choose an editorial from your campus or local newspaper and evaluate it. How successful an argument does it make?
2. Which essay do you find more effective, Schneier's or Isikoff's? Why?
3. Think of some television commercials that have caught your eye. What tactics are used to try to convince you to buy a product or service?

Writing Suggestions

1. Choose an editorial from your campus or local newspaper, and write an objective analysis of it. Your thesis statement will be a claim of fact.
2. Locate two editorials or two articles that take different stands on the same controversial issue. Write an analysis in which you objectively compare the two as examples of argumentation.

3. Locate two editorials or two articles that take different stands on the same controversial issue. Write an essay in which you argue which of the two is a more effective argument and why.

4. Choose a print advertisement to analyze or evaluate in an essay.

RESEARCH ASSIGNMENT ▸ **Incorporating Quotations**

Read each of the following passages. Then for each, write one or two sentences incorporating a quotation. Also incorporate in your sentence(s) the author's name and the title of the work. Choose a different way of incorporating the quote each time so that all three ways are represented: (1) as a grammatical part of your own sentence, (2) with a speech tag such as "he says" or "she writes," and (3) with a complete sentence and a colon.

Put the page number in parentheses, and punctuate correctly according to MLA style.

Passage 1

The school district [in Washington, DC] Michelle Rhee inherited in 2007 was in freefall. Not only had student enrollment plummeted and test scores scraped the bottom of any national rankings, but also many principals had lost control of their schools. Rhee's response to the latter was to eject (or offer voluntary retirement to) nearly fifty principals who had tolerated those conditions.

Her yardstick for progress was basic. In the first year, a principal entering an out-of-control school must succeed in "locking down" the school: seize control of the hallways, bathrooms, lunchrooms, and the nearby city blocks during school dismissal and ensure calm and respect in the classrooms. If principals succeed with that first-year lockdown but test scores still look miserable, they generally got a pass. The second and third years, however, measurable "teaching and learning" was supposed to kick in. If that didn't happen, the principal was "non-reappointed," the district's euphemism for getting fired. Not surprisingly, a lot of principals stumbled along that path, which means a lot of non-reappointments — and a lot of interviews for new principals.

Source: Richard Whitmire, *The Bee-Eater* (San Francisco: Jossey-Bass, 2011): pp. 131–32.

Passage 2

Back in the 1970s, organic food had no such positive image. Many dismissed it as a fringy fad served cold with an eat-your-spinach sermon. How could organic taste good? Indeed, taste was the key challenge. Organic advocates couldn't popularize a cuisine simply by declaring it spiritually and ecologically superior. The world, like my mother, was not waiting for or willing to eat inedible soul food. To win acceptance, it had to be truly delectable.

But that would take a while. Many of us got involved in the organic movement for political reasons — to protest industrial agriculture. Some of us were back-to-the-land rebels with a strong passion for eating locally grown food. Others were food purists, excited by the opportunity to propagate and preserve heirloom varieties of produce and seed stocks. Still others came to the cause simply for the joy of growing our own food, talented amateurs at best who cared more about its appeal to a diner's political conscience than to his or her taste buds.

Luckily, what began as a philosophical fondness for dishes like brown rice and seaweed eventually matured into a tasty cuisine that attracted talented chefs, notably my friend Alice Waters, who called organics "the delicious revolution."

Source: Gary Hirshberg, "Organics — Healthy Food, and So Much More," in Karl Weber, ed., *Food, Inc.: How Industrial Food Is Making Us Sicker, Fatter and Poorer — And What We Can Do about It* (New York: Participant Media, 2009), p. 49.

---

bits   To see what you are learning about argumentation applied to the latest world and national news, read our *Bits* blog, "Argument and the Headlines," at **blogs.bedfordstmartins.com/bits**.

Analyzing the ELEMENTS

Claims: Making a Statement

W hat are you trying to prove? Your claim, or proposition, represents your answer to this question. A claim is the statement that a writer makes about a subject and thus is most closely aligned with the writer-subject leg of the communications triangle.

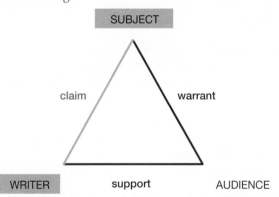

Your **claim** is a conclusion you reach when you are trying to decide what to say about a subject; it becomes your **thesis** when you write about that subject. Claims can be classified as claims of fact, claims of value, and claims of policy, although at times there is a fine line between one type of claim and another.

Claim of fact	States that a condition exists, has existed, or will exist, based on factual evidence.	■ *Excess sun exposure causes skin cancer.* ■ *Environmental policies have slowed the depletion of the Earth's ozone layer.*
Claim of value	Desirable or undesirable based on moral or aesthetic principles.	■ *The most relaxing vacations are spent on the beach.* ■ *Bathing suits have gotten too skimpy.*
Claim of policy	States that a specific course of action should be implemented.	■ *Sunscreen products should be more closely regulated.* ■ *Stricter emissions policies are needed for trucks.*

Claims of Fact

A fact, for the most part, is not a matter for argument — it is an undisputed truth. Many facts can be confirmed by our own senses: *The sun sets in the West. Water freezes at 32 degrees Fahrenheit.* For facts that we cannot confirm for ourselves, we must rely on other sources — reference works, scientific reports, media outlets — for information: *Salmon is rich in omega 3 fatty acids. The United States spent $528 billion on military expenditures in 2011.*

Unlike a simple fact, a **claim of fact** *asserts* that something is true — that a condition has existed, exists, or will exist. An argument built around a claim of fact must convince the reader that the statement is true, usually with the support of factual information such as statistics, examples, and testimony that most responsible observers assume can be verified. (For detailed discussion of support, see Chapter 6.)

Why, you may wonder, would a claim of fact need to be proven, if we all agree on facts? There are several reasons.

Different Interpretations. Facts, while indisputable at their most basic level, may not always be interpreted the same way. Different interpretations lead to different points of view on a subject. Scientists, for example, may look at the same data yet disagree about whether the data indicate a warming of the planet.

> **Claim:** Based on the available evidence, the earth has been undeniably growing warmer for the past fifty years.
>
> **Claim:** The earth's temperatures have remained flat for the past twenty years.

Causal Relationships. A claim of fact may assert a causal relationship based on facts. For example, some researchers may claim that soda consumption is responsible for the rise in the nation's obesity rates, while others may blame the higher obesity rates on Americans' increasingly sedentary lifestyles. Just as different interpretations of facts can lead to different perspectives, a different understanding of cause can lead to a different claim.

> **Claim:** Soda and other sugary drinks are the leading cause of obesity in the United States.
>
> **Claim:** Americans are overweight because they eat too much and exercise too little.

Predictions. A prediction uses known facts to make a claim about the future. Based on available evidence, an analyst may predict that holding teachers accountable for their students' standardized test scores will improve our educational system. This prediction may be disputed by others, who assert that the available evidence indicates the opposite outcome is likely. A prediction can be tested in the future to determine its validity. But even in the future, the results will be subject to interpretation and potential disputes about cause.

Claim: An increased emphasis on standardized testing will lead to higher graduation rates among high school students.

Claim: Too much emphasis on standardized testing will decrease student and teacher morale, leading to higher dropout rates among high school students.

New Data. Scientists and scholars in all fields are constantly working not only to interpret existing data but also to uncover new data. Such new data may change our understanding of history, physics, or biology and cause us to re-evaluate our conclusions. In the health field in particular, researchers regularly uncover new information that may complicate or contradict earlier findings. When new data emerge in a field, it may require some convincing to replace the prevailing viewpoint, such as when the Environmental Protection Agency listed second-hand smoke as a major carcinogen in 1992.

Claim: Although it was once generally believed that cigarette smoke was harmful only to the smoker, researchers now conclude that second-hand smoke poses serious health hazards for nonsmokers as well.

Not all claims are so neatly stated or make such unambiguous assertions. Because we recognize that there are exceptions to most generalizations, we often qualify our claims with words such as *generally, usually, probably,* and *as a rule.* It would not be true to state flatly, for example, *College graduates earn more than high school graduates.* This statement is generally true, but we know that some high school graduates who are electricians or city bus drivers or sanitation workers earn more than college graduates who are schoolteachers or nurses or social workers. In making such a claim, therefore, the writer should qualify it with a word that limits the claim — a **qualifier**. However, watch out for words that overstate your claim. Words like *always, every, all,* and *never* allow for no exceptions.

Remember: Labeling a statement a claim of fact does not make it true. The label simply means that it is worded as though it were a true statement. It is up to the writer to provide support to prove that the statement is indeed true.

ARGUMENT ESSENTIALS Claims of Fact

- Claims of fact assert that a condition has existed, exists, or will exist.
- Claims of fact are supported by factual information such as statistics, examples, and testimony.
- Claims of fact may take one of several forms:
  - a statement in favor of a particular interpretation of data.
  - a suggestion of a causal relationship.
  - a prediction.
  - a case for the acceptance of new evidence.
- Claims of fact may be limited by words such as *generally, usually,* and *probably.*

RESEARCH SKILL ▶ Identifying Your Sources

- Identify the source of any material that you quote, summarize, or paraphrase.
- At a minimum, give the author's last name and the page number in parentheses after the information taken from the source. (There will often not be a page number for online sources.)

- Better: Give the author's full name in your sentence the first time you use that source, and give only the page number in parentheses.
- Briefly identify who the source is, focusing on his or her expertise on the subject at hand.

READING ARGUMENT

Seeing a Claim of Fact

The following essay has been annotated to highlight claims of fact.

Loaded Language Poisons Gun Debate
JOSH LEVS

Opening metaphor: gun debate = Tower of Babel

It's the biggest, fiercest debate taking place across America. But it's poisoned from the get-go by a Tower of Babel predicament.

In disputes over the future of gun laws, people espousing different positions often literally don't understand each other.

Source identified by his claim to authority

"The sides are speaking different languages," says Harry Wilson, author of "Guns, Gun Control, and Elections: The Politics and Policy of Firearms."

Levs's claim of fact and thus his thesis

Many of the most frequently used words and phrases in this debate mean different things to different people — or, in some cases, don't have clear meanings to anyone. From terms like "assault weapons" to the battle between "gun control" and "gun rights," the language in the national conversation is making it tougher to find common ground.

Another source identified by her claim to authority

"What language does is frame the issue in one way that includes some things and excludes others," says Deborah Tannen, a Georgetown University linguistics professor and author of "The Argument Culture: Stopping America's War of Words."

5

Examples

It's a phenomenon that America sees all the time: "pro-life" vs. "pro-choice" in the abortion debate; "marriage equality" vs. "protecting marriage" in the

---

Josh Levs is a CNN journalist. This piece appeared on cnn.com on January 31, 2013.

battle over same-sex marriage. Those who oppose the estate tax have termed it a "death tax."

"The gun control debate is catching up to this now," says Wilson, director of the Institute for Policy and Opinion Research at Roanoke College in Salem, Virginia.

The massacre at an elementary school in Newtown, Connecticut, "was a game changer. It changed the political landscape overnight."

Example

As the debate rages in Washington and throughout the country, here's a look at some of the flashpoint lingo muddying the waters:

Sets up further examples

Gun Control vs. Gun Rights

Headings identify examples developed more fully.

10   When President Obama recently announced plans to sign 23 executive orders on the issue, he avoided the phrase "gun control." Instead, he emphasized the need "to reduce the broader epidemic of gun violence in this country."

"We've seen this transformation from use of the term 'gun control' to 'gun violence,'" says Wilson, "because no one can be in favor of gun violence. That's universal."

"Gun control," to many Americans, is not a positive term, Tannen adds.

The key is "the set of associations people have with a word"—and Americans don't like the idea of the government "controlling" many of their decisions.

That's why "gun rights" works well for the National Rifle Association in pushing against new gun laws. "For Americans, the word 'rights' is always a positive thing. That's not necessarily true in other cultures, but it is for Americans," Tannen says.

15   Wayne LaPierre, executive vice president of the NRA, spoke to those associations this week during his testimony before Congress.

"We believe in our freedom," he said, speaking for gun owners who are NRA members. "We're the millions of Americans from all walks of life who take responsibility for our own safety and protection as a God-given, fundamental right."

While the current debate has its own tenor, the focus on language has been around for decades. It's embodied in the title of one of the best-known gun control groups.

The Brady Campaign to Prevent Gun Violence grew out of an organization called the National Council to Control Handguns.

Common Sense

Listen to any leading voice on this issue, and you're likely to hear that term repeatedly.

President Obama used it to describe the steps he's calling for, including   20
universal background checks for gun owners and legislation prohibiting "further manufacture of military-style assault weapons."

Examples from both sides of the debate

The NRA, meanwhile, announced in December that LaPierre would offer "common sense solutions." He then pushed for armed guards in American schools. Many Americans were angry and argued that was the opposite of common sense. The NRA later said it believes each school should decide for itself.

Former U.S. Rep. Gabby Giffords and her husband, Mark Kelly, have begun a political action committee to take on the gun lobby's influence. In an op-ed in *USA Today*, they said LaPierre's initial remarks showed that "winning even the most common-sense reforms will require a fight."

Wilson says the term seems to be playing well for those pushing for new gun regulations. "It makes people say, 'these are common-sense ideas,'" he says.

Assault Weapons

But what exactly are those ideas? When it comes to the most controversial one being discussed — banning "assault weapons" — it's unclear. That's because the term itself is abstract. There is no clear definition of an "assault weapon."

Definition of a key term is unclear

The 10-year so-called assault weapons ban enacted in 1994 named 19   25
semiautomatic firearms, as well as semiautomatic rifles, pistols, and shotguns with specific features.

"In general, assault weapons are semiautomatic firearms with a large magazine of ammunition that were designed and configured for rapid fire and combat use," the Justice Department said at the time.

That may be the closest thing to a simple explanation the government ever gave, but if you want to see how incredibly complicated the official definition is in the law itself, check out the language.

"I wrote a book on gun control. I don't know what an assault weapon is," Wilson says.

The National Shooting Sports Foundation and other gun enthusiasts complain that what ultimately separated an "assault weapon" from a "nonassault weapon" under the 1994 law was cosmetic.

Some Second Amendment groups and gun retailers prefer the terms "tac-   30
tical rifle" or "modern sporting rifle."

The term "assault rifle" was first used by Germany during World War II, the *New York Times* notes. Later, U.S. manufacturers adopted the words as they began to sell firearms modeled after new military rifles.

In today's parlance, adding "military-style" doesn't draw a clear line either.

Sen. Dianne Feinstein, D-California, who has submitted legislation for a new "assault weapons ban," says it would include, among other things, "all semiautomatic rifles that can accept a detachable magazine and have at least one military feature: pistol grip; forward grip; folding, telescoping, or detachable stock; grenade launcher or rocket launcher; barrel shroud; or threaded barrel." *Some very specific definitions*

The previous ban included semiautomatic pistols with at least two features, including a detachable magazine, threaded barrel, a shroud allowing the shooter to "hold the firearm with the nontrigger hand without being burned," a weight of 50 ounces or more unloaded, or what was described as "a semiautomatic version of an automatic firearm."

Semiautomatic

35   An automatic weapon, as the Justice Department put it, is a machine gun that allows you to fire bullets in succession by holding in the trigger. Fully automatic weapons are severely restricted under existing law, but in some cases they are still legal to own, as the *Los Angeles Times* notes.

They're commonly used in the military but rarely owned by civilians.

A semiautomatic weapon can load bullets automatically, but it fires only once each time you pull the trigger.

In the effort to prevent mass killings, those pushing for a new assault weapons ban want to halt the production and sale of certain semiautomatic weapons and high-capacity "feeding devices"—such as magazines—that allow for a large number of rounds of ammunition.

Feinstein's bill would ban selling, transferring, importing, or manufacturing 120 named firearms, certain semiautomatic rifles, handguns, "shotguns that can accept a detachable magazine and have one military characteristic," and "semiautomatic rifles and handguns with a fixed magazine that can accept more than 10 rounds."

40   During the previous ban, gun manufacturers were able to make cosmetic changes to evade the law. One chief question now is how a piece of legislation could avoid the same happening again.

Can Words Help Bridge the Gap?

New words might help
establish common ground.

"If you get new words, there's a better chance of moving beyond the polarization," says Tannen, who is spending this year at Stanford's Center for Advanced Study in the Behavioral Sciences. But, she warns: "Words don't stay neutral for long — because they quickly get associated with the people that use them."

When asked for a case in which more neutral language may have helped the government reach a consensus on a controversial topic, Tannen said "nothing comes to mind."

Instead, the race is on to control the semantics, which are "crucial," says Wilson.

"In American politics, the person who gets to define the issue wins."

Practice: Claim of Fact

Review the print advertisement on page 157, and answer the questions that follow.

Paper Because
DOMTAR PAPER

Domtar

Reading and Discussion Questions

1. How is the claim qualified?
2. How does this ad use text and picture to reinforce each other?
3. How valid do you feel the text is? (Have you observed scenes like the one depicted in the ad, or perhaps been part of such a scene?)
4. How clear is the connection between what the ad says about social media and what is being advertised? What *is* being advertised?

:e This advertisement is one of a series produced by Domtar Paper and promoted on the company's Web site, paperbecause.com. View more ads like this one, along with Domtar's additional claims about the importance of paper, at **macmillanhighered.com/rottenberg**.

Claims of Value

Unlike claims of fact, which state that something is true and can be validated by reference to the data, claims of value **make a judgment**. They express approval or disapproval. They attempt to prove that some action, belief, or condition is right or wrong, good or bad, beautiful or ugly, worthwhile or undesirable.

Claim: Democracy is superior to any other form of government.

Claim: Killing animals for sport is wrong.

Claim: The Sam Rayburn Building in Washington is an aesthetic failure.

Some claims of value are simply expressions of taste, likes and dislikes, or preferences and prejudices. The Latin proverb *De gustibus non est disputandum* means that we cannot dispute taste. If you love the musical *Wicked*, there is no way for anyone to prove you wrong.

Many claims of value, however, can be defended or attacked on the basis of standards that measure the worth of an action, a belief, a performance, or an object. As far as possible, our personal likes and dislikes should be supported by reference to these standards. Value judgments occur in any area of human experience, but whatever the area, the analysis will be the same. We ask the arguer who is defending a claim of value: *What are the standards or criteria for deciding that this action, this belief, this performance, or this object is good or bad, beautiful or ugly, desirable or undesirable? Does the thing you are defending fulfill these criteria?*

There are two general areas in which people often disagree about matters of value: aesthetics and morality.

Aesthetics

Aesthetics is the study of beauty and the fine arts. Controversies over works of art — the aesthetic value of books, paintings, sculpture, architecture, dance, drama, and movies — rage fiercely among experts and laypeople alike. They may disagree on the standards for judging or, even if they agree about standards, may disagree about how successfully the art object under discussion has met these standards. The Rogerian approach to conflict resolution can be particularly useful in resolving disagreements over the standards for judging. Agreeing on those standards is the first step toward resolving the conflict and is a necessary step before seeking agreement on how well the standards have been met.

Consider a discussion about popular music. Hearing someone praise the singing of Manu Chao, a hugely popular European singer now playing to American crowds, you might ask why he is so highly regarded. You expect Chao's fans to say more than "I like him" or "He's great." You expect them to give reasons to support their claims. They might show you a short review from a respected newspaper that says, "Mr. Chao's gift is simplicity. His music owes a considerable amount to Bob Marley . . . but Mr. Chao has a nasal, regular-guy voice, and instead of the Wailers' brooding, bass-heavy undertow, Mr. Chao's band delivers a lighter bounce. His tunes have the singing directness of nursery rhymes."[1] Chao's fans accept these criteria for judging a singer's appeal.

You may not agree that simplicity, directness, and a regular-guy voice are the most important qualities in a popular singer. But the establishment of standards itself offers material for a discussion or an argument. You may argue about the relevance of the criteria, or you may agree with the criteria but argue about the success of the singer in meeting them. Perhaps you prefer complexity to simplicity. Or even if you choose simplicity, you may not think that Chao has exhibited this quality to good effect.

It is probably not surprising, then, that despite wide differences in taste, professional critics more often than not agree on criteria and whether an art object has met the criteria. For example, almost all movie critics agree that *Citizen Kane* and *Gone with the Wind* are superior films. They also agree that *Plan 9 from Outer Space*, a horror film, is terrible.

Morality

Value claims about morality express judgments about the rightness or wrongness of conduct or belief. Here disagreements are as wide and deep as in the arts — and more significant. The first two examples on page 158 reveal how controversial such claims can be. Although a writer and reader may share many values — among them a belief in democracy, a respect for learning, and a desire for peace — they may also disagree, even profoundly, about other values. The subject of divorce, for example, despite its prevalence in our society, can produce a conflict between people who have differing moral standards. Some people may insist on adherence to absolute standards, arguing that the values they hold are based on immutable religious precepts derived from God and biblical scripture. Since marriage is sacred, divorce is always wrong, they say, whether or not the conditions of society change. Other people may argue that

---

[1] Jon Pareles, *New York Times*, July 10, 2001, p. B1.

values are relative, based on the changing needs of societies in different places and at different times. Since marriage is an institution created by human beings at a particular time in history to serve particular social needs, they may say, it can also be dissolved when other social needs arise. The same conflicts between moral values might occur in discussions of abortion or suicide.

Nevertheless, even where people agree about standards for measuring behavior, a majority preference is not enough to confer moral value. If in a certain neighborhood a majority of heterosexual men decide to harass a few gay men and lesbians, that consensus does not make their action right. In formulating value claims, an arguer should be prepared to ask and answer questions about the way in which those value claims, as well as those of others, have been determined. Lionel Ruby, an American philosopher, sums it up in these words: "The law of rationality tells us that we ought to justify our beliefs by evidence and reasons, instead of asserting them dogmatically."[2]

ARGUMENT ESSENTIALS Claims of Value

- Claims of value make a judgment.
- Claims of value should be supported by reference to standards that measure the worth of an action, belief, performance, or object.
- Claims of value most often are about aesthetics or morality.

READING ARGUMENT

Seeing a Claim of Value

The following essay has been annotated to highlight claims of value.

Morning-After Pill a Boon for Women
DEBORAH NUCATOLA

The context

Last week, a federal judge issued a decision lifting the age and point-of-sale restrictions on emergency contraception, citing solid scientific and medical research showing that it is safe and effective in preventing unintended pregnancy.

Thesis: a claim of value

This is great news for all women because these restrictions created confusion and barriers, and when unprotected sex has occurred, time is a crucial factor. Emergency contraception can prevent pregnancy for up to five days after intercourse, but the sooner it's used the more effective it is.

That's why women's health providers and activists lobbied to make emergency contraception available without a prescription — to reduce delays. And

---

Deborah Nucatola is a physician and the senior director of medical services for Planned Parenthood Federation of America. Her article appeared on cnn.com in April 2013.

---

[2] Lionel Ruby, *The Art of Making Sense* (New York: Lippincott, 1968), p. 271.

because emergency contraception is safe, making it over-the-counter was a big step in creating better access to birth control.

Clearing up confusion about what emergency contraception is and how it works has been more challenging.

5   It's a fact that emergency contraception is birth control. The reality is, pregnancy doesn't happen right after sex. It can take up to six days for the sperm and egg to meet after intercourse. That's why it's possible to prevent pregnancy even after the fact. Emergency contraception postpones ovulation, which prevents sperm from coming in contact with and fertilizing an egg. Pregnancy can't happen if there is no egg to join with sperm.

In contrast, the so-called "abortion pill," mifepristone, works by blocking the hormone progesterone, which is needed for a pregnancy to continue. So there's a big difference between emergency contraception and nonsurgical abortion.

There was much talk last week about the implications of lifting the age restrictions. Some of it was motivated by safety concerns, which is a good and natural question to ask about any medication.

It's a fact that doctors have been prescribing emergency birth control since the 1960s, and there have been no reports of serious complications. More to the point, studies have repeatedly shown that emergency contraception is safe for use by women of all ages, including teens.

Another concern among some is that access to emergency contraception will increase the rates of unprotected sex, especially among teens. There is no evidence to support this.

10   It's a fact that rates of unprotected sex do not increase when there is more access to emergency contraception. Research also indicates that teens understand how to use emergency contraception and that it is not intended for ongoing, regular use.

The bottom line is that the use of reliable birth control is the best way to prevent an unintended pregnancy, but the fact is that unprotected sex does occur and sometimes birth control methods do fail. A condom could break, a woman could forget to take a pill, or nonconsensual sex could occur.

That's why when a woman fears she might become pregnant after her contraceptive has failed or she has had unprotected sex, she needs fast access to emergency contraception, not delays at the pharmacy counter. Lifting these restrictions will allow emergency contraception to be stocked on store shelves, making it more accessible to everyone. It will provide a safe, effective way to prevent pregnancy and reduce the need for abortion.

That's why last week's ruling is so important — it's based on good science and good sense. And that's a fact.

Marginal annotations:

The key term needs to be defined.

What it is

What it isn't

Concerns about the medication

Safety concerns

Concern that it will lead to more unprotected sex

Reiterates values behind her support

Practice: Claim of Value

Movie reviews by definition support claims of value. Analyze the following review, focusing on its claim and support for that claim.

Spike Jonze's *Her* Shows Love's Perils — in Any Form
KENNETH TURAN

Spike Jonze has a knack for disturbing our peace, and his new film *Her* does that with a vengeance.

A different and daring futuristic tale starring Joaquin Phoenix and Scarlett Johansson, *Her* is a look at the pleasures and perils of new technology that's a smart entertainment and a subtle warning, a love story and a horror show. Acerbic, emotional, provocative, it's a risky high dive off the big board with a plot that sounds like a gimmick but ends up haunting, odd, and a bit wonderful.

Previously responsible for the singular *Being John Malkovich* and *Adaptation* as well as the self-indulgent *Where the Wild Things Are*, Jonze is a director who goes his own way with ideas no one else could have imagined.

With *Her*, Jonze for the first time has sole writing credit. He not only came up with a killer idea, he's had the nerve to go all the way with it, to tease out multiple implications of his lightly dystopian "what if" plot all the way to the unforeseen but perfectly logical denouement.

5   What helps Jonze get the most out of his examination of the consequences of a man (Phoenix) falling in love with the voice of his operating system (Johansson, never seen onscreen) is his lack of interest in making *Her* simply an empty Luddite screed.

As Jonze has taken pains to insist in numerous interviews, *Her* in his mind is as much about the nature of individual relationships as it is about a future in which we trust and rely on our devices more than we do our fellow human beings.

Her's fascination with the pending impersonalization of the personal, with a coming world where falsity is the new sincerity, begins with its first sequence, which has Phoenix's Theodore looking directly at the camera and saying with genuine feeling, "I've been thinking of telling you how much you mean to me."

The succeeding dialogue, however, reveals that Theodore is not being emotional, he's just doing his job, working for BeautifulHandwritten Letters.com, a company that makes it its business to compose personal thank you notes for the gratitude impaired.

This slightly futuristic enterprise is set in a slightly futuristic Los Angeles, evocatively photographed by Hoyte Van Hoytema (*Tinker Tailor Soldier Spy*) and smartly constructed out of bits of the real Los Angeles and glimpses of Shanghai's new purpose-built Pudong district by the directors' longtime production designer K. K. Barrett.

10   With glasses and a diffident manner typing him as a bit of a nerd, Theodore doesn't quite know what to do with himself when he's

This review by film critic Kenneth Turan appeared in the *Los Angeles Times* on December 17, 2013.

alone, which is a lot of the time. *Her* gives him a number of options, including unnerving phone sex, happy flashback memories of his former marriage to Catherine (Rooney Mara, softer than we're used to), and a video game featuring a foul-mouthed alien tot (Jonze provides the unnerving voice).

Phoenix does solid work in this poor soul role, but, not surprising for an actor who is most at home with extreme characters like Freddie Quell in *The Master*, he becomes more convincing once *Her* ventures into stranger territory. Once, in other words, Samantha comes into Theodore's life.

It all starts with an ad that catches Theodore's eye, an ad promising "the first artificially intelligent operating system . . . a consciousness that knows you." With nothing else going on in his life, Theodore is ready for something new, so he signs on.

Enter Samantha, with a voice that tells you immediately that this is an entity who really cares about you, you and only you. Theodore is nonplused at first by Samantha's easy familiarity. But he soon gets used to "her" and, given what she brings to his life, that is no surprise.

In short order — Samantha is nothing if not a quick study — she organizes Theodore's schedule, helps him with his writing and his video game playing, laughs at his jokes, and makes some of her own. Samantha also encourages him to seek human companionship beyond his old college pal Amy (a very different Amy Adams from her flashy con woman in *American Hustle*), even pushing him into a problematic blind date (an impressive Olivia Wilde). Is it any wonder that Theodore is soon telling Samantha that he has more fun with her than anyone . . . human?

Key to making this transition work is the exceptional work done by Johansson in a part that was originally acted from start to finish by Samantha Morton before Jonze decided he wanted a different vocal quality in the role. Johansson does a remarkable job using only her voice to create what is in effect a brand new person whose warmth and joy are infectious.

Samantha doesn't stay brand new for long, however. As Theodore gets increasingly attached to her, Samantha is learning more and more about what human life is like. "I have intuition, the ability to grow and evolve through my experiences, just like you," she is continually reminding Theodore, but she is learning at an exponential rate, which leads to problems and situations only Jonze could think up and bring off.

As the relationship deepens, Jonze draws intriguing parallels between the Theodore-Samantha relationship, alternately creepy and sweet, and one between two actual people. If falling in love with anyone is a form of socially acceptable insensitivity, someone asks, how is what these two have that much different?

Finally, however, the questions *Her* poses about the ambivalent potential of personal technology is its most intriguing aspect. This is a film about how we live now and how we might live in the future. We are entering a brave new world and dealing with the consequences is our fate.

15

Reading and Discussion Questions

1. Where does Turan most directly state his claim?
2. What other examples of language from the review are evaluative?
3. What does the reviewer mean when he says that Jonze was not interested in creating "simply an empty Luddite screed"? How does the movie go beyond that focus?
4. How effective do you find Turan in supporting his claim?
5. How effective is Turan in balancing the need to summarize the plot of the movie and the need to evaluate it?

Claims of Policy

Claims of policy argue that certain conditions should exist. As the name suggests, they advocate adoption of policies or courses of action because problems have arisen that call for solution. Almost always, *should* or *ought to* or *must* is expressed or implied in the claim.

Claim: Voluntary prayer should be permitted in public schools.

Claim: A dress code ought to be introduced for all public high schools.

Claim: A law should permit sixteen-year-olds and parents to "divorce" each other in cases of extreme incompatibility.

Claim: Mandatory jail terms must be imposed for drunk driving violations.

Claim-of-policy arguments often begin by attempting to convince the audience that a problem exists. This will require a factual claim that offers data proving that present conditions are unsatisfactory. Claims of value may also be necessary to support the claim of fact. The policy itself is usually introduced after the problem is established; the policy is presented as a viable solution to the problem.

Consider this policy claim: *The time required for an undergraduate degree should be extended to five years.* Immediate agreement with this policy among student readers would certainly not be universal. Some students would not recognize a problem. They would say, "The college curriculum we have now is fine. There's no need for a change. Besides, we don't want to spend more time in school." First, then, the arguer would have to persuade a skeptical audience that there is a problem — that four years of college is no longer enough because the stock of knowledge in almost all fields of study continues to increase. The arguer would provide data to show that students today have many more choices in history, literature, and science than students had in those fields a generation ago and would also emphasize the value of greater knowledge and more schooling compared to the value of other goods the audience cherishes, such as earlier independence. Finally, the arguer would offer a plan for implementing the policy. The plan would have to consider initial psychological resistance, revision of the curriculum, costs of more instruction, and costs of lost production in the workforce. Most important, this policy would point out the benefits for both individuals and society if it were adopted.

In this example, we assumed that the reader would disagree that a problem existed. In many cases, however, the reader may agree that there is a problem but disagree with the arguer about the way to solve it. Most of us, no doubt, agree that we want to reduce or eliminate the following problems: misbehavior and vandalism in schools, drunk driving, crime on the streets, child abuse, pornography, pollution. But how should we go about solving those problems? What public policy will give us well-behaved, diligent students who never destroy school property? safe streets where no one is ever robbed or assaulted? loving homes where no child is ever mistreated? Some members of society would choose to introduce rules or laws that punish infractions so severely that wrongdoers would be unwilling or unable to repeat their offenses. Other members of society would prefer policies that attempt to rehabilitate or reeducate offenders through training, therapy, counseling, and new opportunities.

> **ARGUMENT ESSENTIALS** Claims of Policy
>
> - Claims of policy argue for an action or a change in thinking.
> - Claims of policy express or imply that something should or must be done.
> - Claims of policy usually depend on a factual claim that establishes that present conditions are unacceptable.

READING ARGUMENT

Seeing a Claim of Policy

The following essay has been annotated to highlight claims of policy.

College Life versus My Moral Code
ELISHA DOV HACK

Many people envy my status as a freshman at Yale College. My classmates and I made it through some fierce competition, and we are excited to have been accepted to one of the best academic and extracurricular programs in American higher education. I have an older brother who attended Yale, and I've heard from him what life at Yale is like.

He spent all his college years living at home because our parents are New Haven residents, and Yale's rules then did not require him to live in the dorms.

Background that reveals his respect for Yale and his connection to it through his brother

Elisha Dov Hack was a member of the Yale College freshman class of 1997. This article appeared on September 9, 1997, in the *New York Times*. The case brought by Hack and four other Jewish students remained in court until all but Hack had graduated. Hack went on to marry — and live off campus — before his 2003 graduation in engineering sciences.

But Yale's new regulations demand that I spend my freshman and sophomore years living in the college dormitories.

I, two other freshmen, and two sophomores have refused to do this because life in the dorms, even on the floors Yale calls "single sex," is contrary to the fundamental principles we have been taught as long as we can remember — the principles of Judaism lived according to the Torah and 3,000-year-old rabbinic teachings. Unless Yale waives its residence requirement, we may have no choice but to sue the university to protect our religious way of life.

Bingham Hall, on the Yale quadrangle known as the Old Campus, is one of the dorms for incoming students. When I entered it two weeks ago during an orientation tour, I literally saw the handwriting on the wall. A sign titled "Safe Sex" told me where to pick up condoms on campus. Another sign touted 100 ways to make love without having sex, like "take a nap together" and "take a steamy shower together."

That, I am told, is real life in the dorms. The "freshperson" issue of the *Yale Daily News* sent to entering students contained a "Yale lexicon" defining *sexile* as "banishment from your dorm room because your roommate is having more fun than you." If you live in the dorms, you're expected to be part of the crowd, to accept these standards as the framework for your life.

Can we stand up to classmates whose sexual morality differs from ours? We've had years of rigorous religious teaching, and we've watched and learned from our parents. We can hold our own in the intellectual debate that flows naturally from exchanges during and after class. But I'm upset and hurt by this requirement that I live in the dorms. Why is Yale — an institution that professes to be so tolerant and open-minded — making it particularly hard for students like us to maintain our moral standards through difficult college years?

We are not trying to impose our moral standards on our classmates or on Yale. Our parents tell us that things were very different in college dormitories in their day and that in most colleges in the 1950s students who allowed guests of the opposite sex into their dorm rooms were subject to expulsion. We acknowledge that today's morality is not that of the 1950s. We are asking only that Yale give us the same permission to live off campus that it gives any lower classman who is married or at least twenty-one years old.

Yale is proud of the fact that it has no "parietal rules" and that sexual morality is a student's own business. Maybe this is what Dean Richard H. Brodhead meant when he said that "Yale's residential colleges carry . . . a moral meaning." That moral meaning is, basically, "Anything goes." This morality is Yale's own residential religion, which it is proselytizing by force of its regulations.

We cannot, in good conscience, live in a place where women are permitted to stay overnight in men's rooms, and where visiting men can traipse through

(Margin notes:)

How residency rules have changed

Establishes the problem

Examples of affronts to his religious beliefs

Another example of accepted dorm standards

Challenges whether Yale should make it difficult for students to maintain their morals outside of class

Tries to achieve middle ground by acknowledging that morality has changed, but argues that exceptions to the policy are already made

Claim of policy

Attacks the opposition by defining immorality as Yale's religion

the common halls on the women's floors — in various stages of undress — in the middle of the night. The dormitories on Yale's Old Campus have floors designated by gender, but there is easy access through open stairwells from one floor to the next.

Floors designated by gender are not the solution.

10   The moral message Yale's residences convey today is not one that our religion accepts. Nor is it a moral environment in which the five of us can spend our nights, or a moral surrounding that we can call home.

The source of conflict

Yale sent me a glossy brochure when it welcomed me as an entering student. It said, "Yale retains a deep respect for its early history and for the continuity that its history provides — a continuity based on constant reflection and reappraisal." Yale ought to reflect on and reappraise a policy that compels us to compromise our religious principles.

Uses Yale's own advertising against it

Follow Up

What happened to the lawsuit to which Hack refers? It was tied up in court until 2001, when all of the students involved except Hack had graduated. The students lost the legal battle at all levels, primarily because their case depended on their proving that having to live in a residence hall constituted discrimination based on religion. The university successfully argued that the residence requirement was not discriminatory. Hack graduated from Yale in 2003. All five students chose to live in apartments during their first two years while paying full housing fees for dorm rooms they never occupied.

Practice: Claim of Policy

Read the following essay, and answer the questions at the end.

Your Toxic Beauty Regime
KIARA VENTURA

As I flipped through *Seventeen* magazine, I stopped to look at an ad for Neutrogena's Pink Grapefruit Oil-Free Acne Wash. I'd been getting annoyed at having random pimples on my face, so I was instantly gripped by it. I smelled the scratch-and-stiff that came with the advertisement and agreed that it was an "uplifting blast of naturally derived grapefruit." As added bonuses, two actresses I like, Hayden Panettiere and Miranda Cosgrove, are the brand spokespeople, and when you purchase the product,

Neutrogena will donate $1 to something called Global Giving.

So when I buy this product my skin will be as clear as Miranda's and I will help out a charity? "Wow!" I thought, "that sounds like a plan!" But then I thought a little more, and one thing

When she wrote this article, Kiara Ventura was a participant in a special writing program offered by Youth Communication. The article was posted in the September/October 2012 issue of *YCteen* at youthcomm.org.

stopped me from running to my local Rite-Aid and buying a magical bottle of this stuff—the worry that some of the ingredients in it could be harmful.

I had just read a book called *No More Dirty Looks*, which takes a critical look at the beauty products industry, and I'd interviewed one of the authors, Siobhan O'Connor. During the interview, my friends and I brought in some personal care products like hand lotion, styling gel, deodorant, and shampoo for her to evaluate.

When she started reading the labels on our products, she showed us that many of the ingredients were chemicals that are carcinogens (which means they can cause cancer), neurotoxins (poisons that can mess up your nervous system), and endocrine disrupters (which can screw up how your body regulates hormones). It was hard to believe that we use products every day that could potentially damage our health.

Serious Risks

5   Health problems linked to ingredients in common products include everything from acne and rashes to brain damage, cancer, and nervous system damage. Young people and pregnant women should be especially wary because the harmful ingredients can hurt developing bodies. For example, "scientists are finding that women with high levels of certain chemicals in their blood and urine—BPAs and phthalates are the two big ones—are having babies with genital birth defects in baby boys at much higher rates than people who have low levels of these chemicals," O'Connor said.

So why would companies knowingly put harmful stuff in their products? Well, apparently it's just good for business. These chemicals are generally cheaper and less likely to spoil than natural ingredients, and they give products that feeling, smell, and quality that we consumers love. Certain chemicals make our shampoo lather up nicely, give our perfume that wonderful smell, and make our lotion smooth enough that it absorbs into our skin in seconds. But the truth is that some of the chemicals that improve our consumer experience can hurt our health.

Companies say that the dose of bad chemicals is so tiny that they're not dangerous, which is a convincing argument until you think about how many different products we use—each with its own trace amount of bad chemicals. Most people use about twelve to twenty products a day, including toothpaste, face wash, lotion, perfume, deodorant, ChapStick, soap, shampoo, conditioner, shaving cream, nail polish—and let's not even get started with makeup.

Just imagine how many chemicals our skin absorbs and our noses inhale each and every day of our lives. One product might not be so bad, but some would argue that the cumulative effect of all those chemicals—which is called "bioaccumulation"—is not worth the risk. In addition, no one really knows what constitutes a safe level of many of these chemicals, or how all the chemicals we use interact with each other. Unfortunately, this is something we don't usually think about—until something bad happens.

A Bad Reaction

The authors of *No More Dirty Looks*, best friends Siobhan O'Connor and Alexandra Spunt, first came up with the idea for the book after they got a popular keratin hair-straightening treatment at a salon. O'Connor recalled, "Our eyes were watering, we were coughing, I ended up getting a weird, red rash on my scalp and the back of my neck that has come and gone since then. And it was a reaction, we found out after the fact, to formaldehyde, which is one of the ingredients used to straighten our hair."

10   Formaldehyde (yes, the same stuff used to embalm dead people) is typically used as a preservative in things like nail polish, antiperspirant, makeup, bubble bath, shampoo, baby lotions, and hair dyes. It's also a known carcinogen. It's not that once you use these products you will definitely get cancer. Rather, they add up over a long period, which can increase risk.

After their reaction to the hair straightening treatment, the authors began researching how beauty products are regulated by the FDA (Food and Drug Administration). Their book provides a little history lesson that will not make you snooze. "The laws that govern cosmetics were written in 1938, and it is 2011 and they've barely changed," even though tons of new chemicals and products are being produced every year, O'Connor said.

Scary Secret Ingredients

Because there aren't many laws regulating what companies put into their products, the government has very little power to ensure that the stuff you see on the shelves is safe.

"Let's say we're all using lotion on our bodies and our skin's turning red, or we're getting rashes, or maybe our kids are having asthma reactions, getting really sick when they smell [a certain product] — the FDA cannot tell the company [that makes the product], 'You're not allowed to sell that.' It's not within their rights to do that, which is crazy," O'Connor said. The U.S. is clearly lagging behind in this area: Europe has banned more than 1,000 ingredients for use in personal care products while the United States has only banned nine.

One of the major issues that O'Connor warned us about is a sneaky ingredient called "fragrance." In the book, the authors tell us the story of Betty Bridges, who couldn't breathe when she came in contact with a mysterious substance that seemed to be in several products she used. When she called up the manufacturers to try to figure out what, exactly, she was allergic to, they wouldn't reveal what chemicals were in the fragrances they used in their products.

You see, "fragrance" isn't one particular chemical. It is just a word representing many chemicals. Companies don't list the specific ingredients they use to make their products smell good, because they consider this their secret formula (like SpongeBob's "krabby patty formula"). They don't want other companies to steal the recipe and make the same scent.   15

To protect companies' competitive advantages, the FDA allows them to hide the ingredients in "fragrance," so we basically don't know what chemicals we're using on ourselves. And unfortunately, "fragrance" is in almost everything — even in my friend's Purell Hand Sanitizer. Knowing this made me want to go "all natural" and stop buying products full of chemicals — but figuring out which products are healthy was harder than I thought.

Natural — or Nasty?

In the beauty section of any pharmacy, you see bottles of hair care products decorated with pictures of plants, fruits, and natural scenery. They may claim to be "natural" or "clean," which would make you think that they are safe, or free of synthetic chemicals, right?

Well, the authors warn us that even if a product says "organic" or "sulfate free," it doesn't mean that it is completely innocent. For example, while evaluating a green tea-scented Dove soap my friend brought to the interview, O'Connor pointed out, "There's no green tea anywhere in the whole thing!" In fact, it contained "fragrance" and something called propylene glycol, which animal studies have shown can affect the brain and nervous system and cause endocrine disruption.

"The illusion of something natural sells," said O'Connor. "They're trading on the idea that we don't know any better, because we don't."

20   To help us out, the book lists some dangerous ingredients to look out for (as does our story "Buyer Beware!"), and provides information about alternatives that are made from safer ingredients. O'Connor admitted that natural products can be less appealing in some ways: "Sometimes the packaging looks a little hippy-dippy; it's not as pretty, not as appealing — but it's loaded with ingredients that are ultra-great for your skin and body."

Even if a natural product doesn't feel as good as an artificial one — for example, some natural lotions will be a bit greasier than conventional ones, and natural shampoos will not create that satisfying lather because they don't contain the chemicals that create suds — just know that it is still doing its job and not exposing you to harmful chemicals.

Beauty Background Check

There are also a lot of online resources to help you investigate your beauty products. For example, the fantastically useful Web site ewg.org /skindeep gives products a rating from 1 to 10, and provides information about potential health hazards associated with the product's ingredients. If you are concerned about your products and your health, I recommend the site. You may be surprised by what you find.

In fact, when I looked up that awesome-looking grapefruit-scented Neutrogena face wash, I found out that it had some pretty toxic stuff in it. According to the Web site, it was a "high health concern," mostly because of two ingredients: fragrance and something called PEG-80 sorbitan laurate, which it said could possibly cause "organ system toxicity."

The advertisement for this face wash made it seem so positive, clean, and fresh, but I guess there is an ugly side to most products these days. So, the next time I go to my local pharmacy looking for a new face wash, I will have my glasses on and the bad ingredient list in hand!

Reading and Discussion Questions

1. Remember that a claim of policy may build on claims of fact and of value. What is Ventura's claim of policy? How does she use factual information and evaluation to build toward that claim?

2. One of the strengths of Ventura's article is its specific support. What are some of the most convincing supporting details that she provides?

3. Ventura makes good use of an authority on her subject whom she had interviewed. She also makes use of her own experience. In what sense is she also an "authority" on her subject? Do you find the first person portions of the article effective? Why, or why not?

 View the slide show that accompanies this article at **macmillanhighered** .com/rottenberg.

WRITER'S GUIDE
Stating Your Claim

Whether you are making a claim of fact, a claim of value, or a claim of policy, your claim is the **thesis** of your argument. Here are some tips for writing an effective claim.

All Types of Claims

- Keep your audience and purpose in mind. Whom you are writing for, and why? What are you trying to convince them of? What do you want them to do? To gain your readers' interest, be sure to let them know how the issue pertains to them.

Claims of Fact

- Be sure you will be able to find sufficient supporting evidence to back up your claim.
- Use qualifiers such as *generally, usually,* and *probably* to limit a claim; avoid using words such as *always, every, all,* and *never,* which do not allow for exceptions.
- Be aware of opposing viewpoints, and be prepared to refute them.

Claims of Value

- When writing about an aesthetic issue, be sure you understand the criteria used to measure standards in the field you are writing about: sports, dance, music, photography, and so on.
- When writing about a moral issue, be careful not to alienate or offend readers who may espouse opposing views on the subject.
- As much as possible, provide strong evidence and good reasons for your claims of value, and avoid dogma.

Claims of Policy

- Begin by proving that the problem exists by employing a claim of fact with supporting evidence. (You may also need to include a claim of value to convince readers that something must be done.)
- Use special care to frame your claim of policy in a way that readers will not immediately reject. Depending on your topic, readers may have a high level of emotional involvement on the matter.
- Be aware that alternative solutions to the problem may exist, and be prepared to explain why your proposal is superior.
- Have realistic expectations about what you hope to achieve — what your audience can actually do about the situation. Sometimes you may argue for people to vote a certain way, sign a petition, or write letters to officials. At other times, the most you might hope to accomplish is to get your audience to consider the situation from your perspective.

Assignments for Claims: Making a Statement

Reading and Discussion Questions

1. Find several recent print ads, and explain what their claims are.

2. Notice that Josh Levs's essay "Loaded Language Poisons Gun Debate" does not take a side in the debate. Choose a current controversial issue, and write a claim of fact about it.

3. Locate a movie review online or in hard copy that has a clear claim and is based on clear evaluative criteria. Choose a review that is an essay, not just a single paragraph. Bring it to class, and share it with your class or group. By looking at a range of different reviews, come to some conclusions about the sort of criteria used in making judgment calls about movies and what sort of claims provide good thesis statements for reviews. What are some other characteristics that all or most good movie reviews share?

4. Consider one or more of your school's policies that you would like to see changed. In your opinion, what is wrong with the policy as it currently stands? What exactly would you recommend be done to improve the situation?

Writing Suggestions

1. Choose a controversial issue in the field in which you are majoring or one in which you might major. Practice differentiating among the three types of claims by writing a claim of fact, a claim of value, and a claim of policy on that issue.

2. Choose one of the claims of fact you wrote for #2 above, and write an essay supporting it.

3. Choose a recent print ad, and write an essay explaining how text and pictures work together in it to support a claim.

4. Write a review of a recent movie. Your thesis will be a claim of value.

5. Write a review of a recent play, concert, art exhibit, or similar cultural event. Your thesis will be a claim of value.

6. Using Elisha Dov Hack's essay as a model, write an essay suggesting a change at your school. Write it in the form of a letter to your school's newspaper.

RESEARCH ASSIGNMENT ▶ **Acknowledging Reliable Authorities**

The next page includes a list of quotations and the names of those who are quoted. Do some research to find out what gives the person quoted the authority to speak knowledgeably on the subject of the quotation. Then work the information you found into a lead-in to the quotation, as in the example.

Example

"We are promoting human rights by building homes for people who don't have them."—Jimmy Carter

"We are promoting human rights by building homes for people who don't have them," explains former president Jimmy Carter, who has been involved with Habitat for Humanity International since 1984 and who, with his wife, leads its Jimmy and Rosalynn Carter Work Project one week each year.

1. "Innovation has nothing to do with how many R&D dollars you have. When Apple came up with the Mac, IBM was spending at least 100 times more on R&D. It's not about money. It's about the people you have, how you're led, and how much you get it."—Steve Jobs

2. "If gun laws in fact worked, the sponsors of this type of legislation should have no difficulties drawing upon long lists of crime rates reduced by such legislation. That they cannot do so after a century and a half of trying—that they must sweep under the rug the southern attempts at gun control in the 1870–1910 period, the northeastern attempts in the 1920–1939 period, the attempts at both Federal and State levels in 1965–1976—establishes the repeated, complete, and inevitable failure of gun laws to control serious crime."—Orrin G. Hatch

3. "The old argument that the networks and other 'media elites' have a liberal bias is so blatantly true that it's hardly worth discussing anymore. No, we don't sit around in dark corners and plan strategies on how we're going to slant the news. We don't have to. It comes naturally to most reporters."—Bernard Goldberg

4. "You built a factory and it turned into something terrific or a great idea—God bless! Keep a hunk of it. But part of the underlying social contract is you take a hunk of that and pay forward for the next kid who comes along."—Elizabeth Warren

5. "It takes more courage to send men into battle than to fight the battle yourself."—Colin Powell

6. "I want to state upfront, unequivocally and without doubt: I do not believe that any racial, ethnic, or gender group has an advantage in sound judging. I do believe that every person has an equal opportunity to be a good and wise judge, regardless of their background or life experiences."—Sonia Sotomayor

bits

To see what you are learning about argumentation applied to the latest world and national news, read our *Bits* blog, "Argument and the Headlines," at **blogs.bedfordstmartins.com/bits**.

Support: Backing Up a Claim

Support for a claim represents the answer to the question "What have you got to go on?"[1] All claims in an argument — whether of fact, of value, or of policy — must be supported. Sometimes an author will use his or her own experience as support for a claim. At other times, authors may conduct interviews, field research, lab experiments, or surveys to obtain support for their position. As a student, you will most likely turn primarily to print and electronic sources for your support. (See Chapter 11 for a full discussion of finding sources.)

The emphasis in providing support is on the relationship between writer and audience — the rhetorical leg of the communications triangle:

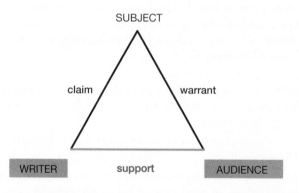

You are presenting **evidence** to an audience in hopes of convincing that audience to see the subject in the same way you do. You may remember from the discussion of Aristotelian rhetoric in Chapter 1 that arguments rely on *ethos*, *logos*, and *pathos* for their effectiveness. You must present your evidence and yourself in such a way that your audience finds you trustworthy (*ethos*). You also have to consider what evidence your audience will find convincing — what

---

[1] Stephen Toulmin, *The Uses of Argument* (Cambridge: Cambridge University Press, 1958), p. 98.

examples, statistics, and opinions will appeal to them logically (*logos*). You are using emotional appeal (*pathos*) in conjunction with other types of appeal when you appeal to your audience's needs and values.

WRITER'S GUIDE
Using Support

---

1. In deciding how much support you need for your claim, it is always a good idea to assume that you are addressing an audience that may be at least slightly hostile to that claim. Those who already agree with you do not need convincing.

2. Keep a mental, if not a written, list of the different types of support you use in an essay. Few essays will use all of the different types of support, but being aware of all the possibilities will prevent you from forgetting to draw on one or more types of support that may advance your argument.

3. In that checklist of types of support, don't forget that there are two main categories: evidence and appeals to needs and values. Appeals to needs and values will generally need the reinforcement that comes from more objective forms of evidence, but the two in combination can often provide the strongest case for your claim.

4. Remember that you will usually need to give credit to your source(s) for information you use as support. See Chapter 13 for complete treatment of how to document sources.

Evidence

When authors provide evidence in support of their claim, they primarily use facts, examples, statistics, opinions (usually the opinions of experts), and images.

Factual Evidence

In Chapter 5, we defined facts as statements possessing a high degree of public acceptance. Some facts can be verified by experience alone.

- Eating too much will make us sick.
- We can get from Hopkinton to Boston in a half hour by car.
- In the Northern Hemisphere it is colder in December than in July.

The experience of any individual is limited in both time and space, so we must accept as fact thousands of assertions about the world that we ourselves can never verify. Thus we accept the report that human beings landed on the moon in 1969 because we trust those who can verify it.

Facts can provide important support for a claim, as shown in the example here. The claim has been underlined.

<u>Nuclear energy has a wide-ranging value proposition.</u> Nuclear energy

- produces large amounts of electricity at industry-leading reliability and efficiency levels
- is affordable and has forward price stability that will be important as our economy continues to bounce back
- provides nearly two-thirds of all carbon-free electricity
- maintains grid stability through voltage support
- contributes to the fuel and technology diversity that is one of the bedrock characteristics of a reliable and resilient electric sector
- is an economic driver through high-paying jobs and taxes in the communities and states where they are located.[2]

Factual evidence appears most frequently as examples and statistics, which are a numerical form of examples.

Examples

Examples are the most familiar kind of factual evidence. In addition to providing support for the truth of a generalization, examples can enliven otherwise dense or monotonous prose. In the following paragraph, the writer supports the claim (underlined in the topic sentence) by offering a series of specific examples.

> <u>You can hardly go anywhere these days and not see or hear an advertisement for college.</u> Throughout Concourse B at Denver International Airport, nearly every other advertisement greeting passengers is for a higher-education institution: Colorado State University, the University of Wyoming, Colorado Mesa College, and the University of Northern Colorado. Airline magazines are filled with promotions for executive MBA programs. At least once an hour on the all-news radio station in Washington, DC, listeners hear about the degree in cybersecurity offered by a University of Maryland campus. Sunday newspapers are filled with details on certificate programs in the latest hot job fields, such as social media and sustainability. Anyone checking e-mail on Google will see ads pop up for the creative writing program at Southern New Hampshire University or the political management degree at George Washington University.[3]

---

[2] Marvin S. Fertel, "United States Energy Association Briefing," Nuclear Energy Institute. nei.org, 16 Jan. 2014. Web.

[3] Jeffrey J. Selingo, *College (Un)Bound: The Future of Higher Education and What It Means for Students* (New York: New Harvest, 2013), p. 6.

Hypothetical examples, which create imaginary situations for the audience and encourage them to visualize what might happen under certain circumstances, can also be effective. The following paragraph illustrates the use of hypothetical examples. (The author is describing megaschools, high schools with more than two thousand students, and her claim is underlined.)

> And in schools that big there is inevitably a critical mass of kids who are neither jocks nor artists nor even nerds, kids who are nothing at all, nonentities in their own lives. . . . The creditable ballplayer who might have made the team in a smaller school is edged out by better athletes. The artist who might have had work hung in a smaller school is supplanted by abler talents. And the disaffected and depressed boy who might have found a niche, or a friend, or a teacher who noticed, falls between the cracks. Sometimes he quietly drops out. Sometimes he quietly passes through. And sometimes he comes to school with a gun.[4]

All claims about vague or abstract terms would be boring or unintelligible without examples to illuminate them. For example, if you claim that a movie contains "unusual sound effects," you will certainly have to describe some of the effects to convince the reader that your generalization can be trusted.

Statistics

Statistics express information in numbers. In the following example, statistics have been used to support the authors' claim, which has been underlined.

> To the kids growing up in a housing project on Chicago's south side, crack dealing was a glamour profession. For many of them, the job of gang boss — highly visible and highly lucrative — was easily the best job they thought they had access to. Had they grown up under different circumstances, they might have thought about becoming economists or writers. But in the neighborhood where J. T.'s gang operated, the path to a decent legitimate job was practically invisible. Fifty-six percent of the neighborhood's children lived below the poverty line (compared to a national average of 18 percent). Seventy-eight percent came from single-parent homes. Fewer than 5 percent of the neighborhood's adults had a college degree; barely one in three adult men worked at all. The neighborhood's median income was about $15,000 a year, well less than half the U.S. average. During the years that Venkatesh lived with J. T.'s gang, foot soldiers often asked his help in landing what they called "a good job": working as a janitor at the University of Chicago.[5]

---

[4] Anna Quindlen, "The Problem of the Megaschool," *Newsweek*, March 26, 2001, p. 68.

[5] Steven D. Levitt and Stephen J. Dubner, *Freakonomics: A Rogue Economist Explores the Hidden Side of Everything* (New York: William Morrow, 2005), p. 105.

Statistics are more effective in comparisons that indicate whether a quantity is relatively large or small and sometimes even whether a reader should interpret the result as gratifying or disappointing. For example, if a novice gambler were told that for every dollar wagered in a state lottery, 50 percent goes back to the players as prizes, would the gambler be able to conclude that the percentage is high or low? Would he be able to choose between playing the state lottery and playing a casino game? Unless he had more information, probably not. But if he were informed that in casino games, the return to the players is over 90 percent and in slot machines and racetracks the return is around 80 percent, the comparison would enable him to evaluate the meaning of the 50 percent return in the state lottery and even to make a decision about where to gamble his money.[6]

Comparative statistics are also useful for measurements over time. For instance, the following statistics show what comparisons based on BMI, or body mass index, reveal about how Miss America contestants have changed over the years.

> Miss America contestants have become increasingly thinner over the past 75 years. In the 1920s, contestants had BMIs in the normal range of 20–25. Since then, pageant winners' body weights have decreased steadily to a level about 12 percent below levels from the mid-1900s. Since 1970, nearly all of the winners have had BMIs below the healthy range, with some as low as 16.9, a BMI that would meet part of the diagnostic criteria for anorexia nervosa.[7]

Diagrams, tables, charts, and graphs can make clear the relations among many sets of numbers. Such charts and diagrams enable readers to grasp the information more easily than if it were presented in paragraph form. For example, Figure 6.1 shows bar graphs used by the Census Bureau to explore the issue of high school education attainment among selected groups. Figure 6.2 is a type of pie chart compiled by the Congressional Budget Office to show the 2011 U.S. Federal Budget.

Expert Opinion

Based on their reading of the facts, experts express opinions on a variety of controversial subjects: whether capital punishment is a deterrent to crime; whether legalization of marijuana will lead to an increase in its use; whether children, if left untaught, will grow up honest and cooperative; whether sex education courses will result in less sexual activity and fewer illegitimate births. The interpretations of the data are often profoundly important because they influence social policy and affect our lives directly and indirectly.

---

[6] Curt Suphee, "Lotto Baloney," *Harper's*, July 1983, p. 201.

[7] S. Rubenstein and B. Caballero, "Is Miss America an Undernourished Role Model?" *JAMA* (2000), p. 1569. Qtd. in Jillian Croll, "Body Image and Adolescents," *Guidelines for Adolescent Nutrition Services*, J. Stang and M. Story, eds. (2005). June 9, 2007. http://www.epi.umn.edu/let/pubs/adol_book.shtm.

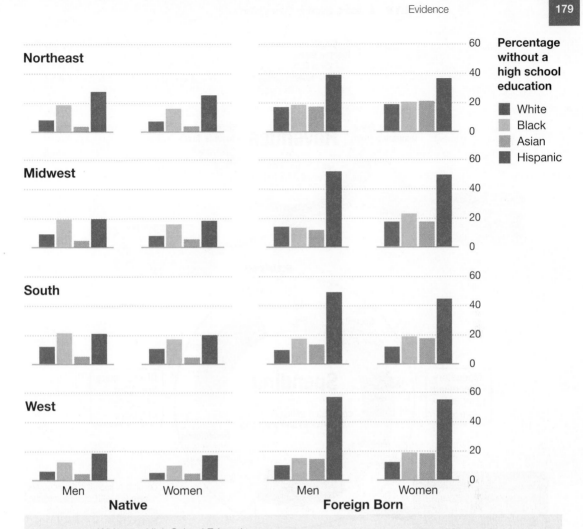

FIGURE 6.1 Without a High School Education. U.S. Census Bureau (census.gov/dataviz/visualizations/035). January 17, 2013.

For the problems mentioned above, the opinions of people recognized as authorities are more reliable than those of people who have neither thought about nor done research on the subject. But opinions may also be offered by student writers in areas in which they are knowledgeable. If you were asked, for example, to defend or refute the statement that work has advantages for teenagers, you could call on your own experience and that of your friends to support your claim. You can also draw on your experience to write convincingly about your special interests.

One opinion, however, is not always as good as another. The value of any opinion depends on the quality of the evidence and the trustworthiness of

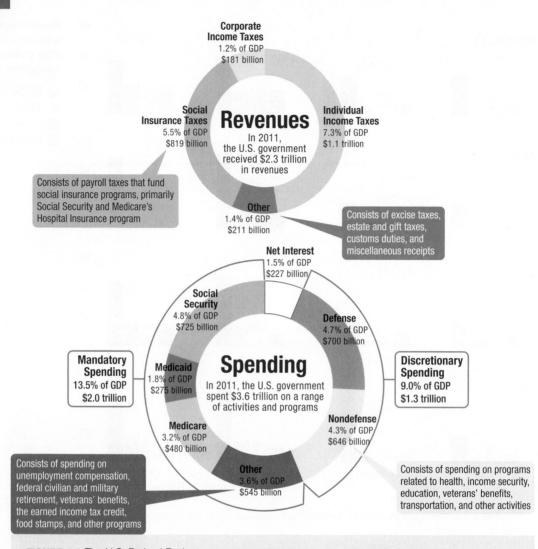

FIGURE 6.2 The U.S. Federal Budget. Congressional Budget Office (cbo.gov/publication/42636).

the person offering it. Clayton M. Christensen and Henry J. Eyring are both experts on the subject of education. Christensen holds a named professorship in Business Administration at the Harvard Business School, and Eyring has been director of Brigham Young University's MBA program and is currently an administrator at BYU–Idaho. In spite of their own credentials, when they wrote their book *The Innovative University: Changing the DNA of Higher Education from the Inside Out* (2011), they were careful to establish the expertise of those whose ideas they drew upon:

No one could doubt that U. S. Education Secretary Margaret Spellings meant business. In upbraiding the nation's universities and colleges, the 2006 report of her commission on the future of higher education used the language of business:

> What we have learned over the last year makes clear that American higher education has become what, in the business world, would be called a mature enterprise: increasingly risk-averse, at times self-satisfied, and unduly expensive. It is an enterprise that has yet to successfully confront the impact of globalization, rapidly evolving technologies, an increasingly diverse and aging population, and an evolving marketplace characterized by new needs and paradigms. . . .

The Spellings Commission was not a lone voice of criticism in 2006. That same year two distinguished academics, Derek Bok and Harry Lewis, both of Harvard, published books critical of higher education.[8]

What happens when authoritative sources disagree? Such disagreement is probably most common in the social sciences. They are called the "soft" sciences precisely because a consensus about conclusions in these areas is more difficult to reach than in the natural and physical sciences. The following two paragraphs show experts disagreeing over the reason for rises in college tuition costs.

> Suppose we asked the president of a public university to explain what he or she sees. Very likely that president would point out the fact that tuition and fees tend to rise very rapidly after decreases in growth in the overall economy. Your attention would be drawn to the rapid tuition increases following the episodes of negative GDP growth in 1982 and 1991 and the very slow GDP growth in 2001. Even the decade of falling tuition in the 1970s was interrupted by the oil shock years around 1974. The university president would say something like this: "When the overall economy slows down, state tax collections fall, and states cut appropriations for universities. As a result public universities have to resort to large tuition increases to make up for lost public funding."
>
> If we asked Representatives Boehner and McKeon to comment on the data, they would focus on an entirely different phenomenon. In *The College Cost Crisis* they say "the facts show tuition increases have persisted regardless of the circumstances such as the economy or state funding, and have far outpaced inflation year after year, regardless of whether the economy has been stumbling or thriving." Essentially, they are looking at the fact that after 1980 the "real" growth in college tuition and fees always has been positive. This means that tuition and

---

[8] Clayton M. Christensen and Henry J. Eyring, *The Innovative University: Changing the DNA of Higher Education from the Inside Out* (Hoboken, NJ: Jossie-Bass, 2011), pp. 4-5.

fees always have grown more rapidly than the CPI (Consumer Price Index). Representatives Boehner and McKeon also claim they know why this has happened. They place the blame squarely on "wasteful spending by college and university management."[9]

But even in the natural and physical sciences, where the results of observation and experiment are more conclusive, we encounter heated differences of opinion. A popular argument concerns the extinction of the dinosaurs. Was it the effect of an asteroid striking the earth? or widespread volcanic activity? or a cooling of the planet? All these theories have their champions among the experts. A debate of more immediate relevance concerns the possible dangers of genetically modified foods, as distinguished from foods modified by traditional breeding practices. Jeffrey M. Smith, director of the Institute for Responsible Technology and author of *Seeds of Deception: Exposing Industry and Government Lies about the Safety of the Genetically Engineered Foods You're Eating* (2003) and *Genetic Roulette: The Documented Health Risks of Genetically Engineered Foods* (2007), presents a different perspective on the issue:

> In addition to unintended changes in the DNA, there are health risks from other aspects of GM crops. When a transgene starts to function in the new cell, for example, it may produce proteins that are different from the one intended. The amino acid sequence may be wrong, the protein's shape may be different, and molecular attachments may make the protein harmful. The fact that proteins act differently in new plant environments was made painfully clear to developers of GM peas in Australia. They cancelled their ten-year, $2 million project after their GM protein, supposedly identical to the harmless natural version, caused inflammatory responses in mice. Subtle, unpredicted changes in molecular attachments might have similarly triggered deadly allergic reactions in people if the peas were put on the market.[10]

In 2000, at a hearing before the U.S. Senate Committee on Foreign Relations, Subcommittee on International Economic Policy, Export and Trade Promotion, Roger N. Beachy made the following statement. Beachy produced the world's first genetically modified tomato and in 2009–2011 was President Obama's director of the National Institute for Food and Agriculture.

> Agricultural producers in the U.S. have a growing awareness of their duties as keepers of the environment; many are actively reducing the use of harmful agrichemicals while maintaining highly efficient production of safe foods. Plant scientists and agriculturists have developed better crops and improved production methods that have enabled

---

[9] Robert B. Archibald and David H. Feldman, *Why Does College Cost So Much?* (New York: Oxford UP, 2010), p. 9.

[10] Jeffrey M. Smith, *Genetic Roulette: The Documented Health Risks of Genetically Engineered Foods* (St. Louis: Yes!, 2007). Web.

farmers to reduce the use of insecticides and chemicals that control certain diseases. Methods such as integrated pest management, no-till or low-till agriculture have been tremendously important in this regard. Some of the success has come through the judicious application of biotechnology to develop new varieties of crops that resist insects and that tolerate certain herbicides. For example, biotechnology was used to develop varieties of cotton and corn that are resistant to attack by cotton bollworm and corn borer. These varieties have allowed farmers to reduce the use of chemical insecticides by between 1.5 and 2 mil gallons, while retaining or increasing crop yields. Crops that are tolerant to certain "friendly" herbicides have increased no-till and low-till agriculture, reducing soil erosion and building valuable topsoil to ensure the continued productivity of our valuable agricultural lands.[11]

How can you choose between authorities who disagree? If you have applied the tests discussed so far and discovered that one source is less qualified by training and experience or makes claims with little support or appears to be biased in favor of one interpretation, you will have no difficulty in rejecting that person's opinion. If conflicting sources prove to be equally reliable in all respects, then you should continue reading other authorities to determine whether a greater number of experts support one opinion rather than another. Although numbers alone, even of experts, don't guarantee the truth, nonexperts have little choice but to accept the authority of the greater number until evidence to the contrary is forthcoming. Finally, if you are unable to decide between competing sources of evidence, you may conclude that the argument must remain unsettled. Such an admission is not a failure; after all, such questions are considered controversial because even the experts cannot agree, and such questions are often the most interesting to consider and argue about.

Images

Evidence does not always have to be verbal. Images can also provide support for an argument. Before there were photographs, paintings and even crude cave drawings provided evidence of the cultures that produced them. A man named Mathew Brady captured the reality of war through his photos of the Civil War and thus earned the title the Father of Photojournalism. Crime scene photos and video surveillance tapes provide evidence on screen and in real life. In April 2013, the Boston Marathon bombers were identified through photos from more than one source, some of them first circulated via reddit.com and Facebook.

---

[11] "World Renowned Plant Scientist Dr. Roger N. Beachy Testifies before U.S. Senate Committee to Explain the Role of Agricultural Biotechnology in the Battle against Poverty and Hunger in Developing Countries," agbioworld.org, 12 Jul. 2000.

FIGURE 6.3 Martian surface. NASA

Images are also critical as evidence in scientific research. Proof of a hypothesis often takes the form of plants and animals viewed in the wild or in the lab, of cells viewed through a microscope, or of distant objects viewed through a telescope. The photo shown in Figure 6.3 was released by NASA in December 2013, as possible evidence of liquid water active on Mars.

 Go to **macmillanhighered.com/rottenberg** to see the complete slideshow.

RESEARCH SKILL ⟩ Evaluating Evidence

Before you begin to write, you must determine whether the evidence you have chosen to support your claim is sound. Can it convince your readers?

Evaluation of Factual Evidence

■ **Are the facts up to date?** The importance of up-to-date information depends on the subject. For many of the subjects you write about, recent research and scholarship will be important, even decisive, in proving the soundness of your data. "New" does not always mean "best," but in fields where research is ongoing — education, psychology, technology, medicine, and all the natural and physical sciences — you should be sensitive to the dates of the research.

■ **Is the factual evidence sufficient?** The amount of factual evidence you need depends on the complexity of the subject and the length of your paper. Given the relative brevity of most of your assignments, you will need to be selective. For the claim that indoor pollution is a serious problem, one supporting fact would obviously not be enough. For a 750- to 1,000-word paper, three or four supporting facts would probably be sufficient. The choice of evidence should reflect different aspects of the problem: in this case, different sources of indoor pollution — gas stoves, fireplaces, kerosene heaters, insulation — and the consequences for health.

- **Are the facts relevant?** All the factual evidence should, of course, contribute to the development of your argument. Also keep in mind that not all readers will agree on what is relevant. Is the unsavory private life of a politician relevant to his or her performance in office? If you want to prove that a politician is unfit to serve because of his or her private activities, you may first have to convince some members of the audience that private activities are relevant to public service.

Examples

- **Are the examples representative?** This question emphasizes your responsibility to choose examples that are typical of all the examples you do not use. If you were trying to build a case about the economic impact of illegal immigrants in the United States but took your statistics from Maine, Vermont, Montana, North Dakota, and West Virginia, your sample would not be representative because these states have the smallest numbers of illegal immigrants, estimated to be less than 0.5 percent of the population for each of the five states.

- **Are the examples consistent with the experience of the audience?** The members of your audience use their own experiences to judge the soundness of your evidence. If your examples are unfamiliar or extreme, they will probably reject your conclusion. If most members of the audience find that your examples don't reflect their own attitudes, they may question the validity of the claim.

Statistics

- **Do the statistics come from trustworthy sources?** You should ask whether the reporter of the statistics is qualified and likely to be free of bias. Among the generally reliable sources are polling organizations such as Gallup, Roper, and Louis Harris and agencies of the U.S. government such as the Census Bureau and the Bureau of Labor Statistics. Other qualified sources are well-known research foundations, university centers, and insurance companies that prepare actuarial tables.

- **Are the terms clearly defined?** The more abstract or controversial the term, the greater the necessity for clear definition. *Unemployment* is an example of a term for which statistics will be difficult to read if the definition varies from one user to another. For example, are seasonal workers employed or unemployed during the off-season? Are part-time workers employed?

- **Are the comparisons between comparable things?** Folk wisdom warns us that we cannot compare apples and oranges. Population statistics for the world's largest city, for example, should indicate the units being compared. Greater London is defined in one way, greater New York in another, and greater Tokyo in still another. The population numbers will mean little unless you can be sure that the same geographical units are being compared.

- **Has any significant information been omitted?** In July 2013, Lifestyle Lift's Web site included this history of the company:

The Origin of a Revolutionary Approach
In 2001, Lifestyle Lift Founder, Dr. David Kent, was determined to find a safer and more affordable approach to facial rejuvenation. He knew there had to be a better alternative to traditional facelift, necklift, minilift, and eyelift procedures — one that eliminated the dangers of general anesthesia, shortened the long recovery times, and substantially reduced the cost. Working closely with his wife, Linda Kent, R.N., Lifestyle Lift was born and together they grew the idea into a nationwide company across the United States. The groundbreaking Lifestyle Lift approach yields amazing, lasting results that

- are customized for each person
- address face, eye, and neck aging
- leave you with a natural, refreshed appearance
- allow for quicker recovery.

continued

What the Web site does not mention is that as a result of a probe in Florida, the company was ordered by Florida's attorney general in June 2013 to stop calling its procedures revolutionary and that a similar probe in New York "found evidence that company employees were posing as satisfied customers." Florida's attorney general ordered the company to make clear whether its satisfied customers were compensated for their testimonials. The Lifestyle Lift company still advertises its procedures as groundbreaking in spite of the fact that they are tried and true plastic surgery methods done with local instead of general anesthesia.

Expert Opinion

- **Is the source of the opinion qualified to give an opinion on the subject?** The discussion of credibility in Chapter 1 (p. 7) pointed out that certain achievements by the interpreter of the data — publications, acceptance by colleagues — can tell us something about his or her competence. The answers to questions you must ask are not hard to find: Is the source qualified by education? Is the source associated with a reputable institution — a university or a research organization? Is the source credited with having made contributions to the field — books, articles, research studies? If the source is not clearly identified, you should treat the data with caution.

  In addition, you should question the identity of any source listed as "spokesperson" or "reliable source" or "an unidentified authority." Even when the identification is clear and genuine, you should ask if the credentials are relevant to the field in which the authority claims expertise. All citizens have the right to express their views, but this does not mean that all views are equally credible or worthy of attention.

- **Is the source biased for or against his or her interpretation?** Even authorities who satisfy the criteria for expertise may be guilty of bias. Bias arises as a result of economic reward, religious affiliation, political loyalty, and other interests. The expert may not be aware of the bias; even an expert can fall into the trap of ignoring evidence that contradicts his or her own intellectual preferences. Before accepting the interpretation of an expert, you should ask: Is there some reason why I should suspect the motives of this particular source?

  This is not to say that all partisan claims lack support. They may, in fact, be based on the best available support. But whenever special interest is apparent, there is always the danger that an argument will reflect this bias.

- **Has the source bolstered the claim with sufficient and appropriate evidence?** An author might claim, "Statistics show that watching violence on television leads to violent behavior in children." But if the author gave no further information — neither statistics nor proof that a cause-effect relation exists between televised violence and violence in children, the critical reader would ask, "What are the numbers? Who compiled them?"

  Even those who are reputed to be experts in the subjects they discuss must do more than simply allege that a claim is valid or that the data exist. They must provide facts to support their interpretations.

Images

- **Is the image relevant?** The photograph or other image should advance your argument. If it doesn't, it is not effective support. If it does, it must deserve the trust put in it as legitimate support. In the 2012 movie *Promised Land*, unscrupulous businessmen posing as environmental activists try to prove that fracking is killing livestock in the surrounding area by showing the locals a photograph of dead cows. They lose local support, however, when a closer look at the photo reveals that it was taken in a completely different part of the country.

- **Are you confident the photograph has not been altered?** It is so easy these days to PhotoShop or otherwise alter images that we can hardly trust what our eyes tell us.
- **Does the image depend too much on emotional appeal?** Emotional appeal is a legitimate form of appeal if it complements, instead of replaces, logic. We have all seen pictures of starving children and abused animals used to move us to donate money to alleviate their suffering. That is a legitimate use of emotional appeal as long as the money really goes to help the suffering children or animals. A little research can reveal what percentage of money donated to a given charity actually reaches those in need.

ARGUMENT ESSENTIALS

Evidence

- Evidence can take the form of facts, or statements possessing a high degree of public acceptance.
- Evidence can take the form of examples, which provide specific support for a generalization and enliven prose.
- Evidence can take the form of statistics, or information expressed in numbers.
- Evidence can take the form of expert opinion, or the interpretations of facts by people recognized as authorities on or at least knowledgeable about the subject.
- Evidence can take the form of images, or nonverbal support for an assertion.

READING ARGUMENT

Seeing Evidence

The following professional essay on sports fans and student essay on organic food have been annotated to highlight the use of evidence. Read each essay, and answer the questions that follow.

Are Sports Fans Happier?

SID KIRCHHEIMER

Let the madness begin!

Some opening statistics

March is the time when vasectomies increase by 50 percent thanks to the much-anticipated opportunity for patients to "recover" in front of their TVs.

March is also the time when workplaces do some real number-crunching: on the expected loss in employee productivity (estimated at 8.4 million hours and $192 million last year); on money bet on office pools (a hefty chunk of the $2.5 billion in total sports wagering each year); and even on the number of times workers hit the so-called "Boss Button" (computer software that instantly hides live video of games with a phony business spreadsheet), which was activated more than 3.3 million times during the first four days of last year's tournament.

His thesis: Fans are winners.

But mostly, the NCAA Basketball Championship — better known as "March Madness" or "The Big Dance" — is a time that gives us something to cheer about beyond the game itself. If history and science hold true, no matter the outcome of the three-week tournament that begins in March, most of the millions who will follow its hard-court action will emerge as winners. "That's because in the long run it's really not the games that matter," says Daniel

Expert opinion

Wann, PhD, a professor of psychology at Murray State University in Kentucky and author of *Sports Fans: The Psychology and Social Impact of Spectators.*

Thesis: Being a fan leads to social connections, which lead to psychological health.

"Being a fan gives us something to talk about, to share and bond with others. And for the vast majority of people, it's psychologically healthier when you can increase social connections with others."

After conducting some 200 studies over the past two decades, Wann, a leading researcher on "sports fandom," finds consistent results: people who identify themselves as sports fans tend to have lower rates of depression and

5

Sid Kirchheimer is a health and medical writer and editor who has written for AARP since 2000. This article appeared in the March 13, 2012, edition of the *Saturday Evening Post.*

higher self-esteem than those who don't. Blame it on our primal nature. "Sports fandom is really a tribal thing," says Wann, a phenomenon that can help fulfill our psychological need to belong — providing similar benefits to the social support achieved through religious, professional, or other affiliations. "We've known for decades that social support — our tribal network — is largely responsible for keeping people mentally sound. We really do have a need to connect with others in some way."

Opinion: causal connection

But when it comes to opportunities to connect, the Big Dance may have a foothold over other sporting events. "The beauty of March Madness is that it attracts people of all levels of sports fandom — and for different reasons," says Edward Hirt, Ph.D., a professor of psychology at Indiana University who researches how fanship affects social identity.

A different expert's opinion

Some watch, whether or not they usually follow sports, because they are alumni or have another previous affiliation to these "tribal networks" — the 60-plus participating college teams. Others connect on the spot, perhaps because it's easier to form emotional allegiances with gutsy amateur athletes who compete with heart and soul (and while juggling mid-term exams) rather than for the paychecks collected by millionaire pros.

Examples of reasons people watch

Also consider the unique nature of the tournament itself — a series of back-to-back games over the course of several weeks with little to no idle time in between during which a casual fan might lose interest. "I have not seen any empirical evidence to support that March Madness is necessarily better than other sports events" for promoting mood and mindset enhancements. "But theoretically I expect it could be," says Wann.

"There are only a couple of events — the Super Bowl also comes to mind — that seem to transcend typical fandom into being akin to a national holiday . . . a reason for people to get together. But with the Super Bowl, everything leads to one game — and most of the time it's an anticlimactic one that's over by half-time."

10 With March Madness, however, Wann notes, "there's a longer, more drawn out event that provides more opportunities to engage in social opportunities and connections. And bonds tend to be stronger with a longer passage of time."

Do the math: More games + more time = more opportunities to share for better bonding. "Because upsets are a normal occurrence, and you get runs by Cinderella teams knocking off the perennial favorites, there's enough uncertainty and unpredictability in this tournament to get people excited — and keep them excited," adds Hirt. "Early games affect later decisions; there's a cascading effect, as opposed to a one-time pick . . . and that allows for the

Examples

pride that comes with someone with no sports expertise being able to win the office pool."

Expert opinion: causal connection

Maybe that's why despite a short-term productivity loss many experts believe that March Madness actually benefits the workplace in the long term. Bonds formed in office pools and post-game water-cooler chatter build morale and inspire teamwork. At afterwork get-togethers in front of the tube, buddies can share chicken wings — and their emotions. "You have guys hugging each other, cursing at the ref, and bonding by sharing a sense of commonality," says Hirt. "Where else can guys express their emotions like that?"

Examples

And those other relationships? Although studies show that two to four percent of marriages are negatively affected when one spouse is an ardent fan (think of the so-called "football widow"), sports fandom has a positive or neutral effect on nearly half of relationships, says Wann. "It gives many couples something to do together or allows one to have time to go off and do their own thing."

Even if you watch in solitude, March Madness and other sporting events provide a diversion from the woes of everyday life — if only for a few hours. "Older people, especially when widowed or physically incapacitated, are more likely than others to relate to televised events," says Stuart Fischoff, Ph.D., senior editor of the *Journal of Media Psychology* and a California State University, Los Angeles, professor emeritus of psychology. "Watching sports helps us get outside ourselves."

Expert opinion

With the thrill of victory, many fans experience bona fide joy — complete with hormonal and other physiological changes such as increased pulse and feelings of elation. And with defeat, the overwhelming majority may initially feel sadness and disappointment, but usually rebound within a day or two, studies show.

Opinion: causal connection

15

However, lest we present too rosy a picture, it must be said that sports fandom can also be a health hazard. In a 2008 study published in the *New England Journal of Medicine*, researchers found that on days when Germany's soccer team played in the World Cup, cardiac emergencies more than tripled for German men and nearly doubled for women. Of course, European soccer fans are an extreme bunch; but even in the U.S., although visits to hospital emergency rooms tend to decrease during a much-anticipated sports game, there's a higher-than-usual surge immediately after the game ends. The explanation: To see a game's final outcome, some die-hard fans delay making that trip to the ER.

Examples of health hazards

And, of course, no story about March Madness would be complete without mention of gambling. The odds of predicting all game winners are about

9.2 quintillion to one. Yet when it comes to sports betting, nothing turns John Q. Fan into Jimmy the Greek more than the NCAA tournament. Workplace camaraderie is one reason. But there's another important factor.

Bragging rights.

With Super Bowl pools there's just a series of boxes with different scores. If you're lucky enough to pick the right one, you win. "But it's a more complex task in filling out all the March Madness brackets, and a seductive pleasure in trying to predict the upsets," says psychologist Edward Hirt.   *Expert opinion*

20   Another reason why nearly twice as much money is wagered on March Madness than the Super Bowl: More than in other events, NCAA tournament fans simultaneously root for more than one team, triggering a greater likelihood of making multiple bets.

With other sports championships you have to wait a week or at least several days between games, but this sports soap opera — with its David versus Goliath battles — continues night and day, providing a stronger hook.

So let the games begin. Whatever the final outcome, odds are good that   *Returns to thesis idea*
the overall advantage — for mind, body, and spirit — is definitely in your court.

Reading and Discussion Questions

1. As you look back over the annotations, what are the types of support used most often by Kirchheimer?

2. If you were going to write an essay analyzing Kirchheimer's use of support, what would your thesis be?

3. Do you find Kirchheimer's essay effective? Why, or why not? If you were going to write an evaluative essay about "Are Sports Fans Happier?" what would its thesis be?

Safer? Tastier? More Nutritious? The Dubious Merits of Organic Foods

KRISTEN WEINACKER

Kristen Weinacker

ENGL 203

Dr. Winchell

October 23, 2013

Safer? Tastier? More Nutritious? The Dubious
Merits of Organic Foods

Causal connections

Organic foods are attractive to some consumers because of the principles behind them and the farming techniques used to produce them. There is a special respect for organic farmers who strive to maintain the ecological balance and harmony that exist among living things. As these farmers work in partnership with nature, some consumers too feel a certain attachment to the earth (Wolf 1–2). They feel happier knowing that these foods are produced without chemical fertilizers, pesticides, and additives to extend their shelf life (Pickrell; Agricultural Extension Service 5). They feel that they have returned to nature by eating organic foods that are advertised as being healthy for maintaining a vigorous lifestyle. Unfortunately,

Claim of fact

research has not provided statistical evidence that organic foods are more nutritious than conventionally grown ones.

The debate over the nutritional benefits has raged for decades. Defenders of the nutritional value of organic foods have employed excellent marketing and sales strategies. First, they freely share the philosophy behind their farming and follow up with detailed descriptions of their management techniques. Second, organic farmers skillfully appeal to our common sense. It seems reasonable to believe that organic foods are more nutritious since they are grown without chemical fertilizers and pesticides. Third, since the soil in which these crops are grown is so rich and healthy, it seems plausible that these crops have absorbed and developed better nutri-

Expert opinion

ents. As Lynda Brown asserts in her book *Living Organic*, "Organic farmers believe that growing crops organically provides the best possible way to produce healthy food" (26). Brown provides beautifully illustrated and enlarged microscopic photographs to show the

At the time she wrote this essay, Kristen Weinacker was an undergraduate at Clemson University.

more developed structure of organic foods compared to conventional products to convince the consumer to believe that organic foods are more nutritious (27). Fourth, many consumers view the higher price tags on organic foods and assume that they must be more nutritious. Generalizations permeate the whole world of organic foods. These marketing strategies persuade the consumer that organic foods are healthier than conventional foods without providing any factual comparisons.

In their book *Is Our Food Safe?* Warren Leon and Caroline Smith DeWaal compare organic and conventionally produced foods. They strongly suggest that consumers buy organic foods to help the environment (68). They believe that organic foods are healthier than conventional ones. However, statistics supporting this belief are not provided. The authors even warn consumers that they need to read product labels because some organic foods may be as unhealthy as conventional ones (68–69). An interesting poll involving 1,041 adults was conducted by ABC News asking, "Why do people buy organic?" Analyst Daniel Merkle concluded that 45 percent of the American public *believes* that organic products are more nutritious than conventionally grown ones. Also, 57 percent of the population maintains that organic farming is beneficial for the environment. According to the pollsters, the primary reason why people bought organic foods is the belief that they are healthier because they have less pesticide residue. However, there has never been any link established between the nutritional value of organic foods and the residue found on them. Clever marketing strategies have made the need for concrete data really not of prime importance for the consumer to join the bandwagon promoting organic foods.

This pervasive belief among the American public that organic foods are probably healthier than conventionally grown foods was reiterated in my telephone interview with Mr. Joseph Williamson, an agricultural county extension agent working with Clemson University. When asked if organically grown foods are more nutritious than those grown conventionally, he replied that they probably were for two reasons. First, organic crops tend to grow more slowly. Therefore, the nutrients have more time to build up in the plants. Second, organic plants are usually grown locally. The fruits and vegetables are allowed to stay on the plants for a longer period of time. They ripen more than those picked green and transported across miles. He contends that these conditions promote a better nutrient

Causal connection: Consumers believe organic foods are healthier because of these marketing strategies.

Expert opinion

Statistics

Expert opinion

Suspected causal connections, but not supported by statistical evidence

buildup. Unfortunately, the extension agent acknowledges that statistical evidence is not available to support the claim that organic products are more nutritious.

Expert opinion

An article entitled "Effect of Agricultural Methods in Nutritional Quality: A Comparison of Organic with Conventional Crops" reports on conclusions drawn by Dr. Virginia Worthington, a certified nutrition specialist. Worthington examines why it is so difficult to ascertain if organic foods are more nutritious. First, "the difference in terms of health effects is not large enough to be readily apparent." There is no concrete evidence that people are healthier eating organic foods or, conversely, that people become more ill eating conventionally grown produce. Second, Dr. Worthington notes that variables such as sunlight, temperature, and amount of rain are so inconsistent that the nutrients in crops vary yearly. Third, she points out that the nutrient value of products can be changed by the way products are stored and shipped. After reviewing at least thirty studies dealing with the question if organic foods are more nutritious than conventionally grown ones, Dr. Worthington concludes that there is too little data available to substantiate the claim of higher nutritional value in organic foods. She also believes that it is an impossible task to make a direct connection between organic foods and the health of those people who consume them.

Causal connections cannot be drawn.

After being asked for thirty years about organic foods by her readers and associates, Joan Dye Gussow, writer for *Eating Well* magazine, firmly concludes that there is "little hard proof that organically grown produce is reliably more nutritious." Reviewing seventy years' worth of studies on the subject, Gussow has no doubt that organic foods should be healthier because of the way they are produced and cultivated. Gussow brings up an interesting point about chemical and pesticide residue. She believes that the fact that organic foods have been found to have fewer residues does not make them automatically more nutritious and healthier for the consumer. As scientific technologies advance, Gussow predicts that research will someday discover statistical data that will prove that organic foods have a higher nutritional value compared to conventionally grown ones.

Another expert opinion that causal connections cannot be drawn

In order to provide the public with more information about the nature of organic foods, the well-known and highly regarded magazine *Consumer Reports* decided to take a closer look at organic foods in their January 1998 magazine, in an article entitled "Organic Foods: Safer? Tastier? More nutritious?" By conducting comparison tests,

5

their researchers discovered that organic foods have less pesticide residue, and that their flavors are just about the same as conventionally grown foods. These scientists came to the conclusion that the "variability within a given crop is greater than the variability between one cropping system and another." *Consumer Reports* contacted Professor Willie Lockeretz from the Tufts University School of Nutrition Science and Policy. He told researchers that "the growing system you use probably does affect nutrition. . . . But it does it in ways so complex you might be studying the problem forever." Keeping in mind these comments made by Dr. Lockeretz, *Consumer Reports* believes it would be an impossible task to compare the nutritional values of organic and conventional foods. Therefore, researchers at *Consumer Reports* decided not to carry out that part of their comparison testing.

Expert opinion

Although statistical evidence is not available at this time to support the claim that organic foods are more nutritious than conventionally grown ones, there is a very strong feeling shared by a majority of the general public that they are. We are called back to nature as we observe the love that organic farmers have for the soil and their desire to work in partnership with nature. We are easily lured to the attractive displays of organic foods in the grocery stores. However, we must keep in mind the successful marketing techniques that have been used to convince us that organic foods are more nutritious than conventionally grown ones. Although common sense tells us that organic foods should be more nutritious, research has not provided us with any statistical data to prove this claim.

Restatement of thesis

Works Cited

Agricultural Extension Service. *Organic Vegetable Gardening.* Knoxville: University of Tennessee. PB 1391. Print.

Brown, Lynda. *Organic Living.* New York: Dorling Kindersley, 2000. Print.

Gussow, Joan Dye. "Is Organic Food More Nutritious?" *Eating Well* (May/June 1997). Web. 27 March 2003. <http://www.prnac.net /rodmap-nutrition.html>.

"Effect of Agricultural Methods on Nutritional Quality: A Comparison of Organic with Conventional Crops." *Alternative Therapies* 4

(1998): 58–69. Web. 18 Feb. 2003. <http://www.purefood.org
/healthier101101.cfm>.

Leon, Warren, and Caroline Smith DeWaal. *Is Our Food Safe?* New
York: Three Rivers, 2002.

Merkle, Daniel. "Why Do People Buy Organic?" abcnews.com.
3 Feb. 2000. Web. 27 March 2003.

"Organic Foods: Safer? Tastier? More Nutritious?" *Consumer Reports.* Jan. 1998. Web. 24 Feb. 2003. <http://www.consumer
reports.org/main/detailsv2.jsp?content%3%ecnt_id+18959&f>.

Pickrell, John. "Federal Government Launches Organic Standards."
Science News 162.17 (Nov. 2002). Web. <http://www.sciencenews
.org/blog/food-thought/federal-government-launches-organic
-standards>.

Williamson, Joseph. Telephone interview. 28 Feb. 2013.

Wolf, Ray, ed. *Organic Farming: Yesterday's and Tomorrow's Agriculture.* Philadelphia: Rodale, 1977. Print.

Reading and Discussion Questions

1. Looking back over the annotations, what types of support did you find noted most often?

2. What is unusual about the use of causal connections in this particular piece? How does that contribute to Weinacker's thesis?

Practice: Evidence

Read the following essay, and answer the questions at the end.

I'm Sorry, Steve Jobs: We Could Have Saved You

SIDDHARTHA MUKHERJEE

On October 5, the night that Steve Jobs died, I ascended 30,000 feet into the thin air above New York on a flight to California. On my lap was a stash of scientific papers. I was reading and taking notes — where else? — on an iPad.

Jobs's death — like a generational Rorschach test — had provoked complex reactions within each of us. There was grief in abundance, of course, admixed with a sense of loss, with deso-

lation and nostalgia. Outside the Apple store in SoHo, New York, that evening, there were bou-

Siddhartha Mukherjee is an Indian-born American oncolo-
gist and hematologist who won the 2010 Pulitzer Prize
for General Nonfiction for his book *The Emperor of All
Maladies: A Biography of Cancer.* Currently he teaches at
Columbia University and practices at Columbia University
Medical Center. This article appeared in *Newsweek* on
October 8, 2012.

quets of white gerberas and red roses. Someone had left a bushel of apples by the doorstep and a sign that read "I-miss . . ."

I missed Jobs, too — but I also felt a personal embarrassment in his death. I am an oncologist and a cancer researcher. I felt as if my profession, my discipline, and my generation had let him down. Steve Jobs had promised — and then delivered — life-altering technologies. Had we, in all honesty, given him any such life-altering technologies back?

I ask the question in all earnestness. Jobs's life ended because of a form of pancreatic cancer called pancreatic neuroendocrine tumor, or PNET. These tumors are fleetingly rare: about five in every million men and women are diagnosed with PNETs each year. Deciphering the biology of rare cancers is often challenging. But the past five years have revealed extraordinary insights into the biology of some rare cancers — and PNETs, coincidentally enough, have led part of that charge. By comparing several such tumors, scientists are beginning to understand the biology of these peculiar tumors.

5 But understanding biology is an abstract activity. Steve Jobs needed more than "biology." He needed medicines. And despite our efforts, we were unable to transform our knowledge about PNETs into medical realities during his lifetime. The question is, are we ready to achieve this transformation sometime in the near future?

Let's take PNETs as a case in point. In 2008 a team of scientists from Johns Hopkins University set out to document all the gene mutations in PNETs — creating a systematic genetic "anatomy" of these tumors. Cancer, of course, is ultimately a disease of mutations in genes. Human cells possess about 23,000 genes in total. In cancer cells some of these genes are changed — mutated — and begin to function abnormally.

Many of the genes that are mutated in various cancers, predictably, control cellular growth. Genes regulate the growth of cells like invisible puppeteers tugging and pushing opposing strings behind curtains. There are genes that command a cell to grow and those that tell a cell to stop growing. Cancer occurs when these growth-control genes are mutated, resulting in the dysregulated growth of a cell.

But the genes most frequently mutated in PNETs are odd. They don't seem to control growth directly; rather they seem to affect the way cells regulate genes. Take a moment to understand this by considering normal development. A cell in the retina possesses the same 23,000 genes as a cell in the skin, yet these two cells barely resemble each other in shape, size, or behavior. How does a cell, then, "know" how to become a retinal cell versus a skin cell? How can the same set of 23,000 genes be used to specify such radically diverse behaviors, functions, and forms?

Part of the answer lies in the way genes are controlled, or regulated. Although a skin cell and a retinal cell inherit the same set of 23,000 genes, a skin cell activates or suppresses a unique subset of the total — say 5,000 of the 23,000 — while a retinal cell activates another subset. It's like an elaborate mix-and-match game: each cell dips into the same box of genes and chooses a unique spectrum of genes for itself, thereby attaining its form, function, and behavior.

10 To use an analogy that Jobs might have used: every human cell contains the same "hardware" of genes. But every individual cell type activates a particular "software" — a program (involving a particular combination of genes) that is unique unto itself to achieve its particular function.

But the answer raises a question: how does the skin cell know how to activate such software? In part through master regulatory genes that accomplish this task. These master-control genes exercise exquisite control on the growth, shape, size, and identity of a cell. They activate entire programs of gene expression; they toggle hundreds of molecular switches to turn "on" and turn "off" programs.

There are many such families of master-control genes, and one such family acts by modifying DNA — the stuff that all genes are made of. And PNETs appear to possess frequent mutations in these DNA-modifying genes. The phenomenon is not unique to PNETs. In my own laboratory we have discovered that leukemias and other blood disorders also possess frequent changes in such DNA-modifying genes. Others have found mutations in DNA-modifying genes in lymphomas and brain tumors, and in colon and stomach cancers.

There is, in short, a novel principle of cancer unfolding here: that DNA-modifying genes can be mutated in certain tumors. But what connects these DNA-modifying genes to the ultimate growth behavior of a cancer cell? Might these genes become targets for new drugs? Might one such medicine be used to treat — or even cure — PNETs?

Indeed, DNA-modifying genes aren't the only new and unusual targets unfolding as we learn more about cancer. There are genes that affect the way cancer cells use glucose or other building blocks, such as amino acids, during their metabolism.

15   This knowledge — gleaned over the past five years — should have accelerated an effort to find medicines that affect these new pathways that seem to control cancer. And indeed, to an extent, it has. Many of these new pathways have become reasonable targets for anti-cancer drugs. Medicines that attack a specific family of genes termed "kinases" — genes dysregulated in blood and lung cancers and melanoma — have made their way into human use. Nearly all of these originated with the discovery of specific gene mutations in particular variants of cancer.

But there are vast gaps in knowledge still, and even larger chasms in drug development. Targeting an errant gene in a cancer cell might sound like a simple, well-defined task, but in fact it is mind-bogglingly complex. Cancer cells arise out of normal cells — and they resemble normal cells so closely that it can be difficult, at times, to tell them apart at a genetic level (of the 23,000 genes in a normal cell, a cancer cell may share 22,962 and have only 38 that are altered).

I wonder whether Jobs himself might have enjoyed the strange challenge of creating anti-cancer drugs: it is, after all, the ultimate design problem. Molecules have to be made to "fit" exactly into unique clefts and pockets of a cell's machinery in order to logjam malignant growth. Extraneous bits and pieces have to be shaved off so that the drug can bind to its intended target with a neat, satisfying click. The human testing and clinical trials that follow drug discovery present peculiar operational challenges. And there's production and safety monitoring that come after. The popular press has adopted the term "designer drugs" for the new generation of molecules that can target cancer cells with exquisite specificity. I like to think that the ultimate designer of our generation might have had something to add to this most profound frontier of design.

Certainly he could have added a plea for adequate resources. The National Cancer Institute (NCI) is the nation's preeminent institution tasked with leading cancer scientists toward new means to prevent, treat, and cure cancers. Its annual budget of about $5 billion is stagnating and threatened. The Food and Drug Administration, charged with ensuring that new cancer medicines are brought effectively and safely to the public, operates on a budget of about $4 billion. If these amounts sound impressive, consider the fact that in 2008 the United States was spending about $12 billion every month on conflict in the Middle East — more than the annual NCI and FDA budgets combined.

If we are truly committed to creating medicines to prevent and treat cancer, we seem to be doing a rather lax job in funding this effort. We cannot continue to develop medicines under these circumstances. The postdoctoral researcher who identified the alterations in DNA-modifying genes in leukemia in my lab is debating whether to continue his research. His bench mate, a talented chemist I hired out of graduate school, is teaching biology at a local night school to supplement her income. Next year, when she runs out of grant funds, she is thinking of returning to Florida to work in a tattoo parlor.

20   The Japanese people speak of a "Lost Decade" — the *Ushinawareta Junen* — a period between 1990 and 2000 when banks collapsed, the economy stagnated, and culture lost its effervescence. Emblematic of this decade was a "lost generation" of Japanese men and women who were unable to contribute to critical problems affecting their generation. My fear is that we too will face a lost generation — of molecules.

Cancer, meanwhile, marches onward. The statistics are stark: in the United States, one in two men and one in three women will encounter it. One in four will die from it. It's important — given the complexity of the problem — not to oversell the speed or effectiveness of cancer research. Creating new medicines for cancer is slow, painstaking, time-consuming work. But that's precisely why we need federal support to keep this process intact. It is exactly why — when Congress chooses to ax the NCI budget — we should take that decision with utmost seriousness. If we don't generate enough political support for cancer research, we will not bring to life the kinds of medicines we need to treat our own cancers in the future — including the kind that killed Jobs. The vast gene-decoding efforts of the last decade will remain abstract, academic exercises — biology without medicine.

On my way back from the airport two days after his death, the signs and the apples were still outside the Apple store. I felt as if I should have added my own: "I'm sorry, Steve. I wish we had done better."

Reading and Discussion Questions

1. How does Mukherjee make use of Steve Jobs's death to advance the point he is trying to make? How did Jobs's death make him feel?
2. What parallels does Mukherjee make between Jobs's career and his own in the article?
3. Because Mukherjee is an oncologist and cancer researcher, he is expressing an expert's opinion. What other types of evidence does he offer?

4. What is Mukherjee's claim?

5. How effective do you find Mukherjee's argument? Does the use of Jobs's death add to its effectiveness? Explain your response.

Appeals to Needs and Values

Good factual evidence is usually enough to convince an audience that your factual claim is sound. Using examples, statistics, and expert opinion, you can prove, for example, that women do not earn as much as men for the same work. But even good evidence may not be enough to convince your audience that unequal pay is wrong or that something should be done about it. In making value and policy claims, an **appeal to the needs and values** of your audience is absolutely essential to the success of your argument. If you want to persuade the audience to change their minds or adopt a course of action — in this case, to demand legislation guaranteeing equal pay for equal work — you will have to show that assent to your claim will bring about what they want and care deeply about.

If the audience concludes that the things you care about are very different from what they care about, if they cannot identify with your goals and principles, they may treat your argument with indifference, even hostility, and finally reject it. But you can hope that decent and reasonable people will share many of the needs and values that underlie your claims. Finding these shared needs and values is what Carl Rogers was advocating when he said that the way to improved communication is to try to express your audience's position fairly and to look for common ground between their position and yours. The appeal to these needs and values was what Aristotle called *pathos*.

Appeals to Needs

The most familiar classification of needs was developed by the psychologist Abraham H. Maslow in 1954.[12] These needs, said Maslow, motivate human thought and action. In satisfying our needs, we attain both long- and short-term goals. Because Maslow believed that some needs are more important than others, he arranged them in hierarchical order from the most urgent biological needs to the psychological needs that are related to our roles as members of a society.

For most of your arguments, you won't have to address the audience's basic physiological needs for nourishment or shelter. The desire for health, however, now receives extraordinary attention. Appeals to buy health foods, vitamin sup-

---

[12] Abraham H. Maslow, *Motivation and Personality* (New York: Harper and Row, 1954), pp. 80–92.

SELF-
ACTUALIZATION
NEEDS
Fulfillment in realizing
one's potential

ESTEEM NEEDS
Material success; achievement;
power, status, and recognition by others

SOCIAL NEEDS
Love within a family and among friends;
roots within a group or a community

SAFETY NEEDS
Security; freedom from harm; order and stability

PHYSIOLOGICAL NEEDS
Basic bodily requirements: food and drink; health; sex

plements, drugs, exercise and diet courses, and health books are all around us. Many of the claims are supported by little or no evidence, but readers are so eager to satisfy the need for good health that they often overlook the lack of facts or authoritative opinion. The desire for physical well-being, however, is not so simple as it seems; it is strongly related to our need for self-esteem and love.

Appeals to our needs to feel safe from harm, to be assured of order and stability in our lives, are also common. Insurance companies, politicians who promise to rid our streets of crime, and companies that offer security services all appeal to this profound and nearly universal need. (We say "nearly" because some people are apparently attracted to risk and danger.) At this writing, those who monitor terrorist activity are attempting both to arouse fear for our safety and to suggest ways of reducing the dangers that make us fearful.

The last three needs in Maslow's hierarchy are the ones you will find most challenging to appeal to in your arguments. It is clear that these needs arise out of human relationships and participation in society. Advertisers make much use of appeals to these needs.

Social Needs

"Whether you are young or old, the need for companionship is universal." (ad for dating service)

"Share the Fun of High School with Your Little Girl!" (ad for a Barbie doll)

Esteem Needs

"Enrich your home with the distinction of an Oxford library."

"Apply your expertise to more challenges and more opportunities. Here are outstanding opportunities for challenge, achievement, and growth." (Perkin-Elmer Co.)

Self-Actualization Needs

"Be all that you can be." (former U.S. Army slogan)

"Are you demanding enough? Somewhere beyond the cortex is a small voice whose mere whisper can silence an army of arguments. It goes by many names: integrity, excellence, standards. And it stands alone in final judgment as to whether we have demanded enough of our-selves and, by that example, have inspired the best in those around us." (*New York Times*)

Of course, it is not only advertisers who use these appeals. We hear them from family and friends, from teachers, from employers, from editorials and letters to the editor, from people in public life.

Appeals to Values

Needs give rise to values. If we feel the need to belong to a group, we learn to value commitment, sacrifice, and sharing. And we then respond to arguments that promise to protect our values. It is hardly surprising that values, the prin-ciples by which we judge what is good or bad, beautiful or ugly, worthwhile or undesirable, should exercise a profound influence on our behavior. Virtually all claims, even those that seem to be purely factual, contain expressed or unex-pressed judgments.

For our study of argument, we will speak of groups or systems of values because any single value is usually related to others. People and institutions are often defined by such systems of values.

Values, like needs, are arranged in a hierarchy; that is, some are clearly more important than others to the people who hold them. Moreover, the arrange-ment may shift over time or as a result of new experiences. In 1962, for example, two speech teachers prepared a list of what they called "Relatively Unchang-ing Values Shared by Most Americans."[13] Included were "puritan and pioneer standards of morality" and "perennial optimism about the future." More than fifty years later, an appeal to these values might fall on a number of deaf ears.

You should also be aware of not only changes over time but also different or competing value systems that reflect a multitude of subcultures in the United

---

[13] Edward Steele and W. Charles Redding, "The American Value System: Premises for Persua-sion," *Western Speech*, 26 (Spring 1962), pp. 83–91.

States. Differences in age, sex, race, ethnic background, social environment, religion, even in the personalities and characters of its members, define the groups we belong to. Such terms as *honor, loyalty, justice, patriotism, duty, responsibility, equality, freedom,* and *courage* will be interpreted very differently by different groups.

All of us belong to more than one group, and the values of the several groups may be in conflict. If one group to which you belong — say, peers of your own age and class — is generally uninterested in and even scornful of religion, you may nevertheless hold to the values of your family and continue to place a high value on religious belief.

How can a knowledge of your readers' values enable you to make a more effective appeal? Suppose you want to argue in favor of a sex education program in the middle school you attended. The program you support would not only give students information about contraception and venereal disease but also teach them about the pleasures of sex, the importance of small families, and alternatives to heterosexuality. If the readers of your argument are your classmates or your peers, you can be fairly sure that their agreement will be easier to obtain than that of their parents, especially if their parents think of themselves as conservative. Your peers are more likely to value experimentation, tolerance of alternative sexual practices, freedom, and novelty. Their parents are more likely to value restraint, conformity to conventional sexual practices, obedience to family rules, and foresight in planning for the future.

Knowing that your peers share your values and your goals will mean that you need not spell out the values supporting your claim; they are understood by your readers. Convincing their parents, however, who think that freedom, tolerance, and experimentation have been abused by their children, will be a far more challenging task. In one written piece you have little chance of changing their values, a result that might be achieved only over a longer period of time. So you might first attempt to reduce their hostility by suggesting that even if a community-wide program were adopted, students would need parental permission to enroll. This might convince some parents that you share their values regarding parental authority and primacy of the family. Second, you might look for other values to which the parents subscribe and to which you can make an appeal. Do they prize maturity, self-reliance, responsibility in their children? If so, you could attempt to prove, with authoritative evidence, that the sex education program would promote these qualities in students who took the course.

But familiarity with the value systems of prospective readers may also lead you to conclude that winning assent to your argument will be impossible. It would probably be fruitless to attempt to persuade a group of lifelong pacifists to endorse the use of nuclear weapons. The beliefs, attitudes, and habits that support their value systems are too fundamental to yield to one or two attempts at persuasion.

Evaluating Appeals to Needs and Values

If your argument is based on an appeal to the needs and values of your audience, the following questions will help you evaluate the soundness of your appeal.

- **Have the values been clearly defined?** Because value terms are abstractions, you must make their meaning explicit by placing them in context and providing examples. If a person values his Second Amendment rights, does that mean he is opposed to any restrictions on gun ownership? Does another's opposition to abortion extend to cases of rape and incest?

- **Are the needs and values to which you appeal prominent in the reader's hierarchy at the time you are writing?** Gun control becomes a focus in the media and on people's minds whenever a mass shooting occurs. The need for election reform is a hot topic every four years but fades from memory in between.

- **Is the evidence in your argument clearly related to the needs and values to which you appeal?** Remember that readers must see some connection between your evidence and their goals. Statistics can be impressive, for example, but your audience must see their relevance.

ARGUMENT ESSENTIALS
Appeals to Needs and Values

- In making value and policy claims, it is essential to appeal to the needs and values of your audience, but first you must identify what those needs and values are.

- Needs can be viewed on a hierarchy developed by psychologist Abraham Maslow.

- Values are the principles by which we judge what is good or bad, beautiful or ugly, worthwhile or undesirable.

READING ARGUMENT

Seeing Appeals to Needs and Values

The following essay on genetics has been annotated to highlight appeals to needs and values. Read the selection, and answer the questions that follow. The numbered annotations in paragraphs 5–9 point out threats to human needs and values posed by reprogenetics. The second set of numbered annotations sum up the author's response.

Building Baby from the Genes Up
RONALD M. GREEN

The two British couples no doubt thought that their appeal for medical help in conceiving a child was entirely reasonable. Over several generations, many female members of their families had died of breast cancer. One or both spouses in each couple had probably inherited the genetic mutations for the disease, and they wanted to use in-vitro fertilization and preimplantation genetic diagnosis (PGD) to select only the healthy embryos for implantation. Their goal was to eradicate breast cancer from their family lines once and for all.

Appeal to physiological need for health

In the United States, this combination of reproductive and genetic medicine — what one scientist has dubbed "reprogenetics" — remains largely unregulated, but Britain has a formal agency, the Human Fertilization and Embryology Authority (HFEA), that must approve all requests for PGD. In July 2007, after considerable deliberation, the HFEA approved the procedure for both families. The concern was not about the use of PGD to avoid genetic disease, since embryo screening for serious disorders is commonplace now on both sides of the Atlantic. What troubled the HFEA was the fact that an embryo carrying the cancer mutation could go on to live for 40 or 50 years before ever developing cancer, and there was a chance it might never develop. Did this warrant selecting and discarding embryos? To its critics, the HFEA, in approving this request, crossed a bright line separating legitimate medical genetics from the quest for "the perfect baby."

Appeal to values: Was it right to reject an embryo that would develop into a person who might never get the disease or live 40 to 50 years without it?

Like it or not, that decision is a sign of things to come — and not necessarily a bad sign. Since the completion of the Human Genome Project in 2003, our understanding of the genetic bases of human disease and non-disease traits

Ronald M. Green is a professor of ethics at Dartmouth College and the author of *Babies by Design: The Ethics of Genetic Choice* (2007). This article was published in the *Washington Post* on April 13, 2008.

has been growing almost exponentially. The National Institutes of Health has initiated a quest for the "$1,000 genome," a 10-year program to develop machines that could identify all the genetic letters in anyone's genome at low cost (it took more than $3 billion to sequence the first human genome). With this technology, which some believe may be just four or five years away, we could not only scan an individual's — or embryo's — genome, we could also rapidly compare thousands of people and pinpoint those DNA sequences or combinations that underlie the variations that contribute to our biological differences.

With knowledge comes power. If we understand the genetic causes of obesity, for example, we can intervene by means of embryo selection to produce a child with a reduced genetic likelihood of getting fat. Eventually, without discarding embryos at all, we could use gene-targeting techniques to tweak fetal DNA sequences. No child would have to face a lifetime of dieting or experience the health and cosmetic problems associated with obesity. The same is true for cognitive problems such as dyslexia. Geneticists have already identified some of the mutations that contribute to this disorder. Why should a child struggle with reading difficulties when we could alter the genes responsible for the problem?

Many people are horrified at the thought of such uses of genetics, seeing   5
echoes of the 1997 science-fiction film *Gattaca*, which depicted a world where parents choose their children's traits. Human weakness has been eliminated through genetic engineering, and the few parents who opt for a "natural" conception run the risk of producing offspring — "invalids" or "degenerates" — who become members of a despised underclass. *Gattaca*'s world is clean and efficient, but its eugenic obsessions have all but extinguished human love and compassion.

These fears aren't limited to fiction. Over the past few years, many bioethicists have spoken out against genetic manipulations. The critics tend to voice at least four major concerns. First, they worry about the effect of genetic selection on parenting. Will our ability to choose our children's biological inheritance lead parents to replace unconditional love with a consumerist mentality that seeks perfection?

Second, they ask whether gene manipulations will diminish our freedom by making us creatures of our genes or our parents' whims. In his book *Enough*, the techno-critic Bill McKibben asks: If I am a world-class runner, but my parents inserted the "Sweatworks2010 GenePack" in my genome, can I really feel pride in my accomplishments? Worse, if I refuse to use my costly genetic endowments, will I face relentless pressure to live up to my parents' expectations?

Appeal to need for health, physical and cognitive

1. Appeal to need for love and community

2. Appeal to need for self-actualization

Third, many critics fear that reproductive genetics will widen our social divisions as the affluent "buy" more competitive abilities for their offspring. Will we eventually see "speciation," the emergence of two or more human populations so different that they no longer even breed with one another? Will we re-create the horrors of eugenics that led, in Europe, Asia and the United States, to the sterilization of tens of thousands of people declared to be "unfit" and that in Nazi Germany paved the way for the Holocaust?

3. Appeal to values — threat of increased social division and a return to the horrors of the Holocaust

Finally, some worry about the religious implications of this technology. Does it amount to a forbidden and prideful "playing God"?

4. Appeal to religious values

10   To many, the answers to these questions are clear. Not long ago, when I asked a large class at Dartmouth Medical School whether they thought that we should move in the direction of human genetic engineering, more than 80 percent said no. This squares with public opinion polls that show a similar degree of opposition. Nevertheless, "babies by design" are probably in our future — but I think that the critics' concerns may be less troublesome than they first appear.

Will critical scrutiny replace parental love? Not likely. Even today, parents who hope for a healthy child but have one born with disabilities tend to love that child ferociously. The very intensity of parental love is the best protection against its erosion by genetic technologies. Will a child somehow feel less free because parents have helped select his or her traits? The fact is that a child is already remarkably influenced by the genes she inherits. The difference is that we haven't taken control of the process. Yet.

1. Author responds with faith in parental love.

Knowing more about our genes may actually increase our freedom by helping us understand the biological obstacles — and opportunities — we have to work with. Take the case of Tiger Woods. His father, Earl, is said to have handed him a golf club when he was still in the playpen. Earl probably also gave Tiger the genes for some of the traits that help make him a champion golfer. Genes and upbringing worked together to inspire excellence. Does Tiger feel less free because of his inherited abilities? Did he feel pressured by his parents? I doubt it. Of course, his story could have gone the other way, with overbearing parents forcing a child into their mold. But the problem in that case wouldn't be genetics, but bad parenting.

2. Author responds that there will be no threat to self-actualization.

Granted, the social effects of reproductive genetics are worrisome. The risks of producing a "genobility," genetic overlords ruling a vast genetic underclass, are real. But genetics could also become a tool for reducing the class divide. Will we see the day when perhaps all youngsters are genetically vaccinated against dyslexia? And how might this contribute to everyone's social betterment?

3. Author responds that some divisions could be reduced.

4. Author responds that religions tend to accept modification for disease cures or prevention but not for other reasons.

As for the question of intruding on God's domain, the answer is less clear than the critics believe. The use of genetic medicine to cure or prevent disease is widely accepted by religious traditions, even those that oppose discarding embryos. Speaking in 1982 at the Pontifical Academy of Sciences, Pope John Paul II observed that modern biological research "can ameliorate the condition of those who are affected by chromosomic diseases," and he lauded this as helping to cure "the smallest and weakest of human beings . . . during their intrauterine life or in the period immediately after birth." For Catholicism and some other traditions, it is one thing to cure disease, but another to create children who are faster runners, longer-lived, or smarter.

But why should we think that the human genome is a once-and-for-all-finished, untamperable product? All of the biblically derived faiths permit human beings to improve on nature using technology, from agriculture to aviation. Why not improve our genome? I have no doubt that most people considering these questions for the first time are certain that human genetic improvement is a bad idea, but I'd like to shake up that certainty.

Human genetic improvement is *not* a bad thing.

Genomic science is racing toward a future in which foreseeable improvements include reduced susceptibility to a host of diseases, increased life span, better cognitive functioning, and maybe even cosmetic enhancements such as whiter, straighter teeth. Yes, genetic orthodontics may be in our future. The challenge is to see that we don't also unleash the demons of discrimination and oppression. Although I acknowledge the risks, I believe that we can and will incorporate gene technology into the ongoing human adventure.

Claim

15

Reading and Discussion Questions

1. Remember that the annotations here focus only on appeals to needs and values because that is the focus of this portion of the chapter. That does not mean that those are the only types of support in the essay. What other types of support did you notice? To begin with, what type of support does the first paragraph provide?

2. The annotations make the organization of most of the essay fairly obvious. Explain the organizational pattern.

3. If you were going to write an essay analyzing Green's use of support, what would your thesis be?

Practice: Appeals to Needs and Values

Analyze the 1948 print advertisement on page 209 using the questions that follow it.

The Baseball Man's Cigarette
CHESTERFIELD CIGARETTES

Getty Images

Reading and Discussion Questions

1. What needs or values does the ad appeal to? How?
2. Do you think the same approach to selling cigarettes would work today? Why, or why not?

Practice: Appeals to Needs and Values

In the following opinion piece, Jeremy Markel takes an insightful look at marketing aimed at "tweens." Read the essay, and answer the questions that follow it.

Marketing to "Tweens" Objectifies Women
JEREMY MARKEL

Last November Victoria's Secret showcased its new "tween" lingerie line at its annual fashion show. The showcase was part of Pink's new marketing campaign intended for what the industry calls "tweens": girls and teens.

Pink, Victoria's Secret's "teen friendly" clothing store, and others like it such as Hot Topic and American Eagle, have created their own lingerie lines and have begun marketing them toward young women. Even Justice, a store that is intended for girls ages 7–12, has begun selling flowered underwear and tie-dye bras online.

In 2011, Walmart launched its makeup line, geoGirl, which is marketed to 8–12 year-old girls. The line has 69 cosmetic products including blush, mascara, and exfoliants.

These marketing trends target younger and younger girls and women; they manipulate them by standardizing certain behaviors and styles of dress, impress upon them the idea that being sexy is necessary, engender an arbitrary and unrealistic idea of what being "sexy" is, and distort their self-concepts.

5   Stuart Burgdoerfer, the chief financial officer of Limited Brands, the parent company of Victoria's Secret, stated that "when somebody's 15 or 16 years old, what do they want to be? They want to be older, and they want to be cool like the girl in college, and that's part of the magic of what we do at Pink."

By "magic," Stuart essentially meant that Pink is manipulating younger generations based upon their ideas of what being older is like and is exploiting a need that it, as well as other clothing and cosmetics stores, helps create.

Victoria's Secret uses college-age models, and defines "sexiness" as being extremely thin, having flawless skin, wearing make-up, and having unnaturally white teeth. It then provides young women with the tools — lingerie, makeup, and perfume — that will help them achieve the unrealistic and arbitrary standard of appearance that it helps create.

The fact that teen heartthrob Justin Bieber was hired to perform during the showcasing of Pink's "tween" lingerie line during the Victoria's Secret fashion show last November clearly illus-

When he wrote this piece, Jeremy Markel was a junior majoring in communication studies at the University of Georgia. The opinion piece was published on March 24, 2013, in the campus newspaper, *Red and Black*.

trates Limited Brands's intention to persuade girls and teens that they need to use Pink's products in order to be appealing.

Even though Hot Topic and American Eagle have not stated that they are targeting the same 15–16 age group as Pink, Marcie Merriman, founder of PrimalGrowth, stated stores are "all going to say they're targeting 18–22 year-olds, but the reality is you're going to get the younger customer."

10   This is especially true in stores that are "teen friendly." Placing clothing that is marketed to 18–22 year-olds alongside clothing intended for younger audiences will attract younger girls and women who, in Burgdoerfer's words, "want to be cool like the girl in college."

In addition to standardizing behaviors and constructing beauty, the increasing number of images that women and girls see of super-thin models have been linked to body image issues in women and girls. Researchers have stated that, "having unrealistic expectation[s] for one's body image creates a greater chance for body dissatisfaction. The media may influence one's body image in such a way through constant portrayal of the 'thin ideal.'"

Walmart's makeup line is a perfect example of the creation of unrealistic and arbitrary ideals of beauty for girls. Marketing cosmetics to any age group implies that one's current appearance needs adjusting, but one striking fact about geoGirl is that it includes exfoliators. "The line's creators claim it's formulated for fresh young skin, with ingredients like willow bark to exfoliate and chamomile to calm, as well as antioxidants, which reportedly prevent aging."

Preventing aging is impossible, however. Entropy cannot be stopped no matter how much willow bark or chamomile one uses. What is even more ridiculous is that we are talking about 8–12 year-olds whose skin is probably in the best condition it will ever be in. Other than "early bloomers" who experience acne at young ages and other similar cases, rarely do cosmetics problems exist for this age group.

Regardless, geoGirl is creating cosmetics problems for 8–12 year-olds, and then providing them with the tools to fix those problems.

What Walmart, Pink, and similar clothing stores are doing is detrimental to the self-esteem, body image, and general well-being of girls and women. Their marketing campaigns and lingerie and cosmetics lines create unrealistic standards by which women and girls are intended to live. Moreover, they objectify and sexualize their own consumers.   15

Reading and Discussion Questions

1. What is the author's claim?
2. Who is the author's audience? How does the author appeal to that audience's needs and values?

Assignments for Support: Backing Up a Claim

Reading and Discussion Questions

1. Consider what types of evidence you find most convincing in an argument. Is the best type of evidence dependent on the topic and the context? Explain.

2. Look for examples in the media of the misuse of evidence. Explain why the evidence is misleading.

3. Use examples to explain which news shows depend on factual evidence and which depend largely on opinion. Do both have a useful role to play in our society? Explain.

4. In the aftermath of the massacre at Sandy Hook Elementary, there was talk of passing laws requiring teachers to carry weapons on school and college campuses. What needs of the people were those who proposed the law appealing to? How could opponents of such laws have used similar types of appeal to argue their case?

5. Consider presidential debates you have seen or other televised coverage of candidates during the months leading up to an election. What are some specific examples of how the candidates try to appeal to the voters' needs and values?

6. The average American citizen is usually ignorant of much of the reality of what goes on in the Islamic world. When Americans take a stand on issues such as U.S. involvement in Afghanistan, to what extent do you believe they are basing that stand on solid supporting evidence?

Writing Suggestions

1. Analyze different television commercials for the same product or similar products. Write an essay supporting a conclusion you are able to draw about the types of appeal used in the commercials.

2. Write a letter about a problem on your campus to the person who is in a position to correct the problem. Provide convincing evidence that a problem exists, and in suggesting a solution to the problem, keep in mind the needs and values of your audience as well as those of others on campus.

RESEARCH ASSIGNMENT

1. Do some preliminary research on the following topics:
   - The link between autism and vaccines
   - The link between cell phones and cancer

- The movement to drop the SAT as a requirement for college admissions
- The environmental impact of plastic water bottles

2. For each of the topics above, track down one or more sources that use each type of evidence and emotional appeal discussed in the chapter:
   - an example
   - a statistic
   - an expert opinion
   - an image
   - an appeal to a need
   - an appeal to a value

3. Evaluate the sources you have found, using the Research Skill boxes on pages 184 and 204.

bits

To see what you are learning about argumentation applied to the latest world and national news, read our *Bits* blog, "Argument and the Headlines," at **blogs.bedfordstmartins.com/bits**.

Warrants: Examining Assumptions

We now come to the third element in the structure of the argument—the warrant. Claim and support, the other major elements we have discussed, are more familiar in ordinary discourse, but there is nothing mysterious or unusual about the warrant. All our claims, both formal and informal, are grounded in warrants: assumptions that the audience must share with us if our claims are to prove to be acceptable.

The arrows in the following diagram illustrate that writer and audience must be looking at the subject with the same underlying beliefs in order for the argument to be persuasive.

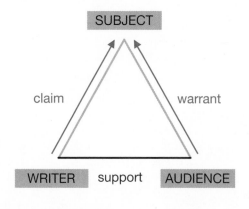

General Principles

The following exercise provides a good starting point for this chapter. Do the assigned task by yourself or in a small group.

Practice: Warrants

A series of environmental catastrophic events has virtually wiped out human life on Earth. The only known survivors in your vicinity are the eleven listed below. There are resources to sustain only seven. Choose seven of the following people to survive. List them in the order in which you would choose them, and be prepared to explain the reasons for your selection: that is, why you chose these particular persons and why you placed them in this certain order.

- Dr. D. — thirty-seven, PhD in history, college professor, in good health (jogs daily), hobby is botany, enjoys politics, married with one child (Bobby).
- Mrs. D. — thirty-eight, rather obese, diabetic, MA in psychology, counselor in a mental health clinic, married to Dr. D., has one child.
- Bobby D. — ten, cognitively deficient with IQ of 70, healthy and strong for his age.
- Mrs. G. — twenty-three, ninth-grade education, cocktail waitress, worked as a prostitute, married at age sixteen, divorced at age eighteen, one son (Joseph).
- Joseph G. — three months old, healthy.
- Mary E. — eighteen, trade school education, wears glasses, artistic.
- Mr. N. — twenty-five, starting last year of medical school, music as a hobby, physical fitness buff.
- Mrs. C. — twenty-eight, daughter of a minister, college graduate, electronics engineer, single now after a brief marriage, member of Zero Population Growth.
- Mr. B. — fifty-one, BS in mechanics, married with four children, enjoys outdoors, much experience in construction, quite handy.
- Father Frans — thirty-seven, Catholic priest, active in civil rights, former college athlete, farming background, often criticized for liberal views.
- Dr. L. — sixty-six, doctor in general practice, two heart attacks in the past five years, loves literature and quotes extensively.

There may have been a great deal of disagreement over which survivors in the above scenario to select. If so, the reason for that disagreement was that in making their choices, different members of your group or of your class as a whole were operating under different assumptions or basing their decisions on different warrants. Some of you may have chosen not to let Mrs. G. survive because she seemed to have nothing particularly vital to offer to the survival of the group as a whole. If you analyzed your claim, support, and warrant in that case, they would look something like the following. Notice the warrant in particular.

Claim: Mrs. G. should not be allowed to survive.

Support: She has no skills vital to the survival of the group.

Warrant: Those chosen to survive must have skills vital to the survival of the group.

Another way of looking at the warrant is to ask yourself this question: **What would I have to believe in order to accept that claim, given the support I have to go on?**

Others may have felt that Mrs. G. should be allowed to survive along with her child, the infant in the group. The reasoning would look like this:

Claim: Mrs. G. should be allowed to survive.

Support: She has an infant son.

Warrant: Those with infants should be allowed to survive.

That assumes, of course, choosing to allow the infant, Jospeh G., to survive. If that was not the case, the warrant behind letting Mrs. G. survive would be invalid.

Did you decide to let Baby Joseph survive? If so, what was your reasoning? How would you fill in the blanks?

Claim: Joseph G. should be allowed to survive.

Support: _____

Warrant: _____

Or if you thought the opposite — that the infant should not be one of the seven allowed to survive — what was your reasoning?

Claim: Joseph G. should not be allowed to survive.

Support: _____

Warrant: _____

You may have felt that an infant had very little chance of survival and therefore his spot should be given to someone more likely to survive. Or you may have thought that the future of the civilization depended on the survival of the young. Or you may just not have liked the thought of killing an infant.

There are few easy answers in this exercise, but behind each choice is a warrant, or underlying assumption. If you chose to kill off Dr. L., it was probably because he had had two heart attacks and was less likely than others to survive. You might have decided that the young Mr. N., a physical fitness buff and a medical student, would be more vital to the survival of the others. Out of compassion, you might have wanted to save Bobby D., or you might have concluded that a cognitively deficient ten-year-old with an IQ of 70 had the least to offer the rest of the group.

Obviously, this is an exercise with no right answer. What it can teach us, however, is to consider the assumptions on which our beliefs are based. There are reasons you might have chosen certain individuals to survive that could be stated as general principles:

Those who are in the best physical condition should be allowed to survive.

Those with the most useful skills should be allowed to survive.

Those who are mentally deficient should not be allowed to survive.

Those who are most likely to reproduce should be allowed to survive.

Fortunately, this is merely an intellectual exercise. Whenever you take a stand in a real-life situation, though, you do so on the basis of certain general principles that guide your choices. Those general principles that you feel most strongly about exist as part of your intellectual and moral being because of what you have experienced in your life thus far. They have been shaped by your observations, your personal experience, and your participation in a culture. Some of the general principles behind your thoughts and actions may be these:

> Cheating is always wrong.
> I have a right to express my opinion.
> Premarital sex is wrong.
> Morality changes with the times.
> Killing under any circumstances is wrong.
> Killing is wrong except in self-defense.
> Killing is wrong except in war.
> Cruelty to animals is wrong.
> Government intrudes too much in my daily life.

All of these are broad statements that could apply in any number of different circumstances. That's why we refer to them as general principles. Your warrants may not always be this broad, but at times they will be. Because the observations, experiences, and cultural associations on which these principles are based vary from one individual to another, your audience may not always agree with your warrants or assumptions. The success of Rogerian argument depends on identifying at least one assumption, or warrant, that opposing sides share. The success of any argument depends on at least understanding your own warrants and those of your audience.

Widely Held Assumptions

Some warrants are so widely accepted that they do not need to be stated or require any proof of their validity. If an argument claims that every new dorm on campus should have a sprinkler system, it probably does not even need to state the warrant. If it did, it would be something like this: *Measures that would increase the likelihood that dorm residents would survive a fire should be implemented in all dorms.*

If your house catches on fire, you call 911. If your car is stolen, you call the police (or 911). You may have never used the term *warrant* in such cases because these assumptions are so widely agreed on that they don't have to be stated. We teach these responses even to young children, who in some cases have saved their own lives and those of others by knowing what to do.

Claim: I should call 911.

Support: I just saw a stranger sneaking around my neighbor's house.

Warrant: If you see a stranger sneaking around the neighborhood, you should call 911.

Other widely held assumptions:

> **Claim:** Michael should get a smoke detector.
>
> **Support:** His new apartment doesn't have a working smoke detector.
>
> **Warrant:** Every apartment needs a working smoke detector.

> **Claim:** I should drive you home.
>
> **Support:** You've been drinking, and I haven't.
>
> **Warrant:** The one who hasn't been drinking should do the driving.

> **Claim:** Ping's mother won't let him visit at Daniel's house.
>
> **Support:** Daniel's parents keep guns that are not locked up in their home.
>
> **Warrant:** People shouldn't let their children visit where guns are not kept locked up.

Notice that a warrant is a broad generalization that can apply to a number of different situations, while the claim is about a specific place and time. It should be added that in other arguments the warrant may not be stated in such general terms. However, even in arguments in which the warrant makes a more specific reference to the claim, the reader can infer an extension of the warrant to other similar arguments. In the sprinkler system example on page 217, the warrant mentions dorms in particular. But it is clear that such warrants can be generalized to apply to other arguments in which we accept a claim based on an appeal to our very human need to feel secure.

What about claims that are more controversial? Why is it so difficult for those who oppose abortion, for example, to communicate with those who favor it, and vice versa? Anyone who believes that abortion is the murder of an unborn child is basing that argument on the warrant that a fetus is a child from conception. Many on the other side of the debate do not accept that warrant and thus do not accept the claim. Obviously, disagreements on such emotionally charged issues are very difficult to resolve because the underlying warrants are based on firmly held beliefs that are resistant to change. It is always better to be aware of your opponent's warrants, however, than to simply dismiss them as irrelevant.

The British philosopher Stephen Toulmin, who developed the concept of warrants, dismissed more traditional forms of logical reasoning in favor of a more audience-based, courtroom-derived approach to argumentation. He refers to warrants as "general, hypothetical statements, which can act as bridges" and "entitle one to draw conclusions or make claims."[1] The word *bridges* to denote the action of the warrant is crucial. We use the word *warrant* to emphasize that in an argument it guarantees a connecting link — a bridge — between the claim and the support. This means that even if a reader agrees that the support is

---

[1] Stephen Toulmin, *The Uses of Argument* (Cambridge: Cambridge University Press, 1958), p. 98.

sound, the support cannot prove the validity of the claim unless the reader also agrees with the underlying warrant.

The following dialogue offers another example of the relationship between the warrant and the other elements of the argument.

> *"Stop talking on the phone, and concentrate on driving!"*
> *"Aw, I always talk on my cell when I'm driving."*
> *"Well, you shouldn't. It's not safe."*
> *"So what?"*
> *"You shouldn't do unsafe things while driving."*

If we put this into outline form, the warrant, or assumption, in the argument is clear.

Claim: You shouldn't talk on your cell phone while you are driving.

Support: Talking on a cell phone while driving is not safe.

Warrant: You shouldn't do unsafe things while driving.

We can also represent an argument in diagram form, which shows the warrant as a bridge between the claim and the support.

```
SUPPORT ───────────────────────▶ CLAIM
                    │
                    │
                    │
                 WARRANT
           (expressed or unexpressed)
```

The argument above can then be written like this:

```
     SUPPORT ──────────────────▶ CLAIM
Talking on a cell phone while       You shouldn't talk on your
   driving is not safe.             cell phone while driving.
                    │
                 WARRANT
            You shouldn't do unsafe
              things while driving.
```

Claim and support (or lack of support) are relatively easy to uncover in most arguments. One thing that makes the warrant different is that it is often unexpressed and therefore unexamined by both writer and reader because they take it for granted. In the argument about using a cell phone while driving, the warrant was stated. Consider another example where the warrant is implied, not stated. What is the implied warrant in the following?

The technological revolution in how information is distributed and consumed holds the promise to scale higher education to serve more students and cut costs. At the same time, the rush to embrace technology as a solution to every problem has created tension on campuses over whether the critical role higher education plays in preparing the whole person to be a productive citizen in a democratic society is at risk. Indeed, in an increasingly complex world, the foundation of learning — a liberal arts education — is more important than ever.[2]

The claim is that traditional higher education has the potential to be transformed by technology. The implied assumption — the implied warrant — is that increasing the number of students receiving a quality liberal arts education in a cost-effective way will lead to a better society.

READING ARGUMENT

Practice: Widely Held Assumptions

Read the following opinion piece by National Public Radio's Scott Simon. It's about one father's change of heart about same-sex marriage. After reading the piece, answer the questions that follow it.

The Power of a Father's Love Overturns His Beliefs
SCOTT SIMON

When Senator Rob Portman of Ohio on Friday became the latest conservative politician to announce his support for same-sex marriage, he disclosed that his son, Will, a junior at Yale University, had told him two years ago that he is gay; and that love and admiration for his son had moved the senator to reflect — and change.

When Mr. Portman was in the House of Representatives, he co-sponsored a 1996 law to prevent same-sex marriage.

"At the time, my position . . . was rooted in my faith tradition," he wrote in Friday's *Co-lumbus Dispatch*. "Knowing that my son is gay prompted me to consider the issue from another perspective: that of a dad who wants all three of his kids to lead happy, meaningful lives with the people they love . . . and my belief that we are all children of God."

A lot of Americans, according to polls, are growing to accept same-sex marriage, whatever

---

Scott Simon is a National Public Radio correspondent and host of NPR's *Weekend Edition Saturday*. This opinion piece aired on March 16, 2013.

---

[2] Jeffrey J. Selingo, *College (Un)Bound: The Future of Higher Education and What It Means for Students* (New York: New Harvest, 2013), p. xvii.

their politics or faith. The politicians of both major parties may simply be trying to keep pace. But many of them have said that personal experience, especially with their children, has caused them to see the issue in a new light.

5   When President Obama told ABC News last May that his position on same-sex marriage was "evolving," he cited his daughters.

"Malia and Sasha," he said, "they've got friends whose parents are same-sex couples. . . . And frankly, that's the kind of thing that prompts a change of perspective."

Former Vice President Dick Cheney was probably the first major political figure to explicitly support same-sex marriage, in 2009, saying, "I think people ought to be free to enter into any kind of union they wish." His daughter, Mary Cheney, lived in a committed relationship for many years and is now married.

Perhaps a politician — or any of us — shouldn't have to feel that our child is directly affected by an issue to take a fresh look. But there is nothing like children to chip away at any hard ideological assumptions we hold, especially if we begin to think that our certitudes may prevent our children from being happy.

In a round of interviews with Ohio newspapers Friday, Senator Portman spoke about how much he admired his son. "He's an amazing young man," he said. "If anything, I'm even more proud of the way he has handled the whole situation."

He sounded like a father who was glad and   10 proud to have learned something from his son. And his son might learn something from his father, too, that can be useful for all of us as we grow older: about keeping an open mind and heart, and being open to change.

Reading and Discussion Questions

1. What is Simon's claim? Is it about Senator Portman, or is it a broader point?
2. What is Simon's support?
3. What generalization is Simon's warrant, or the generalization that links his claim and support? Is there a single sentence that sums up the warrant, or is it unstated?

Recognizing and Analyzing Warrants

There is no simple formula for locating warrants. And, yes, there can be more than one warrant in a single text because different portions of the text may be based on separate warrants. Once you have read a selection, it is a good idea to locate the thesis statement or try to put the thesis into your own words. Then look at the evidence the author offers in support of that thesis. The warrant will be a statement that shows the connection between the claim and support.

Unstated Warrants

We have already noted that sometimes the warrant is unstated. Arguers might neglect to state their warrants for one of two reasons: (1) as in our earlier examples, they may believe that the warrant is obvious and need not be expressed; (2) they may want to conceal the warrant in the hope that the reader will overlook its weakness.

Here are a few more examples of warrants that are so obvious that they need not be expressed:

Mothers love their children.
A good harvest will result in lower prices for produce.
Killing innocent children is wrong.
First come, first served.

These statements seem to embody beliefs that most of us would share and that might be unnecessary to make explicit in an argument. The last statement, for example, is taken as axiomatic, an article of faith that we seldom question in ordinary circumstances. Suppose you hear someone make the claim, *I deserve to get the last ticket to the concert.* If you ask why he is entitled to a ticket that you also would like to have, he may answer in support of his claim, "Because I was here first." No doubt you accept his claim without further argument because you understand and agree with the warrant that is not expressed: *If you arrive first, you deserve to be served before those who come later.*

But even those warrants that seem to express universal truths invite analysis if we can think of claims for which these warrants might not, after all, be relevant. "First in line," for example, may justify the claim of a person who wants a concert ticket, but it cannot in itself justify the claim of someone who wants a vital medication that is in short supply.

Moreover, offering a rebuttal to a long-held but unexamined warrant can often produce an interesting and original argument. If someone exclaims, "All this buying of gifts! I think people have forgotten that Christmas celebrates the birth of Christ," she need not express the assumption — that the buying of gifts violates what ought to be a religious celebration. It goes unstated by the speaker because it has been uttered so often that she knows the hearer will supply it. But one writer, in an essay titled "God's Gift: A Commercial Christmas," argued that contrary to popular belief, the purchase of gifts — which means the expenditure of time, money, and thought on others rather than oneself — is not a violation but an affirmation of the Christmas spirit.[3]

The second reason for refusal to state the warrant lies in the arguer's intention to disarm or deceive the reader, although the arguer may not be aware of this. For instance, failure to state the warrant is common in advertising and politics, where the desire to sell a product or an idea may outweigh the responsibility to argue explicitly. The advertisement below was famous not only for what it said but for what it did not say.

Philip Morris USA

What is the unstated warrant in the ad? The manufacturer of Virginia Slims hoped we would agree that being permitted to smoke cigarettes was a significant sign of female liberation. But many readers would insist that proving "You've come a long way, baby" requires more evidence than women's freedom to smoke (or "serve" the business world). The shaky warrant weakened the claim.

---

[3] Robert A. Sirico, *Wall Street Journal*, December 21, 1993, sec. A, p. 12.

Strategies for Recognizing Warrants

1. In written arguments, locate the one sentence that best states the author's claim. If the argument is unwritten (such as a print advertisement), or if there is no single sentence that sums up the claim, try to express the claim in a single sentence of your own.

2. Think about what audience the author was targeting. How is that audience likely to respond to the claim? The most important question to ask about the audience regarding warrants is this one: What assumption or assumptions must the audience make to be able to accept the claim? The answer to that question will be the warrant or warrants on which the piece is based.

3. Most written arguments include support to strengthen the author's claim. Remember that the warrant is the link between claim and support. It may help to use the formula used in this chapter to think systematically through the argument. Ask yourself what the claim is, what support the author is offering, and what warrant connects the two. Do that for each of the author's major supporting statements.

4. The author may not need to state his or her warrant directly if it is a universally accepted truth that most reasonable readers would agree with. It should be clear to you as a reader, however, what the warrant is.

READING ARGUMENT

Recognizing Unstated Warrants

The following essay was written in August 2013 and examines a judge's ruling concerning the "stop, question, and frisk" policy that the New York Police Department claims has cut down on crime in the city over the last two decades. This is a more complex argument than others we have looked at in this chapter, but it will help if you approach it considering what Terry Eastland's claim of policy is and why.

Don't Stop Frisking
TERRY EASTLAND

Since the early 1990s the New York Police Department has used a crime-prevention strategy that it calls "stop, question, and frisk." Accordingly, officers stop and question a person based on reasonable suspicion and sometimes pat down the clothing of the individual to ensure that he is not armed. The de-

Terry Eastland is an executive editor for the *Weekly Standard*, where this article appeared on August 26, 2013. During the Reagan era, Eastland was Director of Public Affairs for the Justice Department and later was a resident scholar at the Ethics and Public Policy Center. Among his works is *Freedom of Expression in the Supreme Court* (2000).

partment credits the strategy in large part for the huge declines in murder and major crimes over two decades in what is now the nation's safest big city. But the liberal opposition to stop-question-and-frisk has been fighting back, and last week federal district judge Shira A. Scheindlin declared the NYPD's use of the strategy unconstitutional and ordered a set of remedies whose implementation is to be overseen by an independent monitor she has appointed.

During the trial, which ended three weeks ago, a *New Yorker* writer sympathetic to Scheindlin's view of the case observed that the litigation was "rooted in the hope that a single judge can diagnose a complex problem and reform a huge organization like the New York Police Department based on the imperfect medium of trial testimony," and that while the judge's "dedication to protecting citizens' rights is beyond question . . . it is less clear that she has the wisdom, or even the ability, to impose her vision in the real world of New York."

Before the world discovers whether Judge Scheindlin can indeed impose her vision, and with what consequences, it would be good to know whether her decision in the class-action case of *Floyd* v. *New York City* can stand. Fortunately, Mayor Michael Bloomberg has declared that he will appeal. The mayor has said the judge was biased against the city, and on so important an issue as stop-question-and-frisk — public safety long being a top concern of New Yorkers — a fresh set of judicial eyes could help ensure public confidence in the process and what it ultimately yields in this case.

In her decision, Judge Scheindlin did not strike down stop-question-and-frisk as such, which the Supreme Court upheld against constitutional challenge in the 1968 case of *Terry* v. *Ohio*, but instead ruled against the tool "as applied" in the city. The nineteen *Floyd* plaintiffs — each of them black or Hispanic — contended that stop-question-and-frisk violated their constitutional rights in two ways. First, they said they were stopped without a legal basis — that is, without "reasonable suspicion" — in violation of the Fourth Amendment's prohibition against unreasonable searches and seizures. And second, they said they were targeted for stops because of their race and ethnicity in violation of the Fourteenth Amendment's equal protection guarantee.

5   Judging the plaintiffs' "Terry-stop" claims under the Fourth Amendment, Scheindlin concluded that "nine of the stops and frisks were unconstitutional — that is, they were not based on reasonable suspicion." In five others she said the stops were based on reasonable suspicion but the frisks were not and on that account were unconstitutional. And in the remaining five, she said those stopped or frisked failed to prove their claims. By the way, there could

Marginal notes:

The police claim the policy has reduced crime, but Scheindlin has declared it unconstitutional.

Even her sympathizers question Scheindlin's ability to make and enforce the decision alone.

Mayor plans to appeal.

Details of ruling

More details

have been hundreds of plaintiffs, but the nineteen were apparently all the *Floyd* lawyers could find, or were willing to find, and they had mixed results in trying to persuade a sympathetic judge of their claims.

The nineteen stops of the named plaintiffs were a tiny subset of the more than 4.4 million stops made by the NYPD between 2004 and 2012, more than 80 percent of them stops of blacks or Hispanics, with slightly more than 50 percent of them resulting in a frisk, weapons being found in 1.5 percent of the frisks, and some 6 percent of the stops resulting in arrests. It is hard to see how much could be reliably inferred from those numbers about the 4.4 million stops.

Scheindlin recognized as much when she wrote that *Floyd* was "not primarily about the nineteen individual stops that were the subject of testimony at trial." Nor was the case about an actual stop-question-and-frisk law or regulation that the judge found in violation of the Fourth Amendment, for there were no such instruments. What the case was about, the judge wrote, was "whether the City has a *policy* or *custom* [the judge's emphasis] of violating the Constitution by making unlawful stops and conducting unlawful frisks." Weighing "extensive expert submissions and testimony" on various aspects of the department's use of the strategy, she concluded there was. But her assessment of the relevant law and how she looked for it, in a case of such

importance to not just New York City but in municipalities across the country, merits appellate review.

As for the plaintiffs' claims about being targeted by race and ethnicity for stops, here there is an oddity. For while none of the nineteen plaintiffs were able to prove equal protection claims against actual police officers, Scheindlin, using statistics and anecdotal evidence, decided that the class the plaintiffs represented (and which included them) had been discriminated against. As with stop-and-frisk, she said, there was no stated policy that endorsed racial

targeting but an unwritten one, which relied in part upon how crime victims had described those they say committed the crimes against them, descriptions that include the race and ethnicity of the alleged perpetrators.

In concluding that the NYPD was guilty of "indirect racial profiling," Scheindlin made much of one police chief's testimony that officers are to focus their reasonable-suspicion-based stops on "the right people," citing it more than a dozen times, but whether she used those words in context could interest the appeals court. So could her analysis of competing statistical

models, especially since she seems at times to embrace the dubious notion that the racial Terry-stop rates in a given community should be comparable to the percentages by race of the people who live in that community.

10   Judge Scheindlin emphasized throughout *Floyd* that her mandate was to judge the constitutionality of the policy as carried out, not its effectiveness. Evidently constitutionality in the context at hand may not, ever, take into account the first imperative of government, which is to ensure the safety of its citizens. The judge's determination to regulate the NYPD, through ambitious reforms and a monitor reporting to her, may result in less safe streets in the poor and minority communities where crime once thrived and where stop-question-and-frisk has most often been employed. That is why an appeal is necessary — to determine, with so much weighing in the balance, whether the judge's decision is correct or not.

> Support for claim: The policy keeps citizens safe.

> Author expresses why the argument is so important.

Amazing, is it not, that the best hope for continuing one of the most successful anticrime strategies in modern times lies in the U.S. Court of Appeals for the Second Circuit, not exactly a tribunal dominated by judicial conservatives.

Analysis

Using Toulmin's terms, Eastland's argument could be outlined like this.

Claim: Scheindlin's ruling — that the "stop, question, and frisk" policy as applied in New York is unconstitutional — should be appealed.

Support: The current policy is effective at keeping citizens safe.

Implied warrant: The effectiveness of the policy is more important than its constitutionality.

Recognizing the warrant in an argument is a major step toward determining its validity. However, complex arguments require further analysis of the warrant, including its backing, reservation, and qualifiers.

Backing

How do we know if a warrant is valid? We cannot answer this question until we consider the **backing**. Backing is evidence that gives the warrant authority. Backing, or authority, for the warrant in the earlier example about using a cell phone while driving would consist of data proving the danger of doing unsafe things while driving. That particular warrant, we would discover, has backing because (1) there is evidence of the number of accidents that have occurred while the driver was talking on a cell phone or texting, and (2) there are studies showing that reaction time is slower when the driver is distracted. In that case, the evidence guarantees the soundness of the claim.

In Eastland's opinion piece about Scheindlin's ruling, he explicitly provides backing for his warrant when he states, "The first imperative of government is to ensure the safety of its citizens." In charting the elements of Eastland's argument, the backing would be placed below the warrant to show that it is evidence for the warrant:

SUPPORT ————————➤ CLAIM

The current policy is effective
at keeping citizens safe and
should not be changed.

Schleindlin's ruling
should be appealed.

WARRANT

The effectiveness of the policy is more
important than its constitutionality.

BACKING

The first imperative of government is to
ensure the safety of its citizens.

The statement backing Eastland's warrant is problematic in that it suggests that the unconstitutionality of a law doesn't matter if it comes to choosing between what is constitutional and what is effective in fighting crime.

Reservation

What makes Eastland's argument acceptable in this case is that warrants can be modified or limited by **reservations**, which remind the reader that there are conditions under which the warrants will not be relevant. In the cell phone example, a reservation would be that using a cell phone while driving is not as dangerous if you use a hands free option. The reservation in the "stop, question, and frisk" example is that Scheindlin is not actually arguing that the policy is unconstitutional in its wording but in its execution, which is exactly why Eastland feels the ruling should be appealed.

SUPPORT ————————➤ CLAIM

The current policy is effective
at keeping citizens safe and
should not be changed.

Schleindlin's ruling
should be appealed.

WARRANT

The effectiveness of the policy is more
important than its constitutionality.

BACKING

The first imperative of government is to
ensure the safety of its citizens.

RESERVATION

The fact that a policy is not executed
fairly does not make the policy
itself unconstitutional.

Qualifier

A claim is often modified by one or more **qualifiers**, which limit the claim. The qualifier may be a term like *probably*, *most likely*, *in most cases*, or *usually*. In this case, the claim itself contains no qualifiers. Eastland states unequivocally that the ruling needs to undergo appellate review. His hope is that during that review, the policy will be declared constitutional, as it has been previously.

ARGUMENT ESSENTIALS

Analyzing Warrants

- Once you locate the claim in a piece of writing, look for information that **supports** that claim.
- The assumption that a reader has to accept in order to accept the link between claim and support is the **warrant**.
- Any information that supports the warrant is **backing**.
- **Reservations** are limits or modifications of the warrant; that is, conditions under which the warrant would not be relevant.
- **Qualifiers** are words or phrases that limit the claim.

RESEARCH SKILL Finding and Narrowing a Research Topic

When you have a research assignment, you might start with a topic idea that is too broad for the length of the paper you have been assigned. That does not mean that you have to abandon the idea completely. Instead, you can narrow the topic to one that is more manageable, given the length of the paper you will be writing.

1. Try using some of these approaches to identify a part of your broad topic that might be appropriate:

	Instead of	Try
Narrow according to **time**:	The U.S. space program	The U.S. space program in the twenty-first century
Narrow according to **place**:	Same-sex marriage	Same-sex marriage in California
Narrow to one **aspect**:	Abortion	Late-term abortion
Narrow to one **part**:	Obamacare	Insurance for businesses with fewer than fifty employees
Narrow to one **group**:	Immigration reform	Immigration reform and college students
Narrow to a single **problem**:	Standardized testing	Cultural bias in standardized testing

2. You may get some additional ideas by applying to your broad topic the traditional reporter's questions: *who, what, where, when,* and *why.*

3. You may get still different information if you look at your broad subject in terms of *relationships*: How do parts *compare* and *contrast*? What can you discover about *causes* and *effects*? How is the *definition* of your key term different from that of similar terms?

Once you narrow your topic, you can start working toward a thesis. As you do, you will want to consider your purpose and your audience. Part of analyzing your audience should involve trying to understand what their view of the subject is and what warrants underlie their beliefs about it.

READING ARGUMENT

Analyzing Warrants

The following essay has been annotated to highlight claims, supports, and warrants.

The Case for Torture

MICHAEL LEVIN

Introduction: statement of opposing view

It is generally assumed that torture is impermissible, a throwback to a more brutal age. Enlightened societies reject it outright, and regimes suspected of using it risk the wrath of the United States.

Claim of policy: rebuttal of opposing view

I believe this attitude is unwise. There are situations in which torture is not merely permissible but morally mandatory. Moreover, these situations are moving from the realm of imagination to fact.

Support: hypothetical example to test the reader's belief

Suppose a terrorist has hidden an atomic bomb on Manhattan Island which will detonate at noon on July 4 unless . . . (here follow the usual demands for money and release of his friends from jail). Suppose, further, that he is caught at 10 A.M. of the fateful day, but — preferring death to failure — won't disclose where the bomb is. What do we do? If we follow due process — wait for his lawyer, arraign him — millions of people will die. If the only way to save those lives is to subject the terrorist to the most excruciating possible pain, what grounds can there be for not doing so? I suggest there are none. In any case, I ask you to face the question with an open mind.

These questions are warrants that he rejects. His responses are warrants he can accept.

Torturing the terrorist is unconstitutional? Probably. But millions of lives surely outweigh constitutionality. Torture is barbaric? Mass murder is far more barbaric. Indeed, letting millions of innocents die in deference to one who flaunts his guilt is moral cowardice, an unwillingness to dirty one's hands. If *you* caught the terrorist, could you sleep nights knowing that millions died because you couldn't bring yourself to apply the electrodes?

The warrants on which the essay is based

Once you concede that torture is justified in extreme cases, you have admitted that the decision to use torture is a matter of balancing innocent lives against the means needed to save them. You must now face more realistic cases involving more modest numbers. Someone plants a bomb on a jumbo jet. He alone can disarm it, and his demands cannot be met (or if they can, we

Support: hypothetical example

5

Michael Levin is a professor of philosophy at the City University of New York. This essay is reprinted from the June 7, 1982, issue of *Newsweek*.

refuse to set a precedent by yielding to his threats). Surely we can, we must, do anything to the extortionist to save the passengers. How can we tell three hundred, or one hundred, or ten people who never asked to be put in danger, "I'm sorry, you'll have to die in agony, we just couldn't bring ourselves to . . ."

Here are the results of an informal poll about a third, hypothetical, case. Suppose a terrorist group kidnapped a newborn baby from a hospital. I asked four mothers if they would approve of torturing kidnappers if that were necessary to get their own newborns back. All said yes, the most "liberal" adding that she would administer it herself.

Support: informal poll

I am not advocating torture as punishment. Punishment is addressed to deeds irrevocably past. Rather, I am advocating torture as an acceptable measure for preventing future evils. So understood, it is far less objectionable than many extant punishments. Opponents of the death penalty, for example, are forever insisting that executing a murderer will not bring back his victim (as if the purpose of capital punishment were supposed to be resurrection, not deterrence or retribution). But torture, in the cases described, is intended not to bring anyone back but to keep innocents from being dispatched. The most powerful argument against using torture as a punishment or to secure confessions is that such practices disregard the rights of the individual. Well, if the individual is all that important—and he is—it is correspondingly important to protect the rights of individuals threatened by terrorists. If life is so valuable that it must never be taken, the lives of the innocents must be saved even at the price of hurting the one who endangers them.

Defense of the claim: a) Not punishment but protection of the innocent

The warrant for this particular line of defense

Better precedents for torture are assassination and preemptive attack. No Allied leader would have flinched at assassinating Hitler, had that been possible. (The Allies did assassinate Heydrich.) Americans would be angered to learn that Roosevelt could have had Hitler killed in 1943—thereby shortening the war and saving millions of lives—but refused on moral grounds. Similarly, if nation A learns that nation B is about to launch an unprovoked attack, A has a right to save itself by destroying B's military capability first. In the same way, if the police can by torture save those who would otherwise die at the hands of kidnappers or terrorists, they must.

b) Precedents for torture

Basically, the same warrant, reworded

There is an important difference between terrorists and their victims that should mute talk of the terrorists' "rights." The terrorist's victims are at risk unintentionally, not having asked to be endangered. But the terrorist knowingly initiated his actions. Unlike his victims, he volunteered for the risks of his deed. By threatening to kill for profit or idealism, he renounces civilized standards, and he can have no complaint if civilization tries to thwart him by whatever means necessary.

c) Denial that terrorists have rights

Warrants

Just as <u>torture is justified only to save lives</u> (not extort confessions or re-   10
cantations), it <u>is justifiably administered only to those *known* to hold innocent
lives in their hands.</u> Ah, but how can the authorities ever be sure they have the
right malefactor? Isn't there a danger of error and abuse? Won't we turn into
Them?

d) Easy identification of terrorists

Questions like these are disingenuous in a world in which terrorists
proclaim themselves and perform for television. The name of their game is
public recognition. After all, you can't very well intimidate a government into
releasing your freedom fighters unless you announce that it is your group that
has seized its embassy. "Clear guilt" is difficult to define, but when 40 million people see a group of masked gunmen seize an airplane on the evening
news, there is not much question about who the perpetrators are. There will be
hard cases where the situation is murkier. Nonetheless, a line demarcating the
legitimate use of torture can be drawn. Torture only the obviously guilty, and
only for the sake of saving innocents, and the line between Us and Them will
remain clear.

Conclusion warrant:
"Paralysis in the face of evil is the greater danger."

There is little danger that the Western democracies will lose their way if
they choose to inflict pain as one way of preserving order. <u>Paralysis in the face
of evil is the greater danger.</u> Some day soon a terrorist will threaten tens of
thousands of lives, and torture will be the only way to save them. We had better start thinking about this.

Practice: Recognizing and Analyzing Warrants

Read the following argument by Robert A. Sirico. Then summarize the argument in a paragraph. Next, explain what the claim is, what types of support are
used, and what the warrant is. Is the warrant one that you agree with? Explain.

An Unjust Sacrifice
ROBERT A. SIRICO

An appeals court in London has made a Solo-
monic ruling, deciding that eight-week-old
twins joined at the pelvis must be separated. In
effect, one twin, known as Mary, is to be sac-
rificed to save the other, known as Jodie, in an
operation the babies' parents oppose.

The judges invoked a utilitarian rationale,
justified on the basis of medical testimony.
The specialists agreed that there is an 80 to 90
percent chance that the strong and alert Jodie
could not survive more than a few months if she
continued to support the weak heart and lungs
of Mary, whose brain is underdeveloped.

Robert A. Sirico, a Roman Catholic priest, is president of
the Acton Institute for the Study of Religion and Liberty in
Grand Rapids, Michigan. This article appeared in the September 28, 2000, *New York Times*.

This is a heartbreaking case, and the decision of the court was not arrived at lightly. But even the best of intentions, on the part of the state or the parents, is no substitute for sound moral reasoning. Utilitarian considerations like Mary's quality of life are not the issue. Nor should doctors' expert testimony, which is subject to error, be considered decisive.

Here, as in the case of abortion, one simple principle applies: There is no justification for deliberately destroying innocent life. In this case, the court has turned its back on a tenet that the West has stood by: Life, no matter how limited, should be protected.

5   While this case is so far unique, there are guidelines that must be followed. No human being, for instance, can be coerced into donating an organ — even if the individual donating the organ is unlikely to be harmed and the individual receiving the organ could be saved. In principle, no person should ever be forced to volunteer his own body to save another's life, even if that individual is a newborn baby.

To understand the gravity of the court's error, consider the parents' point of view. They are from Gozo, an island in Malta. After being told of their daughters' condition, while the twins were in utero, they went to Manchester, England, seeking out the best possible medical care. Yet, after the birth on August 8, the parents were told that they needed to separate the twins, which would be fatal for Mary.

They protested, telling the court: "We cannot begin to accept or contemplate that one of our children should die to enable the other one to survive. That is not God's will. Everyone has a right to life, so why should we kill one of our daughters to enable the other one to survive?"

And yet, a court in a country in which they sought refuge has overruled their wishes. This is a clear evil: coercion against the parents and coercion against their child, justified in the name of a speculative medical calculus.

The parents' phrase "God's will" is easily caricatured, as if they believed divine revelation were guiding them to ignore science. In fact, they believe in the merit of science, or they would not have gone to Britain for help in the first place.

But utilitarian rationality has overtaken   10
their case. The lawyer appointed by the court to represent Jodie insisted that Mary's was "a futile life." That is a dangerous statement — sending us down a slippery slope where lives can be measured for their supposed value and discarded if deemed not useful enough.

Some might argue that in thinking about the twins, we should apply the philosophical principle known as "double effect," which, in some circumstances, permits the loss of a life when it is an unintended consequence of saving another. But in this case, ending Mary's life would be a deliberate decision, not an unintended effect.

Can we ever take one life in favor of another? No, not even in this case, however fateful the consequences.

Practice: Recognizing and Analyzing Warrants

This photograph was taken during Occupy Wall Street, on November 20, 2011. Study the photo, and then answer the questions that follow it.

Endangered Species
REBECCA DAVIS

HRC WENN Photos/Newscom

Reading and Discussion Questions

1. What point is the person holding the sign trying to make?
2. What warrant underlies the statement on the sign?
3. Write the claim, support, and warrant that constitute the argument being made.

 For more visual analysis of warrants, go to **macmillanhighered** **.com/rottenberg**.

Assignments for Warrants: Examining Assumptions

Reading and Discussion Questions

1. Should students be given a direct voice in the hiring of faculty members? On what warrants about education do you base your answer?

2. Discuss the validity of the warrant in this statement from the *Watch Tower* (a publication of the Jehovah's Witnesses) about genital herpes: "The sexually loose are indeed 'receiving in themselves the full recompense, which was their due for their error' (Romans 1:27)."

3. In 2010, a judge in Saudi Arabia had to make the decision whether or not a man could be intentionally paralyzed as punishment for having paralyzed another man in a fight. His victim had requested this punishment. What would the judge's warrant be if he chose to order the punishment? What would it be if he decided not to honor the victim's request?

4. In view of the increasing interest in health in general, and nutrition and exercise in particular, do you think that universities and colleges should impose physical education requirements? If so, what form should they take? If not, why not? What warrant underlies your position?

5. What are some of the assumptions underlying the preference for natural foods and medicines? Can *natural* be clearly defined? Is this preference part of a broader philosophy? Try to evaluate the validity of the assumption.

6. The author of the following passage, Katherine Butler Hathaway, became a hunchback as a result of a childhood illness. Here she writes about the relationship between love and beauty from the point of view of someone who is deformed. Discuss the warrants on which the author bases her conclusions.

   > I could secretly pretend that I had a lover ... but I could never risk showing that I thought such a thing was possible for me ... with any man. Because of my repeated encounters with the mirror and my irrepressible tendency to forget what I had seen, I had begun to force myself to believe and to remember, and especially to remember, that I would never be chosen for what I imagined to be the supreme and most intimate of all experience. I thought of sexual love as an honor that was too great and too beautiful for the body in which I was doomed to live.

Writing Suggestions

1. Diagram three of the decisions you made about survivors of the imaginary catastrophe in the opening assignment. Show claim, support, and warrant, and if you can identify any, also show backing, reservations, or qualifiers.

2. In "An Unjust Sacrifice," Robert A. Sirico presents a case in which he finds no justification for letting one twin die in order to save the other. His belief

in the sanctity of human life appears to be absolute, even when it will most likely lead to the death of both twins. Write an essay in which you give examples of how your value system underlies your political views.

3. Both state and federal governments have been embroiled in controversies concerning the rights of citizens to engage in harmful practices. In Massachusetts, for example, a mandatory seat-belt law was repealed by voters who considered the law an infringement of their freedom. (It was later reinstated.) Write an essay in which you explain what principles you believe should guide government regulation of dangerous practices.

4. Henry David Thoreau writes, "Unjust laws exist: Shall we be content to obey them, or shall we endeavor to amend them, and obey them until we have succeeded, or shall we transgress them at once?" Write an essay in which you explain under what circumstances you would feel compelled to break the law, or why you feel that you would never do so.

RESEARCH ASSIGNMENT ▷ **Narrowing a Research Topic**

1. Think of three different ways to narrow each of the following broad topics:
   - The effects of stress
   - Eating disorders
   - Presidential elections
   - Genetic engineering
   - Athletes and drugs
   - College admissions tests
   - Suicide in the military
   - Social networking

2. For each broad topic, select one of the narrower topics you came up with. For that narrower topic, identify some widely held assumptions. Then explain what underlying warrants that are not so widely held might make it difficult to reach agreement.

bits To see what you are learning about argumentation applied to the latest world and national news, read our *Bits* blog, "Argument and the Headlines," at **blogs.bedfordstmartins.com/bits**.

Using the
ELEMENTS

Definition: Clarifying Key Terms

The Purposes of Definition

Before we examine the other elements of argument, we need to consider definition, a component you may have to deal with early in writing an essay.

Arguments often revolve around definitions of crucial terms. Consider the following examples. In the gun control debate, there is disagreement over what an assault weapon is. In the debate over euthanasia, it makes a difference whether the issue is passive or active euthanasia. When planning the prosecution of an alleged criminal, whether the accused is defined as an enemy combatant or not determines how he will be tried. In the publicity surrounding the death of Trayvon Martin, it made a difference whether George Zimmerman was viewed as a neighborhood watch leader or as a vigilante. Likewise, it made a difference whether the attack on the U.S. consulate in Benghazi in 2012 was seen as a protest gone wrong or a terrorist attack.

A corrupt use of definition can be used to distort reality. But even where there is no intention to deceive, the snares of definition are difficult to avoid. How do you define *abortion*? Is it "termination of pregnancy"? Or is it "murder of an unborn child"? During a celebrated trial of a physician who performed an abortion and was accused of manslaughter, the prosecution often used the word *baby* to refer to the fetus, but the defense referred to "the products of conception." These definitions of *fetus* reflected the differing judgments of those on opposite sides. Not only do judgments create definitions, but definitions also influence judgments.

Definitions can indeed change the nature of an event or a "fact." How many farms are there in the United States? The answer to the question depends on the definition of *farm*. For example, read the following excerpt:

> Because of a change in the official definition of the word *farm*, New York lost 20 percent of its farms on January 1, with numbers dropping from 56,000 to 45,000....
>
> The U.S. Department of Agriculture (USDA) defines *farm* broadly as any operation with the potential to produce at least $1,000 worth of agricultural goods in a given year. Based on 2006 prices, an operation

could be considered a farm for growing 4 acres of corn, a tenth of an acre of berries, or for owning one milk cow. Consequently, most U.S. establishments classified as a farm produce very little, while most agricultural production occurs on a small number of much larger operations. . . .

USDA's farm definition has remained unchanged since 1975. However, the increasing concentration of agricultural production on large farms and the proliferation of small "rural residence" farms with little or no production have led to proposals to narrow the definition of a farm to more closely target "actively engaged" farmers.

Any change in the farm definition could have far-reaching consequences since the characteristics of farms vary from place to place. For example, changing the annual farm sales threshold to $10,000 would result in a redistribution of the share of farms located in each state. Under this scenario, almost two-thirds of all states would experience changes in their share of farms of less than 0.5 percent (in either direction).[1]

A change in the definition of *poverty* can have similar results. An article in the *New York Times,* under the headline "A Revised Definition of Poverty May Raise Number of U.S. Poor," makes this clear:

> The official definition of *poverty* used by the Federal Government for three decades is based simply on cash income before taxes. But in a report to be issued on Wednesday, a panel of experts convened by the [National] Academy of Sciences three years ago at the behest of Congress says the Government should move toward a concept of poverty based on disposable income, the amount left after a family pays taxes and essential expenses.[2]

The differences are wholly a matter of definition. But such differences can have serious consequences for those being defined, most of all in the disposition of billions of federal dollars in aid of various kinds.

In fact, local and federal courts almost every day redefine traditional concepts that can have a direct impact on our lives. The definition of *family*, for example, has undergone significant changes that acknowledge the existence of new relationships. In January 1990, the New Jersey Supreme Court ruled that a family may be defined as "one or more persons occupying a dwelling unit as a single nonprofit housekeeping unit, who are living together as a stable and permanent living unit, being a traditional family unit or the *functional equivalent* thereof" (italics for emphasis added). This meant that ten Glassboro State College students, unrelated by blood, could continue to occupy a single-family

---

[1] Erik O'Donoghue, "Changing the Definition of a 'Farm' Can Affect Federal Funding," *Amber Waves,* Dec. 2009, p. 7.

[2] *New York Times*, April 10, 1995, sec. A, p. 1.

house despite the objection of the borough of Glassboro.[3] Even the legal definition of *maternity* has shifted. Who is the mother — the woman who contributes the egg or the woman (the surrogate) who bears the child? Several states, acknowledging the changes brought by medical technology, now recognize a difference between the birth mother and the legal mother.

ARGUMENT ESSENTIALS Purposes of Definition

- Controversy often revolves around definitions of crucial terms.
- Effective communication between writer and reader is not possible if they do not have in mind the same definition of a key term.
- Negotiating a definition that all parties can agree on is the starting point to resolving conflict.

READING ARGUMENT

Seeing Definition

The following essay illustrates how definition can aid argumentation.

GOP Fear of Common Core Education Standards Unfounded

MICHAEL GERSON

Modern conservatism comes in two distinct architectural styles. The first seeks to build from scratch, using accurate ideological levels and plumb lines, so every wall is straight and every corner squared. The goal of politics is to apply abstract principles in their purest form. But there is another type of conservatism, often practiced at the state level, which attempts to build out of flawed, existing materials, resulting in some odd angles and incongruous additions. These conservative reformers assemble unexpected alliances, accept reasonable compromises, and welcome incremental progress.

Gerson uses analogy to explain two types of conservatism.

This contrast is increasingly evident in the debate over the Common Core State Standards. To ideological conservatives, it is the "Obamacore"; an "unprecedented federal intervention into education"; a "threat to the American tradition of individual liberty and limited government." According to a recent

How the first of the two types defines the Common Core

Michael Gerson is an op-ed columnist for the *Washington Post* and a former top speechwriter for George W. Bush. This opinion piece was published on May 20, 2013.

---

[3] *New York Times*, February 1, 1990, sec. B, p. 5.

How the RNC defines it, in a
derogatory manner
resolution passed by the Republican National Committee, the Common Core
is "a nationwide straightjacket on academic freedom and achievement."

The actual definition
This is mostly a projection of baseless political fears. The Common Core
standards are actually an attempt by governors — including many conservative, Republican governors — to set some coherent standards on what children
should know about math and English by various grade levels. It emphasizes
analytic reasoning and the interpretation of "informational texts," including
historical documents such as the Constitution and the Gettysburg Address.

More details about the
Common Core
The Common Core standards "are rigorous, they are traditional," says
Michael Petrilli of the Fordham Institute; "one might even say they are 'conservative.' They expect students to know their math facts, to read the nation's
founding documents, and to evaluate evidence and come to independent
judgments. In all of these ways, they are miles better than three-quarters of
the state standards they replaced — standards that hardly deserved the name
and that often pushed the left-wing drivel that Common Core haters say they
abhor."

It's not perfect and not
enough, but it's better than
what we have.
The Common Core is neither perfect nor sufficient. The math standards,   5
according to some analysts, are set one or two years behind international
levels. But it says something about the American educational system that, by
global standards, mediocrity would be a distinct improvement. And higher
standards, of course, don't guarantee better student achievement, which depends on effective curricula, quality teaching, useful assessment, and rigorous
accountability.

Higher standards are only potentially helpful. But low standards are uniformly destructive. And the Common Core generally raises standards. The approach was crafted by states. It is voluntary. It provides some common metrics
to compare the performance of schools and districts across the country. And
if this is a conspiracy against limited government, it has somehow managed
to recruit former governors Mitch Daniels and Jeb Bush, current governors
Bobby Jindal and Chris Christie, and the U.S. Chamber of Commerce. A plot
this vast is either diabolical or imaginary.

Clarifies part of the definition
The conservative reformers who helped shape the Common Core are
trying to make incremental improvements in a deeply flawed system. Many
of their conservative opponents are applying a single, abstract principle — an
ideological commitment to localism in education. They distrust the federal
government, which is understandable in the Obama era. But the Common
Core is not a federal approach. It is a national approach created by institutions
outside the federal government.

The alternative to this reform is not an ideal ideological world in which state and local control has resulted in excellence. The main problem of American primary and secondary education is one that conservatives should understand: It is a market with insufficient information and choices, resulting in poor quality. We don't have standards and measurements that allow us to adequately compare the outcomes between students, between schools, and between states. So, many states can hide behind dumbed-down standards. Many school districts can betray minority children for generations without scrutiny or consequence. And the whole system can get away with leaving millions of American students unprepared for global competition.

The alternative is not ideal.

Conservatives should stand for political principle. They should also reject the temptation to elevate one principle above all others, regardless of conditions and circumstances. Localism is not the answer to all our educational problems. And resistance to standards puts ideological conservatives in some questionable company. In fighting the Common Core, some tea party activists have made common cause with elements of the progressive education blob that always resist rigor, measurement, and accountability. This alliance increasingly constitutes the mediocrity caucus in American politics.

Claim

10   Localism is an important conservative principle, but so is excellence. And the measure of a successful education policy is the demonstrated presence of actual education.

Practice: Definition

Consider what Charles's purpose is in using definition. Read the essay, and answer the questions that follow it.

Stop Calling Quake Victims Looters
GUY-URIEL CHARLES

To define someone as a looter is not simply to describe him, or her, through an act, it is to make a moral judgment. It is to characterize the person as lawless and criminal. It connotes someone who is without self-restraint; an animal; wanton and depraved.

It is a description that is void of empathy for someone who is consciously or subconsciously viewed as "the other." Tragically, it fits into the stereotype that many have about people of African descent, be they African Americans or Haitian Americans.

The news media have to stop describing starving Haitians who are simply trying to survive the earthquake and aftershocks that took their

Guy-Uriel Charles is a law professor at Duke Law School and founder of Duke's Center on Law, Race, and Politics. He is Haitian American. The article appeared on cnn.com on January 21, 2010.

homes, their loved ones, and all their possessions by this highly derogatory term.

It's a lesson they should have learned covering the devastation wrought by Hurricane Katrina. I remember the news accounts then that described black residents of New Orleans as "looters," but used benign words to describe white residents engaged in the same action: "taking things."

5 Academics have found repeated instances of this in media content analyses after disasters. One example, widely disseminated on the Web post-Katrina, juxtaposed an Associated Press photo that showed a young black man wading through chest-high water "after looting a grocery store" (said the caption), with an AFP/Getty photo of a white woman in the same position, although the caption this time described her "finding" food "from a local grocery store."

It is time to put this practice to rest.

Put yourself in the position of the average Haitian in Port-au-Prince. One minute you were going about your business, the next minute the earth shook and literally your world crumbled all around you. But you were one of the lucky ones, you survived the earthquake. Injured? Yes. But alive.

Your first thought is to cry out for your family, especially your kids. But most of your family is buried under a rubble pile somewhere. You had four children but only one survived the earthquake. You have spent the last few days, along with your fellow survivors, digging through the rubble trying to find them.

It is now a week after the earthquake, and you have eaten little or nothing. You are hungry and thirsty, and while you hear rumors of aid coming, you have not seen any evidence of it.

You have not heard from the president and 10 indeed you've heard rumors that his wife is dead. Perhaps he left the country; you would too, if you could. There is no police presence at all. No governmental authority to provide support. There are no markets.

This photo was taken on January 18, 2010, in Port-au-Prince, Haiti, in the aftermath of a devastating earthquake. Gallo Images/Alamy

The only money you have are the few gourdes (Haitian dollars) that you have in your pockets. The rest of your money is in the safe place you always kept it — but it is now buried with your food. The banks are not open. There is no one to borrow from; they are all in the same boat as you. There are no functioning institutions.

You have family in the United States and they are desperately trying to get you some help. They have contacted all of the big aid agencies, but those agencies have issues of their own. Some have lost staff members. They are doing the best they can, but they have no idea that you exist and you have no way of finding them. The roads are impassable, and they can't get clearance from whoever is in charge of the airport to land their planes, which bring much needed supplies.

They're afraid to go anywhere without security because they've heard that the people are becoming restless. Indeed, though you do not know this, the U.S. military is also worried that citizens will get violent and start stealing. The United Nations is waiting for more troops, and the doctors have stopped treating patients because of those same fears: violence, looting.

Under normal circumstances you would not think of taking food without paying for it. You are what other Haitians would call "bien eleve" not "mal eleve." By that they mean you were well-raised, with manners and dignity.

15 Haitians put a strong premium on dignity. To take something for which you have not paid does not only offend your sense of legality but also your sense of personhood. It is undignified. But not only are you starving, so is your only surviving child. You would prefer to pay, but whom? What would you pay with? You'd prefer to wait, but for whom? How long can you afford to wait?

You feel that your desperate state is evidence that you have been abandoned by your family, your country, the international community, and Bondié (God). (The Creole word for God literally means "good God.")

So you take. You take just enough for a couple of days and a couple of family members. You take and you run to feed those for whom the only measure of fortune is survival in Haiti, post-earthquake. You take and you run.

Are you a looter? Try as we might to prevent it, the answer to that question is inevitably racialized. We cannot separate the word looting from its racial implications or the supposed crime of looting from its racial origins. In the throes of the civil rights movement in the United States, many states made looting a crime. Almost all of these states were southern states that had a history of criminalizing behavior that they associated more with African Americans than with whites.

Even so, the criminal law, for all of its shortcomings, is often more sophisticated than we are. It recognizes that context matters. It has been developed with concepts — such as necessity and justification — to identify the circumstances under which a person who would normally be held culpable can be held either less culpable or not at all culpable. Taking food is different than taking a television.

It is past time for our news media to develop similar sophistication. It is time to stop characterizing black people trying to survive in dire circumstances as looters. Are they takers? Yes. Are they looters? Let's wait for a criminal conviction first.

Reading and Discussion Questions

1. What is Charles's claim in the article?

2. How is what happened in Haiti after the earthquake similar to what happened in New Orleans after Hurricane Katrina? (See also pp. 63–67.)

3. What support does Charles offer for his contention that the answer to the question of whether or not a person is considered a looter "is inevitably racialized" (para. 18)?

4. Why is *looter* not an appropriate term to use to describe those in Haiti who took food and other goods without paying?

5. What does Charles mean when he says that criminal law "is often more sophisticated than we are" (para. 19)?

Defining the Terms in Your Argument

In some of your arguments, you will introduce terms that require definition. We've pointed out that a definition of *poverty* is crucial to any debate on the existence of poverty in the United States. The same may be true in a debate about the legality of euthanasia, or mercy killing. Are the arguers referring to passive euthanasia (the withdrawal of life-support systems) or to active euthanasia (the direct administration of drugs to hasten death)? It is not uncommon, in fact, for arguments about controversial questions to turn into arguments about the definition of terms.

An argument can end almost before it begins if writer and reader cannot agree on definitions of key terms. While clear definitions do not guarantee agreement, they do ensure that all parties understand the nature of the argument. In the Rogerian approach to argumentation, negotiating a definition that all parties can accept is the starting point to resolving conflict.

The Limitations of Dictionary Definitions

Reading a dictionary definition is the simplest and most obvious way to learn the basic definition of a term. An unabridged dictionary is the best source because it usually gives examples of the way a word can be used in a sentence; that is, it furnishes the proper context.

In many cases, the dictionary definition alone is not sufficient. It may be too broad or too narrow for your purpose. Suppose, in an argument about pornography, you want to define the word *obscene*. *Webster's New International Dictionary* (3rd edition, unabridged) gives the definition of *obscene* as "offensive to taste; foul; loathsome; disgusting." But these synonyms do not tell you what qualities make an object or an event or an action "foul," "loathsome," and "disgusting." In 1973 the Supreme Court, attempting to narrow the definition of *obscenity*, ruled that obscenity was to be determined by the community in accordance with local standards. One person's obscenity, as numerous cases have demonstrated, may be another person's art. The celebrated trials in the early twentieth century about the distribution of novels regarded as pornographic — D. H. Lawrence's *Lady Chatterley's Lover* and James Joyce's *Ulysses* — emphasized the problems of defining obscenity.

Another dictionary definition may strike you as too narrow. *Patriotism*, for example, is defined in one dictionary as "love and loyal or zealous support of one's country, especially in all matters involving other countries." Some readers may want to include an unwillingness to support government policies they consider wrong.

These limitations illustrate why opening an essay with a dictionary definition is often not a very effective strategy, although many beginning writers use it. In order to initiate the effective discussion of a key term, you should be able to define it in your own words.

Stipulation and Negation: Stating What a Term *Is* and *Is Not*

Since definitions can vary so much and well-meaning writers want their readers to understand their arguments, it is often necessary to establish from the beginning what definition a writer is using for the purposes of a particular argument. That means writers may **stipulate** the definition that they are using, knowing that other people in other contexts may define the term differently. In some cases, one way to clarify how a term is being used is to stipulate what it is not. This is called **negation**.

In stipulating the meaning of a term, the writer asks the reader to accept a definition that may be different from the conventional one. The writer does this to limit or control the argument. A term like *national security* can be defined by a nation's leaders in such a way as to sanction persecution of citizens and reckless military actions. Likewise, a term such as *liberation* can be appropriated by terrorist groups whose activities often lead to oppression rather than liberation.

Even the word *violence*, which the dictionary defines as "physical force used so as to injure or damage" and whose meaning seems utterly clear and uncompromising, can be manipulated to produce a definition different from the one that most people normally understand. Some pacifists refer to conditions in which "people are deprived of choices in a systematic way" as "institutionalized quiet violence." Even where no physical force is employed, this lack of choice in schools, in the workplace, in black neighborhoods is defined as violence.[4]

A writer and an audience cannot agree on a solution to a problem if they cannot even agree on what they are talking about. Carl Rogers's advice applies here: Listen to how your audience defines a key term. Make clear how you

---

[4] Newton Garver, "What Violence Is," in James Rachels, ed., *Moral Choices* (New York: Harper & Row, 1971), pp. 248–49.

define it. Then work from there toward a definition that you can stipulate as the agreed-upon definition that you will use as you move toward resolution.

In *Through the Looking-Glass*, Alice asked Humpty Dumpty "whether you can make words mean so many different things."

> "When *I* use a word," Humpty Dumpty said scornfully, "it means just what I choose it to mean — neither more nor less."[5]

A writer, however, is not free to invent definitions that no one will recognize or that create rather than solve problems between writer and reader.

To avoid confusion, it is sometimes helpful to tell the reader what a term is *not*. In discussing euthanasia, a writer might say, "By euthanasia I do not mean active intervention to hasten the death of the patient." Another example: "Patients are diagnosed with PDD-NOS (Pervasive Developmental Disorder-Not Otherwise Specified) if they have some behaviors seen in autism but do not meet the full criteria for having an autistic disorder." A negative definition may be more extensive, depending on the complexity of the term and the writer's ingenuity.

Defining Vague and Ambiguous Terms

You will need to define other terms in addition to those in your claim. If you use words and phrases that have two or more meanings, they may appear vague and ambiguous to your reader. In arguments of value and policy, abstract terms such as *freedom of speech, justice,* and *equality* require clarification. Despite their abstract nature, however, they are among the most important in the language because they represent the ideals that shape our laws. When conflicts arise, the courts must define these terms to establish the legality of certain practices. Is the Ku Klux Klan permitted to make disparaging public statements about ethnic and racial groups? That depends on the court's definition of *free speech*. Can execution for some crimes be considered cruel and unusual punishment? That, too, depends on the court's definition of *cruel and unusual punishment*.

Consider the definition of *race*, around which so much of U.S. history has revolved, often with tragic consequences. Until recently, the only categories listed in the census were white, black, Asian-Pacific, and Native American, "with the Hispanic population straddling them all." But rapidly increasing intermarriage and ethnic identity caused a number of political and ethnic groups to demand changes in the classifications of the Census Bureau. Some Arab Americans, for example, prefer to be counted as "Middle Eastern" rather than white. Children of black-white unions are defined as black 60 percent of the time, while children of Asian-white unions are described as Asian 42 percent of the time. Research has been conducted to discover how people feel about the terms that are used to define them. As one anthropologist pointed

[5] Lewis Carroll, *Alice in Wonderland and Through the Looking-Glass* (New York: Grosset & Dunlap, 1948), p. 238.

out, "Socially and politically assigned attributes have a lot to do with access to economic resources."[6]

"Socially and politically assigned attributes" can also be the basis for judging others. The definition of *success*, for example, varies among social groups as well as among individuals within the group. So difficult is the formulation of a universally accepted measure for success that some scholars regard the concept as meaningless. Nevertheless, we continue to use the word as if it represents a definable concept because the idea of success, however defined, is important for the identity and development of the individual and the group. It is clear, however, that when crossing subcultural boundaries, even within a small group, we need to be aware of differences in the use of the word. If contentment — that is, the satisfaction of achieving a small personal goal — is enough, then a person making a minimal salary but doing work that he or she loves may be a success. But you should not expect all your readers to agree that these criteria are enough to define *success*.

Abstract terms can be one source of vagueness in writing. Concrete examples usually help to define an abstraction. Abstract and concrete terms are treated more fully in the Language chapter on pages 282–83.

RESEARCH SKILL ▶ Using Encyclopedias

When there is disagreement about the definition of a term, you may need more than a dictionary definition to clarify the points on which the disagreement occurs. Often an encyclopedia can give a much fuller discussion of the complexities of defining terms that defy simple, clear-cut definitions. The more specialized the encyclopedia, the more useful the information — unless it uses so much jargon that it is useful only to specialists.

For example, *abortion* is defined in the *Encyclopedia Britannica Online* like this:

> **Abortion** — the expulsion of a fetus from the uterus before it has reached the stage of viability (in human beings, usually about the 20th week of gestation). An abortion may occur spontaneously, in which case it is also called a miscarriage, or it may be brought on purposefully, in which case it is often called an induced abortion.

A specialized encyclopedia may provide more detailed information by discussing different positions in the debate for or against abortion. What follows is only a portion of an article from the *Encyclopedia of Philosophy*, which also includes a list of works cited that leads to other possible sources:

> The claims to which partisans on both sides of the "abortion" issue appeal seem, if one is not thinking of the abortion issue, close to self-evident, or they appear to be easily defensible. The case against abortion (Beckwith 1993) rests on the proposition that there is a very strong presumption that ending another human life is seriously wrong. Almost everyone who is not thinking about the abortion issue would agree. There are good arguments for the view that fetuses are both living and human. ("Fetus" is generally used in the philosophical literature

continued

---

[6] *Wall Street Journal*, September 9, 1995, sec. B, p. 1.

on abortion to refer to a human organism from the time of conception to the time of birth.) Thus, it is easy for those opposed to abortion to think that only the morally depraved or the seriously confused could disagree with them. Standard pro-choice views appeal either to the proposition that women have the right to make decisions concerning their own bodies or to the proposition that fetuses are not yet persons. Both of these propositions seem either to be platitudes or to be straightforwardly defensible. Thus, it is easy for pro-choicers to believe that only religious fanatics or dogmatic conservatives could disagree. This explains, at least in part, why the abortion issue has created so much controversy. The philosophical debate regarding abortion has been concerned largely with subjecting these apparently obvious claims to the analytical scrutiny philosophers ought to give to them.

Consider first the standard argument against abortion. One frequent objection to the claim that fetuses are both human and alive is that we do not know when life begins. The reply to this objection is. . . .

You may find that your library has a database — such as Gale Virtual Reference Library — that lets you search a number of different encyclopedias at the same time. Just the first six entries from the list generated by that database lead to a range of encyclopedias you can investigate:

1. Abortion: I. Medical Perspectives. Allan Rosenfield, Sara Iden, and Anne Drapkin Lyerly. *Encyclopedia of Bioethics*. Ed. Stephen G. Post. Vol. 1. 3rd ed. New York: Macmillan Reference USA, 2004. p. 1–7.

2. Abortion. Menachem Elon. *Encyclopaedia Judaica*. Ed. Michael Berenbaum and Fred Skolnik. Vol. 1. 2nd ed. Detroit: Macmillan Reference USA, 2007. p. 270–273.

3. Abortion. Don Marquis. *Encyclopedia of Philosophy*. Ed. Donald M. Borchert. Vol. 1. 2nd ed. Detroit: Macmillan Reference USA, 2006. p. 8–10.

4. Abortion. *National Survey of State Laws*. Ed. Richard A. Leiter. 6th ed. Detroit: Gale, 2008. p. 339–371.

5. Abortion. *West's Encyclopedia of American Law*. Ed. Shirelle Phelps and Jeffrey Lehman. Vol. 1. 2nd ed. Detroit: Gale, 2005. p. 13–26.

6. Abortion. Mark R. Wicclair and Gabriella Gosman. *Encyclopedia of Science, Technology, and Ethics*. Ed. Carl Mitcham. Vol. 1. Detroit: Macmillan Reference USA, 2005. p. 1–6.

Note: Wikipedia is a convenient source that often appears as the first source listed in the results from an online search, but it should be used with caution, if at all, for serious research. The information it contains can be written by anyone, no matter what their credentials may be. However, it may serve as a good source of references and links to more reputable sources.

Definition by Example

One of the most effective ways of defining terms in an argument is to use examples. Both real and hypothetical examples can bring life to abstract and ambiguous terms. The writer in the following passage defines *cognate* in the first two sentences through negation and then by means of examples:

At some colleges and universities, a cognate is a personalized alternative to a minor. Where a minor is a cluster of courses from one department that a student takes in addition to a major as a secondary emphasis area, a cognate lets a student, with the approval of an advisor, choose a cluster of courses from different departments that serve as a secondary emphasis area to complement his or her minor. For example, a film studies major might take a course in the Foreign Languages department about how foreign cultures are represented through film, a course in the anthropology department focusing on anthropology in film, a course in the English department about film adaptation of novels, and a course in the psychology department on the representation of abnormal psychology in film. A student interested in the environment might major in biology and put together a cognate from courses in law, economics, geography, and history.

> **ARGUMENT ESSENTIALS**
> ## Defining the Terms in Your Argument
>
> - You and your reader must agree on definitions of key terms if your argument is to be effective.
> - In most cases, a dictionary definition is not sufficient.
> - Stipulate the definition of key terms that you are using because other people in other contexts may define the term differently.
> - In some cases, you may clarify a term by stipulating what it is not, or by negation.
> - Avoid vague and ambiguous terms, or take the time to explain which of two or more possible meanings is the one you intend.

Writing Extended Definitions

When we speak of an extended definition, we usually refer not only to length but also to the variety of methods for developing the definition. The argumentative essay can take the form of an extended definition. This type of definition essay is appropriate when the idea under consideration is so controversial or so heavy with historical connotations that even a paragraph or two cannot make clear exactly what the arguer wants his or her readers to understand. For example, if you were preparing a definition of *patriotism,* you would probably use a number of methods to develop your definition: personal narrative, examples, stipulation, comparison and contrast, and cause-and-effect analysis.

WRITER'S GUIDE
Writing a Definition Essay

The following are important steps to take when you write an essay of definition.

1. **Choose a term that needs definition** because it is controversial or ambiguous, or because you want to offer a personal definition that differs from the accepted interpretation. Explain why an extended definition is necessary. Or choose an experience that lends itself to treatment in an extended definition. One student defined *culture shock* as she had experienced it while studying abroad in Hawaii among students of a different ethnic background.

2. **Decide on the thesis** — the point of view you wish to develop about the term you are defining. If you want to define *heroism*, for example, you may choose to develop the idea that this quality depends on motivation and awareness of danger rather than on the specific act performed by the hero.

3. **Distinguish wherever possible between the term you are defining and other terms with which it might be confused.** If you are defining *love*, can you make a clear distinction between the different kinds of emotional attachments that the word conveys?

4. **Try to think of several methods of developing the definition** — using examples, comparison and contrast, analogy, cause-and-effect analysis. However, you may discover that one method alone — say, use of examples — will suffice to narrow and refine your definition.

5. **Arrange your supporting material** in an order that gives emphasis to the most important ideas.

READING ARGUMENT

Seeing an Extended Definition

In the United States, terrorism has received unprecedented attention since the tragic events of September 11, 2001. You may be surprised to learn that the essay that follows was written in May of that year, before planes crashing into the World Trade Center, the Pentagon, and a field in Pennsylvania gave the term new meaning for Americans forever. Just as the problem of terrorism has not yet been solved, the problem of defining terrorism remains unsolved as well. The essay has been annotated to highlight the use of definition.

The Definition of Terrorism
BRIAN WHITAKER

Decide for yourself whether to believe this, but according to a new report there were only 16 cases of international terrorism in the Middle East last year.

That is the lowest number for any region in the world apart from North America (where there were none at all). Europe had 30 cases — almost twice as many as the Middle East — and Latin America came top with 193.

This article was published May 7, 2001, in *Guardian Unlimited,* the daily online version of the British newspaper the *Guardian.* Whitaker is a former editor on Comment Is Free, the *Guardian's* Web expansion.

The figures come from the U.S. State Department's annual review of global terrorism, which has just been published on the Internet. Worldwide, the report says confidently, "there were 423 international terrorist attacks in 2000, an increase of 8% from the 392 attacks recorded during 1999."

Statistics on terrorism from before 9/11

No doubt a lot of painstaking effort went into counting them, but the statistics are fundamentally meaningless because, as the report points out, "no one definition of terrorism has gained universal acceptance."

Problems with attempts to define terrorism

5   That is an understatement. While most people agree that terrorism exists, few can agree on what it is. A recent book discussing attempts by the UN and other international bodies to define terrorism runs to three volumes and 1,866 pages without reaching any firm conclusion.

Using the definition preferred by the state department, terrorism is: "Pre-meditated, politically motivated violence perpetrated against noncombatant* targets by subnational groups or clandestine agents, usually intended to influence an audience." (The asterisk is important, as we shall see later.)

U.S. State Department's definition

"International" terrorism — the subject of the American report — is defined as "terrorism involving citizens or the territory of more than one country."

Definition of "international" terrorism

The key point about terrorism, on which almost everyone agrees, is that it's politically motivated. This is what distinguishes it from, say, murder or football hooliganism. But this also causes a problem for those who compile statistics because the motive is not always clear — especially if no one has claimed responsibility.

Main point of agreement is motivation.

So the American report states — correctly — that there were no confirmed terrorist incidents in Saudi Arabia last year. There were, nevertheless, three unexplained bombings and one shooting incident, all directed against foreigners.

Example of incidents with no known motivation

10   Another essential ingredient (you might think) is that terrorism is calculated to terrorize the public or a particular section of it. The American definition does not mention spreading terror at all, because that would exclude attacks against property. It is, after all, impossible to frighten an inanimate object.

Another part of the definition

Among last year's attacks, 152 were directed against a pipeline in Colombia which is owned by multinational oil companies. Such attacks are of concern to the United States and so a definition is required which allows them to be counted.

For those who accept that terrorism is about terrorizing people, other questions arise. Does it include threats, as well as actual violence? A few years ago, for example, the Islamic Army in Yemen warned foreigners to leave the country if they valued their lives but did not actually carry out its threat.

Questions about which examples meet the criteria

More recently, a group of Israeli peace activists were arrested for driving around in a loudspeaker van, announcing a curfew of the kind that is imposed on Palestinians. Terrifying for any Israelis who believed it, but was it terrorism?

Another characteristic of terrorism, according to some people, is that targets must be random — the intention being to make everyone fear they might be the next victim. Some of the Hamas suicide bombings appear to follow this principle but when attacks are aimed at predictable targets (such as the military) they are less likely to terrorize the public at large.

Definitions usually try to distinguish between terrorism and warfare. In   15
general this means that attacks on soldiers are warfare and those against civilians are terrorism, but the dividing lines quickly become blurred.

The state department regards attacks against "noncombatant* targets" as terrorism. But follow the asterisk to the small print and you find that "noncombatants" includes both civilians and military personnel who are unarmed

or off duty at the time. Several examples are given, such as the 1986 disco bombing in Berlin, which killed two servicemen.

The most lethal bombing in the Middle East last year was the suicide attack on USS *Cole* in Aden harbor which killed 17 American sailors and injured 39 more.

As the ship was armed and its crew on duty at the time, why is this classified as terrorism? Look again at the small print, which adds: "We also consider as acts of terrorism attacks on military installations or on armed military personnel when a state of military hostilities does not exist at the site, such as bombings against U.S. bases."

A similar question arises with Palestinian attacks on quasi-military targets such as Israeli settlements. Many settlers are armed (with weapons supplied by the army) and the settlements themselves — though they contain civilians — might be considered military targets because they are there to consolidate a military occupation.

If, under the state department rules, Palestinian mortar attacks on settle-   20
ments count as terrorism, it would be reasonable to expect Israeli rocket attacks on Palestinian communities to be treated in the same way — but they

are not. In the American definition, terrorism can never be inflicted by a state.

Israeli treatment of the Palestinians is classified as a human rights issue (for which the Israelis get a rap over the knuckles) in a separate state department report.

Denying that states can commit terrorism is generally useful, because it gets the U.S. and its allies off the hook in a variety of situations. The disadvantage is that it might also get hostile states off the hook — which is why there has to be a list of states that are said to "sponsor" terrorism while not actually committing it themselves.

Interestingly, the American definition of terrorism is a reversal of the word's original meaning, given in the *Oxford English Dictionary* as "government by intimidation." Today it usually refers to intimidation of governments.

The term's original meaning

The first recorded use of "terrorism" and "terrorist" was in 1795, relating to the Reign of Terror instituted by the French government. Of course, the Jacobins, who led the government at the time, were also revolutionaries and gradually "terrorism" came to be applied to violent revolutionary activity in general. But the use of "terrorist" in an anti-government sense is not recorded until 1866 (referring to Ireland) and 1883 (referring to Russia).

Its history

25   In the absence of an agreed meaning, making laws against terrorism is especially difficult. The latest British anti-terrorism law gets round the problem by listing 21 international terrorist organizations by name. Membership of these is illegal in the UK.

The difficulty of making laws against terrorism

There are six Islamic groups, four anti-Israel groups, eight separatist groups, and three opposition groups. The list includes Hizbullah, which though armed, is a legal political party in Lebanon, with elected members of parliament.

Among the separatist groups, the Kurdistan Workers Party — active in Turkey — is banned, but not the KDP or PUK, which are Kurdish organizations active in Iraq. Among opposition groups, the Iranian People's Mujahedeen is banned, but not its Iraqi equivalent, the INC, which happens to be financed by the United States.

Issuing such a list does at least highlight the anomalies and inconsistencies behind anti-terrorism laws. It also points toward a simpler — and perhaps more honest — definition: terrorism is violence committed by those we disapprove of.

This author's stipulated definition

Practice: Extended Definition

Like most extended definitions, the definition of "conscientious objection" in the essay beginning on page 256 uses several of the means of defining a term that this chapter has covered. Which of them do you see, and where? Read the essay, and answer the questions that follow it.

Conscientious Objection in Medicine: A Moral Dilemma

ISHMEAL BRADLEY

Consider this: what would you do if a patient with terminal pancreatic cancer told you, his primary care doctor of twenty years, that he wanted your help to end his life? Or, what if a woman in her first trimester who contracted an infection that threatened the health of her fetus asked you, her obstetrician, to perform an abortion? Ethical questions like these are encountered not infrequently today. However, they can pose a moral dilemma for the physician. Where are the boundaries between professional obligations and personal morality? Can personal morality override professional duty when it comes to patient care?

Conscientious objection in medicine is the notion that a health care provider can abstain from offering certain types of medical care with which he/she does not personally agree. This includes care that would otherwise be considered medically appropriate. An example would be a pro-life obstetrician who refuses to perform abortions or sterilizations. On the one hand, there is the argument that physicians have a duty to uphold the wishes of their patients, as long as those wishes are reasonable. On the other is the thought that physicians themselves are moral beings and that their morality should not be infringed upon by dictates from the legislatures, medical community or patient interests.

Several states in the last few years have passed laws that protect health care providers from retribution if those providers, who invoke their conscience, refuse to provide medical care. One example is the Michigan Conscientious Objector Policy Act of 2004 which allows providers to decline offering care if that care compromises the provider's beliefs, except in the event of an emergency.[1] Furthermore, a state law in Georgia extends conscientious objection to pharmacists by allowing them to refuse to fill a prescription for emergency contraception, even to a victim of sexual assault.[2]

This issue was reignited in December 2008 by the passage of the Medical Conscience Rule by the Department of Health and Human Services in the closing weeks of the Bush administration. Then-Secretary Michael Leavitt sought to expand the scope of several laws passed by Congress in the 1970s, 1990s, and 2000s.[3] Those previous laws were designed to protect health care entities — individual providers, insurance companies, hospitals, charitable organizations providing medical care — who received any form of federal funding from reprisal if they chose not to provide certain medical services that violated their conscience, most notably abortion services.

Specifically, the goal of the new law is to "prohibit recipients of certain federal funds from coercing individuals in the health care field into participating in actions they find religiously or morally objectionable" and to "prohibit discrimination on the basis of one's objection to, participation in, or refusal to participate in, specific medical procedures, including abortion and sterilization."[4] Also, the new regulation aims to educate the health care community about the protections afforded by federal law, ensure

5

Ishmeal Bradley is a doctor of internal medicine in New York. His article was posted on May 28, 2009, on *Clinical Correlations: The NYU Langone Online Journal of Medicine.*

compliance with current federal law, hear grievances brought to the Department's attention by plaintiffs, and to "take an active role in promoting open communication within the health care field [in order to foster] a more inclusive, tolerant environment . . . than [what] may currently exist."[4] Any health care entity found to be in violation of the new law would be subject to a termination of federal support and repayment of funds already received.

In a statement released on the DHHS website, Secretary Leavitt expressed that "health care providers should not be forced to choose between good professional standing and violating their conscience." Critics say that there are already federal and state laws on this issue, and that the Secretary was acting more out of ideology than for concern for the actual dilemma. Also, the language of the Medical Conscience Rule is so broad that it could seriously hinder patient access to health care. Opposing the new law are the American Hospital Association and the American Medical Association, while faith-based organizations, like the Catholic Health Association, support it. Although the AMA's guidelines do say that a physician can choose whom to serve in non-emergent situations, they also emphasized that the "responsibility to the patient is paramount." In a letter to the DHHS last fall, the AMA expressed concern about the wording of the new law, feeling that it was "overly broad and could lead to differing interpretations causing unnecessary confusion and disruption among health care institutions and professionals," thereby hindering patient access to care.[5] Despite opposition from several prominent professional organizations, the new law went into effect on January 20, 2009. Responding to pressure from the new Obama administration and patient advocacy groups, the new DHHS is currently taking steps to rescind the law.[6, 7]

Since the 1970s, Congress has passed several laws to protect health care entities from perceived discrimination. In 1973 Congress passed the Church Amendments in response to *Roe v. Wade*. The first amendment stated that any entity that received federal support from the DHHS could not compel employees to perform sterilization or abortion procedures, make their facilities available for such procedures, or provide personnel for such procedures if doing so would be contrary to the entity's religious beliefs.[4] The second and third amendments outlawed job discrimination on the basis of personal convictions regarding these reproductive matters.

Then came the Public Health Service Act of 1996, which was both more specific and expansive about reproductive rights than the earlier Church Amendments. It explicitly forbade federal, state, and local agencies that received federal funding from discriminating against any health care entity that refused to provide abortion services, training for such services, or referrals for patients to other agencies that did perform those services, and outlawed health care organizations from requiring their physicians from being trained in abortions.[4] Similarly, the Weldon Amendment, a rider on the 2005 appropriations bill for the DHHS, reiterated that no funds from the Department would be provided to an agency if that agency subjected a "health care entity to discrimination on the basis that the health care entity [did] not provide, pay for, provide coverage of, or refer for abortions."[4]

Against this backdrop of the Medical Conscience Rule, the question remains, is there a place for conscientious objection in medicine? Is it acceptable for a health care provider to deny appropriate and legal medical care to a patient when asked to do so? Critics cite the supremacy of patient autonomy and the professional duty of a physician as reasons to oppose conscientious objection. On the other side, those in favor stress that the morality of the physician is an integral part in the doctor–patient relationship and should not be ignored.

10   In a controversial article published in 2006, Julian Savulescu, a medical ethicist from Oxford, wrote that the "primary goal of a health service is to protect the health of its recipients."[8] Furthermore, he wrote that doctors should not be able to "offer partial medical services or partially discharge their obligations to care for their patients" because they are not ready to offer legal and beneficial, but controversial, care. He argues that the personal beliefs and morality of the physician should not enter into medical decision-making. The only thing that matters is what is "best" for the patient as both the patient and the law see fit.

This paradigm is unabashedly absolutist. Critics of his have mentioned that in his reasoning, physicians would be forced to perform procedures or services that they may view as immoral. According to Savulescu, what some of his critics may not fully appreciate is that there is no question of personal morality in this model. To appreciate this, one has to accept a priori several fundamental premises. One, that patients can make reasonable decisions when presented with all the data. Two, that the duty of a physician is to honor a patient's wishes, if those wishes are within reason. And three, that patient autonomy and the right to guide one's own medical care are universal truths. Conscientious objection

inherently takes the decision-making power away from the patient and places it in the hands of the physician.

The professional duty of the physician is a subject of debate, too. Whereas Savulescu argues that duty is absolute and unwavering, those in favor of conscientious objection feel that duty is malleable and can change depending on the situation at hand.

Proponents of this case-specific model argue that conscientious objection does have a place in medicine and that the individual health care provider can decide what he or she will or will not offer to a patient. The patient's requests are only one part of the decision-making process, the other part being the will of the health care provider. They contend that every controversial situation should be viewed uniquely and judged on its own singular status. Along these lines, Plato once said that "prudence is not concerned with universals only; it must also take cognizance of particulars." However, disregard for "universals" can introduce an element of caprice into the health care community, which would only create more confusion and inconsistencies.[6]

One potential solution for conscientious objection is the so-called "physician-referral policy." If a patient requests something that the physician feels uncomfortable providing, the physician can refer the patient to someone else who will honor that request. However, for this system to function, there must be enough providers available to perform those services. If there are not, then patients are needlessly harmed by not having access to appropriate medical care.

The Medical Conscience Rule complicates   15 this policy because it exempts physicians from the requirement of referring patients to other providers. The patient, who relies on the physician for his or her expert advice and referrals to other providers, is left without recourse. Furthermore, the physician referral policy can damage the notion of informed consent. The physician may not present the patient with all the available options, especially if some of those options are not in line with the physician's beliefs, like abortion or withdrawing life support.[9] Or, the physician may present or withhold the data in such a way as to push the patient towards one course of action that may be more acceptable to the physician but not in the interest of the patient.

Unfortunately, difficult decisions will always arise in the practice of medicine, and when they do, doctors should work with patients to determine the best option specific to that patient and his or her circumstance. We must all remember, patients and doctors together, that no pro-choice physician is pro-abortion, that no doctor is pro-death. But sometimes, physicians must perform certain tasks for the ultimate good of their patient, even if one has to take the plunge and place one's personal convictions aside.

On a personal note, I believe myself to be a moral and religious man. I use those values to guide my own personal decision-making, but I try to stop short of imposing those rules on another person — including a patient — who may have a very different set of values. Furthermore, I took an oath on the day that I graduated from medical school that obligated me to offer, to the best of my abilities, appropriate, uncompromised medical care without bias. There will certainly be times when I will be faced with a request from a patient or patient's representative that I will personally find morally difficult, but one that is still legally and ethically acceptable. I hope that those instances are few and

far between; when they do arrive, I expect that I will be able to take a step back and fully take on the mantle of the physician and act for the good of my patients, respecting their values as well as medical evidence, never putting my own interests before those of my patients.

Notes

1. Michigan Conscientious Objector Policy Act of 2004, HB-5006. 11 Mar. www .legislature.mi.gov/documents/2003-2004 /billengrossed/house/htm/2003-HEBH -5006.htm.
2. National Women's Law Center, "Pharmacy Refusals: State Laws, Regulations, and Policies," 6 Apr. 2009. www.nwlc.org/pdf /pharmacyrefusalpoliciesapril2009.pdf.
3. David Stout, "Medical 'Conscience Rule' Is Issued," *New York Times,* 19 Dec. 2008.
4. United States Dept. of Health and Human Services, "Ensuring That Department of Health and Human Services Funds Do Not Support Coercive or Discriminatory Policies or Practices in Violation of Federal Law," 45 CFR Part 88. Federal Register, 19 Dec. 2008, Vol. 73, no. 245, 78071–78101. http:// edocket.access.gpo.gov/2008/E8-30134.htm.
5. Amy Lynn Sorrel, "Revised Language in Proposed HHS Rule Still Bolsters Abortion Conscience Laws," *American Medical News*, 22.29, Sept. 2008.
6. Julie D. Cantor, "Conscientious Objection Gone Awry — Restoring Selfless Professionalism in Medicine," *NEJM* 360.15 (2009): 1484–85.
7. Most parts of the Medical Conscience Rule were rescinded in 2011. — Eds.
8. Julian Savulescu, "Conscientious Objection in Medicine," *BMJ* 332 (2006): 294–97.
9. Karen E. Adams, "Moral Diversity among Physicians and Conscientious Refusal of Care in the Provision of Abortion Services," *J Am Med Womens Assoc,* 58 (2003): 223–26.

Reading and Discussion Questions

1. Where does Bradley most concisely state his definition of conscientious objection in medicine?
2. Why is conscientious objection in medicine so controversial?
3. What was the goal of the Medical Conscience Rule? What were some of the different reactions to that law?
4. What is Bradley's personal opinion regarding conscientious objection in medicine? Do you agree? Why, or why not?

Assignments for Definition: Clarifying Key Terms

Reading and Discussion Questions

1. Why is definition such a crucial element in argumentation? In what ways can it help resolve issues? How can it lead to problems?
2. Who has the power to stipulate how a term is defined? The government? The media? Society in a broader sense? Where have you seen examples of each in the readings in this chapter?

Writing Suggestions

1. Narrate an experience you have had in which you felt either aided or hindered by being defined as a member of a specific group. It could be a group defined by gender, race, religious affiliation, or membership on a team or in a club.
2. Would adoption at the state level of a policy prohibiting classifying people by race, color, ethnicity, or national origin be beneficial or pernicious for the individual and for society? In other words, what is good or bad about classifying people?
3. Find a subject for which definition is critical to how statistics are interpreted and for which you can make a successful argument in a 750- to 1,000-word paper. Your essay should provide proof for a claim.
4. Write about an important or widely used term whose meaning has changed since you first learned it. Such terms often come from the slang of particular groups: drug users, rock music fans, musicians, athletes, computer programmers, or software developers.
5. Write an essay in which you provide specific examples of how government officials sometimes use euphemisms and other careful word choices to disguise the truth.

RESEARCH ASSIGNMENT ▸ **Using Encyclopedias**

1. Find out what encyclopedias your library has to offer. A librarian may be able to give you a list. Some may be in print and others online. If there is no list, you can search under "encyclopedia" and scan the list for relevant titles.

2. Now choose one of the controversial subjects listed below, and investigate what you can learn about it from three different encyclopedias. Do not use more than one general encyclopedia. Cut, paste, and print; photocopy; or take notes on the three sources and be prepared to discuss what you found. One question you should consider is how useful each encyclopedia would be to a researcher.

   - Solar power
   - Undocumented workers
   - Current legal status of same-sex marriage
   - Sexual harassment

bits

To see what you are learning about argumentation applied to the latest world and national news, read our *Bits* blog, "Argument and the Headlines," at **blogs.bedfordstmartins.com/bits**.

Language: Using Words with Care

The Power of Words

Words play such a critical role in argument that they deserve special treatment. An important part of successful writers' equipment is a large and active vocabulary, but no single chapter in a book can give this to you; only reading and study can widen your range of word choices. Even in a brief chapter, however, we can point out how words influence the feelings and attitudes of an audience, both favorably and unfavorably.

One kind of language responsible for shaping attitudes and feelings is **emotive language**, language that expresses and arouses emotions. Understanding it and using it effectively are indispensable to the arguer who wants to move an audience to accept a point of view or undertake an action.

Nowhere is the power of words more obvious and more familiar than in advertising, where the success of a product may depend on the feelings that certain words produce in the prospective buyer. Even the names of products may have emotive significance. Although most manufacturers agree that a good name won't save a poor product, they also recognize that the right name can catch the attention of the public and persuade people to buy a product at least once. According to an article in the *Wall Street Journal,* a product name not only should be memorable but also should "remind people of emotional or physical experiences."[1]

Practice

Careful thought and extensive research go into the naming of automobiles, a "big ticket" item for most consumers. What reasoning might have gone into the naming of the models, old and new, listed on page 263? What response do the names Mercedes-Benz and Rolls-Royce evoke?

---

[1] *Wall Street Journal,* August 5, 1982, p. 19.

Aspen	Infinity	Matrix	Rendezvous
Dart	Jaguar	Mustang	Sequoia
Eclipse	Land Rover	Nova	Taurus
Fusion	Leaf	Odyssey	Trailblazer
Grand Prix	Liberty	Quest	Tundra
Impala	Malibu	Regal	Viper

Even scientists recognize the power of words to attract the attention of other scientists and the public to discoveries and theories that might otherwise remain obscure. A good name can even enable the scientist to visualize a new concept. One scientist says that "a good name," such as "quark," "black hole," "big bang," "chaos," or "great attractor," "helps in communicating a theory and can have a substantial impact on financing." Certainly the subatomic particle that gives mass to matter attracts more attention when called the "God particle" than when referred to as the "Higgs boson."

It is not hard to see the connection between the use of words in conversation and advertising and the use of emotive language in the more formal arguments you will be writing. Emotive language reveals your approval or disapproval, assigns praise or blame—in other words, makes a judgment about the subject. Keep in mind that unless you are writing purely factual statements, such as scientists write, you will find it hard to avoid expressing judgments. Neutrality does not come easily, even where it may be desirable, as in news stories or reports of historical events. For this reason, you need to attend carefully to the statements in your argument, making sure that you have not disguised judgments as statements of fact. In Rogerian argument, you need to remain neutral as you summarize your opponent's argument as well as your own.

Of course, in attempting to prove a claim, you will not be neutral. You will be revealing your judgment about the subject—first in the selection of facts and opinions and the emphasis you give to them, and second in the selection of words.

Like the choice of facts and opinions, the choice of words can be effective or ineffective in advancing your argument, moral or immoral in the honesty with which you exercise it. After the readings that follow, the remaining sections of this chapter offer some insights into recognizing and evaluating the use of emotive language in the arguments you read, as well as into using such language in your own arguments where it is appropriate and avoiding it where it is not. Your decisions about language determine the voice you project in your writing. You do not use the same voice in everything you write, but in formal written arguments you will want to be especially mindful of using a voice appropriate for your intended audience.

READING ARGUMENT

Practice: The Power of Words
Analyze the use of language in this Stihl ad.

Consumer Confidence
STIHL

You won't find STIHL in Lowe's®, The Home Depot® or on Wall Street. We keep it in the family. You will find us where there's a proud commitment to customer service—at over 8,000 independent STIHL dealers nationwide. In 2008, their dedication helped us achieve our 17th consecutive year of record growth. You'll also find us in the hands of millions of hard-working folks who are truly passionate about a job done right. Who use real power tools, not toys that need to be replaced. People who like to roll up their sleeves when the cuff links are off. Who know a sharp investment when they see one.

Invest in a STIHL today. You can count on us to help you do more. Visit STIHLUSA.com

Number 1 Worldwide **STIHL**®

Stihl Inc.

Practice: The Power of Words

In one of the most memorable speeches in the history of the United States, President Franklin D. Roosevelt asked the country both to accept a point of view and to prepare to take action. Read Roosevelt's speech and our brief analysis, and then answer the questions that follow.

Address to Congress, December 8, 1941
FRANKLIN D. ROOSEVELT

Yesterday, December 7, 1941 — a date which will live in infamy — the United States of America was suddenly and deliberately attacked by naval and air forces of the Empire of Japan.

The United States was at peace with that nation, and, at the solicitation of Japan, was still in conversation with its government and its Emperor looking toward the maintenance of peace in the Pacific.

Indeed, one hour after Japanese air squadrons had commenced bombing in the American island of Oahu, the Japanese Ambassador to the United States and his colleague delivered to our Secretary of State a formal reply to a recent American message. And, while this reply stated that it seemed useless to continue the existing diplomatic negotiations, it contained no threat or hint of war or of armed attack.

It will be recorded that the distance of Hawaii from Japan makes it obvious that the attack was deliberately planned many days or even weeks ago. During the intervening time the Japanese Government has deliberately sought to deceive the United States by false statements and expressions of hope for continued peace.

5   The attack yesterday on the Hawaiian Islands has caused severe damage to American naval and military forces. I regret to tell you that very many American lives have been lost. In addition, American ships have been reported torpedoed on the high seas between San Francisco and Honolulu.

Yesterday the Japanese Government also launched an attack against Malaya. Last night Japanese forces attacked Hong Kong. Last night Japanese forces attacked Guam. Last night Japanese forces attacked the Philippine Islands. Last night the Japanese attacked Wake Island. And this morning the Japanese attacked Midway Island.

Japan has therefore undertaken a surprise offensive extending throughout the Pacific area. The facts of yesterday and today speak for themselves. The people of the United States have already formed their opinions and well understand the implications to the very life and safety of our nation.

As Commander-in-Chief of the Army and Navy I have directed that all measures be taken for our defense, that always will our whole nation remember the character of the onslaught against us.

No matter how long it may take us to overcome this premeditated invasion, the American people, in their righteous might, will win through to absolute victory.

Franklin D. Roosevelt was president of the United States from 1933 to 1945. He gave this speech the day after the Japanese attack on the U.S. Naval Base at Pearl Harbor in Hawaii, which was then a U.S. territory.

10   I believe that I interpret the will of the Congress and of the people when I assert that we will not only defend ourselves to the uttermost but will make it very certain that this form of treachery shall never again endanger us.

Hostilities exist. There is no blinking at the fact that our people, our territory, and our interests are in grave danger.

With confidence in our armed forces, with the unbounding determination of our people, we will gain the inevitable triumph, so help us God.

I ask that the Congress declare that since the unprovoked and dastardly attack by Japan on December 7, 1941, a state of war has existed between the United States and the Japanese Empire.

Analysis

In his brief speech to Congress, Roosevelt captured some of the grief and the feeling of outrage Americans were experiencing. Except for the most famous phrase in the speech, in which he declares December 7, 1941, a "date which will live in infamy," most of the first portion of the speech establishes the facts. A turning point in the speech comes when he shifts from facts to implications. The speech then builds to its emotional climax, in the next-to-last paragraph, before he concludes with a declaration of war.

Reading and Discussion Questions

1. Describe Roosevelt's language in the first five paragraphs. How does it compare with the language he uses in the second half of the speech?
2. What is the effect of the repetition in paragraph 6?
3. Beginning in paragraph 8, what specific words start to build an emotional response to Japan's actions?
4. What is the significance of the verb tense that Roosevelt uses in the last sentence?

Connotation

The **connotations** of a word are the meanings we attach to it apart from its explicit definition. Because these added meanings derive from our feelings, connotations are one form of emotive language. For example, the word *rat* denotes or points to a kind of rodent, but the attached meanings of "selfish person," "evil-doer," "betrayer," and "traitor" reflect the feelings that have accumulated around the word.

In Chapter 8, we observed that definitions of controversial terms, such as *poverty*, may vary so widely that writer and reader cannot always be sure that they are thinking of the same thing. A similar problem arises when a writer assumes that the reader shares his or her emotional response to a word. Emotive meanings originate partly in personal experience. The word *home*, defined merely as "a family's place of residence," may suggest love, warmth, and security to one person; it may suggest friction, violence, and alienation to another. The values of the groups to which we belong also influence meaning. Writers and speakers count on cultural associations when they refer to our country, our flag, and heroes and enemies we have never seen. The arguer must also be aware that some apparently neutral words trigger different responses from different groups — words such as *cult, revolution, police,* and *beauty contest.*

Various reform movements have recognized that words with unfavorable connotations have the power not only to reflect but also to shape our perceptions of things. In 2007, the NAACP went so far as to hold a "funeral for the N — word." The women's liberation movement also insisted on changes that would bring about improved attitudes toward women. The movement condemned the use of *girl* for a female over the age of eighteen and the use in news stories of descriptive adjectives that emphasize the physical appearance of women. And the homosexual community succeeded in reintroducing the word *gay,* a word current centuries ago, as a substitute for words they considered offensive.

Members of certain occupational groups have invented terms to confer greater respectability on their work. The work does not change, but the workers hope that public perceptions will change

— if janitors are called *custodians.*
— if garbage collectors are called *sanitation engineers.*
— if undertakers are called *morticians.*
— if people who sell makeup are called *cosmetologists.*

Events considered unpleasant or unmentionable are sometimes disguised by polite terms, called **euphemisms**. For example, many people refuse to use the word *died* and choose *passed away* instead. Some psychologists and physicians use the phrase *negative patient care outcome* for what most of us would call *death.* Even when referring to their pets, some people cannot bring themselves to say *put to death* but substitute *put to sleep* or *put down.* In place of a term to describe an act of sexual intercourse, some people use *slept together* or *went to bed together* or *had an affair.*

Polite words are not always so harmless. If a euphemism disguises a shameful event or condition, it is morally irresponsible to use it to mislead the reader into believing that the shameful condition does not exist. An example of such usage was cited by a member of Amnesty International, a group monitoring human rights violations throughout the world. He objected to a news report describing camps in which the Chinese government was promoting "reeducation through labor." This term, he wrote, "makes these institutions seem like a cross between Police Athletic League and Civilian Conservation Corps camps." On the contrary, he went on, the reality of "reeducation through labor" was that the victims were confined to "rather unpleasant prison camps." The details he offered about the conditions under which people lived and worked gave substance to his claim.[2]

Perhaps the most striking examples of the way that connotations influence our perceptions of reality occur when people respond to questions posed by poll-takers. Sociologists and students of poll-taking know that the phrasing of a question, or the choice of words, can affect the answers and even undermine the validity of the poll. In one case, poll-takers first asked a selected group of people if they favored continuing the welfare system. The majority answered no. But when the poll-takers asked if they favored government aid to the poor, the majority answered yes. Although the terms *welfare* and *government aid to the poor* refer to essentially the same forms of government assistance, *welfare* has acquired for many people negative connotations of corruption and shiftless recipients.

In 2013, Michael Dimock, director of the Pew Research Center for the People & the Press, provided an excellent example of how much difference the wording of a survey question can make. It had just been made public that the Department of Justice had subpoenaed the phone records of AP journalists. The following bar graphs show how three different polling organizations worded their questions about the action by the Justice Department—and the responses. Dimock called his report "a case study in the challenges pollsters face in a breaking news environment when public attention and information is relatively limited."[3]

Three Questions on the Department of Justice/AP Issue

Do you approve or disapprove of the Justice Department's decision to subpoena the phone records of AP journalists as part of an investigation into the disclosure of classified information? (Pew Research)

Approve	36
Disapprove	44
No opinion	20

The AP reported classified information about U.S. anti-terrorism efforts and prosecutors have obtained AP's phone records through a court order. Do you think this action by federal prosecutors is or is not justified? (*Washington Post*/ABC News)

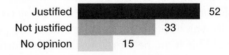

Justified	52
Not justified	33
No opinion	15

---

[2] Letter to the *New York Times*, August 30, 1982, p. 25.
[3] Michael Dimock, "Polling When Public Attention Is Limited: Different Questions, Different Results," pewresearch.org. Original charts provided by Pew Research Center.

As you may know, after the AP ran news stories that included classified information about U.S. anti-terrorism efforts, the Justice Department secretly collected phone records for reporters and editors who work there. Do you think that the actions of the Justice Department were acceptable or unacceptable? (CNN/ORC)

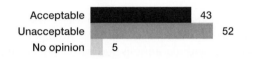

Acceptable 43
Unacceptable 52
No opinion 5

Fox News began its own survey two days later and concluded it one day later than the other polling organizations. The slight delay in timing raises the possibility that opinions in this fourth poll had shifted over time — even just a few days.

Fox News Question and Context

Does it feel like the federal government has gotten out of control and is threatening the basic civil liberties of Americans, or doesn't it feel this way to you?

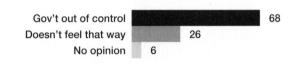

Gov't out of control 68
Doesn't feel that way 26
No opinion 6

As you may have heard, the U.S. Justice Department secretly seized extensive telephone records of calls on both work and personal phones for reporters and editors working for the Associated Press in the spring of 2012. At the time, the news organization, using government leaks, had broken a story about an international terrorist plot. The government obtained the phone records without giving the news organization prior notice, as is customary. Do you think the government was probably justified in taking these actions or does this sound more like the government went too far? (Fox News)

Justified 31
Went too far 60
No opinion 8

Polls concerning rape address another highly charged subject. Dr. Neil Malamuth, a psychologist at the University of California at Los Angeles, says, "When men are asked if there is any likelihood they would force a woman to have sex against her will if they could get away with it, about half say they would. But if you ask them if they would rape a woman if they knew they could get away with it, only about 15 percent say they would." The men who change their answers aren't aware that "the only difference is in the words used to describe the same act."[4]

The wording of an argument is crucial. Because readers may interpret the words you use on the basis of feelings different from your own, you must support your word choices with definitions and with evidence that enables readers to determine how and why you made them.

---

[4] *New York Times*, August 29, 1989, sec. C, p. 1.

READING ARGUMENT

Practice: Connotation

Read and analyze the following commentary. Pick out specific words and phrases that have negative connotations.

Why Keep Athletes Eligible but Uneducated?
FRANK DEFORD

So much about big-time college sports is criticized. But the worst scandal is almost never mentioned; the academic fraud wherein the student-athletes, so-called, are admitted without even remotely adequate credentials and then aren't educated so much as they are just kept eligible.

The reason this shameful practice seldom surfaces is because all the major conference schools are guilty and everybody — presidents, trustees, coaches, media, fans — everybody accepts the corruption. Only occasionally does the truth bubble up. Enter Mary Willingham at the University of North Carolina. She was a learning specialist, working with the Tar Heel athletes who needed study help. And invariably, almost all of the most unqualified were from the revenue sports, football and basketball. She was so appalled at the academic inability of so many players that she began to speak out about the terrible hypocrisy.

Meanwhile, the university removed her from working with athletes, reduced her title and, she says, "doubled my workload. They're trying to get rid of me," she told me. Fans of the Tar Heel teams treat her unkindly. This invariably happens to college sports whistleblowers who dare

---

Frank Deford is a commentator for NPR's *Morning Edition*. His peers have voted him the U.S. Sportswriter of the Year six times. These comments aired on *Morning Edition* on September 4, 2013.

reveal what is called a dirty little secret, wink-wink; but which is, in fact, a filthy, big lie.

Imagine, showing up at college, Ms. Willingham says, with reading, writing, and vocabulary skills so below your classmates that nothing makes sense. She found some athletes admitted to Chapel Hill, one of the most elite public universities in the country, with fourth-grade reading skills. Worse, some are, simply, non-readers. More upsetting, she found cheating rampant. It troubles her, she admits, that she herself lied about that, filling out boilerplate NCAA forms that affirmed that there was no cheating. But everybody does it. Just tell the NCAA what it wants, and sell more tickets.

5   What is so sad, Ms. Willingham says, is that almost all the academically deficient players whom she worked with wanted to learn, wanted an education. But their time and energy were eaten up by their sport. There wasn't enough time left over for the student-athletes to try to become students.

But understand, as another college year begins — or, more visibly, as another college football season begins — that what goes on at Chapel Hill is substantially no different than the way athletic programs are run across the country. It's the only way to win. As Ms. Willingham says she's been told so often: Athletics is in charge of the university. She doesn't want to believe that because among other things, she says that she loves the University of North Carolina. She loves that place of learning.

Practice: Connotation

The following passage comes from the January 2007 issue of the *International Journal of Inclusive Democracy*. Read the passage, underlining any words that have negative connotations. Then rewrite the passage using neutral language.

Dispatches from a Police State: Animal Rights in the Crosshairs of State Repression
STEVEN BEST

Welcome to the post-constitutional America, where defense of animal rights and the earth is a terrorist crime.

In the wake of 9/11, and in the midst [of] the neoliberal attack on social democracies, efforts to grab dwindling resources, and [to] crush dissent of any kind, the U.S. has entered a neo-McCarthyist period rooted in witch-hunts and political persecution. The terms and players have changed, but the situation is much the same as the 1950s: The terrorist threat has replaced the communist threat, Attorney General Alfred [sic] Gonzalez dons the garb of Sen. Joseph McCarthy, and the Congressional Meetings on Eco-Terrorism stand in for the House Un-American Activities Committee. The Red Scare of communism has morphed into the Green Scare of ecoterrorism, where the bad guy today

Steven Best is an associate professor of humanities and philosophy at the University of Texas at El Paso. His books include (with Anthony J. Nocella II) *Terrorists or Freedom Fighters? Reflections on the Liberation of Animals* (2004). This article appeared in the January 2007 issue of the *International Journal of Inclusive Democracy*.

is not a commie but an animal, environmental, or peace activist. In a nightmare replay of the 1950s, activists of all kinds today are surveilled, hassled, threatened, jailed, and stripped of their rights. As before, the state conjures up dangerous enemies in our midst and instills fear in the public, so that people willingly forfeit liberties for an alleged security that demands secrecy, nonaccountability, and centralized power. . . .

The bogus "war on terror" has served as a highly effective propaganda and bullying device to ram through Congress and the courts a pro-corporate, anti-environmental, authoritarian agenda. Using vague, catch-all phrases such as "enemy combatants" and "domestic terrorists," the Bush administration has rounded up and tortured thousands of non-citizens (detaining them indefinitely in military tribunals without right to a fair trial) and surveilled, harassed, and imprisoned citizens who dare to challenge the government or corporate system it protects and represents.

Slanting

Slanting, says one dictionary, is "interpreting or presenting in line with a special interest." The term is almost always used in a negative sense. It means that the arguer has selected facts and words with favorable or unfavorable connotations to create the impression that no alternative view exists or can be defended. For some questions, it is true that no alternative view is worthy of presentation, and emotionally charged language to defend or attack a position that is clearly right or wrong would be entirely appropriate. We aren't neutral, nor should we be, about the tragic abuse of human rights anywhere in the world or even about infractions of the law such as drunk driving or vandalism, and we should use strong language to express our disapproval of these practices.

Most of your arguments, however, will concern controversial questions about which people of goodwill can argue on both sides. In such cases, your own judgments should be restrained. Slanting will suggest a prejudice — that is, a judgment made without regard to all the facts. Unfortunately, you may not always be aware of your bias or special interest; you may believe that your position is the only correct one. You may also feel the need to communicate a passionate belief about a serious problem. But if you are interested in persuading a reader to accept your belief and to act on it, you must also ask: If the reader is not sympathetic, how will he or she respond? Will he or she perceive my words as "loaded" — one-sided and prejudicial — and my view as slanted?

R. D. Laing, a Scottish psychiatrist, defined *prayer* in this way: "Someone is gibbering away on his knees, talking to someone who is not there."[5] This description probably reflects a sincerely held belief. Laing also clearly intended it for an audience that already agreed with him. But the phrases "gibbering away" and "someone who is not there" would be offensive to people for whom prayer is sacred. Consider the effect on an audience of such statements as these:

---

[5] "The Obvious," in David Cooper, ed., *The Dialectics of Liberation* (Harmondsworth, U.K./Baltimore, MD: Penguin Books, 1968), p. 17.

- Any senator who would vote for this bill is ignoring the most basic rights of humanity.
- It is selfish for gun owners to think only of their own desires.
- The children had the misfortune of being raised by a single mother.
- Drug company executives who refuse dying children the compassionate use of experimental drugs have no conscience.
- The current level of airport security is an insult to the law-abiding citizens who are delayed by it.
- No one who values human life would text while driving.

You can slant an argument by means of the facts you choose to include or leave out as well as by means of word choice.

- During the search for Malaysia Airlines Flight 370, one reporter made headlines with the report that one of the pilots had been having marital difficulties. What he did not offer was any proof whatsoever that the pilot's personal life had any bearing on the plane's disappearance.
- A defense sometimes offered when a young person is accused of a crime is that he is a straight-A student, a fact that is irrelevant to his guilt or innocence.
- The fact that a defendant does not testify in her own defense is often assumed to be a sign of guilt when there may be a number of reasons why she does not take the stand. That fact may override, for some, other facts that are clearly in evidence.
- An argument might be made that a man has never been indicted for abusing his wife. Other records may reveal, however, that the police have been called to the home on numerous occasions to investigate domestic violence but no charges have been filed.
- In the movie *The Hunt*, a kindergarten teacher is accused of molesting a little girl because she describes the teacher's anatomy in language it is assumed she would not know otherwise. What the viewers know is that she has heard her older brother and his friends using such language while looking at sexually explicit pictures.

RESEARCH SKILL ▶ Evaluating Language in Sources

The sources you use are in a sense "witnesses" on behalf of your argument. Some sources are believable and trustworthy, just as some witnesses are. However, your argument is weakened by any hint that your sources are unreliable. Be sure that your sources do not weaken your argument by

- using so many words with negative connotations that there seems to be a clear and unfair bias.

- using such inflammatory language that ideas get lost in the emotion.
- using language that builds on hidden assumptions.
- using language that would be offensive to your intended audience.

Practice

Locate specific examples of slanted language in the first of these two excerpts. What effect does the word choice have in the first piece? How does it compare to the word choice in the second passage, on the same topic?

1. Grandstanding politicians love to rail against the gun. Inanimate objects are good targets to beat up on. That way, politicians do not have to address the real problems in our society. We pay a price for this craven misdirection, though, in thousands of murders, muggings, rapes, robberies, and burglaries.

    Yet that is not the greatest danger we face. The Founding Fathers knew that *governments* could turn criminal. That is the principal reason they wanted every man armed: An armed citizenry militates against the development of tyranny. The Founding Fathers did not want every man armed in order to shoot a burglar, although they had nothing against doing so. The Founding Fathers did not want every man armed in order to shoot Bambi or Thumper, although they had nothing against doing so. The Founding Fathers wanted every man armed in order to shoot soldiers or police of tyrannical regimes who suppress the rights of free men.[6]

2. Americans also have a right to defend their homes, and we need not challenge that. Nor does anyone seriously question that the Constitution protects the right of hunters to own and keep sporting guns for hunting game any more than anyone would challenge the right to own and keep fishing rods and other equipment for fishing — or to own automobiles. To "keep and bear arms" for hunting today is essentially a recreational activity and not an imperative of survival, as it was 200 years ago; "Saturday night specials" and machine guns are not recreational weapons and surely are as much in need of regulation as motor vehicles.

    Americans should ask themselves a few questions. The Constitution does not mention automobiles or motorboats, but the right to keep and own an automobile is beyond question; equally beyond question is the power of the state to regulate the purchase or the transfer of such vehicle and the right to license the vehicle and the driver with reasonable standards. In some places, even a bicycle must be registered, as must some household dogs.[7]

Figurative Language

Figurative language consists of words that produce images in the mind of the reader. Students sometimes assume that vivid picture-making language is the exclusive instrument of novelists and poets, but writers of arguments can also avail themselves of such devices to heighten the impact of their messages.

---

[6] Roger McGrath, "A God-Given Natural Right," *Chronicles*, October, 2003, p. 425.
[7] Warren Burger, "The Right to Bear Arms," *Parade*, January 14, 1990, p. 419.

Figurative language can do more than render a scene. It shares with other kinds of emotive language the power to express and arouse deep feelings. Like a fine painting or photograph, it can draw readers into the picture where they partake of the writer's experience as if they were also present. Such power may be used to delight, to instruct, or to horrify. In 1741, the Puritan preacher Jonathan Edwards delivered his sermon "Sinners in the Hands of an Angry God," in which people were likened to repulsive spiders hanging over the flames of Hell to be dropped into the fire whenever a wrathful God was pleased to release them. The congregation's reaction to Edwards's picture of the everlasting horrors to be suffered in the netherworld included panic, fainting, hysteria, and convulsions. Subsequently Edwards lost his pulpit in Massachusetts, in part as a consequence of his success at provoking such uncontrollable terror among his congregation.

Language as intense and vivid as Edwards's emerges from very strong emotion about a deeply felt cause. In the following paragraph, Lavina Melwani uses figurative language to call attention to some of the problems faced daily by undocumented workers.

> The rats — bold, tenacious, and totally fearless — are what bothered him the most. Prem, who requested his last name not be used, says the rodents have the run of the old apartment he shares in Baltimore City, Maryland, with five other Nepali men, most of them undocumented. "It is impossible to have beds for six people in two rooms," he says. "So we have small roll-out beds or mattresses on the floor. There are many rats running around the apartment and it's difficult to catch them. We can't complain. The landlord doesn't care. He knows we have to live here and have no choice."[8]

You are familiar with some of the most common figures of speech. You know that you can occasionally add creativity and sensory appeal to your writing by means of metaphors and similes. A famous **simile** — a comparison using *like* or *as* — comes from the acceptance speech that George H. W. Bush gave before the Republican convention in 1988:

> For we are a nation of communities, of thousands and tens of thousands of ethnic, religious, social, business, labor union, neighborhood, regional and other organizations, all of them varied, voluntary, and unique.
>
> This is America: the Knights of Columbus, the Grange, Hadassah, the Disabled American Veterans, the Order of Ahepa, the Business and Professional Women of America, the union hall, the Bible study group, LULAC, "Holy Name" — a brilliant diversity spread like stars, like a thousand points of light in a broad and peaceful sky.

---

[8] Lavina Melwani, "No Roof No Roots No Rights," *Little India*, April 12, 2006, p. 42.

Had Bush simply left out the word *like* in the last sentence, he would have been using a **metaphor**.

Another quote from the same speech illustrates another use of language that comes in handy at times in writing an argument: the analogy. An **analogy** is like a metaphor or simile in that it compares; but it is generally more complex, drawing parallels between two things that are similar in some ways but dissimilar in others. At times, an analogy is useful in explaining something unknown or less well known in terms of something else the audience is more familiar with.

In this particular analogy, Bush was comparing the economy to a patient. In comparing the economy to a human being, he was also making use of **personification**:

> My friends, eight years ago this economy was flat on its back — intensive care. We came in and gave it emergency treatment: Got the temperature down by lowering regulation, got the blood pressure down when we lowered taxes. Pretty soon the patient was up, back on his feet, and stronger than ever.
>
> And now who do we hear knocking on the door but the doctors who made him sick. And they're telling us to put them in charge of the case again. My friends, they're lucky we don't hit them with a malpractice suit!

The rules governing the use of figurative language are the same as those governing other kinds of emotive language. Is the language appropriate? Is it too strong, too colorful for the purpose of the message? Does it result in slanting or distortion? What will its impact be on a hostile or indifferent audience? Will they be angered, repelled? Will they cease to read or listen if the imagery is too disturbing?

READING ARGUMENT

Practice: Figurative Language

Read the excerpted speech by former president Ronald Reagan on pages 277–81. Analyze the figurative language used in the speech, and answer the questions that follow.

Excerpt from "The 'Evil Empire' Speech"

RONALD REAGAN

... I tell you there are a great many God-fearing, dedicated, noble men and women in public life, present company included. And, yes, we need your help to keep us ever mindful of the ideas and the principles that brought us into the public arena in the first place. The basis of those ideals and principles is a commitment to freedom and personal liberty that, itself, is grounded in the much deeper realization that freedom prospers only where the blessings of God are avidly sought and humbly accepted.

The American experiment in democracy rests on this insight. Its discovery was the great triumph of our Founding Fathers, voiced by William Penn when he said: "If we will not be governed by God, we must be governed by tyrants." Explaining the inalienable rights of men, Jefferson said, "The God who gave us life, gave us liberty at the same time." And it was George Washington who said that "of all the dispositions and habits which lead to political prosperity, religion and morality are indispensable supports."

And finally, that shrewdest of all observers of American democracy, Alexis de Tocqueville, put it eloquently after he had gone on a search for the secret of America's greatness and genius—and he said: "Not until I went into the churches of America and heard her pulpits aflame with righteousness did I understand the greatness and the genius of America. . . . America is good. And if America ever ceases to be good, America will cease to be great."

Well, I'm pleased to be here today with you who are keeping America great by keeping her good. Only through your work and prayers and those of millions of others can we hope to survive this perilous century and keep alive this experiment in liberty, this last, best hope of man.

I want you to know that this administration is motivated by a political philosophy that sees the greatness of America in you, her people, and in your families, churches, neighborhoods, communities—the institutions that foster and nourish values like concern for others and respect for the rule of law under God.

Now, I don't have to tell you that this puts us in opposition to, or at least out of step with, a prevailing attitude of many who have turned to a modern-day secularism, discarding the tried and time-tested values upon which our very civilization is based. No matter how well intentioned, their value system is radically different from that of most Americans. And while they proclaim that they're freeing us from superstitions of the past, they've taken upon themselves the job of superintending us by government rule and regulation. Sometimes their voices are louder than ours, but they are not yet a majority.

... Freedom prospers when religion is vibrant and the rule of law under God is acknowledged. When our Founding Fathers passed the first amendment, they sought to protect churches from government interference. They never intended to construct a wall of hostility between government and the concept of religious belief itself.

5

Ronald Reagan was president of the United States from 1981 to 1989. He made this speech at the Annual Convention of the National Association of Evangelicals in Orlando, Florida, on March 8, 1983.

The evidence of this permeates our history and our government. The Declaration of Independence mentions the Supreme Being no less than four times. "In God We Trust" is engraved on our coinage. The Supreme Court opens its proceedings with a religious invocation. And the Members of Congress open their sessions with a prayer.

. . . Now, I'm sure that you must get discouraged at times, but you've done better than you know, perhaps. There's a great spiritual awakening in America, a renewal of the traditional values that have been the bedrock of America's goodness and greatness.

10   One recent survey by a Washington-based research council concluded that Americans were far more religious than the people of other nations; 95 percent of those surveyed expressed a belief in God and a huge majority believed the Ten Commandments had real meaning in their lives. And another study has found that an overwhelming majority of Americans disapprove of adultery, teenage sex, pornography, abortion, and hard drugs. And this same study showed a deep reverence for the importance of family ties and religious belief.

I think the items that we've discussed here today must be a key part of the Nation's political agenda. For the first time the Congress is openly and seriously debating and dealing with the prayer and abortion issues — and that's enormous progress right there. I repeat: America is in the midst of a spiritual awakening and a moral renewal. And with your Biblical keynote, I say today, "Yes, let justice roll on like a river, righteousness like a never-failing stream."

Now, obviously, much of this new political and social consensus I've talked about is based on a positive view of American history, one that takes pride in our country's accomplishments and record. But we must never forget that no government schemes are going to perfect man. We know that living in this world means dealing with what philosophers would call the phenomenology of evil or, as theologians would put it, the doctrine of sin.

There is sin and evil in the world, and we're enjoined by Scripture and the Lord Jesus to oppose it with all our might. Our nation, too, has a legacy of evil with which it must deal. The glory of this land has been its capacity for transcending the moral evils of our past. For example, the long struggle of minority citizens for equal rights, once a source of disunity and civil war, is now a point of pride for all Americans. We must never go back. There is no room for racism, anti-Semitism, or other forms of ethnic and racial hatred in this country.

I know that you've been horrified, as have I, by the resurgence of some hate groups preaching bigotry and prejudice. Use the mighty voice of your pulpits and the powerful standing of your churches to denounce and isolate these hate groups in our midst. The commandment given us is clear and simple: "Thou shalt love thy neighbor as thyself."

But whatever sad episodes exist in our past,   15 any objective observer must hold a positive view of American history, a history that has been the story of hopes fulfilled and dreams made into reality. Especially in this century, America has kept alight the torch of freedom, but not just for ourselves but for millions of others around the world.

And this brings me to my final point today. During my first press conference as President, in answer to a direct question, I pointed out that, as good Marxist–Leninists, the Soviet leaders have openly and publicly declared that the only morality they recognize is that which will further their cause, which is world revolution. I think I should point out I was only quoting Lenin, their guiding spirit, who said in 1920 that they repudiate all morality that proceeds from supernatural ideas — that's their name for religion — or ideas that are outside class conceptions. Morality is entirely subordinate to the interests of class war. And everything is moral that is necessary for the annihilation of the old, exploiting social order and for uniting the proletariat.

Well, I think the refusal of many influential people to accept this elementary fact of Soviet doctrine illustrates an historical reluctance to see totalitarian powers for what they are. We saw this phenomenon in the 1930's. We see it too often today.

This doesn't mean we should isolate ourselves and refuse to seek an understanding with them. I intend to do everything I can to persuade them of our peaceful intent, to remind them that it was the West that refused to use its nuclear monopoly in the forties and fifties for territorial gain and which now proposes a 50 percent cut in strategic ballistic missiles and the elimination of an entire class of land-based, intermediate-range nuclear missiles. At the same time, however, they must be made to understand we will never compromise our principles and standards. We will never give away our freedom. We will never abandon our belief in God. And we will never stop searching for a genuine peace. But we can assure none of these things America stands for through the so-called nuclear freeze solutions proposed by some.

The truth is that a freeze now would be a very dangerous fraud, for that is merely the il-lusion of peace. The reality is that we must find peace through strength.

I would agree to a freeze if only we could freeze the Soviets' global desires. A freeze at current levels of weapons would remove any incentive for the Soviets to negotiate seriously in Geneva and virtually end our chances to achieve the major arms reductions which we have proposed. Instead, they would achieve their objectives through the freeze.

A freeze would reward the Soviet Union for its enormous and unparalleled military buildup. It would prevent the essential and long overdue modernization of United States and allied defenses and would leave our aging forces increasingly vulnerable. And an honest freeze would require extensive prior negotiations on the systems and numbers to be limited and on the measures to ensure effective verification and compliance. And the kind of a freeze that has been suggested would be virtually impossible to verify. Such a major effort would divert us completely from our current negotiations on achieving substantial reductions.

A number of years ago, I heard a young father, a very prominent young man in the entertainment world, addressing a tremendous gathering in California. It was during the time of the cold war and communism and our own way of life were very much on people's minds. And he was speaking to that subject. And suddenly, though, I heard him saying, "I love my little girls more than anything." And I said to myself, "Oh, no, don't. You can't — don't say that." But I had underestimated him. He went on: "I would rather see my little girls die now, still believing in God, than have them grow up under communism and one day die no longer believing in God."

20

There were thousands of young people in that audience. They came to their feet with shouts of joy. They had instantly recognized the profound truth in what he had said, with regard to the physical and the soul and what was truly important.

Yes, let us pray for the salvation of all of those who live in that totalitarian darkness — pray they will discover the joy of knowing God. But until they do, let us be aware that while they preach the supremacy of the state, declare its omnipotence over individual man, and predict its eventual domination of all peoples on the Earth, they are the focus of evil in the modern world.

25   It was C. S. Lewis who, in his unforgettable "Screwtape Letters," wrote: "The greatest evil is not done now in those sordid 'dens of crime' that Dickens loved to paint. It is not even done in concentration camps and labor camps. In those we see its final result. But it is conceived and ordered (moved, seconded, carried, and minuted) in clear, carpeted, warmed, and well-lighted offices, by quiet men with white collars and cut fingernails and smooth-shaven cheeks who do not need to raise their voice."

Well, because these "quiet men" do not "raise their voices," because they sometimes speak in soothing tones of brotherhood and peace, because, like other dictators before them, they're always making "their final territorial demand," some would have us accept them at their word and accommodate ourselves to their aggressive impulses. But if history teaches anything, it teaches that simple-minded appeasement or wishful thinking about our adversaries is folly. It means the betrayal of our past, the squandering of our freedom.

So, I urge you to speak out against those who would place the United States in a position of military and moral inferiority. You know, I've always believed that old Screwtape reserved his best efforts for those of you in the church. So, in your discussions of the nuclear freeze proposals, I urge you to beware the temptation of pride — the temptation of blithely declaring yourselves above it all and label both sides equally at fault, to ignore the facts of history and the aggressive impulses of an evil empire, to simply call the arms race a giant misunderstanding and thereby remove yourself from the struggle between right and wrong and good and evil.

I ask you to resist the attempts of those who would have you withhold your support for our efforts, this administration's efforts, to keep America strong and free, while we negotiate real and verifiable reductions in the world's nuclear arsenals and one day, with God's help, their total elimination.

While America's military strength is important, let me add here that I've always maintained that the struggle now going on for the world will never be decided by bombs or rockets, by armies or military might. The real crisis we face today is a spiritual one; at root, it is a test of moral will and faith.

Whittaker Chambers, the man whose own   30 religious conversion made him a witness to one of the terrible traumas of our time, the Hiss–Chambers case, wrote that the crisis of the Western World exists to the degree in which the West is indifferent to God, the degree to which it collaborates in communism's attempt to make man stand alone without God. And then he said, for Marxism–Leninism is actually the second oldest faith, first proclaimed in the Garden of Eden with the words of temptation, "Ye shall be as gods."

The Western World can answer this challenge, he wrote, "but only provided that its faith in God and the freedom He enjoins is as great as communism's faith in Man."

I believe we shall rise to the challenge. I believe that communism is another sad, bizarre chapter in human history whose last pages even now are being written. I believe this because the source of our strength in the quest for human freedom is not material, but spiritual. And because it knows no limitation, it must terrify and ultimately triumph over those who would enslave their fellow man. For in the words of Isaiah: "He giveth power to the faint; and to them that have no might He increased strength. . . . But they that wait upon the Lord shall renew their strength; they shall mount up with wings as eagles; they shall run, and not be weary. . . ."

Yes, change your world. One of our Founding Fathers, Thomas Paine, said, "We have it within our power to begin the world over again." We can do it, doing together what no one church could do by itself.

God bless you, and thank you very much.

Go to **macmillanhighered.com/rottenberg** to view and listen to the entire Reagan speech online.

Reading and Discussion Questions

1. In spite of the positive things that Reagan says about America in the first two paragraphs, what specific words suggest a threat to America?

2. Reagan says that our Founding Fathers did not to intend to build a wall of hostility between government and religion. What does the First Amendment say that could be construed that way?

3. What support does Reagan offer for his claim that America was undergoing a spiritual awakening in the early 1980s? Could the same thing be said of America today?

4. What is the legacy of evil to which Reagan refers?

5. What does Reagan hope to achieve by pointing out that the Soviets' name for religion is "supernatural ideas"?

6. This speech is called Reagan's "evil empire" speech. How does Reagan use the description of the Soviet Union as an evil empire to justify opposing a freeze on nuclear weapons?

Concrete and Abstract Language

Unlike **concrete words**, which point to real objects and real experiences, **abstract words** express qualities apart from particular things and events.

Concrete	*Abstract*
Velvety, dark red roses	Beauty
Returning money found in the street to the owner, although no one has seen the discovery	Honesty

Although they also rely on the vividness of concrete language, arguments use abstract terms far more extensively than other kinds of writing. Using abstractions effectively, especially in arguments of value and policy, is important for two reasons:

1. Abstractions represent the qualities, characteristics, and values that the writer is explaining, defending, or attacking.
2. Abstractions enable the writer to make generalizations about his or her data.

Abstractions tell us what conclusions we have arrived at; details tell us how we got there. Look at the following paragraph by Michael Pollan.

> Domestication is an evolutionary, rather than a political, development. It is certainly not a regime humans somehow imposed on animals some ten thousand years ago. Rather, domestication took place when a handful of especially opportunistic species discovered, through Darwinian trial and error, that they were more likely to survive and prosper in an alliance with humans than on their own. Humans provided the animals with food and protection in exchange for which the animals provided the humans their milk, eggs, and — yes — their flesh. Both parties were transformed by the new relationship: The animals grew tame and lost their ability to fend for themselves in the wild (natural selection tends to dispense with unneeded traits) and the humans traded their hunter-gatherer ways for the settled lives of agriculturists. (Humans changed biologically, too, evolving such new traits as the ability to digest lactose as adults.)[9]

Taken by itself, Pollan's first sentence (or topic sentence) is a bit general, relying heavily on the abstract word *evolutionary* to describe *domestication*. The rest of the paragraph, however, supports the first sentence with concrete details. Just as definitions are needed for vague or ambiguous terms (see Chapter 8), an arguer must use concrete language to provide readers with a clear understanding of an abstract concept.

---

[9] Michael Pollan, *The Omnivore's Dilemma* (New York: Penguin, 2006), p. 320.

A common problem in using abstractions is omission of details. Either the writer is not a skilled observer and cannot provide the details, or the writer believes that such details are too small and quiet compared to the grand sounds made by abstract terms. These grand sounds, unfortunately, cannot compensate for the lack of clarity and liveliness. Lacking detailed support, abstract words may be misinterpreted. They may also represent ideas that are so vague as to be meaningless.

Practice

Write three to five specific details to support one of these topic sentences that use abstract language.

1. High school students often live with a lot of stress.
2. Much of the coursework in high school is not relevant to students' future plans.
3. Bipartisanship has hampered the passage of legislation that would improve the quality of life of the average American.
4. Our campus should work toward sustainability.
5. Social networking encourages relationships that are very superficial.
6. Shoppers have to admit that healthy food choices are available if they take the time to look for them.

Shortcuts

Shortcuts are abbreviated substitutes for argument that avoid the hard work necessary to provide facts, expert opinion, and analysis of warrants. Even experts, however, can be guilty of using shortcuts, and the writer who consults an authority should be alert to that authority's use of language. Two of the most common uses of shortcuts are clichés and slogans.

Clichés

A cliché is an expression or idea grown stale through overuse. Clichés in language are tired expressions that have faded like old photographs; readers no longer see anything when clichés are placed before them. Some phrases are so obviously clichés and so old-fashioned that you are not likely to use them in your writing:

Thick as thieves	As old as the hills
Opposites attract	Time heals all wounds
Read between the lines	Live and learn
Age before beauty	Avoid like the plague
Dry as a bone	Fit as a fiddle

All bets are off	All bent out of shape
Caught me off guard	Clean bill of health
Take it from me	Takes its toll on you
Par for the course	Pass the buck
Fall through the cracks	Make a federal case of it
First things first	Made of money
More than meets the eye	A half-baked idea

Others are a bit more likely to slip into your writing because they are almost filler in sentences, empty words:

All in due time	A bad call
Back against the wall	The bottom fell out
Boils down to	By the book
Business as usual	Call the shots
Call it a day	Cut your losses
Close rank	From day one
Go downhill	Raise the bar
In this day and time	

Another category of phrases has been labeled *thought-terminating clichés*. These clichés represent ready-made answers to questions, stereotyped solutions to problems, "knee-jerk" reactions:

God moves in mysterious ways.

You don't always get what you want.

To each his own.

We will have to agree to disagree.

Because that is our policy.

I'm the parent, that's why.

There's no silver bullet.

You're either with us or against us.

Certain cultural attitudes encourage the use of clichés. The liberal American tradition has been governed by hopeful assumptions about our ability to solve problems. A professor of communications says that "we tell our students that for every problem there must be a solution."[10] But real solutions are hard to come by. In our haste to provide them, to prove that we can be decisive, we may be tempted to produce familiar responses that resemble solutions. All reasonable solutions are worthy of consideration, but they must be defined and supported if they are to be used in a thoughtful, well-constructed argument.

Attitudes toward certain cultures also encourage the use of clichéd language and thought. When we accept a worn-out and overused perception of an ethnicity, nationality, or any other group, we are viewing individuals as **stereotypes**.

---

[10] Malcolm O. Sillars, "The New Conservatism and the Teacher of Speech," *Southern Speech Journal* 21 (1956), p. 240.

Avoid stereotypes in your writing, and be wary of other writers who employ them to further an argument.

Slogans

Slogans, like clichés, are short, undeveloped arguments. They represent abbreviated responses to often complex questions. As a reader, you need to be aware that slogans merely call attention to a problem; they cannot offer persuasive proof for a claim in a dozen words or less. As a writer you should avoid the use of slogans that evoke an emotional response but do not provide a reason for that response.

Advertising slogans are the most familiar. These may give us interesting and valuable information about products, but most advertisements give us slogans that ignore proof — shortcuts substituting for argument.

Walmart: Save money. Live better.

FedEx: When there is no tomorrow.

Red Cross: The greatest tragedy is indifference.

PlayStation: Live in your world. Play in ours.

Disneyland: The happiest place on earth.

Ajax: Stronger than dirt.

IBM: Solutions for a small planet.

McDonald's: i'm lovin' it.

Hallmark: When you care enough to send the very best.

DeBeers: A diamond is forever.

Levi's: Quality never goes out of style.

Subway: Eat fresh.

The persuasive appeal of advertising slogans heavily depends on the connotations associated with products. In Chapter 6, we discussed the way in which advertisements promise to satisfy our needs and protect our values (see p. 200, "Appeals to Needs and Values"). Wherever evidence is scarce or nonexistent, the advertiser must persuade us through skillful choice of words and phrases (as well as pictures), especially those that produce pleasurable feelings. "Let it inspire you" is the slogan of a popular liqueur. It suggests a desirable state of being but remains suitably vague about the nature of the inspiration. Another familiar slogan — "Noxzema, clean makeup" — also emphasizes a quality that we approve of, but what is "clean" makeup? Since the advertisers are silent, we are left with warm feelings about the word and not much more. What feelings are evoked by the slogans listed above?

Advertising slogans are persuasive because their witty phrasing and punchy rhythms produce an automatic *yes* response. We react to them as we might react to the lyrics of popular songs, and we treat them far less critically than we treat more straightforward and elaborate arguments. Still, the consequences of failing to analyze the slogans of advertisers are usually not serious. You may be tempted to buy a product because you were fascinated by a brilliant slogan, but if the product doesn't satisfy, you can abandon it without much loss. However, ignoring ideological slogans coined by political parties or special-interest groups may carry an enormous price, and the results are not so easily undone.

Ideological slogans, like advertising slogans, depend on the power of connotation, the emotional associations aroused by a word or phrase. American political history is, in fact, a repository of slogans:

1864	Abraham Lincoln	Don't Swap Horses in the Middle of the Stream
1900	William McKinley	A Full Dinner Pail
1916	Woodrow Wilson	He Kept Us Out of War
1924	Calvin Coolidge	Keep Cool with Coolidge
1928	Herbert Hoover	A Chicken in Every Pot and a Car in Every Garage
1964	Lyndon B. Johnson	The Stakes Are Too High for You to Stay at Home
1980	Ronald Reagan	Are You Better Off Than You Were Four Years Ago?
1988	George Bush	A Kinder, Gentler Nation
1992	Bill Clinton	Putting People First
2000	George W. Bush	Leave No Child Behind
2008	Barack Obama	Change We Can Believe In

Over time, slogans, like clichés, can acquire a life of their own and, if they are repeated often enough, come to represent an unchanging truth we no longer need to examine. "Dangerously," says Anthony Smith, "policy makers become prisoners of the slogans they popularize."[11]

WRITER'S GUIDE
Choosing Your Words Carefully

1. **Strive for a voice that is appropriate for your intended audience.** Following the rest of these suggestions will help you achieve that goal. Think about the type of *ethos* you want to present to your readers by means of the language you use.

2. **Avoid language with connotations that might produce a negative reaction in your audience.** Even if you do not agree with your audience, you want your case to be heard. Let your ideas speak for you, and don't let your word choice alienate your audience.

3. **If you have used slanted language, consider whether it will advance or weaken your argument.** Your argument will be an opinion. You don't want to seem so opinionated that no one will listen.

---

[11] "Nuclear Power — Why Not?" *The Listener*, October 22, 1981, p. 463.

4. **Use figurative language where appropriate for your purposes.** It can produce images in the minds of audience members and can arouse emotion when doing so is appropriate.

5. **Support abstract language with concrete language.** Concrete details can convey to your readers exactly what you have in mind much more precisely than abstract language.

6. **Edit out any clichés or slogans from your early drafts.** Clichés and slogans are stale, unoriginal language or catchphrases that are too brief to convey complex ideas.

Slogans also have numerous shortcomings as substitutes for the development of an argument. **First, their brevity presents serious disadvantages.** Slogans necessarily ignore exceptions or negative instances that might qualify a claim. They usually speak in absolute terms without describing the circumstances in which a principle or idea might not work. Their claims therefore seem shrill and exaggerated. In addition, brevity prevents the sloganeer from revealing how he or she arrived at conclusions.

Second, slogans may conceal unexamined warrants. When Japanese cars were beginning to compete with American cars, the slogan "Made in America by Americans" appeared on the bumpers of thousands of American-made cars. A thoughtful reader would have discovered in this slogan several implied warrants: *American cars are better than Japanese cars; the American economy will improve if we buy American; patriotism can be expressed by buying American goods.* If the reader were to ask a few probing questions, he or she might find these warrants unconvincing.

Silent warrants that express values hide in other popular and influential slogans. "Pro-life," the slogan of those who oppose abortion, assumes that the fetus is a living being entitled to the same rights as individuals already born. "Pro-choice," the slogan of those who favor abortion, suggests that the freedom of the pregnant woman to choose is the foremost or only consideration. The words *life* and *choice* have been carefully selected to reflect desirable qualities, but the words are only the beginning of the argument.

Third, although slogans may express admirable sentiments, they often fail to tell us how to achieve their objectives. They often address us in the imperative mode, ordering us to take an action or refrain from it. But the means of achieving the objectives may be nonexistent or very costly. If sloganeers cannot offer workable means for implementing their goals, they risk alienating the audience. Sloganeering is one of the recognizable attributes of propaganda. Propaganda for both good and bad purposes is a form of slanting, of selecting language and facts to persuade an audience to take a certain action. Even a good cause may be weakened by an unsatisfactory slogan. If you assume that your audience is sophisticated and alert, you will probably write your strongest arguments devoid of clichés and slogans.

> **ARGUMENT ESSENTIALS**
> ## Evaluating Language
>
> - The writer's choice of words should advance the writer's argument.
> - Emotive language may be used appropriately to express and arouse emotions.
> - Words with positive and negative connotations should be used with care.
> - Avoid using one-sided and prejudicial language.
> - Words that produce images in the mind of the reader can heighten the impact of the message.
> - Use concrete language to support abstract language.
> - Clichés and slogans are no substitutes for facts, expert opinion, and analysis.

READING ARGUMENT

Seeing Language

The following selection incorporates all of the aspects of language discussed in this chapter. As you read it, consider connotation, slanting, figurative language, concrete versus abstract language, and shortcuts. After reading the article and the accompanying annotations, answer the questions that follow.

Food for Thought (and for Credit)
JENNIFER GROSSMAN

Humorous tone; speaks directly to audience with *you* and *we*

Want to combat the epidemic of obesity? Bring back home economics. Before you choke on your 300-calorie, trans-fat-laden Krispy Kreme, consider: Teaching basic nutrition and food preparation is a far less radical remedy than gastric bypass surgery or fast-food lawsuits. And probably far more effective.

Jennifer Grossman is vice president of the Dole Nutrition Institute, which distributes health information to the public through lectures and publications. Formerly, she was director of Education Policy at the Cato Institute and a speechwriter for President George H. W. Bush. She has written editorials for the *New York Times*, where this column appeared on September 2, 2003; the *Wall Street Journal*; the *Los Angeles Times*; the *New York Post*; the *Weekly Standard*; the *National Review*; and the *Women's Quarterly*.

Obesity tends to invite such drastic solutions because it is so frustratingly difficult to treat. This intractability, coupled with the sad fact that obese children commonly grow up to be obese adults, argues for a preventative approach. As the new school year begins, we need to equip kids with the skills and practical knowledge to take control of their dietary destinies.

Despite its bad rep as Wife Ed 101, home economics has progressive roots. At the turn of the century it "helped transform domesticity into a vehicle to expand women's political power," according to Sarah Stage in *Rethinking Home Economics: Women and the History of a Profession*. In time, focus shifted from social reform to the practical priorities of sanitation and electrification, and then again to an emphasis on homemaking after World War II — giving ammunition to later critics like Betty Friedan who charged home ec with having helped foster the "feminine mystique."

Banished by feminists, Becky Home-ecky was left to wander backwater school districts. For a while it seemed that mandating male participation might salvage the discipline while satisfying political correctness. By the late 1970s one-third of male high school graduates had some home-ec training, whereas they comprised a mere 3.5 percent of home-ec students in 1962. Since then, "home economics has moved from the mainstream to the margins of American high school," according to the United States Department of Education, with even female participation — near universal in the 1950s — plummeting by 67 percent.

What has happened since? Ronald McDonald and Colonel Sanders stepped in as the new mascots of American food culture, while the number of meals consumed outside the home has doubled — from a quarter in 1970 to nearly half today. As a result, market economics has increasingly determined ingredients, nutrient content, and portion size. Agricultural surpluses and technological breakthroughs supplied the cheap sweeteners and hydrogenated oils necessary for food to survive indefinitely on store shelves or under fast-food heat lamps.

5   Unsurprisingly, the caloric density of such foods soared relative to those consumed at home. Good value no longer meant taste, presentation, and proper nutrition — but merely more-for-less. Thus, the serving of McDonald's French fries that contained 200 calories in 1960 contains 610 today. The lure of large was not limited to fast-food, inflating everything from snack foods to cereal boxes.

But the hunger for home economics didn't die with its academic exile. Martha Stewart made millions filling the void, vexing home-ec haters like Erica Jong for having "earned her freedom by glorifying the slavery of home."

Starts with slang (*rep*); moves into more formal language

Loaded language

Concrete data back up abstractions.

Concrete example

Home and Garden TV, the Food Network, and countless publications thrive on topics once taught by home ec.

All of which begs the question: If the free market has done such a good job of picking up the slack, why bring home ec back? Because much of the D.I.Y. (do-it-yourself) culture is divorced from the exigencies of everyday life. It's more like home rec: catering to pampered chefs with maids to clean up the kitchen.

The new home economics should be both pragmatic and egalitarian. Traditional topics — food and nutrition, family studies, home manage-

ment — should be retooled for the twenty-first century. Children should be able to decipher headlines about the dangers of dioxin or the benefits of anti-oxidants. Subjects like home finance might include domestic problem-solving: How would you spend $100 to feed a family of four, including a diabetic, a nursing mother, and infant, for one week?

While this kind of training might most benefit those low-income minority children at highest risk of obesity, all children will be better equipped to make smart choices in the face of the more than $33 billion that food companies spend annually to promote their products. And consumer education is just part of the larger purpose: to teach kids to think, make, fix, and generally fend for themselves.

Some detractors will doubtless smell a plot to turn women back into stitching, stirring Stepford Wives. Others will argue that schools should focus on the basics. But what could be more basic than life, food, home, and hearth?   10

A generation has grown up since we swept home ec into the dust heap of history and hung up our brooms. It's time to reevaluate the domestic discipline, and recapture lost skills.

Reading and Discussion Questions

1. How would the students at the high school you attended have responded to a course such as the one Grossman describes?
2. Do you think that offering such a course would be a good idea? Why, or why not?
3. How convincing is Grossman's argument that there is a need for consumer education?
4. How does Grossman's use of language add or detract from her argument?

Practice: Examining Language

Use the questions following this film review to guide your analysis of its author's use of language.

Flood the Zone

JOHN PODHORETZ

First and foremost, *Noah* is a movie, and the first question about a movie is whether it is good or bad as a movie. That turns out to be a difficult one to answer.

On the one hand, *Noah* is ridiculous in every sense of the word. It is entirely possible that you will get the giggles about 30 seconds in — specifically, at the moment when cowriter/director Darren Aronofsky dubs in the sound of a hearty crunch and slurp as he shows a silhouette of Eve biting into the forbidden fruit — and you may never stop giggling until the closing titles.

Pauline Kael once wrote about an inadvertently hilarious exchange in a terrible movie called *Slow Dancing in the Big City* (1978). A man tells his girlfriend he's flying to Europe, and she responds by asking, "On a plane?" Kael observed that the director must have heard this exchange a thousand times as his movie was being edited: Did he never think to cut her line? Similarly, one has to wonder about Aronofsky and that crunch-and-slurp. Didn't he have a friend to whom he showed an early cut who could have told him to take the sound out?

If you do get the giggles, you will roar with laughter a few minutes later when you meet the fallen angels who end up helping Noah build the ark, for God has sent them to earth and encrusted them with mud and turned them into computer-generated ROCK MONSTERS! The campy guffaws will just keep coming, as when one of Noah's sons meets the girl of his dreams . . . in an open pit full of corpses.

5   But here's the thing: If you don't start giggling, you might well find yourself gripped by *Noah*. I have to admit I was. It is a deadly serious portrait of the burdens that moral responsibility places on a good man, particularly as enacted by a magnificent Russell Crowe, in the best performance he has given in more than a decade. He is once again teamed with Jennifer Connelly, with whom he made *A Beautiful Mind* (2001) and who has been brought back to life as an actress just as Noah brings Crowe back to life as an actor.

The movie has generated some controversy because it strays significantly from the biblical account; indeed, it seems to be based less on Genesis than on a work of ancient apocrypha called the Book of Enoch — from which Aronofsky and cowriter Ari Handel derived Noah's relationship with the fallen angels, called Watchers.

The Book of Enoch describes how the corruption of man rendered the earth barren and lifeless, and Aronofsky uses this as the source material for an explicitly environmentalist message. But *Noah* is no simple tract; indeed, if you take it seriously, it is also a portrait of the spiritual danger of environmentalist extremism. (Spoilers from here on out.)

Halfway through the movie, Noah becomes convinced that God wants to wipe all of mankind from the earth because of humanity's foulness, and that he only wants Noah and his family to survive to shepherd the innocent animals safely through the flood. Noah declares

John Podhoretz is the editor of *Commentary* and the *Weekly Standard*'s movie critic. His review appeared in the *Weekly Standard* on April 14, 2014.

that his youngest son, Japheth, is to be "the last man," and he is prepared to commit infanticide to achieve his aim. And not merely infanticide, but the murder of his own grandchildren.

It's ludicrous to have a debate about how faithful *Noah* is to the original Genesis story; after all, according to the old song taught at countless Bible camps, the Lord told Noah to make the ark out of hickory "barky-barky," while the King James version says "gopher wood." There is no requirement for absolute fidelity to the text when trying to turn a biblical tale into a full-blown narrative.

10   Those upset about *Noah* supposedly playing fast-and-loose with the Bible should actually be more deeply offended by the movie's truly anti-religious core: It depicts a God who is nothing less than demonic in his cruelty. He punishes the fallen angels in horrific ways for taking pity on Adam and Eve. He then deserts mankind entirely and leaves humans to their own devices, yet has the nerve to blame them for not behaving as he wishes they would. And, as Noah was right about the opaque messages he received from "the Creator" (as God is known here) about the coming end of the world and the need for an ark, so he is presumably also right that he is supposed to kill his grandchildren and end the human race.

Even more audaciously, it is not the Almighty who ultimately tells Noah's descendants to be fruitful and multiply, but Noah. Thus, at the very beginning of civilization itself, man, not God, is placed at the center of the moral universe — for it is Noah writing the rules, not the Creator. Darren Aronofsky then blesses his own astonishing inversion of the moral frame of Western civilization with a 360-degree special-effects rainbow.

Directors are always accused of playing God, but this is ridiculous — whether or not you get the giggles.

Reading and Discussion Questions

1. At what point do you realize that Podhoretz's language is not completely objective? What are other examples from the review of language with either negative or positive connotations?
2. How does Podhoretz's choice of words capture the humorous approach he takes to some of Aronofsky's decisions?
3. What clichés do you find in the review?
4. Do Podhoretz's word choices strengthen the review or weaken it? Explain.

Practice: Examining Language

Analyze Whitney Smith's language use in this op-ed piece for her school newspaper.

USC Course Evaluations Need New Strategy
WHITNEY SMITH

There is nothing quite as obnoxious as receiving five e-mails at 3 a.m. urging students to evaluate their professors. What the university fails to understand is that students are bombarded with assignments as well as expectations to pour in countless hours in the library to study for finals. Meanwhile, they are pestered to complete these evaluations as well.

The evaluations that students do take the time to fill out are the ones that berate professors they hate. However, nothing that I have seen makes it apparent that there has been action taken against said professors. Instead, these professors turn up year after year, continuing to lash out with their most gruesome tactics. The evaluations that are forced upon students in class are answered with a sea of all "5's" and a gaggle of blank responses to the open-ended questions so that the student may leave the class sooner.

If the evaluations were not shoved down students' throats, they would serve their intended purpose. The biggest change that would encourage more students to take the time to fill out the evaluation would be making sure the timing didn't interfere with the last few weeks' workload. Placing course evaluations at the very end of the year, or even handing them out at the end of each exam, would make students less likely to feel apathetic toward yet another "assignment" that they are required to complete. Instead of assailing students with e-mails, a friendly reminder at the end of class would allow students to feel less irked and give professors a more accurate understanding of their strengths and weaknesses.

Whitney Smith was a student at the University of South Carolina when this piece was published in the campus newspaper on April 25, 2013.

Assignments for Language: Using Words with Care

Reading and Discussion Questions

1. Listen to or read the "I Have a Dream" speech by Martin Luther King Jr., noting its uses of figurative language.
2. Look back at the company slogans on page 285, and explain what each means.

3. Examine a few periodicals from fifty or more years ago. Select either an advertising or a political slogan in one of them, and relate it to beliefs or events of the period. Alternatively, tell why the slogan is no longer relevant.

4. Make up a slogan for a cause that you support. Explain and defend your slogan.

5. In watching television dramas about law, medicine, or criminal or medical investigation, do you find that the professional language, some of which you may not fully understand, plays a positive or negative role in your enjoyment of the show? Explain your answer.

Writing Suggestions

1. Analyze a print ad of your choosing, explaining how text and visuals work together to support a claim. Your essay can be analytical or evaluative.

2. Write two paragraphs about your roommate, a family member, or a former teacher, making one balanced and the other either negatively slanted or positively slanted. Make the two distinctive through the facts you choose to include or omit, not the words you choose.

3. Write two paragraphs, one a positive and one a negative description of either a fictional person or someone you know. The facts should be essentially the same, but you will use charged words to make the difference.

4. Locate a speech by Martin Luther King Jr. such as "I Have a Dream" (choose a short one), and write an essay analyzing its use of figurative language. You'll need a thesis that holds your examples together.

5. Choose a popular slogan from advertising or politics. Write a paragraph explaining how it appeals to needs and/or values.

6. Explain in an essay why shortcuts are a natural result of our technological age.

7. Analyze a presidential or other debate using some of the terms discussed in this chapter.

8. Locate a copy of President Bush's first speech after the attacks of 9/11, and compare it to President Roosevelt's after the bombing of Pearl Harbor.

RESEARCH ASSIGNMENT **Evaluating Language**

In the following passages, locate words with negative connotations, inflammatory language, language that builds on hidden assumptions, or offensive language.

Passage 1

Until we have universal background checks, better reporting from the states, and more — just more safety across the board, maybe a presence in schools is worth considering. I know that there is a police presence in the new location of the Sandy Hook school, and it certainly does reassure me when I drop my daughters off to see that there is that level of protection.

> — Veronique Pozner, mother of one of the children killed at Sandy
> Hook Elementary

(Source: *Anderson Cooper 360 Degrees*, "Guns under Fire Town Hall." CNN, 31 Jan. 2013.)

Passage 2

The Three Percent movement I founded has been denounced by that paragon of moral virtue, Bill Clinton, and I am a perennial "honorable mention" on the Southern Poverty Law Center's list of dangerous folks. I have even been the subject of an eighteen and a half minute rant by Rachel Madcow on MSNBC, and the current attorney general of the United States knows — and despises — me by name because of the Fast and Furious scandal that, with my friend David Codrea, I broke the news of on the Internet. Eric Holder would not be surprised to know that the feeling is mutual.

> — Speech at a Hartford firearm rights rally, April 20, 2013

(Source: Mike Vanderboegh, "My Name Is Mike Vanderboegh & I Am an Arms Smuggler." Sipseystreetirregulars.blogspot.com, 20 Apr. 2013.)

Passage 3

The rapidity of change and the speed with which new situations are created follow the impetuous and heedless pace of man rather than the deliberate pace of nature. Radiation is no longer merely the background radiation of cosmic rays, the ultraviolet of the sun that have existed before there was any life on earth; radiation is now the unnatural creation of man's tampering with the atom. The chemicals to which life is asked to make its adjustment are no longer merely the calcium and silica and copper and all the rest of the minerals washed out of the rocks and carried in rivers to the sea; they are the synthetic creations of man's inventive mind, brewed in his laboratories, and having no counterparts in nature.

(Source: Rachel Carson, "The Obligation to Endure," *Silent Spring*. New York: Houghton Mifflin, 1962, p. 7.)

bits

To see what you are learning about argumentation applied to the latest world and national news, read our *Bits* blog, "Argument and the Headlines," at **blogs.bedfordstmartins.com/bits**.

Logic: Understanding Reasoning

Throughout the book, we have pointed out the weaknesses that cause arguments to break down. In the vast majority of cases, these weaknesses represent breakdowns in logic or the reasoning process. We call such weaknesses **fallacies**, a term derived from Latin. Sometimes these false or erroneous arguments are deliberate; in fact, the Latin word *fallere* means "to deceive." But more often these arguments are either carelessly constructed or unintentionally flawed. Thoughtful readers learn to recognize them; thoughtful writers learn to avoid them.

As discussed in Chapter 1, the reasoning process was first given formal expression by Aristotle. In his famous treatises, he described the way we try to discover the truth — observing the world, selecting impressions, making inferences, generalizing. In this process, Aristotle identified two forms of reasoning: induction and deduction. Both forms, he realized, are subject to error. Our observations may be incorrect or insufficient, and our conclusions may be faulty because they have violated the rules governing the relationship between statements. Induction and deduction are not reserved only for formal arguments about important problems; they also represent our everyday thinking about the most ordinary matters. As for the fallacies, they, too, unfortunately, may crop up anywhere, whenever we are careless in our use of the reasoning process.

In this chapter, we examine some of the most common fallacies. First, however, a closer look at induction and deduction will make clear what happens when fallacies occur.

Induction

Induction is the form of reasoning in which we come to conclusions about the whole on the basis of observations of particular instances. For example, two friends decided to do some price comparisons.[1] They went to four popular stores, and at each one they checked the prices of the same four items: Sunbeam Giant Bread, Charmin Ultra Strong 9 Pack MegaRoll toilet paper, a gallon of store-brand whole milk, and a 12-pack of Cherry Coke Zero.

These shoppers were using the inductive method to determine which store is the least expensive. They studied the prices of individual items at individual stores and used that information to arrive at a generalization. They were moving from specifics — the prices of specific items at specific stores — to general observations. They compared the prices at the four stores and concluded that Walmart is the least expensive.

They were using induction, but how accurate was their conclusion? In inductive reasoning, the reliability of your conclusion depends on the quantity and quality of your observations. Were four items out of the thousands available at these four stores a sufficiently large sample? Would the friends' conclusion have been the same if they had chosen fifty items? One hundred? Even without pricing every item in all four stores, you would be more confident of your generalization as the quality and quantity of your samples increased.

Bloomberg Industries did a study of prices at Walmart and Target that made headlines in *Time* magazine.[2] The headline read, "Target Battles Walmart for Low-Price Supremacy." Who won the battle? Target did, but by only 0.46 percent. That means that for every $100 spent at Target, shoppers save $0.46 over Walmart for the same items. In this study, researchers compared prices on 150 similar items at the two stores, a much more convincing sample size than in our previous example. In this case, there were far more specific pieces of information to put together in reaching a generalization. Again, the process represents inductive reasoning because the researchers moved from specifics to generalizations. Later in the chapter, we will discuss a fallacy called "hasty generalization" that occurs when a generalization is based on too little evidence.

In some cases, you can observe all the instances in a particular situation. For example, by acquiring information about the religious beliefs of all the residents of a dormitory, you can arrive at an accurate assessment of the number of Buddhists. But since our ability to make definitive observations about everything is limited, we must make an inductive leap about categories of things that we ourselves can never encounter in their entirety. We make a leap when we have to accept less than absolute certainty or complete data and conclude that we have enough information on which to generalize. It is too much of a leap to conclude from a study of four items that one store is less expensive than another. It is less of a leap to conclude on the basis of 150 items.

Generalizations can also be complicated by other factors. Walmart recently aired television commercials citing specific items to prove that its prices on

---

[1] Amanda Miller, "Shop-o-nomics: 'Which Grocery Store Has the Lowest Prices?'" getoutofdebt.org. 20 Sept. 2010.

[2] Brad Tuttle, "Target Battles Walmart for Low-Price Supremacy." business.time.com. 27 Aug. 2012.

ARGUMENT ESSENTIALS
Induction

- Induction is the process of arriving at a generalization based on the observation of a number of particular instances.

- The accuracy of the generalization depends on the quantity and quality of the particular instances observed.

- In most cases, the generalization will be a probability, not a certainty.

- Arriving at a generalization based on too few particular instances is a logical fallacy called "hasty generalization."

groceries are better than those at Publix. A blogger on Iheartpublix.com responded with her own list of prices on 53 items, showing that Publix prices are better.[3] How can both be true? The blogger acknowledges that her prices were drawn from Publix's weekly ads. In other words, she compared Publix's sale prices with Walmart's everyday prices. (Her argument was that at least some of the Walmart items in the commercial were on sale and that smart shoppers buy when an item is on sale.)

In other cases, we may rely on a principle known in science as "the uniformity of nature." We assume that certain conclusions about oak trees in the temperate zone of North America, for example, will also be true for oak trees growing elsewhere under similar climatic conditions. We also use this principle in attempting to explain the causes of behavior in human beings. If we discover that the institutionalization of some children from infancy results in severe developmental delay, we think it safe to conclude that under the same circumstances all children would suffer the same consequences. As in the previous example, we are aware that certainty about every case of institutionalization is impossible. With rare exceptions, the process of induction can offer only probability, not certain truth.

Keep in mind that induction is a reasoning process, not an organizational pattern for academic essays. An author may make use of inductive reasoning to arrive at a generalization that then becomes the thesis of an essay. It may not always be obvious that the author used induction to arrive at his or her thesis. In the essay that follows, however, the author discloses how he arrived at his thinking about big businesses and their attitude toward the environment. Jared Diamond did not start out thinking that big businesses are active in preserving the environment. A number of specific instances of actions by these companies changed his thinking; thus by the process of inductive reasoning he arrived at his thesis. He provides detailed examples of the environmentally responsible acts by big businesses that shaped his opinion.

---

[3] Michelle, "See the Real Difference — Publix vs. Walmart Shopping." iheartpublix.com. 16 July 2012.

READING ARGUMENT

Seeing Induction

The following excerpted essay has been annotated to show inductive reasoning. Read the essay, and answer the questions that follow.

Will Big Business Save the Earth?

JARED DIAMOND

There is a widespread view, particularly among environmentalists and liberals, that big businesses are environmentally destructive, greedy, evil, and driven by short-term profits. I know — because I used to share that view.

But today I have more nuanced feelings. Over the years I've joined the boards of two environmental groups, the World Wildlife Fund and Conservation International, serving alongside many business executives.

As part of my board work, I have been asked to assess the environments in oil fields, and have had frank discussions with oil company employees at all levels. I've also worked with executives of mining, retail, logging, and financial services companies. I've discovered that while some businesses are indeed as destructive as many suspect, others are among the world's strongest positive forces for environmental sustainability.

Claim: the generalization he arrived at over time

The embrace of environmental concerns by chief executives has accelerated recently for several reasons. Lower consumption of environmental resources saves money in the short run. Maintaining sustainable resource levels and not polluting saves money in the long run. And a clean image — one attained by, say, avoiding oil spills and other environmental disasters — reduces criticism from employees, consumers, and government.

Reasons CEOs are embracing environmental concerns

5   What's my evidence for this? Here are a few examples involving three corporations — Walmart, Coca-Cola, and Chevron — that many critics of business love to hate, in my opinion, unjustly.

He will use three companies to illustrate the evidence that led him (inductively) to his generalization.

Let's start with Walmart. Obviously, a business can save money by finding ways to spend less while maintaining sales. This is what Walmart did with fuel costs, which the company reduced by $26 million per year simply by changing the way it managed its enormous truck fleet. Instead of running a truck's

First example: Walmart

Four paragraphs of specifics on how Walmart shows concern for the environment

Jared Diamond is a professor of geography at the University of California, Los Angeles, and winner of the 1998 Pulitzer Prize for general nonfiction for his book *Guns, Germs, and Steel*. His most recent book is *The World until Yesterday* (2012). This piece appeared in the *New York Times* on December 6, 2009.

engine all night to heat or cool the cab during mandatory 10-hour rest stops, the company installed small auxiliary power units to do the job. In addition to lowering fuel costs, the move eliminated the carbon dioxide emissions equivalent to taking 18,300 passenger vehicles off the road.

Walmart is also working to double the fuel efficiency of its truck fleet by 2015, thereby saving more than $200 million a year at the pump. Among the efficient prototypes now being tested are trucks that burn biofuels generated from waste grease at Walmart's delis. Similarly, as the country's biggest private user of electricity, Walmart is saving money by decreasing store energy use.

Another Walmart example involves lowering costs associated with packaging materials. Walmart now sells only concentrated liquid laundry detergents in North America, which has reduced the size of packaging by up to 50 percent. Walmart stores also have machines called bailers that recycle plastics that once would have been discarded. Walmart's eventual goal is to end up with no packaging waste.

One last Walmart example shows how a company can save money in the long run by buying from sustainably managed sources. Because most wild fisheries are managed unsustainably, prices for Chilean sea bass and Atlantic tuna have been soaring. To my pleasant astonishment, in 2006 Walmart decided to switch, within five years, all its purchases of wild-caught seafood to fisheries certified as sustainable.

Coca-Cola's problems are different from Walmart's in that they are largely   10 long-term. The key ingredient in Coke products is water. The company produces its beverages in about 200 countries through local franchises, all of which require a reliable local supply of clean fresh water.

But water supplies are under severe pressure around the world, with most already allocated for human use. The little remaining unallocated fresh water is in remote areas unsuitable for beverage factories, like Arctic Russia and northwestern Australia.

Coca-Cola can't meet its water needs just by desalinizing seawater, because that requires energy, which is also increasingly expensive. Global climate change is making water scarcer, especially in the densely populated temperate-zone countries, like the United States, that are Coca-Cola's main customers. Most competing water use around the world is for agriculture, which presents sustainability problems of its own.

Hence Coca-Cola's survival compels it to be deeply concerned with problems of water scarcity, energy, climate change, and agriculture. One company goal is to make its plants water-neutral, returning to the environment water in quantities equal to the amount used in beverages and their production.

Second example: Coca-Cola

Five paragraphs of specifics about Coca-Cola

Another goal is to work on the conservation of seven of the world's river basins, including the Rio Grande, Yangtze, Mekong, and Danube — all of them sites of major environmental concerns besides supplying water for Coca-Cola.

These long-term goals are in addition to Coca-Cola's short-term cost-saving environmental practices, like recycling plastic bottles, replacing petroleum-based plastic in bottles with organic material, reducing energy consumption, and increasing sales volume while decreasing water use.

15   The third company is Chevron. Not even in any national park have I seen such rigorous environmental protection as I encountered in five visits to new Chevron-managed oil fields in Papua New Guinea. (Chevron has since sold its stake in these properties to a New Guinea–based oil company.) When I asked how a publicly traded company could justify to its shareholders its expenditures on the environment, Chevron employees and executives gave me at least five reasons.

Third example: Chevron — three paragraphs

First, oil spills can be horribly expensive: it is far cheaper to prevent them than to clean them up. Second, clean practices reduce the risk that New Guinean landowners become angry, sue for damages, and close the fields. (The company has been sued for problems in Ecuador that Chevron inherited when it merged with Texaco in 2001.) Next, environmental standards are becoming stricter around the world, so building clean facilities now minimizes having to do expensive retrofitting later.

Also, clean operations in one country give a company an advantage in bidding on leases in other countries. Finally, environmental practices of which employees are proud improve morale, help with recruitment, and increase the length of time employees are likely to remain at the company.

Reading and Discussion Questions

1. Diamond has changed his mind about big businesses. What has changed his mind?
2. What is his belief now about big businesses and the environment, which is also his thesis?
3. If that thesis is Diamond's major premise, explain how the essay is based on the inductive process. What are the specifics from which this generalization was drawn?
4. Considering Walmart as an example, are you convinced by the details Diamond presents to prove that the company is sincere about the environment? Identify a couple of examples showing the difference that a single large company can make when it takes the protection of the environment seriously.

Deduction

It is useful to think of deduction as working in the opposite direction from induction. With deductive reasoning, an arguer essentially starts with a general statement that would apply to a number of specific situations. Then the arguer applies that generalization to one specific instance. Unlike the conclusions from induction, which are only probable, the conclusions from **deduction** are certain. The simplest deductive argument consists of two premises and a conclusion. In outline form, such an argument looks like this:

Major premise: All students with 3.5 averages and above for three years are invited to become members of Kappa Gamma Pi, the honor society.

Minor premise: George has had a 3.8 average for over three years.

Conclusion: Therefore, he will be invited to join Kappa Gamma Pi.

This deductive conclusion is *valid,* or logically consistent, because it follows necessarily from the premises. No other conclusion is possible. **Validity**, however, refers only to the form of the argument. The argument itself may not be satisfactory if the premises are not true — if Kappa Gamma Pi has imposed other conditions or if George has only a 3.4 average. The difference between truth and validity is important because it alerts us to the necessity for examining the truth of the premises before we decide that the conclusion is sound.

One way of discovering how the deductive process works is to look at the methods used by Sherlock Holmes, that most famous of literary detectives, in solving his mysteries. On one occasion, Holmes observed that a man sitting opposite him on a train had chalk dust on his fingers. From this observation, Holmes deduced that the man was a schoolteacher. If his thinking were outlined, it would take the form of a **syllogism**, the classic form of deductive reasoning:

Major premise: All men with chalk dust on their fingers are schoolteachers.

Minor premise: This man has chalk dust on his fingers.

Conclusion: Therefore, this man is a schoolteacher.

The major premise offers a generalization about a large group or class. This generalization has been arrived at through inductive reasoning, or observation of particulars. The minor premise makes a statement about a specific member of that group or class. The third proposition is the conclusion, which links the other two propositions, in much the same way that a warrant links support and a claim.

But although the argument may be logical, it is faulty. A deductive argument is only as strong as its premises. In this case, the major premise, the generalization that all men with chalk dust on their fingers are schoolteachers, is not true. Perhaps all the men with dusty fingers whom Holmes had so far observed had turned out to be schoolteachers, but his sample was not sufficiently large to

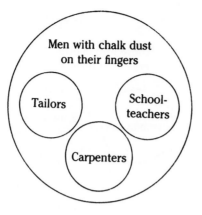

enable him to conclude that all dust-fingered men are teachers. In Holmes's day, draftsmen or carpenters or tailors might have had fingers just as white as those of schoolteachers. Sometimes it is helpful to draw a Venn diagram, circles representing the various groups in their relation to the whole.

If the large circle above represents all those who have chalk dust on their fingers, we see that several different groups may be contained in this universe. To be safe, Holmes should have deduced that the man on the train *might have been* a schoolteacher; he was not safe in deducing more than that. Obviously, if the inductive generalization or major premise is false, the conclusion of the particular deductive argument is also false or invalid.

The deductive argument may also go wrong elsewhere. What if the *minor* premise is untrue? Could Holmes have mistaken the source of the white powder on the man's fingers? Suppose it was not chalk dust but flour or confectioner's sugar or talcum or heroin. Any of these possibilities would weaken or invalidate Holmes's conclusion.

Another example, closer to the kinds of arguments you will examine in your academic work, reveals the flaw in the deductive process.

Major premise: All Communists oppose organized religion.

Minor premise: Robert Roe opposes organized religion.

Conclusion: Therefore, Robert Roe is a Communist.

The fact that two things share an attribute does not mean that they are the same thing. The following diagram makes clear that Robert Roe and Communists do not necessarily share all attributes. Remembering that Holmes may have misinterpreted the signs of chalk on the traveler's fingers, we may also want to question whether Robert Roe's opposition to organized religion has been misinterpreted.

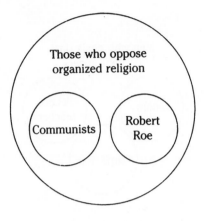

Some deductive arguments give trouble because one of the premises, usually the major premise, is omitted. As in the warrants we examined in Chapter 7, a failure to evaluate the truth of an unexpressed premise may lead to an invalid conclusion. When only two parts of a syllogism appear, we call the resulting form an **enthymeme**. Suppose we overhear the following bit of conversation:

> "Did you hear about Jean's father? He had a heart attack last week."
> "That's too bad. But I'm not surprised. I know he always refused to go for his annual physical checkups."

The second speaker has used an unexpressed major premise, the cause-and-effect warrant *If you have annual physical checkups, you can avoid heart attacks.* He does not express it because he assumes that it is unnecessary to do so. The first speaker recognizes the unspoken warrant and may agree with it. Or the first speaker may produce evidence from reputable sources that such a generalization is by no means universally true, in which case the conclusion of the second speaker is suspect.

A knowledge of the deductive process can help guide you toward an evaluation of the soundness of your reasoning in an argument you are constructing. A syllogism is often clearer than an outline in establishing the relations between the different parts of an argument.

Setting down your own or someone else's argument in this form will not necessarily give you the answers to questions about how to support your claim, but it should clearly indicate what your claims are and, above all, what logical connections exist between your statements.

ARGUMENT ESSENTIALS
Deduction

- Deduction is the process of applying a generalization to a particular instance.
- The simplest deductive argument consists of two premises and a conclusion — a syllogism.
- The conclusions from deduction are certain if both premises are true.

Resources for Teaching

Eleventh Edition

Elements *of* Argument

A TEXT AND READER

Annette T. Rottenberg

Donna Haisty Winchell

RESOURCES FOR TEACHING

ELEMENTS OF ARGUMENT

A Text and Reader

ELEVENTH EDITION

RESODORCES FOR TEACHING

ELEMENTS OF ARGUMENT

A Text and Reader

ELEVENTH EDITION

PREPARED BY

Annette T. Rottenberg

Donna Haisty Winchell

Clemson University

With an essay by

Gail Stygall
University of Washington

BEDFORD/ST. MARTIN'S   BOSTON ◆ NEW YORK

Manufactured in the United States of America.

9 8 7 6 5 4
f e d c b a

For information, write: Bedford/St. Martin's, 75 Arlington Street, Boston, MA 02116
    (617-399-4000)

ISBN 978-1-4576-6259-1

Preface

In these notes we have assembled some of the assignments and classroom activities that have proved successful over the years in illuminating the elements of argument and eliciting thoughtful student response. Every teacher will have a collection of favorite devices, and we claim no superiority for ours. If some of the materials are not suitable for some classes, they may, however, suggest other kinds that are. Together with the writing suggestions in the text, they should provide an ample repertory of things to do for every day of the course. Clearly there will be more material than any single class can profitably use.

Part One, "Understanding Argument," includes an overview of the various approaches to argument—Aristotelian, Rogerian, and Toulmin, as well as treatment of how to read critically, how to examine multimodal arguments, and how to write analytically. Part Two, "Analyzing the Elements," devotes one chapter apiece to the chief elements of argument—claim, support, and warrant. Part Three, "Using the Elements," covers definition, language, and logic.

Part Four, "Researching and Crafting Arguments," treats the writing process itself, analyzing its parts and providing guidelines for organizing, developing, and researching. A portion of Chapter 12 focuses on oral argument and presentation aids. We hope to enable students to become not only more proficient public speakers but also more knowledgeable members of an audience.

Throughout Parts 1 through 4, free online resources extend the book beyond the printed page. Students can examine multimodal arguments such as speeches, blogs, slideshows, and videos; they can get in-depth help with reading, writing, and research tutorials; and they can engage in a wide variety of interactive practice exercises.

The first four parts of the text also include several types of apparatus to help students develop their writing and argumentation skills. Essentials boxes—23 total—briefly summarize and reinforce important argument concepts. One or more Research Skills boxes in each of the first twelve chapters teach valuable research topics. A related practice exercise on each research skill is included at the end of each chapter. "Writer's Guide" boxes give practical advice on how to write effective arguments and response essays; "Strategies" boxes provide more in-depth information on important skills such as prereading and annotating texts.

The remainder of the text is devoted to readings. A new Part Five draws together a collection of five debates, which were previously included as part of the text chapters. Each chapter focuses on a current issue and features two contrasting opinions. Part Six, "Multiple Viewpoints," lends itself to formal and informal classroom debate and longer papers that incorporate research. This section can also be used throughout the course as a reference guide for papers that fulfill different kinds of writing assignments, especially those that call for in-depth analysis of opposing arguments. The most ambitious use of "Multiple Viewpoints" is as a source of information and opinion for the research paper. For shorter papers, students can limit their reading to material in the text. For longer papers, they can conduct research for additional sources. Part Seven, "Classic Arguments," presents a set of time- and class-tested readings.

The linear organization of the course should pose no problems. It is true that from the first assignment students will be writing arguments—before they have completed the study of the elements of argument. This practice, however, is the same as that of any other composition course where the process is one of deepening, widening, and enriching a first draft or a series of undeveloped generalizations. Many teachers of composition believe that students should begin to write whole essays from the beginning of the course. Attention to the components of argument follows when students attempt to make their essays stronger by concentrating on the particular areas that need development and revision.

Gail Stygall's essay at the beginning of this manual provides an overview of some of the special concerns and problems that instructors should anticipate when teaching a course in argument, as well as practical general suggestions that might be useful in dealing with these concerns and problems.

Contents

PART THREE
Using the Elements   29

PART FOUR
Researching and Crafting Arguments   36

PART FIVE
Debating the Issues   45

Strategies for Teaching Argumentation: An Overview

INTRODUCTION

One of the joys we experience in teaching argumentation is seeing our students take a step into the real world of rhetoric and argument. After a semester in the argumentation classroom, students often find they now have a means for articulating the opinions, views, and knowledge that they feel belong in the public discussion. Moreover, the informal logic model, once understood, may be taken into other classrooms as a means for analyzing readings and writing. With the flexibility of *Elements of Argument* and with the dialogue of argument in the classroom, students have access to a practical, everyday logic, so often missing in public discussions of issues. Argument diminishes the instructor's struggle to create a real audience. Students may participate immediately, whether the forum is the classroom, campus wide issues, or national elections, and they can see that their writing can make a difference with a real audience.

STUDENTS' EXPERIENCE WITH ARGUMENT

Although many aspects of a process writing curriculum have been developed in the elementary and secondary schools, we still may not take it for granted that our students have had prior practice in argument. A related problem is that students doubt that we really want their opinions; in high school, they probably experienced institutional constraints on their views. Even if they offered their opinions, they may have had those opinions rejected and may now hesitate to trust us. Moreover, prior to college their basic belief systems have probably gone unchallenged. They may offer what appears to them to be the wisdom of a community, but they have not yet had to maintain that wisdom in the face of a decidedly different community, such as the college classroom.

SETTING THE TONE FOR THE CLASSROOM

Because students have often had so little practice in oral or written argument, we must try to maintain a classroom in which open discussion and debate are the standard procedure. Many instructors use debate as a model to set the necessary atmosphere. Instructors may record sessions of *Face the Nation, Meet the Press, The McLaughlin Group,* or *Crossfire* for classroom discussion. Other instructors arrange for their classes to hear a full intercollegiate debate.

Setting the tone, however, goes beyond having students observe impersonal or distanced third-person demonstrations of debate and argumentation. Students need to hear one another assert and defend arguments, and they must have the opportunity to respond to one another face-to-face. Scheduling discussion time is a useful strategy, following selected reading assignments. Students may be asked to come to class with brief responses to a particular essay, responses that include the students' own arguments about the topic at issue. Arranging for these reaction discussions places tolerance at a premium in the argumentative writing classroom, and the instructor often becomes the immediate arbiter of conflicting views and opinions. You should expect students to ask for your opinion on the various topics, as they invariably will; prepare your own reactions and responses accordingly.

1

MAINTAINING THE FORUM: DEBATES ON PAPER

Many instructors continue the open forum by shifting their focus to actual writing assignments, arranging assignments so that one student is graded for responding directly to another student's paper. Argument becomes quite real when a student sees that his or her reasoning does not convince a classmate. Even a skilled writer learns from this assignment that a good argument acknowledges alternative views. Students who quote out of context, don't order their arguments well, or use logical fallacies without understanding what they represent often see during the refutation process what effect these practices have on the audience. Some instructors extend the dialogue even further by requiring a rebuttal paper in response to the refutation paper. For instructors who have been using a process approach to writing, this paper exchange is a means of helping students recognize the value of audience. In a direct exchange of papers, students cannot help being reminded of the dialogic nature of argumentation.

USING PEER RESPONSES

Process approaches can be further adapted for the argumentation classroom through the use of the audience questionnaire, as suggested in Chapter 1 of this manual. Instead of distributing generic peer-response forms, instructors may ask students to evaluate one another's work in terms of the results of class opinions, requiring students to write briefly about which segments of the class a particular essay will convince, harden, or fail to move. These same peer responders can explore in writing why they think the paper will succeed or fail by pointing to specific parts of the argument and evaluating the strategies informing its delivery. Peer responders may also list and develop counterarguments and offer counterevidence, keeping the focus on the dialogue between writer and reader.

Peer-response exercises can also be used effectively with Part One of *Elements of Argument*. In conjunction with specific chapters, instructors can design peer-response forms for assigned student essays that direct the student responders to the important aspects of argument covered in those chapters. Instructors need to know that students who are inexperienced at focused response may need support in the form of a guided response sheet. Early in the semester, an instructor might ask both the student writer and the peer responder to answer the following questions about the student's essay:

- What is the claim being made here? Write several sentences explaining your answer. You may want to quote from the text of the essay.
- Is this an argument? Use evidence from Chapter 1 of your text to support your answer.
- What type of claim is being made? Explain your answer based on what is said about claims in Chapter 5.
- As writer, describe the purpose or the effect you believe your claim will have on the reader.
- As reader, describe the actual effect of the claim. Do you agree? Did you agree before you started reading? Did your opinion change? Why, or why not?
- Describe the representative person who you believe would be convinced by this essay. Include several characteristics such as age, sex, education, and family background.

Later in the semester, instructors can include further questions that ask students to evaluate the writer's use of definitions or to provide counterdefinitions in response to inadequately developed definitions. Chapter 6 on support and Chapter 7 on warrants also provide opportunities for students to integrate the material of the text with what they are attempting in their own writing.

PROVIDING BACKGROUND INFORMATION TO AID CRITICAL READING

Although peer-response exercises, discussion, and debate can promote critical reading, instructors should expect some students to lack knowledge about the issues presented in the readings in the text. Instructors should anticipate that some or all of the students will know little about the issues involved. This cannot be attributed, in our view, to cultural "illiteracy," but rather to reasons of age or development. An issue may simply be one that we do not seek out until it affects us. That is not to say, however, that in an argumentation class we exempt our students from that issue because of their lack of experience. Instead, we simply need to be prepared to support their reading. For example, students may need contextual information to understand how what we eat affects the environment.

If you have chosen to make "Multiple Viewpoints" the core of your course, you may find it useful before you begin assigning the sections to survey your students on the knowledge they have about the particular issue. Often gaps in knowledge revealed by the survey can be filled with very little discussion. But without the knowledge necessary to evaluate fully the arguments in question, students can have more difficulty than is necessary in discerning even the structure or main points of the essays.

TEACHING WARRANTS AND ASSUMPTIONS

At least partly because our students have had so little practice in argument, they may have problems understanding what we mean by warrants and assumptions. Conflating the terms *warrant* and *assumption* for the purposes of an introductory class, you may want to illustrate the terms by beginning with the exercise that opens Chapter 7. A further step in that exercise would be to ask students to rank survivors in order of their correspondence with students' value systems. Invariably, students are unable to reach a consensus, revealing underlying assumptions that they hold about human behavior.

Instructors can also begin teaching warrants by asking students to complete statements beginning with the following leads: *All lawyers*...; *All English teachers*...; *All students*.... Such statements allow students to begin to see the kinds of assumptions they use implicitly every day. What they say in a discussion about what all lawyers do often reveals what they believe about the criminal justice system or about the civil recovery system. Their beliefs about English teachers are interesting and sometimes disheartening. Students report that they speak more carefully in front of an off-duty English teacher, reveal less about whether they read "popular" fiction, think we value grammar above everything, or believe we are the classic ivory tower type of teacher. Inevitably, students begin to recognize warrants and assumptions. Students realize that they have operating warrants about English teachers: that English teachers are always, and on every occasion, English teachers; that English teachers read only canonical literature; that grammar is all that counts in an English class; and that English classes have little to do with real life.

These discussions, however time-consuming, are a necessary part of introducing warrants to students. While the terminology may be foreign to students, the process of using warrants is not, and with very little practice students can learn the appropriate questions to ask themselves as they try to discern warrants in their own work and the work of others.

Students can also practice adding a series of *because* clauses to the main points of their papers as a way of clarifying their assumptions. For example, a student writing a paper about how television viewing negatively affects children cited passivity, exposure to violence, and fear as her main points. When in an in-class exercise she was asked to identify her warrants with a *because* clause for each, she wrote, "because interaction, not passivity, is a better learning experience" in response to her first point, and "because violence and fear are poor standards for society" to the second and third. Not only did the student gain valuable experience in identifying the warrants behind her claims, she also learned a powerful revision strategy. As her peers pointed out to her, she had grouped two of the points together, with the third being entirely separate. In revising her paper, she concentrated on the last two points, eliminated the first, and turned in a more coherent paper, which included a now-explicit discussion of her warrant.

DIFFERENT WORDINGS OF CLAIMS AND WARRANTS

Students will often propose several versions of claim and warrant for the same essay. Often one group of students will select as claim a very narrow assertion, while another group will select a generalization, perhaps an inference from the text. Likewise, students will show variation in their wording of warrants. As long as students do not go beyond what claims and warrants a particular author might make, some variation in wording not only is acceptable, but also is helpful to students working in an argumentative setting. They will learn that the rhetorical effect of different wording is intrinsic to assessing and addressing their audience.

TEACHING FALLACIES: THE EDITORIAL JOURNAL

Another tool for generating material for argument is the editorial journal. Instructors can require students to maintain a weekly folder containing several examples of what they think are successful and unsuccessful editorials and letters from local or campus newspapers and to record their responses to those editorials and letters in an editorial journal. Students assigned this exercise soon develop a standard against which they judge effective and ineffective arguments. It is then often useful to have students use their developing standard in combination with their knowledge of logical fallacies from Chapter 10. Students can submit for group discussion the most effective and least effective examples they have culled from editorial pages. Asking students to respond to the most troubling and fallacious letters and editorials often bridges the gap between classroom writing and the "real world" of discourse. Many students take the additional step of sending their responses to the local or campus newspaper and sometimes experience the delight of seeing their names in print in those pages.

A variation on this same exercise is an in-class letter-writing task in which students select the most troubling problem on campus and attempt to persuade the appropriate administrator to respond. The instructor may ask different groups to vary their approaches by assigning, for example, one group to argue a claim of fact, another a claim of value. Groups may assess the effectiveness of the arguments of other groups, with the entire class selecting the best letter for the particular audience.

DISTINGUISHING BETWEEN INDUCTION AND DEDUCTION: RESEARCH ASSIGNMENTS

One other aspect of teaching an informal logic model in the writing classroom bears discussion. Many traditional argumentative writing courses have assigned induction and deduction separately. In teaching with an informal Toulmin model, the differences between the traditional and informal approaches often become blurred. Students who have become adept in using the informal model complain vigorously that there is no such thing as a truly inductive paper. Arguing that the Toulmin model requires that warrants be acknowledged, whether the paper is inductive or deductive, students assert that the differences are minimal. For the standard student paper, in which a thesis appears early in the essay, students are indeed correct, and the distinction is difficult to make. A so-called inductive paper with a thesis indicates that the writer has already drawn a conclusion, thus making it less than purely inductive in nature.

If the course you are teaching requires separate inductive and deductive papers, consider making the distinction on the basis of the style of research supporting the paper. For example, assign one essay that focuses on an inductive style of research as a primary research project. These projects, chosen in collaborative groups, may include student-designed surveys of their classmates; observations of behavior on campus, in parking lots, and in shopping malls; and interviews. Essays can be developed from student observations of people's behavior while standing in line, from student interviews with hard-core video game players, and from student surveys addressing the necessity of improving the food available in campus vending machines. Because inferences and the "inductive leap" are highlighted with this approach, students can more easily see the differences between induction and deduction. For a deductive paper, on the other hand, you can stress a secondary research approach, having students begin from basic assumptions about a subject and then examine a particular instance.

Many philosophers and historians of science have made the same point: that observations are always guided by a particular framework. The informal Toulmin model makes this point quite clear to students. What counts as a fact or as an observation is already warranted before the search for facts and observations begins.

We hope our suggestions will be useful for planning a forum on issues in your writing classroom. It is probable that many of your students will have only the composition classroom in which to engage in written debates on public policy issues. Becoming engaged in the consideration, analysis, and argument of various positions, students truly prepare to take their place in civic discussions. As instructors of written argument, we hold a unique position by virtue of our providing the forum in which this process takes place. Few students leave the argumentation classroom without having experienced a change of some kind, and few teachers can resist that kind of opportunity. By providing a model of analysis of argument useful both inside and outside the classroom and by providing the forum for an exchange of views, we can emphasize the uses of writing in unexpectedly productive ways.

— Gail Stygall
University of Washington

PART ONE

UNDERSTANDING ARGUMENT

CHAPTER 1

Approaches to Argument
(text pages 3–33)

Although the Toulmin model gives structure to the text, this chapter introduces it alongside Aristotelian and Rogerian argument, two other approaches used in teaching argumentation courses. Doing so places the Toulmin model in historical context, but more importantly reveals some of the complexity of analyzing and producing argumentative discourse. A basic overview here allows us to return to Aristotle's and Carl Rogers's theories from time to time later in the text.

The chapter provides one essay as an example in introducing each rhetorical approach. Students should realize, however, that any of the three methods could be applied to any of the examples. Returning to Richard J. Davis's essay to analyze it from the perspective of Rogerian argument or the Toulmin model, for example, could work well as a class discussion to help students become more familiar with the different theories and with their terminology.

The research activities in the first twelve chapters are linked to the content of the chapters in which they appear; they also help the students review or learn skills they will need in writing a research paper. In this first chapter, for instance, students review how to use databases.

After discussion of the chapter, assign a brief search through newspapers and magazines (beginning perhaps with the school newspaper) for arguments about current affairs. You may also wish to consult our blog, "Argument in the Headlines," which features regularly updated posts that frame issues in the news using argument concepts. You can find the blog at macmillanhighered.com/bits /argument. Working with current events enables students to arrive at several important conclusions.

1. The most obvious one is that arguments of the kind they will be reading and writing in class are to be found everywhere and that they are the foundation of the democratic process. Students will also discover that a good deal of the factual reporting about political events is reporting of controversies or arguments.

2. Without much familiarity with formal arguments, students may at first regard them all as vehicles of reasoned analysis. As they reflect on their examples, they will recognize that passion and ideology are formidable— sometimes the only—components of many arguments.

3. Many, perhaps most, freshman students believe that hard-core problems in our society remain unsolved because at best we lack the will to solve them, or at worst evil people conspire to frustrate attempts at solution.

6

One other explanation of our failures may not readily occur to them: lack of knowledge. We may ask: What kind of knowledge — that is, data and interpretation of data — do we need in order to solve apparently intractable problems of poverty, war, prejudice, crime, and mental illness? When we introduce this question, we may find that some students think that these problems are new and peculiar to American society. Much of the information needed will turn out to be psychological, the kind most difficult to discover or verify. You can use this discussion to encourage a reflective caution when evaluating and advocating solutions.

4. Not all arguments have two equally valid sides. Some have multiple sides. Others may be said to have only one morally acceptable side. Ask students to suggest subjects that exemplify these conclusions.

Students may be asked to keep informal journals that list controversial subjects appearing online, in newspapers and magazines, on TV and radio, on the campus, and in town. For each subject they may set down some of the important facts, values, and general principles underlying the claims. The journal entries can then serve as a source of subjects for assignments or discussion in class and in conferences with the instructor. A worthwhile dividend of such journal keeping is an increase in the practice of reading and listening, of becoming familiar with the sources and subjects of public controversies.

We suggest leaving discussion and analysis of the three major elements of argument — claim, support, and warrant — to the subsequent chapters. At this point we would require only that students show understanding of the definitions.

In speech classes, students sometimes analyze their audience, i.e., their classmates, before making a proposal that might be unpopular. They distribute questionnaires that they themselves have constructed in an effort to discover the social and political preferences of their classmates. The results of the questionnaire help them to choose an argumentative strategy that will persuade this audience to look more favorably on the proposition being argued.

An application of this procedure for a writing class might work as follows: At the beginning of the semester, a small group of students, perhaps four or five, makes up an informal questionnaire that is filled out by the members of the class. The results of the questionnaire are tabulated and distributed to the class. Later in the semester, for selected papers (for example, arguments of policy) the writers are encouraged to examine the results and add a note describing how and why they have adapted their arguments to the values of this particular audience.

CHAPTER 2
Examining Written Arguments
(text pages 34–60)

This chapter emphasizes that critical reading is essential to the mastery of the elements of argument. Most of us are familiar with the problems encountered by students in reading and responding to a difficult text. The problems are multiple: unfamiliarity with the subject, limited vocabulary, weak sense of metaphor, inability to recognize clues of organization and development. Many of these problems are clearly the result of too little practice — not enough careful attention to hard texts, not enough instruction in the mechanics of reading such material. It's also possible, as Sven Birkerts suggests in *The Gutenberg Elegies* (Faber and Faber 1994), that reading is becoming more tedious as electronic communication effects a radical change in consciousness and literacy. But so far, there is no real substitute for reading in the print media. (Even Bill Gates and Nicholas Negroponte write books to tell us about computers.) Diagnosing the reading difficulties at the beginning of the course—through short quizzes and discussions—can tell us where to offer help.

Several online resources are available to help students improve their critical reading skills. The Web content for *Elements of Argument* includes a tutorial on Active Reading Strategies as well as three LearningCurve exercises on Critical Reading, Topic Sentences and Supporting Details, and Topics and Main Ideas.

Elsewhere in this manual we have suggested calling attention to the vocabulary of an assigned reading *before* students read it. Pointing out the clues that reveal the organization and development of a long, complex argument, again before students read the whole piece, can help them read it more effectively and with greater confidence. Most students find outlining tiresome and unenlightening, partly because they do not do it well, partly because many long articles defy conventional outlining. But early in the course, outlining one or two pieces on the board as students follow the text of an assigned essay can give a sense of what organization means and how it controls the development of the argument. Whether or not they outline their assignments, almost all students will find it useful to write a brief summary of an argument as a means of review.

The primary goals of critical reading, of course, are, first, understanding the argument and, then, determining how effectively the arguer supported his or her claim. But there are additional benefits to be derived from careful reading, benefits that can directly affect the student's writing. Critical reading, which often means over-reading, invites an appreciation of language. Winston Churchill spoke of the advantages of having been a relatively slow learner who had to repeat his lessons: "I got into my bones the essential structure of the ordinary British sentence—which is a noble thing."

This is where annotation pays off for the prospective writer. Students who must respond physically as well as mentally, by writing in the margins, should become more careful readers—more sensitive to diction and to the rhythms of a variety of styles and modes of organization that can be adapted for their own papers.

If you have asked students to write marginal notes while doing a critical reading of a piece, you may want to ask them to go back to the same piece and annotate it from the perspective of a writer. (It may help if they do so in a different colored ink to see the difference.) This time they will be noticing the writer's techniques more than the ideas, although the two necessarily overlap.

Many school libraries have collections of recorded speeches and debates. Tapes, CDs, or DVDs allow replay of portions for class analysis. Just as students gloss a written text, they can annotate an oral presentation, expressing approval or disapproval, asking questions when they hear a doubtful statement. The instructor can model critical listening by stopping the recording at relevant intervals and offering a running commentary. She explains the reasons for her judgments and encourages additional response from the class. Students can listen for examples of logical argument and persuasive language. They can also learn to recognize clichés, slogans, and other departures from clear thinking (see Chapter 10). With relatively little practice, students can become adept at the art of listening.

Deborah Tannen, professor of linguistics at Georgetown University, has written several books that interpret the conversational styles of different cultures as well as of men versus women, among them *You Just Don't Understand: Women and Men in Conversation* (Ballantine 1991) and *The Argument Culture: Moving from Debate to Dialogue* (Random House 1998). Tannen's discussions emphasize the failure to listen attentively and with a will to understand as a major impediment to fruitful communication.

Careful listening plays a significant role in jury trials and formal investigations. In some celebrated cases, jurors seemed to have listened selectively. Students may be surprised to learn that jurors are not permitted to take notes during a trial. A lawyer who has proposed changes in the jury system says, "Jurors often ignore the instructions or misapply them." We can ask students to be alert to televised trials or congressional committee hearings as sources of exercises in careful listening. Courtrooms, as Toulmin observed, are model venues of argumentation.

In learning to listen with attention to the speech of others, students may also improve their ability to hear their own language in writing. Because many students are able to hear errors in grammar and usage that escape the eye, we often ask them to read their papers aloud before submitting them.

CHAPTER 3
Examining Multimodal Arguments
(text pages 61–109)

If the amount of reading many of us do has declined, the amount of listening has greatly increased. But instruction in listening has not kept pace. Jay Heinrichs, author of "How Harvard Destroyed Rhetoric" (*Harvard Magazine*, July–August 1995), deplores the scarcity of serious academic interest in public speech. Rhetoric at Harvard was once, of course, the study of persuasive oratory. And rhetorical theory, whether or not we use the vocabulary of Aristotle or the Sophists, still animates any study of formal argument. Today the proliferation of "undisciplined argument" has convinced Heinrichs that the study of public speech should be restored. "Too few citizens," he says, "know how to listen critically." Chapter 3 provides guidance on critical approaches to audiovisual media such as broadcast news, radio shows, and multimodal Web sites.

This chapter also examines the visual arguments in commercial advertisements, cartoons, and photographs. Students are often unaware of the messages that even the simplest landscape or interior is capable of delivering — claims of fact, value, and policy. The great Hungarian photographer André Kertesz, whose reception in New York was less than friendly, was told, "Your pictures talk too much." And, in fact, his photographs of people reading (*On Reading*, Penguin 1982) are exquisite examples of value claims.

The pictures on TV and in newspapers and magazines that document the damage wrought by terrorist attacks on September 11, 2001, are powerful arguments that seem to need no verbal text. Several publications, including *Newsweek: America Under Attack* (Extra Edition 2001), *New York Times Magazine* (23 Sept. 2001), and *The Day That Changed America* (American Media, Inc.) offered searing photographs of destruction and suffering. See also "The Expression of Grief and the Power of Art" (*New York Times* 13 Sept. 2001: F1), which is a collection of comments on the subject by art, movie, television, and theatre critics.

Students in the class who know something about photography can be asked to explain the way in which composition, color, and other attributes work to convey a point of view. Or a member of the school art department can be invited to speak on the subject of visual argumentation in ads and photojournalism. Explaining the implicit argument in an ad that relies largely on visual imagery is an obvious subject for oral presentation in which visual aids can be used to good effect.

Some students may be interested in examining the implied claims in movie posters, such as those at movie theaters. Several critics have suggested interpretations that are not so obvious to the untrained eye. They are entertainingly summarized in *Civilization* (Apr./May 1999: 35+).

Another accessible subject is fashion advertising, which has come under fire in recent years. Some of the most provocative ads, by companies such as Abercrombie & Fitch and Victoria's Secret, are directed at young people of college age who will probably recognize the implied claims.

For this chapter, two online tutorials provide general help for students working with visuals: "Reading Visuals: Purpose" and "Reading Visuals: Audience." In addition, several online e-readings illustrate concepts and build skills that cannot be demonstrated on the printed page.

CHAPTER 4

Responding to Arguments
(text pages 110–146)

While students are still working through the chapters that introduce the elements of argument, they can practice applying those terms to the arguments of others. The claim for an essay about an argument can be either a claim of fact or a claim of value. It would be rare for an analysis of an argument to support a claim of policy. After reading an essay like Michael Isikoff's "The Snitch in Your Pocket," students can practice writing claims of fact and claims of value about the essay, understanding that a claim of fact objectively analyzes one or more elements of the essay while a claim of value evaluates one or more element. One would explain the types of support used in the essay, for example, while the other would evaluate the effectiveness of the support.

This chapter is a good place to introduce the use of paraphrase, summary, and direct quotation as a means of supporting a thesis. Later, in writing a research paper, your students will most likely all be drawing on different sources—but for now, they can write about a limited number of sources, and the instructor can easily check their use of sources while they are all drawing on the same ones. The ability to work source material into one's own text is a learned skill and one that many students need to practice in order to master. In teaching the use of sources the instructor can also stress the importance of identifying the author of the source and some ways of expressing that author's authority on the subject. Students tend to include the author's name and a page number in parentheses and feel that is adequate documentation. Technically, it may be, but most often much of the impact of quoted or paraphrased material depends on who wrote it. While writing about the arguments of others, students can practice identifying the authors of the quoted or paraphrased material and using their authority as a means of strengthening an argument. Students can also make use of an online tutorial on documenting sources: "Do I Need to Cite That?"

A good beginning exercise on the use of sources is to ask students to summarize an essay and, in doing so, to correctly incorporate at least one direct quotation. The first sentence can identify the author and his or her claim to authority.

This is also a good place to bring in the results of a survey, such as the brief ones reported frequently in magazines such as *Time* and *Newsweek*. Students can be asked to draw a conclusion from the data in the survey and then to write a paragraph supporting that conclusion and drawing on the survey for support.

Alan Noble's "Valedictorian Prays but Should Christians Rejoice?" (Chapter 3) is a good one to ask students to evaluate because there is likely to be a good bit of disagreement. Whether students agree with Noble's argument or not, they have to understand his argument well enough to either support or attack it, and they must be able to argue why they evaluate it in the way that they do.

PART TWO

ANALYZING THE ELEMENTS

CHAPTER 5

Claims: Making a Statement

(text pages 149–173)

CLAIMS OF FACT

1. Students have little difficulty understanding claims of fact. But before giving an assignment, you may want to offer a dozen or more examples of such claims to make clear what kinds of arguments they produce. These are in addition to examples in the book.

2. If students have already elected a major or are about to do so, they can find subjects in their areas of specialization. At this point research need not be emphasized. Students are often able to find sufficient factual data in their memories or their notes. (Wherever possible, they should, of course, give credit to their sources, even to a lecturer in an academic course.)

    The reports they may be asked to make on the job are often claims of fact, in which they will have to provide proof that a condition exists or that something has been found to be true as a result of research. The claims, or thesis statements of their essays, correspond to the conclusions of their reports, which, like the claims, may appear first. *Example* (in an article about food colorants): "The development of organic chemistry produced a series of compounds that are well suited to coloring food. Today most of the food colorants are chemicals produced by synthesis from simple basic materials" (*A Progress Report*, Massachusetts Agricultural Station, July–Aug. 1974).

    Such straightforward factual reports are not likely to be models of creativity, but they emphasize other important qualities of good writing: adequate support; a direct, unadorned style; and clear transitions between ideas. They offer practice in the kind of clear exposition that all writers are well advised to master before they go further.

3. More challenging are factual claims that are clearly controversial. Some will require only reflection on personal observation as support; others will need objective data. *Examples:* "The students on this campus are increasingly conservative." "Children are now judged to be reliable witnesses in child-abuse cases." "Attractive people are regarded by others as more intelligent and sensitive than unattractive people."

    Encourage students to stick to the facts and avoid direct expression of value judgments (although, of course, these may be implicit).

4. Another source of assignments may be Part Five's debates and Part Six's "Multiple Viewpoints." Ask students to choose one of the subjects and, after reading all or most of the selections, derive a limited factual claim. *Example:* "Human stem cells are readily available and easily harvested."

   The supporting materials will not be original. This assignment tests the writer's ability to extract relevant data in support of a thesis, express the facts in his or her own language, and organize them logically.

5. In our culture ads are the most prominent examples of abbreviated arguments that often conceal as much as they reveal, and students enjoy uncovering the missing elements. One caution: Although students may have studied ads in high school and can analyze them with some sophistication, they are disposed to treat all advertisement as untruthful. Ads that conceal or distort are usually the most interesting to examine, but try to get students to make careful distinctions between the ads that support their claims, or seem to, and those that don't.

6. Inevitably, controversial claims will move student writers to ascribe causes.

   A number of tragic school shootings have occurred in recent years, both in the United States — Arkansas, Kentucky, Colorado, Virginia, and Connecticut — and abroad, in Scotland and Canada. They occasioned an outpouring of analyses, impassioned attempts to discover the *causes* of such aberrant behavior in children.

   Students probably have discussed these events in their high school classes. They have also expressed their opinions about the causes to newspaper and television viewers. The social and psychological conditions that may have contributed to these tragedies are subjects for written assignments. So are suggested solutions as claims of policy.

7. Students must be cautioned to avoid assuming that explanations imply justification. For example, according to psychology professor Erwin Staub, the atrocities that occurred in Kosovo province can be explained: "[E]ven violent leaders often express and even share needs of their people. The needs of the Serbs for a feeling of security and for identity as a people are intense." But, he goes on to say, although these needs help to explain Serb behavior, "they cannot justify it."[1]

CLAIMS OF VALUE

1. As they begin to write, students will discover that the line between claims of fact and claims of value is often blurred, but in real-life arguments outside the classroom, these distinctions are not crucial. We make them in the classroom largely because they allow us to examine the elements more closely.

2. Claims of value are more demanding than claims of fact. Facts remain important, but now students must express an attitude toward them. Despite the fact that values are a part of almost every argument — even in claims of fact they may be implicit in the choices of subjects and data — students are sometimes unclear about how to uncover and express them. These approaches may be helpful:

   a. *Ask personal questions.* What do you want out of life? Do you dislike anything about yourself? Do you have religious beliefs? If so, how do they

[1]*The Campus Chronicle* [University of Massachusetts, Amherst] 23 Apr. 1999: 1.

influence your behavior? What are the good things about your family? What are the most valuable things you own? What kind of country do you want the United States to be? And so on. (Of course, for purposes of the exercise the answers need not be true, and it should be clear to students that they are under no obligation to bare their souls. On the other hand, most students, like the rest of us, enjoy talking about themselves.)

The answers that emerge can be written on the board, listed as positive and negative values. You will probably have to change the language, finding more precise terms than the ones that the students offer. This exercise defines values and value systems in a readily understandable way. Values as a form of support will be discussed more fully in Chapter 6, but this discussion should assist students to find the values that can be defended in their value claims.

b. *Analyze one or two essays in the text to discover the values of the author.* What values seem to underlie, for example, Deborah Nucatola's "Morning-After Pill a Boon for Women"?

Students can be asked to answer such questions in short, in-class assignments—fifteen minutes—for which they must produce a well-organized paragraph: clear topic sentence and sufficient supporting material. Because they stress economy and directness, such assignments are useful for teaching some elements of style.

3. As with claims of fact, students can draw on campus experience for subjects that lend themselves to class discussion, outlining, and reinforcing the ways in which claims of value differ from claims of fact. *Examples:* "Student evaluations of teachers are worthless." "Funds for Gay Awareness Week are unjustified."

4. In this unit, too, you might want to point out that claims of value are often required on the job in the form of personnel reports or reports that evaluate marketing strategies and campaigns. If students are interested, topics for such papers can be obtained from books on technical writing or from the business departments of the school.

5. A ready-to-use anthology of material for claims of value appears in a special supplement of the *Wall Street Journal* (5 Mar. 1998), called "Divining the American Character." It includes more than a dozen articles on how "the bedrock morals co-exist uneasily with a desire 'to live and let live.'" An interesting exercise would be to compare the values described in the article and current American values, almost twenty years later.

CLAIMS OF POLICY

1. Since claims of policy assert that something should or should not be done, they presuppose the existence of a problem needing a solution. Both facts and values are indispensable to defense of a policy claim because in many arguments students will first have to establish that a problem exists, then underscore how the desired values will be served by adoption of the proposed solution.

2. As an introduction to this unit, short problems, either real or hypothetical, can test the ability of students to find solutions—that is, to defend claims of policy. The facts are clearly laid out in the summary of the problem. In order to justify the solution, students will need to expose the values that underlie their claims. *Example of a real problem:*

The Plagiarism Problem

John Jones, a senior at U M, was enrolled in a writing course, *Writing about Film*. A few weeks before the end of the semester he suffered a crisis in his love life. The woman who had been his inseparable companion suddenly informed him that she was no longer interested in continuing their friendship. John lost control of himself for a few weeks; he stayed in his room brooding, drank heavily every night, and stopped going to classes. Three days before the end of the semester, he found out that in order to pass the film course and then to graduate, he had to fulfill a final assignment—attend a film and write a review of it. Frantic, John went to the library, copied out a review of a film by a professional critic, and submitted it to the instructor. The instructor recognized the plagiarism and failed John for the course. The failure meant that John could not graduate despite the fact that he had a job waiting for him in Seattle. He argued with the instructor to no avail. The instructor said that he had made it very clear from the beginning of the semester that any plagiarism would result in a failure for the course. John appealed to the provost, who had the authority to grant a Pass for the course.

Question: Should the provost rule that John need not do anything more to fulfill the writing course and allow him to graduate?

3. We have called attention to this problem in the text, but perhaps it bears repeating. In defending claims of policy, students must guard against offering solutions for enormous problems that have defied solution for decades or even centuries. Their ambitions may be laudable, but nevertheless they should be urged to confine themselves to solutions that can be defended in 750 words.

4. "Multiple Viewpoints" is a collection of problems in search of solutions. Assign readings in any of the subjects and ask students to propose solutions based on their evaluations of the arguments.

In defending their claims of policy students should try to use the pattern of organization we call *defending the stock issues*—need, plan, and advantage (see Chapter 11, "Planning and Research"). This pattern permits them to be exhaustive without becoming confused by a multitude of details and a variety of possible approaches.

5. Policy claims are, of course, inherent in any business or professional activity. Ask students who have job experience to write out short summaries of specific problems they remember having encountered on the job, either their own or someone else's. The problems should be substantive, and the facts should be clearly stated. Then ask other students to suggest solutions. Students may also ask for examples of problems from the business departments of the school.

These short writing exercises emphasize clarity, accuracy, and a sensitivity to the audience—the employer, supervisor, or other employees—who will act on the decision.

If the solutions differ, students may discuss the differences and try to uncover the reasons for them. Do the differences derive from lack of sufficient data or from conflicting values? Can the differences be reconciled?

6. The Netherlands has long tolerated euthanasia, but not many people are aware that only in 2001 did the practice become legal. The legalization aroused intense condemnation in other countries but especially in Germany. Students working toward an evaluation of euthanasia should inform themselves about its use by the Nazis, who put to death about 100,000 "men, women, and children who were physically and mentally handicapped. The aim was to improve

what they called the Aryan race by eradicating those who doctors decided had congenital defects." ("Horror Expressed in Germany over Dutch Euthanasia," *New York Times* 11 Apr. 2001: A15.)

Students may also be interested to know that under Dutch law, when their children reach the ages of sixteen and seventeen, "parents must be informed but no longer have the right to decide." Do students think that doctors and others should be able to assist teenagers to commit suicide? If not, why not? If yes, under what circumstances?

7. Should mentally unstable people be allowed to own guns?

Bibliography

Humphry, Derek. *Let Me Die before I Wake.* Eugene, OR: Hemlock Soc., 1991.

McHugh, Paul R. "Dying Made Easy." *Commentary* Feb. 1999: 13–17.

Miniter, Richard. "The Dutch Way of Death." *Wall Street Journal* 25 Apr. 2001: A20.

CHAPTER 6

Support: Backing Up a Claim

(text pages 174–213)

EVIDENCE

1. Students seem to subscribe to the belief that a knowledge of the facts is sufficient to induce a change in our habits and attitudes, but there is plenty of expert evidence that the plain truth is not enough. Robert Sternberg, a Yale University psychologist, says, "People will go to great lengths to avoid information that contradicts their original stories. There's a lot of research that shows that people seek to confirm what they think, rather than disconfirm what they think" (*Boston Globe*, 21 Aug. 1993: 7).

    An interesting area for research by students is the relationship between facts about food and the choices people make. Several studies over the years suggest that the facts do not cause most people to alter their eating habits. Students can survey classmates to determine if their behavior confirms the results of these studies.

2. Assign reading of the following passage. Ask students to write either a short or a long essay that summarizes some of the inferences we draw from observing what people wear. Since the subject is so large (this excerpt is part of a book about clothing), this exercise gives students practice in narrowing the subject of discussion and choosing a thesis statement or paragraph that can be adequately developed in the number of words assigned.

    > For thousands of years human beings have communicated with one another first in the language of dress. Long before I am near enough to talk to you on the street, in a meeting, or at a party, you announce your sex, age, and class to me through what you are wearing—and possibly give me important information (or disinformation) as to your occupation, origin, personality, opinions, tastes, sexual desires, and current mood. I may not be able to put what I observe into words, but I register the information unconsciously, and you simultaneously do the same for me.

> By the time we meet and converse we have already spoken to each other in an older and more universal tongue.

> —Alison Lurie
> *The Language of Clothes*
> (Random House 1981)

3. On September 15, 1995, the *New York Times* published a report giving several different versions of an alleged crime: the shooting of a black police officer by a white police officer (p. B1). The white officer argued that he had mistaken the victim for a criminal. The *Times* summarized the disputed accounts in a chart labeled "Sorting It Out." The chart included three different views of the shooting by witnesses and participants and three different opinions of the wound by medical examiners.

   A written assignment on this story calls for a clear thesis statement or paragraph, extraction of the most important data, and arrangement of materials in an orderly and emphatic way. Above all, it calls for an acknowledgment of the distinctions between facts and inferences in the testimony reported in the article and in the students' interpretations of the testimony. Not least, the students find this assignment interesting and provocative.

4. Ask students to look up information by advocates on both sides of the controversies surrounding one of the popular natural mysteries: the Loch Ness monster, the Bermuda Triangle, Findhorn, Bigfoot, or Sasquatch, etc. Then assign a paper, short or long, that reviews the data on both sides and tries to come to a conclusion regarding the validity of the respective claims. Have students justify their conclusions by defending the evidence. If students find that they cannot make up their minds, this is also a conclusion, but they should be prepared to say why the evidence on both sides proved equally strong or equally weak.

5. From the first paper students have been required to use evidence. Having now read the more elaborate explanations of both factual and opinion evidence in Chapter 6, students can return to their claims of fact, value, and policy and reevaluate the facts and opinions in their essays. Would more data strengthen their claim? If so, what kind? Where can it be found? Would additional expert opinion make their arguments more convincing? If so, whose opinions? Where can they be found?

   If the students show some interest in revising their papers to include more data, encourage them to do so.

6. A popular exercise calls on students to look up the *New York Times* edition that appeared on their birthdays and write a paper that emphasizes straightforward presentation of data to support their claims. Students must find a thesis around which the information can be organized—about the kinds of films being shown, the nature of women's fashion, advertisements for jobs, scientific discoveries of the day, crimes, etc.

7. Advertisements again. This time students choose ads that offer information about the products. They then evaluate the data. In some cases, of course, they will be unequipped to decide whether the data are accurate or sufficient, but if the ads are directed to a lay audience, readers have a right to ask questions about the sufficiency, relevance, and timeliness of the data. In other words, if readers think that evidence for the virtues of the product is inadequate, what else would they want to know?

8. Students sometimes approach the subject of information in ads with the preconception that ads do not offer information—only slogans. Students may therefore be asked to contrast two or more ads that offer different amounts

and qualities of information. Is information more important in some kinds of ads than others—for example, in automobile advertisements, which are often dense with facts?

9. If there is time for lengthier papers, ask students to examine the evidence in the following cases (or any others that remain controversial):

   a. Sacco–Vanzetti, 1921
   b. Kidnapping and murder of the Lindbergh baby, 1932
   c. Kidnapping of Patty Hearst, 1974
   d. Bernhard Goetz, 1987
   e. Rodney King, 1991
   f. O. J. Simpson, 1994
   g. Louise Woodward, 1998
   h. Scott Peterson, 2004
   i. Assassination of Benazir Bhutto, 2007

10. In leading students to examine the credentials of experts, ask them to consider the authors throughout the text as "experts." It will be easy enough to identify Siddhartha Mukherjee, an oncologist, as an authority in his field. Even in more problematic disciplines, such as gun control, we recognize the authority of Richard J. Davis, for example, who, as an attorney and former Assistant Treasury Secretary for Enforcement and Operations, has witnessed decades of failed attempts at creating a federal database of firearms transactions.

    But what are we to say of writers who reflect on their personal experience or expound their philosophies? Why do we think Elisha Dov Hack's views are worth reading? After all, he is no more an "expert" on sexual mores than many of his readers. It might come as a small revelation to students, and pertinent to their participation in a writing course, to recognize that the credibility of Hack and other nonprofessional "experts" is based largely on their excellence as writers. They can discover interesting propositions, and organize, develop, and express them in spirited and highly readable prose. They are intelligent, of course, but also curious about most subjects and well informed about many.

11. *The Science of Conjecture* by James Franklin (Johns Hopkins UP 2001) "provides a history of the rational techniques that mankind has developed to acquire knowledge when certainty is not available—which is most of the time."

12. Students usually need practice in reporting statistics—extracting them from news stories and arranging them in interesting and readable form. Students can research the following subjects and report the information as data that might support a claim. They should, of course, limit the time period for the data. Have them submit their prose summaries to their classmates. Are the data clear and accessible to these readers?

   a. World population growth
   b. Teenage pregnancies
   c. Women in the labor market
   d. Growth of ethnic populations in the United States
   e. American marriage patterns
   f. Dimensions of poverty
   g. Voting patterns in the 2008 elections

13. The three books and one article mentioned below are entertaining and informative references for both teachers and students. They are full of useful

examples that should help students avoid some of the common pitfalls in interpreting and reporting statistical evidence.

Campbell, Stephen K., *Flaws and Fallacies in Statistical Thinking.* Englewood Cliffs, NJ: Prentice-Hall, 1974.

Huff, Darrell. *How to Lie with Statistics.* New York: Norton, 1954.

Paulos, John Allen. *Innumeracy: Mathematical Illiteracy and Its Consequences.* New York: Hill, 1988.

"Fright by the Numbers: Alarming Disease Data Are Frequently Flawed." *Wall Street Journal*, 12 Apr. 1996: B1.

Most of the numbers are extrapolations or estimates—at best. Yet as the media report them, often uncritically and without context, these conjectures assume the mantle of quantifiable fact.

14. Some students may be interested in and sufficiently informed about polling techniques to evaluate some of the famous polling gaffes: the *Literary Digest* poll of 1936 that predicted that Alfred Landon would defeat Franklin D. Roosevelt, the 1948 Gallup poll that predicted Thomas E. Dewey would defeat Harry S. Truman, or the 2000 announcement by most major news networks that Al Gore had defeated George W. Bush.

APPEALS TO NEEDS AND VALUES

1. A lively and immediate source of appeals to needs and values is found in speeches—students may be directed to *Vital Speeches of the Day*, which publishes speeches from a variety of speechmakers.

   Martin Luther King Jr.'s "I Have a Dream" is an outstanding example of spoken discourse that makes a profoundly emotional appeal. Other famous speeches for the purposes of this unit include:

   a. Clarence Darrow's "Address to the Prisoners of Cook County Jail" in 1902
   b. Vice President Richard Nixon's "Checkers" speech in 1952
   c. President John F. Kennedy's Inaugural Address in 1961 (included in Chapter 3 of the text)
   d. Senator Edward Kennedy's TV address explaining to the people of Massachusetts his behavior during and after the accident at Chappaquiddick in 1969

   For example, Darrow's speech is remarkable for the inconsistency of his argument and its numerous fallacies, both of which have been overlooked by textbooks that reprint the address. Edward Kennedy's speech makes a personal appeal, arousing sympathy for his suffering and inducing guilt in the listener for having accused him unjustly.

   Since 1980, the *New York Times* has published "Basic Speeches," delivered by the major candidates in presidential campaigns. These appear in October of the campaign year. All the speeches contain copious and specific references to the values held by the candidates and, presumably, their audiences. The inaugural speeches are also revealing of the attention to values. In his inaugural speech on January 20, 2001, President George W. Bush spoke of America's commitment to "civility, courage, compassion, and character." "Our public interest," he said, depends on "private character, on civic duty and family bonds and basic fairness, on uncounted, unhonored acts of decency. . . ."

2. Advertisements by large corporations (GE, Microsoft, Walmart) appearing frequently in newspapers and magazines comment on political and social issues rather than the merits of the companies' products. As short essays they can be useful for examination of values based on what is perceived to be common consent.

    a. What values do the advertisers assume that we share?
    b. What evidence (examples, facts, statistics) do they offer to convince the reader that their proposals will support our values?
    c. What tones are used in the essays (reasonable, generous, angry, sarcastic, humorous)?

3. Also useful are the ads that promise power, riches, great beauty, etc. Many of the most outrageous ones appear in *The National Enquirer* and similar publications.

    a. Can you infer to what audience they make a strong appeal?
    b. What fears, needs, desires do they appeal to?
    c. What attempts are made to provide credibility?

CHAPTER 7

Warrants: Examining Assumptions

(text pages 214–236)

1. Although the definition of the warrant in Toulmin's *The Uses of Argument* is more complicated than we have made it appear, for the purposes of an undergraduate composition course, those of us who have used the Toulmin model with some success believe that the model works best if we define the warrant as synonymous with assumption, a belief we take for granted, or a general principle underlying other beliefs and attitudes. If students raise questions, we can always widen the definition.

    For obvious reasons the concept of the warrant is more difficult for students to assimilate than that of support, in part because they have seldom been required to make their assumptions explicit. Fortunately for teaching purposes, the examples that we can use are so numerous and so varied that we may call attention to the warrant repeatedly without losing student interest.

2. Advertisements offer a rich and accessible source of material. Students may choose their own ads for analysis and write or speak about them to the class. The exercise should emphasize discussion of a controversial warrant. For an oral presentation, an ad that contains more than a paragraph of text can be duplicated for distribution, and the whole class can participate in a discussion of the validity of the warrant.

3. Subjects for examination of warrants appear almost every day in school newspapers. Sometimes the subjects are about education or other matters relevant to the function and management of the school; sometimes they respond to the world outside. Below are some current issues on college campuses today:

    a. A proposal to introduce a core diversity requirement. (What assumptions about education underlie this proposal?)
    b. A proposal in the South Carolina legislature to cut funding for summer reading programs at some state universities because those schools chose "gay-themed" books to assign.
    c. The idea of a "green" campus.

4. Other sources of analysis of warrants:

    a. *Advice columns in newspapers and magazines.* What assumptions about marriage, sexual problems, child rearing, religion, etc. underlie the advice of the columnists?

    b. *Magazines for teenagers.* Have they changed in the last fifteen or twenty years? On what assumptions about the lives and values of teenagers have the publishers based their changes?

    c. *Arguments in magazines and newspapers that make a controversial or unpopular claim.* The views of Peter Singer, a professor of philosophy at Princeton University, are always good for an argument and the unearthing of warrants held by a very small minority. "The Singer Solution to World Poverty" (*New York Times Magazine* 5 Sept. 1999) explores Singer's claim that Americans are obligated to help support the world's poor: "Whatever money you're spending on luxuries, not necessities, should be given away." If students don't agree, they should try to defend the warrants that underlie their claims. And how do students define luxuries and necessities?

5. Go back to the earlier papers of definition and defense of value and policy claims and examine the warrants, expressed or unexpressed. *Example:* In defending his decision never to marry, a student writes that he values his freedom. What does he assume about marriage, love, individuality, commitment, etc.?

ADDITIONAL TYPES OF WARRANTS

Ehninger and Brockriede (1953) discuss three main categories of warrants: *authoritative, substantive*, and *motivational* warrants. If you would like to introduce your students to an even more complex range of warrants, all of which are subtypes of the three main categories, we have provided discussions of each of seven types below: *authority, generalization, sign, cause and effect, comparison, analogy*, and *values*. A warrants chart on pages 26–27 shows in schematic form the types of warrants, with examples and critical questions that may help students detect them in arguments. If you do choose to teach these additional types of warrants to your students, you may wish to photocopy and distribute the chart.

Authority

Arguments from authority depend on the credibility of their sources, as in this example.

> [Benjamin] Bloom maintains that most children can learn everything that is taught them with complete competence.[1]

Because Benjamin Bloom was a professor of education at the University of Chicago and a widely respected authority on educational psychology, his statement about the educability of children carried considerable weight. Notice that Professor Bloom has qualified his claim by asserting that "most" children, but not all, can learn everything. The reader might also recognize the limits of the warrant—the authority could be mistaken, or there could be disagreement among authorities.

Claim: Most children can learn everything that is taught them with complete competence.

Support: Professor Bloom attests that this is so.

[1]Michael Alper, "All Our Children Can Learn," *University of Chicago Magazine* 1982: 3.

| **Warrant:** | Professor Bloom's testimony is sufficient because he is an accepted authority on educational achievement. |
| **Reservations:** | Unless the data for his studies were inaccurate, unless his criteria for evaluation were flawed, and so on. |

Generalization

Arguments from generalization are based on the belief that a general principle can be derived from a series of examples. But these warrants are credible only if the examples are representative of the whole group being described and not too many contradictory examples have been ignored. In the following excerpt the author documents the tragic effects for children born without knowledge of their fathers.

> For years I've collected bits of data about certain unfortunate people in the news: Son of Sam, the Hillside strangler, the Pennsylvania shoemaker who raped and brutalized several women, a Florida man who killed at least thirty-four women, the man sought in connection with the Tylenol scare. All of them grew up not knowing at least one of their natural parents; most knew neither.[2]

In outline the argument takes this form:

Claim:	People brought up without a sense of identity with their natural parents will respond to the world with rage and violence.
Support:	Son of Sam, the Hillside strangler, the Pennsylvania shoemaker, the Florida murderer, the man in the Tylenol scare responded to the world with rage and violence.
Warrant:	What is true of this sample is true for others in this class.
Reservations:	Unless this sample is too small or exceptions have been ignored.

Sign

As the name suggests, in arguments based on sign the arguer offers an observable datum as an indicator of a condition. The warrant that a sign is convincing can be accepted only if the sign is appropriate, if it is sufficient, and if other indicators do not dispute it (for example, an argument in which the enjoyment of Virginia Slims is presented as a sign of female liberation). In the following example the warrant is stated:

> There are other signs of a gradual demoting of the professions to the level of ordinary trades and businesses. The right of lawyers and physicians to advertise, so as to reintroduce money competition and break down the "standard practices," is being granted. Architects are being allowed to act as contractors. Teachers have been unionized.[3]

Here, too, a reservation is in order.

| **Claim:** | Professions are being demoted to the level of ordinary trades and businesses. |

---

[2]Lorraine Dusky, "Brave New Babies?" *Newsweek* 6 Dec. 1982: 30.
[3]Jacques Barzun, "The Professions under Siege" *Harper's* 6 Oct. 1978: 66.

Support:	Lawyers and physicians advertise, architects act as contractors, teachers have been unionized.
Warrant:	These business practices are signs of the demotion of the professions.
Reservations:	Unless these practices are not widespread.

Cause and Effect

Causal reasoning assumes that one event or condition can bring about another. One can reason from the cause to the effect or from the effect to the cause. The following is an example of reasoning from effect (the claim) to cause (the warrant). The quotation is taken from the famous Supreme Court decision of 1954, *Brown v. Board of Education*, which mandated the desegregation of public schools throughout the United States.

> Segregation of white and colored children in public schools has a detrimental effect upon the colored children. The impact is greater when it has the sanction of the law; for the policy of separating the races is usually interpreted as denoting the inferiority of the Negro group. A sense of inferiority affects the motivation of a child to learn. Segregation with the sanction of law, therefore, has a tendency to [retard] the educational and mental development of Negro children and to deprive them of some of the benefits they would receive in a racial[ly] integrated school system.[4]

The outline of the argument would take this form:

Claim: (Effect):	Colored children have suffered mental and emotional damage in legally segregated schools.
Support:	They suffer from feelings of inferiority, which retard their ability to learn. They are being deprived of important social and educational benefits.
Warrant: (Cause):	Legal segregation has a tendency to retard the emotional and mental development of Negro children.

In cause-effect arguments, the reasoning may be more complicated than an outline suggests. For one thing, events and conditions in the world are not always the result of single causes, nor does a cause necessarily produce a single result. It is probably more realistic to speak of chains of causes as well as chains of effects. A recent headline emphasizes this form of reasoning: "Experts Fear That Unpredictable Chain of Events Could Bring Nuclear War." The article points to the assassination of Archduke Francis Ferdinand of Austria-Hungary in the Bosnian city of Sarajevo in 1914, which "set in motion a series of events that the world's most powerful leaders could not stop" — that is, World War I.

Or, as another example, opinion polls a few years ago indicated Americans' unwillingness to "approve any bellicose activity, unless US interests are seen as truly vital and are clearly defined."[5] The immediate cause of this isolationism is usually attributed to the "Vietnam syndrome," the relic of a bitter experience in an unpopular war. But this single cause, according to some students of the problem, is insufficient to explain the current mood. History, they say, reveals "decades of similar American resistance to foreign involvements." Needless to say, the "Vietnam syndrome" no longer prevails in the wake of the attacks on September 11, 2001, and the very real possibility of further attacks in the future. Some students may

[4]*Brown v. Board of Education of Topeka*, 347 U.S. 487–96 (May 17, 1954)
[5]*Public Opinion*, Apr.–May 1982: 16

want to examine the causes of the furious hatred of the United States that triggered the September 11 attacks and to evaluate the plausibility of those causes.

Causes can also be either *necessary* or *sufficient*. That is, to contract tuberculosis, it is necessary to be exposed to the bacillus, but this exposure in itself may not be sufficient to bring on the disease. However, if the victim's immune system is depressed for some reason, exposure to the bacillus will be sufficient to cause the illness. Or, to make an example from law and politics: To reduce the incidence of drunk driving, it would be necessary to enact legislation that penalized the drunk driver. But that would not be sufficient unless the police and the courts were diligent in making arrests and imposing sentences.

Comparison

In some arguments, characteristics and circumstances in two or more cases are compared to prove that what is true in one case ought to be true in another. Unlike the elements in analogies, the things being matched in comparison belong to the same class. The following is a familiar argument based on a comparison of similar activities in different countries at different times. On the basis of these apparent similarities, the author makes a judgment about America's future.

> Perhaps I'm wrong, but the auguries seem to me threatening. Like the bourgeoisie of pre–World War I in Europe, we are retreating into our well-furnished houses, hoping the storm, when it comes, will strike someone else, preferably the poor. Our narcissistic passion for sports and fitness reminds me of Germany in the twenties and early thirties, when the entire nation turned to hiking, sun-bathing, and the worship of the body beautiful, in part so as not to see what was happening to German politics — not to speak of the family next door. The belief that gold in the garden is more important than government helped to bring France to defeat in 1940 and near civil war in the 1950s. When the middle class stops believing in government or in the future, it's all over, time truly to sew the diamonds in the lining of your coat and make a run for it.[6]

This is the argument in outline form:

Claim:	The behavior of many middle-class Americans today threatens our future.
Support:	The same kind of behavior by the Germans in the twenties and thirties and by the French in the thirties and forties led to disaster.
Warrant:	Because such behavior brought disaster to Germany and France, it will bring disaster to America.

But is this warrant believable? Are the dissimilarities between the United States now and these European countries in earlier decades greater than the similarities? For example, if the present American passion for sports and fitness is caused by very different social forces than those that operated in Germany in the twenties and thirties, then the comparison warrant is too weak to support the author's claim.

Analogy

An analogy warrant assumes a resemblance in some characteristics between dissimilar things. Analogies differ in their power to persuade. Some are explanatory; others are merely descriptive. Those that describe are less likely to be useful

---

[6]Michael Korda, "The New Pessimism," *Newsweek* 14 June 1982: 10.

in a serious argument. In conversation, human beings are often likened to other animals — cows, pigs, rats, chickens. Or life and happiness are compared to a variety of objects: "Life is a cabaret," "Life is just a bowl of cherries," "Happiness is a warm puppy." But such metaphorical uses are more colorful than precise. In those examples, one quality is abstracted from all the others, leaving us with two objects that remain essentially dissimilar. Descriptive analogies promise immediate access to the reader, as do paintings or photographs. Such shortcuts are tempting, but descriptive analogies are seldom enough to support a claim. Consider the following example, which appears in a speech by Malcolm X, the black civil rights leader, criticizing the participation by whites in the march on Washington in 1962 for black rights and employment:

> It's just like when you've got some coffee that's too black, which means it's too strong. What do you do? You integrate it with cream, you make it weak. But if you pour too much cream in it, you won't even know you ever had coffee.[7]

This is the outline of the argument:

Claim:	Integration of black and white people in the march on Washington weakened the black movement for rights and jobs.
Support:	Putting white cream into black coffee weakens the coffee.
Warrant:	Weakening coffee with cream is analogous to weakening the black rights movement by allowing white people to participate.

The imagery is vivid, but the analogy does not represent convincing proof. The dissimilarities between whitening coffee with cream and integrating a political movement are too great to convince the reader of the damaging effects of integration. Moreover, words like *strong* and *weak* as they apply to a civil rights movement need careful definition. To make a convincing case, the author would have to offer not imagery but facts and authoritative opinion.

The following analogy is more successful because it is explanatory rather than descriptive. The elements on both sides of the analogy are failing or sick human beings and less than productive tests. This excerpt appears in an article by Albert Shanker, late president of the American Federation of Teachers, deploring the low scores of American students in national tests.

> It's not the first time we've heard about the dismal performance of US students in math: NAEP [National Assessment of Educational Progress] has been giving us the same bad news for twenty years. So it should come as no surprise that our kids are nowhere near "first in the world." What can we expect now? Only, I'm afraid, that another test will be administered two years from now to see if we're doing any better.
>
> Suppose you were feeling terrible and went to a doctor who tested you, said you had a fever, and asked you to come back in two weeks. And suppose you returned every couple of weeks for a year or so to be tested, and every time, you got the same bad news but still no diagnosis and no advice. Few of us would think much of a doctor who did nothing but test us and give us bad news. But that's what's been going on in education for twenty years.[8]

---

[7]"Message to the Grass Roots," *Roots of Rebellion*, ed. Richard P. Young (New York: Harper, 1970) 357.
[8]"Testing Is Not Enough," *New York Times* 20 Oct. 1991: E7.

WARRANTS CHART

Type of Warrant	Subtype	Example
Authoritative Warrants are based on the credibility of a source		**Claim:** Cigarette smoking is harmful.
Substantive Warrants are based on beliefs about the reliability of factual evidence	A **Generalization Warrant** is a substantive warrant based on the belief that it is possible to derive a general principle from a series of examples.	**Claim:** Marijuana is a potent medicine for relief of pain in seriously ill patients.
	A **Sign Warrant** is a substantive warrant based on the belief that an observable datum is an indicator of a particular condition.	**Claim:** Press reports and TV news programs deal in lies and deception.
	A **Cause-and-Effect Warrant** is a substantive warrant that assumes that one event or condition can bring about another.	**Claim:** Giving free food to poor countries can be counter-productive.
	A **Comparison Warrant** is a substantive warrant that assumes that what is true in one case ought to be true in another.	**Claim:** The United States should set an annual budget for physician spending, then let doctors do their work.
	An **Analogy Warrant** is a substantive warrant that assumes a resemblance in some characteristics between dissimilar things.	**Claim:** Sports have become the secular religion of America.
Motivational Warrants are based on the values of the arguer and the audience.		**Claim:** People in this country work too hard to enjoy God and family.

SUPPORT:	WARRANT:	CRITICAL QUESTIONS
The surgeon general has determined that cigarette smoking is hazardous to your health.	The surgeon general is a reliable medical authority.	Could the authority be mistaken in this case? Do other reputable authorities disagree?
SUPPORT: In controlled experiments marijuana has reduced severe side effects and pain of illness and cancer therapy in several patients.	WARRANT: What was true for the patients in the experiments will undoubtedly be true for many more.	Are the examples representative of the whole group being described? Have contradictory examples been ignored?
SUPPORT: In 1992, NBC faked exploding gas tanks in an exposé of GM trucks. In the past journalists greatly exaggerated the dangers of dioxin and radon.	WARRANT: Such fakery is a sign of the deceptive practices of the media.	Is the sign appropriate? Is the sign sufficient? Do other indicators dispute the sign?
SUPPORT: Poor farmers plant fewer crops if farming becomes unprofitable.	WARRANT: People will lack incentive to provide for themselves if others provide for them.	Is the cited cause sufficient to bring about the effect? Have other possible causes been overlooked?
SUPPORT: This practice has enabled Canada to save money without reducing the pay of doctors.	WARRANT: Because this practice is successful in Canada, it should be successful in the United States.	Are the dissimilarities between the things being compared greater than the similarities? Have all or only a few of the important characteristics been compared?
SUPPORT: Both sports and religion have gods, saints, houses of worship, and "true believers."	WARRANT: The feelings of veneration for the spectacle and values of sports are analogous to the feelings of adherents of formal religion.	Is the analogy explanatory or merely descriptive? Are there sufficient similarities between the two elements to make the analogy appropriate?
SUPPORT: Americans work 20 percent more today than in 1973 and have 32 percent less free time per week.	WARRANT: Work should not be an end in itself but a means to enjoyment of "mental culture, moral and social progress, and the Arts of Living." (J. S. Mill)	Might some people disagree with the arguer's values? Is the value relevant to the claim?

Shanker's argument may be outlined like this:

Claim: Testing students in math year after year without proposing remedies is fruitless.

Support: Testing a sick person again and again without offering a diagnosis or treatment would be considered unacceptable medical practice.

Warrant: Math tests which fail to diagnose the problem and propose remedies are analogous to medical tests which offer no diagnosis or treatment for the patient.

This analogy, however, suffers from the weakness of all analogies—dissimilarities between the objects being compared. Many physical illnesses may be easier to diagnose and cure than deficiencies in math. The latter are certainly due to a variety of social, economic, and personal problems that are difficult or impossible for the educational system to treat.

Values

Warrants may also reflect needs and values, and readers accept or reject the claim to the extent that they find the warrants relevant to their own goals and standards. The persuasive appeal of advertisements, as we know, leans heavily on value warrants, which are often unstated. Sometimes they include almost no printed message except the name of the product accompanied by a picture. The advertisers expect us to assume that if we use their product, we can acquire the desirable characteristics of the attractive people shown using it.

Value warrants are indispensable in arguments on public policy. In the following excerpt from a radio debate, a professor of statistics at Berkeley argues in favor of affirmative action policies to promote the hiring of women faculty. Her claim has been made earlier, but her warrant and any reservations remain unstated. This is her supporting material.

> 6.9 percent is [a] very tiny proportion of the faculty. You still have to go a long ways to see a woman teaching in this university. Most all of the students go to this university and never, ever have a woman professor, a woman associate professor, even a woman assistant professor teaching them. There's a lack of role models, there's a lack of teaching, and it brings a lack of breadth into the teaching.[9]

The Berkeley professor's argument may be outlined like this:

Claim: The proportion of women on the Berkeley faculty should be increased.

Support: Because women are only 6.9 percent of the faculty, most students never have a woman teacher.

Warrant: Exposure of students to women faculty is a desirable educational goal.

Reservation: Unless individual women faculty members are significantly less competent than men.

[9]Elizabeth Scott, quoted in "Affirmative Action: Not a Black and White Issue," National Public Radio, week of 25 Apr. 1977: 7.

PART THREE

USING THE ELEMENTS

CHAPTER 8
Definition: Clarifying Key Terms
(text pages 239–261)

You might want to begin this unit by dividing the class into four or five groups and assigning to each group the definition of a common object—book, bed, chair, cup, shoe. The definitions that emerge from the group are then compared to those in the dictionary. (The definitions by students are often remarkably close.)

After this exercise, ask students to describe the process of definition they have just engaged in. As the discussion proceeds, students discover, first of all, that in matters of definition we know more than we can tell. (See Michael Polanyi's fascinating examination of this in *The Tacit Dimension*, Routledge & K. Paul, 1967.) Apart from this philosophical dilemma, the attempt to define these familiar objects gives practice in distinguishing the properties that separate similar objects or objects belonging to the same genres. Equally important, students must think of examples if they are to make useful distinctions—between a shoe and a boot, between a chair and a stool, between a book and a magazine. The same necessity to resort to examples will become even clearer when they define abstract terms.

You may assign a single vague or ambiguous term, on which there is sure to be disagreement, for an extended discussion by each member of the class: success; the good life; normal sexuality; maturity; heroism; and necessities, comforts, and luxuries. Some or all of the completed papers may be duplicated and distributed to the whole class or made available online. Through a discussion or written assignment, the class may examine the criteria governing the different definitions. Can we reach a consensus? Why, or why not? What are the implications of success or failure in reaching consensus about these particular terms?

Students can also tackle the definitions of words that have acquired several, sometimes contradictory, meanings. *Example: discrimination.* For most students, this word carries a negative connotation. You might also offer the following example:

> A young woman who knows nothing about the mechanics of a car finds herself stranded in a parking lot because the engine of her car will not start. Passing near her are two people—a young man and a young woman. The car owner ignores the young woman and turns to the young man, asking him if he can identify and perhaps solve the problem of the stalled car.

Does this action represent *discrimination* in the negative sense? Students must explain their answers in such a way as to make clear how they define the term.

They might also be directed to examine the use of the word in aesthetic criticism. Why has the word taken on negative connotations in other areas of discourse?

29

Students can find examples of implicit definitions even in their popular songs. Example: Pink Floyd in "The Wall": "We don't need no education. We don't need no thought control. . . . Teachers, leave us kids alone." How is education defined in this song?

Stereotype has suffered the same fate as *discrimination*. We've discussed with students a different perception of a word almost always treated nowadays as a reflection of prejudice. From *The Biosexual Factor* by Richard Hagen:

> Stereotypes are the stuff of prediction. Used correctly, they can save us a great deal of grief. If ignored, they may exact a price. The teenage girl who hitchhikes alone because she doesn't accept stereotypic warnings about male sexual behavior is likely to learn a lot about stereotypes.

In recent years, the definition of *disability* has received critical attention from the medical and legal professions. The American Psychiatric Association lists more than three hundred illnesses, among them "road rage" and "jury duty disorder" (Week In Review, *New York Times* 28 Sept. 1997). Students can look up rulings on the Americans with Disabilities Act in *Facts on File* for June 27, 1998. More recent cases include the rights of near-sighted pilots and tournament golfers who cannot walk, among others. See "What Is Golf? What Is a Disability?" (*New York Times* 3 June 2001: Wk. 18).

Bibliography

Rosenbaum, Ron. "Degrees of Evil." *The Atlantic Monthly* Feb. 2001: 63–68. "Some thoughts on Hitler, bin Laden, and the hierarchy of wickedness."

CHAPTER 9
Language: Using Words with Care
(text pages 262–295)

1. Again we turn to advertisements for their use of slogans, clichés, and emotive language. Advertising claims in airline ads, we are told by a national advertising group, "promise great buys and then dissolve into airline jargon filled with restrictions." Ask students to examine some airline ads for jargon and code words that are meaningless or slippery.

   A paperback entitled *I Can Sell You Anything* by Carl P. Wrighter (Ballantine 1984) offers a popular attack on techniques of advertising. Wrighter supports his claims by offering dozens of examples of "weasel words" in specific commercial advertisements. The claims of each ad are clearly stated. Often the argument is exaggerated, and some of the ads will no longer be familiar to students, but they can use Wrighter's formulas as a model, choosing their own ads and substituting their own weasel words.

   An article in the *New York Times* (26 Nov. 1998), "A Name So Smooth, the Product Glides In," by J. C. Herz, describes in fascinating detail how products are named, that is, how the sounds of letters like z, "one of the fastest sounds in the alphabet," can influence the choice of name for the product. "Orwell was dead wrong," says the author. "The language isn't being crushed under the weight of oppression. It is experiencing an algal bloom of new vocabulary." Students need not be linguists to try to uncover—or imagine—the origins of product names which seem to come out of nowhere—Advil, Skype, Splenda.

2. Have students collect literature from various politically active groups on campus. Assign a study of the language based on some of the categories in the text: connotations, euphemisms, clichés, slogans, slanted language, picturesque language.

   a. Is the message persuasive? How much of the persuasive effect is due to the way that language is used?

   b. Identify terms that you consider effective and tell why.

   c. Identify terms that you consider ineffective and tell why.

3. Students can find slogans everywhere. The slogans, of course, will differ from year to year and from place to place, depending on the emergence of new issues. Ask students to compose their own political slogans and defend them. To whom does the slogan appeal? What shortcuts have been taken; that is, what questions about your abbreviated argument might be asked by an unfriendly reader?

4. There are clichés—statements of obvious ideas—everywhere. Students can examine some recent speeches for examples of clichés. They might consider answers to the following questions: Can the use of clichés be justified? What would be the effect of substituting unusual ideas, even a surprising and perhaps unpleasant truth?

5. Have students examine some of the classic speeches of the past: Patrick Henry's speech before the Virginia Convention of 1775, Abraham Lincoln's Gettysburg Address, Winston Churchill's address to the Congress of the United States of America on December 26, 1941. Students will notice that all of these speeches contain memorable phrases. Ask whether they think that the language differs in any significant way from the language of the 21st century. Have them explain any differences and describe how they contribute to the success or failure of particular speeches.

6. Below is a passage from a Protestant historian, G. M. Trevelyan, about the English Reformation. Students may be asked to pick out the words and phrases that indicate slanting.

   > It is often falsely asserted that the [Protestant] Reformation was a plunder of the poor; that it dispossessed them of their heritage in favor of a squirearchy [landed proprietor class]. The fact is that the medieval Church, on its financial side, was a squirearchy richer and more jealous of its possessions than any which had existed since the Reformation. What the revolution did was to transfer enormous wealth from one squirearchy to another; from a squirearchy which, in its very nature, was intensely conservative and seldom let go of anything in its possessions, to another which lived far more among the people, and whose extravagances often led to the division of the land, so that there grew up in Elizabethan and Jacobean times a whole class of small yeoman farmers.
   >
   > The medieval Church was, no doubt, more friendly to the poor than any State Institution of those days would have been. But it was far from that Christian fraternity and generous beneficence which is often claimed for it, and which the earliest Christianity had actually displaced. It was deeply feudalized; it was no longer a really democratic institution in any strict sense of the word. Popes were the most absolute sovereigns of their day, and sometimes the most luxurious and most directly responsible for those wars which were chronic in Christendom.

We have tried to encourage students to uncover other examples in their own texts, but they find this difficult to do. The exercise above will at least induce a healthy caution about the objectivity of textbook writers, even distinguished historians.

7. The use of computers has clearly influenced language, perhaps in ways that are not so benign. In "When the Geeks Get Snide, Computer Slang Scoffs at Wetware (the Humans)" (*New York Times* 27 June 2000: C1), Michiko Kakutani argues that "geek-speak is flush with disparaging or defensive references to the real world and flesh-and-blood human beings." Students can probably provide examples of her thesis and argue for or against it.

8. One writer yearns for the return of "proper letter-writing" (Tunku Varadarjan, "Spilling Words and Hitting 'Send'—Not Letter-Perfect," *Wall Street Journal* 21 Sept. 2000: A19) as opposed to instantaneous and casual e-mail. Do students feel that the language of e-mail and texting has drawbacks as a mode of communication? Does "proper" letter-writing have a place in their lives?

9. What about names of military operations? We are mostly unaware of the importance that leaders of government attach to the naming of wartime activities. The name first suggested for the war against the Taliban was *Infinite Justice*; then, after criticism, it became *Enduring Freedom*. Winston Churchill said names should not have "an air of despondency, they should not be frivolous and ordinary, and they should not be a target for fun." The decisions about naming offer fascinating excursions into psychology and language. See "Operation Moniker: Military Name Game" (*New York Times* 13 Oct. 2001: A15).

CHAPTER 10

Logic: Understanding Reasoning

(text pages 296–334)

1. The teaching of fallacies poses special, though not insuperable, problems. Some fallacious statements by public figures are obvious, like those in the list of exercises in the text. But arguments by professional writers often contain concealed fallacies or fallacies that uninformed students are unable to identify. One example that comes immediately to mind is Ashley Montagu's "Man, the Ignoble Savage?" (from *The Nature of Human Aggression*). This essay, reprinted in several readers, purports to be an attack on the use of examples by others, but Montagu offers only one example in rebuttal, and this example is a scarcely credible rumor that remains unsubstantiated. (An interesting assignment would ask students to look for more convincing research to support Montagu's claim.)

   The rule for all of us—teachers and students alike — is to cultivate fearlessness in our criticism of articles by putative experts. Since freshman students are naturally disinclined to be critical of their mentors (publicly, at least), we may risk overzealousness in uncovering faulty arguments in textbooks, newspapers, and magazines. Advertisers are not the only arguers guilty of concealment or distorted reasoning.

2. Students should be on the alert for dubious arguments in what they read and hear and bring them in for examination by the class. If they are keeping journals, they may record these fallacies or what they interpret as fallacies in their journals. The nomenclature is not important. Some of their entries will turn out to be examples of sound reasoning after all, but no matter. The objective of the exercise is increased alertness. Sensitive discrimination will, we hope, come later.

In some cases, students will be lucky to find explicit references to fallacies, as in the beginning of this letter (*Wall Street Journal* 15 Nov. 1983): "Your editorial is an illustration of the slippery slope argument." Less explicitly, the writer will say (*Wall Street Journal* 7 Dec. 1983): "Your editorial was critical of Surgeon General C. Everett Koop for 'citing particularly egregious magazine articles and medical cases as proof that the United States could easily slip into some Nazi-like approval of general euthanasia.' I, for one, would not dismiss Dr. Koop's concern quite so readily."

3. Some school newspapers are rife with weak and fallacious arguments in the editorials and letters to the editor. As a source of fallacies, they have two advantages: They are easily available, and students probably feel fewer inhibitions in attacking their peers.

RECOGNIZING COMMON FALLACIES: ANSWERS

Students generally have no difficulty recognizing and explaining these fallacies even when they cannot find the names for them.

1. *Begging the question.* The judge is assuming the answer to the very question that a trial is supposed to answer.

2. *Non sequitur.* It doesn't follow that because something is good for us the government should enforce compliance.

3. *Post hoc fallacy.* There is no proof that watching these particular TV shows is the cause of high or low school grades. It is more reasonable to suppose that children who do well or poorly in school select one show or the other because of its appeal to their level of intelligence and achievement.

4. *Hasty generalization or small sample.* A faulty prediction for one month is not enough for an accusation of unreliability.

5. *Two wrongs don't make a right.* The writer thinks that death and danger are unacceptable for men in combat, but subjecting women to death and danger doesn't make these "wrongs" more acceptable.

6. *Faulty use of authority.* Taste is a matter of individual preference. It would be hard to prove that Cher, however gifted an actress, is superior to anybody else in her choice of a sweetener. (Of course, we also know that she is only posing for a paid advertisement.)

7. *Two wrongs don't make a right.* The arguer seems to infer that gambling is wrong, but legalizing it won't make it morally right. (This is what Norman Cousins calls "cop-out realism," or "If you can't beat 'em, join 'em.")

8. *Post hoc.* What was money spent for in the past? Have conditions changed that may make the expenditure of more money appropriate now?

9. *Non sequitur.* It does not follow that campus newspapers select the best or even good writers. They usually have to settle for those who make themselves available.

10. *Begging the question.* The arguer assumes that standard English is necessary only for certain kinds of employment, but that remains to be proved. Standard English has other uses unrelated to employment.

11. *Non sequitur.* In this case, discrimination means making judicious choices. It should not be considered pejorative. To perform their duties, which may involve physical exertion, police officers should be required to fulfill certain physical standards.

12. *Faulty comparison or begging the question.* Qualified doctors and medical students are different. By definition a medical student is still being tested, and access to information in books during the testing process may defeat the purposes of testing.

13. *Non sequitur.* Chemicals are the building blocks of nature. Some may be unsafe, but they are not all synonymous with poisons by any means.

14. *Begging the question.* The arguer assumes that the only relevant criterion for choosing courses is payment of tuition. But a student enters into an implicit contract when he or she enrolls in the college or university and accepts the criteria laid down by the institution for the granting of a diploma.

15. *False dilemma.* The writer assumes that there are only two alternatives available to those who want to marry. But there is at least one more — marriages freely chosen that are not based on romantic love. Besides, we have no way of knowing how well arranged marriages worked. Staying married when divorce is difficult or unavailable doesn't prove the success of the marriage.

16. *Hasty generalization or small sample.* Three examples are not sufficient to support a generalization about a population of hundreds of thousands or millions.

17. *Hasty generalization or small sample.* One example of a highly intelligent athlete is not enough to prove the intelligence of a large population.

18. *Begging the question.* One indictment does not lead to filling the prisons.

19. *False analogy.* Harris is making an analogy between inanimate objects — buildings, cars, ham — and animate objects or students. Students, after all, have choices and some control over their education.

20. *Post hoc fallacy.* There is no evidence here that doctrines of feminism have caused women to turn to crime. Anyway, crime is usually the result of many factors that are difficult to separate.

21. *Non sequitur.* It doesn't follow that just because an activity is healthful the university should require it. (There are a number of things that are good for us that a center of academic learning does not choose to introduce into its curriculum.)

22. *Ad hominem.* Meany is attacking the habits of the younger generation, not their views, which remain unknown.

23. *Non sequitur.* It doesn't follow that early poverty makes a candidate sympathetic to the problems of the poor. In fact, the opposite may be true.

24. *False analogy.* In the European cases troops were engaged in crushing freedom; in the Little Rock case they were engaged in extending it.

25. *Post hoc fallacy.* There is no evidence that the election of Governor Jones is the cause of the corruption. His election and government corruption may be coincidental. In fact, he may be uncovering — and ending — corruption that existed before he took office.

26. *False dilemma.* These may not be the only alternatives for the voters. There may be ways to improve education without a pay increase.

27. *Post hoc fallacy.* It would be hard to prove a cause-effect relation.

28. *False analogy.* The dissimilarities between the two states are probably much greater than the similarities.

29. *Post hoc fallacy.* Self-explanatory.

30. *Faulty use of authority*. Even Galileo should have asked for stricter evidence than the great Aristotle could provide on the subject of natural science.

31. *Slippery slope fallacy*. The progression projected by Brustein—from Congress curtailing grants to artists whose work is controversial to Congress ordering the execution of artists whose work is deemed blasphemous—is hardly inevitable.

PART FOUR

RESEARCHING AND CRAFTING ARGUMENTS

INTRODUCTION

Part Four is meant to complement all writing assignments throughout the semester. It is one thing for students to grasp the concept of a claim of fact, for example, but writing an essay in which they demonstrate their ability to communicate that understanding is quite another. Chapter 11, then, instructs students in the processes of planning and researching an argumentative paper. Chapter 12 addresses drafting, revising, and presenting arguments. A portion of the chapter provides guidelines for oral argument. In a course that emphasizes written discourse, defending a claim before a live audience encourages awareness of the differences between speech and writing. Students must learn to accommodate both language and organization to the differing needs of listeners and readers. They already know the importance of acquiring proficiency in speech, and, despite some initial misgivings, find the speech assignments a useful and enlightening experience. Chapter 13 covers documenting sources. These three chapters present writing the research paper as a culmination of a course in argumentative writing. Although students in all their papers so far have been demonstrating their mastery of the elements of argument and the process of composition, the research paper will put their skills to a more demanding test. In these chapters, we discuss the purposes of the research paper and the procedures for helping students to produce interesting and authoritative documents. We have also provided two student research papers which have been annotated to show students exactly how the authors proceed in defending a claim.

CHAPTER 11
Planning and Research
(text pages 337–371)

Unlike many upper-level courses, in which the only writing may be an examination and a research paper, our course requires writing from the very first week of class, and students practice research skills at some level throughout the semester. The research paper serves not to introduce but to bring together in a more ambitious exercise the principal elements of argument. But it is only one among many papers.

The purposes of the research paper are twofold: (1) mastering a long paper—perhaps three times longer than any of the weekly writing students have done so far—with its special and more demanding problems of organization; (2) learning how to substantiate more extensive claims of fact, value, and policy that require the data and authoritative opinion the writer cannot supply — in other words, more practice in organization, development, and documentation.

New teachers who are introducing the research paper for the first time may find suggestions in the following outline that can be adapted to their particular programs.

1. Assign a fast reading of Chapter 11. Take ten or fifteen minutes to turn pages with students, pointing out what they will find and which parts deserve a slightly longer glance.

    At the next class, go over the important parts of the chapter. Concentrate on the tasks that must be accomplished first. Encourage questions. Reassure students that the assignment is not as daunting as they think it is. It might even be fun, and you are ready to help.

2. In class, discuss finding a topic. The commonly quoted advice to graduate students about to embark on a dissertation still holds true: Choose something that really interests you, because you'll have to live with it for a while.

    The first and most obvious source of subjects will be in "Debating the Issues" and "Multiple Viewpoints," Parts Five and Six of the text. Topics are suggested for each chapter, but students may think of others that interest them more. Other subjects may be found in personal experience, at home and at school, and in the neighborhood, in town, or on campus.

3. Work out a schedule for the project. Freshman students need help in managing time, and they are grateful for a structure that defines their responsibilities. We favor making the time available for the research paper no longer than a month. (We've found that allowing more time for research and writing doesn't produce better papers.) Set deadlines for specific stages of the project:

    a. The choice of topic
    b. A briefly annotated list of five sources examined in the first week or ten days. Two of the items may be taken from the text book; the other three from other sources. (All of these may not appear in the final bibliography, but they represent a start.)
    c. The final paper

4. Announce the availability of teacher conferences at any point during the research and writing. Early in the project we schedule one conference with each student. Later conferences can be based on individual need. Some students will have trouble refining and narrowing the topic. Others will need help finding sources. And still others will encounter problems in organizing and in using the sources appropriately.

5. While students work on their research papers outside of class, you can ask for short papers, sometimes in class, which introduce an idea or present a piece of evidence that is part of the longer paper. Some papers will suggest the need for a conference. If not, papers should be returned promptly with comments relevant to the research paper. Needless to say, attention to the ongoing process of the paper should also make plagiarism more difficult.

6. Unless you anticipate and address the problem, some students, drunk with their newly acquired knowledge of the research tool, will produce a series of quotations, sometimes as many as twenty in a six-page paper, tightly strung together like a well-made necklace, with nothing visible between the pearls. This is *not* a research paper. We need to make clear to students that *they* are the authors and that the materials derived from other sources must be used *only* to support their claims. We should emphasize that too much research material

can be as fatal as too little. The two sample research papers give students models for the intelligent use of quotations.

The digital age has changed the nature of research. The library will not be the first place most students will look for information on a topic. It is much easier to look online. If you want your students to include anything other than online sources, you will need to make that a clear requirement for the research paper. You will also need to take time to go over with your students the information in this chapter about how to evaluate sources. There is the temptation for them to believe that information is valid merely because it is on the Internet, but if they stop and think about it, anyone with access to a computer can post to the Web. The challenge comes in locating good information amid all of the "garbage" elicited by an online search. Refer to the tutorial "Online Research Tools" on the book's Web site for further help in this area.

In this edition we follow one student, Katie, as she works through some of the steps in the research process in much the same way each student in your class will. We also include interactive online exercises to help students working in either MLA or APA style.

CHAPTER 12
Drafting, Revising, and Presenting Arguments
(text pages 372–399)

Success in teaching composition, like success in parenting, has its mysteries. Good writers and good children emerge from all kinds of environments — authoritarian, permissive, and unlikely combinations of the two. The suggestions that follow have been tested in a wide variety of programs — from some in which an activity and an assignment were designated for each day of the semester to others in which no structure was provided and floundering was a rite of passage.

When we supervise new teaching assistants, we always advise them to teach from their strengths, which might not be the same as ours, and if necessary to adapt any suggestions for assignments and classroom management to ones with which they feel more secure. New teachers who read these ideas will, we hope, be able to make similar adjustments.

COMPOSITION: ORGANIZATION AND DEVELOPMENT

Unlike the arrangement of ideas in description, which may be spatial, or in narration, which may be chronological, the arrangement of ideas in argument is logical, and has, therefore, wide application. We can try to make clear to students that the modes of organization outlined in the text are exactly the same as those they will be expected to use for their writing in the workplace or any activities that call for reports, evaluations, and recommendations.

If students have trouble arranging the materials of an argument, you can ask them first to establish the nature of their claims, and then to examine essays in the book that exemplify an appropriate organization. Often the first paragraph of an essay serves as an introduction to the kind of organization. Most beginning writers are glad to learn that these forms exist and are ready for use in any argument.

As they gain power in using these conventional forms, they will be free to modify them — for example, withholding the main idea until the end.

As for development and support, you can stress this throughout the semester in every piece students read and write, pointing out varied strategies that good writers use to convince readers of the soundness of their claims.

In introducing or summarizing the concepts of organization and development, you may want to use the blackboard, SMART Board, or computer. You can write down the claim or thesis statement for an argument suggested by a student — for example, "Schools should remove vending machines of unhealthful snack food" — and then ask students to suggest topic sentences for three paragraphs and the means of supporting the ideas summarized in the topic sentences. You can use this device for the three ways of organizing a claim and can make ample reference to the forms of support that are treated in Chapter 6.

From time to time, you may want to duplicate good student papers, sometimes from a previous semester, for distribution to the class and discuss the successful use of the different ways of organizing and supporting a particular argument. Duplication of less successful papers — without names — can also work if the problems are not severe and the instructor can call attention to some strengths as well.

AVOIDING PLAGIARISM

There is no foolproof way of preventing plagiarism. But a few precautions can reduce the number of incidents.

1. Make sure that students understand the nature of the offense. Many students are genuinely ignorant of the necessity for crediting sources. Review the examples in the text. Some instructors warn students at the beginning of the semester that a finding of plagiarism will result in an F for the course. Urge students to ask questions about citation if they are in doubt.

2. Keep an impromptu paper, one written on the first or second day of class, as a sample of the student's style and thinking. (We assign a short essay in class on a subject that allows students to develop a simple argument.) This paper serves primarily as a test of the skills — or lack of skills — that students bring with them. However, if a subsequent paper exhibits a radical departure in vocabulary, syntax, and development of ideas, the instructor should inquire about the differences. A few judicious questions, starting perhaps with vocabulary, will lead to an acknowledgment of help. This works best, of course, when the source is a professional writer with clearly superior skills.

3. Avoid "free" assignments. Whatever their merits, they may tempt students who have difficulty finding subjects to "borrow" papers from friends or the library.

4. Vary assignments from year to year. It is time-consuming to think of variations on previous assignments, but it should go without saying that if the same assignment is peddled year after year, some student papers will also make the rounds.

5. If your program calls for reviewing several drafts of a paper, you should be able to notice any abrupt changes in the final draft. But be prepared to find that some ambitious plagiarists are not daunted and will manufacture drafts of another student's essay.

EVALUATION AND GRADING

1. Before assigning the first paper, it is a good idea to discuss with students the criteria for grading. As an introduction, ask them to list in order of importance the elements of composition that ought to enter into an evaluation. In some classes, half of the students will head their lists with spelling, punctuation, or grammar. What is probably already obvious to them but what they are afraid to say, knowing how perverse English teachers can be, usually comes as a relief — that nobody reads an essay merely for spelling or punctuation. The criteria ought to be (1) an interesting and important idea; (2) clarity of expression; (3) adequate development; (4) clear organization; (5) correct spelling, grammar, and punctuation. In class discussion, you can try to elicit the reasons for this list and the order in which the items appear. Students need to see how these criteria are justified by their claims on the reader. (If the reader of an essay cannot understand what the writer is trying to say, a good outline and a lot of data will be powerless to save the argument.)

2. Although the emphasis in evaluation rests on the elements of argument, we do not ignore grammar and mechanics in considering the grade. For many students, accuracy will be a hallmark of their professions. In a class of mechanical engineers to whom one of us taught writing, students were told by the engineer who directed the course that sloppy letters of application were routinely discarded by most companies. Employers would infer that an engineer who was careless about spelling and punctuation might also be careless about specifications for a machine. In a real sense, then, matters of spelling, grammar, and punctuation are an integral part of the argument, and not only for engineers. Although the treatment of grammar in our text is brief, students may benefit from several interactive online exercises on topics such as comma usage, fragments, appropriate language, and subject-verb agreement.

3. What students do read with high interest is the paragraph or two that instructors write in summing up their evaluation of the whole paper. Comments and questions in the margin are helpful but no substitute for this final evaluation, which for students represents part of the ongoing dialogue initiated by their arguments.

    As an example, we reproduce here a student paper followed by the sort of evaluation one of us would write. The essay is above average in style, freedom from mechanical errors, organization, and attention to development. But it is weakened by flaws that are typical of many good student arguments. Here is the essay:

The New Drinking Laws: A Sour Taste

All I wanted was an Amaretto sour. To get it, I had to have the little black stamp on the back of my hand that told the bartender I was at least twenty-one. I was only twenty and a half. So there I sat at a North Carolina nightspot with my brother and his girlfriend Debbie, sipping a soda. Six months made the difference between a watery Coke and a taste of liquor.

Debbie had a solution. She led me back to the ladies' room, licked the black stamp on the back of her hand, and pressed it onto my hand. It was light, so I darkened it with black eyeliner.

"It's backwards, but they won't notice," Debbie assured me. "It's dark in here."

Well, the bartender did notice, and I didn't get the Amaretto sour. "This is a fake," he said. "You have to come with me." He walked around to my side of the bar, grabbed my arm, and led me to a small office at the front of the bar. There, he took a bottle of rubbing alcohol out of the desk, wet a piece of cotton with it, and wiped the stamp from my hand. "Now get out of here," he said.

At first, I wanted to cry. But as I walked to the car with Debbie and Grant, I became angry. I was a responsible person, and I had never taken a drink and gotten behind the wheel. I rarely had more than two drinks at a time. Sure, I had skirted the law, but the law was unfair.

Now young people across the country are getting a taste of that unfairness.

Under pressure from special-interest groups and a federal government that has threatened to take away their highway funds, every state in the country has raised the legal age for buying and drinking alcohol to twenty-one. I argue that, in raising the drinking age, states have violated the rights of a large group of people. Further, I believe that increasing the age is not the best way to deter drunken driving and reduce traffic fatalities.

Supporters of the current drinking laws question the ability of eighteen-year-olds to drink responsibly. These people need to take a look at the other responsibilities that rest with eighteen-year-olds now. Under United States law, an eighteen-year-old can vote, go to war, get married, and have a family, but cannot legally enjoy a beer. The implication is that people who are under the age of twenty-one are mature enough to assume the responsibilities of adulthood but are not responsible enough to enjoy its pleasures. I find this judgment arbitrary and unfair. Once we have decided what the age of majority should be (and we seem to have decided on the age of eighteen for most activities) we should apply that standard uniformly.

Other supporters of new laws argue that when drinking ages go up, traffic fatalities go down. In fact, studies have indicated that in states where the drinking age has been increased, fatalities have dropped by as much as 10 percent. This is good news, but it does not prove that the new drinking laws are entirely responsible for the drop in traffic fatalities. Tougher drunk driving laws and stepped-up efforts to educate the public about the dangers of drinking and driving could also have been major factors in the drop in fatalities.

In the last several years, drunk driving laws and penalties have been made tougher throughout the nation. That is good: Rigorous enforcement of these laws is what we need. Also, education is always a positive force. The better the general public understands the damage that irresponsible drinking can do to individuals and society, the better off everyone will be. There are problem drinkers in all age groups. The law should go after them instead of using an arbitrary age limit that restricts the rights of citizens.

Finally, I do not believe that the higher drinking age will deter people under the age of twenty-one from drinking. Those under the legal age have always found ways to skirt the law and get their hands on alcohol, and they will continue to do so. The quest for the pleasure of intoxication is part of our nature. Restricting the supply of alcohol might make it harder for eighteen-year-olds to get, but it will not make it less desirable.

I wasn't deterred from drinking the night that I got kicked out of that bar in North Carolina. After leaving there, we drove a few miles down the road to another bar, and my brother bought me my Amaretto sour. It might have been more satisfying had it been legal.

The written evaluation would say:

> I think this is a hard claim to defend, but you've handled several things very well. The organization is tight, and you make excellent transitions between ideas. I liked the introduction; it's a lively, well-told personal anecdote, and your reference to it at the end makes clear that it was an integral part of your argument. Even more important, in the body of your argument you offer other kinds of support: an appeal to fairness and data about drinking and driving.
>
> But some changes and additions might have made your argument even stronger. (1) You are probably right that the laws alone have not been responsible for the big drop in alcohol-related deaths—among fifteen- to nineteen-year-olds they have plunged from a peak of 6,281 in 1982 to 2,170 in 1988—but most experts agree that the laws are at least partly responsible. So you would have to argue that the death rate won't rise if the drinking age is lowered. Can you find data and expert opinion to support that view? You say you are a responsible driver—good point—but are you typical? (2) The analogy with other rights granted to eighteen-year-olds is somewhat shaky. Couldn't someone argue that granting those rights to teenagers was a mistake and that we should raise the ages for all the activities you cite? There's nothing special about age eighteen that guarantees maturity. After all, most eighteen-year-olds don't vote, most marriages at eighteen aren't notably successful, and as soldiers in the army, eighteen-year-olds are under strict supervision. (3) Finally, I wonder who your audience is. Are you writing for adults who might be persuaded to change the laws? I'm not sure that your attempts to evade the law would convince them that you are mature and responsible, or that pleading for the "pleasure of intoxication"—at a time when drinking by young people is declining, for good reasons—will be very persuasive. If you like, we can talk more about this in conference, and I can show you the sources of my data.

PEER EVALUATION

Peer review is less useful in argumentation courses than in courses that emphasize other modes of discourse. That is because the student reviewer often lacks sufficient knowledge of the subject of the argument to make informed comment. An example: A student writing about prisons had taken all his data from a *Time* magazine article of about fifteen years ago. The paper was well written, but the student reading it had no way of knowing that the data had changed so greatly that the claims were no longer valid. If instructors want to give students practice in evaluating arguments of classmates—a potentially valuable exercise—they are well advised, I think, to limit the areas on which the critic is asked to comment.

It is true, of course, that instructors can also be ignorant of areas of knowledge investigated by a student writer. But most of us have sufficient experience as laborers in various fields of scholarship to know which questions to ask.

CONFERENCES

Some programs mandate a specific number of conferences during the semester. Some even prescribe the amount of time to be spent. One guide for teachers calls for an initial conference of two minutes! Other syllabi leave the number of conferences to the instructor. But why conferences at all?

1. One teacher of composition at a prestigious university says frankly that his function in a conference is to rewrite the student's paper, explaining the point of his revision as he goes. In fact, such an extreme strategy may work in some cases—if the student is alive to nuances of vocabulary and tone and can understand and accept the changes, if he or she learns by imitation, and has sufficient confidence to take issue with some of the teacher's revisions. Most of us, however, see the conference at its best as a dialogue or a conversation which either the teacher or the student may initiate.

    Arguments, we have told our students, are implicit dialogues, and a conference represents not only our opportunity to respond at greater length to the student's argument but also the student's opportunity to respond to *us*—to the written comments, for example—and to talk about the process of composition. As the students articulate their theses, answering our questions and explaining what they tried to do and why they chose to do it this way, some things may become clear that remained opaque when they were engaged in a monologue. Conferences can also function as mini-workshops for two, three, or four students who share a composition problem or have argued the same subject with varying degrees of success.

2. In part, conferences also function as kinder, gentler substitutes for written comments. One instructor wrote, "Think More!" across the top of a student paper. It might be harder to give such peremptory and humiliating advice in person.

    Poor writers, although they may come reluctantly to a conference, may profit most from these sessions. They may be unwilling to pay the necessary attention to largely negative written comments, but at a conference, they must confront them, and the comments can be prefaced, softened, and modified to accommodate a vulnerable human presence. These students may also be more articulate in speech than in writing and better able to assist the instructor by giving a clearer sense of what they really wanted to argue.

3. Finally, conferences allow student and teacher to look at mechanical errors and their corrections in a different way. Corrections on the student essay of spelling, grammar, and punctuation errors don't always produce improvement; many students won't—or can't—read them. And a multitude of correction results in a trail of red ink that signifies a disaster. A conference has the virtue of allowing you to ask questions, listen to answers, offer explanations, and, most of all, point out with pencil and finger the things that need change. For such problems a small physical demonstration has an impact that the written correction does not.

ORAL ARGUMENT

1. An introduction to speeches by the class might include a student guest speaker whose argument can be evaluated in a class discussion following the speech. Criticism should be based on criteria laid out earlier in the chapter. The speaker need not be perfect but should demonstrate abilities against which students in the class can measure their own. An outside speaker allows students to offer a frank evaluation, which they are sometimes reluctant to do openly for a classmate. In many schools with debate clubs and speech or drama departments, instructors can find willing candidates for the role of guest speaker. The instructor should suggest the kind of speech that fulfills the objectives of the speech unit, preferably a claim of policy that will include both facts and values.

2. Students can fill out an evaluation form for each speech, briefly commenting on the main elements. (You can make copies of a simple form with spaces for comment.) Before turning the evaluations over to the speakers, you can read them to make sure that they are serious and respectful and then remove the names of the critics.

3. When guest speakers appear to address either the whole school or an organization on campus, you can sometimes assign attendance for the class. As with the speeches in their own class, students can fill out evaluation forms. The objectives of any speech unit should, of course, include not only proficiency in delivering a speech, but the critical ability to evaluate an oral argument.

4. "Words Go Right to the Brain, But Can They Stir the Heart?: Some Say Popular Software Debases Public Speaking" discusses the influence of software on oral presentation, especially in business (*New York Times* 17 Apr. 1999: A17). Some critics think that PowerPoint and other software presentation aids "contribute to the debasement of rhetoric." A professor of communication asks us to imagine Martin Luther King Jr.'s "I Have a Dream" speech with PowerPoint.

5. But Stephen Pinker, professor of cognitive science and the author of *The Language Instinct* (Morrow 1994), argues that human beings are visual creatures. "If anything," he says, "PowerPoint, if used well, would ideally reflect the way we think." Pinker served on a committee at Massachusetts Institute of Technology that "updat[ed] the traditional writing requirement to include both speech and graphic communication."

6. Further guidance on oral arguments and presentations can be found on our online tutorial, "Presentations."

CHAPTER 13

Documenting Sources

(text pages 400–440)

Students can use this chapter as a handy reference to the most common types of sources that they will be using in their papers. In addition to the many examples printed in the text, online tutorials are available that detail how to cite books, articles, Web sites, and databases in both MLA and APA styles.

Complete student research papers exemplify how to format an essay, cite sources, and construct an argument.

PART FIVE

DEBATING THE ISSUES

INTRODUCTION

Debate may be considered an extension of a problem-solving analysis. The debaters are considering the merits of a solution to some problem, for example, a plan to restrict government agencies in their investigations of private citizens.

The formal debate proposition is always a two-sided question; it can be answered yes or no.

The proposition is worded so that the affirmative (yes) side will be arguing for a change in policy, or, in the case of value questions, a new idea. (The argument that torture is justified in terrorism cases is an example of the latter.) Because the affirmative is arguing for a change, they are said to have the *burden of proof*, while the negative has only to defend the status quo.

The affirmative argument usually centers around three *stock issues* that grow out of the problem-solving analysis. The affirmative will argue

1. that there is a need for a change;

2. that their proposal will meet the need;

3. that their proposal is the best solution to the problem. These stock issues are referred to as need, plan, and advantages.

The negative may answer the affirmative case in a number of ways.

1. They may *debate* every issue. "There is no problem, and even if there were, your plan is expensive, inefficient, and undesirable."

2. They may *waive* an issue. "Yes, indeed, we agree there is a serious problem, but your proposed solution is useless."

3. They may propose a *counterplan*. "Things are bad all right, but I have a better idea for improving them than yours." Tournament debaters do not do this too often for strategic reasons: It means the negative must assume part of the burden of proof.

Following are some questions you might consider as you listen to or read a debate:

1. How important is definition of terms? Does it become an issue in the debate?

2. Does the negative attack the affirmative argument on every point, or does the debate narrow to one or two issues?

3. Do the speakers base their arguments on any generally accepted principles or values, such as justice, individual freedom, constitutional guarantees?

4. Do you find examples of causal argument, argument from example, or argument from analogy?

5. How important is evidence in the debate? Do the authors question the credibility of each other's sources? To what extent, if any, does the argument center around evidence?

6. Which author do you think presented a stronger case, and why?

The pairs of articles here do not always express diametrically opposed positions, so they do not follow the rigid rules of formal debates. Each, however, provides a different perspective on the issue.

CHAPTER 14

What's in a Word? Should We All Pledge to End Derogatory Use of the Word *Retard*?
(text pages 443–451)

This pair of essays is a good example of how very differently two authors can approach a subject. As will always be the case with these debates, the two discuss the same issue but represent very different points of view. Neither author comes across as cruel or unfeeling. Each simply takes a stand based on what he or she values most. Students can analyze each author's tactics by considering questions such as these:

1. Bauer is clearly writing on a much more personal level. How do you respond to her argument? Why do you think you respond in that way?

2. Have you ever been with people who treated someone like the group of girls at the theater treated Margaret? Why might they have done what they did? Is there any validity to the claim that people really don't mean anything by it when they use the word *retard*? Could the girls Bauer describes have honestly claimed that they were just joking?

3. Why was there such a reaction to the use of the word *retard* in *Tropic Thunder*? Do you feel that it was an overreaction?

4. Why does Fairman oppose banning the use of the word *retard*? Is such a thing really possible? To what extent is it possible to make people stop using an offensive term?

5. What values does Fairman base his opinion on? What is more important to him than the potential pain that the use of the word *retard* causes individuals like Margaret? Is there validity to his point of view? Explain.

6. Are there differences, in your opinion, between the use of the word *retard* and the use of the "N-word"?

Why is it okay for African Americans to use a demeaning term in referring the other African Americans when it is not okay for whites to use the same word? By the same logic, would it be okay for Margaret Bauer to call her friends with Down syndrome *retards*?

Bibliography

"Special Olympics Fights Use of Word 'Retard.'" March 31, 2009. msnbc.com
Park, Madison. "Congress Eliminates The R-Word." September 27, 2010. cnn
    .com.

Senator, Susan. "What's Missing in R-Word Debate." washingtonpost.com, August 29, 2008.

CHAPTER 15

Social Responsibility: Do Businesses Have an Obligation to Society?

(text pages 452–457)

1. These two articles are part of a larger debate that includes Milton Friedman and that was published in October 2005 on reason.com under the title "Rethinking the Social Responsibility of Business." You might want to look at, or have your students look at, the whole debate since it provides more than is mentioned here, including rebuttal.

2. One question you might like to consider with your students is how the consumer is affected by a business's philosophy regarding philanthropy. How is the shopper walking into the store affected by the beliefs held at corporate headquarters regarding the social responsibility of business?

3. In some stores like Walmart, you will see bulletin boards showing news about the store's charitable giving. Do you think that such displays affect a shopper's decision to shop there or otherwise affect his or her attitude toward the store? Why? In what ways? How are customer relations affected when a business links its name with a major charitable endeavor like the Susan B. Komen Foundation or the Salvation Army?

4. Whole Foods has grown to be an extremely successful business. What is the connection between that success and the business's philanthropy? Can a smaller business afford to be philanthropic, even on a smaller scale?

CHAPTER 16

Science and Morality: Should Human Stem Cells Be Used for Research?

(text pages 458–466)

1. Because of the speed with which both scientific advances and public policy are being made for human stem cells, this is a good topic to approach by having the students research the most recent developments in the ongoing debate. This topic works well for instructors who like to have their students do two or more papers using the same basic research to better understand the different types of claims. Students could be asked to write a claim-of-fact paper on the issue of embryonic stem-cell research and then follow up with a second one supporting a claim of policy regarding such research. The first would be objective and the second, subjective.

2. The two essays can be used effectively side by side to discuss argumentative strategy because both consider the hope that stem-cell research offers patients suffering from a range of different illnesses and their families, but each reaches

a different conclusion nonetheless. Students can analyze what those conclusions are and how each was arrived at.

3. Both authors make use of emotional appeal. Ask students to consider how that appeal differs in the two essays.

4. Some readings will lead to a discussion of problems that depend on information unfamiliar to most students. As citizens and voters, however, they will be increasingly concerned with questions generated by advances in biology, for example. For learners there is plenty of information available. An introduction to the stem-cell debate appears in an issue of *The Science Times* (18 Dec. 2000: sec. D), an eight-page summary of the facts that underlie the controversy. It contains clear definitions, diagrams, photographs, and expert opinion.

5. It is not surprising that the decision of the government to fund stem-cell research, however limited, should have roused some religious organizations to respond. Perhaps some students can speak or write on the positions taken by their churches or temples.

Bibliography

Daley, George Q. "Missed Opportunities in Embryonic Stem-Cell Research." *New England Journal of Medicine* 351.7 (2004): 627–28.

Fox, Cynthia. "Why Stem Cells Will Transform Medicine." *Fortune* 11 June 2001: 159–62.

Friedrich, M. J. "Researchers Make the Case for Human Embryonic Stem Cell Research." *JAMA* 292.7 (2004): 791–92.

"New Study Shows Most Americans Support Embryonic Stem Cell Research." *Stem Cell Week* 8 Nov. 2004: 35.

"Science Magazine Hosts Discussion of Debate on Embryonic Stem Cell Research." *Gene Therapy Weekly* 4 Nov. 2004: 69.

"'Snowflakes' Bring an Early Winter to Washington, D.C.: Meet the 'Faces' of Embryonic Stem-Cell Research." *US Newswire* 22 Sept. 2004: n. pag.

"The New Animal Farm." *Newsweek* 2 Apr. 2001: 42–45.

CHAPTER 17

Gender Stereotypes: Is the "Princess" Phenomenon Detrimental to Girls' Self-Image?

(text pages 467–473)

1. If your students are not familiar with the Disney princesses, there is a whole Web site devoted to them at princess.disney.com. One way to start a discussion of these essays is to ask what familiarity your students have with the "princess" phenomenon through their own childhood movie viewing or through family connections. Do they feel that the movies and the related marketing campaigns taught the wrong values? Why, or why not?

2. You might want to ask your students how they respond to these words from a Disney ad campaign: *"I am a Princess. I am brave sometimes, I am scared sometimes. Sometimes I am brave even when I am scared. I believe in loyalty and trust. I believe loyalty is built on trust. I try to be kind, I try to be generous. I am kind even*

when others are not so generous. I am a Princess. I think standing up for myself is important. I think standing up for others is more important, but standing with others is most important. I am a Princess. I believe compassion makes me strong. Kindness is power. And family is the tightest bond of all. I have heard I am beautiful, I know I am strong. I am a Princess. Long may I reign."

3. Monika Bartyzel's criticism of the Disney princesses is similar to criticism of Barbie, whom some have criticized for providing little girls with an unrealistic role model. You might ask your students if they are aware of any changes that have been made in the Barbie collection to make Barbie a better role model. Many will probably know that the doll's measurements have been adjusted to more nearly reflect the shape of real women, and over the years Barbie has been outfitted for numerous careers, including some that are not traditionally associated with women.

4. The Bartyzel and Leichty articles provide a good context in which to discuss appeal to needs and values. What does each author value, as reflected in her view of the princesses?

CHAPTER 18

Economics and College Sports: Should College Athletes Be Paid?

(text pages 474–478)

1. There are factual claims in these two essays that are contradictory. This is a good place to remind students that what classifies a claim as a claim of fact is its form, but not necessarily its truthfulness. Students could do research to see which author's claim about the graduation rate of student athletes is valid. (They can't both be correct.)

2. These articles also offer an opportunity to recognize fallacies. For example, Hartenstine is guilty of an *ad hominem* argument when he brings in the fact that Marx was a benchwarmer while in college, which is irrelevant to the accuracy of his argument.

3. An even more recent related topic in the news is the push for the unionization of college athletes. You could ask your students to do some research on this possibility and discuss their opinions. Would unionization be a middle ground between the current situation and one in which college athletes were not even students?

PART SIX

MULTIPLE VIEWPOINTS

INTRODUCTION

1. The debates, articles, and visuals in this section represent the argumentative process in its clearest and most understandable form. If throughout the semester we have emphasized that arguments are dialogues, the selections given here will show students how the dialogues work, that is, how people on opposing sides actually respond to each other, whether well or poorly. Where it is clear that the response is not direct, that there is no clash, the debates can be equally instructive.

2. "Multiple Viewpoints" may be used as a discrete unit or as a source of materials for assignments in the text.

   a. If it is used as a self-contained unit, the introduction and the questions that precede it suggest a number of ways of examining the material and writing about it.

   b. "Multiple Viewpoints" also lends itself to use as a source of data, expert opinion, motivational appeals, warrants, and ethical and unethical use of language. In fulfilling assignments that call for supporting materials, students may find material here, either as a substitute for, or in addition to, library or online research. In several places in these notes we have suggested assignments that give students the opportunity to find support for their claims among the selections in "Multiple Viewpoints."

   c. In addition, as pointed out earlier, "Multiple Viewpoints" can furnish the material for a research paper. Longer papers may require supplementary research, but there is probably sufficient material in each section for a paper of six to seven pages.

3. Some of these subjects will be more effective than others for a given group of students, depending on their experience with and knowledge of the subject. When time does not permit using all the subjects, we choose the most provocative ones, those that will produce, as far as we can tell, the liveliest feelings, both for and against.

4. Given the timeliness of these subjects, research to discover whether changes have occurred since the articles and letters in the book were written will be indispensable. Students must be encouraged to read at least one full-coverage daily newspaper, watch TV newscasts and special reports, and listen to radio news programs. Surveys show that most college students don't read newspapers or listen to TV newscasts. Some of them do, however, read *Time* or *Newsweek*. These students can be asked to report to the class on the ways in which the same stories are treated in different news magazines.

5. An enormously productive unit may be organized around formal classroom debate. Although debate is almost always an oral exercise, there is plenty of

opportunity in a writing class for students to commit their outlines to paper, develop major points that cannot be adequately treated in the five minutes allotted to oral presentation, and make extended critiques of the debates of their classmates.

Each debate usually requires four people, two on the affirmative side, two on the negative, although the Lincoln–Douglas format—one debater on each side—is also possible. If time does not permit a round of formal debates, the class may choose four or five debate subjects, with each team producing an argument that will be duplicated or read aloud for consideration by the whole class. This organization reduces the arguments to one on each side and eliminates rebuttal time. After reading or hearing the arguments, the class may write evaluations based on answers to the questions on the debate sheet.

For supporting materials, students could confine themselves to the data in this section. Their efforts will involve extracting the relevant issues and organizing them in a succinct and understandable way. They may also, of course, need to do further research for more recent data.

CHAPTER 19

Social Networking: What Are the Consequences of Becoming an Online Society?

(text pages 481–499)

1. The issue of social networking is one that is close to the hearts of most college freshmen these days. A prewriting assignment for this unit might ask students to freewrite about what specific functions social networking serves in their lives. A second or alternate topic could be the dangers of social networking.

2. There is a good deal of material in these essays for a discussion of how social networking is changing young people and the pros and cons of such change.

3. Some students may have seen the film version of the founding of Facebook, *The Social Network*. They should be able to shed some light on why the site was originally created.

4. Students will come to this unit with their own notions of some of the dangers of social networks. Some of the essays can add to their understanding of those dangers. A good in-class exercise is to have the students come up with claims about the dangers: claims of fact, claims of value, and claims of policy.

Bibliography

"Innovating for Development: Accidental Activists: Using Facebook for Change—An Interview with Randi Zuckerberg." *Journal of International Affairs* 64.1 (2010): 177+. *Academic OneFile*. Web. 11 Jan. 2011.

Kaya, Travis. "New College Networks, Unlike Facebook, Connect 'Social' to Studies." *The Chronicle of Higher Education* 57.08 (2010). *Academic OneFile*. Web. 11 Jan. 2011.

Powell, Russell S. "Who Is on the Other End of Facebook?" *The Chronicle of Higher Education* 56.08 (2009). *Academic OneFile*. Web. 11 Jan. 2011.

CHAPTER 20

Violence on Campus: How Far Will We Go to Keep Our Schools Safe?

(text pages 500–511)

1. Unfortunately, this is a topic that is not fading from the headlines. Students are likely to have some strong feelings about the subject. One news commentator recently pointed out how appalling it is that we are now able to predict how these events will play out because we have seen them so often. Some argued after Sandy Hook that the aftermath of such a tragedy is not the time to make a decision about gun control. Others clearly think that is exactly the time to act to make guns less accessible. Students can discuss whether emotions cloud the issue or if an emotional response is just what is called for in such cases.

2. This is a difficult subject on which to find common ground, but those on both sides of the gun control issue have the best interests of students at heart, even if they disagree completely on the best way to keep them safe. That shared concern is at least a starting point for discussion. One benefit of approaching the issue from the Rogerian point of view is that it forces one side to accurately sum up the other position. Lots of people condemn the NRA, for example, without being able to state what exactly the NRA's official position is on school safety. (It can be found at nraschoolshield.com/nss_final_full.pdf.) There are excellent articles articulating both points of view, plus dozens of others that provide all of the examples of logical fallacies that you could use in teaching those.

3. One way of looking at gun control that gets less attention is the different needs of schools in different locations and the resulting need to let gun control be a local issue. An example can be found in the article by State Senator Dan Lederman from South Dakota: yankton.net/opinion/editorials/article _e87a9e96-8cef-5248-89b8-a802813e770e.html.

4. Another issue that gets less attention than school shootings is the general category of violence against teachers. Teachers and administrators are sometimes victims of school shooting sprees, and in one particularly well publicized case recently, a teacher was the sole target of a violent student. A little research would reveal that violence against teachers is a more widespread problem than many would suspect.

5. The bullying issue raised in the last reading in this chapter has received a lot of press. Susan Eva Porter is probably in the minority in her position on bullying. Bullying in our schools is another rich subject for research and discussion.

CHAPTER 21

Food Matters: How Do Politics and the Economy Affect What We Eat?

(text pages 512–527)

1. Since students may never have considered the ethical costs related to what they eat, you might want to have them do an informal prewriting assignment

speculating about what some of those costs might be. You will most likely get a range of different answers that can open your discussion of the readings in this unit.

2. Some of these essays are easily analyzed in terms of cause/effect relationships. For example, Greenaway's essay explores the effects a pathway to citizenship will have on our food supply, Astyk and Newton discuss the causes of starvation, and Pollan explores the effects of low food prices.

3. The essays by Astyk and Newton and by Holt-Giménez can be discussed together in terms of the human suffering caused by decisions about food production and distribution.

4. Other essays can be linked by the fact that the motivation behind decisions regarding food production seem to spring from worthy motives, but upon further reflection, can be traced to less noble ones.

5. A broad topic that would let students draw on several of these essays is the complexity of the relationship between food production methods and the consequences of those methods. The bottom line may be that there is no easy solution to the problems highlighted in the unit (although human greed leads to some of them).

Bibliography

Frieden, Thomas R., William Dietz, and Janet Collins. "Reducing Childhood Obesity through Policy Change: Acting Now to Prevent Obesity." *Health Affairs* 29.3 (2010): 357–63. *EBSCOhost*. Web. 15 Sept 2010.

von Braun, Joachim, and Mary Ashby Brown. "Ethical Questions of Equitable Worldwide Food Production Systems." *Plant Physiology* 133: 1040–45. *EBSCOhost*. Web. 22 Sept. 2010.

Young, Stephen B., and Jeanette Leehr. "It's Time to Talk about the Ethics of Food." *StarTribune.com*. Web. 26 December 2010.

CHAPTER 22

Competitive Sports: What Risks Should Athletes Be Allowed to Take?

(text pages 528–545)

1. Current and former professional athletes are speaking out about the concussions they have suffered. This is a subject that is easy to find opinions about. The Sepkowitz and Blecher essays are good starting points because they discuss why concussions so often go unreported—and why they shouldn't. The controversy provides good examples of the values underlying claims. What is so important, for example, that athletes will risk their future health for their sport?

2. Two other essays, those by Brody and Golinkin, look at sports injuries in children. The two authors' opinions can be contrasted and, as with the Sepkowitz and Blecher pieces, can be analyzed in terms of the underlying values. What is so important in this case that parents would risk their children's health and safety?

CHAPTER 23

Freedom of Speech: Are Limitations on Our Rights Ever Justified?

(text pages 546–558)

1. Freedom of speech on campus and on the Internet may be of most relevance to students, especially if there have been incidents of abusive language at their own schools and censorship of material on school-based Web sites. Students ought to examine any policy statements on their own campuses that define *racism*, *sexism*, or *homophobia* and threaten punishment for their expression. If examples do not exist or are difficult to find, students can be encouraged to supply them. As they do so, they should keep in mind that some schools have been forced to modify their guidelines after courts have ruled that strict speech codes violated the First Amendment.

    Arguers may find themselves walking a narrow line between truth and offense. Students should consider this question: If the truth is offensive to some groups, should it nevertheless be expressed? The issue is complicated by the very nature of the academic purpose, which is usually defined as freedom in the search for truth. And there is another question: Do people have a right to express their feelings even if the expression is morally repugnant? Overtly racist speech or arguments that attempt to prove the superiority of the white race and the inferiority of all others can still be encountered in books and on the Internet. See J. Philippe Rushton's *Race, Evolution, and Behavior: A Life History Perspective* (Port Huron, MI, Charles Darwin Research Institute, 2000). This book, by a professor of psychology at the University of Western Ontario, argues for the superiority of "Orientals" and "whites" in intelligence and other vaguely defined characteristics, such as personality. Ask students to defend or attack the proposition that Rushton, who lectures widely, should be allowed to expound his views at a school assembly.

    At the University of Massachusetts, a speech code proposal ensured freedom from harassment based on race, color, national or ethnic origin, gender, sexual orientation, age, religion, marital status, military service status, and disability. The Graduate Employees Organization wanted the policy extended to include citizenship, culture, HIV status, language, parental status, political affiliation or belief, and pregnancy status. A number of faculty members protested the expansion of "protected categories" as a serious impediment to free discussion of social issues in the classroom.

2. Is freedom of speech on campus different from freedom of speech on the street? The president of Emory University argues that free speech does not protect "vicious epithets," because universities are places where "the habits and manners of our civil society" are passed on to the next generation. But on the street there may be different rules. In New York State, the highest court ruled that abusive speech was protected under federal and state constitutional guarantees of free speech. The case arose when a woman and her son, both mentally retarded, were verbally harassed by a neighbor.

    In February 1998, nine teenagers in a Miami high school went to jail for publishing and circulating a pamphlet, "First Amendment Rights," which included a veiled death threat to the black principal, racist comments, and obscene cartoons (*New York Times*, 4 March, 1998: A25). The Miami American

Civil Liberties Union defended the students, terming the pamphlet "a satire . . . in terms you hear on late-night stand-up comedy." The deputy superintendent of schools argued that "free speech doesn't give anyone the right to use a word that would inflame."

The newspaper article points out: "While the US Supreme Court has upheld students' right to political expression, it has also permitted school officials to censor student newspapers and to discipline a student who made suggestive comments in a speech."

Discuss with the class the limits to free speech in publications written and distributed by students.

Revisionist history has emerged as a new and troubling issue. It expresses itself not only in denial of the Holocaust but also in new interpretations of ancient history. Students, of course, will not find it easy to marshal and examine all the facts in these debates, but they can attempt to assess the advantages and disadvantages of an academic freedom that gives college instructors the right to espouse any theory. (This freedom might also encompass the right to teach creationism.) Are there just and reasonable limits to such freedom?

In January 2001, an appeals court in Pennsylvania ruled that a school district's antiharassment policy violated First Amendment rights of free speech. The policy prohibited "jokes, name-calling, graffiti, innuendo, making fun of a student's clothing, social skills, or surname." The ruling was a response to a lawsuit by two students who feared they would be punished for expressing their religious belief that homosexuality is a sin. If asked to defend or attack the appeals court ruling, how would students define the kind of speech that should be punished?

3. The reference to lyrics in popular music should be of special interest to students. They will almost certainly know some of the offensive lyrics that could provoke some parents. Is labeling of albums a denial of free speech, a form of censorship? A distinction can be made between censure and censorship, a distinction often ignored in the debate over works of art considered offensive. Students can offer examples that clarify the definitions of these terms.

In the wake of the terrorist attack on September 11, 2001, some radio executives asked program directors not to broadcast certain songs which might be "taken the wrong way," for example, "When You're Falling" by Peter Gabriel. Other executives feared that such action heralded the suppression of free speech in popular music. Is the decision to honor the request a dangerous precedent or a responsible action demanded by a nation at war?

4. In 1996, Congress passed the Communications Decency Act, which forbade distribution of indecent material to minors on the Internet. But in 1999, the ban was ruled unconstitutional by the Supreme Court. Senator John McCain sponsored a bill to require antipornography filters on computers in schools and libraries that might receive federal funds for Internet hookups.

Ask students how they would respond to this kind of censorship. Is it feasible? Is there a better way to control children's access to obscene material on the Internet?

Thousands of underground high school newspapers are now on the Web. To what extent should school authorities be permitted to control or censor them? "Of greater concern," says a newspaper report, "are the Web sites created by students at home to post threats against or mock the teachers." A problem arises, says the deputy chief counsel for the Pennsylvania School Boards

Administration, "if students are openly spilling hatred or contemplating violence against the staff" (*New York Times* 7 June 2001: E6).

5. What about terrorists on the Web? Guerrilla groups now use the Internet to disseminate propaganda and plan attacks. Should they be controlled or censored? Or would this violate their rights to freedom of speech? See "Terrorists on the Web: Electronic 'Safe Haven' " (*U.S. News & World Report* 22 June 1998: 46).

Bibliography

Coles, Robert. "Safety Lessons for the Internet." *New York Times* 11 Oct. 1997: A23. Asks for some legal protection for children from pornography on the Internet.

Hanna, Judith Lynne. "Wrapping Nudity in a Cloak of Law." *New York Times* 29 July 2001: E14.

Hentoff, Nat. *Living the Bill of Rights: How to Be an Authentic American.* New York: HarperCollins, 1998.

Tribe, Laurence H. "The Internet vs. The First Amendment." *New York Times* 28 Apr. 1999: A27. The lessons of Littleton, Colorado: "It would be a mistake to think that good surveillance or control [of the Internet] can play an important role in preventing violent crimes."

CHAPTER 24

Advancements in Medicine: What Are the Ethical Costs of Modern Health?

(text pages 559–576)

As advances in the fields of medicine make possible things once thought impossible, questions arise about where to draw the line between what is possible and what is right. Should parents be able to choose the gender of their children? Should they undergo medical tests that might reveal abnormalities and thus might lead to an abortion? Should parents have a child in order to save the life of an older sibling? Should adopted children have the right to their birth parents' medical records? Students can readily add to this list. The list grows with every advance in medicine, so television, online, and print news sources should be watched for the latest in issues of medical ethics.

It is difficult to discuss medical ethics without discussing students' personal belief systems. The most devoutly religious students will want to turn to biblical authority as their primary or most significant source on such issues. Nowhere is it more important to discuss audience than where students most strongly feel their value systems are under attack or where they feel so strongly about their value system that they are not even willing to listen to other points of view. In teaching argument, you have probably stressed that there is little point in writing for those who agree with you. Assuming that their audience is at least mildly hostile to their point of view forces them to consider their opponent's side of the argument and try to counter that opponent with the best support possible. This is a place where the results from a poll done at the beginning of the term or a more focused one given at this point in the term can be used to find out what the students in the class feel about medical ethics.

Writers and movie makers have long realized the attraction of speculating about science out of control. A classic like *Frankenstein* (the book and the movie) illustrates the danger of a scientist playing God. A movie as recent as *Contagion* (2011) is based on the premise that a virus has gone out of control and is destroying most of the inhabitants of the United States. A subject that students enjoy discussing but that can also make them aware of some of the ethics involved in medical research is how close we have come to doing some of the things that were once possible only in novels or movies. Endless numbers of identical twins, for example, were a staple of society in Aldous Huxley's *Brave New World* (1932). Now we have clones.

Peter Singer's article "The 'Unnatural' Ashley Treatment Can Be Right for Profoundly Disabled Children," in Chapter 1, clearly illustrates how what is medically possible is not necessarily ethical. Students can be asked to analyze the warrants implicit in the two sides of the debate over stunting the growth of a disabled individual.

Eric Schulzke's "Pro-Life Health Professionals in Conflict between Conscience and Career" considers whether health professionals should be required to perform medical procedures that violate their own religious beliefs. This article also can lead to a fruitful discussion of warrants and thus of the ethical complexity of the field of medicine.

PART SEVEN

CLASSIC ARGUMENTS

INTRODUCTION

"Reading requires more than words." This observation serves as a partial text for the comments that follow on the use of the "Classic Arguments" section. To understand and enjoy the selections in this section, students will need not only the ability to decode the linguistic symbols but also information—about historical events and figures.

There are two sources for the background information and the interpretation of that information: the library and the instructor. Use of the library needs no recommendation from me, but I should like to put in a word for the instructor as a resource. Notwithstanding the prevailing distaste for lecturing in composition courses, it seems to me perfectly legitimate for instructors to give students the information they need in a short summary before they proceed, and even to interpret the data if necessary, whenever such an introduction saves valuable time, enlivens the information, and arouses student interest as library research often does not.

Since each selection in "Classic Arguments" is followed by questions and writing suggestions, I have offered here only occasional questions and suggestions for classroom activities. Instead I have written about these essays largely as I myself have responded to them—sometimes in full agreement, sometimes in partial acquiescence—and as I have discussed them with students, who have often disagreed with me.

A Modest Proposal (p. 578)

JONATHAN SWIFT

1. If students are reading this essay for the first time without preparation or warning, some of them will take Swift's proposal literally. But, then, so did some eighteenth-century readers with perhaps less justification. Some teachers think that the multiple horrors of organized cruelty and genocide in the twentieth century have made Swift's proposal at least marginally credible. We hope not.

2. Students should be able to describe the person ostensibly making the "modest" proposal, since the proposer himself calls attention to his characteristics: compassionate but disinterested, thoughtful, reasonable, temperate, well-informed. The question is whether such a person—one who is compassionate and reasonable—could make a proposal to breed human infants for food. If students agree that he could not, then why has he done so? If his reasons are not those that he alleges them to be, what can they be?

    There are several ways of deciding on the answers. One is to examine the language. Does the voice of the proposer—formal, detached, heavy with statistical data—suggest one who is passionately distressed by the suffering of the Irish? Why does the proposer refer to the Irish in terms descriptive of animals rather than human beings? Is there any place in which the voice and language of the author seem to change, where he offers solutions entirely different in kind from the breeding of children for food? How are we to interpret the difference in these two voices? In the next-to-last paragraph, even the voice of the proposer begins to change; to urge that Irish adults would have been fortunate to die within the first year of life is a judgment that can be offered only in bitter irony.

3. It is not just the language or the disparity between the voices that can give away the ironic stance. There are also the external criteria, including the subject itself. Are there people in Swift's audience, no matter how indifferent to the fate of the Irish, who would enjoy the prospect of eating human infants? Would an Anglican dean be likely to make such a suggestion in the expectation that reasonable people would find it acceptable? Why would an essay outlining a serious proposal to breed children for food survive for more than two hundred years not as a curiosity but as a model of expository prose for readers throughout the English-speaking world? Consideration of these questions ought to lead to a suspicion, even in the most undiscerning reader, that some other interpretation than the literal one must exist.

The Declaration of Independence (p. 585)
THOMAS JEFFERSON

Today's students need some help with Jefferson's language, and one way to approach the document is to ask them to look at how it is organized and what its purpose is. The title makes clear that it is a declaration, but in declaring the colonies' independence, Jefferson wanted to be very sure to justify the break with England to the king and his supporters and also to future readers.

Civil Disobedience (p. 588)
HENRY DAVID THOREAU

Thoreau's classic defense of civil disobedience is the antithesis of Socrates' defense of the rights of the state. Thoreau believes that "that government is best which governs least" or not at all. He denies the authority of government to command the allegiance of an individual who does not wish to concede it. Civil disobedience is justified when conscience dictates that a greater harm will result from compliance with the law than from refusal to obey.

1. Students will need information about the Mexican War of 1846–1848, to which Thoreau makes a number of references. We may assume that students know something about slavery (although a study by the National Endowment for the Humanities revealed that 80 percent of college seniors were ignorant of what the Emancipation Proclamation did). They will also need to know that Massachusetts was not a slave state that Thoreau was objecting to an implicit sanction of slavery for economic reasons.

2. Thoreau uses the term "unjust laws," but he fails to define it. Throughout the essay he speaks of "right" and "wrong," "conscience," "a higher law." In the next-to-last paragraph he mentions the New Testament. Students can profitably wrestle with a summary of Thoreau's criteria for judgment. They

can uncover clues in his opinions of slavery, the Constitution of the United States, the majority in a democracy, voting, soldiers, imprisonment, and Daniel Webster.

3. Discussing the relevance of Thoreau's ideas and actions to present-day issues — civil rights, racism, U.S. foreign policy, taxation — can test and sharpen student understanding of civil disobedience. What kind of protest would Thoreau engage in today? (His own protest ended after one day in jail when an aunt bailed him out.) What specific issues would be likely to arouse him? If he were a college student today, would he resort to protests against some college rules and activities? Many student protesters who engage in unlawful activities insist on amnesty as a condition of their surrender to the authorities. What would Thoreau have said about the refusal to accept punishment?

    What would Thoreau say about the growth of government since his day? Students might speculate on the state of individual rights 150 years after Thoreau. What examples can they offer of restrictions on individual rights? Can these restrictions be justified by taking into account population growth and the increasing complexity of life?

    Can the acts of civil disobedience by Thoreau and Martin Luther King Jr. be compared or contrasted? Students should take into consideration the causes for which each was jailed and the principles on which each based his defense.

4. This essay is like a rich cake, studded with unexpected treats. Students may find it indigestible at first, but they can be helped to enjoy it. The claim will be perfectly comprehensible to anyone who is familiar with protests against unjust laws or an unjust government. It is Thoreau's discursive organization and sonorous prose that prevent average or slow readers from appreciating the force of his ideas. Since there is hardly time in one semester to read and discuss a long essay like this one with the thoroughness it deserves, we shall have to settle for an understanding of its major ideas. Fortunately, Thoreau includes homely examples of his most abstract utterances in almost every paragraph. These examples provide the key to decoding the generalizations students may find difficult.

    The essay suggests opportunities for short, in-class exercises to increase student comprehension. (1) Paraphrase an important idea. (2) Offer examples for one of Thoreau's generalizations.

Ain't I a Woman (p. 604)
SOJOURNER TRUTH

An interesting approach to this short speech by Truth is to ask students to look at different versions of it. Because there is no written draft by Truth, readers today have to depend on newspaper accounts, which record her words differently. For example, most versions do not even include the words that give the piece its accepted title. Students can discuss how changes in the language from one version to another affect their reading of the speech and what they might reflect about the biases of the reporters.

A broader topic to consider is where and how the abolitionist movement and the women's movement overlap. Truth was speaking not only as a former slave but also as a former female slave. What difference does that make in her comments about slavery?

The Obligation to Endure (p. 605)
RACHEL CARSON

The book *Silent Spring* from which this essay comes is considered one of the most influential early works of the environmental movement. Carson's earlier works had popularized science, making the world of the sea in particular accessible to laypeople, but with her 1962 work she sounded a warning about the dangers of pesticides that proved very accurate. *Silent Spring* as well was accessible to the average citizen with no scientific training, but the picture it presented of the future of the earth was indeed bleak.

An interesting subject for research would be just how accurate Carson's dire predictions have proved to be.

Reflections on the Bicentennial of the United States Constitution (p. 611)
THURGOOD MARSHALL

On the occasion of the bicentennial of the U.S. Constitution, speakers throughout the year and across the country had glowing things to say about this founding document. As an African American, and the first African American justice of the U.S. Supreme Court, Marshall looked at the Constitution from a different perspective. For him, a document that counted each American slave as three fifths of a human being was seriously flawed. The strength of the document, from Marshall's perspective, was that it is a living document that has changed with the times to meet the needs of a changing nation.

Appendix: Sample Syllabus (15-week Semester)

Week 1: **Chapter 1: Approaches to Argument**

Chapter 2: Examining Written Arguments

Week 2: Chapter 2 continued; practice writing summaries

Week 3: Draft of Essay #1 due (Examining a Written Argument—supporting claim of fact)

Feedback from peers

Chapter 5: Claims: Making a Statement

Week 4: Final draft of Essay #1 due

Chapter 3: Examining Multimodal Arguments

Week 5: **Chapter 4: Responding to Arguments**

Begin work on Essay #2 (Responding to Argument—supporting claim of fact or value about one or two readings from chapters covered thus far or a debate from one of Chapters 14–18 of instructor's or student's choice)

Week 6: Continue work on Essay #2

Chapter 6: Support: Backing Up a Claim

Readings from one of Chapters 19–24, instructor's choice

Week 7: Essay #2 due

Continue readings from choice of Chapters 19–24

Week 8: **Chapter 7: Warrants: Examining Assumptions**

Apply information in Chapters 6 and 7 to essays read earlier

Work on Essay #3 (Responding to Argument—supporting claim of value or policy, based on readings)

Week 9: Essay #3 due

Introduction to Research: Overview of Chapters 11–13

[Over the course of weeks 10–15, students will be working on two essays based on their research topic. In class they can be applying the concepts in Chapters 8–10 to any readings of the instructor's choice—from those chapters, the debates (Chapters 14–18), the multiple viewpoints (Chapters 19–24), or the classics (Part 7)—but also to the essays they are writing.]

Week 10: **Chapter 8: Definition: Clarifying Key Terms**

Research: Topic proposal due

Week 11: **Chapter 9: Language: Using Words with Care**

Research: Working bibliography due—5–7 possible sources, listed in proper form

Week 12: **Chapter 10: Logic: Understanding Reason**

Week 13: Essay #4 due (First Research Essay—supporting a claim of fact about their topic)

Week 14: Go over samples of Essay #4, noting strengths and weaknesses and suggesting how to change the claim into a claim of policy for Essay #5

Week 15: Essay #5 due (Second Research Essay—supporting a claim of policy about their topic)

READING ARGUMENT

Seeing Deduction

The following essay has been annotated to show deduction.

It's All about Him

DAVID von DREHLE

My reporter's odyssey has taken me from the chill dawn outside the Florida prison in which serial killer Ted Bundy met his end, to the charred façade of a Bronx nightclub where Julio Gonzalez incinerated eighty-seven people, to a muddy Colorado hillside overlooking the Columbine High School library, in which Eric Harris and Dylan Klebold wrought their mayhem. Along the way, I've come to believe that we're looking for why in all the wrong places.

The author establishes his knowledge of mass murders, his "claim to authority."

I've lost interest in the cracks, chips, holes, and broken places in the lives of men like Cho Seung-Hui, the mass murderer of Virginia Tech. The pain, grievances, and self-pity of mass killers are only symptoms of the real explanation. Those who do these things share one common trait. They are raging narcissists. "I died—like Jesus Christ," Cho said in a video sent to NBC.

Thesis statement (and major premise): Mass murderers are narcissists.

Psychologists from South Africa to Chicago have begun to recognize that extreme self-centeredness is the forest in these stories, and all the other things — guns, games, lyrics, pornography — are just trees. To list the traits of the narcissist is enough to prove the point: grandiosity, numbness to the needs and pain of others, emotional isolation, resentment, and envy.

The traits of the narcissist

In interviews with Ted Bundy taped a quarter-century ago, journalists Stephen Michaud and Hugh Aynesworth captured the essence of homicidal narcissism. Through hour after tedious hour, a man who killed 30 or more young women and girls preened for his audience. He spoke of himself as an actor, of life as a series of roles, and of other people as props and scenery. His desires were simple: "control" and "mastery." He took whatever he wanted, from shoplifted tube socks to human lives, because nothing mattered beyond his desires. Bundy said he was always surprised that anyone noticed his victims had vanished. "I mean, there are so many people," he explained. The only death he regretted was his own.

Major premise applied to Ted Bundy

5   Criminologists distinguish between serial killers like Bundy, whose crimes occur one at a time and who try hard to avoid capture, and mass killers like

---

David von Drehle is editor-at-large for *Time* magazine. His most recent book is *Abraham Lincoln and America's Most Perilous Year* (2012). This article appeared in *Time* on April 30, 2007.

Cho. But the central role of narcissism plainly connects them. Only a narcissist could decide that his alienation should be underlined in the blood of strangers. The flamboyant nature of these crimes is like a neon sign pointing to the truth. Charles Whitman playing God in his Texas clock tower, James Huberty spraying lead in a California restaurant, Harris and Klebold in their theatrical trench coats — they're all stars in the cinema of their self-absorbed minds.

Freud explained narcissism as a failure to grow up. All infants are narcissists, he pointed out, but as we grow, we ought to learn that other people have lives independent of our own. It's not their job to please us, applaud for us, or even notice us — let alone die because we're unhappy.

A generation ago, the social critic Christopher Lasch diagnosed narcissism as the signal disorder of contemporary American culture. The cult of celebrity, the marketing of instant gratification, skepticism toward moral codes, and the politics of victimhood were signs of a society regressing toward the infant stage. You don't have to buy Freud's explanation or Lasch's indictment, however, to see an immediate danger in the way we examine the lives of mass killers. Earnestly and honestly, detectives and journalists dig up apparent clues and weave them into a sort of explanation. In the days after Columbine, for example, Harris and Klebold emerged as alienated misfits in the jock culture of their suburban high school. We learned about their morbid taste in music and their violent video games. Largely missing, though, was the proper frame around the picture: the extreme narcissism that licensed these boys, in their minds, to murder their teachers and classmates.

Something similar is now going on with Cho, whose florid writings and videos were an almanac of gripes. "I'm so lonely," he moped to a teacher, failing to mention that he often refused to answer even when people said hello. Of course he was lonely.

In Holocaust studies, there is a school of thought that says to explain is to forgive. I won't go that far. But we must stop explaining killers on their terms. Minus the clear context of narcissism, the biographical details of these men can begin to look like a plausible chain of cause and effect — especially to other narcissists. And they don't need any more encouragement.

There's a telling moment in Michael Moore's film *Bowling for Columbine*,   10
in which singer Marilyn Manson dismisses the idea that listening to his lyrics contributed to the disintegration of Harris and Klebold. What the Columbine killers needed, Manson suggests, was for someone to listen to them. This is the narcissist's view of narcissism: Everything would be fine if only he received more attention. The real problem can be found in the killer's mirror.

Marginal notes:

Other examples of narcissistic mass murderers

Freud said narcissists never grow up. They put their happiness over others' lives.

Investigators have failed to recognize narcissism as the real motivation in mass murder cases.

Major premise applied to Cho

Outside the context of narcissism, the murderers' actions can seem too logical.

The author reiterates that the killer's problem is not lack of attention but how the killer sees himself.

Analysis

Von Drehle wrote "It's All about Him" shortly after the 2007 massacre at Virginia Tech. Although we cannot know exactly how he arrived at the thesis, we can reasonably assume he went through something of an inductive process on the way to writing this deductive essay. Perhaps he read and watched enough about Cho, the shooter at Virginia Tech, to hypothesize about Cho's motivation. His earlier observations of other mass murderers led him to notice similarities among them. Once he arrived at a theory about what they had in common, he had the major premise for a deductive argument that he could test out on other mass murderers. He was able to construct an argument that could be summarized in syllogistic form:

Major premise: Mass murderers are narcissistic.
Minor premise: Cho was a mass murderer.
Conclusion: Cho was narcissistic.

In his essay, he presents his major premise early and then applies it to other U.S. mass murderers: Ted Bundy, Charles Whitman, James Huberty, Eric Harris, and Dylan Klebold.

If von Drehle's major and minor premises are true, then the conclusion, of necessity, must be true. That Cho was a mass murderer is an indisputable fact; thus the minor premise is true. But what of the major premise? If we applied the deduction that mass murderers are narcissistic to mass murderers not mentioned by von Drehle, would the conclusion be the same in each case? In other words, is it true that all mass murderers are narcissistic?

Because it would be virtually impossible to apply von Drehle's deduction to all mass murderers, he would have built a more convincing case had he restricted his thesis statement with a word like most or many. That, however, would have invalidated the deductive logic that tells us that a syllogism's conclusion must be true. As it is, the examples he offers are not enough to convince all readers that his theory of narcissism is valid. Still, he offers a unique look at the motivation of mass murderers and one that makes it impossible for anyone else to be blamed for the crimes that these men and boys have committed. Behind his argument are his many years of journalistic experience and his opening revelation that he has been on the scene during the aftermath of many of the crimes to which he refers.

Practice: Deduction

The excerpt below exemplifies former Secretary of State Hillary Clinton's frequent use of deduction. Read the excerpt, and answer the questions that follow it.

Excerpt from Remarks at the Asia Pacific Economic Cooperation Women and the Economy Summit
HILLARY CLINTON

Integrating women more effectively into the way businesses invest, market, and recruit also yields benefits in terms of profitability and corporate governance. In a McKinsey survey, a third of executives reported increased profits as a result of investments in empowering women in emerging markets. Research also demonstrates a strong correlation between higher degrees of gender diversity in the leadership ranks of business and organizational performance. The World Bank finds that by eliminating discrimination against female workers and managers, managers could significantly increase productivity per worker by 25 to 40 percent. Reducing barriers preventing women from working in certain sectors would lower the productivity gap between male and female workers by a third to one half across a range of countries.

Hillary Clinton served as Secretary of State for President Barack Obama from 2009 to 2013. The speech was given in September 2011.

Reading and Discussion Questions

1. What is the major premise in this passage from Clinton's speech?
2. What is the relationship between the first sentence and the rest of the paragraph?

Common Fallacies

In this necessarily brief review it would be impossible to discuss all the fallacies listed by logicians, but we can examine the ones most likely to be found in the arguments you will read and write. Fallacies are difficult to classify, first, because there are literally dozens of systems for classifying, and second, because under any system there is always a good deal of overlap. It's helpful to remember that even if you cannot name the particular fallacy, you can learn to recognize it and not only refute it in the arguments of others but avoid it in your own as well.

RESEARCH SKILL ▸ Identifying Reliable Authorities

We all like to think that if information is in print, it is reliable. Unfortunately, that is not always the case. People with unjust biases and even those who want to sow hatred often find a way to get their opinions into print. In general, works that appear in print go through a much more extensive vetting process than what appears online, but there are so-called vanity presses that will publish pretty much anything if the author will pay the cost. There are also all sorts of periodicals that express slanted — and often conflicting — points of view, some of them offensive to many of us. That's what comes of freedom of the press. Whether in print, online, or in audiovisual sources, you should always look for well-known, credentialed authors and speakers who employ logical reasoning and avoid inflammatory language.

Hasty Generalization

Many of our prejudices are a result of **hasty generalization**. A prejudice is literally a judgment made before the facts are in. On the basis of experience with two or three members of an ethnic group, for example, we may form the prejudice that all members of the group share the characteristics that we have attributed to the two or three in our experience.

Superstitions are also based in part on hasty generalization. As a result of a very small number of experiences with black cats, broken mirrors, Friday the thirteenth, or spilled salt, some people will assume a cause-and-effect relation between these signs and misfortunes. *Superstition* has been defined as "a notion maintained despite evidence to the contrary." The evidence would certainly show that contrary to the superstitious belief, in a lifetime hundreds of such "unlucky" signs are not followed by unfortunate events. To generalize about a connection is therefore unjustified.

Any generalization based on too few particular instances is a hasty generalization. Since we seldom have the chance to observe every possible instance before arriving at a generalization, we have to interpret what "too few" means in a particular context.

- I got a parking ticket for parking on the street before I got my permit and another ticket for parking facing the wrong way on the street. These police in Columbia are just out to make money off of college students!
- That driver who cut me off was an old lady. Old people shouldn't be allowed to drive.
- I studied for my first two statistics tests and still failed. I'm not going to even bother to study for the final because I'm going to fail it anyway.
- I've got to wear my lucky Clemson shirt! We never lose when I wear it!
- It made me really nervous having that family of Muslims on my flight.

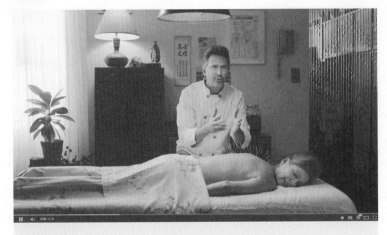

FIGURE 10.1 Holiday Inn Express commercial. Holiday Inn

Faulty Use of Authority

The use of authority—the attempt to bolster claims by citing the opinions of experts—was discussed in Chapter 6. Experts are a valuable source of information on subjects we have no personal experience with or specialized knowledge about. Properly identified, they can provide essential support. The **faulty use of authority** occurs when individuals are presented as authorities in fields in which they are not. An actor who plays a doctor on television may be hired to advertise the latest sleep medicine but actually has no more expertise with medications than the average consumer. The role that he plays may make him appear to be an authority but does not make him one. No matter how impressive credentials sound, they are largely meaningless unless they establish relevant authority.

Vintage ads are a rich source of false use of authority:

- More doctors smoke Camels than any other cigarettes. (1949)
- For Sun Giant Raisins: Horror film star Vincent Price says, "Around my kitchen this is raisin time of year . . . because raisins are good, and good for you." (1974)
- The Soda Pop Board of America claimed that laboratory tests have proven that babies who start drinking soda early have a much higher chance of gaining acceptance and "fitting in" during the preteen years. (2002 parody)

In a series of popular television commercials for Holiday Inn Express that ran for eleven years starting in 1998 and then were started again in 2013, ordinary people step in to perform the role of professionals. When it is discovered that they are not professionals as others assumed, the retort is always the same: "But I stayed at a Holiday Inn Express last night." In one of the ads a woman relaxes under what she assumes to be the talented hands of a skilled acupuncturist, only to find that his sole claim to authority is what hotel he stayed at the night before. (See Figure 10.1.)

Post Hoc or Doubtful Cause

The entire Latin term for this fallacy is *post hoc, ergo propter hoc,* meaning, "After this, therefore because of this." The arguer infers that because one event follows another event, the first event must be the cause of the second. But proximity of events or conditions does not guarantee a causal relation.

- The rooster crows every morning at 5:00 and, seeing the sun rise immediately after, decides that his crowing has caused the sun to rise.
- A month after A-bomb tests are concluded, tornadoes damage the area where the tests were held, and residents decide that the tests caused the tornadoes.
- After the school principal suspends daily prayers in the classroom, acts of vandalism increase, and some parents are convinced that failure to conduct prayer is responsible for the rise in vandalism.

In each of these cases, the fact that one event follows another does not prove a causal connection. The two events may be coincidental, or the first event may be only one — and an insignificant one — of many causes that have produced the second event. The reader or writer of causal arguments must determine whether another more plausible explanation exists and whether several causes have combined to produce the effect. Perhaps the suspension of prayer was only one of a number of related causes: a decline in disciplinary action, a relaxation of academic standards, a change in school administration, and changes in family structure in the school community.

In the social sciences, cause-and-effect relations are especially susceptible to challenge. Human experiences can seldom be subjected to laboratory conditions. In addition, the complexity of the social environment makes it difficult, even impossible, to extract one cause from among the many that influence human behavior.

False Analogy

Many analogies are merely descriptive and offer no proof of the connection between the two things being compared. An analogy is called a **false analogy** when two things are compared to each other on the basis of superficial similarities while significant dissimilarities are ignored.

- Bill Clinton had no experience of serving in the military. To have Bill Clinton become president, and thus commander-in-chief of the armed forces of the United States, was like electing some passer-by on the street to fly the space shuttle.
- Students should be allowed to look at their textbooks during examinations. After all, surgeons have X-rays to guide them during an operation; lawyers have briefs to guide them during a trial; carpenters have blueprints to guide them when building a house. Why, then, shouldn't students be allowed to look at their textbooks during an examination?
- Education cannot prepare men and women for marriage. Trying to educate them for marriage is like trying to teach them to swim without allowing them to go into the water. It can't be done.
- People are like dogs. They respond best to clear discipline.

Ad Hominem

The Latin term *ad hominem* means "against the man" and refers to an attack on the person rather than on the argument or the issue. The assumption in such a fallacy is that if the speaker proves to be unacceptable in some way, his or her statements must also be judged unacceptable. Attacking the author of the statement is a strategy of diversion that prevents the reader from giving attention where it is due — to the issue under discussion.

You might hear someone complain, "What can the priest tell us about marriage? He's never been married himself." This ad hominem accusation ignores the validity of the advice the priest might offer. In the same way, an overweight patient might reject advice on diet by an overweight physician. In politics, it is not uncommon for antagonists to attack each other for personal characteristics that may not be relevant to the tasks they will be elected to perform. They may be accused of infidelity to their partners, homosexuality, atheism, or a flamboyant social life. Even if certain accusations should be proved true, voters should not ignore the substance of what politicians do and say in their public offices.

- I wouldn't vote for Higgins because he left his wife and three kids to run off with his secretary.
- The CEO of that company is gay, so I wouldn't buy its products.
- She shouldn't serve on the school board; she had her first child before she was married!

Ad hominem accusations against the person do *not* constitute a fallacy if the characteristics under attack are relevant to the argument. If the politician is irresponsible and dishonest in the conduct of his or her personal life, we may be justified in thinking that the person will also behave irresponsibly and dishonestly in public office.

False Dilemma

As the name tells us, the **false dilemma**, sometimes called the "black-white fallacy," poses an either-or situation. The arguer suggests that only two alternatives exist, although there may be other explanations of or solutions to the problem under discussion. The false dilemma reflects the simplification of a complex problem. Sometimes it is offered out of ignorance or laziness, sometimes to divert attention from the real explanation or solution that the arguer rejects for doubtful reasons.

You may encounter the either-or situation in dilemmas about personal choices. "At the University of Georgia," says one writer, "the measure of a man was football. You either played it or worshipped those who did, and there was no middle ground."[4] Clearly, this dilemma — playing football or worshiping those who do — ignores other measures of manhood.

Politics and government offer a wealth of examples.

---

[4] Phil Gailey, "A Nonsports Fan," *New York Times Magazine*, December 18, 1983, sec. 6, p. 96.

©David J. & Janice L. Frent Collection/CORBIS

- U.S.A.: Love it or leave it.
- If we don't end our dependence on oil, we will destroy our children's future.
- Either you are with us, or you are with the terrorists.

In an interview with the *New York Times* in 1975, the Shah of Iran was asked why he could not introduce into his authoritarian regime greater freedom for his subjects. His reply was, "What's wrong with authority? Is anarchy better?"

Slippery Slope

If an arguer predicts that taking a first step will lead inevitably to a second, usually undesirable step, he or she must provide evidence that this will happen. Otherwise, the arguer is guilty of a **slippery-slope** fallacy.

Predictions based on the danger inherent in taking the first step are commonplace. In a speech to Congress on October 27, 1999, Independent presidential candidate Ron Paul said, "I am strongly pro-life. I think one of the most disastrous rulings of this century was *Roe versus Wade*. I do believe in the slippery-slope theory. I believe that if people are careless and casual about life at the beginning of life, we will be careless and casual about life at the end. Abortion leads to euthanasia. I believe that."[5] Here are other examples:

- The Connecticut law allowing sixteen-year-olds and their parents to divorce each other will mean the death of the family.
- If we ban handguns, we will end up banning rifles and other hunting weapons.

Slippery-slope predictions are simplistic. They ignore not only the dissimilarities between first and last steps but also the complexity of the developments in any long chain of events.

---

[5] Quoted in "Protect All Human Life." ronpaul.com.

Begging the Question

If the writer makes a statement that assumes that the very question being argued has already been proved, the writer is guilty of **begging the question**. In a letter to the editor of a college newspaper protesting the failure of the majority of students to meet the writing requirement because they had failed an exemption test, the writer said, "Not exempting all students who honestly qualify for exemption is an insult." But whether the students are honestly qualified is precisely the question that the exemption test was supposed to resolve. The writer has not proved that the students who failed the writing test were qualified for exemption. She has only made an assertion *as if* she had already proved it.

Circular reasoning is an extreme example of begging the question: "Women should not be permitted to join men's clubs because the clubs are for men only." The question to be resolved first, of course, is whether clubs for men only should continue to exist.

Other examples:

- I hate soccer because it's a sport I just don't like.
- The reason these clubs are in such demand is that everyone wants to get in them.
- Freedom of speech is important because people should be able to speak freely.

Straw Man

The **straw-man** fallacy consists of an attack on a view similar to but not the same as the one your opponent holds. It is a familiar diversionary tactic. The name probably derives from an old game in which a straw man was set up to divert attention from the real target that a contestant was supposed to knock down.

Notice how in the following passage about New York mayor Michael Bloomberg's proposed ban on the sale of sugary drinks larger than sixteen ounces, conservative pundit George Will shifts the focus from that proposed restriction to global warming:

> "That's modern liberalism: They delight in bossing people around," Will complained to ABC's George Stephanopoulos. "What Bloomberg is saying [is] the government helps with your health care, the government's implicated in your health. Therefore, we own you. Therefore, the government can fine tune all the decisions you make pertinent to your health."
>
> "This is one of the reasons liberals are so enamored over the issue of climate change," Will continued. "They say all our behaviors in some way affect the climate, therefore, the government — meaning, we liberals, the party of government — can fine tune all your behavior right down to the light bulbs you use."[6]

---

[6] David Edwards, "George Will Uses Bloomberg's Soda Ban to Blast Climate Change Laws," rawstory.com, 3 June 2012.

Red Herring

Another diversionary tactic is the **red herring**. The straw man is an attempt to draw an opponent's attention to an issue similar to but not exactly what the opponent was talking about that the speaker or writer can better address. A red herring is an attempt to divert attention away from the subject at hand to *any* other subject, not just one related to the original subject.

An outstanding example of the red herring fallacy occurred in the famous Checkers speech of Senator Richard Nixon. In 1952, during his vice-presidential campaign, Nixon was accused of having appropriated $18,000 in campaign funds for his personal use. At one point in the radio and television speech in which he defended his reputation, he said:

> One other thing I probably should tell you, because if I don't they will probably be saying this about me, too. We did get something, a gift, after the election.
>
> A man down in Texas heard Pat on the radio mention the fact that our two youngsters would like to have a dog, and, believe it or not, the day before we left on this campaign trip we got a message from Union Station in Baltimore saying they had a package for us. We went down to get it. You know what it was?
>
> It was a little cocker spaniel dog, in a crate that he had sent all the way from Texas, black and white, spotted, and our little girl, Tricia, the six-year-old, named it Checkers.
>
> And, you know, the kids, like all kids, loved the dog, and I just want to say this, right now, that regardless of what they say about it, we are going to keep it.[7]

Of course, Nixon knew that the issue was the alleged misappropriation of funds, not the ownership of the dog, which no one had asked him to return.

Two Wrongs Make a Right

The **two-wrongs-make-a-right** fallacy is another example of the way in which attention may be diverted from the question at issue.

After President Jimmy Carter in March 1977 attacked the human rights record of the Soviet Union, Russian officials responded:

> As for the present state of human rights in the United States, it is characterized by the following facts: millions of unemployed, racial discrimination, social inequality of women, infringement of citizens' personal freedom, the growth of crime, and so on.[8]

---

[7] Radio and television address of Senator Nixon from Los Angeles on September 23, 1952.

[8] The *New York Times*, March 3, 1977, p. 1.

The Russians made no attempt to deny the failure of *their* human rights record; instead they attacked by pointing out that the Americans are not blameless either.

Other examples:

- Anyone who killed those innocent children deserves the death penalty.
- It's ok to use chemical weapons against the U.S., since the U.S. used them against Viet Nam.
- I had every right to take his Blu-ray player. He broke mine!

Non Sequitur

The Latin term **non sequitur**, which means "it does not follow," is another fallacy of irrelevance. An advertisement for a book, *Worlds in Collision*, whose theories about the origin of the earth and evolutionary development have been challenged by almost all reputable scientists, states:

> Once rejected as "preposterous"! Critics called it an outrage! It aroused incredible antagonism in scientific and literary circles. Yet half a million copies were sold and for twenty-seven years it remained an outstanding bestseller.

Joel Pett, *Lexington Herald-Leader*, CartoonArts International, Inc.

We know, of course, that the popularity of a book does not bestow scientific respectability. The number of sales, therefore, is irrelevant to proof of the book's theoretical soundness—a non sequitur.

Other examples sometimes appear in comments by politicians and political candidates. In June 2010, President Obama said, "After all, oil is a finite resource. We consume more than 20 percent of the world's oil, but have less than 2 percent of the world's oil reserves."[9] This is a non sequitur because the relevant relationship would be between the U.S. percentage of world *population* (not oil reserves) and the U.S. percentage of world oil consumption.

Ad Populum

Arguers guilty of the **ad populum** fallacy make an appeal to the prejudices of the people (*populum* in Latin). They assume that their claim can be adequately defended without further support if they emphasize a belief or attitude that the audience shares with them. One common form of ad populum is an appeal to patriotism, which may enable arguers to omit evidence that the audience needs for proper evaluation of the claim. In the following advertisement, the makers of Zippo lighters made such an appeal in urging readers to buy their product:

> It's a grand old lighter. Zippo—the grand old lighter that's made right here in the good old U.S.A.
>
> We truly make an all-American product. The raw materials used in making a Zippo lighter are all right from this great land of ours.
>
> Zippo windproof lighters are proud to be Americans.

Other examples:

- But you have to let me go to the party! *Everyone* will be there!
- Everybody drives a little over the speed limit. If I drove the speed limit, I would get rear-ended!
- Lipton Ice Tea. Join the Dance.

Appeal to Tradition

In making an **appeal to tradition**, the arguer assumes that what has existed for a long time and has therefore become a tradition should continue to exist *because* it is a tradition. If the arguer avoids telling his or her reader *why* the tradition should be preserved, he or she may be accused of failing to meet the real issue.

The following statement appeared in a letter defending the membership policy of the Century Club, an all-male club established in New York City in

---

[9] Glen Kessler, "U.S. Oil Resources: President Obama's 'Non Sequitur Facts,'" *Washington Post Online*, washingtonpost.com, 15 Mar. 2012.

Strategies for Uncovering Logical Fallacies

1. If your source is making use of induction — that is, drawing a conclusion based on a number of individual examples — does it have enough examples with variety to justify the conclusion? In other words, will your readers be able to make the inductive leap from examples to the conclusion you are asking them to make?

2. If your source is making use of deduction, is its conclusion a logical one based on the premises underlying it? To be sure, write out its argument in the form of a syllogism, and confirm that both the major and the minor premises are true.

3. Avoid sources that word their thesis statements in absolute terms like *all, every, everyone, everybody,* and *always.*

4. Use the list of fallacies in this chapter as a checklist while you read each of your sources with a critical eye, looking for any breakdown in logic.

1847 that was under pressure to admit women. The writer was a Presbyterian minister who opposed the admission of women.

> I am totally opposed to a proposal which would radically change the nature of the Century. . . . A club creates an ethos of its own over the years, and I would deeply deplore a step that would inevitably create an entirely different kind of place.
>
> A club like the Century should surely be unaffected by fashionable whims. . . .[10]

Numerous activities continue "because it's always been done that way." They range from debutante balls that may seem out of sync with modern times to football traditions. Texas A&M students were so devoted to the massive bonfire that marked the approach of their game with rival University of Texas that it was continued off campus, unsanctioned by the school, even after eleven students and one former student died during a collapse of the stacked wood in 1999. Tradition in and of itself is not a bad thing, but discrimination, injustice, and unsafe behaviors have often been prolonged in the name of tradition.

Practice

Decide whether the reasoning in the following examples is faulty. Use the common fallacies presented in the previous pages to explain your answers.

1. The presiding judge of a revolutionary tribunal, being asked why people are being executed without trial, replies, "Why should we put them on trial when we know that they're guilty?"

---

[10] David H. C. Read, letter to the *New York Times,* January 13, 1983, p. 14.

2. The government has the right to require the wearing of helmets while operating or riding on a motorcycle because of the high rate of head injuries incurred in motorcycle accidents.

3. Children who watch game shows rather than situation comedies receive higher grades in school. So it must be true that game shows are more educational than situation comedies.

4. The meteorologist predicted the wrong amount of rain for May. Obviously, the meteorologist is unreliable.

5. Women ought to be permitted to serve in combat. Why should men be the only ones to face death and danger?

6. If Lady Gaga uses Truvia, it must taste better than Splenda.

7. People will gamble anyway, so why not legalize gambling in this state?

8. Because so much money was spent on public education in the last decade while educational achievement declined, more money to improve education can't be the answer to reversing the decline.

9. He's a columnist for a campus newspaper, so he must be a pretty good writer.

10. We tend to exaggerate the need for Standard English. You don't need much Standard English for most jobs in this country.

11. It's discriminatory to mandate that police officers must conform to a certain height and weight.

12. A doctor can charge for a missed appointment, so patients should be charged less when a doctor keeps them waiting.

13. Because this soft drink contains so many chemicals, it must be unsafe.

14. Core requirements should be eliminated. After all, students are paying for their education, so they should be able to earn a diploma by choosing the courses they want.

15. We should encourage a return to arranged marriages in this country since marriages based on romantic love haven't been very successful.

16. I know three redheads who have terrible tempers, and since Annabel has red hair, I'll bet she has a terrible temper, too.

17. Supreme Court Justice Byron White was an all-American football player while in college, so how can you say that athletes are dumb?

18. Benjamin H. Sasway, a student at Humboldt State University in California, was indicted for failure to register for possible conscription. Barry Lynn, president of Draft Action, an antidraft group, said, "It is disgraceful that this administration is embarking on an effort to fill the prisons with men of conscience and moral commitment."

19. James A. Harris, former president of the National Education Association: "Twenty-three percent of schoolchildren are failing to graduate and another large segment graduates as functional illiterates. If 23 percent of anything else failed—23 percent of automobiles didn't run, 23 percent of the buildings fell down, 23 percent of stuffed ham spoiled—we'd look at the producer."

20. A professor at Rutgers University: "The arrest rate for women is rising three times as fast as that of men. Women, inflamed by the doctrines of feminism, are pursuing criminal careers with the same zeal as business and the professions."

21. Physical education should be required because physical activity is healthful.

22. George Meany, former president of the AFL-CIO, in 1968: "To these people who constantly say you have got to listen to these younger people, they have got something to say, I just don't buy that at all. They smoke more pot than we do and if the younger generation are the hundred thousand kids that lay around a field up in Woodstock, New York, I am not going to trust the destiny of the country to that group."

23. That candidate was poor as a child, so he will certainly be sympathetic to the poor if he's elected.

24. When the federal government sent troops into Little Rock, Arkansas, to enforce integration of the public school system, the governor of Arkansas attacked the action, saying that it was as brutal an act of intervention as Russia's sending troops into Hungary to squelch the Hungarians' rebellion. In both cases, the governor said, the rights of a freedom-loving, independent people were being violated.

25. Governor Jones was elected two years ago. Since that time, constant examples of corruption and subversion have been unearthed. It is time to get rid of the man responsible for this kind of corrupt government.

26. Are we going to vote a pay increase for our teachers, or are we going to allow our schools to deteriorate into substandard custodial institutions?

27. You see, the priests were right. After we threw those virgins into the volcano, it quit erupting.

28. The people of Rome lost their vitality and desire for freedom when their emperors decided that the way to keep them happy was to provide them with bread and circuses. What can we expect of our own country now that the government gives people free food and there is a constant round of entertainment provided by television?

29. From Mark Clifton, "The Dread Tomato Affliction" (proving that eating tomatoes is dangerous and even deadly): "Ninety-two point four percent of juvenile delinquents have eaten tomatoes. Fifty-seven point one percent of the adult criminals in penitentiaries throughout the United States have eaten tomatoes. Eighty-four percent of all people killed in automobile accidents during the year have eaten tomatoes."

30. From Galileo, *Dialogues Concerning Two New Sciences*: "But can you doubt that air has weight when you have the clear testimony of Aristotle affirming that all elements have weight, including air, and excepting only fire?"

31. Robert Brustein, artistic director of the American Repertory Theater, commenting on a threat by Congress in 1989 to withhold funding from an offensive art show: "Once we allow lawmakers to become art critics, we take the first step into the world of Ayatollah Khomeini, whose murderous review of

The Satanic Verses still chills the heart of everyone committed to free expression." (The Ayatollah Khomeini called for the death of the author Salman Rushdie because Rushdie had allegedly committed blasphemy against Islam in his novel.)

READING ARGUMENT

Seeing Logical Fallacies

The following essay has been annotated to point out places where the author finds logical fallacies with cyclists' demands for road privileges. Annotations also note logical problems with the author's argument.

Drivers Get Rolled
CHRISTOPHER CALDWELL

Late last August, along the coast of New Hampshire, Kevin Walsh, police chief in the town of Rye, got a lecture on law enforcement from a bunch of grown-up bicyclists. Local law requires bikers to ride single-file when there is traffic. But this day, a pack of a dozen or so bikers were racing down Ocean Boulevard, at high speed, up to five abreast, according to an interview the chief later gave. Walsh decided to flag them down and tell them what they were doing was unsafe, "out of control," and "an accident waiting to happen." He stood in the middle of Ocean Boulevard and signaled them to stop. The bikers blew past him in a whoosh! of Lycra, sweat, and profanity. Walsh got in his cruiser and cut off the bikers four miles up the road. When he stopped them, they began to chew him out. "You almost killed somebody back there, standing in the middle of the road," one of them screamed at the cop. "Do you understand we can't stop? Do you understand we can't stop like a car?"

The bikers are setting up a straw man to divert blame from themselves.

Shows the false analogy: If they can't stop like a car, they shouldn't expect the rights of drivers.

Like many episodes in the world of adult recreational cycling, this one breaks new ground in the annals of chutzpah. Few non-cyclists would think to scold a law enforcement official for having nearly been run over by them. Fewer still would release to the news media a video of the incident — which came from a camera mounted on the handlebars of one of the bikers — in the almost demented belief that it constituted a vindication rather than an incrimination. And yet you can see it online.

Christopher Caldwell is a senior editor at the *Weekly Standard*. His article appeared on weeklystandard.com on November 18, 2013.

Incidents like this now happen every day. Laws governing bikes on roads have never been crystal-clear, and have always been marked by a degree of common sense and compromise. An increase in racing and commuting bikers has altered what passes for common sense. Cyclists like the ones in New Hampshire, whose reckless riding and self-righteousness have earned rolled eyes nationwide and the nickname of "Lycra louts" in England, have tested the public's willingness for compromise. As bicyclists become an ever more powerful lobby, ever more confident in the good they are doing for the environment and public health, they are discovering — to their sincere surprise — that they are provoking mistrust and even hostility among the public.

Transported

When there are more bicyclists on the road, when most bicyclists are no longer children and teens, and when well-built bikes can easily descend a hill at 50 miles an hour, new questions come up. The first is how we are to think of bikes. Are they like really fast pedestrians? Or like cars with a lower maximum speed? The law's general view is that they are vehicles. But what the law really means is not that bikes are exactly like cars but that they are analogous. You don't need to get a license to ride a bike, you don't need your vehicle inspected to put it on the road, and you aren't charged tax for the upkeep of highways. There is considerable ambiguity here, and activist bikers, with lawyerly sophistication, almost unfailingly claim the best of both worlds. Consider the guy we mentioned above who insisted police chief Walsh give him all the rights of the road for a vehicle he claimed to be unable to stop. Bicyclists are exactly like cars when it suits them — as when they occupy the middle of a lane in rush hour. But they are different when it suits them — going 18 mph in that very same lane even though the posted speed is 45, riding two abreast, running red lights if there's nothing coming either way, passing vehicles on the right when there's a right turn coming up. This makes bikes a source of unpredictability, frustration, and danger.

Shows why the analogy between cars and bikes works only part of the time

This should not alarm us unduly. Bicyclists sometimes do require the middle of the roadway, and do need special consideration. The rightmost part of the road is often punctuated with old-fashioned sewer grates that will swallow a tire whole and fling you over the handlebars. There are broken bottles, dropped hypodermic needles, oil slicks that have drained off the road's crown, and places where the road is frittered away. The right side of the road is also where passenger doors get flung open, sometimes suddenly, and one piece of bad timing will send you to kingdom come. Almost 700 cyclists died on the road in the United States in 2011. Let us not forget the environmental,

A reminder of the dangers of bicycling

5

aesthetic, and health benefits of cycling over driving, which are obvious and undeniable.

The problem is that our transportation network, built at the cost of trillions over the decades, is already over capacity, as the Obama administration was fond of reminding us when arguing for the 2009 stimulus package. It is not so easily rejiggered. Unquestionably we have misbuilt our transport grid. It makes us car-dependent. It should better accommodate bikers and walkers. But for now it can't. Unless you want to cover much more of the country in asphalt — which is far from the professed wishes of bikers — lane space is finite. There are few places in America where public transportation can serve as a serious alternative to driving. In only five metropolitan areas — Boston, New York, Washington, Chicago, and San Francisco — do as many as 10 percent of commuters take public transportation.

A simple if unfortunate fact: Our transportation network was not built to accommodate bicycles.

So, except in a few spots where roads were built too wide and can now accommodate bike paths, adding bicycles to the mix means squeezing cars. Bike-riders don't "share" the road so much as take it over. Their wish is generally that the right-hand lane of any major or medium-sized road be turned into a bike lane or, at best, a shared-use lane. This would place drivers in a position of second-class citizenship on roads that were purpose-built for them. There are simply not enough cyclists to make that a reasonable idea. What is going on is the attempt of an organized private interest to claim a public good. Cyclists remind one of those residents in exurban subdivisions who, over years, allow grass and shrubbery to encroach on dirt public sidewalk until it becomes indistinguishable from their yards, and then sneakily fence it in.

False dilemma: Private interest and public good do not have to be mutually exclusive.

Our numbers about how many people bike and how often are relatively imprecise. The best estimates come from counting commutes and accidents. According to the U.S. census, 120 million people drive to work every weekday, and 750,000 bike. In other words, there are 160 drivers for every biker. Bike use is growing — but even at 40 times the present level it would still not be sensible public policy to squander a quarter, a third, or half of the lane space on a busy rush-hour artery for a bike lane.

Bike riding could be the wave of the future, or it could be a sports fad, the way tennis was in the 1970s or skateboarding in the 1980s or golf in the 1990s. It is hard to tell, since bike riding is now the beneficiary of vast public and private subsidies and massive infrastructure projects, from Indianapolis's $100 million plan to add bike lanes and other nonauto byways to Citibank's underwriting of the New York City bike-share program. "Subsidize it and they will come," could be the motto. Drivers are being taxed to subsidize their own eviction.

High Rollers

There are a number of internationally recognized signals through which   10
bicyclists convey their intentions to drivers. The raised left hand means a right
turn, the dropped left hand means slowing down, and so on. I have never
seen either of these gestures used. Instead, cyclists tend to communicate with
motorists through a simpler, all-purpose gesture, the raised middle finger.
The self-righteousness, the aplomb, of bicyclists is their stereotypical vice and

> Hasty generalization: Not all bikers are rude.

quirk, like the madness of hatters, the drunkenness of poets, and the communism of furriers.

The attitude was nicely captured in a pro-biking letter to the editor in
the *Brookline TAB*, the community paper for Boston's richest neighborhoods:
"Whenever someone bikes or walks to the store or to work," the writer began,
"he or she is taking one automobile off the road and making a significant contribution both to Brookline's safety and to reducing the carbons so dangerous
to life on earth." You see? It only looks like I'm having a midlife crisis — I'm

> The virtues of biking are irrelevant to the issue of biking safely.

actually on a rescue mission! The question of what courtesy the cyclist owes
the community is immediately taken off the table, replaced by the question of
what the community can possibly do to repay its debt to the cyclist.

All of us who care about the environment have a sense — even a conviction — that biking is more virtuous than driving. What distinguishes the biking enthusiast is that he is just as convinced that biking is more virtuous than
walking: "While riding," another *TAB* correspondent wrote, "I have encountered pedestrians who are texting. They are a danger to themselves and others,
because they sometimes make erratic movements and often ignore requests to
step to the side so a bicycle can pass." By "request," the writer probably means
a barked command of "On your right!" or "On your left!" made by a cyclist approaching from behind at 30 mph.

If bicyclists have a more highly developed sense that they can boss others around, this is because they disproportionately belong to the classes from
which bosses come. They are, to judge from their blogs, more aggrieved by
delivery trucks parked in bike lanes than drivers are by delivery trucks parked
in car lanes. This may be because proportionately fewer of them have ever met
a person who drives a delivery truck. The 2011 accident data of the National
Highway Traffic Safety Administration give us a hint that ardent bicycling
is not, for the most part, a youthful avocation, as those whose biking days
ended in the 1970s or '80s might assume. The average age of those killed
cycling — presumably a rough proxy for those doing the most grueling road
riding — has been rising by close to a year annually. In 2003 it was 36; in 2011
it was 43. Cyclists are heavily weighted towards the baby boom generation.

The group involved in the most fatal accidents in 2011 is ages 45–54, followed by ages 55–64. The two cohorts make up those born between 1947 and 1966.

This generation is at the height of its earning power, and bikers are drawn from the very richest part of it. Shortly after Birmingham, England, got almost $30 million from the government to make itself more bike-friendly, the *Birmingham Post* researched who was building bike spaces in London. Topping the list were the Gherkin, the ghastly Norman Foster–designed skyscraper in the financial district that houses a lot of London's financial-services industry; Goldman Sachs's Fleet Street headquarters; and London Wall Place, a high-end office building slated for construction in the City. This helps explain why Portland, Oregon, is so proud of its status as the country's most "bicycle-friendly" city, and why Las Vegas, Louisville, and other places are vying to outdo it. City officials want to be "bicycle-friendly" for the same reason they want to be "gay-friendly" or "Internet-friendly," and for the same reason they built opera houses in the nineteenth century and art museums in the twentieth — it is a way of telling investors: "Rich people live here."

> Doubtful cause: Is that why cities want to be bicycle friendly?

15   Once you understand that bicycling is a rich person's hobby, you can understand the fallacy that *Slate* editor David Plotz, an ardent bicyclist, committed when he asked why such a large number of dangerous drivers he encountered while cycling to work drove the same make of car. Of the twenty scares he's had in his life, ten came from BMWs. "In other words," Plotz wrote, "the BMW, a car that has less than 2 percent market share in the United States, was responsible for 50 percent of the menacing." Why, he wondered? Was it a sense of entitlement, or were BMW-drivers just "assholes"? Probably neither — it is that luxury-car-driving and bike-commuting are heavily concentrated in the same very top sliver of the American class hierarchy. The percentage of BMWs driving between where the average cyclist lives to where the average cyclist works is a heck of a lot higher than 2 percent. It may not be 50 percent — the Help, after all, needs to use these roads, too — but it is high.

> False dilemma: Feeling entitled and being assholes are not the only alternatives.

Wheel Estate

If bike-friendly areas are rich neighborhoods, they are a particular kind of rich neighborhood. They are college towns, or at least "latte towns," to use the term David Brooks coined in these pages. The top cities for cycling commuters, according to the U.S. census, are Corvallis and Eugene in Oregon, Fort Collins and Boulder in Colorado, and Missoula, Montana. The census notes that Portland, Oregon, is the only metropolitan area in which at least 2 percent of commutes are by bike.

Its concentration in cultural hubs has consequences. Bicycling's apostles have behind them not just the economic and lobbying power of the "One Percent," but also the cultural and intellectual power of its most sophisticated members. The idea that there might be alternative social goods competing with cycling, or any reason not to offer cyclists as much leeway and indulgence as they might demand, seems scarcely to have occurred to anybody who discusses it in public. That, surely, is why a cyclist might think that posting a video of a cyclist scolding a well-meaning New Hampshire police chief might help the cycling cause. The promotion of cycling is open to discussion as to means, but not as to ends. The question is how, not whether, to build more bike infrastructure; and how, not whether, to educate motorists about their responsibilities to bikers. It is never about educating bicyclists on how to find alternative modes of transport.

Bicyclists expect privileges.

Leaders of the biking community, though, most often try to cast themselves as an underprivileged minority. Ian Walker, a "traffic psychologist" from the University of Bath, describes cyclists as a "minority outgroup"— they suffer in a society that "views cycling as anti-conventional and possibly even infantile." In an August editorial calling for an end to "anti-cyclist bias," the *San Francisco Bay Guardian* opined: "To focus exclusively on the behavior of cyclists is like blaming a rape victim for wearing a short skirt."

False analogy

As is not uncommon when progressive utopias are being constructed, there are a number of informal activist groups for enforcing opinion. The Twitter feed CycleHatred was founded in Britain to expose those who wrote negative things about cyclists, although recent press reports have implicitly questioned whether such exposure might do the anti-cycling cause more good than harm. The cycling journalist Peter Walker of the *Guardian* commented on a Tweet (probably good-humored) attacking Britain's Olympic gold medalist Bradley Wiggins for having made cycling popular ("If Wiggins came in here, I'd give him a piece of my mind"). Ian Walker responded:

Walker points out the hasty generalization.

> This is a fantastic example of what is sometimes called the "cyclists should get their house in order" argument — that people who have nothing in common except choosing cycling as one of their several regular forms of transport are nonetheless necessarily defined by it, and are somehow responsible for the worst actions by others on bikes.

But this is a category error. That our road system cannot provide the resources to support cyclists in the style to which they would like to become accustomed is a matter of policy and limited resources, not of civil rights and   20 prejudice. An action that is ignorable at the individual level — such as cycling down the middle of the street at high speed — can become a problem when the masses do it. That is why, for instance, people have been forbidden to burn leaves in their backyard for the past half-century. One pile of leaves is a beautiful smell. Several are a pollution problem, or so they tell us. Right or wrong, those who consider leaf burning a problem are not making a bigoted assessment of the personalities of the individual leaf-burners.

Bikers' unmet needs, in terms of both infrastructure and law, are limitless. A common trope is to compare America's spending on bikes with that of the Netherlands. Amsterdam spends $39 per resident on bike trails, laments the *Boston Globe*, while Boston spends under $2. Until we shell out as much as the Dutch, there can be no such thing as misspent money. Pointing to areas, mostly poor, in which Washington, D.C.'s Capital Bikeshare program has failed to win a following, the director of the program assured the *Washington Post* that "those areas where the bike community is not yet self-sustaining" are "precisely where the District Department of Transportation needs to double its efforts."

> The analogy is incomplete unless the number of bikers is also compared.

The bicycle agenda is coming to resemble the feminist agenda from the 1970s, when previously all-male universities went co-ed. Everything that was ever off-limits to the aggrieved minority must be opened up, while sancta established for the minority in the old days must be preserved, and new ones founded. So bikers must have access to roads and hiking trails, but also get their own new "bike boulevards." Having a special bike-friendly highway, such as Route 9W, west of the Hudson River, does not mean that certain other highways will ever be closed off to bikes in the interest of efficiency or fairness.

> The analogy is not clear.

While it is wrong to call bicyclists a downtrodden minority, they are a minority in one sense. They are one of those compact, issue-oriented small groups that, as the economist Mancur Olson warned in his classic *The Logic of Collective Action* (1965), generally take unmotivated majorities to the cleaners. There are probably a million dedicated cyclists in this country, bent on taking over a quarter or a third of the nation's road space, built at the price of, let us repeat, trillions. They are ranged against the 200 million drivers who have a vague sense they are being duped. But this sense is only vague, and because motorists, like other American voters, have developed the habit of being talked into giving up what is theirs, any wise person would bet on the bicyclists' winning all they ask for. A small collection of elite hobbyists will continue, as Tacitus might have put it, to make a traffic jam and call it peace.

Reading and Discussion Questions

1. Explain why the anecdote in the first paragraph is an example of the straw man fallacy.
2. Explain one or more of the examples of false analogy in the article.
3. How convincing is Caldwell's argument that bicyclists are among our richest citizens? Does your experience seem to support that claim? Explain.
4. Have you experienced or witnessed the sorts of problems between bikers and drivers that Caldwell describes? If so, give an example.
5. In spite of the focus in the annotations on logical fallacies, what strengths does the article have?

Practice: Uncovering Logical Fallacies

Read the speech below, and answer the questions that follow.

On Nation and Race
ADOLF HITLER

There are some truths which are so obvious that for this very reason they are not seen or at least not recognized by ordinary people. They sometimes pass by such truisms as though blind and are most astonished when someone suddenly discovers what everyone really ought to know. Columbus's eggs lie around by the hundreds of thousands, but Columbuses are met with less frequency.

Thus men without exception wander about in the garden of Nature; they imagine that they know practically everything and yet with few exceptions pass blindly by one of the most patent principles of Nature's rule: the inner segregation of the species of all living beings on this earth.

Even the most superficial observation shows that Nature's restricted form of propagation and increase is an almost rigid basic law of all the innumerable forms of expression of her vital urge. Every animal mates only with a member of the same species. The titmouse seeks the titmouse, the finch the finch, the stork the stork, the field mouse the field mouse, the dormouse the dormouse, the wolf the she-wolf, etc.

Only unusual circumstances can change this, primarily the compulsion of captivity or any other cause that makes it impossible to mate within the same species. But then Nature begins to resist this with all possible means, and her most visible protest consists either in refusing further capacity for propagation to bastards or in limiting the fertility of later offspring; in most cases, however, she takes away the power of resistance to disease or hostile attacks.

This is only too natural.

Any crossing of two beings not at exactly the same level produces a medium between the level of the two parents. This means: The

5

Adolf Hitler (1889–1945) became the Nazi dictator of Germany in the mid-1930s. "On Nation and Race" (editor's title) begins Chapter 11 of *Mein Kampf (My Struggle)*, vol. 1, published in 1925.

offspring will probably stand higher than the racially lower parent, but not as high as the higher one. Consequently, it will later succumb in the struggle against the higher level. Such mating is contrary to the will of Nature for a higher breeding of all life. The precondition for this does not lie in associating superior and inferior, but in the total victory of the former. The stronger must dominate and not blend with the weaker, thus sacrificing his own greatness. Only the born weakling can view this as cruel, but he after all is only a weak and limited man; for if this law did not prevail, any conceivable higher development of organic living beings would be unthinkable.

The consequence of this racial purity, universally valid in Nature, is not only the sharp outward delimitation of the various races, but their uniform character in themselves. The fox is always a fox, the goose a goose, the tiger a tiger, etc., and the difference can lie at most in the varying measure of force, strength, intelligence, dexterity, endurance, etc., of the individual specimens. But you will never find a fox who in his inner attitude might, for example, show humanitarian tendencies toward geese, as similarly there is no cat with a friendly inclination toward mice.

Therefore, here, too, the struggle among themselves arises less from inner aversion than from hunger and love. In both cases, Nature looks on calmly, with satisfaction, in fact. In the struggle for daily bread all those who are weak and sickly or less determined succumb, while the struggle of the males for the female grants the right or opportunity to propagate only to the healthiest. And struggle is always a means for improving a species' health and power of resistance and, therefore, a cause of its higher development.

If the process were different, all further and higher development would cease and the opposite would occur. For, since the inferior always predominates numerically over the best, if both had the same possibility of preserving life and propagating, the inferior would multiply so much more rapidly that in the end the best would inevitably be driven into the background, unless a correction of this state of affairs were undertaken. Nature does just this by subjecting the weaker part to such severe living conditions that by them alone the number is limited, and by not permitting the remainder to increase promiscuously, but making a new and ruthless choice according to strength and health.

No more than Nature desires the mating of weaker with stronger individuals, even less does she desire the blending of a higher with a lower race, since, if she did, her whole work of higher breeding, over perhaps hundreds of thousands of years, might be ruined with one blow.

10

Historical experience offers countless proofs of this. It shows with terrifying clarity that in every mingling of Aryan blood with that of lower peoples the result was the end of the cultured people. North America, whose population consists in by far the largest part of Germanic elements who mixed but little with the lower colored peoples, shows a different humanity and culture from Central and South America, where the predominantly Latin immigrants often mixed with the aborigines on a large scale. By this one example, we can clearly and distinctly recognize the effect of racial mixture. The Germanic inhabitant of the American continent, who has remained racially pure and unmixed, rose to be master of the continent; he will remain the master as long as he does not fall a victim to defilement of the blood.

The result of all racial crossing is therefore in brief always the following:

(a) Lowering of the level of the higher race;

(b) Physical and intellectual regression and hence the beginning of a slowly but surely progressing sickness.

To bring about such a development is, then, nothing else but to sin against the will of the eternal creator.

And as a sin this act is rewarded.

15   When man attempts to rebel against the iron logic of Nature, he comes into struggle with the principles to which he himself owes his existence as a man. And this attack must lead to his own doom.

Here, of course, we encounter the objection of the modern pacifist, as truly Jewish in its effrontery as it is stupid! "Man's role is to overcome Nature!"

Millions thoughtlessly parrot this Jewish nonsense and end up by really imagining that they themselves represent a kind of conqueror of Nature; though in this they dispose of no other weapon than an idea, and at that such a miserable one, that if it were true no world at all would be conceivable.

But quite aside from the fact that man has never yet conquered Nature in anything, but at most has caught hold of and tried to lift one or another corner of her immense gigantic veil of eternal riddles and secrets, that in reality he invents nothing but only discovers everything, that he does not dominate Nature, but has only risen on the basis of his knowledge of various laws and secrets of Nature to be lord over those other living creatures who lack this knowledge — quite aside from all this, an idea cannot overcome the preconditions for the development and being of humanity, since the idea itself depends only on man. Without human beings there is no human idea in this world; therefore, the idea as such is always conditioned by the presence of human beings and hence of all the laws which created the precondition for their existence.

And not only that! Certain ideas are even tied up with certain men. This applies most of all to those ideas whose content originates, not in an exact scientific truth, but in the world of emotion, or, as it is so beautifully and clearly expressed today, reflects an "inner experience." All these ideas, which have nothing to do with cold logic as such, but represent only pure expressions of feeling, ethical conceptions, etc., are chained to the existence of men, to whose intellectual imagination and creative power they owe their existence. Precisely in this case the preservation of these definite races and men is the precondition for the existence of these ideas. Anyone, for example, who really desired the victory of the pacifistic idea in this world with all his heart would have to fight with all the means at his disposal for the conquest of the world by the Germans; for, if the opposite should occur, the last pacifist would die out with the last German, since the rest of the world has never fallen so deeply as our own people, unfortunately, has for this nonsense so contrary to Nature and reason. Then, if we were serious, whether we liked it or not, we would have to wage wars in order to arrive at pacifism. This and nothing else was what Wilson, the American world savior, intended, or so at least our German visionaries believed — and thereby his purpose was fulfilled.

In actual fact the pacifistic-humane idea is   20 perfectly all right perhaps when the highest type of man has previously conquered and subjected the world to an extent that makes him the sole ruler of this earth. Then this idea lacks the power of producing evil effects in exact proportion as its practical application becomes rare and finally impossible. Therefore, first struggle and then we shall see what can be done. Otherwise mankind has passed the high point of its development and the end is not the domination of any ethical idea but barbarism and consequently chaos. At this point someone or other may laugh, but this planet once moved through the ether for millions of years without human beings and it can do so again some day if men forget that they owe their higher existence, not to the ideas of a few crazy ideologists, but to the knowledge and ruthless application of Nature's stern and rigid laws.

Everything we admire on this earth today—science and art, technology and inventions—is only the creative product of a few peoples and originally perhaps of one race. On them depends the existence of this whole culture. If they perish, the beauty of this earth will sink into the grave with them.

However much the soil, for example, can influence men, the result of the influence will always be different depending on the races in question. The low fertility of a living space may spur the one race to the highest achievements; in others it will only be the cause of bitterest poverty and final undernourishment with all its consequences. The inner nature of peoples is always determining for the manner in which outward influences will be effective. What leads the one to starvation trains the other to hard work.

All great cultures of the past perished only because the originally creative race died out from blood poisoning.

The ultimate cause of such a decline was their forgetting that all culture depends on men and conversely; hence that to preserve a certain culture the man who creates it must be preserved. This preservation is bound up with the rigid law of necessity and the right to victory of the best and strongest in this world.

Those who want to live, let them fight, and those who do not want to fight in this world of eternal struggle do not deserve to live. 25

Even if this were hard—that is how it is! Assuredly, however, by far the harder fate is that which strikes the man who thinks he can overcome Nature, but in the last analysis only mocks her. Distress, misfortune, and diseases are her answer.

The man who misjudges and disregards the racial laws actually forfeits the happiness that seems destined to be his. He thwarts the triumphal march of the best race and hence also the precondition for all human progress, and remains, in consequence, burdened with all the sensibility of man, in the animal realm of helpless misery.

It is idle to argue which race or races were the original representative of human culture and hence the real founders of all that we sum up under the word *humanity*. It is simpler to raise the question with regard to the present, and here an easy, clear answer results. All the human culture, all the results of art, science, and technology that we see before us today, are almost exclusively the creative product of the Aryan. This very fact admits of the not unfounded inference that he alone was the founder of all higher humanity, therefore representing the prototype of all that we understand by the word *man*. He is the Prometheus of mankind from whose bright forehead the divine spark of genius has sprung at all times, forever kindling anew that fire of knowledge which illumined the night of silent mysteries and thus caused man to climb the path to mastery over the other beings of this earth. Exclude him — and perhaps after a few thousand years darkness will again descend on the earth, human culture will pass, and the world turn to a desert.

Reading and Discussion Questions

1. Find places in the essay where Hitler attempts to emphasize the scientific objectivity of his theories.

2. Are some passages difficult to understand? (See, for example, para. 11.) How do you explain the difficulty?

3. In explaining his ideology, how does Hitler misinterpret the statement that "Every animal mates only with a member of the same species" (para. 3)? How would you characterize this fallacy?

4. Hitler uses the theory of evolution and his interpretation of the "survival of the fittest" to justify his racial philosophy. Find the places in the text where Hitler reveals that he misunderstands the theory in its application to human beings.

5. What false evidence about race does Hitler use in his assessment of the racial experience in North America? Examine carefully the last sentence of paragraph 11: "The Germanic inhabitant of the American continent, who has remained racially pure and unmixed, rose to be master of the continent; he will remain the master as long as he does not fall a victim to defilement of the blood."

6. What criticism of Jews does Hitler offer? How does this criticism help to explain Hitler's pathological hatred of Jews?

7. Hitler believes that pacifism is a violation of "Nature and reason" (para. 19). Would modern scientists agree that the laws of nature require unremitting struggle and conflict between human beings — until the master race conquers? Explain your response.

Assignments for Logic: Understanding Reasoning

Reading and Discussion Questions

1. How do the inductive and deductive reasoning processes relate to the scientific method?

2. Look at an issue of *Consumer Reports* or at the *Consumer Reports* Web site. Pick a general category like laptop computers, SUVs, or digital cameras. Explore how the researchers arrive at their recommendations. Do they use induction or deduction?

3. Why is it difficult to read an essay and tell whether the writer approached the topic through induction or deduction?

4. Do you feel that Jared Diamond's essay "Will Big Business Save the Earth?" is effective? Why, or why not?

5. Locate print ads to illustrate some of the fallacies covered in this chapter.

Writing Suggestions

1. Do some research on the other side of the issue that Diamond addresses. Choose a company that is not doing its part environmentally, and write an essay similar to Diamond's treatment of one company in his essay.

2. Using David von Drehle's essay as a model, write an essay supporting one of these thesis statements or a similar one:

   Those who do these things share one common trait. They are eternal optimists.
   Those who do these things share one common trait. They are eternal pessimists.
   Those who do these things share one common trait. They are tireless workers.
   Those who do these things share one common trait. They are selfless givers.

3. Write an essay in which you analyze one or more fallacies in a single print ad or use several ads to illustrate logical fallacies.

RESEARCH ASSIGNMENT

1. Go to *Google* or another general search engine that you are familiar with. Do a search for either "autism and vaccines" or "cell phones and cancer." (You may have used one of these subjects for an earlier exercise.) Before you click on a link, examine the first ten to fifteen entries in the resulting list. Look at each URL, and see what you can learn from it. Also notice any other information that might affect your opinion of the source's reliability or objectivity.

   - Are there sources that you immediately trust as reliable? Which ones, and why?
   - Are there any that you immediately assume will present a biased perspective? Which ones, and why?
   - Are there any that are completely unfamiliar to you? If so, choose two or three, and speculate what type of source each might be.

2. Now click on a couple of the sources that you trusted as being reliable. Identify exactly who wrote the document that you have accessed. If you cannot find an author, what does that suggest? If there is an author, search that person's name. See if you find convincing credentials that support the assumption that he or she is qualified to write on the subject at hand.

3. Do the same with at least two sources that you predicted would be biased. Does further investigation support your assumption? If so, how?

4. Go to at least one of the sources that were unfamiliar to you. Once you look more closely at the source, do you find any evidence of its reliability or lack thereof? Explain.

bits

To see what you are learning about argumentation applied to the latest world and national news, read our *Bits* blog, "Argument and the Headlines," at **blogs.bedfordstmartins.com/bits**.

RESEARCHING
and Crafting Arguments

Planning and Research

By now, you should be fairly adept at supporting claims. The next step is to apply your skills to writing an argument of your own on a subject of your choice or for an assignment on a topic other than those covered in this text.

In this chapter, we move through the various stages involved in preparing to write an argument: choosing a topic, locating and evaluating sources, and taking notes.

Finding an Appropriate Topic

To write an argument, you first must identify your topic. This is a relatively easy task for someone writing an argument as part of his or her job — a lawyer defending a client, for example, or an advertising executive presenting a campaign. For a student, however, it can be daunting. Which of the many ideas in the world worth debating would make a good subject?

Several guidelines can help you evaluate the possibilities. Perhaps your assignment limits your choices. If you have been asked to write a research paper, you obviously must find a topic on which research is available. If your assignment is more open-ended, you need a topic that is worth the time and effort you expect to invest in it. In either case, your subject should be one that interests you. Don't feel you have to write about what you know — very often, finding out what you don't know will turn out to be more satisfying. You should, however, choose a subject that is familiar enough for you to argue about without fearing you're in over your head.

In this chapter, we will follow a student, Katie, who has been assigned a research paper for her first-year English class. In preparation for the assignment, the class has viewed the movie *Food, Inc.* This is the assignment that Katie must complete:

> The movie *Food, Inc.* raises a multitude of questions about food: the link between the corporate world and our food supply, organic foods, world hunger, alternative fuels, farm workers, childhood obesity. These

are just a sampling of the issues raised. For your research essay, choose an argumentative topic related in some way to the issues discussed in the film. Your thesis should be either a claim of value or a claim of policy. Your essay should be 6–8 double-spaced pages and must use at least six sources. There should be some variety in type of sources — books, articles, electronic journals, etc. Use MLA guidelines for documentation.

Invention Strategies

As a starting point, think of conversations you've had in the past few days or weeks that have involved defending a position. Is there some current political issue you're concerned about? some dispute with friends that would make a valid paper topic? One of the best sources is controversies in the media. Keep your project in mind as you watch TV, read print or online sources, or listen to the radio. You may even run into a potential subject in your course reading assignments or classroom discussions. Fortunately for the would-be writer, nearly every human activity includes its share of disagreement.

As you consider possible topics, write them down. One that looks unlikely at first glance may suggest others or may have more appeal when you come back to it later. Further, simply putting words on paper has a way of stimulating the thought processes involved in writing. Even if your ideas are tentative, the act of converting them into phrases or sentences can often help in developing them.

When student researcher Katie began thinking about her research assignment, she made the following entry in her journal:

I have started thinking about a topic related to food. I knew that there is also a book called *Food, Inc.*, so I went to the library's Web site and looked it up. It is a collection of essays edited by Karl Weber. It looked like a source worth investigating, so I checked it out.

The subtitle of the book is *How Industrial Food Is Making Us Sicker, Fatter, and Poorer — And What We Can Do about It.* That's what the film was about too. I don't have time to read the whole book for this assignment, but I looked at the preface and table of contents to get ideas about how to find a narrow enough subject. One subject that I thought might be interesting is today's epidemic of childhood obesity. There is one chapter in the part of the book that suggests solutions that's called "Improving Kids' Nutrition: An Action Tool Kit for Parents." There is also another essay paired with that one entitled "Childhood Obesity: The Challenge."

When I skimmed the second one, I could tell immediately that it has some good statistics about how bad the problem of childhood obesity is. I know that childhood obesity is too large a subject, and I have to come up with a thesis that is either a claim of value or a claim of policy. I don't think there is much controversy that a problem exists, and that would be a claim of fact. In the first essay I read about something I had never heard of — competitive foods. I found out that competitive foods are the "extras" sold to students in addition to or instead of the nutritious food served in the cafeteria. That has to be a controversial subject.

Evaluating Possible Topics

As you consider possible topics, you must, of course, follow any guidelines provided by your instructor. Not every topic is appropriate for an argumentative essay. Some would be difficult or impossible to find support for; others would make your job as a researcher more difficult than it has to be. The Writer's Guide below describes some characteristics of effective research paper topics.

WRITER'S GUIDE
Effective Research Paper Topics

Keep the following points in mind when settling on a topic for your research paper.

- **Interesting.** Your topic must interest your audience. Who is the audience? For a lawyer, it is usually a judge or jury; for a columnist, anyone who reads the newspaper in which his or her column appears. For the student writer, the audience is to some extent hypothetical. You should assume that your paper is directed at readers who are reasonably intelligent and well informed, but who have no specific knowledge of the subject. It may be useful to imagine you are writing for a local or school publication.

Less Interesting	More Interesting
Nice places to go bird watching	The effect of increasing feral cat population on native song birds
Which college has the best basketball team	The debate over whether schools should drop their intercollegiate sports program in favor of improved health and wellness for all students

- **Debatable.** The purpose of an argument is to defend or refute a thesis, so you should choose a topic that can be seen from more than one perspective. In evaluating a subject that looks promising, ask yourself: Can a case be made for other views? If not, you have no workable ground for building your own case.

Less Debatable	More Debatable
Shoplifting (Nobody would disagree that it is wrong.)	The increased use of security cameras in public spaces
Popularity of electronic tablets (Nobody would disagree that these have become enormously popular.)	The inability to share e-books, which cost just as much as print books

- **Not Too Broad.** Consider how long your paper will be and whether you can do justice to your topic in that amount of space. Your essay will not be very effective if you are able to cover your subject in only a general way with no specifics. As a general rule, the more specific your topic, the better the resulting essay.
- **Not Too Narrow.** In contrast, if you can cover your subject in a paragraph or even in a single page, it clearly is too narrow to be the subject for an argumentative essay.

Too Broad	Too Narrow	Appropriate
Nuclear energy around the world	Why a hybrid car made sense to me	Why the United States should invest in solar energy

- **Not Too Unconventional.** When offering an explanation, especially one that is complicated or extraordinary, look first for a cause that is not too difficult to accept — one that doesn't strain credibility. A reasonable person interested in the truth would search for more conventional explanations before accepting the bizarre or the incredible. Looking for a supernatural explanation for the disappearance of ships in the Bermuda Triangle or a new conspiracy theory to explain the assassination of John F. Kennedy is probably not the best use of your research time and would lead to a claim that would be difficult if not impossible to support.

Even if you start out with a topic that does not meet these criteria, you can use that as a starting point and move toward one that does, as in the examples above. Don't discard a topic that you are interested in until you have tried reworking and improving it. A topic that is too broad can be narrowed down; one that is too narrow can become part of a larger argument. A shift in focus can sometimes make a topic that is not debatable or interesting into one that is.

At this preliminary stage, don't worry if you don't know exactly how to word your thesis. It's useful to write down a few possible phrasings to be sure your topic is one you can work with, but you need not be precise. The information you unearth as you do research will help you to formulate your ideas. Also, stating a thesis in final terms is premature until you know the organization and tone of your paper. If your topic or assignment does not require research, you may want to move ahead to Chapter 12. Student researcher Katie focused her initial topic idea like this:

> I narrowed my topic first to childhood obesity and then to competitive foods in schools. I think that I would like my claim to be that competitive foods should not be allowed in schools, but I will have to see if I can find enough good sources to support that claim.

Initiating Research

The success of any argument, short or long, depends in large part on the quantity and quality of the support behind it. Research, therefore, can be crucial for any argument outside your own experience.

Keeping Research on Track

You should prepare for research by identifying potential resources and learning how they work. Make sure you know how to use the library's catalog and other databases available either in the library or through the campus network. For each database that looks useful, explore how to execute a subject search, how to refine a search, and how to print out or download results. Make sure you know how to find books, relevant reference materials, and journals. Find out whether interlibrary loan is an option and how long it takes. If you plan to use government publications, find out if your library is a depository for federal documents. Identify relevant organizations using the *Encyclopedia of Associations*, and visit their Web sites. Finally, discuss your topic with a librarian at the reference desk to make sure you haven't overlooked anything.

WRITER'S GUIDE
Keeping Your Research on Track

1. **Focus your investigation on building your argument,** not merely on collecting information about the topic. Do follow any promising leads that turn up from the sources you consult, but don't be diverted into general reading that has no direct bearing on your thesis.
2. **Look for at least two pieces of evidence to support each point you want to make.** If you cannot find sufficient evidence, you may need to revise or abandon the point.

3. **Use a variety of sources.** Seek evidence from different kinds of sources (books, magazines, Web sites, government reports, even personal interviews with experts) and from different fields.

4. **Be sure your sources are authoritative.** Articles and essays in scholarly journals are more authoritative than articles in college newspapers or in magazines. Authors whose credentials include many publications and years of study at reputable institutions are probably more reliable than newspaper columnists and the so-called man in the street. However, you can judge reliability much more easily if you are dealing with facts and inferences than with values and emotions.

5. **Don't let your sources' opinions outweigh your own.** Your paper should demonstrate that the thesis and ideas you present are yours, arrived at after careful reflection and supported by research. The thesis need not be original, but your paper should be more than a collection of quotations or a report of the facts and opinions you have been reading.

6. **Don't ignore information that opposes the position you plan to support.** Your argument is not strengthened by pretending such information does not exist. You may find that you must revise or qualify your position based on what your research reveals. Your readers may be aware of other positions on the issue and may judge you to be unreliable, careless, or dishonest if you do not acknowledge them. It is far better to fairly summarize opposing arguments and refute them than to ignore them.

7. **Be sure to use the right number of sources.** Review your assignment to see if the instructor has provided guidelines. Eight sources is about right for a 1,500-word paper, unless your assignment states otherwise. That means sources that you actually use, not ones that you examine but never use ideas or wording from. You want to have enough sources, but not too many. Don't place so much weight on any single source that your paper seems to be mostly a rehash of one author's ideas.

RESEARCH SKILL What Is Common Knowledge?

Common knowledge is information so widely known that you do not need to identify a source. How do you decide?

- One rule that some writers follow is to classify information as common knowledge if at least three to five general reference works such as dictionaries or encyclopedias provide the same information. A more general guideline is to consider it common knowledge if the average reader would be familiar with it.

- It is not necessary to document common knowledge because it is readily available information.

- If you are in doubt as to whether certain information is common knowledge, it is better to identify your source.

Sketching a Preliminary Outline

An outline is usually not written in complete sentences, but some instructors prefer complete sentences, so check your assignment. If your outline is written in sentence form, it will pretty closely match the topic sentences in your paper. If not, the ideas in the outline will provide the organization of the ideas in your paper. Ideas represented by Roman numerals are parallel in significance; the same is true for items represented by *A, B, C*, and so on. You would never have a *I* without a *II*. The same is true at the next level: You wouldn't have an *A* without a *B*. The logic behind that guideline is that there is no reason for breaking a category into only one subordinate category. If your outline needs to be more detailed, *A*-level heads are broken down using *1, 2, 3*, and so on. Those heads can be further broken down into *a, b, c* heads if necessary. You will most likely not need that level of specificity in your outline unless your instructor requires it.

Save the Roman numeral heads for the major divisions of your paper. Use the *A*-level heads for paragraph-level ideas. Make the wording of each level as nearly parallel as possible, as in the following preliminary outline:

Thalidomide: Changing a Drug's Reputation

  I. Thalidomide's history: a promising drug but a medical nightmare
   A. Explain how drug was developed
   B. Explain the medical disaster it caused
  II. New look at thalidomide: its potential to effectively treat cancer and other diseases
   A. Discuss how it first worked to treat leprosy
   B. Support how it can treat cancer
   C. Support how it can treat other diseases
  III. Conclusion

Now you are ready to begin the search for material that will support the argument you have outlined. Remember that your plan for your paper may change depending on what your research reveals. Be prepared to change your outline as necessary so that the outline you turn in with your final draft matches the paper you eventually write.

Student researcher Katie's preliminary outline looked like this:

At this point, I can sketch only a very rough outline of the shape my essay may take. My thesis and my outline may have to change as I continue my research.

Competitive Food in Schools

  I. The history of competitive food in schools
    A. Explain what competitive food is
    B. Explain why competitive food is allowed
 II. The dangers of competitive food in schools
    A. Explain the immediate effect on school performance
    B. Explain the long-term health effects
III. Suggested solutions
IV. Conclusion

Types of Sources

There are two principal ways of gathering supporting evidence for your argument — primary research and secondary research.

Primary Research

Primary sources are firsthand information. By *firsthand* we mean information taken directly from the original source, including field research (interviews, surveys, personal observations, or experiments). If your topic relates to a local issue involving your school or community, or if it focuses on a story that has never been reported by others, field research may be more valuable than anything available in the library. However, the library can be a source of firsthand information. Memoirs and letters written by witnesses to past events, photographs, contemporary news reports of historical events, or expert testimony presented at congressional hearings are all primary sources that may be available in your library. The Internet, too, can be a source of primary data. A discussion list, newsgroup, or chat room focused on your topic may give you a means to converse with activists and contact experts. Web sites of certain organizations provide documentation of their views, unfiltered by others' opinions. The text of laws, court opinions, bills, debates in Congress, environmental impact statements, and even selected declassified FBI files can be found through government-sponsored Web sites. Other sites present statistical data or the text of historical or political documents. Be aware that primary sources do not have to be print sources. Photographs, posters, advertisements, and other visuals can also serve as raw material to be interpreted. Student researcher Katie came up with the following list of possible primary sources:

I want to find at least two good primary sources on my topic. Here is a list of possibilities:

Interview with parents of school-age children

Interview with students

Interview with school cafeteria workers/manager

Printed regulations governing school lunches

Statistics about school nutrition

Statistics about competitive foods

School menus

Poster advertising competitive foods

Letter to the editor

One of the rewards of primary research is that it often generates new information, which in turn produces new interpretations of familiar conditions. It is a favored method for anthropologists and sociologists, and most physical and natural scientists use observation and experiment at some point as essential tools in their research.

The information gleaned from primary research can be used directly to support your claim, or it can provide a starting point for secondary research.

Secondary Research

Secondary sources provide commentary on and analysis of a topic. In addition to raw evidence found in primary sources, secondary sources provide a sense of how others are examining the issues and can yield useful information and analysis. Secondary sources may be written for a popular audience, ranging from news coverage, to popular explanations of research findings, to social analysis, to opinion pieces. Or they may be scholarly publications — journals in which experts present their research and theories to other researchers. (For more on popular and scholarly sources, see the Research Skill box on page 346.) These sources might also take the form of analytical reports written to untangle possible courses of action, such as a report written by staff members for a congressional committee or an analysis of an issue by a think tank that wants to use the evidence it has gathered to influence public opinion.

You can find both primary and secondary sources in your school library and online. For example, you can find journal articles in a library database and statistics on a government Web site.

RESEARCH SKILL ▶ Popular vs. Scholarly Articles

Popular Articles (Magazines)

- Are often written by journalists or professional writers for a general audience
- Use language easily understood by the general public
- Rarely give full citations for sources
- Tend to be shorter than journal articles

Scholarly Articles (Journals)

- Are written by and for faculty, researchers, or scholars (chemists, historians, doctors, artists, etc.)
- Use scholarly or technical language
- Tend to be longer articles about research
- Include full citations for sources
- Are often refereed or peer-reviewed (articles are reviewed by an editor and other specialists before being accepted for publication)
- Book reviews and editorials are not considered scholarly articles, even when found in scholarly journals.

Some Points to Remember

- Both magazine and journal articles can be good sources for your work.
- When selecting articles, think about how you intend to use the information:
    - Do you want background on a topic that is new to you? **(use magazines)**
    - Did your instructor say to cite scholarly resources? **(use journals)**
- Often a combination of the two will be most appropriate for undergraduate research.

Source: Adapted from the University of Arizona Library Web site, www.library.arizona.edu/help /tutorials/scholarly/guide.html. Copyright Arizona Board of Regents for the University of Arizona.

Popular magazines.   Richard B. Levine/Newscom

The American Economic Review

ARTICLES

JAMES HECKMAN, RODRIGO PINTO, AND PETER SAVELYEV
    Understanding the Mechanisms Through Which an Influential Early Childhood
    Program Boosted Adult Outcomes

DAMON CLARK AND HEATHER ROYER
    The Effect of Education on Adult Mortality and Health: Evidence from Britain

DAVID H. AUTOR, DAVID DORN, AND GORDON H. HANSON
    The China Syndrome: Local Labor Market Effects of Import Competition in the
    United States

AMIT K. KHANDELWAL, PETER K. SCHOTT, AND SHANG-JIN WEI
    Trade Liberalization and Embedded Institutional Reform: Evidence from Chinese
    Exporters

ERICA FIELD, ROHINI PANDE, JOHN PAPP, AND NATALIA RIGOL
    Does the Classic Microfinance Model Discourage Entrepreneurship Among the Poor?
    Experimental Evidence from India

NICO VOIGTLÄNDER AND HANS-JOACHIM VOTH
    How the West "Invented" Fertility Restriction

MICHAEL J. ROBERTS AND WOLFRAM SCHLENKER
    Identifying Supply and Demand Elasticities of Agricultural Commodities:
    Implications for the US Ethanol Mandate

KLAUS DESMET AND ESTEBAN ROSSI-HANSBERG
    Urban Accounting and Welfare

JIN LI AND NIKO MATOUSCHEK
    Managing Conflicts in Relational Contracts

PHILIPPE GAGNEPAIN, MARC IVALDI, AND DAVID MARTIMORT
    The Cost of Contract Renegotiation: Evidence from the Local Public Sector

GIACOMO CALZOLARI AND VINCENZO DENICOLÒ
    Competition with Exclusive Contracts and Market-Share Discounts

MARCIN PĘSKI AND BALÁZS SZENTES
    Spontaneous Discrimination

PAOLO BUONANNO AND STEVEN RAPHAEL
    Incarceration and Incapacitation: Evidence from the 2006 Italian Collective Pardon

ARTHUR CAMPBELL
    Word-of-Mouth Communication and Percolation in Social Networks

LEVON BARSEGHYAN, FRANCESCA MOLINARI, TED O'DONOGHUE,
AND JOSHUA C. TEITELBAUM
    The Nature of Risk Preferences: Evidence from Insurance Choices

SHORTER PAPERS: J. A. Parker, N. S. Souleles, D. S. Johnson, and R. McClelland; S. Dhingra; E. E. Schlee;
A. Kurmann and C. Otrok; A. Ziegelmeyer, C. March, and S. Krügel

OCTOBER 2013

Scholarly journal. Cover image of the American Economic Review, October 2013, Vol. 103, No. 6. *American Economic Association*

Finding Sources

The nature of your topic will determine which route you follow to find good sources. If the topic is current, you may find it more important to use articles than books and might bypass the library catalog altogether. If the topic has to do with social policy or politics, government publications may be particularly useful, though they would be unhelpful for a literary paper. If the topic relates to popular culture, the Internet may provide more information than more traditional publications. Consider what kinds of sources will be most useful as you choose your strategy. If you aren't certain which approaches fit your topic best, consult with a librarian at the reference desk.

Databases

You will most likely use one or more databases (online catalogs of reference materials) to locate books and articles on your topic. The library catalog is a database of books and materials owned by the library; other databases may cover articles in popular or specialized journals and may even provide the full text of articles. Some databases may be available only in the library; others may be accessible all over campus.

To search for books, videos, or periodical publications, use the library catalog. For every book in the library, there is an entry in the catalog that gives the book's author, title, publisher, date, length, and subject headings and perhaps some notes about its contents. The catalog entry also gives the call number or location on the shelf and may offer some indication as to the book's availability. Remember when searching the catalog, though, that entries are for whole books and not specific parts of them. If you use search terms that are too narrow, you may not find a book that has a chapter on exactly what you are looking for. Plan to browse the shelves and examine the tables of contents of the books that you find through the catalog to see which ones, in fact, are most helpful for your topic. Student researcher Katie's catalog search is described and illustrated on pages 348–49.

When I did a keyword search of the university library catalog for *competitive foods,* I got 22 results, but most of them had nothing to do with competitive foods in schools. I tried putting the term in quotation marks, and the number was reduced to 5:

Clemson University

This is a listing from the library catalog for a publication that looks promising. I can access the whole publication online by way of the link in the listing:

Corporate author	United States. General Accounting Office.
Title	**School meal programs [electronic resource] : competitive foods are available in many schools : actions taken to restrict them differ by state and locality.**
Publication info.	[Washington, D.C.] : U.S. General Accounting Office, [2004]
Links	
	Connect to http://purl.access.gpo.gov/GPO/LPS48829
Description	p. ; cm.
System details	Mode of access: Internet from GPO Access web site. Address as of 5/13/04: http://frwebgate.access.gpo.gov/cgi-bin/getdoc.cgi?dbname=gao&docid=f:d04673.pdf; current access available via PURL.
Note	Title from title screen (viewed on May 13, 2004).
	"April 2004."
	Paper version available from: U.S. General Accounting Office, 441 G St., NW, Rm. LM, Washington, D.C. 20548.
	"GAO-04-673."
Bibliography	Includes bibliographical references.
Subject	School children -- United States -- Nutrition.
	Nutrition policy -- United States.
	National school lunch program.
Added title	**Competitive foods** are available in many schools : actions taken to restrict them differ by state and locality
Gov't document no.	0546-D (online)

Clemson University

To search for articles, use a generalized database of periodicals. Online indexes such as *EBSCOhost, Infotrac, Searchbank, Readers' Guide Abstracts,* and *ProQuest* may include citations, citations with abstracts (brief summaries), or the entire text of articles. Ask the librarian what is available in your school's library. Student researcher Katie's database search is included on page 350.

I used *Academic OneFile* to search for articles about competitive foods in schools. When I searched *competitive foods,* I got 2,200 results! When I put *competitive foods* in quotation marks, that number was reduced to 50. When I added the search word *school,* the number was still 49. When I clicked the options for peer-reviewed only and full text only, and subject "school food services," I ended up with a more manageable list of 8, including these 3 that look promising:

1. The National School Lunch and competitive food offerings and purchasing behaviors of high school students. Alyvia Burkey, Casey Korba, and Anastasia M. Snelling. *Journal of School Health.* 77.10 (Dec. 2007) p701. Word Count: 3101. BACKGROUND: Across the nation, schools have become actively involved in developing obesity prevention strategies both in classrooms and in cafeterias. We sought to determine the type of foods being offered during lunch . . .

2. Food fight: the battle over redefining competitive foods. Sheila Fleischhacker. *Journal of School Health.* 77.3 (Mar. 2007) p147. Word Count: 4543. BACKGROUND: Environmental and policy influences are potentially the most powerful — and yet the least understood — strategies for reversing the current childhood obesity epidemic. METHODS: This essay focuses on the school . . .

3. The effects of competitive foods promoted in schools. Donald Siegel. JOPERD — *The Journal of Physical Education, Recreation & Dance.* 77.9 (November–December 2006) p12. Word Count: 717. What Was the Question? Recently there has been a great deal of concern about childhood obesity and the role of foods consumed during and after school in mediating a child's weight. While noting that federal guidelines . . .

In addition to these general databases, you may find you need to delve deeper into a particular subject area. **Every academic discipline has some sort of in-depth index to research in that field,** and though the materials these indexes cover tend to be highly specialized, they can provide more substantial support for your claims because they usually include sources written by experts in their fields. These resources may be available in electronic or print form. Here are some examples:

> *Art Index*
> *Biological Abstracts* (the online version is known as *Biosis*)
> *Business Periodicals Index*
> *ERIC* (focused on education research)
> *Index Medicus* (*Medline* or *PubMed* online)

Modern Language Association International Bibliography
    (*MLA Bibliography* online)
Psychological Abstracts (*PsychInfo* or *PsychLit* online)
Sociological Abstracts (*Sociofile* online)

Check with a librarian to find out which specialized databases or indexes that relate to your topic are available in your school's library.

Here are some common features that appear in many databases.

Keyword or Subject Searching. You might have the option of searching a database by *keyword*—using the words that you think are most relevant to your search—or by subject. Typically, a keyword search will search for any occurrence of your search term in titles, notes, or the descriptive headings provided by database catalogers or indexers. The advantage to keyword searching is that you can use terms that come naturally to mind so that you cast your net as widely as possible. The disadvantage is that there may be more than one way to express your topic and you may not capture all the relevant materials unless you use the right keywords.

With *subject searching*, you use search terms from a list of subject headings (sometimes called "descriptors") established by the creators of the database. To make searching as efficient as possible, they choose one word or phrase to express a subject. Every time a new source is entered into the database, the indexers describe it using words from the list of subject headings: When you use the list to search the database, you retrieve every relevant source. You might find that a database lists these subject headings through a thesaurus feature. The sophisticated researcher will always pay attention to the subject headings or descriptors generally listed at the bottom of a record for clues to terms that might work best and for related terms that might be worth trying.

Searching for More Than One Concept. Most database searches allow you to combine terms using the connectors *and, or,* and *not.* These connectors (also known as *Boolean operators*) group search terms in different ways. If you search for "zoos *and* animal rights," for example, the resulting list of sources will include only those that deal with both zoos and animal rights, leaving out any that deal with only one subject and not the other. If you connect terms with *or,* your list will contain sources that deal with either concept: A search for "dogs *or* cats" will create a list of sources that cover either animal. *Not* excludes concepts from a search. A search for "animal rights *not* furs" will search for the concept animal rights and then cut out any sources that deal with furs.

Limiting a Search. Most databases have options for limiting a search by a number of variables:

- Publication date
- Language

- Format
- Peer-reviewed (scholarly works chosen for publication by other scholars)
- Full-text (instead of simply a brief abstract)
- Includes images

Truncating Search Terms with Wild Cards. At times, you will search for a word that has many possible endings. A wild card is a symbol that, placed at the end of a word root, allows for any possible ending for a word. For example, *animal** will allow a search for *animal* or *animals.*

Options for Saving Records. You may have the opportunity to print, download, or e-mail to yourself the citations you find in a database. Many databases have a feature for marking just the records you want so you save only those of interest.

Encyclopedias

General and specialized encyclopedias offer quick overviews of topics and easy access to factual information. They also tend to have excellent selective bibliographies, pointing you toward useful sources. You will find a wide variety of encyclopedias in your library's reference collection; you may also have an online encyclopedia, such as *Britannica Online,* available through the Web anywhere on campus. Some specialized encyclopedias include the following:

> *Encyclopedia of African American History and Culture*
> *Encyclopedia of American Social History*
> *Encyclopedia of Bioethics*
> *Encyclopedia of Educational Research*
> *Encyclopedia of Hispanic Culture in the United States*
> *Encyclopedia of International Relations*
> *Encyclopedia of Philosophy*
> *Encyclopedia of Sociology*
> *Encyclopedia of the United States in the Twentieth Century*
> *Encyclopedia of World Cultures*
> *International Encyclopedia of Communications*
> *McGraw-Hill Encyclopedia of Science and Technology*

Statistical Resources

Often statistics are used as evidence in an argument. If your argument depends on establishing that one category is bigger than another, that the majority of people hold a certain opinion, or that one group is more affected by something than another group, statistics can provide the evidence you need. Of course, as with any other source, you need to be sure that your statistics are as reliable as possible and that you are reporting them responsibly.

It isn't always easy to find things counted the way you want. If you embark on a search for numbers to support your argument, be prepared to spend some time locating and interpreting data. Always read the fine print that explains how and when the data were gathered. Some sources for statistics include these:

U.S. Bureau of the Census. This government agency produces a wealth of statistical data, much of it available on CD-ROM or through the Web at www .census.gov. A handy compilation of the agency's most useful tables is found in the one-volume annual handbook *Statistical Abstract of the United States*, which also includes statistics from other government sources.

Other Federal Agencies. Numerous federal agencies gather statistical data. Among these are the National Center for Education Statistics, the National Center for Health Statistics, the National Bureau of Labor Statistics, and the Federal Bureau of Investigation, which annually compiles national crime statistics. One handy place to find a wide variety of federal statistics is the Web site *FedStats* at www.fedstats.gov.

United Nations. Compilations of international data published by the United Nations include the *Demographic Yearbook and Statistical Yearbook*. Some statistics are also published by U.N. agencies such as the Food and Health Organization. Some are available from the U.N. Web site at www.un.org.

Opinion Polls. Several companies conduct opinion polls, and some of these are available in libraries. One such compilation is the Gallup Poll series, which summarizes public opinion polling from 1935 to the present. Other poll results are reported by the press. Search a database that covers news publications by using your topic and "polls" as keywords to locate some summaries of results.

Government Resources

Beyond statistics, government agencies compile and publish a wealth of information. For topics that concern public welfare, health, education, politics, foreign relations, earth sciences, the environment, or the economy, government documents may provide just the information you need.

The U.S. federal government is the largest publisher in the world. Its publications are distributed free to libraries designated as document depositories across the country. If your library is not a depository, chances are there is a regional depository somewhere nearby. Local, state, and foreign governments are also potential sources of information.

Federal documents distributed to depository libraries are indexed in *The Monthly Catalog of U.S. Government Documents*, available in many libraries as an electronic database. These include congressional documents such as hearings and committee reports, presidential papers, studies conducted by the Education Department or the Centers for Disease Control, and so on. Many government documents are available through the Internet. If you learn about a government publication through the news media, chances are you will be able to obtain a copy at the Web site of the sponsoring agency or congressional body. In fact, government publications are among the most valuable of resources available on the Web because they are rigorously controlled for content. You know you are looking at a U.S. federal government site when you see the domain suffix *.gov* in the URL.

Web-Based Sources

The World Wide Web is an important resource for researchers. It is particularly helpful if you are looking for information about organizations, current events, political debates, popular culture, or government-sponsored research and activities. It is not an especially good place to look for literary criticism, historical analysis, or scholarly research articles, which are still more likely to be published in traditional ways. Biologists reporting on an important experiment, for example, are more likely to submit an article about it to a prestigious journal in the field than simply post their results on the Web.

Because anyone can publish whatever they like on the Web, searching for good information can be frustrating. Search engines operate by means of automated programs that gather information about sites and match search terms to whatever is out there, regardless of quality. A search engine may locate thousands of Web documents on a topic, but most are of little relevance and dubious quality. The key is to know in advance what information you need and who might have produced it. For example, if your topic has to do with some aspect of free speech and you know that the American Civil Liberties Union is involved in the issue, a trip to the ACLU home page may provide you with a wealth of information, albeit from a particular perspective. If your state's pollution control agency just issued a report on water quality in the area, you may find the report published at the agency's Web site or the e-mail address of someone who could send it to you. The more you know about your topic before you sit down to surf, the more likely you will use your time productively.

If you have a fairly broad topic and no specific clues about where it might be covered, you may want to start your search by using a selective guide to good sites. For example, the University of Texas maintains an excellent directory to sites relating to Latin America. Subject guides that selectively list valuable sites can be found at the University of California's *Infomine* at http://infomine.ucr .edu and the *World Wide Web Virtual Library* project at www.vlib.org/Home .html. Reference librarians will also be able to point you to quality sites that relate to your topic.

If you have a fairly specific topic in mind or are looking for a particular organization or document on the Web, a search engine can help you find it. *Google* is one of the best. No matter what search engine you choose, find out how it works, how it ranks results, and how deeply it indexes Web pages. Some search engines will retrieve more results than others simply because of the way the program gathers information from sites. As with databases, there are usually ways to refine a search and improve your results. Many search engines offer an advanced search option that may provide some useful options for refining and limiting a search.

It is important to know what will not be retrieved by a search engine. Because publishing and transmitting texts on the Web are relatively easy, it is becoming more common for libraries to subscribe to databases and electronic journals that are accessed through a Web browser. You may have *Britannica Online* and *LexisNexis* as options on your library's home page. However, the contents of those subscriptions will be available only to your campus community and will not be searched by general Web search engines.

Student researcher Katie's Web search on "school nutrition" produced the following results.

> I clicked on the fourth site, "Child Nutrition Programs/Food and Nutrition Service." This looked good because it had a *.gov* domain. The link took me here:

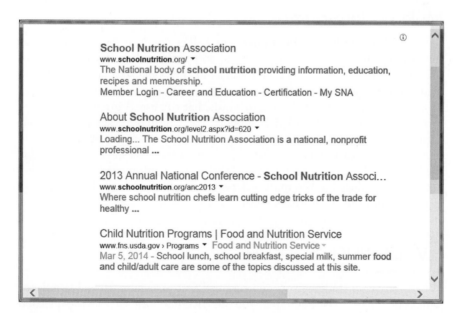

Google

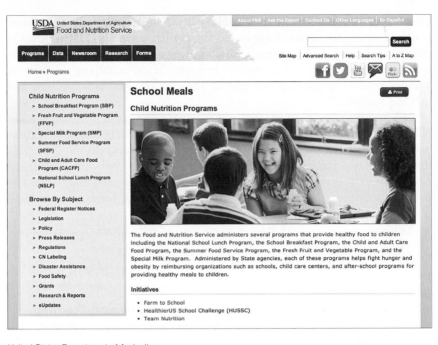

United States Department of Agriculture

Multimodal Sources

Since the Internet is a world of images as well as words, it may give you ideas for livening up your own work with all sorts of visuals — if your instructor allows it. You may also find useful visuals in the books and articles that you read. Don't forget, though, that you are obligated to give credit to the source of your visuals along with the ideas and words that you use. A graph or chart may provide just the sort of statistical support that will make a key point in your argument, and it can be easily cut and pasted into your electronic text, but you must document that graph or chart as you would text. You should acknowledge the location where you found the visual and as much information as is provided about who produced it. You must seek permission to use visuals that you intend to publish in print or electronic form.

Evaluating Sources

When you begin studying your sources, read first to acquire general familiarity with your subject. Make sure that you are covering both sides of the question as well as facts and opinions from a variety of sources. As you read, look for what seem to be the major issues. They will probably be represented in all or most of your sources. Record questions as they occur to you in your reading. It may be useful to review Chapters 2 and 3 for more help with reading critically.

Evaluating Sources for Relevance

The sources you find provide useful information that you need for your paper and help you support your claims. One key to supporting claims effectively is to make sure you have the best evidence available. It is tempting when searching a database or the Web to take the first sources that look good, print them or copy them, and not give them another thought until you are sitting down to compose your argument—only to discover that the sources aren't as valuable as they could be. Sources that looked pretty good at the beginning of your research may turn out to be less useful once you have learned more about the topic. And a source that seems interesting at first glance may turn out to be a rehash or digest of a much more valuable source, something you realize only when you sit down and look at it carefully.

To find the right material, be a critical thinker from the start of your research process. Scan and evaluate the references you encounter throughout your search. As you examine options in a database, choose sources that use relevant terms in their titles, seem directed to an appropriate audience, and are published in places that will look credible in your Works Cited list. For example, a Senate Foreign Relations Committee report will carry more weight as a source than a comparable article in *Good Housekeeping.* An article from the scholarly journal *Foreign Affairs* will carry more clout than an article from *Reader's Digest,* even if they are on the same subject. (For more on popular versus scholarly sources, see the Research Skill box on page 346.)

Skim and quickly evaluate each source that looks valuable.

- Is it relevant to your topic?
- Does it provide information you haven't found elsewhere?
- Can you learn anything about the author, and does what you learn inspire confidence?

As you begin to learn more about your topic and revise your outline as necessary, you can use sources to help direct your search. If a source mentions an organization, for example, you may use that clue to run a search on the Web for that organization's home page. If a newspaper story refers to a study published in a scientific journal, you may want to seek out that study to see the results of the research firsthand. And if you have a source that includes references to other publications, scan through them to see which ones might also prove helpful to you. When you first started your research, chances are you weren't quite sure what you were looking for. Once you are familiar with your topic, you need to concentrate on finding sources that will best support the claims you want to make, and your increasing familiarity with the issue will make it easier to identify the best sources. That may mean a return trip to the library.

Practice: Evaluate Sources for Relevance

Look at the entries in the list from *LexisNexis*, an academic database. The topic being researched was competitive foods in schools. (Competitive foods are those sold in schools other than foods provided through the federally funded school lunch program.) The search terms were *competitive foods* and *school*.

Reprinted with the permission of LexisNexis, a division of Reed Elsevier Inc.

1. You can tell immediately that some entries are clearly not relevant to the topic competitive foods in school. Which ones?
2. Which ones seem most directly relevant to the topic?
3. Item #6 seems unrelated at first, perhaps, but how might it be relevant?
4. Are there any articles that might be too narrow in their focus? Why?

Evaluating Sources for Reliability

Once you have selected some useful sources to support your claims, it is time to make a more in-depth evaluation to be sure you have the best evidence available.

- Is it current enough? Have circumstances changed since this text was published?
- Is the author someone you would want to call on as an expert witness? Does the author have the experience or credentials to make a solid argument that will carry weight with your readers?

- Is it reliable information for your purposes? It may be highly opinionated, but are the basic facts it presents confirmed in other sources? Is the evidence presented in the text convincing?

These questions are not always easy to answer. In some cases, articles will include some information about the author, such as where he or she works. In other cases, no information or even an author's name is given. In that case, it may help to evaluate the publication and its reputation. If you aren't familiar with a publication and don't feel confident making your own judgment, see if it is described in Katz's *Magazines for Libraries*, which evaluates the reputation and quality of periodicals.

Web sites pose challenges and offer unique opportunities for researchers, for one reason because they are part of a developing genre of writing. When evaluating a Web site, first examine what kind of site you are reading.

- Is the Web page selling or advertising goods or services (a business site)?
- Is it advocating a point of view (an advocacy site) or providing relatively neutral information, such as that found in the yellow pages (an informative or educational site)?
- Is the Web site addressing the interests of people in a particular organization or with common interests (an information-sharing site)?
- Is it reporting up-to-the-minute news (a news site) or appealing to some aspect of an individual's life and interests (a personal site)?

Useful information for a research paper may be obtained from any of these kinds of Web pages, but it is helpful to know what the main purpose of the site is — and who its primary audience is — when determining how productive it will be for your research.

RESEARCH SKILL ▸ Evaluating Web-Based Sources

- **Authority.** Is the author an expert in the field or otherwise qualified through experience to write about the subject? Be wary of a source if no author is listed.

- **Accuracy.** Does the support the author offers for his or her ideas convince you that the major ideas expressed are valid and accurate? Factual information can often be checked by finding another source that provides the same information.

- **Objectivity.** Does the author reveal bias that could keep the content from being reliable? You do not want to build your case on someone else's unsupported opinion.

- **Currency.** Is the information recent unless there is a reason for using a source from an earlier period? You do not want to build your case on information that has been superseded by more recent sources.

- **Coverage.** Does the author provide enough information about the subject, in enough detail, to be useful for your purposes? If not, you might find other sources to be more useful.

Source: Adapted from Wolfgram Memorial Library (Widener University, Chester, PA) Web site, www.widener.edu/about/campus_resources/wolfgram_library/evaluate/info.aspx. Copyright Jan Alexander and Marsha Ann Tate, 1996–2005.

As you weigh the main purpose of the site, evaluate its original context. Does the site originate in a traditional medium, such as a print journal or an encyclopedia? Is the site part of an online journal, in which case its material had to go through a screening process? Or is the site the product of one individual's or organization's desire to create a Web page, which means the work may not have been screened or evaluated by any outside agency? In that case, the information may still be valuable, but you must be even more careful when evaluating it.

To find answers to many of the questions in the Research Skill box, make a brief overview of the site itself by looking, for example, at the clues contained in the Web address. That is, *.com* in the address means a business or commercial site; *.edu* is a site sponsored by a university or college; *.k12* is a site associated with a primary or secondary school; *.gov* indicates that the federal government sponsored the site; and *.org* suggests that the site is part of a nonprofit or noncommercial group. Sites originating outside the United States have URLs that end with a two-letter country abbreviation, such as *.uk* for United Kingdom. Although these address clues can reveal a great deal about the origins and purposes of a Web site, remember that personal Web sites may also contain some of these abbreviations. Institutions such as schools and businesses sometimes sponsor individuals' personal Web sites (which are often unscreened by the institution) as well as official institutional sites. One possible key to determining whether a Web site is a personal page, however, is to look for a tilde (~) plus a name or part of a name in the address. Finally, if you are unsure of the sponsoring organization of a page, try erasing all the information in the URL after the first slash (/) and pressing the "Enter" key. Doing so often brings you to the main page of the organization sponsoring the Web site. For more help with evaluating online sources, see page 94.

Most Web sites include a way to contact the author or sponsoring organization of the site, usually through e-mail. This is often a quick and easy way to get answers to the preliminary questions. If the site contains an address or phone number as part of its contact information, this means the organization or individual is available and probably willing to stand behind the site's content.

RESEARCH SKILL Evaluating Multimodal Sources

Whether you find them in print or online, sources that include a mix of images, audio, video, and even text require special attention. Keep the following questions in mind.

- **Audio.** How does the sound affect what is being shown or spoken? Is there a speaker? Does the speaker shout or use any specific style or tone? Is there music or noise? How does the noise or music affect the mood? Do you think this was intentional?

- **Images.** How does color (or lack of color) affect the presentation of the image? What effect does image size and quality have on the message? What effect does the composition as a whole have (cropping, focus, angle, etc.)?

- **Film/Video.** Is the production quality slick or rough? Do you think the quality reflects the limitations of the filmmaker or an intentional creative choice? What is the perspective of the film? Do you feel like a participant in the action or a viewer? How does the use of close-ups,

long shots, color, lighting, and other visual effects affect the mood? How does sound affect the mood?

- **Other Multimodal Sources.** Consider the mood or tone that the creator is trying to achieve through sound, pictures, and video. Think about pace, volume, and imaging. Do they play on emotions with fear, humor, guilt, or sadness? How do these factors influence the content?

ARGUMENT ESSENTIALS
Evaluating Sources

Check All Sources for Relevance

- Be critical of your sources from the beginning of your research. Look for the best sources, not the first ones you can locate.
- Look for sources that use relevant terms in their titles, are directed to an appropriate audience, and are published in reputable places.
- Skim possible sources for relevance, usefulness (not information you already have), and informative value.
- Let your sources lead you to other possible sources.

Check All Sources for Reliability

- Check each source for currency.
- Check the authority of the author(s).
- Check whether the information is reliable for your purposes.

Use Special Care with Web-Based Sources

- Consider what type of site it is. Is it trying to sell something, advocating a point of view, providing information, reporting the news?
- Consider its original context. Is it, for example, a journal article available through a database? A site created and maintained by a single person?
- Is it a *.gov, .com, .edu,* or *.org* site? What does that tell you?

Special Considerations for Multimodal Sources

- Consider livening up your work with visuals if your instructor allows it.
- Be sure to give your source for information in modes other than text just as conscientiously as you would for text.

Practice: Evaluating Web-Based Search Results

Look at the entries from a *Google* search of the terms *competitive foods* and *school*. Use the questions that follow to consider how reliable these potential sources might be.

Google

1. The first entry is a publication of the CDC and has a *.gov* URL. What is the CDC, and what does that suggest to you about how reliable the source might be?

2. The fourth entry is also a .gov source. What do the acronyms *FNS* and *USDA* stand for? What does that suggest about the reliability of the sources?

3. There are two sources here that are from organizations' sites. Go to the articles, and see what you can determine about the organizations that would suggest they are trustworthy sources.

READING ARGUMENT

Seeing Evaluation of a Web-Based Source

The annotations here show how student researcher Katie evaluated a Web-based source using the five characteristics listed in the Research Skill box on page 359: authority, accuracy, objectivity, currency, and coverage.

Child Nutrition Programs
UNITED STATES DEPARTMENT OF AGRICULTURE

United States Department of Agriculture

1 Authority: This should be a trustworthy site because it is maintained by the Food and Nutrition Service of the U.S. Department of Agriculture.

2 Objectivity: This tab provides links to data and research regarding USDA Nutrition Assistance programs.

3 Accuracy: This and the data tab link to evidence-based analysis and rigorous evaluation, "critical tools to promote effective policies and strong management in the Federal nutrition assistance programs."

4 Coverage: The site provides links to each of the school nutrition programs funded by the federal government.

5 Currency: Links provide information about the subjects listed. Information is usually listed in reverse chronological order and is current to at least the last six months.

e-Practice: Evaluating a Web-Based Source

National Vaccine Information Center Web Site
NATIONAL VACCINE INFORMATION CENTER

Go to **macmillanhighered.com/rottenberg**, and evaluate this Web site using the five characteristics listed in the Research Skill box on page 359: authority, accuracy, objectivity, currency, and coverage.

This screenshot of the National Vaccine Information Center's (NVIC) homepage is reproduced with the permission of NVIC and can be accessed at www.nvic.org. Use of it in this book does not imply an NVIC endorsement of statements or opinions of the authors. NVIC is a charitable nonprofit organization founded in 1982 to prevent vaccine injuries and deaths through public education and advocates for the inclusion of informed consent protections in public health policies and laws.

Taking Notes

While everyone has methods of taking notes, here are a few suggestions that should be useful to research writers who need to read materials quickly, comprehend and evaluate the sources, use them as part of a research paper assignment, and manage their time carefully. If you need more detailed help with quoting, paraphrasing, and summarizing, review pages 119–123 in Chapter 4.

When taking notes from a source, summarize instead of quoting long passages. Summarizing as you read saves time. If you feel that a direct quote is more effective than anything you could write and provides crucial support for your argument, copy the material word for word. Leave all punctuation exactly as it appears, and insert ellipsis points (. . .) if you delete material. Enclose all quotations in quotation marks, and copy complete information about your source, including the author's name, the title of the book or article, the journal name if appropriate, page numbers, and publishing information. If you quote an article that appears in an anthology, record complete information about the book itself.

If you aren't sure whether you will use a piece of information later, don't copy the whole passage. Instead, make a note of its bibliographic information so that you can find it again if you need it. Taking too many notes, however, is preferable to taking too few, a problem that will force you to go back to the source for missing information.

One of the most effective ways to save yourself time and trouble when you are ready to write your research paper is to document your research as you go along. That way, when the time comes to create your Works Cited page, you will be ready to put the works you used in alphabetical order — or let your computer do it for you — and provide a list of those works at the end of your paper. Some instructors may require a bibliography, or a list of all of the works you consulted (sometimes titled simply Works Consulted), but at a minimum you will need a Works Cited page. As that title indicates, the list will include only those works that you quote, paraphrase, or summarize in your paper.

Once you are fairly certain that you will use a certain source, go ahead and put it in proper bibliographic form. That way, if the citation form is complicated, you can look it up or ask your instructor before the last minute. Also, you will realize immediately if you are missing information required by the citation and can record it while the source is still at hand. See Chapter 13 for complete details about what information you will need and the proper form for it.

Note Taking and Prewriting

Use the note-taking process as a prewriting activity. Often when you summarize an author's ideas or write down direct quotes, you see or understand the material in new ways. Freewrite about the importance of these quotes, paraphrases, or summaries, or at least about those that seem especially important. If nothing else, take a minute to justify in writing why you chose to record the notes. Doing so will help you clarify and develop your thoughts about your argument.

Taking this prewriting step seriously will help you analyze the ideas you record from outside sources. You will then be better prepared for the more formal (and inevitable) work of summarizing, paraphrasing, and composing involved in thinking critically about your topic and writing a research paper. Maybe most important, such work will help with that moment all writers face when they realize they "know what they want to say but can't find the words to say it." Overcoming such moments does not depend on finding inspiration while writing the final draft of a paper. Instead, successfully working through this common form of writer's block depends more on the amount of prewriting and thoughtful consideration of the notes done early in the research process.

Working with Your Outline

As you take notes, also remember to refer to your outline to ensure that you are acquiring sufficient data to support all the points you intend to raise. Of course, you will be revising your outline during the course of your research as issues are clarified and new ideas emerge, but the outline will serve as a rough guide throughout the writing process. Keeping close track of your outline will also prevent you from recording material that is interesting but not relevant. It may help to label your notes with the heading from the outline to which they are most relevant.

Relying on the knowledge of others is an important part of doing research; expert opinions and eloquent arguments help support your claims when your own expertise is limited. But remember, this is *your* paper. Your ideas and insights into other people's ideas are just as important as the information you uncover at the library or through reputable online sources. When writing an argument, do not simply regurgitate the words and thoughts of others in your essay. Work to achieve a balance between providing solid information from expert sources and offering your own interpretation of the argument and the evidence that supports it.

Managing and Documenting Sources

Using word-processing software can invigorate the processes of note taking and of outlining. Taking notes using a computer gives you more flexibility than using pen and paper alone. For example, you can save your computer-generated notes and your comments on them in numerous places (at home, school, or work, or on a disk); you can cut and paste the text into various documents; you can add to the notes or modify them and still revert to the originals with ease.

You can also link notes to background material on the Web that may be useful once you begin writing drafts of your paper. For example, you could create links to an author's Web page or to any of his or her other works published on the Web. You could create a link to a study or an additional source cited in your notes, or you could link to the work of other researchers who support or argue against the information you recorded.

Because you can record information in any number of ways on your computer, your notes act as tools in the writing process. One of the best ways to start is to open a file for each source; enter the bibliographic information; directly type into the file a series of potentially useful quotations, paraphrases, and summaries; and add your initial ideas about the source. (For each entry, note the correct page references as you go along, and indicate clearly whether you are quoting, paraphrasing, or summarizing.) You can then use the capabilities of your computer to aid you in the later stages of the writing process. For example, you can collect all your research notes into one large file in which you group similar sources, evaluate whether you have too much information about one issue or one side of an argument, or examine sources that conflict with one another. You can imagine various organizational schemes for your paper based on the central themes and issues of the notes you have taken, and you can more clearly determine which quotes and summaries are essential to your paper and which ones may not be needed.

When you're ready to begin your first draft, the computer enables you to readily integrate material from your source notes into your research paper by cutting and pasting, thus eliminating the need to retype and reducing the chance of error. Be sure, though, that cutting and pasting do not lead you to plagiarize inadvertently. Any wording taken from your sources that you use in your paper must be placed in quotation marks and attributed to the source. You can also combine all the bibliographic materials you have saved in separate files and then use the computer to alphabetize your sources for your final draft.

Although taking notes on the computer does not dramatically change the research process, it does highlight the fact that taking notes, prewriting, drafting a paper, and creating a Works Cited page are integrated activities that should build from one another. When you take notes from a journal, book, or Web site, you develop your note-taking abilities so that they help with the entire writing process.

ARGUMENT ESSENTIALS
Taking Notes

- Summarize instead of quoting long passages.
- If you do quote a passage, copy it word for word in quotation marks, using ellipsis points (. . .) to indicate any words that you left out (but only if the omission does not change the essential meaning of the passage).
- Write down all the bibliographic information (in proper form) that you will need for your Works Cited page. (See Chapter 13 for details.)
- Jot down a few notes to yourself about why these notes are important.
- Label notes according to the part of your rough outline they support.
- When taking notes on your computer, start a new file for each potential source.
- When cutting and pasting information from a source, be sure not to plagiarize unintentionally.
- Put each source's bibliographic information in proper form while you are taking notes on it.

READING ARGUMENT

Seeing How to Take Notes

Read the following essay, and then read student researcher Katie's notes following it as an example of how to take notes on your reading. Katie's notes (p. 369) begin with the label "IIB — Long-term health effects." This label is referencing her outline, shown on page 344. Katie's notes also include page references to the original source.

Childhood Obesity: The Challenge
THE ROBERT WOOD JOHNSON FOUNDATION

Childhood obesity is a serious public health problem in the United States. Over the past three decades, obesity rates have soared among all age groups, increasing more than four times among children ages six to eleven. Today, more than twenty-three million children and teenagers are overweight or obese. That's nearly one in three young people. Even among ages two to five, a quarter of children are now overweight or obese. Among certain racial and ethnic groups, the rates are still higher.

The ramifications are alarming. If we don't succeed in reversing this epidemic, we are in danger of raising the first generation of American children who will live sicker and die younger than their parents' generation.

Preventing obesity during childhood is critical because habits formed during youth frequently continue well into adulthood:

- Research shows that obese adolescents have up to an eighty percent chance of becoming obese adults. Overweight and obese children are at higher risk for a host of serious illnesses, including heart disease, stroke, asthma, and certain types of cancer.

- Increasing numbers of children are being diagnosed with health problems once considered to be adult ailments, including high blood pressure, type 2 diabetes, and gallstones.

- Obesity poses a tremendous financial threat to our economy and our health-care system. It's estimated that the obesity epidemic costs our nation $117 billion annually in direct medical expenses and indirect costs, including lost productivity. Childhood obesity alone carries a huge price tag — up to $14 billion annually in direct health-care costs.

How did we get to this point? There's a simple explanation for the childhood obesity epidemic: our children are consuming far more

The Robert Wood Johnson Foundation is the largest philanthropic organization in the country devoted exclusively to improving the health and health care of all Americans. The group spearheaded the establishment of 911 emergency telephone service throughout the United States. Now it is focusing much of its efforts on the childhood obesity epidemic. This essay appeared in *Food, Inc.: How Industrial Food Is Making Us Sicker, Fatter, and Poorer — And What You Can Do about It* (2009).

calories than they burn. Today's obese teenagers consume between 700 and 1,000 more calories per day than what's needed for the growth, physical activity, and body function of a normal-weight teen. Over the course of ten years, that "energy gap" is enough to pack an average of fifty-eight extra pounds on an obese adolescent.

5   As a society, we've dramatically altered the way we live, eat, work, and play — creating an environment that fuels obesity:

■ On average, today's young people spend more than four hours per day using electronic media, including television, DVDs, and video games.

■ A generation ago, about half of all school-aged children walked or biked to school. Today, nearly nine out of ten are driven to school. And once they get there, there aren't many opportunities for exercise — fewer than four percent of elementary schools provide daily physical education.

■ At the same time, children are eating more unhealthy foods in ever-larger sizes. In recent decades, the typical calorie content of menu items like French fries and sodas has increased approximately fifty percent. Children consume these high-calorie, low-nutrient foods not only in restaurants, but also in their homes and schools.

■ In communities hardest hit by obesity, families frequently have little access to affordable healthy foods. There often are no grocery stores, only convenience marts that rarely stock fresh fruits and vegetables. There aren't enough safe places for kids to play or programs to help them be physically active every day.

To reverse the childhood obesity epidemic, we must remove these barriers by creating policies and environments that provide families with better access to healthy foods and opportunities for physical activity.

IIB — Long-term health effects

Robert Wood Johnson Foundation. "Childhood Obesity: The Challenge." *Food, Inc.: How Industrial Food Is Making Us Sicker, Fatter and Poorer — and What You Can Do about It*. Ed. Karl Weber. New York: PublicAffairs, 2009. 259–61. Print.

Link to Foundation: www.rwjf.org

Might need to lead in to quotes: The Foundation is "the nation's largest philanthropy devoted exclusively to improving the health and health care of all Americans." 259

In three decades, the obesity rate has quadrupled for those age 6–11. 259

"If we don't succeed in reversing this epidemic, we are in danger of raising the first generation of American children who will live sicker and die younger than their parents' generation." 259

Because of the difference between calorie intake and the physical activity needed to burn those calories, in ten years an adolescent could gain 58 pounds. 260

50% of children a generation ago walked to school. Now 90% ride. 260

"fewer than four percent of elementary schools provide daily physical education" 260

In some places where obesity is worst, the people can't afford healthy foods, there are convenience stores instead of grocery stores, and it is not safe for children to play outside. 261

Practice: Taking Notes
Using Katie's notes as a model, take notes on the following essay.

To Curb School Lunch Waste, Ease the Fruit and Vegetable Rules
LOS ANGELES TIMES EDITORIAL BOARD

No one should have expected that putting more vegetables in front of elementary school students would instantly turn them into an army of broccoli fans. Plenty of food has been thrown out since new federal rules took effect in 2011 requiring students in the subsidized school lunch program to choose a fruit or vegetable each day. Nevertheless, studies find that continued exposure to produce is resulting in more children eating at least some of it.

That's worth a certain amount of wasted food. The new lunch rules, pushed by the Obama administration and passed by Congress, provide better nutrition and introduce more students to healthful eating habits that they will, it's hoped, carry into adulthood.

Still, the program is afflicted by rigid, over-reaching regulations that defy common sense.

Schools must provide items from five food groups, including a fruit and a vegetable, every day. Students must choose three items, even if they're not hungry enough for all of them, and at least one must be produce. But fruits and vegetables rank as the least popular items, so requiring schools to offer one of each for each student practically guarantees that an enormous amount of fruits and vegetables will go to waste.

Even worse are the rules about what kinds of produce must be offered and in what form. They make it nearly impossible, for example, to hide the vegetables in soups or lasagna, where they might be more palatable to students. It took a

This editorial appeared in the *Los Angeles Times* on April 8, 2014.

long, intense lobbying effort for schools to get permission to serve smoothies; even though cafeterias are encouraged to serve yogurt and fruit, they weren't allowed until just recently to combine them into a healthful drink.

5   The federal rules even prohibit students from taking food out of the cafeteria to eat later.

No wonder so much ends up in garbage cans. In the Los Angeles Unified School District, as the *Times* recently reported, it adds up to $100,000 in wasted food each day.

Congress is supposed to reauthorize the school lunch bill in 2015, and there are many changes it should make. Though the law should continue to require all students to take a fruit or vegetable, it should allow them to take only as much food as they want. Children should be able to pick two fruits or two vegetables in a day, which they can't do now, and eat their leftovers later. Schools should be free to mix vegetables together in appealing and healthful dishes. Lawmakers need to think more like budget-conscious parents and less like detail-obsessed regulators.

bits

To see what you are learning about argumentation applied to the latest world and national news, read our *Bits* blog, "Argument and the Headlines," at **blogs.bedfordstmartins.com/bits**.

12

Drafting, Revising, and Presenting Arguments

Chapter 11 discusses the planning of an argumentative paper and the process involved in researching topics that require support beyond what the writer knows firsthand. This chapter discusses moving from the planning and researching stage into the actual writing of the paper or presentation.

Reviewing Your Research

Making a preliminary outline before you conduct any needed research gives direction to your research. If your topic requires no research, a preliminary outline helps you to organize your own thoughts on the subject. Preliminary outlines can change, however, in the process of researching and writing the paper. As you begin drafting the paper, be sure you have a solid thesis and strong and plentiful evidence for each topic in your preliminary or revised outline.

Once you are satisfied that you have identified all the issues that will appear in your paper, you should begin to determine what kind of organization will be most effective for your argument. Now is the time to organize the results of your thinking into a logical and persuasive form. If you have read about your topic, answered questions, and acquired some evidence, you may already have decided on ways to approach your subject. If not, you should look closely at your outline now, recalling your purposes when you began your investigation, and develop a strategy for using the information you have gathered to achieve those purposes.

Be mindful of the context in which the argument is taking place, and try this procedure for tackling the issues in any controversial problem.

1. Raise the relevant issues, and omit those that would distract you from your purpose. Plan to devote more time and space to issues you regard as crucial.
2. Produce the strongest evidence you can to support your factual claims, knowing that the opposing side or critical readers may try to produce conflicting evidence.

3. Defend your value claims by finding support in the fundamental principles with which most people in your audience would agree.
4. Explain as specifically as possible what you want your audience to think or do when you are arguing a policy claim.
5. Argue with yourself. Try to foresee what kinds of refutation are possible. Try to anticipate and meet the opposing arguments.
6. Consider the context in which your argument will be read, and be sensitive to the concerns of your audience.

RESEARCH SKILL ▶ Reviewing Your Research

- Is your thesis the right scope — not too broad or too narrow?

- Does your working outline show any gaps in your argument?

- Does your research show enough counterarguments? If not, your thesis may not be debatable and may need to be changed.

- Does your research show strong counterarguments that might make you want to change your thesis or shift the perspective of your argument?

- Have you identified the warrants linking your claim with data and ensured that these warrants, too, are adequately documented?

- Have you found sufficient data to support your claim?

- Is your research varied enough and not too reliant on one source or source type? Have you met your instructor's guidelines for number and type of sources?

- If you intend to quote or paraphrase sources in your paper, do your notes include exact copies of all statements you may want to use? Do your notes include complete references?

- Have you answered all the relevant questions that have come up during your research?

- Do you have enough information about your sources to document your paper?

Student researcher Katie applied the six steps in the review process to her topic like this:

1. The relevant issue for my thesis is that competitive foods should not be in schools. I need to establish that there is an obesity epidemic, which is a factual claim, but that is not my main focus. Competitive foods are one thing that contributes to the obesity epidemic, and it is one that something could be done about. I need to spend most of my time focusing on what is wrong with competitive foods and what should be done about the problem.
2. My thesis will be a claim of policy, but along the way I will establish that competitive foods are one factor that leads to childhood obesity. I think I have enough evidence to support that.
3. I am not supporting a values claim, but behind my thesis, anyone should agree that we should do what we can to stop the increase

in childhood obesity. Everyone should be in favor of good health for children.

4. What I want to happen is for all competitive foods to be removed from schools.

5. Some people would argue that the competitive foods are what the kids want to eat, or they would already be eating the cafeteria food. I have also discovered that some people think there are economic reasons for letting these vendors sell their products in the schools. I will have to argue that that is not as important as the children's health.

6. People who have children in school or will have should be concerned. One thing that makes my argument stronger is that people are already starting to read and hear more and more about healthy eating. It's in the news a lot.

Organizing the Material

The first point to establish in organizing your material is what type of thesis you plan to present. Is your intention to make readers aware of some problem? to offer a solution to the problem? to defend a position? to refute a position held by others? The way you organize your material will depend to a great extent on your goal. With that goal in mind, look over your outline and reevaluate the relative importance of your issues. Which ones are most convincing? Which are backed up by the strongest support? Which ones relate to facts, and which ones concern values?

With these points in mind, let's look at various ways of organizing an argumentative paper. You won't know in advance how many paragraphs your paper ought to have, but you can choose a general strategy before you begin writing. Here are four possibilities:

- Defending the main idea
- Refuting an opposing view
- Finding the middle ground
- Presenting the stock issues

Your thesis should introduce a claim that can be adequately supported in the space available to you. If your research has opened up more aspects than you anticipated, you may want to narrow your thesis to one major subtopic. Or you could emphasize only the most persuasive arguments for your position (assuming these are sufficient to make your case) and omit the others. In a brief paper (three or four pages), three issues are probably all you have room to develop. However, if you suspect your thesis can be proved in one or two pages, look for ways to expand it. What additional issues might be brought in to bolster your argument? Alternatively, is there a larger issue for which your thesis could become a supporting idea?

You will also want to choose the order in which to present your thesis and supporting ideas to determine which of your points will receive the most emphasis.

Defending the Main Idea

All forms of organization will require you to defend your main idea, but one way of doing this is simple and direct. Early in the paper, state the main idea that you will defend throughout your argument. You can also indicate here the two or three points you intend to develop in support of your claim, or you can raise these later as they come up. Suppose your thesis is that widespread vegetarianism would solve a number of problems. You could phrase it this way:

If the majority of people in this country adopted a vegetarian diet, we would see improvements in the economy, in the health of our people, and in moral sensitivity. You would then develop each of the claims in your list with appropriate data and warrants. Notice that the thesis statement in the first (thesis) paragraph has already outlined your organizational pattern. However, if you find that listing your two or three main ideas in the thesis leads to too much repetition later in the paper, you can introduce each one as it arises in your discussion of the topic. Your thesis would remain more general: *If the majority of people in this country adopted a vegetarian diet, there would be noticeable improvement.*

Defending the main idea is effective for factual claims as well as policy claims, in which you urge the adoption of a certain policy and give the reasons for its adoption. It is most appropriate when your thesis is straightforward and can be readily supported by direct statements.

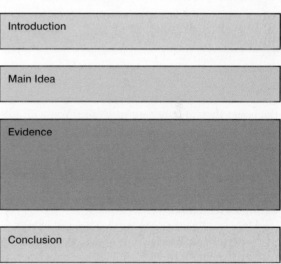

Defending the Main Idea

Introduction

Main Idea

Evidence

Conclusion

Refuting an Opposing View

Refuting an opposing view means attacking it in order to weaken, invalidate, or make it less credible to a reader. Since all arguments are dialogues or debates — even when the opponent is only imaginary — refutation of another point of view is always implicit in your arguments. As you write, keep in mind

Strategies for Refuting an Opposing View

1. **Read the argument carefully,** noting the points with which you disagree. You must be familiar with your opponent's argument in order to refute it.

2. **Summarize an opposing view at the beginning of your paper** if you think your audience may be sympathetic to it or unfamiliar with it. Give readers enough information to understand what you plan to refute. Be respectful of the opposition's views. You do not want to alienate readers who might not agree with you at first.

3. **If your argument is long and complex, choose only the most important points to refute.** Otherwise, the reader who does not have the original argument on hand may find a detailed refutation hard to follow. If the argument is short and relatively simple — a claim supported by only two or three points — you may decide to refute them all, devoting more space to the most important ones.

4. **Attack the principal elements in the argument of your opponent.**

   a. Question the evidence. (See Chapter 6.) Question whether your opponent has proved that a problem exists.

   b. Attack the warrants or assumptions that underlie the claim. (See Chapter 7.)

   c. Attack the logic or reasoning of the opposing view. (Refer to the discussion of fallacious reasoning in Chapter 10.)

   d. Attack the proposed solution to a problem, pointing out that it will not work.

5. **Be prepared to do more than attack the opposing view.** Supply evidence and good reasons in support of your own claim.

the issues that an opponent may raise. You will be looking at your own argument as an unsympathetic reader may look at it, asking yourself the same kinds of critical questions and trying to find its weaknesses in order to correct them. In this way, every argument you write becomes a form of refutation.

Here is a sentence form that might help you write a thesis for this type of essay:

> On the topic of _____, X claims that _____. However, _____.

See pages 116–119 for additional sentence forms.

Refuting an Opposing View

Introduction

Summary of Opposing View

Refutation of Opposing View

Conclusion

Finding the Middle Ground

Although an argument, by definition, assumes a difference of opinion, we know that opposing sides frequently find accommodation somewhere in the middle. As you mount your own argument about a controversial issue, you need not confine yourself to support of any of the differing positions. You may want to acknowledge that there is some justice on all sides and that you understand the difficulty of resolving the issue.

Here is a sentence form that might help you write a thesis for this type of essay:

On the topic of _____, X claims that _____. In contrast, Y argues that _____. They agree that _____, a view that deserves consideration.

Finding the Middle Ground

Introduction

Presentation of Various Viewpoints

Proposal of Middle Ground

Conclusion

Strategies for Finding the Middle Ground

Consider these guidelines for an argument that offers a compromise between or among competing positions:

1. **Explain the differing positions** early in your essay. Make clear the major differences separating the two (or more) sides.

2. **Point out, whenever possible, that the differing sides already agree** to some exceptions to their stated positions. Such evidence may prove that the differences are not so extreme as their advocates insist.

3. **Make clear your own moderation and sympathy,** your own willingness to negotiate.

4. **Acknowledge that opposing views deserve to be considered,** if you favor one side of the controversy.

5. **Provide evidence that accepting a middle ground can offer marked advantages** for the whole society. Whenever possible, show that continued polarization can result in violence, injustice, and suffering.

6. **Be as specific as possible** in offering a solution that finds a common ground, emphasizing the part that you are willing to play in reaching a settlement.

Presenting the Stock Issues

Presenting the stock issues, or stating the problem before the solution, is a type of organization borrowed from traditional debate format. It works for policy claims when an audience must be convinced that a need exists for changing the status quo (present conditions) and for introducing plans to solve the problem. You begin by establishing that a problem exists (need). You then propose a solution (plan), which is your thesis. Finally, you show reasons for adopting the plan (advantages). These three elements — need, plan, and advantages — are called the *stock issues*.

For example, suppose you wanted to argue that measures for reducing acid rain should be introduced at once. You would first have to establish a need for such measures by defining the problem and providing evidence of damage. Then you would present your thesis, a means for improving conditions. Finally you would suggest the benefits that would follow from implementation of your plan. Notice that in this organization your thesis paragraph usually appears toward the middle of your paper, although it may also appear at the beginning.

A sentence form such as the following can guide you in writing an appropriate thesis:

> _____ is a problem, but _____ can help resolve it.

A sample thesis statement might look like this:

> Traffic congestion around the stadium on game days is a problem, but temporarily limiting University Avenue to eastbound traffic would allow for a smoother and faster flow of traffic.

Student researcher Katie looked at the four ways of organizing an argumentative paper and decided that the best one for her topic was Presenting Stock Issues:

Presenting the Stock Issues

Introduction

Establishment of Problem (Need)

Proposal of Solution (Plan)

Explanation of Advantages

Conclusion

> I need to show that there is a **need** to do something to combat the problem of competitive foods, then what **plan** might help solve the problem, and then the **advantages** of the plan I suggest. My thesis might look like this: *Childhood obesity is increasing at an alarming rate, but schools can help by eliminating competitive foods.*

Ordering Material for Emphasis

Whichever way you choose to work, you should revise your outline to reflect the order in which you intend to present your thesis and supporting ideas. Not only the placement of your thesis paragraph but also the wording and arrangement of your ideas will determine what points in your paper receive the most emphasis.

Suppose your purpose is to convince the reader that cigarette smoking is a bad habit. You might decide to concentrate on three unpleasant attributes of cigarette smoking: (1) It is unhealthy; (2) it is dirty; (3) it is expensive. Obviously, these are not equally important as possible deterrents. You would no doubt consider the first reason the most compelling, accompanied by evidence to prove the relationship between cigarette smoking and cancer, heart disease, emphysema, and other diseases. This issue, therefore, should receive greater emphasis than the others.

There are several ways to achieve emphasis:

- Make the explicit statement that you consider a certain issue the most important.

  > Finally, and *most important,* revealing too much personal information on social media can put the user's safety at risk.

- Placing the material to be emphasized in an emphatic position, either first or last in the paper. The end position, however, is generally more emphatic.
- Elaborate on the material to be emphasized, treating it at greater length, offering more data and reasons for it than you give for the other issues.

WRITER'S GUIDE

Organizing an Argument Paper

The organizing steps that come between preparation and writing are often neglected. Careful planning at this stage, however, can save much time and effort later. As you prepare to start writing, you should be able to answer the following questions:

1. Is the purpose of my paper to persuade readers to accept a potentially controversial idea, to refute someone else's position, to find middle ground, or to propose a solution to a problem?
2. Can or should my solution also incorporate elements of compromise and negotiation?
3. Have I decided on an organization that is likely to accomplish this purpose?
4. Does my outline arrange my thesis and issues in an appropriate order to emphasize the most important issues?
5. Does my outline show an argument whose scope suits the needs of this paper?

Writing

Beginning the Paper

Having found a claim you can defend and the voice you will adopt toward your audience, you must now think about how to begin. An introduction to your subject should consist of more than just the first paragraph of your paper. It should invite the reader to give attention to what you have to say. It should also point you in the direction you will take in developing your argument.

Consider the kind of argument you intend to present. Does your paper make a factual claim? Does it address values? Does it recommend a policy or action? Is it a rebuttal of some current policy or belief? The answers to those questions will influence the way you introduce the subject.

If your thesis makes a factual claim, you may be able to summarize it in one or two opening sentences. *Whether we like it or not, money is obsolete. The currency of today is not paper or coin, but plastic.* Refutations are easy to introduce in a brief statement: *Contrary to popular views on the subject, America is not as competitive in the cyber world as its citizens would like to believe.*

A thesis that defends a value is usually best preceded by an explanatory introduction. *Sending troops to Iraq was the best decision Bush could have made at the time* is a thesis that can be stated as a simple declarative opening sentence. However, readers who disagree may not read any further than the first line. Someone defending this type of claim is likely to be more persuasive if he or she presents the thesis less directly.

> "When 9/11 happened I thought I'm not hearing from Muslims like ourselves," she says, meaning liberal and moderate *Saturday Evening Post* types. "I'd only hear from the old men and the conservative women. So I started writing opinion pieces. I wanted to get another voice out there to show that, look, 9/11 doesn't represent all Islam."[1]

One way to keep a thesis from alienating the audience is to phrase it as a question.

> How do you know you can trust what you read? Start by recognizing that there is no such thing as completely unbiased news. No one can report any news story without encapsulating complicated events, deciding what's really important, leaving out what the reporter thinks are insignificant details, and adopting a point of view that makes it possible to stitch together all the elements and tell a story. Therefore no two people will ever report any news story the same way. So there is no such thing as a single objective telling of a news event.[2]

---

[1] Mona Eltahawy, qtd. in Ron Rosenbaum, "The Next Revolution," *Smithsonian,* May 2013, p. 30.

[2] *Post* Editors, "Balancing Act," *Saturday Evening Post*, May/June 2013, p. 46.

For any subject that is highly controversial or emotionally charged, especially one that strongly condemns an existing situation or belief, you may sometimes want to express your indignation directly. Of course, you must be sure that your indignation can be justified. The author of the following introduction, a physician and writer, openly admits that he is about to make a case that may offend readers.

> Is there any polite way to introduce today's subject? I'm afraid not. It must be said plainly that the media have done about as sorry and dishonest a job of covering health news as is humanly possible, and that when the media do not fail from bias and mendacity, they fail from ignorance and laziness.[3]

If your thesis advocates a policy or makes a recommendation, it may be a good idea, as in a value claim, to provide a short background.

> Competitive foods in schools are the soft drinks, sugary snacks, and chips that we were not allowed to buy in the school cafeteria but that today's public school students are. These foods that are largely lacking in nutrition contribute to the overall problem of obesity among children and youth. We may not be able to control what young children eat at home or what teenagers eat when they are out with their friends, but we can control what they eat while at school. For the good of the next generation, all competitive foods should be banned from the public schools.

There are also other ways to introduce your subject. One is to begin with an appropriate quotation or indirect quotation.

> "Land is the only thing in the world that amounts to anything, for 'tis the only thing in this world that lasts. . . . 'Tis the only thing worth working for," says Gerald O'Hara to daughter Scarlett in *Gone with the Wind*.
>   Wise words. Real estate was on an upward surge for decades. It seemed unstoppable. Then, along came the disastrous collapse of the housing bubble in 2007. Six years later, we're seeing a good rebound in real estate prices, and that has many, perhaps you, wondering if land is once again, if not worth fighting and dying for, at least worth investing in.[4]

Or you may begin with an anecdote:

> As a child, Kamala accompanied her parents to civil rights marches in Oakland. She's been making strides for justice — and breaking down barriers — ever since.[5]

---

[3] Michael Halberstam, "TV's Unhealthy Approach to Health News," *TV Guide*, September 20–26, 1980, p. 24.

[4] Russell Wild, "Land Ho!," *Saturday Evening Post*, May/June 2013, p. 36.

[5] Nancy Pelosi, "Kamala Harris: California's Triple Threat," *Time*, April 29–May 6, 2013, p. 64.

Or you may begin with a statement meant to capture your readers' attention — maybe even shock them a bit — in order to make them read on.

> North Korea's Supreme Leader Kin Jong Un is the world's youngest head of state — and behaves like it.[6]

Building an Effective Argument

In general, the writer of an argument follows the same rules that govern any form of expository writing. Your style should be clear and readable, your organization logical, your ideas connected by transitional phrases and sentences, your paragraphs coherent. The main difference between an argument and expository writing is the need to persuade an audience to adopt a belief or take an action. You should assume your readers will be critical rather than neutral or sympathetic. Therefore, you must be equally critical of your own work. Any apparent gap in reasoning or ambiguity in presentation is likely to weaken the argument.

The style and tone you choose depend not only on the nature of the subject but also on how you can best convince readers that you are a credible source. **Style** in this context refers to the elements of your prose — simple versus complex sentences, active versus passive verbs, metaphors, analogies, and other literary devices. It is usually appropriate in a short paper to choose an expository style, which emphasizes the elements of your argument rather than your personality. You can discover some helpful pointers on essay style by reading the editorials in newspapers such as the *New York Times,* the *Washington Post,* and the *Wall Street Journal.* The authors are typically addressing a mixed audience comparable to the hypothetical readers of your own paper. Though their approaches vary, each writer is attempting to portray himself or herself as an objective analyst whose argument deserves careful attention. **Tone** is the approach you take to your topic — solemn or humorous, detached or sympathetic. Style and tone together compose your **voice** as a writer.

Remember too that part of establishing your credibility as a writer is to document your sources with care. You will need to use a combination of quotations, paraphrases, and summaries to support your points. See Chapter 4 for guidance on how to incorporate these elements into your paper. See Chapter 13 for advice on how to cite these sources.

Concluding the Paper

You may have heard the advice to tell your readers in the introduction what you are going to say, then say it in the body of your paper, and then in your con-

---

[6] Barbara Demick, "Kim Jong Un: Asia's Nuclear Bully," *Time,* April 29–May 6, 2013, p. 68.

clusion tell them what you have said. That doesn't mean to repeat your thesis statement word for word, although you will want to return to your thesis idea. Here are a few other don'ts for conclusions:

- Don't begin with "In conclusion," "In summary," "To conclude," or some other similar but unnecessary transition.
- Don't switch into first person with "I think," "I feel," or another similar personalization.
- Unless your paper is over ten pages long, your instructor requires it, or the conventions of your field require it, don't summarize your main points.
- Don't start a new topic.
- Don't let a concluding quotation replace your own concluding thoughts.
- Don't have a one-sentence conclusion.
- Don't use vague platitudes such as "Only time will tell" or "History will be the judge."

Here are some strategies to consider as you conclude your paper:

- Answer the question "So what?" What is the significance of your argument? Point out how the future may be affected or what other implications there might be.
- Issue a call for action. Make clear to your readers what they can do about the situation.
- Generalize about your subject's broader applications or what the next step might be.
- Bring all of your ideas into a coherent whole. Make clear how all of the pieces fit together.
- Use a relevant quotation in conjunction with, but not in place of, your own concluding ideas.

In any case, you will want to return to your thesis idea and be sure your conclusion encompasses the whole essay, not just part of it. The conclusion establishes the impression that your readers are left with, and you want it to be a good one.

WRITER'S GUIDE
Dos and Don'ts of Effective Writing

DO

- Present your thesis clearly in the introduction
- Consider your purpose and audience
- Vary sentence structure
- Use rich, standard vocabulary
- Support your points with details and examples

- Use a clear and appropriate expository style
- Make your text unified
- Emphasize the most important points
- Include a conclusion
- Proofread

DON'T

- Repeat unnecessarily
- Exaggerate
- Use short, choppy paragraphs
- Pad your writing
- Generalize

Revising

The final stage in writing an argument is revising. The first step is to read through what you have written to be sure your paper is complete and well organized. Have you omitted any of the issues, warrants, or supporting evidence on your outline? Is each paragraph coherent in itself? Do your paragraphs work together to create a coherent paper? All the elements of the argument—the issues raised, the underlying assumptions, and the supporting material—should contribute to the development of the claim in your thesis statement. Any material that is interesting but irrelevant to that claim should be cut. See the Writer's Guide: Organizing an Argument Paper (page 379) for reminders of effective organization.

Next, be sure that the style and tone of your paper are appropriate for the topic and the audience. Remember that people choose to read an argument because they want the answer to a troubling question or the solution to a recurrent problem. Besides stating your thesis in a way that invites the reader to join you in your investigation, you must retain your audience's interest through a discussion that may be unfamiliar or contrary to their convictions. The outstanding qualities of argumentative prose style, therefore, are clarity and readability. In addition your paper should reach a clear conclusion that reinforces your thesis.

ARGUMENT ESSENTIALS
Checklist for Effective Arguments

- Interesting and debatable thesis
- All claims supported with documented evidence
- No unsupported controversial warrants
- Appropriate organization
- Opposing arguments refuted

Style is obviously harder to evaluate in your own writing than organization. Your outline provides a map against which to check the structure of your paper. Clarity and readability, by comparison, are somewhat abstract qualities. Two procedures may be helpful. The first is to read two or three (or more) essays by authors whose style you admire and then turn back to your own writing. Awkward spots in your prose are sometimes easier to see if you get away from it and respond to someone else's perspective than if you simply keep rereading your own writing.

The second method is to read aloud. If you have never tried it, you are likely to be surprised at how valuable this can be. Again, start with someone else's work that you feel is clearly written, and practice until you achieve a smooth, rhythmic delivery that satisfies you. And listen to what you are reading. Your objective is to absorb the patterns of English structure that characterize the clearest, most readable prose. Then read your paper aloud, and listen to the construction of your sentences. Are they also clear and readable? Do they say what you want them to say? How would they sound to a reader? According to one theory, you can learn the rhythm and phrasing of a language just as you learn the rhythm and phrasing of a melody. And you will often *hear* a mistake or a clumsy construction in your writing that has escaped your eye in proofreading.

Use the spell-check and grammar-check functions of your word-processing program, but keep in mind that correctness depends on context. A spell-check program will not flag a real word that is used incorrectly, such as the word *it's* used where the word *its* is needed. Also, a grammar-check function lacks the sophistication to interpret the meaning of a sentence and may flag as incorrect a group of words that is indeed correct while missing actual errors. It is ultimately up to you to proofread the paper carefully for other mistakes. Correct the errors, and reprint the pages in question. See the Writer's Guide: Dos and Don'ts of Effective Writing (pp. 383–84) and Argument Essentials: Checklist for Effective Arguments (page 384) for reminders of what you need to check as you revise.

Oral Arguments

You will often be asked to make oral presentations in your college classes. Many jobs, both professional and nonprofessional, will call for speeches to groups of fellow employees or prospective customers, to community groups, and even to government officials. Wherever you live, there will be controversies and public meetings about schooling and political candidates, about budgets for libraries and road repairs and pet control. The ability to rise and make your case before an audience is one that you will want to cultivate as a citizen of a democracy.

Some of your objectives as a writer will also be relevant to you as a speaker: making the appropriate appeal to an audience, establishing your credibility, finding adequate support for your claim. But other elements of argument will be different: language, organization, and the use of visual and other aids.

The Audience

Most speakers who confront a live audience already know something about the members of that audience. They may know why the audience is assembled to hear the particular speaker, their vocations, their level of education, and their familiarity with the subject. They may know whether the audience is friendly, hostile, or neutral to the views that the speaker will express. Analyzing the audience is an essential part of speech preparation.

In college classes, students who make assigned speeches on controversial topics are often encouraged to first survey the class. Questionnaires and interviews can give the speaker important clues to the things he should emphasize or avoid: They will tell him whether he should give both sides of a debatable question, introduce humor, use simpler language, and bring in visual or other aids.

If you know something about your audience, ask yourself what impression your clothing, gestures and bodily movements, voice, and general demeanor might convey. Make sure, too, that you understand the nature of the occasion — is it too solemn for humor? too formal for personal anecdotes? — and the purpose of the meeting, which can influence your choice of language and the most effective appeal.

Credibility

Credibility, as you learned in Chapter 1, is another name for *ethos* (the Greek word from which the English word *ethics* is derived) and refers to the honesty, moral character, and intellectual competence of the speaker.

Public figures, whose speeches and actions are reported in the media, can acquire (or fail to acquire) reputations for being endowed with those characteristics. And there is little doubt that a reputation for competence and honesty can incline an audience to accept an argument that would be rejected if offered by a speaker who lacks such a reputation.

How, then, do speakers who are unknown to the audience or who boast only modest credentials convince listeners that they are responsible advocates? From the moment the speaker appears before them, members of the audience begin to make an evaluation based on external signs such as clothing, mannerisms, and body language. But the most significant impression of the speaker's credibility will be based on what the speaker says — and how. Does the speaker give evidence of knowing the subject? of being aware of the needs and values of the audience? Especially if arguing an unpopular claim, does the speaker seem modest and conciliatory?

Unknown speakers are often advised to establish their credentials in the introduction to their speech, to summarize their background and experience as proof of their right to argue the subject they have chosen.

Speakers often use an admission of modesty as proof of an honest and unassuming character, presenting themselves not as experts but as speakers well aware of their limitations. Such an appeal can generate sympathy in the audience (if they believe the speaker) and a sense of identification with the speaker.

Organization

A well-planned speech has a clearly defined beginning, middle, and end. The beginning, which offers the introduction, can take a number of forms, depending on the kind of speech and its subject. Above all, the introduction must win the attention of the audience, especially if they have been required to attend, and encourage them to look forward to the rest of the speech. The authors of *Principles of Speech Communication* suggest seven basic attention-getters:

- referring to the subject or occasion
- using a personal reference
- asking a rhetorical question
- making a startling statement of fact or opinion
- using a quotation
- telling a humorous anecdote
- using an illustration[7]

The middle or body of the speech is, of course, the longest part. It is devoted to development of the claim that appears at the beginning. The length of the speech and the complexity of the subject determine how much support you provide. Some points are more important than others and should therefore receive more extended treatment. Unless the order is chronological, it makes sense for the speaker to arrange the supporting points in emphatic order, that is, the most important at the end because this may be the one that listeners will remember.

The conclusion should be brief; some rhetoricians suggest that the ending should constitute 5 percent of the total length of the speech. For speeches that contain several main points with supporting data, you may need to summarize. Or you may return to one of the attention-getters mentioned earlier. One writer recommends this as "the most obvious method" of concluding speeches, "particularly appropriate when the introduction has included a quotation, an interesting anecdote, a reference to an occasion or a place, an appeal to the self-interest of the audience, or a reference to a recent incident."[8]

The speaker must also ensure the smooth flow of argument throughout. Coherence, or the orderly connections between ideas, is even more important in speech than in writing because the listener cannot go back to uncover these connections. The audience listens for expressions that serve as guideposts — words, phrases, and sentences to indicate which direction the argument will take. Words such as *next, then, finally, here, first of all, whereas, in addition, second, in fact, now,* and *in conclusion* can help the listener to follow the argument's development.

---

[7] Bruce E. Gronbeck et al., *Principles of Speech Communication,* 13th brief ed. (New York: Longman, 1998), pp. 243–47.

[8] James C. McCroskey, *An Introduction to Rhetorical Communication* (Englewood Cliffs, NJ: Prentice-Hall, 1968), p. 204.

Language

> It should be observed that each kind of rhetoric has its own appropriate style. That of written prose is not the same as that of spoken oratory.
>
> — Aristotle

In the end, your speech depends on the language you use. No matter how accurate your analysis of the audience, how appealing your presentation of self, how deep your grasp of the material, if the language does not clearly and emphatically convey your argument, the speech will probably fail. Fortunately, the effectiveness of language does not depend on long words or complex sentence structure — quite the contrary. Most speeches, especially those given by beginners to small audiences, are distinguished by an oral style that respects the rhythms of ordinary speech and sounds spontaneous.

- Use words that both you and your listeners are familiar with, language that convinces the audience you are sharing your knowledge and opinions, neither speaking down to them nor talking over their heads. You never want to use language that makes the audience appear ignorant or unreasonable.
- Make sure that the words you use will not be considered offensive by some members of your audience. Today we are all sensitive, sometimes hypersensitive, to terms that were once used freely if not wisely. One word, improperly used, can cause some listeners to reject the whole speech. This is particularly true of terms that suggest bias based on gender, race, or sexual orientation.
- Consider whether the subject is one that the particular audience you are addressing is not likely to be familiar with. If this is the case, then explain even the basic terms. In one class, a student who had chosen to discuss a subject about which he was extremely knowledgeable, betting on horse races, neglected to define clearly the words *exacta, subfecta, trifecta, parimutuel,* and others, leaving his audience fairly befuddled.
- Wherever it is appropriate, use concrete language with details and examples that create images and cause the listener to feel as well as think. One student speaker used strong words to good effect in providing some unappetizing facts about hot dogs: "In fact, the hot dog is so adulterated with chemicals, so contaminated with bacteria, so puffy with gristle, fat, water, and lacking in protein, that it is nutritionally worthless."[9]
- Because the audience must grasp the grammatical construction without the visual clues of punctuation available on the printed page, use short, direct sentences. Use subject-verb constructions without a string of phrases or

---

[9] Donovan Ochs and Anthony Winkler, *A Brief Introduction to Speech* (New York: Harcourt, Brace, Jovanovich, 1979), p. 74.

clauses preceding the subject or interrupting the natural flow of the sentence. Use the active voice frequently.

- Consider a popular stylistic device — repetition and balance, or parallel structure — to emphasize and enrich parts of your message. Almost all inspirational speeches, including religious exhortation and political oratory, take advantage of such constructions, whose rhythms evoke an immediate emotional response. It is one of the strengths of Martin Luther King Jr.'s "I Have a Dream" speech, which you can read and listen to online. Keep in mind that the ideas in parallel structures must be similar and that, for maximum effectiveness, they should be used sparingly in a short speech. Not least, the subject should be weighty enough to carry this imposing construction.

Support

The support for a claim is essentially the same for both spoken and written arguments. Factual evidence, including statistics and expert opinion, as well as appeals to needs and values, is equally important in oral presentations. But time constraints will make a difference. In a speech, the amount of support that you provide will be limited to the capacity of listeners to digest and remember information that they cannot review. This means that you must choose subjects that can be supported adequately in the time allotted.

While both speakers and writers use logical, ethical, and emotional appeals in support of their arguments, the forms of presentation can make a significant difference. The reasoning process demanded of listeners must be relatively brief and straightforward, and the supporting evidence readily assimilated. The ethical appeal or credibility of the speaker is affected not only by what is said but also by the speaker's appearance, bodily movements, and vocal expressions. And the appeal to the sympathy of the audience can be greatly enhanced by the presence of the speaker. Take the example of former U.S. congresswoman Gabrielle Giffords, shot in the head in 2012 and slowly recovering movement and speech. Written descriptions of pain and heartbreak are very moving, but place yourself in an audience, looking at Giffords and imagining her suffering. No doubt the effect would be deep and long-lasting, perhaps more memorable even than the written word.

Because the human instrument is so powerful, it must be used with care. You have probably listened to speakers who used gestures and voice inflections that had been dutifully rehearsed but were obviously contrived and worked, unfortunately, to undermine rather than support the speaker's message and credibility. If you are not a gifted actor, you should avoid gestures, body language, and vocal expressions that are not truly authentic.

Some speeches, though not all, can be enhanced by visual and other aids: charts, graphs, maps, models, objects, handouts, recordings, and computerized images. These aids, however, no matter how visually or aurally exciting, should not overwhelm your own oral presentation. The objects are not the stars of the show. They exist to make your spoken argument more persuasive.

Presentation Aids

Charts, Graphs, Handouts

Charts and graphs, large enough and clear enough to be seen and understood, can illuminate speeches that contain numbers of any kind, especially statistical comparisons. You can make a simple chart yourself, on paper for use with an easel or on a computer to be projected or to be printed for presentation to an audience. Enlarged illustrations or a model of a complicated machine — say, the space shuttle — would help a speaker to explain its function. You already know that photographs or videos are powerful instruments of persuasion, above all in support of appeals for humanitarian aid, for both people and animals.

The use of a handout also requires planning. It's probably unwise to put your speech on hold while the audience reads or studies a handout that requires time and concentration. Confine the subject matter of handouts to material that can be easily grasped as you discuss or explain it.

Audio

Audio aids may also enliven a speech or even be indispensable to its success. One student played a recording of a scene from *Romeo and Juliet,* spoken by a cast of professional actors, to make a point about the relationship between the two lovers. Another student chose to define several types of popular music, including rap, goth, heavy metal, and techno. But he used only words, and the lack of any musical demonstration meant that the distinctions remained unclear.

Video

With sight, sound, and movement, a video can illustrate or reinforce the main points of a speech. A speech warning people not to text while driving will have a much greater effect if enhanced by a video showing the tragic and often gruesome outcome of car accidents caused by distracted driving. Schools that teach driver's education frequently rely on these bone-chilling videos to show their students that getting behind the wheel is a serious responsibility, not a game. If you want to use video, check to make sure that a computer, Blu-ray, or DVD player and television are available to you. Most schools have an audio-visual department that manages the delivery, setup, and return of all equipment.

Multimedia

Multimedia presentation software programs enable you to combine several different media such as text, charts, sound, and still or moving pictures into one unit. In the business world, multimedia presentations are commonly used in situations where there is a limited amount of time to persuade or teach a fairly large audience.

Though effective when done well, technically complicated presentations require careful planning. First you need to familiarize yourself with the program. Most presentation software programs come equipped with helpful tutorials. If the task of creating your own presentation from scratch seems overwhelming, you can use one of the many preformatted presentation templates: You will simply need to customize the content.

You also need to make sure the equipment you need (computer, projector, connection cords, etc.) will be available. Robert Stephens, founder of the Geek Squad, a Minneapolis-based business that provides on-site emergency response to computer problems, gives the following tips for multimedia presentations:

1. In case of equipment failure, always bring two of everything.
2. Back up your presentation on CD-ROM or a Zip drive.
3. Avoid live visits to the Internet. Because connections can fail or be painfully slow, and sites can move or disappear, if you must visit the Internet in your presentation, download the appropriate pages onto your hard drive ahead of time. It will still look like a live visit.
4. In the end, technology cannot replace creativity. Make sure that you are using multimedia to reinforce, not replace, your main points.[10]

If you have never used the devices you need for your presentation, practice using them before the speech. Few things are more disconcerting for the speechmaker and the audience than a speaker who is fumbling with his or her materials, unable to find the right picture or to make a machine work.

READING ARGUMENT

Examining a Speech

Read the following excerpts from a speech by Anna Maria Chávez, the CEO of the Girl Scouts of the USA, to get a better understanding of audience, credibility, organization, language, and support. The first two paragraphs (in italic) provide background on Chávez and the speech.

 Go to **macmillanhighered.com/rottenberg** to view a video of the speech.

---

[10] Robert Stephens as paraphrased in Eric Matson, "When Your Presentation Crashes . . . Who You Gonna Call?," *Fast Company*, February/March 1997, p. 130.

Address to the National Council Session/ 52nd Convention of the Girl Scouts of the USA

Anna Maria Chávez

The following speech was presented by Girl Scouts of the USA national CEO Anna Maria Chávez to delegates of the organization's 2011 National Council Session/52nd Convention in Houston, Texas. The speech served to introduce Ms. Chávez as the nineteenth CEO of the national organization of the Girl Scout Movement, and the first Latina to lead the organization. Chávez was addressing more than 15,000 members of the 112 local Girl Scout councils across the country, in addition to Girl Scout alumnae, current and prospective donors, and active girl members of the Movement.

The triennial convention also celebrated the 100th Anniversary of the Girl Scouts, and Ms. Chávez used her address to talk about how far the Movement had come in its first 100 years and the opportunities and challenges it faced as it stood on the doorstep of its second century. In her remarks, Ms. Chávez suggests that Girl Scouts are at a pivotal and transitional moment in its history and positions herself as a change-agent who would bring a new kind of dynamism and leadership to bear in propelling the Girl Scouts into their second century of service to girls.

Support: Personal example of how scouting influenced her

Audience: Identifies with Girl Scouts and leaders who are her audience

... One day my parents took me on a picnic, and I found this cave and it had really important Native American hieroglyphics, and these kids had graffitied all over it. And I was mad. So I stomped back down that hill with my little science kit. And I ran up to my mother and I said, "Mother, this isn't fair! They destroyed this wonderful cave and the environment, and the Girl Scouts taught me that we need to cherish the environment. This has to stop." And she looked at me very calmly and said, "Well, Anna Maria, what do we do in these instances?" And she said to me, and I repeated to her, "Well, I've got to do something. I've got to change this." And she said, "Okay, how are you going to do that? Who does these things?" I said, "Well, people who make laws and change the world, and lawyers." And she goes, "Okay, so what happens next?" "Well, if I want to be a lawyer, I must go to law school," so as a Girl Scout, by then the age of twelve, I was headed to law school.

Support: Another personal example of a helpful lesson learned through scouting

Credibility: Establishes that she is well educated and resourceful

And that courage kept me well, because I went to Yale because they invited me. They sent me a brochure, so I'd assumed they wanted me. So I went. I

In 2011, the Girl Scouts of the USA welcomed Anna Maria Chávez as the organization's CEO. The excerpts are from the speech Chávez gave at its National Council Session/52nd Convention in Houston, in November 2011.

hadn't even gone, and my parents go, "Do you want us to take you?" "No, I got this." I get there, and I discovered a whole new environment. I was a kid from a small town on scholarship, and I worked two jobs to scrape by. And I remember one December my scholarship was running out, and I had one dollar left, so I went and I took that dollar and I taped it to the wall above my desk where I studied every night, and I stared at it. And it had to last me about four weeks because if I missed dinner, because of my second job, I had to pay for it. So every night I would run home from work to get to that dining hall. But it taught me, as we are taught in Girl Scouts, to use our resources wisely. So I saved that dollar, and I thought, you know, I can do this. And I went on to law school and after that I went to Washington, and that is where this Girl Scout learned how to take a few hard knocks. But that was okay, because I eventually got to advise a U.S. president, a vice president, two cabinet secretaries, three federal administrators, two governors, and a husband. And that's when the Girl Scouts of Southwest Texas called. And they said, "You know, we would really be interested for you to come work with us."

And I took that leap of chance, and I went out there, and I took that opportunity — who wouldn't? — to take the opportunity to champion such a noble cause, to play a role in changing lives and through their lives change a nation. So in just two years, our team in Southwest Texas established unprecedented partnerships with school districts and leading businesses to serve more girls than ever. And that really shows the success we can have in building strategic partnerships to offer the Girl Scout leadership experience to as many girls as we can. I love working for girls. They make our job fun, and they keep us real, and the exuberance they bring to their daily work really energizes me, which is my secret of energy. And they motivate me every day to jump out of bed. . . .

[These girls] need encouragement. They need someone to tell them that anything is possible. Because they can. All of you, I know, can share a story of Girl Scouts who are doing great things. Maybe your story is about a group of ten Brownies from Worcester, Massachusetts, who, through examples in *The Wild Journey*, worked through their local TV station to produce and air PSAs that educated their community on water conservation. Or maybe your story can be taken from the amazing girls we have seen this week here in Houston. They are leading the nation in making the world a better place, one project at a time.

5   But I want to tell you about a young lady I met in San Antonio because the teens in our council came to me and said, ". . . You need to help us bring more teenaged girls into our system, and you need to retain us as well." So they created a program, a new pathway called Gamma Sigma girls, and it was

Support/credibility: Uses herself as an example of leadership

Audience: Praises her audience

Support: Other examples of Girl Scouts as leaders

targeted toward high school girls that didn't have an opportunity to be Girl Scouts in their younger years. And in that program, Irene saw things she had never seen before. She was so energized, and even though she was a senior, she felt that she could give back to her community, and she was a positive force in her school. She did everything she could to help her Girl Scout sisters. Irene is a bright girl who has unfortunately faced some challenges. And at the end of the year — the Girl Scout year — I learned that through all of this, Irene, since the age of nine, had been homeless, and since the age of fourteen had been in twelve schools. Now, even with all of this going against her, she felt she had found a home with Girl Scouts. She felt she was in a safe environment with other girls to help other people change the world.

Support: One specific extended example

As a Girl Scout, Irene has blossomed. She is doing amazing things in her community, she graduated in the top ten of her graduating class, and she now goes across the country to talk to other teens and children about the ability to express your views, to live through barriers, and make a difference to others. She's created a close-knit friend group at school, and I don't think we can ever underestimate the importance of what our program and Girl Scouts meant to her and to other girls. She used to wake up every day at 5:00 a.m. to get to school, ride an hour and a half on the bus just to see her Girl Scout sisters. Today Irene is a freshman at Texas State University in San Marcos. She is the first in her family to graduate from [high school], and she is here with us today. . . I am in awe of her and the thousands of girls she represents. She is really an important part of our history.

Organization: She generalizes from one example to the thousands in attendance, but also to the millions not yet reached by her organization.

Now, forever, we will have a lifelong circle of friends. There are ten thousand of us here today in this room alone. What breaks my heart and keeps me moving forward is that Irene was almost never a Girl Scout. Because of limited funds, she almost was unable to become a member of our organization. And there are millions of girls outside our movement just like Irene, because of lack of funding, not enough volunteer support, [who] have yet to join our movement. Those girls are the ones I worry about the most, the ones who need us. These are the girls that literally keep me up late at night but motivate me to wake up in the morning to keep going. That is why I took on this important yet daunting role. Like Irene, I too faced obstacles, but Girl Scouts gave me the hope to push through them, and I wanted to make sure our important work continued.

Right now, Girl Scouts reaches about ten percent of the girls in our country, and that is not enough. Today there is a girl out there who is searching for a place where she feels at home. Do you see her? Somewhere in this country there is a teenager who really needs the guidance and confidence that she can gain through Girl Scouts. Can you hear her?

We need to reach out to these girls. We need to let them know we're here for them. To do that, we need to turn ourselves outward and address the world about our movement. In the next hundred years—because we are experts at mobilizing and grassroots organization—we can unite our members to make a difference. Now, let's ask the world to imagine their communities without Girl Scouts. Imagine the thousands of food drives, clothing and toy collections that would never take place were it not for Girl Scouts. Imagine the hundreds of thousands of hours spent on take-action projects, to plant trees, adopt pets, and build gardens, projects that would have never happened if not for Girl Scouts. And the most terrifying of all, imagine this world without Girl Scout cookies.

Organization: She starts to address the solution to the problem.

Language: She uses everyday language throughout and occasional humor.

10   We need to step forward and shout from the rooftops: the time is now, the time is right. The question of female leadership has moved onto the front pages. There is enormous and growing understanding of what it can mean for women to really play a role in leading our society. And there is greater and greater awareness of the benefit of teaching girls to lead, so that they can be the leaders in their lives no matter what they do.

Organization: She generalizes about the increased awareness of women as leaders.

Now, I'm not just talking about executives or judges or scientists. I'm also talking about the women that go out and get their degrees so they can stay home and raise their children. Any girl deserves a chance to be what she wants to be because that is her choice. That's something you give girls, and they know it. Why do you think Irene woke up at 5:00 a.m. so she could tolerate a long bus ride to go to a Girl Scout meeting. Because, my friends, we have something precious, we are something precious. The world is waiting for a leader to step forward in the name of girls and women. We are that leader. With three million members in the United States, ten million sisters worldwide, and fifty million alumnae, we are bigger than we recognize. We are turning a hundred years old, and the eyes of the world are upon us. So let's show them what we've got. Let's tell **everybody** about it. We're going to stand up and say, "This is who we are, and this is who we are not." This is what we are going to say to the country and the world: "Girl Scouts is developing the female leaders of tomorrow with the courage, confidence, and character they will need to help make this world a better place."

Organization: Her claim

This is what we are going to say to parents: "Girl Scouts will open the doors of possibilities for your daughter—or your niece—that life has to offer, and we will provide them the leadership skills that they will need to navigate their own paths to success.

Organization/language:
Parallel order, repeated
language

And this is what we are going to say to the girls: "We are proud to renew our promise to you. The recognition you receive for making things better in your school, in your place of worship, in your community all contribute to the lifting up of your voices to signal a brand new day for an impatient world waiting for the goodness you bring. We know that you are capable, you are strong, you are smart, you are beautiful, you are bold. Your family recognized your greatness as soon as they called you by your name for the very first time. Juliette[11] recognized it as soon as she called you by your name. She called you Girl Scout. You must know that your time is now."

Audience: She draws in her
audience by asking questions
to which they shout answers.

Our time is now, so here's what I want from everybody in this room here today. Will you help me? Will **you** be the force that propels this movement further than even Juliette could imagine? Will you? Will you tell your stories so that we are no longer the best kept secret? Will you raise your voices so that all girls can raise theirs? Well, to paraphrase Juliette Gordon Low, we've got something for the girls of Houston and all of America and all of the world, and we are going to start today. Thank you.

---

[11] Juliette Gordon Low founded the Girl Scouts in 1912.

Practice: Examining a Speech

Read the following speech given at Georgetown University on May 18, 2012, by U.S. Department of Health and Human Services secretary Kathleen Sebelius, and answer the questions that follow it.

Remarks to Georgetown University's Public Policy Institute
KATHLEEN SEBELIUS

Dean Montgomery, members of the faculty, family, friends, and graduates: It's an honor to be with you this morning. And let me start with some well-earned congratulations. Last weekend, on Mother's Day, I was at the University of Kansas when my younger son received his Master's degree. So I know the hard work and effort that got you here today.

I married a Georgetown law graduate and am a Hoya Mom — the mother of a double Georgetown graduate. So in my family, Hoya Saxa comes second only to Rock Chalk Jayhawk.

Kathleen Sebelius served as governor of Kansas from 2003 to 2009, when she became the secretary of the U.S. Department of Health and Human Services.

And I was especially pleased to be invited to speak to you, the public policy graduates. Having spent my entire life in public service, I believe you've chosen the most challenging, frustrating, exciting, consequential, and rewarding career there is. And today, I want to share a few lessons from my career that I hope will be useful as you begin yours.

I started out as an "unpaid volunteer." My dad got into politics when I was five, so for most of my childhood, I spent my fall days putting up yard signs and going door to door.

5 Actually, the more accurate term might be forced labor. There wasn't a lot of choice in the matter. (It was only later that I discovered that other families were going to football games and picnics while I was attending political rallies.)

But what I got from those fall outings, and from our conversations around our dinner table, was a deep belief in the value of public service. And throughout my career, it's been that unwavering belief that's carried me to my highest points—and gotten me through my lowest.

I know you share that belief. If you didn't, you wouldn't be here today. You wouldn't have suffered through regression analysis. You wouldn't have passed up bigger salary possibilities in other fields.

So my first hope for you today is that you always hold on to your commitment to work for the common good. If you let that focus guide you, you will never go off course.

I learned the second lesson when I came to Washington in the late 60s to attend Trinity College. Those were tumultuous times in our nation's history, and DC was right in the middle of it. During my college years, the draft was reinstated, as the government ramped up the war in Vietnam. Racial tensions, that had been smoldering, erupted after the assassination of Martin Luther King Jr., and neighborhoods in DC were burned to the ground.

What was striking at the time is how young people were driving these national debates. There was a feeling not just that young people could change the world—but that we had to.

Robert Kennedy spoke about those times in a famous speech. He said: "This world demands the qualities of youth. Not a time of life, but a state of mind, a temper of the will, a quality of the imagination, a predominance of courage over timidity, of the appetite for adventure over the life of ease."

As you set out on your careers, you may find yourselves tempted to defer to those who are older or have more experience. And on behalf of the parents in the audience, I want to be clear that even though we may not know who Kim Kardashian is, or why everyone is always so angry about her, we do still have some wisdom to share. You still need to call your mom! (In fact, after this ceremony ends, the first thing you should do is thank the parents, teachers, mentors, and friends who supported your journey to this graduation day.)

But the truth is, wisdom isn't the only thing that comes with age. Growing older can also bring complacency and cautiousness.

I know Georgetown hasn't trained you to sit on the sidelines. You've studied under leading policy-makers. You've proven your skills, not just on tests and papers, but in the real world through programs like Project Honduras.

15 So my second piece of advice is: Don't wait. Go ahead and do it yourself—because if you don't, it might never happen.

Now, I wish I could give you a roadmap for exactly how to do that. But the truth is that career paths are usually only visible looking backwards, like the tracks we make in the snow.

I'm an accidental feminist who learned that girls can do anything by attending an all-girls school where we had to do everything. I ended up in Kansas because that's where my husband grew up. I began my political career because our part-time legislature was a better fit for me, as a mother with two young children, than the 60-hour-a-week job I had.

As I moved along, I sought out opportunities to learn new skills and new subject areas. I started out working in corrections. Later, I worked on everything from education, to children and family issues, to the budget, to jobs and economic development, to rural challenges.

One of the issues I kept coming back to was health care, culminating in my current position. And now, I have the extraordinary opportunity to help implement legislation that is finally, after seven decades of failed debate, ensuring that all Americans have access to affordable health coverage.

20   But I never would have been here if I hadn't taken some chances. For me, the biggest risk was running for Kansas Insurance Commissioner. The indicators were not promising. The statewide office had never been held by a woman or a Democrat. The previous three commissioners had close ties to the insurance industry and had served nearly fifty years combined. And it was 1994, when running for office as a Democrat was the basic equivalent of wearing a Georgetown jersey in the Syracuse student section.

But I went for it and won. And I ended up not just getting an incredible opportunity to make a difference, but also gaining invaluable experience for the job I have now. (Who knew?)

All of you are going to face similar choices in your careers. It might be taking a more senior position at a much smaller organization. It might be moving abroad to work. It might be going from running a campaign to becoming a candidate.

And when you do encounter these opportunities, I encourage you take a deep breath and seize them.

And that brings me to the final lesson I want to leave with you today, which is that no matter what path you choose, it's going to be hard.

Ultimately, public policy is about mak-   25
ing difficult choices. Today, there are serious debates under way about the direction of our country — debates about the size and role of government, about America's role as a global economic and military leader, about the moral and economic imperative of providing health care to all our citizens. People have deeply held beliefs on all sides of these discussions, and you, as public policy leaders, will be called on to help move these debates forward.

These are not questions with quick and easy answers. When I was in junior high, John Fitzgerald Kennedy was running for president. I wasn't old enough to vote, but it was the first national campaign I really remember. Some of then-Senator Kennedy's opponents attacked him for his religion, suggesting that electing the first Catholic president would undermine the separation of church and state, a fundamental principle of our democracy. The furor grew so loud that Kennedy chose to deliver a speech about his beliefs just seven weeks before the election.

In that talk to Protestant ministers, Kennedy talked about his vision of religion and the public square, and said he believed in an America, and I quote, "where no religious body seeks to impose its will directly or indirectly upon the general populace or the public acts of its officials—and where religious liberty is so indivisible that an act against one church is treated as an act against us all."

Kennedy was elected president on November 8, 1960. And more than fifty years later, that conversation, about the intersection of our nation's long tradition of religious freedom with policy decisions that affect the general public, continues.

Contributing to these debates will require more than just the quantitative skills you have learned at Georgetown. It will also require the ethical skills you have honed—the ability to weigh different views, see issues from other points of view, and in the end, follow your own moral compass.

These debates can also be contentious. But 30 this is a strength of our country, not a weakness. In some countries around the world, it is much easier to make policy. The leader delivers an edict and it goes into effect. There's no debate, no criticism, no second guessing.

Our system is messier, slower, more frustrating, and far better. It requires conversations that can be painful, and it almost always ends in compromise. But it's through this process of conversation and compromise that we move forward, together, step by step, toward a "more perfect union."

Looking out on you this morning, I feel very optimistic about the future of that union. If you hold on to your idealism, resist complacency, take chances, and engage thoughtfully with the difficult challenges of our time, you will succeed. And I can't wait to see what you will accomplish.

Congratulations and good luck!

Reading and Discussion Questions

1. How does Sebelius attempt to relate to audience members and thus draw them into her speech?
2. What did Sebelius learn from her early involvement in her father's campaigns? How does that relate to her audience on this occasion?
3. What advice does she offer the graduates?
4. Why does she feel that the jobs the graduates will enter will require ethical skills? Does she come across as an ethical person herself? Why, or why not?

---

bits

To see what you are learning about argumentation applied to the latest world and national news, read our *Bits* blog, "Argument and the Headlines," at **blogs.bedfordstmartins.com/bits**.

Documenting Sources

As you write your paper, anytime that you make use of the wording or ideas of one of your sources, you must document that use. Two of the most common methods of crediting sources are the Modern Language Association (MLA) and American Psychological Association (APA) systems. The MLA system consists of two main components: the in-text citations (explained below) and the list of Works Cited (shown on pages 403–412).

MLA In-Text Citations

In the text of your paper, immediately after any quotation, paraphrase, or idea you need to document, simply insert a parenthetical mention of the author's last name and the page number(s) on which the material appears. You don't need a comma after the author's name or an abbreviation of the word *page* or *p.* For example, the following sentence appears in the sample MLA paper later in this chapter:

> Although there are nutritious competitive options, those do not sell as well as the ones high in sugar, salt, and calories (Hartline-Grafton 2–3).

The parenthetical reference tells the reader that the information in this sentence came from pages of the book or article that appears in the Works Cited at the end of the paper. The complete reference on the Works Cited page provides all of the information readers need to locate the original source:

> Hartline-Grafton, Heather. "How Competitive Foods in Schools Impact Student Health, School Meal Programs, and Students from Low-Income Families." *Issue Briefs for Child Nutrition Reauthorization 5.* Washington, D.C.: Food Research and Action Center, 2010. EBSCOhost. Web. 22 Sept. 2010.

If the author's name is mentioned in the same sentence, it is also acceptable to place only the page numbers in parentheses; it is not necessary to repeat the author's name. For example:

According to Heather Hartline-Grafton, although there are nutritious competitive options, those do not sell as well as the ones high in sugar, salt, and calories (2–3).

Remember, though, that a major reason for using qualified sources is that they lend authority to the ideas expressed. The first time an author is mentioned in the paper, he or she — or they — should be identified by full name and by claim to authority:

Parke Wilde and Mary Kennedy, both researchers in the Friedman School of Nutrition Science and Policy at Tufts University in Boston, explain some of the complexities in an article entitled "The Economics of a Healthy School Meal."

A last name and page number in parentheses do not carry nearly the same weight as a full name and credentials. You should save the former for subsequent citations once the author has been fully identified. If more than one sentence comes from the same source, you do not need to put parentheses after each sentence. One parenthetical citation at the end of the material from a source is enough if it is clear from the way you introduce the material where your ideas end and the source's begin.

According to the Robert Wood Johnson Foundation, a charitable organization whose goal is to improve the health of all Americans, the rate of obesity for those between the ages of six and eleven has quadrupled in three decades. Children are being diagnosed with what used to be considered adult diseases, like high blood pressure, adult-onset diabetes, and gallstones. The Foundation reports, "If we don't succeed in reversing this epidemic, we are in danger of raising the first generation of American children who will live sicker and die younger than their parents' generation" (259–60).

If you are using more than one work by the same author, you will need to provide in the parentheses the title or a recognizable shortened form of the title of the particular work being cited. If the author's name is not mentioned in the sentence, you should include in parentheses the author's last name, the title, and the page number, with a comma between the author's name and the title. If both the author's name and the title of any work being cited are mentioned in the sentence, the parentheses will include only the page number. Had two works by Hartline-Grafton been listed in the Works Cited in the sample paper, the first example on page 400 would have looked like this:

Although there are nutritious competitive options, those do not sell as well as the ones high in sugar, salt, and calories (Hartline-Grafton, "How Competitive Foods" 2–3).

If there is more than one author, don't forget to give credit to all. Two or three authors are acknowledged by name in the parentheses if not in your own sentence: (Harmon, Livesy, and Jones 23). With four or more authors, use *et al.*, the Latin term for *and others*: (Braithwaite et al. 137).

Some sources do not name an author. To cite a work with an unknown author, give the title, or a recognizable shortened form, in the text of your paper. If the work does not have numbered pages, which is often the case in Web pages or nonprint sources, do not include page numbers. For example:

> In some cases Sephardic Jews, "converted" under duress, practiced Christianity openly and Judaism in secret until recently ("Search for the Buried Past").

Direct quotations should always be introduced or worked into the grammatical structure of your own sentences. If you need help introducing quotations, refer to the Writer's Guide in Chapter 4 (pp. 123–125). Remember, however, that you need to provide parenthetical documentation not only for every direct quotation but also for every paraphrase or summary. Document any words or ideas that are not your own.

As a general rule, you cannot make any changes in a quotation. Two exceptions must be clearly marked when they occur. At times, you may use brackets to make a slight change that does not alter the meaning of the quotation. For example, a pronoun may need to be replaced by a noun in brackets to make its reference clear. Or a verb tense may be changed and bracketed to make the quotation fit more smoothly into your sentence. An ellipsis (...) is used when you omit a portion of the quotation that does not change the essential meaning of the quote. You do not need to use ellipses at the beginning or end of a direct quotation. If the omitted portion included the end of one sentence and the beginning of another, there should be a fourth period (....).

If a quotation is more than four typed lines long, it needs to be handled as a block quotation. A block quotation is usually introduced by a sentence followed by a colon. The quotation itself is indented one inch or ten spaces from the left margin. No quotation marks are necessary since the placement on the page informs the reader that it is a quotation. The only quotation marks in a block quotation would be ones copied from the original, as in dialogue. A paragraph break within a block quotation is indented an additional five spaces. The parenthetical citation is the same as with a quotation run into your text, but the period appears before the parenthesis.

With print sources in particular, you will often need to cite one work that is quoted in another or a work from an anthology. For the former, the parenthetical documentation provides the name and page number of the source you actually used, preceded by the words "qtd. in":

> The National School Lunch Program has been in existence since 1946 "as a measure of national security, to safeguard the health and well-being of the Nation's children and to encourage the domestic consumption of nutritious agricultural commodities and other food" (qtd. in Center for Science 230).

A work in an anthology is cited parenthetically by the name of the author of the work, not the editor of the anthology: (Simkovich 3).

The list of Works Cited includes all material you have used to write your research paper. This list appears at the end of your paper and always starts on a new page. Center the title Works Cited, double-space between the title and the first entry, and begin your list, which should be arranged alphabetically by author. Each entry should start at the left margin; indent all subsequent lines of the entry five spaces or one-half inch. Number each page, and double-space throughout.

One more point: *Content notes,* which provide additional information not readily worked into a research paper, are indicated by superscript numbers. Content notes are included on a Notes page before the list of Works Cited.

MLA Works Cited Entries

Following are examples of the citation forms you are most likely to need as you document your research. In general, for both books and magazines, information should appear in the following order: author, title, and publication information. Each item should be followed by a period. When using as a source an essay that appears in this book, follow the citation model for "Material Reprinted from Another Source," unless your instructor indicates otherwise. Consult the *MLA Handbook for Writers of Research Papers,* Seventh Edition (2009), for other documentation models and a list of acceptable shortened forms of publishers' names.

Directory of MLA Works Cited Entries

Print Sources

1. A Book by a Single Author

   Edsel, Robert M. *Saving Italy: The Race to Rescue a Nation's Treasures from the Nazis.* New York: W. W. Norton, 2013. Print.

2. Two or More Works by the Same Author or Authors

   Rashid, Ahmed. *Pakistan on the Brink: The Future of America, Pakistan, and Afghanistan.* New York: Penguin, 2012. Print.

   ---. *Taliban: The Power of Militant Islam in Afghanistan and Beyond.* 2nd ed. New Haven, CT: Yale UP, 2008. Print.

   For the second and subsequent books by the same author, replace the author's name with three hyphens, followed by a period and the title.

3. A Work with Two Authors

   Alderman, Ellen, and Caroline Kennedy. *The Right to Privacy.* New York: Vintage, 1995. Print.

   NOTE: This form is followed even for two authors with the same last name.

   Ehrlich, Paul, and Anne Ehrlich. *Extinction: The Causes and Consequences of the Disappearance of Species.* New York: Random, 1981. Print.

The Elements of Citation

BOOK (MLA)

When you cite a book using MLA style, include the following:

1 Author

2 Title and subtitle

3 City of publication

4 Publisher

5 Date of publication

6 Medium

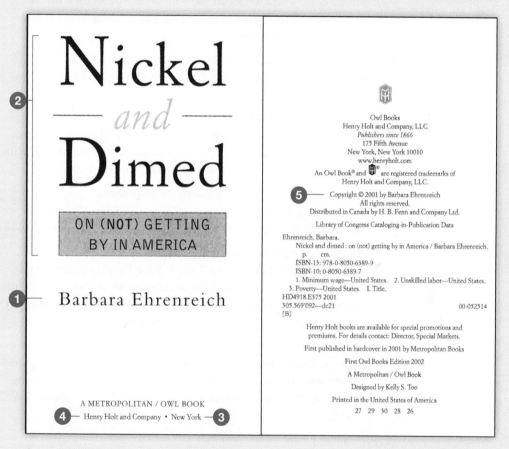

Works Cited entry for a book in MLA style

Ehrenreich, Barbara. *Nickel and Dimed: On (Not) Getting by in America.* New York:

Holt, 2001. Print.

4. A Work with Three or More Authors

Fry, Tony, Susan Stewart, and Clive Dilnot. *Design and the Question of History.* London: Bloomsbury Academic P, 2015. Print.

If there are more than three authors, name only the first and add "et al." (meaning "and others").

5. A Work with a Corporate Author

Cracked.com. *The De-Textbook: The Stuff You Didn't Know about the Stuff You Thought You Knew.* New York: Plume-Penguin, 2013. Print.

6. An Anthology or a Compilation

Dark, Larry, ed. *Prize Stories 1997: The O. Henry Awards.* New York: Anchor, 1997. Print.

7. A Work in an Anthology

Head, Bessie. "Woman from America." *Wild Women: Contemporary Short Stories by Women Celebrating Women.* Ed. Sue Thomas. Woodstock: Overlook, 1994. 45–51. Print.

8. An Introduction, Preface, Foreword, or Afterword

Buatta, Mario. Foreword. *George Stacey and the Creation of American Chic.* By Maureen Footer. New York: Rizzoli, 2014.

9. Material Reprinted from Another Source

Pollan, Michael. "Food Fight." *New York Review of Books* 24 Sept. 2010. Rpt. in *Elements of Argument: A Text and Reader.* Annette T. Rottenberg and Donna Haisty Winchell. 10th ed. Boston: Bedford/St. Martin's, 2012. 576–79. Print.

10. A Multivolume Work

Corcoran, Kevin, and Joel Fischer, eds. *Couples, Families, and Children.* Oxford, UK: Oxford UP, 2013. Print. Vol. 1 of *Measures for Clinical Practice and Research: A Sourcebook.* 2 vols. 2013.

11. An Edition Other Than the First

Charters, Ann, ed. *The Story and Its Writer: An Introduction to Short Fiction.* 8th ed. Boston: Bedford/St. Martin's, 2011. Print.

12. A Translation

Modi, Narendra. *A Journey: Poems by Narendra Modi.* Trans. Ravi Mantha. New Delhi: Rupa Publications, 2014. Print.

13. A Republished Book

Bellamy, Edward. *Looking Backward.* 1888. Charleston, SC: BiblioBazaar, 2008. Print.

NOTE: The only information about original publication you need to provide is the publication date, which appears immediately after the title.

14. A Book in a Series

Sutton, Matthew Avery. *Jerry Falwell and the Rise of the Religious Right: A Brief History with Documents.* Boston: Bedford/St. Martin's, 2013. Print. The Bedford Series in History and Culture.

The series title goes after the publication information and the medium.

15. An Article from a Journal

Manzi, Jim. "The New American System." *National Affairs* 1.19 (Spring 2014): 3–24. Print.

16. An Article from a Daily Newspaper

Doctorow, E. L. "Quick Cuts: The Novel Follows Film into a World of Fewer Words." *New York Times* 15 Mar. 1999, sec. B: 1+. Print.

17. An Article from a Magazine

Schulhofer, Stephen. "Unwanted Sex." *Atlantic Monthly* Oct. 1998: 55–66. Print.

18. An Unsigned Editorial

"Better Rules for Bad Lawyers." Editorial. *New York Times* 15 Apr. 2014, sec. B: 12. Print.

19. Anonymous Works

Citation World Atlas. Maplewood: Hammond, 1999. Print.

"The March Almanac." *Atlantic Monthly* Mar. 1995: 20. Print.

20. A Review

Jackson, Lawrence. "The Vampire: The Fickle Career of Carl Van Vechten." Rev. of *The Tastemaker: Carl Van Vechten and the Birth of Modern America*, by Edward White. *Harper's Magazine* Apr. 2014: 89–94. Print.

21. An Article in a Reference Work

"Child Abuse." *Mosby's Medical Dictionary.* St. Louis, MO: Elsevier, 2013. Print.

22. A Government Document

United States. National Endowment for the Arts. *2006 Annual Report.* Washington: Office of Public Affairs, 2007. Print.

Frequently the Government Printing Office (GPO) is the publisher of federal government documents.

23. An Unpublished Manuscript

> Leahy, Ellen. "An Investigation of the Computerization of Infor-
> mation Systems in a Family Planning Program." MS thesis.
> U of Massachusetts, Amherst, 2010. Print.

24. A Letter to the Editor

> Flannery, James W. Letter. *New York Times Book Review* 28 Feb.
> 1993: 34. Print.

25. Personal Correspondence

> Bennett, David. Letter to the author. 3 Mar. 2010. TS.

> Include the medium of the correspondence at the end of the entry. Use
> TS for typescript and MS for manuscript (for handwritten letters).

26. A Cartoon or a Comic Strip

> Ziegler, Jack. "Tai Chi vs. Chai Tea." Cartoon. *New Yorker*
> 14 Apr. 2014: 51. Print.

> Henley, Marian. "Maxine." Comic strip. *Valley Advocate* 25 Feb.
> 2010: 39. Print.

Electronic Sources

27. A Web Site

> Heiner, Heidi Anne. *SurLaLune Fairy Tales.* Heidi Anne Heiner,
> 3 Sept. 2009. Web. 9 Sept. 2013.

> Include the name of the author or editor of the Web site when this
> information is available; otherwise, begin the entry with the name of
> the Web site in italics, followed by a period; the publisher or sponsor
> of the Web site (usually found near the copyright information on the
> site's home page) followed by a comma and the date of publication or
> last update. Then add the medium (Web), a period, and the date you
> accessed the site.

28. A Page or Article within a Web Site

> Goodale, Wing, and Tim Divoll. "Birds, Bats and Coastal
> Wind Farm Development in Maine: A Literature Review."
> *BioDiversity Research Institute.* BioDiversity Research Inst.,
> 29 May 2009. Web. 25 Aug. 2013.

29. A Book Available on the Web

> Kramer, Heinrich, and James Sprenger. *The Malleus Malefi-
> carum.* Trans. Montague Summers. New York, 1971.
> MalleusMaleficarum.org. Web. 14 Dec. 2013.

> In this case, the book had been previously published, and information
> about its original publication was included at the site.

The Elements of Citation

ARTICLE FROM A WEB SITE (MLA)

When you cite a brief article from a Web site using MLA style, include the following:

1 Author

2 Title of work

3 Title of Web site

4 Sponsor of site

5 Date of publication or latest update

6 Medium (Web)

7 Date of access

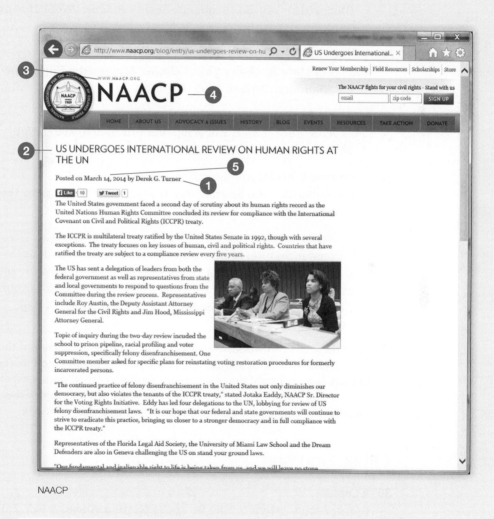

NAACP

Works Cited entry for a brief article from a Web site in MLA style

┌─── 1 ───┐ ┌─────────────────── 2 ───────────────────┐
Turner, Derek G. "US Undergoes International Review on Human Rights at the UN."

┌── 3 ──┐ ┌─ 4 ─┐ ┌─── 5 ───┐ ┌─ 6 ─┐ ┌─── 7 ───┐
NAACP.org. NAACP, 14 Mar. 2014. Web. 24 Apr. 2014.

30. An Article from an Electronic Journal

> Minow, Mary. "Filters and the Public Library: A Legal and
>   Policy Analysis." *First Monday* 2.12 (1997): n. pag. Web.
>   28 Nov. 2013.

31. An Article from a Database

> Afifi, Tamara D., et al. "Analyzing Divorce from Cultural
>   and Network Approaches." *Journal of Family Studies* 19.3
>   (Dec. 2013): 240–53. *Academic Search Premier.* Web. 16 Apr.
>   2014.

32. A CD-ROM

> Corcoran, Mary B. "Fairy Tale." *Grolier Multimedia Encyclope-*
>   *dia.* Danbury: Grolier, 1995. CD-ROM.

33. An Article from an Electronic Reference Work

> "Folk Arts." *Britannica.* Encyclopedia Britannica, 2007. Web.
>   14 Dec. 2013.

34. A Personal E-mail Communication

> Franz, Kenneth. "Re: Species Reintroduction." Message to the
>   author. 12 Oct. 2013. E-mail.

35. A Posting to a Discussion List, Web Forum, or Newsgroup

> Lee, Constance. "Re: Mothers and Stepmothers." *Folklore Dis-*
>   *cussion List.* Texas A&M U, 10 Sept. 2007. Web. 24 Oct. 2008.
> House, Ron. "Wind Farms: Do They Kill Birds?" *Google Groups:*
>   *Rec.Animals.Wildlife.* Google, 7 Sept. 2009. Web. 14 Sept.
>   2013.

Treat these as short works from a Web site. Include the author of the
posting and the title or subject line of the posting in quotation marks
(if there is no title, use the designation "Online posting" without quotation marks). Then add the name of the Web site, the sponsor of the
site, the date of the posting, the medium, and your date of access.

Other Sources

36. A Lecture

> Grant, Adam. "Giving: The Secret of Getting Ahead." 92Y Talks.
>   92nd Street Y, New York. 16 Apr., 2014. Lecture.

The Elements of Citation

ARTICLE FROM A DATABASE (MLA)

When you cite an article from a database using MLA style, include the following:

1 Author

2 Title of article

3 Title of periodical, volume and issue numbers

4 Date of publication

5 Inclusive pages

6 Name of database

7 Medium (Web)

8 Date of access

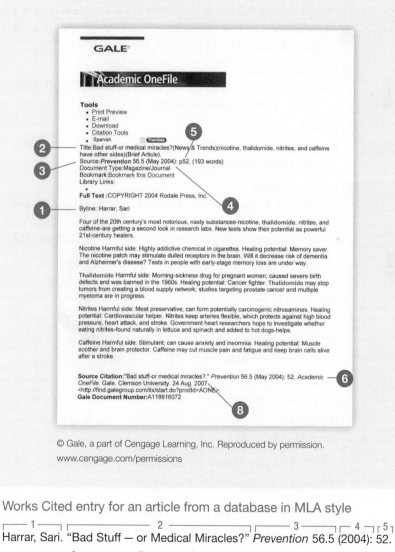

Works Cited entry for an article from a database in MLA style

Harrar, Sari. "Bad Stuff — or Medical Miracles?" *Prevention* 56.5 (2004): 52.

Academic OneFile. Web. 24 Aug. 2007.

37. A Film

> *Jerusalem.* Dir. Daniel Ferguson. Writ. Sheila Curran Bernard
> and Daniel Ferguson. Cosmic Picture/Arcane Pictures, 2013.
> Film.

Other pertinent information to give in film references, if available, is
the writer and director (see model for radio/television program for
style).

38. A Television or Radio Program

> "The London Season." *Downton Abbey.* Masterpiece Classic.
> Perf. Shirley MacLaine and Elizabeth McGovern. PBS. WXEL,
> Palm Beach, FL, 23 Feb. 2014.

39. A Videocassette

> *Style Wars!* Prod. Tony Silver and Henry Chalfont. New Day
> Films, 1985. Videocassette.

40. A DVD

> *Harry Potter and the Order of the Phoenix.* Prod. David Barron
> and David Heyman. Warner Bros., 2007. DVD.

41. A Performance

> *Quilters: A Musical Celebration.* By Molly Newman and Barbara
> Damashek. Dir. Joyce Devlin. Musical dir. Faith Fung.
> Mt. Holyoke Laboratory Theatre, South Hadley, MA. 26 Apr.
> 1991. Performance.

42. An Interview

> Bacharach, Sam. "Where Money Meets Morale." Interview by
> Alexa Von Tobel. *Inc.* Apr. 2014: 48–49. Print.

If the interviewer's name is not given or if there is no title to the interview, these elements may be left out.

> Phillips, Adam. "The Art of Nonfiction No. 7." Interview. *The*
> *Paris Review* (Spring 2014): 29–54.

An interview conducted by the author of the paper would be documented as follows:

> Hines, Gregory. Personal interview. 29 Mar. 1987.

A broadcast interview would be documented as follows:

> Hines, Gregory. Interview by Charlie Rose. *Charlie Rose.* PBS.
> WGBH, Boston. 30 Jan. 2001. Television.

MLA-Style Annotated Bibliography

An annotated bibliography is a list of sources that includes the usual bibliographic information followed by a paragraph describing and evaluating each source. Its purpose is to provide information about each source in a bibliography so that the reader has an overview of the resources related to a given topic.

For each source in an annotated bibliography, the same bibliographic information included in a Works Cited or References list is provided, alphabetized by author. Each reference also has a short paragraph that describes the work, its main focus, and, if appropriate, the methodology used in or the style of the work. An annotation might note special features such as tables or illustrations. Usually an annotation evaluates the source by analyzing its usefulness, reliability, and overall significance for understanding the topic. An annotation might include some information on the credentials of the author or the organization that produced it.

A Sample Annotation Using the MLA Citation Style

Warner, Marina. "Pity the Stepmother." *New York Times* 12 May 1991, late ed.: D17. *LexisNexis Universe*. Web. 12 Dec. 2013.

The author asserts that many fairy tales feature absent or cruel mothers, transformed by romantic editors such as the Grimm brothers into stepmothers because the idea of a wicked mother desecrated an ideal. Warner argues that figures in fairy tales should be viewed in their historical context and that social conditions often affected the way that motherhood figured in fairy tales. Warner, a novelist and author of books on the images of Joan of Arc and the Virgin Mary, writes persuasively about the social roots of a fairy-tale archetype.

APA style does not call for annotated citations. However, some instructors may require an annotated bibliography, so with either MLA or APA, follow your instructor's guidelines.

MLA Paper Format

Print your essay on one side of 8½-by-11-inch white computer paper, double-spacing throughout. Leave margins of 1 to 1½ inches on all sides, and indent each paragraph one-half inch or five spaces. Unless a formal outline is part of the paper, a separate title page is unnecessary. Instead, beginning about one inch from the top of the first page and flush with the left margin, type your name, the instructor's name, the course title, and the date, each on a separate line; then double-space and type the title, capitalizing the first letter of the words of the title except for articles, prepositions, and conjunctions. Double-space and type the body of the paper.

Number all pages at the top right corner, typing your last name before each page number in case pages are mislaid. If an outline is included, number its pages with lowercase roman numerals.

MLA-Style Sample Research Paper

Hedden 1

Kathleen Hedden

Mrs. Swanson

English 102-14

October 29, 2010

Competitive Foods and the Obesity Epidemic

It is difficult these days to watch television or read a newspaper without hearing about the problem of childhood obesity in the United States. Opinions differ as to the best solution for dealing with this problem that threatens the health of a rising generation, but few would deny that it is a problem.

Thomas R. Frieden, head of the Centers for Disease Control and Prevention in Atlanta and thus one of the leading health officials in the country, is among those who have used the term *epidemic* to describe what is happening: "What has changed, in just the course of a generation, is that childhood obesity has become an epidemic," he says. "In the 1960s, 5 percent of children were overweight. Today, nearly 20 percent are" (Frieden, Dietz, and Collins). Concern about obesity is concern not just for how our children — and our future adults — look, but for their present and future health. According to the Robert Wood Johnson Foundation, a charitable organization whose goal is to improve the health of all Americans, the rate of obesity for those between the ages of six and eleven has quadrupled in three decades. Children are being diagnosed with what used to be considered adult diseases, like high blood pressure, adult-onset diabetes, and gallstones. The Foundation reports, "If we don't succeed in reversing this epidemic, we are in danger of raising the first generation of American children who will live sicker and die younger than their parents' generation" (259–60).

The problem of childhood obesity will have to be attacked on several fronts. Parents and other caregivers have to be educated and motivated to control children's diet and physical activity. Because of the number of hours that most children spend in school five days a week for a large part of the year, however, the CDC's *Morbidity and*

Hedden follows "presenting stock issues" approach.

Frieden's name and position lend authority to the quotation.

Defining the problem (presenting evidence)

Frieden is quoted, but all three authors need to be cited.

Establishing a need for a solution

Foundation as author, mentioned in text, so page number only needed in parentheses

Hedden 2

Mortality Weekly Report has stated that "schools are in a unique position to help improve youth dietary behaviors and prevent and reduce obesity" (Centers for Disease Control).

The federal government has long subsidized the nation's school lunch program. The National School Lunch Program has been in existence since 1946 "as a measure of national security, to safeguard the health and well-being of the Nation's children and to encourage the domestic consumption of nutritious agricultural commodities and other food" (qtd. in Center for Science 230).

One problem now is the sale of what are called competitive foods, or those foods and beverages sold in schools but outside of the meal program supported by the federal government. They may be sold through vending machines, snack bars, school stores, or in a la carte lines, but they do not have to meet the nutrition standards that must be met by cafeteria food. They are not supposed to be available in the food service area during lunch, but they sometimes are and in other cases are close by.

Dr. Heather Hartline-Grafton, Senior Nutrition Policy Analyst for the Food Research and Action Center (FRAC), explains how this competitive food contributes to the obesity epidemic:

> Competitive foods are often energy-dense, nutrient-poor items, and their availability at school undermines efforts to promote healthy diets and prevent obesity. Not only do the sales of competitive foods and beverages decrease participation in the school meal programs, but the sales are often subsidized by school meal reimbursements. (1)

Competitive foods are a widespread presence in schools: They are available in 73% of elementary schools, 97% of middle schools, and 100% of high schools, most often in the form of vending machines and a la carte lines. Although there are nutritious competitive options, those do not sell as well as the ones high in sugar, salt, and calories (Hartline-Grafton 2–3).

While the U.S. Department of Agriculture has the power to regulate the food served in the school lunch program, it currently has little power to regulate competitive foods. That power depends in

The organization is the author. No page number because accessed online.

Claim

Support

One work quoted in another. The citation is to the work Katie actually used.

Support

Support

Support

Author not mentioned in text, so her name is included with page number in parentheses.

Hedden 3

part on what foods are defined as foods of minimal nutritional value (FMNVs). Hartline-Grafton explains:

Block
quotation.
Notice that
the whole
quotation
is indented,
there are no
quotation
marks, and the
period comes
before the
parenthesis.

> FMNVs are defined as foods providing less than five percent of recommended intakes for eight key nutrients. Examples include carbonated soda, gum, hard candies, and jelly beans. Other competitive foods, including candy bars, chips, and ice cream, are not considered FMNVs (and therefore not under USDA authority) and may be sold in the cafeteria during meal periods. In short, unlike the federal school lunch and breakfast programs, competitive foods are, for the most part, exempt from federal nutrition standards and regulation. (2)

If it is obvious that many competitive foods are a danger to our children's health and well-being and that they are beyond the control of even the USDA's regulations, why are these foods not removed from schools?

Explains
why prob-
lem exists

One simple answer is because students like them and buy them. Most students are in the habit of eating fast food away from school and see no problem eating it at school. They like the high-fat, high-sugar foods that do not conform to the regulations that school cafeterias must follow.

If students are not willing to monitor their own food intake and the USDA cannot, why do schools continue to allow these foods lacking in nutritional value to be sold? Part of the answer is that some school districts in some states have chosen to regulate the competitive foods sold in the district or to eliminate them entirely. The economics of school meals, however, are much more complicated than one might think. Parke Wilde and Mary Kennedy, both researchers in the Friedman School of Nutrition Science and Policy at Tufts University in Boston, explain some of the complexities in an article entitled "The Economics of a Healthy School Meal." Schools are reimbursed a set amount for each lunch subsidized by the federal government. Even when better-off students pay for their lunch, the federal government pays its part. Other students, depending on their parents' income, pay a reduced rate or nothing at all. Even that set formula, however, is affected by competitive foods. Students and their parents

Hedden 4

are pushing for more nutritious foods than are required by the federal government, and the districts must balance the money lost when students don't eat school lunches with that gained by selling competitive foods. Wilde and Kennedy write,

> Any successful business must understand the economic interactions across its product lines, but these interactions are particularly intense for a school food service. A child who consumes a reimbursable lunch and breakfast will have lower demand for *a la carte* items, while a child who skips a real meal may be hungrier for a snack. This interaction means that school food service decisions about competitive foods strongly affect the federal school meals program, and vice versa.

By that logic, if competitive foods were not available, students might opt for the healthier alternative of the school meal.

In September 2010, Congress passed the Healthy, Hunger-Free Kids Act of 2010, a huge step forward in schools' ability to control the foods served at school. The act was designed to "commit an additional $4.5 billion to child-nutrition programs over the next 10 years and implement the most sweeping changes to those programs in decades." In response to the problem of competitive foods, it "directs the U.S. Department of Agriculture to set new nutrition standards for all food served in schools, from lunchrooms to vending machines" (Eisler).

Ironically, it is not a foregone conclusion that all schools will benefit from this new legislation. They have to adopt the new nutrition standards, which the Institute of Medicine will recommend and the U.S. Department of Agriculture will write. Schools that adopt the new nutrition requirements will get an increase of six cents per meal in their federal reimbursement rate, the first increase since 1973 and one that has long been needed (Eisler). Stipends are also available for those schools that need to upgrade their kitchens to accommodate preparing the more nutritious meals (Wilde and Kennedy).

It seems obvious that all school districts across the country should adopt the new nutritional standards that are being presented to them with the additional incentive of getting more money per meal for school lunches and breakfasts than they currently get. The new

No page number because an electronic source.

Solution

Author not identified in text. No page number because electronic source.

Hedden 5

Conclusion

standards will remove from schools competitive foods that are particularly unhealthy and replace them with foods that fall under the nutrition guidelines of the new act. Students may not get all of the choices
of foods that they would like, but parents, teachers, and school
officials—and the students themselves—will know that schools are
contributing less to the problem of childhood and adolescent obesity.

Hedden 6

Begin Works
Cited on a new
page.

Works Cited

Center for Science in the Public Interest. "Improving Kids' Nutrition:
    An Action Kit for Parents and Citizens." *Food, Inc.: How Indus-
    trial Food Is Making Us Sicker, Fatter and Poorer—And What You
    Can Do about It*. Ed. Karl Weber. New York: PublicAffairs, 2009.
    227–57. Print.

Centers for Disease Control and Prevention. "Competitive Foods and
    Beverages Available for Purchase in Secondary Schools—Se-
    lected Sites, United States, 2006." *MMWR Weekly* 29 Aug. 2008:
    935–38. *EBSCOhost*. Web. 16 Sept. 2010.

Eisler, Peter. "Sweeping School Lunch Bill Clears Senate Panel."
    usatoday.com. USA Today, 24 Mar. 2010. Web. 22 Sept. 2010.

Frieden, Thomas R., William Dietz, and Janet Collins. "Reducing
    Childhood Obesity through Policy Change: Acting Now to Pre-
    vent Obesity." *Health Affairs* 29.3 (2010): 357–63. *EBSCOhost*.
    Web. 15 Sept 2010.

Hartline-Grafton, Heather. "How Competitive Foods in Schools
    Impact Student Health, School Meal Programs, and Students
    from Low-Income Families." *Issue Briefs for Child Nutrition Reau-
    thorization 5*. Washington, DC: Food Research and Action Center,
    2010. *EBSCOhost*. Web. 22 Sept. 2010.

Robert Wood Johnson Foundation. "Childhood Obesity: The Chal-
    lenge." *Food, Inc.: How Industrial Food Is Making Us Sicker, Fat-
    ter and Poorer—And What You Can Do about It*. Ed. Karl Weber.
    New York: PublicAffairs, 2009. 259–61. Print.

Wilde, Parke, and Mary Kennedy. "The Economics of a Healthy
    School Meal." *Choices* 24.3 (2009): n. pag. *EBSCOhost*. Web.
    21 Sept. 2010.

A work in an
anthology

A journal article
accessed
online

A newspaper
article ac-
cessed online

A document
accessed
online

APA In-Text Citations

Instructors in the social sciences might prefer the citation system of the American Psychological Association (APA), which is used in the sample paper on women in the military (pp. 430–39). Like the MLA system, the APA system calls for a parenthetical citation in the text of the paper following any quotations from your sources. The APA only recommends that page numbers be included for paraphrases or summaries, but you should provide page numbers for these anyway unless your instructor advises you that they are not necessary. In the text of your paper, immediately after any quotation, paraphrase, or idea you need to document, insert a parenthetical mention of the author's last name and the page number on which the material appears. Unlike the MLA system, the APA system also includes the year of publication in the parenthetical reference, using a comma to separate the items within the citation and using "p." or "pp." before the page number(s). Even if the source has a month of publication, only the year is included in the parenthetical citation. Here is an example:

> As of now, women are restricted from 30% of Army assignments and 1% of Air Force assignments (Baer, 2003, p. 1A).

The parenthetical reference tells the reader that the information in this sentence comes from page 1A of the 2003 work by Baer that appears on the References page at the end of the paper. The complete publication information that a reader would need to locate Baer's work will appear on the References page:

> Baer, S. (2003, March 3). In Iraq war, women would serve closer to front lines than in past. *The Baltimore Sun*, p. 1A.

If the author's name is mentioned in the same sentence in your text, the year in which the work was published follows it, in parentheses, and the page number only is placed in parentheses at the end of the sentence.

> According to Baer (2003) of *The Baltimore Sun,* as of now, women are restricted from 30% of Army assignments and 1% of Air Force assignments (p. 1A).

In the APA system, it is appropriate to include only the last name of the author unless you have more than one author with the same name in your list of references, in which case you would include the first initial of the author.

If your list of references includes more than one work written by the same author in the same year, cite the first work as "a" and the second as "b." For example, Baer's second article of 2003 would be cited in your paper like this: (Baer, 2003b).

If a work has two authors, list both in your sentence or in the parentheses, using "and" between them. In these examples from the women in combat paper, there is no page number because the source is a short work from a Web site:

> The fall 2000 suggestion from DACOWITS included a possible re-
> cruiting slogan: "A gynecologist on every aircraft carrier!" (Yoest &
> Yoest, 2002).

> Yoest and Yoest (2002) recall the fall 2000 suggestion from
> DACOWITS for a possible recruiting slogan: "A gynecologist on
> every aircraft carrier!"

If there are three to five authors, list them all by last name the first time they are referred to, and after that, by the last name of the first author and the term "et al." (meaning "and others"): (Sommers, Mylroie, Donnelly, & Hill, 2001); (Sommers et al., 2001). Also use the last name of the first author and "et al." when there are more than five authors, which is often the case in the sciences and social sciences.

If no author is given, use the name of the work where you would normally use the author's name, placing the names of short works in quotation marks and italicizing those of book-length works.

When using electronic sources, follow as much as possible the rules for parenthetical documentation of print sources. If no author's name is given, cite by the title of the work. If no date is given, use the abbreviation "n.d." instead. For a long work, if there are no page numbers, as is often the case with electronic sources, give paragraph numbers if the work has numbered paragraphs, or, if the work is divided into sections, the paragraph number within that section:

> Jamison (1999) warned about the moral issues associated with stem
> cell research, particularly the guilt that some parents felt about let-
> ting their children's cells be used (Parental Guilt section, para. 2).

Remember that the purpose of parenthetical documentation is to help a reader locate the information that you are citing.

At times, you will need to cite one work that is quoted in another or a work from an anthology. For the former, the parenthetical documentation provides author's name, year of publication, and page number of the source you actually used, preceded by the words "as cited in":

> The female soldier "is, on the average, about five inches shorter than
> the male soldier, has half the upper body strength, lower aerobic
> capacity and 37 percent less muscle mass" (as cited in Owens, 1997,
> Anatomy section, para. 2).

A work in an anthology is cited parenthetically by the name of the author of the work, not the editor of the anthology.

APA List of References

Following are examples of the bibliographical forms you are most likely to employ if you are using the American Psychological Association (APA) system for documenting sources. If you need the format for a type of publication not listed here, consult the *Publication Manual of the American Psychological Association*, Sixth Edition (2010).

If you are used to the Modern Language Association (MLA) system for documenting sources, take a moment to notice some of the key differences. In APA style, authors and editors are listed by last name and initials only, and the year comes immediately after the author's or editor's name instead of at or near the end of the entry. Titles in general are not capitalized in the conventional way. The overall structure of each entry, however, will be familiar: author, title, publication information.

Directory of APA Reference Entries

Print Sources

1. A Book by a Single Author

Isreal, J. (2012). *Democratic enlightenment: Philosophy, revolution, and human rights, 1750–1790.* Oxford, England: Oxford University Press.

2. Multiple Works by the Same Author in the Same Year

Gardner, H. (1982a). *Art, mind, and brain: A cognitive approach to creativity.* New York, NY: Basic Books.

Gardner, H. (1982b). *Developmental psychology: An introduction* (2nd ed.). Boston, MA: Little, Brown.

3. A Work by Two to Seven Authors or Editors

Lester, D., & Rogers, J. R. (2012). *Crisis intervention and counseling by telephone and the Internet* (3rd ed.). Springfield, IL: Charles C. Thomas.

NOTE: List the names of *all* the authors or editors, with an ampersand before the last one. For eight or more authors, list the first six authors followed by an ellipsis (three dots), and then list the last author's name. In these citations, there is no ampersand before the last author.

4. A Work by a Corporate Author

Congressional Quarterly, Inc. (2014). *Issues for debate in American public policy: selections from* CQ Researcher (14th ed.). Los Angeles, CA: CQ Press.

5. An Anthology or Compilation

Strayed, C., & Atwan, R. (Eds.). (2013). *The best American essays 2013.* New York, NY: Houghton Mifflin Harcourt.

6. A Work in an Anthology

Yang, V. W. (2013). Field notes on hair. In J. C. Oates & R. Atwan (Eds.), *Best American essays 2013* (pp. 217–224). Boston, MA: Houghton Mifflin Harcourt.

7. An Introduction, Preface, Foreword, or Afterword

Atwan, R. (2013). Foreword. In J. C. Oates & R. Atwan (Eds.), *Best American essays 2013* (pp. ix–xiv). Boston, MA: Houghton Mifflin Harcourt.

8. An Edition Other Than the First

Litin, S. (Ed.). (2009). *Mayo Clinic family health book* (4th ed.). Des Moines, IA: Time Inc. Home Entertainment.

The Elements of Citation

BOOK (APA)

When you cite a book using APA style, include the following:

1 Author

2 Date of publication

3 Title and subtitle

4 City and state of publication

5 Publisher

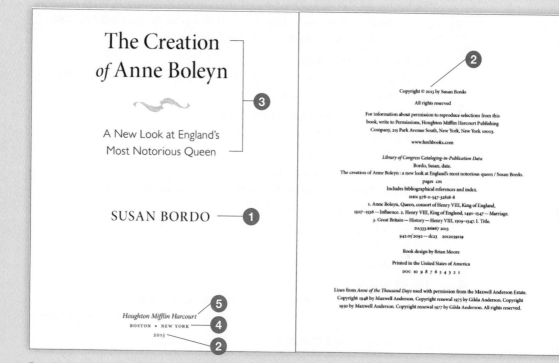

From *The Creation of Anne Boleyn: A New Look at England's Most Notorious Queen* by Susan Bordo. Copyright © 2013 by Susan Bordo. Reprinted by permission of Houghton Mifflin Harcourt Publishing Company. All rights reserved.

Reference list entry for a book in APA style

┌─1─┐ ┌─2─┐ ┌──────────────── 3 ─────────────────

Bordo, S. (2013). *The creation of Anne Boleyn: A new look at England's most*

┌──── 4 ────┐ ┌──── 5 ────┐

notorious queen. Boston, MA: Houghton Mifflin Harcourt.

9. A Translation

Khalifa, K. (2008). *In praise of hatred* (L. Price, Trans.). New York, NY: Thomas Dunne Books-St. Martin's Press.

10. A Republished Book

Dickens, C. (2013). *Great expectations.* New York, NY: Penguin. (Original work published 1861)

11. A Book in a Series

Stone, M. (2013). *The Fascist revolution in Italy: A brief history with documents. The Bedford series in history and culture.* Boston, MA: Bedford/St. Martin's.

12. A Multivolume Work

Helfgott, J. B. (Ed.). (2013). *Criminal psychology* (Vols. 1–4). Santa Barbara, CA: Praeger.

13. An Article from a Daily Newspaper

Yeginsu, C., & Arango, T. (2014, 17 Apr.). Turkey greets Twitter delegation with list of demands. *New York Times*, p. A6.

14. An Article from a Magazine

McWilliams, J. (2014, Spring). Loving animals to death. *The American Scholar*, 18–30.

15. An Article from a Journal

Purchase, H. C. (2014). Twelve years of diagrams research. *Journal of Visual Languages & Computing, 25*(2), 57–75.

16. An Article in a Reference Work

Chichinguane (2014). In P. Mohaghan, *Encyclopedia of goddesses and heroines* (p. 6). Novato, CA: New World Library.

17. A Government Publication

U.S. Department of Homeland Security, Federal Emergency Management Agency (2009, August). *Flood insurance claims handbook* (FEMA F-687). Washington, DC: Government Printing Office.

18. An Abstract

Fritz, M. (1990/1991). A comparison of social interactions using a friendship awareness activity. *Education and Training in Mental Retardation, 25,* 352–359. Abstract retrieved from *Psychological Abstracts*, 1991, 78. (Abstract No. 11474)

When the dates of the original publication and of the abstract differ, give both dates separated by a slash.

19. An Anonymous Work

The status of women: Different but the same. (1992–1993). *Zontian, 73*(3), 5.

20. A Review

Huff, T. E. (2013). Why some nations succeed. [Review of the book *Why nations fail: The origins of power, prosperity & poverty*, by D. Acemoglu & J. A. Robinson]. *Contemporary Sociology, 42*(1), 55–59.

Start with the author of the review, followed by the year and the title (if any). Provide the title of the book or film being reviewed in brackets, along with the title of the book or the year of the film.

21. A Letter to the Editor

Pritchett, J. T., & Kellner, C. H. (1993). Comment on spontaneous seizure activity [Letter to the editor]. *Journal of Nervous and Mental Disease, 181,* 138–139.

22. Personal Correspondence

B. Ehrenreich (personal communication, August 7, 2010).
(B. Ehrenreich, personal communication, August 7, 2010.)

Cite all personal communications to you (such as letters, memos, e-mails, and telephone conversations) in text only, *without* listing them among the references. The phrasing of your sentences will determine which of the two above forms to use.

23. An Unpublished Manuscript

McIntosh, P. (2008). *White privilege and male privilege: A personal account of coming to see correspondences through work in women's studies.* Working Paper 189. Unpublished manuscript, Center for Research on Women, Wellesley College, Wellesley, MA.

24. Proceedings of a Meeting, Published

Guerrero, R. (1972/1973). Possible effects of the periodic abstinence method. In W. A. Uricchio & M. K. Williams (Eds.), *Proceedings of a Research Conference on Natural Family Planning* (pp. 96–105). Washington, DC: Human Life Foundation.

If the date of the symposium or conference is different from the date of publication, give both, separated by a slash. If the proceedings are published annually, treat the reference like a periodical article.

Electronic Sources

25. An Article from an Online Periodical with a DOI

Chattopadhyay, P. (2003). Can dissimilarity lead to positive outcomes? The influence of open versus closed minds.

Journal of Organizational Behavior, 24, 295–312. doi:10.1002
/job.118

If the article duplicates the version that appeared in a print periodical, use the same basic primary journal reference. See "An Article from
a Periodical." Some online articles have a "digital object identifier"
(DOI). Use the DOI at the end of the entry in place of the URL.

26. An Article from an Online Periodical without a DOI

Riordan, V. (2001, January 1). Verbal-performance IQ discrepan-
cies in children attending a child and adolescent psychiatry
clinic. *Child and Adolescent Psychiatry On-Line.* Retrieved
from http://www.priory.com/psych/iq.htm

If an article does not have a DOI, after the publication information
add the exact URL for the article or the URL of the home page of the
journal.

27. A Nonperiodical Web Document

Munro, K. (2001, February). *Changing your body image.* Retrieved from http://www.kalimunro.com/article_changing
_body_image.html

In general, follow this format: author's name, the date of publication (if
no publication date is available, use "n.d."), the title of the document in
italics, and the source's URL.

28. A Chapter or Section in a Web Document

National Council of Welfare, Canada. (1998). Other issues related to poverty lines. In *A new poverty line: Yes, no or
maybe?* (chap. 5). Retrieved from http://www.ncwcnbes.net
/htmdocument/reportnewpovline/chap5.htm

29. An E-mail

Do not include personal communications such as e-mails in your list of
references. See "Personal Correspondence."

30. A Message Posted to a Newsgroup

Isaacs, K. (2008, January 20). Re: Philosophical roots of
psychology [Electronic newsgroup message]. Retrieved from
news://sci.psychology.psychotherapy.moderated

Include an online posting in your reference list only if the posting
is archived and is retrievable. Otherwise, cite an online posting as a
personal communication and do not include it in the list of references.
Care should be taken when citing electronic discussions. In general,
they are not scholarly sources.

The Elements of Citation

ARTICLE FROM A WEBSITE (APA)

When you cite an article from a website using APA style, include the following:

1 Author

2 Date of publication or most recent update

3 Title of document on website

4 Title of section (if any)

5 Date of access (only if content is likely to change)

6 URL of document

Common Sense Media

Reference list entry for a brief article from a website in APA style

┌── 1 ──┐ ┌──── 2 ────┐ ┌──────────────── 3 ────────────────┐
Mendoza, K. (2014, March 31). Webinar rewind: How to implement digital citizenship

┌──────────────────────── 4 ────────────────────────┐
districtwide. In *Common Classroom: A Community for Common Sense Educators.*

┌──────────────── 6 ────────────────┐
Retrieved from http://www.commonsensemedia.org/educators/blog/webinar

-rewind-how-to-implement-digital-citizenship-districtwide

The Elements of Citation

ARTICLE FROM A DATABASE (APA)

When you cite an article from a database using APA style, include the following:

1 Author

2 Date of publication

3 Title of article

4 Name of periodical

5 Volume and issue numbers

6 Page numbers

7 DOI (if available)

8 URL for journal's home page (if no DOI)

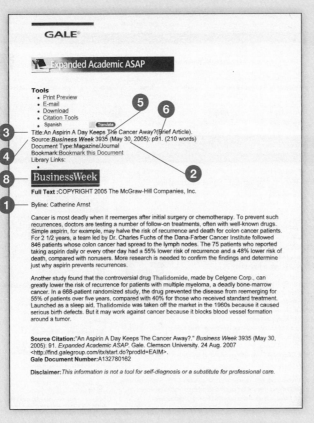

© Gale, a part of Cengage Learning, Inc. Reproduced by permission.
www.cengage.com/permissions.

Reference list entry for an article from a database in APA style

┌─ 1 ─┐ ┌─── 2 ────┐ ┌──────────────── 3 ────────────────┐ ┌──── 4 ────┐
Arnst, C. (2005, May 30). An aspirin a day keeps the cancer away? *Business Week*

┌ 5 ┐┌ 6 ┐   ┌──────── 8 ────────┐
3935, 91. Retrieved from http://businessweek.com/

31. An Article from a Database

Lopez, F. G., Melendez, M. C., Sauer, E. M., Berger, E., & Wyss-mann, J. (1998). Internal working models, self-reported problems, and help-seeking attitudes among college students. *Journal of Counseling Psychology, 45,* 79–83. Retrieved from http://www.apa.org/journals/cou

To cite material retrieved from a database, follow the format appropriate to the work retrieved. If the article has a DOI, include this at the end of the entry. If the article does not have a DOI, include the URL of the periodical's home page at the end of the entry.

Other Sources

32. A Film

Wachowski, A., & Wachowski, L. (Writers/Directors), & Silver, J. (Producer). (1999). *The matrix* [Motion picture]. United States: Warner Bros.

Include the name and the function of the originator or primary contributor (director or producer). Identify the work as a motion picture, or if you viewed a videocassette or DVD, include the appropriate label in brackets. Include the country of origin and the studio. If the motion picture is of limited circulation, provide the name and address of the distributor in parentheses at the end of the reference.

33. A Television Series

Jones, R. (Producer). (1990). *Exploring consciousness* [Television series]. Boston, MA: WGBH.

APA-Style Sample Research Paper

The following paper shows APA citations in the context of an actual text and the format for several different entries on the References page. Angela has used quotations sparingly and has instead made extensive use of summary and paraphrase. Often there is no page number in her parenthetical citations. That is because she was drawing from short online sources in which the paragraphs are not numbered but in which it is easy to find the material she refers to.

The format of the title page illustrates APA guidelines, as does the running head that is on each page.

Notice that Angela's thesis appears as the last sentence in her first paragraph. She carefully documents the restrictions on women in the U.S. military and argues why those restrictions are appropriate.

Women in Combat 1

The Controversy over Women in Combat

Angela Mathers
English 103-13
Ms. Carter
April 7, 2011

Women in Combat 2

Abstract

Women have served in the U.S. military since World War I. Although many barriers to their complete participation in all phases of military service have been broken, women are still appropriately restricted from direct ground combat assignments. Because women are held to a lower physical standard than men, men in their units cannot trust their ability to perform on the battlefield. One argument in favor of combat assignments for women has been that the lack of combat experience stands in the way of their progressing through the ranks. Such careerism, however, goes against a soldier's sworn duty, and there are ways to advance in the military other than through combat service. The social and logistical problems created are an argument against women's serving in close quarters with men. Pregnancy among some enlisted women is also highly likely and poses its own medical and logistical problems. Combat assignments for women would be a threat to the effectiveness and readiness of American troops.

The Controversy over Women in Combat

Throughout the history of the military, the role of women has changed and adapted as the needs of the country have. From Molly Pitcher to Rosie the Riveter, women have always held a place in making the military what it is today. Issues have surfaced in the modern military about the current role of female service members with regard to combat assignments. Positions on submarines, small destroyers, specialized combat teams, and a handful of other assignments are restricted to men-only clubs. The factors determining why women are restricted from these assignments include physical ability, deployability, the cost effectiveness of providing the facilities that women need, and the effect on the overall readiness of the military. Women who desire these assignments, and other opponents of these restrictions, have retorted with reasons that they should be included, the foremost being women's rights and their desire to advance up the ranks of the military. However, women are rightly restricted from direct ground combat assignments to ensure the readiness of the military and the effectiveness of these combat units.

Women were first recruited, and began serving, in the military during World War I because they were needed to fill the clerical, technical, and health care jobs that were left vacant as more men were drafted. All these women, however, were discharged as soon as the war ended. The Women's Army Corps (WAC) was founded during World War II and gave women their own branch of the military. They served in the same jobs as they did in World War I but with the addition of noncombatant pilot assignments. Women did not get their permanent place in the ranks until 1948 when the Women Armed Services Integration Act was passed through Congress, allowing them to serve under the conditions that they were not to hold any rank above colonel, were limited mostly to clerical or health-care jobs, and were not to make up more than 2% of the entire military. They were still limited to their own female-only corps until 1978, when the military was fully integrated and women were allowed to hold any assignment that their male counterparts could except for

Overview of the controversy

Opposing view

Thesis

A history of women in the military from a source accessed through a subscription service

Women in Combat 4

combat roles. The rules have been relaxed over the years as women have proven themselves in combat support missions, especially in the Persian Gulf War in 1991 ("Women," 2000). They continue to push to be allowed into every job that men hold, and the effect this is having on the military is a fiery issue. According to Baer (2003) of *The Baltimore Sun,* as of now, women are restricted from 30% of Army assignments, 38% of Marine assignments, and 1% of Air Force assignments. From the Navy, women are excluded from the special operations SEAL groups. These exclusions are from Military Occupational Specialities (MOS) "whose primary mission is ground combat" as defined by the Pentagon. They are also excluded from Navy submarines and small battleships that do not have the facilities to accommodate women (p. 1A).

There have been many advancements for combat-seeking women since the Persian Gulf War. McDonough (2003), writing for the Associated Press, reports that females are now allowed to fly combat missions in fighter jets and bombers for the Air Force and Navy. They can serve in many combat support roles such as combat Military Police companies. They can also be assigned to chemical specialist units that clean up contaminated areas on the battlefield, and to engineering units that build and repair bridges and runways in high-risk areas. Women can also pilot the Army's Apache assault helicopters over the battlefield during high risk conditions, and pilot troop-carrying helicopters onto the battlefield to deliver troops for a rescue mission during an assault. However, none of these MOSs are in selective special operations units such as Marine Force Recon or Army Airborne Rangers, who serve as the "tip of the spear" in ground combat for missions like Operation Enduring Freedom in Afghanistan or Operation Iraqi Freedom.

The federal government and military have been under pressure from several sides on the issue of women serving in combat roles in the military. There are those that believe that all assignments, no matter how demanding of time, body, talent, and mind, should be open to women as well as men. According to Gerber (2002) of the

The parenthetical citation shows where paraphrase ends and her ideas begin.

Source and year included in text

Page only in parentheses

Author and year in text; no page number because electronic version

A Web site

Women in Combat 5

James MacGregor Burns Academy of Leadership, this is the general consensus of the Defense Advisory Committee on Women in the Services (DACOWITS). It was established in 1951 by General George Marshall but was disbanded when Secretary of Defense Donald Rumsfeld let its charter run out when it came up for renewal in 2002. However, its motives could be called into question as to whether it is rallying for the good of the military and its purposes or pushing its own platform that women should be integrated in all parts just because they believe it is deserved. Former DACOWITS Chairperson Vickie McCall even told the U.S. Air Force in Europe News Service, "You have to understand. We don't report facts, we report perception" (as qtd. in Yoest & Yoest, 2002). DACOWITS has often teamed up with other private women's rights activist groups that believe that the military should be an "equal opportunity employer" along with all other private and public employers.

One cause of concern over women's inclusion in combat units has been the rigorous physical standards these troops must meet in training and in turn on the battlefield. Many studies have been done to prove or disprove a distinction between men's and women's physical capabilities. In the quest for evidence, Col. Patrick Toffler, Director of the United States Military Office of Institutional Research, reported that it had identified 120 physical differences (Owens, 1997, p. 40). The female soldier "is, on the average, about five inches shorter than the male soldier, has half the upper body strength, lower aerobic capacity and 37 percent less muscle mass" (as qtd. in Owens, 1997, p. 38). Leo (1997) reports in *U.S. News and World Report* that the way that the military accommodates for these differences is called "gender norming" and works by lowering the standards that women have to reach to pass the physical fitness tests. For instance, in the Marines, men are required to climb the length of a rope and females are only required to climb to a point below that marked with a yellow line (p. 14). These standards are mostly for people to enlist in the services; so the bar is significantly raised for those that choose to compete for a MOS in special operations or combat units. Females

One source quoted in another; source with two authors

A journal paginated by issue

A magazine

enrolled in Army Jump School to be paratroopers are still not required to run as far or do as many push-ups or sit-ups as their male
counterparts. When this double standard is employed in the military,
it blurs the distinction as to which soldiers actually have the physical
ability to perform on the battlefield.

When there is a question as to the physical abilities of a fellow
soldier in a unit, there can be no guarantee that everyone can cover
your back as well as you could for them. When there is no trust in a
unit, it breaks down. Take, for example, the Marine ideology that no
one is left behind on the battlefield. Imagine an officer trying to motivate his troops to jump out of a helicopter in the heat of battle. Some
of the soldiers may doubt a female comrade's capability to carry
them to safety should they be injured, because she does not have
to meet the same physical standards as her male counterparts do.
The training is not only meant to prepare the troops for war combat
and to show the officers that they meet the physical requirements. It
is also a time to begin to build the trust that binds the troops' lives
together and prove to each other they have the physical and mental toughness to accomplish the mission and bring each other back
safely. How can this trust be established when male soldiers witness
some female soldiers being excused from throwing live grenades in
practice because they cannot throw the dummy ones far enough to
keep from being blown to shreds? "The military should be the real
world," said Jeanne Holm, retired two-star General of the Air Force.
"The name of the game is putting together a team that fits and
works together. That is the top priority, not social experimentation"
(as qtd. in Yoest & Yoest, 2002). The military studies prove that a female body is not equipped to perform the same physical rigors as the
male body; therefore, women should not be put in the position where
impossible war-fighting demands are put on them.

When left out of selective combat positions, there is the possibility that women cannot advance up the ranks because they would
not get ample opportunity to prove themselves on the battlefield and
gain combat experience. This experience goes a long way because

One source
quoted in
another

Women in Combat 7

it stands to prove that an officer has the leadership ability to command troops under fire and accomplish the mission. Experience can be gained in many ways, though, since America is not always at war. All officer career fields are necessary to the overall success of the mission, and in order to be promoted every officer must pull his or her weight. Even though the proceedings of the promotion committees are supposed to be kept private, it is no secret that combat experience weighs heavily on promotion picks (Nath, 2002). In a military that is centered on the chain of command, seniority is the most valuable commodity for any member, especially officers. The practice of officers' jockeying for promotions to further their career, stature, and income is called "careerism" (Nath, 2002). This is supposedly prohibited under the Air Force's second core value of "Service Before Self," and similar pledges in the other branches. The argument lies in the conflict between the career ambition of female officers seeking a combat MOS and the needs of a ready military to support the mission.

No page
number given

The truth is, however, that the United States Armed Forces is not an "equal opportunity employer" as many other public and private organizations are. The military is not out to make a profit or provide a ladder to corporate success. Instead, military officers swear to "support and defend the Constitution of the United States against all enemies, foreign and domestic; that I will bear the true faith and allegiance to the same" (Oath of Office, 2003). This oath states they are to uphold the best interest of the mission that the Commander in Chief charges them with. Careerism is not an option under this oath because it is only serving the individual's ambition, not the mission of the military. Elaine Donnelly, President of the Center for Military Readiness, says, "Equal opportunity is important, but the armed forces exist to defend the country. If there is a conflict between career opportunities and military necessity, the needs of the military must come first" (as qtd. in "Women," 2000).

Another concern with females in combat is their deployability, or their availability to be deployed. Because the very nature of combat units is being the "tip of the spear" in battle, they are deployed and

Women in Combat 8

away from home much of the year and are used for an indefinite period of time during the war. Donnelly explains that "if you have a pregnancy rate and it's constant, 10 or 15%, you know that out of 500 women on a carrier at least 50 are going to be unavailable before or during the six-month deployment" (Sommers, Mylroie, Donnelly, & Hill, 2001). This pregnancy issue is not just applicable for conception before the deployment, but during deployment, as is evident on Navy aircraft carriers and destroyers that house women. Even though fraternization, defined as "sexual relationships between service members" (Nath, 2002), is illegal, many ships such as the U.S.S. *Lincoln* "report a dozen [pregnancies] a month" (Layton, 2003). In a close-quarters environment, where combat units are together every hour of the day, this kind of problem distracts from the mission. Also, sailors on submarines sleep in what they call "hot beds," which are rotating shifts for sleep in the few available beds, and changing this system to accommodate separate quarters for females would not be cost effective. Also, pregnant females aboard aircraft carriers are being taken from their duty, and they must be replaced, which is a costly endeavor for the military and throws off the working relationship between service members.

When men and women are put in close quarters, it is just human nature that sexual relationships will begin to develop. This fact has been proven all around the military from the pregnancies on board naval ships all the way up to the Navy's "Tailhook Convention," where in Las Vegas in 1991 dozens of female officers reported being openly sexually assaulted by male officers, both married and unmarried ("Women," 2000). If there were this kind of distraction within special operation ground combat units, the mission would suffer greatly because fraternization would become a huge issue, for favoritism would ensue. When the mission is not the first thing on these troops' minds, the morale, and most important, the trust breaks down.

Another very real barrier to the inclusion of women in these units and on small battleships and submarines is the medical needs of the female body. The fall 2000 suggestion from DACOWITS included as

First reference to source with four authors

Different parts of the same sentence cited to different sources

a possible recruiting slogan "A gynecologist on every aircraft carrier!" (Yoest & Yoest, 2002). This is a possibility on every base and possibly on huge aircraft carriers, but these needs of women cannot be met in the field hospitals in the deserts of Iraq and Afghanistan, where the only goal is to keep soldiers from dying long enough to get them to a base hospital. Another dilemma on forty- to fifty-person submarines is that if a woman were to get pregnant, as is the proven trend, the vessel would have to make a risky surface to get her off to be cared for and find a replacement for her job on board. DACOWITS also suggested to "ensure an adequate supply of hygiene products during deployment" (Yoest & Yoest, 2002), which is a far cry from reality when Marines who are currently in Iraq already march with a 130-pound rucksack holding their bare living necessities. The military certainly does not have the money to cover these hygiene and medical needs when in high-risk areas simply because the resources must go to fulfilling the mission.

Conclusion

As the way we do battle continues to change, so will the roles of males and females; and the military will always have to come up with the best solution to accommodate these differences. As for now, the restrictions that are placed on women's assignments are based in sound reasoning. For the military's purposes, women do not have the physical abilities to fill combat-oriented jobs, and the military does not have the resources to make these assignments available to them. The military needs to be aware of and most concerned with the effectiveness and readiness of its troops and figure out the best way to accomplish its mission and preserve America's freedom and sovereignty.

Women in Combat 10

References

Baer, S. (2003, March 3). In Iraq war, women would serve closer to front lines than in past. *The Baltimore Sun,* p. 1A. Retrieved from http://www.baltimoresun.com

Gerber, R. (2002, September 23). Don't send military women to the back of the troop train. *USA Today.* Retrieved from http://www .usatoday.com

Layton, L. (2003, March 15). Navy women finding ways to adapt to a man's world. *The Washington Post,* p. A15. Retrieved from http://www.washingtonpost.com

Leo, J. (1997, August 11). A kinder, gentler army. *U.S. News and World Report, 123*(6), 14.

McDonough, S. (2003, February 10). More U.S. military women edging closer to combat positions in preparation for Iraq war. *The Associated Press.* Retrieved from http://www.ap.org/

Nath, C. (2002). *United States Air Force Leadership Studies.* Washington, DC: Air Education and Training Command, United States Air Force.

Oath of office: U.S. federal and military oath of office. (2003). Retrieved from http://www.apfn.org/apfn/oathofoffice.htm

Owens, M. (1997, Spring). Mothers in combat boots: Feminists call for women in the military. *Human Life Review, 23*(2), 35–45.

Sommers, C., Mylroie, L., Donnelly, E., & Hill, M. (2001, October 17). IWF panel: Women facing war. *Independent Women's Forum.* Retrieved from RDS Contemporary Women's Issues.

Women in the military. (2000, September 1). *Issues and Controversies.* Retrieved from http://www.2facts.com

Yoest, C., & Yoest, J. (2002, Winter). Booby traps at the Pentagon. *Women's Quarterly.* Retrieved from http://www.bnet.com

DEBATING
the Issues

The chapters in Part Five contain pairs of articles on five controversial questions. These questions generate conflict among experts and laypeople alike for two principal reasons: First, even when the facts are not in dispute, they may be interpreted differently. Second, and more difficult to resolve, equally worthwhile values may be in conflict.

There are not always two diametrically opposed views of the same controversial issue. This will occur when there are only two options: A certain bill should or should not be passed. The president should or should not be impeached. This medical procedure should or should not be allowed. Often, however, there are more than two possible solutions to a problematic situation, or more than two possible views of an issue are worth considering. Here we have chosen to present only two opposing responses to each question.

Debating the Issues lends itself to classroom debates, both formal and informal. It can also serve as a useful source of informed opinions, which can lead to further research. For each of the topics that follow, read both articles and consider the following questions:

1. Are there two — and only two — possible points of view on the subject? Does each author make clear what he or she is trying to prove? What is each author's claim?

2. How important is the evidence in support of the claims? Does the support fulfill the appropriate criteria? If not, what are its weaknesses? Do the authorities have convincing credentials?

3. What stated or unstated assumptions (warrants) are the claims based on? Are the warrants widely accepted? If they need to be defended or qualified, have the authors done so?

4. How important is the definition of key terms? Does definition become a significant issue in the controversy?

5. Other than definition, what role does language play in the authors' arguments?

6. Do the arguments have any flaws in inductive or deductive reasoning? Do they contain any logical fallacies?

What's in a Word?

Should We All Pledge to End Derogatory Use of the Word *Retard*?

CHAPTER

14

The passage of time can often change our perception of what words are offensive. Some words become more acceptable, while others fall increasingly out of favor and are replaced by others with fewer negative connotations. One example would be the changes in terms that refer to African Americans. Another would be terms that refer to sexual orientation. The following articles explore the terminology used to refer to individuals with intellectual disabilities. The term *mentally retarded* replaced more derogatory earlier terms, but now the word *retard* has come under attack. Patricia Bauer and Christopher Fairman debate its use.

A Movie, a Word, and My Family's Battle
PATRICIA E. BAUER

Margaret and I were lingering in front of the multiplex one evening last summer, a mom and her adult daughter laughing about the movie we'd just seen, when a gaggle of cute pre-teen girls sauntered past.

The one in the lead jerked a thumb in our direction and made a goofy face to her friend. "Look. Retard," we heard her say, and Margaret wilted. Her chin trembled. One by one, the other girls turned to look, nudging one another and whispering. The last girl spun all the way around as she slowly walked by, eyes fixed on my daughter.

In her size 6 jeans and Old Navy shirt, Margaret hadn't done anything to attract that

unwanted attention. But then, my blond, blue-eyed daughter lives every day behind a face that can be a lightning rod for such talk. The beautiful face I've loved for 24 years displays some of the characteristic signs of Down syndrome, a chromosomal anomaly associated with varying degrees of cognitive impairment.

Last week lightning struck again, not just for Margaret, but for millions of Americans with intellectual disabilities. Ben Stiller's highly

---

Patricia E. Bauer, a former *Washington Post* reporter, edits patriciaebauer.com, a Web site of news and commentary on issues related to disability. This article appeared in the August 17, 2008, edition of the *Washington Post*.

anticipated *Tropic Thunder* hit screens across the country. The film packs a powerful combination of explosions, irreverence, crudity, and political incorrectness. It also features many iterations of the word "retard."

5   With the film's release, the public has plunged headlong into an overheated argument about the borders between comedy and hate speech, political correctness and oversensitivity. I know, because posts that I put on my blog, drawing attention to the movie's marketing and discussion of a character with an intellectual disability, have set off a firestorm in Hollywood and the disability community. Protesters picketed *Tropic Thunder*'s premiere last week, while the film's high-profile stars defended it as a parody aimed at the movie industry.

The film features Stiller, Robert Downey Jr., and Jack Black as unsavory actors who are thrust into a real conflict while filming a war movie. Stiller's character is an actor who previously sought Oscar glory by portraying Simple Jack, a man with an intellectual disability, a bowl haircut reminiscent of state institutions, and few relatable qualities. Cue the retard jokes.

The original marketing campaign, featured on a Web site that was taken down in response to complaints, included an image of Stiller as Simple Jack bearing the memorable tagline, "Once upon a time . . . There was a retard." Another marketed scene depicts Downey uttering the line that will undoubtedly launch a thousand T-shirts: "Never go full retard."

For years I've tried to figure out how to handle moments like these, when the word "retard" crash-lands at our feet, either aimed directly at Margaret or tossed around as an all-purpose weapon. It has become a routine epithet, used to describe something or someone

stupid or worthless or pathetic. For my daughter and my family, it's more like a grenade, and we're the collateral damage. "It's not a good word," Margaret says. "It's mean, it's insulting, and it hurts people's feelings."

As the word has seemingly become increasingly pervasive in recent years, I've tried gently to let others know that it heaps scorn on people who are already stigmatized and may not be in a position to defend themselves. The responses I've gotten? *Gosh, everybody says it. It's just a joke.* Or: *I didn't mean it like that.* Or: *Lighten up. It doesn't mean anything.* People reacted as if I'd offended them when I told them that they were insulting my daughter and others like her; they would never insult such people, they said.

10   Discouraged, I started letting it pass, gritting my teeth, wishing it would go away. Not everyone uses it, and sometimes I wonder whether I'm overreacting. But I hear it at every turn. A clerk in a store apologizes for being "such a retard" when she can't find an item for me. Ouch. Kids at the mall call one another "you big retard." Ouch. A friend tells a long, involved story at my dinner table about her recent fender bender, with a punchline about "some retard" who parked behind her. Ouch. Ouch. Ouch.

With each of these incidents, I hear what others perhaps don't hear. This word, derived from a clinical term used to describe people like my daughter, carries a cultural subtext so huge that we don't even notice it. By using it, we threaten years of progress toward a society that accepts and values all its citizens, including the 14.3 million with cognitive disabilities.

When I was young, kids like my daughter were kept at home or, worse, sent to institutions by the hundreds of thousands. They had no legally guaranteed right to an education.

A man my age who grew up in a small town in Georgia told me about a boy with Down syndrome who lived down the street. The boy wasn't allowed to go to school and was kept behind a board fence in the backyard; neighborhood kids used to climb a tree to spy on him. The man wept as he recalled the view from an overhanging branch.

Over the past 35 years, the legal landscape has been transformed. In 1975, the Individuals with Disabilities Education Act granted children with disabilities the right to a public education, and the federal government pledged to pay a substantial portion of local special-education costs. The Americans with Disabilities Act of 1990 prohibited discrimination against the disabled. A group of people who'd been invisible emerged to work toward taking their rightful place in society.

15   We've come a long way, but we still have far to go. There are still 38,000 people with intellectual and developmental disabilities housed in institutions nationwide. The federal government hasn't kept its promise to fund special education, and millions of children across the country remain poorly served or not served at all.

Meanwhile, adults with intellectual disabilities are on waiting lists for independent living services all over the country; one recent report estimated more than 100,000 in Texas alone. These adults are largely unemployed and frequently live in poverty. Experts estimate that fewer than 20 percent of those of working age are employed, even though research shows that they are reliable and effective workers when given support and matched with appropriate jobs.

Without a coherent federal policy for providing community services and support, millions of families across the country are left to take care of their loved ones on their own. Parents have little assurance that their adult children will be cared for after they die. At last count, 715,000 people were residing with caregivers age 60 and older. As life expectancies increase, that number grows.

On top of all this is the problem of negative public attitudes. Recent research conducted by the University of Massachusetts found that, if given a choice, more than half of young people wouldn't spend time with a student with an intellectual disability. More than half of parents didn't want such students at their children's school. Almost half of the young people surveyed wouldn't sit next to a student like Margaret on a school bus.

I find these facts and statistics terrifying. My husband and I have spent much of the past two decades doing all we can to shield Margaret from the effects of what I've just described. With a lot of hard work on her part, and with the active support of family and friends, she's faring far better than doctors predicted when she was born. She's a high school graduate, works part-time at a Mediterranean restaurant, takes care of her own apartment, and volunteers at her local hospital and senior center. She's a regular at the gym. She has a lively social network, a cellphone, an e-mail address. That's not to say that her life is rosy all the time, but it seems to be working.

I'd like to hold on to the hope that Margaret's journey reflects our steady national progress   20
toward respecting and valuing all our citizens. But I'm stopped cold by the thought of a major studio constructing an ad campaign and film that prominently feature the word "retard" without a thought to the consequences.

According to the nonprofit Arc of the United States, people with developmental disabilities are 4 to 10 times more likely to be victims of violence than those without. There are always people looking to pick on other people. With the introduction of "Never go full retard" into the lexicon, I can't help thinking that those people have been handed both a weapon and a target.

DreamWorks and the actors in *Tropic Thunder* have already said that this is not their problem. They say that the movie targets Hollywood and seeks to criticize past exploitation of people with disabilities in stereotype-filled blockbusters such as *Rain Man* and *Forrest Gump.*

Such criticism is surely present, and it's not wide of the mark. The film is rated "R" for a reason. It's art, even if crude and distasteful, and it's entitled to this country's broad protections for freedom of speech and expression.

Yet *Tropic Thunder* provides another example of the unthinking acceptance of language that promotes oppression. Anticipating public scrutiny, the studio was careful to build nuance and subtlety into the film's racial humor. A white actor who uses blackface to portray a black character is countered at every turn by a black actor critiquing his actions. But there's no on-screen presence countering the Simple Jack portrayal, nor did the filmmakers consult people with intellectual disabilities or their families about the script.

It seems that the studio never considered that its portrayal of people with disabilities would touch a nerve farther below the skin than it would want to go. Again we hear: I didn't mean it like *that,* and lighten up. It doesn't mean anything.

For millions of Americans like Margaret and me, it does.

25

The Case against Banning the Word *Retard*
CHRISTOPHER M. FAIRMAN

Does the word "retard" have less than three weeks to live?

Long before Rahm Emanuel, Sarah Palin, and Rush Limbaugh made the word fodder for political controversy and late-night punch lines, a movement was under way to eliminate it from everyday conversation. Saying, irrefutably, that the word and its variations are hurtful to many, the Special Olympics is leading a campaign to end its use and is promoting a national awareness day on March 3. Nearly 60,000 people have signed on to the following promise on www.r-word.org: "I pledge and support the elimination of the derogatory use of the R-word from everyday speech and promote the acceptance and inclusion of people with intellectual disabilities."

I sympathize with the effort, but I won't be making that pledge. It's not that I've come to praise the word "retard"; I just don't think we should bury it. If the history of offensive terms in America shows anything, it is that words themselves are not the culprit; the meaning we

Christopher M. Fairman is a professor at the Moritz College of Law at Ohio State University. He is the author of a book subtitled *Word Taboo and Protecting Our First Amendment Liberties* (2009). This article appeared in the *Washington Post* on February 14, 2010.

attach to them is, and such meanings change dramatically over time and across communities. The term "mentally retarded" was itself introduced by the medical establishment in the 20th century to supplant other terms that had been deemed offensive. Similarly, the words "gay" and "queer" and even the N-word can be insulting, friendly, identifying, or academic in different contexts.

The varied and evolving uses of such words ultimately render self-censorship campaigns unnecessary. And restricting speech of any kind comes with a potential price — needlessly institutionalized taboos, government censorship, or abridged freedom of expression — that we should be wary of paying.

5　The latest battle over the R-word kicked into high gear with a Jan. 26 *Wall Street Journal* report that last summer White House Chief of Staff Rahm Emanuel blasted liberal activists unhappy with the pace of health-care reform, deriding their strategies as "[expletive] retarded." Palin, the mother of a special-needs child, quickly took to Facebook to demand Emanuel's firing, likening the offensiveness of the R-word to that of the N-word. Limbaugh seized the low ground, saying he found nothing wrong with "calling a bunch of people who are retards, retards," and Palin rushed to his defense, saying Limbaugh had used the word satirically. Comedy Central's Stephen Colbert took her up on it, calling Palin an "[expletive] retard" and adding, with a smile: "You see? It's satire!"

Emanuel apologized and promised to take the Word.org pledge, but as March 3 nears, the word may already be an endangered species. Forty-eight states have voted to remove the term "mental retardation" from government agencies and state codes, and legislation is pending in Congress to strike it from any federal statutes that still use it, such as the Individuals with Disabilities Education Act. The largest advocacy group for the intellectually disabled, the Association for Retarded Citizens, is now simply the Arc. Similarly, the American Association of Mental Retardation is now the American Association on Intellectual and Developmental Disabilities. The Centers for Disease Control and Prevention now use "intellectual disability" in place of "mental retardation." The diagnostic manuals used by medical professionals also embrace "intellectual disability" as the official label. Behind the changes is the belief that "retardation" doesn't communicate dignity and respect.

The irony is that the use of "mental retardation" and its variants was originally an attempt to convey greater dignity and respect than previous labels had. While the verb "retard" — meaning to delay or hinder — has roots in the 15th century, its use in reference to mental development didn't occur until the late 19th and early 20th centuries, when medical texts began to describe children with "retarded mental development," "retarded children" and "mentally retarded patients." By the 1960s, "mental retardation" became the preferred medical term, gradually replacing previous diagnostic standards such as "idiot," "imbecile," and "moron" — terms that had come to carry pejorative connotations.

As I was growing up in the 1970s, my father worked for the Texas Department of Mental Health and Mental Retardation, one of the now-renamed state agencies. The term "retardation" was common in my home and life, but it was sterile and clinical. It is only in the past generation that the medical term turned into the slang "retard" and gained power as an insult.

The shift is even apparent in popular movies. There was little public controversy when Matt Dillon tried to woo Cameron Diaz in the 1998 hit comedy *There's Something about Mary* by confessing his passion: "I work with retards." (Diaz's character, Mary, had a mentally disabled brother.) But 10 years later, in the comedy *Tropic Thunder,* Robert Downey Jr.'s use of the phrase "full retard" led to picketing and calls for a boycott.

What happened to make the word a target for extinction?

10   All cultures have taboos. Western culture, particularly in the United States, has several taboos surrounding sexuality, grounded largely in a subconscious fear of the parade of horribles — adultery, unwanted pregnancy, incest, venereal disease — that might befall us because of some sexual behaviors. Sometimes the taboo extends to even uttering the words that describe certain behaviors. You can see word taboo at work in the way Emanuel's blunder was reported: "[expletive] retarded." It's still okay to print the R-word. The F-word? Forget it.

For years, I've been researching taboo language and its interaction with the law, and I have written a law review article and recently a book, both titled with the unprintable four letter F-word. The resilience of word taboos, the multiple usages and meanings of a single word, the rise of self-censorship, and the risks of institutionalized taboo and ultimately censorship are all core issues surrounding the F-word, and they help explain what is happening — and may happen still — with the R-word.

Mental disorders also carry cultural taboos. For centuries, mental illness and disability were poorly understood; as recently as the 1800s, they were thought to be the work of devils and demons. Because the origins of mental illness were a mystery, fears that such conditions could be contagious led to isolation through institutionalization. Shame was often attached to individuals and their families, and the result was stigma.

Fortunately, we've come a long way from those days. It's precisely the new enlightenment and openness about mental disabilities that allow Palin to launch the controversy over "retard." But at a subconscious level, the underlying taboo may explain why we constantly seek new terms for this type of disability, new ways to avoid the old stigmas. Invariably, negative connotations materialize around whatever new word is used; "idiot" becomes an insult and gives way to "retardation," which in turn suffers the same fate, leading to "intellectual disability." This illustrates one of the recurring follies of speech restriction: While there may be another word to use, a negative connotation eventually is found. Offense — both given and taken — is inevitable.

Whatever future offensiveness may emerge, though, are we not better off by purging today's insulting language and making our discourse a little kinder? That is the argument of self-censorship advocates such as Palin, who draws parallels between the use of the R-word and the N-word — the most powerful and insulting of all racial epithets. In some respects, the comparison seems overblown. The N-word invokes some of the foulest chapters in our nation's history; "retard," however harsh, pales in comparison. But there still may be some guidance to be gleaned.

While the N-word endures as an insult, it is   15 so stigmatized that its use is no longer tolerated in public discourse. This is a positive step for us all, of course, but its containment does not come without costs. As Harvard law professor Randall

Kennedy described in his 2002 book on the subject, stigmatizing the word has elicited new problems, including an overeagerness to detect insult where none is intended and the use of excessively harsh punishment against those who use the word wrongly.

I've coined a term for overzealous or extreme responses to insulting words: "word fetish." Those under the influence of word fetish aren't content to refrain from using a certain word; they are set on eradicating any use by others. A classic example was the plight of David Howard, a white employee in the D.C. mayor's office in 1999. Howard told staff members that because of budget cuts, he would have to be "niggardly" with available funds. Wrongly believing "niggardly" was a variation of the N-word, black subordinates lobbied for his resignation. Howard ultimately resigned after public protests, though he was soon reinstated. If the campaign against "retard" is successful, an identical risk of word fetish exists. (Imagine that Emanuel had spoken of "retarding the opposition" — would that be unacceptable?)

Like virtually every word in our language, the N-word has multiple uses. While its use as an insult has decreased, there has been a resurgence of the word as a term of identification, even affection, among some African Americans. But should certain groups of people, to the exclusion of others, be allowed to reclaim certain words? If "retard" or "retarded" were similarly restricted, could intellectually disabled individuals appropriate the term for self-identification, essentially reclaiming its original use or developing a new one?

Over time, word fetish can evolve into censorship among private organizations and ultimately direct government control of lan-

guage and institutionalized word taboo. During the 1980s and 1990s, for example, many colleges and universities sought to reduce discrimination by developing speech codes, often targeting racial hate speech such as the N-word. Even with the most combustible insults, however, there must be some accommodation to their continued use; freedom of expression surely embraces unpopular, even insulting, speech. Luckily, speech codes that have been challenged in court have generally lost because they violated the First Amendment.

The risk of direct government censorship of the word "retard" is real. The New Zealand chapter of the Special Olympics is already calling on the country's Broadcasting Standards Authority (equivalent to our Federal Communications Commission) to deem the word "retard" unacceptable for broadcast. This plea is based upon a single incident involving New Zealand television personality Paul Henry, who described the runner-up in the *Britain's Got Talent* competition, Susan Boyle, as retarded. It is not difficult to imagine calls for a similar broadcast ban emerging here.

The current public awareness campaign surrounding the use of the word "gay" offers better lessons and parallels for the R-word debate. Advocacy groups contend that the phrase "that's so gay" fosters homophobia and that anti-gay language is directly related to violence and harassment against homosexuals. At the same time, there is recognition that much anti-gay language is uttered carelessly and isn't necessarily intended as hurtful — as is probably the case with uses of "retard." The Ad Council and the Gay, Lesbian, and Straight Education Network have developed a Web site, ThinkB4YouSpeak .com, that, much like R-Word.org, encourages

20

the public to sign a pledge to cease using the phrase. (The slogan: "Saying that's so gay is so yesterday.")

By increasing sensitivity and awareness, the campaign hopes to encourage people to think about the possible consequences of their word choices. Such reflection would presumably lead individuals to censor themselves once they understand that others can be hurt by their language.

Inherent in this idea is the realization that words have multiple meanings and that those meanings depend on the context and circumstances surrounding any particular statement. For example, "gay" is a term of identification for homosexuals, but it also can be used as an all-purpose put-down: "That's so gay." Those using it as an insult don't intend to say "that's so homosexual," nor do they necessarily make the conscious leap that homosexuality is bad. (Indeed, the success of the ThinkB4YouSpeak .com campaign depends on this distinction.)

Similarly, the R-word has multiple usages. When Emanuel calls fellow Democrats "retarded" for jeopardizing a legislative plan, the term is a stand-in for "stupid" or "misguided" or "dumb" — it obviously does not mean that they meet the IQ diagnostic standard for intellectual disability. It is quite another thing to look at a person with Down syndrome and call him or her a "retard." So, if there are readily identifiable alternate meanings, what is the reason for censorship?

Differing usages also give rise to reclaiming — when words that have an offensive meaning are deliberately given a new spin. The putative slur is captured, repurposed, and owned by the target of insult. We see this when an African American uses the N-word as a term of identification for his friends, or when the word "queer" is reclaimed for TV shows such as *Queer Eye for the Straight Guy* and *Queer as Folk,* and for queer studies and queer theory in university courses. Reclaiming the word "retard" is an option that should involve no risk to freedom of expression.

If interest groups want to pour resources into cleaning up unintentional insults, more power to them; we surely would benefit from greater kindness to one another. But we must not let "retard" go without a requiem. If the goal is to protect intellectually disabled individuals from put-downs and prejudice, it won't succeed. New words of insult will replace old ones.

Words are ideas, and we should be reluctant to surrender any of them. Freedom of expression has come at a dear price, and it is not worth abridging, even so we can get along a little better. That's one F-word we really can't do without.

25

Discussion Questions

1. Is it acceptable, in your opinion, to use the word *retard*? What if you are just among your friends? Explain your answer.

2. In what contexts is Bauer opposed to the use of the word *retard*? Is her position justified? Explain your answer.

3. What claims does Bauer make about the harm that results from the use of *retard*?

4. What emotional appeals does Bauer make in her argument? How persuasive do you find them?

5. What is Fairman's position on the use of the word *retard*?

6. In paragraph 2 of Fairman's piece, he cites a pledge from www.r-word.org. In the pledge, what does *derogatory use* mean? Why is that important?

7. Why won't Fairman be making the pledge?

8. Is Fairman making a claim of fact, value, or policy? Explain.

9. Who makes a more compelling case, Bauer or Fairman? Why?

15

Social Responsibility

Do Businesses Have an Obligation to Society?

John Mackey, cofounder and co-CEO of Whole Foods Market, and Thurman John Rodgers, founder and CEO of Cypress Semiconductor, are both successful businessmen whose companies make profits for their investors. What the two disagree about is the relationship between a company's profits and its responsibility to other stakeholders — customers, employees, vendors, communities, and the environment. Mackey does not agree with American economist Milton Friedman that (in Mackey's words) "the only social responsibility a law-abiding business has is to maximize profits." Rodgers argues that Mackey sacrifices his responsibilities as a businessman to altruism.

Putting Customers ahead of Investors
JOHN MACKEY

In 1970 Milton Friedman wrote that "there is one and only one social responsibility of business — to use its resources and engage in activities designed to increase its profits so long as it stays within the rules of the game, which is to say, engages in open and free competition without deception or fraud." That's the orthodox view among free market economists: that the only social responsibility a law-abiding business has is to maximize profits for the shareholders.

I strongly disagree. I'm a businessman and a free market libertarian, but I believe that the enlightened corporation should try to create value for all of its constituencies. From an investor's perspective, the purpose of the business is to maximize profits. But that's not the purpose for other stakeholders — for customers, employees, suppliers, and the community. Each of those groups will define the purpose of the business in terms of its own needs and desires, and each perspective is valid and legitimate.

John Mackey was the cofounder in 1980 of Whole Foods Market and is now its CEO. He supports free market economics and the movement for organic food. His article and T. J. Rodgers's, which follows, were part of a debate on the social responsibility of business that appeared in the October 2005 issue of *Reason* magazine.

My argument should not be mistaken for a hostility to profit. I believe I know something about creating shareholder value. When I co-founded Whole Foods Market 27 years ago, we began with $45,000 in capital; we only had $250,000 in sales our first year. During the last 12 months we had sales of more than $4.6 billion, net profits of more than $160 million, and a market capitalization over $8 billion.

But we have not achieved our tremendous increase in shareholder value by making shareholder value the primary purpose of our business. In my marriage, my wife's happiness is an end in itself, not merely a means to my own happiness; love leads me to put my wife's happiness first, but in doing so I also make myself happier. Similarly, the most successful businesses put the customer first, ahead of the investors. In the profit-centered business, customer happiness is merely a means to an end: maximizing profits. In the customer-centered business, customer happiness is an end in itself, and will be pursued with greater interest, passion, and empathy than the profit-centered business is capable of.

5   Not that we're only concerned with customers. At Whole Foods, we measure our success by how much value we can create for all six of our most important stakeholders: customers, team members (employees), investors, vendors, communities, and the environment. . . .

There is, of course, no magical formula to calculate how much value each stakeholder should receive from the company. It is a dynamic process that evolves with the competitive marketplace. No stakeholder remains satisfied for long. It is the function of company leadership to develop solutions that continually work for the common good.

Many thinking people will readily accept my arguments that caring about customers and employees is good business. But they might draw the line at believing a company has any responsibility to its community and environment. To donate time and capital to philanthropy, they will argue, is to steal from the investors. After all, the corporation's assets legally belong to the investors, don't they? Management has a fiduciary responsibility to maximize shareholder value; therefore, any activities that don't maximize shareholder value are violations of this duty. If you feel altruism toward other people, you should exercise that altruism with your own money, not with the assets of a corporation that doesn't belong to you.

This position sounds reasonable. A company's assets do belong to the investors, and its management does have a duty to manage those assets responsibly. In my view, the argument is not wrong so much as it is too narrow.

First, there can be little doubt that a certain amount of corporate philanthropy is simply good business and works for the long-term benefit of the investors. For example: In addition to the many thousands of small donations each Whole Foods store makes each year, we also hold five 5% Days throughout the year. On those days, we donate 5 percent of a store's total sales to a nonprofit organization. While our stores select worthwhile organizations to support, they also tend to focus on groups that have large membership lists, which are contacted and encouraged to shop our store that day to support the organization. This usually brings hundreds of new or lapsed customers into our stores, many of whom then become regular shoppers. So a 5% Day not only allows us to support worthwhile causes, but is an excellent marketing strategy that has benefited Whole Foods investors immensely.

10   That said, I believe such programs would be completely justifiable even if they produced no profits and no P.R. This is because I believe the entrepreneurs, not the current investors in a company's stock, have the right and responsibility to define the purpose of the company. It is the entrepreneurs who create a company, who bring all the factors of production together and coordinate it into viable business. It is the entrepreneurs who set the company strategy and who negotiate the terms of trade with all of the voluntarily cooperating stakeholders — including the investors. At Whole Foods we "hired" our original investors. They didn't hire us.

We first announced that we would donate 5 percent of the company's net profits to philanthropy when we drafted our mission statement, back in 1985. Our policy has therefore been in place for over 20 years, and it predates our IPO [Initial Public Offering] by seven years. All seven of the private investors at the time we created the policy voted for it when they served on our board of directors. When we took in venture capital money back in 1989, none of the venture firms objected to the policy. In addition, in almost 14 years as a publicly traded company, almost no investors have ever raised objections to the policy. How can Whole Foods' philanthropy be "theft" from the current investors if the original owners of the company unanimously approved the policy and all subsequent investors made their investments after the policy was in effect and well publicized?

The shareholders of a public company own their stock voluntarily. If they don't agree with the philosophy of the business, they can always sell their investment, just as the customers and employees can exit their relationships with the company if they don't like the terms of trade. If that is unacceptable to them, they always have the legal right to submit a resolution at our annual shareholders meeting to change the company's philanthropic philosophy. A number of our company policies have been changed over the years through successful shareholder resolutions.

Another objection to the Whole Foods philosophy is where to draw the line. If donating 5 percent of profits is good, wouldn't 10 percent be even better? Why not donate 100 percent of our profits to the betterment of society? But the fact that Whole Foods has responsibilities to our community doesn't mean that we don't have any responsibilities to our investors. It's a question of finding the appropriate balance and trying to create value for all of our stakeholders. Is 5 percent the "right amount" to donate to the community? I don't think there is a right answer to this question, except that I believe 0 percent is too little. It is an arbitrary percentage that the co-founders of the company decided was a reasonable amount and that was approved by the owners of the company at the time we made the decision. Corporate philanthropy is a good thing, but it requires the legitimacy of investor approval. In my experience, most investors understand that it can be beneficial to both the corporation and the larger society.

That doesn't answer the question of why we give money to the community stakeholder. For that, you should turn to one of the fathers of free market economics, Adam Smith. *The Wealth of Nations* was a tremendous achievement, but economists would be well served to read Smith's other great book, *The Theory of Moral Sentiments*. There he explains that human nature isn't just about self-interest. It also includes sympathy, empathy, friendship, love, and the desire for social approval. As motives for human behavior, these are at least as important as self-interest. For many people, they are more important.

15   When we are small children we are egocentric, concerned only about our own needs and desires. As we mature, most people grow beyond this egocentrism and begin to care about others — their families, friends, communities, and countries. Our capacity to love can expand even further: to loving people from different races, religions, and countries — potentially to unlimited love for all people and even for other sentient creatures. This is our potential as human beings, to take joy in the flourishing of people everywhere. Whole Foods gives money to our communities because we care about them and feel a responsibility to help them flourish as well as possible.

The business model that Whole Foods has embraced could represent a new form of capitalism, one that more consciously works for the common good instead of depending solely on the "invisible hand" to generate positive results for society. The "brand" of capitalism is in terrible shape throughout the world, and corporations are widely seen as selfish, greedy, and uncaring. This is both unfortunate and unnecessary, and could be changed if businesses and economists widely adopted the business model that I have outlined here.

To extend our love and care beyond our narrow self-interest is antithetical to neither our human nature nor our financial success. Rather, it leads to the further fulfillment of both. Why do we not encourage this in our theories of business and economics? Why do we restrict our theories to such a pessimistic and crabby view of human nature? What are we afraid of?

Put Profits First
T. J. RODGERS

John Mackey's article attacking corporate profit maximization could not have been written by "a free market libertarian," as claimed. Indeed, if the examples he cites had not identified him as the author, one could easily assume the piece was written by Ralph Nader. A more accurate title for his article is "How Business and Profit Making Fit into My Overarching Philosophy of Altruism."

Mackey spouts nonsense about how his company hired his original investors, not vice versa. If Whole Foods ever falls on persistent hard times — perhaps when the Luddites are no longer able to hold back the genetic food

revolution using junk science and fear — he will quickly find out who has hired whom, as his investors fire him.

Mackey does make one point that is consistent with, but not supportive of, free market capitalism. He knows that shareholders own his stock voluntarily. If they don't like the policies of his company, they can always vote to change those policies with a shareholder resolution or simply sell the stock and buy that of another

Thurman John Rodgers is the founder and CEO of Cypress Semiconductor. He is a strong advocate of laissez-faire capitalism.

company more aligned with their objectives. Thus, he informs his shareholders of his objectives and lets them make a choice on which stock to buy. So far, so good.

It is also simply good business for a company to cater to its customers, train and retain its employees, build long-term positive relationships with its suppliers, and become a good citizen in its community, including performing some philanthropic activity. When Milton Friedman says a company should stay "within the rules of the game" and operate "without deception or fraud," he means it should deal with all its various constituencies properly in order to maximize long-term shareholder value. He does not mean that a company should put every last nickel on the bottom line every quarter, regardless of the long-term consequences.

5   My company, Cypress Semiconductor, has won the trophy for the Second Harvest Food Bank competition for the most food donated per employee in Silicon Valley for the last 13 consecutive years (1 million pounds of food in 2004). The contest creates competition among our divisions, leading to employee involvement, company food drives, internal social events with admissions "paid for" by food donations, and so forth. It is a big employee morale builder, a way to attract new employees, good P.R. for the company, and a significant benefit to the community — all of which makes Cypress a better place to work and invest in. Indeed, Mackey's own proud example of Whole Foods' community involvement programs also made a profit.

But Mackey's subordination of his profession as a businessman to altruistic ideals shows up as he attempts to negate the empirically demonstrated social benefit of "self-interest" by defining it narrowly as "increasing short-term profits." Why is it that when Whole Foods gives money to a worthy cause, it serves a high moral objective, while a company that provides a good return to small investors — who simply put their money into their own retirement funds or a children's college fund — is somehow selfish? It's the philosophy that is objectionable here, not the specific actions. If Mackey wants to run a hybrid business/charity whose mission is fully disclosed to his shareholders — and if those shareholder-owners want to support that mission — so be it. But I balk at the proposition that a company's "stakeholders" (a term often used by collectivists to justify unreasonable demands) should be allowed to control the property of the shareholders. It seems Mackey's philosophy is more accurately described by Karl Marx: "From each according to his ability" (the shareholders surrender money and assets); "to each according to his needs" (the charities, social interest groups, and environmentalists get what they want). That's not free market capitalism.

Then there is the arrogant proposition that if other corporations would simply emulate the higher corporate life form defined by Whole Foods, the world would be better off. After all, Mackey says corporations are viewed as "selfish, greedy, and uncaring." I, for one, consider free market capitalism to be a high calling, even without the infusion of altruism practiced by Whole Foods.

If one goes beyond the sensationalistic journalism surrounding the Enron-like[1] debacles, one discovers that only about 10 to 20 public corporations have been justifiably accused of

---

[1] Enron was a Houston energy company that was forced to declare bankruptcy in 2001 after years of fraudulent accounting.

serious wrongdoing. That's about 0.1 percent of America's 17,500 public companies. What's the failure rate of the publications that demean business? (Consider the *New York Times* scandal involving manufactured stories.) What's the percentage of U.S. presidents who have been forced or almost forced from office? (It's 10 times higher than the failure rate of corporations.) What percentage of our congressmen have spent time in jail? The fact is that despite some well-publicized failures, most corporations are run with the highest ethical standards — and the public knows it. Public opinion polls demonstrate that fact by routinely ranking businessmen above journalists and politicians in esteem.

I am proud of what the semiconductor industry does — relentlessly cutting the cost of a transistor from $3 in 1960 to three-millionths of a dollar today. Mackey would be keeping his business records with hordes of accountants on paper ledgers if our industry didn't exist. He would have to charge his poorest customers more for their food, pay his valued employees less, and cut his philanthropy programs if the semiconductor industry had not focused so relentlessly on increasing its profits, cutting his costs in the process. Of course, if the U.S. semiconductor industry had been less cost-competitive due to its own philanthropy, the food industry simply would have bought cheaper computers made from Japanese and Korean silicon chips (which happened anyway). Layoffs in the nonunion semiconductor industry were actually good news to Whole Foods' unionized grocery store clerks. Where was Mackey's sense of altruism when unemployed semiconductor workers needed it? Of course, that rhetorical question is foolish, since he did exactly the right thing by ruthlessly reducing his recordkeeping costs so as to maximize his profits.

I am proud to be a free market capitalist. 10 And I resent the fact that Mackey's philosophy demeans me as an egocentric child because I have refused on moral grounds to embrace the philosophies of collectivism and altruism that have caused so much human misery, however tempting the sales pitch for them sounds.

Discussion Questions

1. What does Mackey think the social responsibility of business should be? How does this differ from Milton Friedman's belief?

2. How does Whole Foods "create value for all of its constituencies"?

3. Why is Rodgers so vehemently opposed to Mackey's philosophy of the social responsibility of business?

4. How does Rodgers feel that his company aids society, not just its investors?

5. Which of the two do you feel presents a more convincing argument? Why?

Science and Morality

Should Human Stem Cells Be Used for Research?

As scientific advances make possible what once seemed impossible, questions arise about whether we should go everywhere that science leads us. Stem cell research promises thrilling advances in the ability to repair the human body, but tempting as the prospects are, one must question at what cost we tamper with human cells. There are moral issues involved in using "discarded" fetal tissue, but these are often answered with praise for all the good that can come from that use. Advances in the use of adult stem cells have made the issue even more complex, as is revealed in these articles written by physicians with opposing views.

Embryonic Stem Cell Research: A Moral Evil or Obligation?

BEAU WATTS

Imagine a world without diabetes, where Parkinson's disease is as easily treatable as an inflamed appendix, and where cancer and paralysis disappear as quickly as the common cold. With the current potential of embryonic stem cell research, this world is all too imaginable. Tremendous strides have been made in this area, but the manners in which these strides have been made have aroused the concern of many. The most promising source for stem cells comes from the destruction of an embryo, which many consider to be deserving of the same rights as any other human being. Others believe that the embryonic cells themselves should be morally protected. With embryos from in vitro fertilization being the current source for embryonic stem cells, the research should be considered morally justifiable. As long as the embryos are the results of other procedures deemed legal, society is obligated to proceed with embryonic stem cell research in an effort to improve the overall quality of life for the population.

The issue of stem cell research can become even more confusing if one becomes lost in

---

Beau Watts is an emergency room physician in Kansas City, Missouri. His essay appeared on the Drury University Web site in December 2011.

the scientific rhetoric. Stem cells describe any precursor cells that have the ability to divide and give rise to multiple tissue and specialized cell types. The idea of stem cells can best be understood when taken into terms of embryonic development. When sperm fuses with an egg, a zygote, or fertilized egg, is formed. A zygote is considered totipotent, meaning its cells can give rise to any other cell type as well as to an entire organism. Within hours of fertilization, the cell begins to divide rapidly. After several cell divisions a hollow ball of cells known as a blastocyst is formed. The blastocyst consists of an outer layer of cells which surround another cluster of cells known as the inner cell mass. It is this inner cell mass that contains stem cells considered to be pluripotent; which are those cells that may also give rise to any other cell type, but independently are unable to give rise to a functional organism (National Institutes of Health 1). These pluripotent stem cells will undergo further development and give rise to another type of stem cell, known as multipotent. These multipotent cells are specialized stem cells that are predetermined to give rise only to cells that maintain a particular function. These cells are found in the body from infanthood onward. An example of a multipotent cell would be a blood stem cell, which can give rise to both red and white blood cells as well as platelets. This knowledge has provided scientists with ideas for three potential stem cell types for experiments: embryonic stem cells, embryonic germ cells, and adult stem cells (Chapman, Frankel, and Garfinkle 134).

Embryonic stem cells, or es cells, are those cells derived from the inner cell mass of the blastula. These stem cells are considered to be the most promising, since they are pluripotent and completely undifferentiated. Another stem cell source is embryonic germ cells. These cells are derived from the gonadal ridge of aborted fetal tissue. These cells are also pluripotent, but may be limited in some replacement therapies because they may already have taken on certain characteristics of their destined function (National Institutes of Health 4). The final type of stem cells currently being used in experimentation is adult stem cells. These are the multipotent cells that are found in certain tissues of the adult body. Since they are multipotent and have not been found to exist in every tissue type, many consider these cells to be of least scientific help in terms of their potential to treat disease (Green 135).

The current source of embryonic stem cells comes from embryos created during the process of in vitro fertilization. During this process embryos are created in the lab, with one becoming implanted into the mother's womb. Because the process is quite costly, several embryos are created at one time to insure a quality of selection. Also, couples requiring this technology may wish to have more than one child, and will thus have spare embryos on hand. The surplus embryos are kept frozen and, if not used, usually discarded at a later date. In some countries such as Britain, the Human Fertilization and Embryology Authority require that the embryos be destroyed if not used within five years of production (Green 148). Couples now have the option of donating their excess embryos for use in medical research, which is currently our best es cell source. Since these embryos, which are by-products of a perfectly legal and genuinely ethically acceptable medical practice, are being destroyed on a considerably large scale, it would seem logical that they be used in a manner that could benefit humanity tremendously. There are, however, those that would disagree with this conclusion (Chapman, Frankel, and Garfinkle viii).

5   Many argue that using es cells for research is morally unacceptable on the basis that they themselves possess the potential to become a living organism. Those that consider an embryo to have full moral status point to two sets of criteria: "possession of a unique human genome and the potential for development into a human being" (Chapman, Frankel, and Garfinkle 11). It is a scientific certainty that the blastocysts indeed contain a unique genetic code. This is unarguable. In regard to the issue of potentiality, proponents of protecting the status of es cells point to an experiment in which individual stem cells were taken from a mouse embryo and used to grow entire mice by injecting the stem cells into an existing embryo whose own cells were genetically engineered to self-destruct in a short period of time (Green 136). Although these stem cells have the potential to develop into a living being, this is by no means achieved through any natural process. With today's technology almost any cell in the body maintains the potential to develop into a living organism. Cloning can perceivably allow any somatic cell in the body the potential to develop into a person. Using potentiality as definition of what cells should be morally protected would have a dramatic effect on many seemingly commonplace medical procedures. In order to clarify the idea of potentiality, one must look at it in terms of natural versus interferential. Embryos are cells that have the natural tendency to develop into a person, whereas embryonic stem cells must be altered or engineered in some manner to generate the same effect. Using the term *natural*, although still open to subjectivity, will

help rational decisions to ethical scientific questions become more easily clarified (Green 136).

Now that it can reasonably be inferred that es cells do not warrant ethical obligation, the moral status of the embryo from which it is derived should be evaluated. Every time embryonic stem cells are obtained it is the result of the destruction of a very early embryo. Should not embryos be held with some type of moral regard? They do have the natural potential to become a human being. Despite this obvious concern, many argue that the embryo be denied moral consideration. As discussed earlier, an embryo is the result of the fusion of sperm and egg. It does not, however, contain any individualized components until after implantation into the uterus. The embryo itself is completely undifferentiated and may not develop into a human until implantation. The embryos used in the derivation of es cells never reach this stage in embryonic development. This is a fact that allows many who oppose abortion to morally accept the idea of a "morning after" pill administered before the zygote becomes implanted into the uterus. Regardless, there are many who still claim this early embryo has moral rights. The National Bioethics Advisory Committee concluded that "the blastocyst must be treated with the respect appropriate to early human embryonic tissue," but its use in research could be justified when that research "aims ultimately to save or heal human life" (Green 134). Also, many religious traditions assume a developmental view of what constitutes a person, believing that the embryo becomes a full person only after a gradual process and thus may not merit the same protection early in its development (Chapman, Frankel, and Garfinkle viii). Whether or not an individual agrees with this argument may, however, prove to be irrelevant in regard to supporting embryonic stem cell research.

It has been established that many individuals find the destruction of the embryo for medical research to be morally reprehensible. Many of these would also argue that it is in turn wrong to benefit from this moral evil. An issue that has long been debated in our society is the culpability involved in the cooperation with evil. The main concern shared by these individuals is that through their support the evil would in turn be encouraged to continue. Pertaining to embryonic stem cell research, those who hold the embryo with high moral regard wonder if they can support research from its destruction in good conscience. United States Catholic Conference spokesperson on bioethics Richard Doerflinger would claim they could not. In response to President Bush's decision to fund research on existing cell lines based on the notion that the embryos have already been destroyed, Doerflinger believes that "(Bush's) moral principle seems to be, if the killing has already been done, we can fund this research. But by the time the scientists come forward with the next group of cell lines, that destruction will already have been done, too. And on we go. Where is the moral limit? On what basis will the president say no? I think this is an untenable and unstable policy" (Shannon 820).

The question of what constitutes immoral cooperation with evil deeds has undergone such strong analysis that philosophers have derived four different manners in which one could be guilty of such cooperation. The first is direct involvement, where the beneficiary is the individual who actually commits the evil. The second pertains to direct encouragement, where the beneficiary persuades an individual to perform the immoral task. The third involves indirect cooperation, where the beneficial consequences of the act lead to a broader acceptance of the wrongful practice. The final way concerns that in the absence of encouragement, there is still the appearance of endorsing the evil deed (Chapman, Frankel, and Garfinkle 14). Considering the proposed source of es cells comes from embryos derived from in vitro fertilization, criteria one and two can be eliminated, since through no involvement of their own have the beneficiaries caused the destruction of the embryo. The third is also easily escapable when considering that the practice of in vitro fertilization is already generally morally acceptable and certainly legal. The fourth, however, requires further analysis.

Examining the debate on the use of aborted fetal tissue for research can shed light on this topic. Russel Smith, author of a volume endorsed by the Roman Catholic Church on the subject, claims that it would be unethical for Catholic researchers to participate in such research (Green 150). His reasons for claiming this, however, leave the door open for debate. Smith claims the wrongfulness does not stem from the act itself, but rather from the possibility of "scandal" from benefiting from such an act. The argument's weakness lies within the fact that there are many ethical acts that, if misinterpreted, could lead to scandal. Adopting this philosophy would surely deprive our society of many beneficial innovations (Green 151). One must also consider the fact that we frequently harvest organs for transplant after an individual has passed on. If the individual were a victim of murder, an immoral act, receiving his or her donated liver does not make the recipient culpable in the crime. There are numerous things we can do for the deceased, including honoring them by insuring that they not die in vain. President Bush's defense of es cell research included the example of the development of the live chickenpox vaccine from aborted human fetal tissue that has provided tremendous health benefits (Shannon 819). When viewed under different terms the idea of benefiting from certain evils that are relatively beyond control appears to be morally acceptable.

10   Another argument offered by those morally opposed to the use of embryonic stem cell research is that adult stem cells could be used just as effectively in their place. The main argument, as presented by the Coalition of Americans for Research Ethics, is that "adult stem cell research is a preferable alternative for progress in regenerative medicine and cell-based therapies for disease because it does not pose the medical, legal, and ethical problems associated with destructive human embryonic stem cell research" (The Coalition of Americans for Research Ethics 293). Proponents for this research argue that adult stem cells, unlike embryonic stem cells, are currently being used and enjoying success in clinical trials. These include effective treatments in spinal cord damage, retinal damage, Parkinson's disease, and diabetes in animal models. Another benefit of the use of adult stem cells is that when used upon the individuals from whom they are derived, they eliminate the threat of immune rejection and tumor formation associated with embryonic stem cells. Although not found in every tissue type, adult stem cells are known to exist in many, including the brain, muscle, retina, and blood vessels. This evidence has led many to believe that adult stem cells provide equal potential for treating disease, less the stigma attached to embryonic stem

cell research (The Coalition of Americans for Research Ethics 293–307).

It is important that the shortcomings of adult stem cells also be addressed. The National Institute of Health has concluded that adult stem cells are inferior to es cells because they have not been found in every cell type, are difficult to harvest and have limited numbers, have a high potential to pass on genetic defects, and simply do not have the pluripotency that es cells contain (The Coalition of Americans for Research Ethics 294). Despite these limits, opponents of es cell research, Doerflinger included, would endorse using only adult stem cell research at the cost of pursuing a less promising directive. While both sides of the debate maintain valid arguments, pursing only one potential treatment is at the least scientifically nonsensical. When searching for cures for disease it is imperative that any possible alternative be explored. The opinions of many panels and leading scientists, including Brigid Hogan of the National Bioethics Advisory Commission, are that adult stem cells have serious limits, and that research on all cell types is needed to better assess their comparative value (Green 158).

Embryonic stem cell research has given society a glimpse of a world where any disease can be treated. From Parkinson's to diabetes, nothing appears to be out of the jurisdiction of this technology. Yet this blockbuster breakthrough has been met with as much adversity as it has enthusiasm. Since the sources of embryonic stem cells are destroyed embryos, many believe the research to be unethical. Embryonic stem cells are considered by some to be a living organism based on their potentiality, but with today's technology almost any cell in the body has the potential to develop into a living being.

Others hold that the embryo be held with moral status, and that benefiting from its death is an unacceptable evil. However, the actual moral obligation to the embryo is highly subjective, since it does not contain any individualized components before becoming implanted into the uterus. Even if one does believe the embryo to have moral claim, benefiting from its destruction does not necessarily make one culpable in the crime, according to guidelines established by many philosophers. Others claim that this debate be altogether avoided by using adult stem cells in place of es cells. Proponents of es cell research boast of the advantages of es cells to adult stem cells, citing the reduced potential of adult stem cells and the need to explore more than one scientific option. With two sides split down the middle, it seems a solution will be a difficult one to find.

Through this heated debate concerning the moral status of the embryo and the potential for a medical revolution, the most important fact seems to have slipped through the cracks. The focus has been aimed toward uncertainties that in all probability will never have answers. Does an embryo warrant moral protections? This question contains a level of such subjectivity that a common resolution seems altogether impossible. Technology has provided us with more information about when life begins than ever before, and society is still no closer to the answer. Instead of devoting so much time to debating this question, the issue that should be considered foremost is where the embryos for es cell research come from. The fact remains that the practice of infertility medicine will continue to lead to the creation and potential destruction of embryos. This, unlike the moral status of the embryo, is a certainty. When these embryos have only the option of being destroyed, the rationale for preventing their use in life-improving research is non-existent. Society is obligated to use these embryos to help improve the quality of life for its fellow man.

Works Cited

Chapman, Audrey R., Mark S. Frankel, and Michele S. Garfinkle. "Stem Cell Research and Applications: Monitoring the Frontiers of Biomedical Research." Washington, DC: American Association for the Advancement of Science, November 1999.

Green, Ronald. *The Human Embryo Research Debates: Bioethics in the Vortex of Controversy.* Oxford: Oxford University Press, 2001.

National Institutes of Health. "Stem Cells: A Primer." May 2000. 10 Sept. 01.

Shannon, Thomas A. "Human Embryonic Stem Cell Therapy." *Theological Studies* 62.4 (Dec. 2001): 811–24.

The Coalition of Americans for Research Ethics. "A Review of the National Institute of Health's 'Guidelines for Research Using Human Pluripotent Stem Cells.'" *Issues in Law and Medicine* 17.3 (Spring 2002): 293–307.

I'm Pro-Life and Oppose Embryonic Stem Cell Research

J. C. WILLKE

Much has been said and written about "stem cell" research. Unfortunately, a number of biologic inaccuracies continue to be promulgated and, as a result, have colored decision making for many people. The first thing to distinguish is the fact that ethically we can experiment on human tissue, but we should not experiment on human beings. Accordingly, it is perfectly ethical to proceed with any and all type of stem cell research as long as this is human tissue, but it is completely unethical to do embryonic stem cell research, which of its very nature necessitates the killing of a living human embryo to obtain that stem cell.

To understand this we must first review early developmental biology. Human life begins at the union of sperm and ovum. During that first day, this is properly termed a "fertilized egg." However, this single-celled human body divides, divides, and divides again, so that nearing the end of the first week this embryo, now called a "blastocyst," numbers several hundred cells. To obtain an embryonic stem cell, the researcher must cut open this embryo, thereby killing him or her and extracting stem cells.

After the first day, a number of names apply to various developmental stages of the same living human, fertilized egg or zygote (a single cell), a blastocyst (many cells), embryo, fetus, infant, child, adolescent, etc. During the first week, this tiny new human floats freely down his or her mother's tube, dividing and sub-dividing as the journey is made. At about one week of life, he or she plants within the nutrient lining of the woman's uterus. In about three more days, having sent roots into the wall of the uterus, this new human sends a chemical hormonal message into the mother's blood stream and this stops her menstrual period. Four days later, the embryonic heart begins to beat and three weeks after that, brain waves are measurable. The biologic fact is that from day one, inside and then outside of the uterus, this is one continuous, uninterrupted period of growth and development. It is impossible to draw a line in time and to say that before this time, this was not a living human, and after this, it is. This is, in fact, a living human at the first cell stage and remains so until the old man dies. Accordingly, killing this living human embryo at day four or five, at week four or five, or at year four or five is, in fact, killing a living human.

At the first cell stage, you were everything you are today. You were already male or female. You were alive, not dead. You were certainly human as you had 46 human chromosomes (you were not a carrot or a rabbit); and most importantly, you were complete. For nothing has been added to the single cell whom you once were, from then until today, nothing except food and oxygen. You were all there then, and to termi-

---

J. C. Willke was an obstetrician for forty years before giving up his practice to devote his time to anti-abortion activism. He helped found the International Right to Life Federation, has served as president of the U.S. National Right to Life Committee, and is president of the Life Issues Institute. He and his late wife have written some of the world's most widely read anti-abortion books. He gained national attention in 2012 when he argued publicly that a woman has natural defenses against getting pregnant as a result of rape. This article appeared on the Web site for the Life Issues Institute.

nate your life at any stage of that can be called nothing other than killing.

5   Note that Senator Mack in his *Wall Street Journal* column repeats the biologic error seen almost everywhere. He speaks constantly of stem cells from "fertilized eggs." That stage lasts only one day. You cannot take a stem cell from a fertilized egg which itself is only one cell. Rather what he is advocating is killing a human embryo and extracting stem cells from the inside of that new living human. He attempts to distinguish between "a frozen fertilized egg" and a fetus. Actually the only difference is location, size, age, and degree of development as the one is just a bit younger than the other.

I can understand why a pro-abortion Senator Jeffords or Chafee would favor destructive embryonic stem cell research, for they are strongly pro-abortion and have demonstrated many times their support for killing babies in the womb. What I don't understand is pro-life Senator Orin Hatch, who "insisted" that a frozen embryo was not the equivalent of an embryo or a fetus in the womb. I've known Senator Hatch well for twenty years. He's pro-life, but on this he has his facts dead wrong, and it's a tragedy that he would lend his undoubted prestige to destructive stem cell research by repeating an obvious biologic falsehood.

To say that these tiny humans will be "discarded" and not used and therefore should be "used" is a fallacious argument. Why then don't we use the tissues of a criminal who has been legally executed? Why did we universally condemn the Nazi doctors who used Jewish subjects because they were going to be killed anyway? Why is it that we cannot cannibalize a person's body who was killed in an accident? It's

because we have respected the human body, an absolute necessity in a civilized nation.

But are there other options? Certainly, there are. There have been marvelous and well-publicized advances in the last year. We now have scientific data showing that stem cells can be obtained from fat. They can be obtained from cord blood. They can be obtained from neural tissue, from bone marrow, muscle, placental, and skin cells. We have reports of bone marrow stem cells being changed into liver cells. We have a report of skin cells being changed into heart cells. We have a report of cord blood promising to possibly create neural cells.

Almost every month we receive reports of new advances in this field. One of the latest is from Congressman Ron Lewis (R-KY), in a letter to HHS Secretary Tommy Thompson. He urges him to consider a "tobacco based adult stem cell alternative to embryonic stem cell research." He notes the leadership of plant protein assisted stem cell research, which has identified the genes in proteins that cause self-renewal of adult stem cells. He points to the fact that certain plant proteins found in tobacco can stimulate such changes. And much more. This is yet the latest revelation. Rest assured there is much more to come.

10   There is a possibility, perhaps a probability that adult stem cells may function more efficiently and more safely than embryonic stem cells. Adult stem cells are increasingly being shown to have a similar and perhaps an identical capacity to become cells of other types. They can be taken from the patient himself, then re-injected, thus eliminating the problem of immune rejection, which is a real problem in using tissues from another human, even from an embryonic human. There is no question but

that there is probably an immense potential of use for stem cells. But this increasingly is being shown to not be exclusive for embryonic stem cells. In fact, adult stem cells may prove to be superior because they don't suffer the problem of rejection.

As for public opinion polls, as usual the wording of the question leads the answer. When the poll speaks of "fertilized eggs" and doesn't mention the destruction of human embryos, you get one kind of an answer. In comparison, a recent poll by International Communications Research of over 1,000 adults was worded more objectively. Its question was as follows: "Stem cells are the basic cells from which all of a person's tissues and organs develop. Congress is considering whether to provide federal funding for experiments using stem cells from human embryos. The live embryos would be destroyed in their first week of development to obtain these cells. Do you support or oppose using your federal tax dollars for such experiments?" The results were: Support – 24%, Opposed – 70%, Don't Know and Refused – 6%. Further, only 18% supported "all stem cell research" while 67% supported "only adult stem cell research."

Finally, can embryonic stem cells be said positively to be able to cure diseases that stem cells from other ethical sources would be unable to? No one can make that statement. Let us by all means pursue aggressive research with stem cells, but there are some bridges that we, in a civilized society, should not cross. We should not deliberately kill one living human to possibly benefit another. Use stem cells? Yes, but don't kill to get them.

Discussion Questions

1. Both articles begin with the morality of stem cell research. How does Watts bring in the legality of it?
2. What are the different types of stem cells used in research, and how does each of the two articles address the differences?
3. Much of Willke's argument depends on the warrant that to destroy an embryo is to kill a human being. Explain to what extent that line of reasoning is largely a matter of definition.
4. What does Watts mean by the term *obligation* in his title? How can stem cell research be considered an obligation?
5. What is the claim in each of the two articles?
6. Which of the two arguments do you find more convincing? Explain why.

Gender Stereotypes

Is the "Princess" Phenomenon Detrimental to Girls' Self-Image?

Some parents make an effort not to box their children into stereotyped gender roles by choosing "boy toys" or "girl toys." Even some of those enlightened parents, though, find themselves with daughters who want to live in a world of tiaras, pink evening gowns, castles, and "happily ever after." Many of these little girls get their notion of being a princess from movies, and that notion is reinforced through multimillion-dollar marketing campaigns. It can be expensive for Mom and Dad, but is it truly harmful? That is the question debated in these articles by Monika Bartyzel and Crystal Liechty.

Girls on Film: The Real Problem with the Disney Princess Brand
MONIKA BARTYZEL

Disney built its massive Princess empire — which now stretches from 1937's Snow White to 2012's Merida — by sanitizing the stories of the past. From "Snow White" to "The Frog Prince," Disney excised fairy tales of their inherent horror — the rampant cannibalism, torture, and bloody mayhem characteristic of most traditional stories — in favor of a blanket policy of "happily ever after." The literary darkness was cleansed, but despite the company's best efforts, a social darkness has remained.

Disney has a sad history of gross racial stereotypes (from *Dumbo*'s crows to *Aladdin*'s ear-cutting barbarians) and highly problematic female characterizations and storylines (from

Snow White's servitude to the Little Mermaid giving up her voice for love). The company's latest in a long string of controversies came last week with the news that Merida, the heroine at the heart of last year's *Brave*, was becoming a certified Disney Princess.

Last weekend, the fiery Scottish lass from the film received an official coronation at the Magic Kingdom — not as the rebellious girl introduced in *Brave*, but as a sparkling,

Monika Bartyzel is a freelance writer who created Girls on Film, a weekly feature on "femme-centric film news and concerns" at theweek.com. This article appeared there on May 17, 2013.

made-over princess. Disney's redesign of the character tamed her unruly hair, expanded her breasts, shrank her waist, enlarged her eyes, plastered on makeup, pulled her (now-glittering) dress off her shoulders, and morphed her defiant posture into a come-hither pose. The bow-wielding Merida of *Brave* — a character who explicitly fought against the princess world her mother tried to push her into in the film — was becoming what she hated, and inadvertently revealing the enormously problematic nature of Disney's Princess line.

Let's rewind. Disney began its empire with three princesses, Snow White, Cinderella, and Aurora, the Sleeping Beauty. Then, when Aurora woke from her slumber in the 1959 film, Disney began a slumber of its own: Three decades passed until Disney used a princess as a main character again, in 1989's *The Little Mermaid.* At first, the princess revival hinged on the same, tired narrative: the hunt for a prince, which required a young woman to give up her own voice and passions for the love of a man. But the arrival of Aladdin in 1992 showed that Disney's princess world could actually expand. There were still a number of problematic aspects in each film, but Disney's scope began to stretch beyond the lily-white princesses of its earlier films: Aladdin, Pocahontas, and Mulan brought new visions of what a "Disney Princess" could be, with the latter even stretching the barriers to show that Mulan — a princess in principle, if not in title — could also be a fierce warrior.

5   The evolution of Disney's princesses was stymied by the arrival of the Disney Princess line in the late 1990s. The Disney Princess franchise doesn't celebrate the increasingly diverse world of princesses; instead, it pulls back the progress the company had made, pushing the more forward-thinking female characters back into the reductive feminine stereotypes of the past.

Author Peggy Orenstein — the force behind the initial backlash to Merida's coronation — revealed the impact of "princess culture" on young women with her 2006 *New York Times* article "What's Wrong with Cinderella?" and subsequent book, 2011's *Cinderella Ate My Daughter: Dispatches from the Front Lines of the New Girlie-Girl Culture.* As a mother, Orenstein wrote about how excessive repetition of Princess products, which encompassed everything from pens to Band-Aids, had a significant effect on her daughter. It even informed how adults interacted with her child, offering "princess pancakes," pink balloons, and even a "princess chair" at the dentist's office.

Orenstein's experiences revealed not only the reductive world of pastel pink princesses, but also the growing struggle for mothers to create worlds of diverse opportunity for their daughters. Orenstein's own daughter read her distaste for what Cinderella represented as hatred for a woman: "There's that princess you don't like, Mama! . . . Don't you like her blue dress, Mama? . . . Then don't you like her face?"

Psychotherapist Mary Finucane, meanwhile, struggled with her daughter's even darker concerns. "She began refusing to do or wear things that princesses didn't do or wear," Finucane said of her 3-year-old daughter. "She had stopped running and jumping because princesses didn't do those things. That was about the time I stopped waiting for the phase to pass — when she stopped running." As Orenstein explains, princess culture was no longer just about fairy tale magic, but "a constant narrowing of what it means to be feminine."

Last year, *Brave*'s Merida arrived as a character specifically designed to combat Disney's increasingly reductive princess archetype. In a petition drafted to fight Merida's redesign, A Mighty Girl founder Carolyn Danckaert includes *Brave* creator Brenda Chapman's inspiration for the film:

> Because of marketing, little girls gravitate toward princess products, so my goal was to offer up a different kind of princess — a stronger princess that both mothers and daughters could relate to, so mothers wouldn't be pulling their hair out when their little girls were trying to dress or act like this princess. Instead they'd be like, "Yeah, you go girl!"

10   Instead of celebrating the fiery spirit that made *Brave* the eighth top-grossing film of 2012, however, Disney chose to do the opposite, making her into exactly what Chapman (and Merida) were fighting against and ignoring Disney's own promotional video about "What it truly means to be a Princess."

Unfortunately, Merida isn't the only victim. Virtually every Disney princess has received a redesign that makes her look more like the others: narrower jaws, larger eyes, smaller noses, and waists narrowed so drastically that the characters look as if Disney has marched them into a plastic surgeon's office for liposuction and rib removal. The characters of color have it even worse, with their features audaciously whitewashed: Mulan changes from a young Chinese woman into a girl with white, ruddy skin and plump lips; Pocahontas, meanwhile, gets lighter skin, chin implants, larger eyes and lips, and a much smaller nose. (Jasmine's makeover is more subdued — but like Mulan and Pocahontas, her skin lightens with every updated look.)

These redesigns are in conflict with the films, which show Mulan hating the matchmaking makeup put on her, or Merida violently tugging at the oppressive fashions she has to wear. The redesigns come after the films — which means that the ultimate message is that these characters have found happiness in this restrictive femininity, as the nonstop Disney marketing that young children are subjected to on a daily basis begins to act as a real-world sequel to the films themselves.

Fortunately — though without taking any responsibility — Disney has started to quietly backtrack on some of these changes. Mulan's skin was darkened a touch on her official webpage (although it's still a far cry from the "reflection" video from the original film that's viewable just underneath her introduction), and Merida's 2-D redesign was not included on her official Princess webpage at all.

After a week of silence, Disney finally responded to criticism at Disney-themed website Inside the Magic on Wednesday. In a statement, Disney Consumer Products says the controversy has been "blown out of proportion," since Merida's new look wasn't an official redesign, but a "one-time stylized version" to fit the specific needs of the coronation. (DCP goes as far as saying that Merida herself wanted to "dress up" for the coronation — conveniently ignoring that *Brave* specifically emphasized her distaste for that sort of thing.)

The company claims that the image used   15 on the invitation is only the "official" version used for the ceremony, and not any other image circulating on the web. Unfortunately, even that limited qualification proves inaccurate. In the same statement, DCP admits there are other variations of Merida's coronation redesign being used for various retail stores, and the article includes a picture of a T-shirt emblazoned with the new version of the character.

As always, Disney is testing the limits of its consumers, with the pitch and ferocity of public unrest serving as the sole compass guiding the company's decisions. The Merida controversy mimics the arrival of *The Princess and the Frog* a few years ago. Before the film starred Tiana, the budding restaurantress of the final cut, it was supposed to be about Maddy, a chambermaid working for a rich white family, until backlash led to creative tweaks. When Disney Television's Princess Sofia was introduced as a Latina last year by the executive producer, the company backtracked, linking her ethnicity to a fictional kingdom to dodge growing questions about the young princess. Earlier this month, Disney actually planned to trademark the holiday Dia de los Muertos for an upcoming Pixar film, until protests made them change course.

But regardless of Disney's characteristic backpedaling, there are many who wish for the world of Disney Princesses to die altogether. That's an unrealistic goal in this market; as Orenstein once wrote: " 'Princess,' as some Disney execs call it, is not only the fastest-growing brand the company has ever created; they say it is on its way to becoming the largest girls' franchise on the planet." Fortunately, there's no reason this behemoth of a brand can't learn the same lesson Disney's film division is slowly learning: that stories for young girls and boys alike can thrive by depicting young women who are interested in more than princes and pretty dresses. Many hate the term "princess" for what the brand currently represents: one very narrow version of femininity that has a significant impact on its young consumers' visions of themselves. But it's well within Disney's power to continue its successful brand while reflecting the lessons and diversity the films offer.

Creatives like *Brave*'s Brenda Chapman have given Disney the opportunity to make "princess" a term encompassing many different embodiments of young women that live all kinds of "happy endings." *Brave*'s young protagonist is a young princess who hates being forced to dress up and act regal. She just wants to shoot her bow and arrow and be brave like her dad — and ultimately, her happiness has nothing to do with finding a prince. (Some have chastised Disney for turning her into a princess, but let's not forget: She already was one!)

The truth is that, just as there are all kinds of women, there can be all kinds of princesses. We live in a world where even Barbie was an executive, astronaut, and surgeon in her early days, and can now be anything from a military officer to a race car driver to a computer engineer. So far, no matter how many adventures they've had on screen, the Disney Princess line has taken its characters and whittled them into uniform fembots. There's nothing brave about that — but it's not too late for Disney to accept its responsibility as a creator of family-friendly products and work not to narrow the worldview of young girls, but to expand it.

In Defense of Princess Culture
CRYSTAL LIECHTY

Let me preface this with the disclaimer that the following is my opinion and only my opinion and I realize sane, intelligent women can have other opinions on this topic. Yadda, yadda, yadda. Whatever. Here goes.

I was reading a blog the other day. In it, a mother talked about her daughter's love of princess culture — the movies, the dresses, the stories, and all that goes with it. To paraphrase her, this particular mom was pretty disappointed in this. She "hates" the princess stories. She "really, really" does.

But she was sucking it up and supporting her daughter, anyway (kudos for that). Though it killed her to do so, this mother allowed her daughter to tiptoe through the magical world of castles and happy endings.

But when she had to read the story of Cinderella to her daughter's Kindergarten class, she (and this is where she lost me) adjusted the story to suit herself: Cinderella's stepsisters? "Jealous and misunderstood." The stepmother: "lonely, rather than cruel." Cinderella's prince? A "like-minded partner."

5 Um . . .

SERIOUSLY!?!

My daughter also loves princess culture, as anyone who has met her is aware. She loves the dresses and the stories and the books and the PRINCES and the LOVE! It's all so wonderful and magical! The funny thing is, when she was born, I had it in my mind she'd be a tomboy, following after her brother in dirty overalls and messy pigtails.

That is not how things played out. And at first I wasn't sure how I felt about it.

After seeing my daughter decked out in her princess best, someone asked me, "Were you into princesses when you were little, too?"

"I don't know," I said, realizing I really didn't 10 know. "I was never given the chance."

I grew up with hand-me-downs and once-a-year trips to Walmart. I'd never really been presented with a princess dress. But thinking back, if I had been, I'm pretty sure I would've been STOKED.

Somewhere along the way, I'd come to believe princesses were a bad thing. Degrading to women; a symbol of being spoiled and superficial (thanks, Paris Hilton); a precursor to those sad little girls in beauty pageants.

But is any of that actually true?

Because, ladies, have you watched Disney's Snow White lately? That girl had someone try to KILL her, yo. And she got away and survived! And the whole time, she was really, really NICE about it.

And Cinderella? Talk about work ethic. Plus 15 she had a good attitude, even when people were completely awful to her — she remained honest and sweet. And it was because of that goodness that she was rewarded with a happy ending.

So what's so offensive about this? We don't want our daughters learning that if you work hard and are good and sweet, even in the face of difficult circumstances, you'll find happiness?

I already know the rebuttal to this question: it's the idea that a woman needs a prince to

---

Crystal Liechty is a mom from Utah. She posted these comments on the blog *The Unexceptional Mom* on February 7, 2013.

rescue her in order for her to be happy that women find so offensive.

To which I have one question:

WHAT'S SO AWFUL ABOUT THAT?

20   Why is it offensive that a woman might need a man to be happy? I can tell you, I wouldn't be happy without MY man. Does this make me weak? Or just honest with myself? I know, I know, there are a lot of women out there without men in their lives and they're doing just fine. Great. Good for them.

But why does that mean I should shield my daughter from the idea of finding love? I'm kind of hoping she finds a "prince" to take care of her one day. And these princess movies give me a great chance to talk to her about what kind of guy she should marry: namely someone who is courteous, gallant, willing to do anything for her; to protect her from the bad things in the world.

Which brings me to my next point: lonely stepmothers and misunderstood stepsisters?? I'm sorry but if you're bullying someone and treating them like a slave, I don't care WHY you're doing it — you're a bad guy.

And I want my daughter to understand that there are BAD people out there in the world. If someone hurts her or treats her badly, I don't want her to try understanding where they're coming from. I want her running in the other direction.

And my final point: as far as role models go, do you have any better ideas!?

25   Would you rather your daughter dress up as and admire Bratz dolls?

Or Katy Perry and Ke$ha? I'm racking my brain, scanning popular culture, trying to find a better avenue to direct my daughter down. There are options — but not a lot.

If my daughter knows all the words to every song in *The Little Mermaid,* so what? It's better than her singing along with Rihanna's latest ode to promiscuity.

And if she hopes to someday find a gallant man to marry, awesome! I hope she finds him. And if she loves wearing princess dresses and crowns and jewels, guess what? Those dresses are pretty classy. She could do worse.

I have another daughter. She's just learning how to be alive right now (dude, getting a toy into your mouth with brand new hands is HARD WORK) but when she's old enough to care, will I steer her in the same direction? No, I won't. If she's into pirates or animals or ninja spies, I will totally support her in that. And use that culture to teach her the values I want her to learn.

30   But in the meantime, I ain't hating on the princesses and I don't think you should either.

Discussion Questions

1. Why does Monika Bartyzel find Disney's re-creation of Merida such a violation of the spirit of the movie *Brave*?

2. What is Bartyzel's problem with the Disney princesses in general?

3. How is Crystal Liechty's style different from Bartyzel's? Is it an effective style for her purposes? Explain.

4. Why does Liechty feel different from Bartyzel about her daughter's love of the princess way of life? Does she offer evidence for her position other than her personal feelings? Explain.

5. Which of the two articles do you find more convincing, and why?

6. Does either author's view of the princess phenomenon coincide with memories you have of children you grew up with — or of your own childhood? Explain.

Economics and College Sports

Should College Athletes Be Paid?

What once might have been dismissed as a ridiculous question is now the stuff of cover stories of leading periodicals. How have sports changed to the point that there is now serious discussion of paying college athletes? Revenue sports bring in millions of dollars. Star athletes are more likely to leave college for the pros before finishing their degrees, lured by the prospect of huge salaries. And many athletes who don't make it to the pros never graduate anyway, but instead play out their eligibility and drop out of sight. The best coaches make millions of dollars while strict rules prohibit their players from earning money signing autographs or from accepting even small gifts from donors. The discrepancy is being noted more and more by the athletes who bring in those millions of dollars and who also bring fame to their schools. Paul Marx and Warren Hartenstine look at two sides of the question.

Athlete's New Day

PAUL MARX

College football is heading for a new day. It won't be long before the players on the field are going to receive more than a pittance. The present structure governed by the rules of the National Collegiate Athletic Association is beginning to crack.

There is the O'Bannon suit against the NCAA challenging its right to prohibit college athletes from sharing in the profits from sales of their names and images. There is the new attention to concussions, often resulting in lifelong disabilities for which the athletes are meagerly compensated. There is the growing awareness that college football is not an amateur sport, as the NCAA insists that it is. And there is the players' growing resentment of the huge gap between their compensation and that of their coaches.

The four highest coaches' salaries for 2012 were $5.2 million for the University of Texas's

Paul Marx is a retired English professor from Maryland. His article appeared in the *Baltimore Sun* on October 30, 2013.

Mack Brown, $4.2 million for Ohio State's Urban Meyer, $3.8 million for the University of Iowa's Kirk Ferentz, and $3.7 million for Louisiana State University's Les Miles. It is rare for any head coach at a major football school to have a base salary of less than half a million. The compensation for the best college football players, on the other hand, is the traditional tuition and fees, room and board, and books. Never is there spending money.

Players are not happy about these disparities, and a protest movement is beginning. As things stand now players put in a full work week of games, practices, meetings, body-building sessions, and travel. There's not much time for, or interest in, school work.

5   But not everyone is cut out to be a student; most football players are not. Most do not meet their college's admission standards. Nevertheless, they are enrolled, as "special admits." At Georgia and Texas A&M, not untypically, 94 percent of freshman football players were special admits. Even with gut courses and special tutoring, barely 50 percent of college football players graduate.

Why can't these athletes play for a college without having to abide by anachronistic NCAA rules? On their recruiting trips, what do coaches tell high school stars? Most often the selling point is simply that playing at his school will enhance the player's chances of being noticed by an NFL team. At the football factories, most players are full-time students, as the NCAA requires, only on paper.

How would a pay-the-player system come about? The key is to get all the schools in one major conference to go ahead and make the change. Already, players at Georgia in the Southeastern Conference and Georgia Tech

in the Atlantic Coast Conference have made protests on the field. The protests will spread to teams in other major conferences — the Big 10, the Big 12, the PAC-12.

With more player protests, students will begin to sympathize with the players, and they too will protest. College presidents will sympathize with their students, and they will bring the issue to their conference. The conference will realize that if its schools pay, the best players available will gravitate to that conference. Because their games will be played by the best players out there, broadcasters will pay the conference more to get their games. The necessity of football membership in the NCAA will be gone. To be competitive other major conferences will begin to pay their players.

Enrolling as a full-time student and working on a degree should be optional, not compulsory. Players' relationships to the schools they play for should be spelled out in an individualized pay-for-service contract rather than an NCAA-standardized letter of intent that impinges on basic freedoms. In any case, on game days, paid players would take the field in the school's traditional colors. The cheerleaders would perform, just as they do now. Stadiums would still ring with fight songs and the brass of marching band.

Every two weeks players would receive a   10
paycheck, the amount determined by the demand for a player's services. If players sold their autographs, there would be no penalty. If they wanted to accept free tattoos, they could do so without fear. If automobile dealers wanted to give them breaks on the purchase of new cars, they could accept the deal. Boosters who wanted to help players out financially could do so above board. The injustices of fake amateurism would be gone.

College Athletes Should Not Be Paid
WARREN HARTENSTINE

In ["Athlete's New Day"], Paul Marx demonstrates an embarrassing lack of knowledge and research about his subject. The graduation rate by 2011 for all freshmen entering all U.S. colleges and universities in 2005 was 59 percent, 61 percent for women, and 56 percent for men. Meanwhile, "[a]ccording to the most recent Graduation Success Rate data 82 percent of Division I freshmen scholarship student-athletes who entered college in 2004 earned a degree. In Division II, 73 percent of freshmen student-athletes who entered college in 2004 graduated. The graduation rate data are based on a six-year cohort prescribed by the U.S. Department of Education."

Yes, a small percentage of student athletes are admitted as "exceptional admits." But these numbers speak to the success of standards that indicate a high probability of success and the tutoring programs that exist in today's programs, not unlike programs in place for many high potential, non-athletes admitted to every institution.

While Mr. Marx was attending every home game at Michigan and Iowa, I was playing Division I football at one of the other Big Ten institutions with an annual graduation success rate in the top 10 percent nationally, at 85 percent. While he was teaching English, I spent the early years of my career as an assistant dean at a large East Coast state university. Of the 800 living football lettermen from my alma mater who listed a career, the most common professions indicated enormous success. Some 15 percent played professional football as a first career, but 15 percent were corporate executives,

13 percent were K–12 educators, 13 percent were corporate sales executives, and 10 percent were professionals (doctors, lawyers, dentists, financial services, etc.).

I think contemporary college football players are still motivated by winning the game and earning opportunities to play at the next level. Like us, I seriously doubt that players in at least 100 of the Division I schools even know how much their coaches earn. And I would bet those who do see the high salaries as an institutional investment in their success as players.

In the 1960s when Mr. Marx was presumably warming a bleacher in the Big House, the NCAA scholarship cap provided for tuition, room, board, books and $15 per month "laundry money," period. Fifty years later, with 50-week football programs, no opportunities for summer employment and players predominantly from poorer families, the cap has not changed at $15, period. And scholarship student athletes do not qualify for any additional forms of aid, leaving their parents to sacrifice to subsidize their education.

For those of you who want to cheer for paid college athletes, contact Mr. Marx for more information on Michigan and Iowa. Or better yet, buy Orioles or Ravens tickets. For those of us who want to cheer for student athletes, 85 percent of whom graduate and two-thirds of whom

5

Warren Hartenstine is a Penn State graduate who played football for Coach Joe Paterno. The article appeared in the *Baltimore Sun* on November 2, 2013, in response to Marx's.

become professional and community leaders, yes, speak up for fairer allowances but stay true to the principles of the self discipline and dual success of those who actually pay a huge price to represent and succeed in your favorite institution of higher education.

Discussion Questions

1. Do you find Marx's argument in favor of paying student athletes convincing? Why, or why not?
2. How do you respond to both writers' comments about the high salaries paid to college coaches?
3. Short of paying college football players a salary, what change does Hartenstine suggest in how athletes are compensated?
4. Critique Hartenstine's argument. Do you find it more or less effective than Marx's? Why?
5. Do you personally feel that college athletes should be paid? Why, or why not?

Multiple VIEWPOINTS

The following section contains readings expressing a variety of viewpoints on six controversial questions. These questions generate conflict among experts and laypeople alike for two principal reasons. First, even when the facts are not in dispute, they may be interpreted differently. Second, and certainly more difficult to resolve, equally worthwhile values may be in conflict.

Multiple Viewpoints lends itself to classroom debates, both formal and informal. It can also serve as a useful source of informed opinions, which can lead to writing or to further research. The collection also provides opportunities to apply the concepts taught throughout this text.

- Consider how an Aristotelian approach can lend insight into the argument. Apply the terms *logos, ethos,* and *pathos.*
- Consider where authors have tried to establish **common ground,** as suggested by a **Rogerian** approach.
- Consider each piece in terms of **claim, support,** and **warrant,** and consider how these elements of argument can be used to compare or contrast different pieces.
- Consider the use of logic in each reading or visual and how logical **fallacies,** if any, detract from its message.
- Consider how language affects the way you read each piece.
- Consider how the selections as a whole give insight into the broader question raised in the chapter.

Social Networking

What Are the Consequences of Becoming an Online Society?

The impact of social networking is not to be confused with the impact of the World Wide Web. In the first of these essays, Alfredo Lopez argues that where the Web is expansive and freeing, social networks are restrictive and limiting. There are times, however, when young people need to limit what they reveal about themselves through social networking. It can be chilling to learn how much a social networking company can know about its users and who might gain access to that information. Parents are becoming aware of the dangers that too much of a presence on social networking sites can pose for their children. College students need to be aware that graduate schools and potential employers may look at online information about an applicant in addition to what is in a résumé. Both college and professional athletes' social networking is now usually monitored to be sure that "poor social media judgment" does not lead to "lost scholarships, lost endorsement deals, and lost fans" (see p. 497).

Are sites such as Facebook a place where the lonely can find a solution to their isolation, or do such sites merely remind them of just how alone they really are? Can a long list of online "friends" take the place of real-world contacts, or is it primarily those who make friends easily offline who do so online as well? For many people today, social networking sites have changed the dynamics of social interaction. They can enrich the social lives of those who use them, but they must be used with caution.

Social Networking and the Death of the Internet
ALFREDO LOPEZ

Before Reading: How do the Internet and social networking sites differ in purpose? Which offer the most potential benefit to humankind?

This summer, a team at the European Organization for Nuclear Research (CERN) has undertaken a remarkable project: to recreate the first Web site and the computer on which it was first seen.

It's a kind of birthday celebration. Twenty years ago, software developers at the University of Illinois released a Web browser called Mosaic in response to work being done at CERN. There, a group led by Tim Berners-Lee had developed a protocol (a set of rules governing communications between computers) that meshed two basic concepts: the ability to upload and store data files on the Internet and the ability of computers to do "hypertext," which converts specific words or groups of words into links to other files.

They called this new development the "World Wide Web."

When you read Berners-Lee's original proposal you get a feeling for the enthusiasm and optimism that drove this work, and since it's all very recent, the people who did it are still around to explain why. In interviews, Sir Tim (Berners-Lee is now a Knight) insists he could not foresee how powerful his new project would be but he knew it would make a difference. For the first time in history, people could communicate as much as they want with whomever they want wherever they want. That, as he argued in a recent article, is the reason why it's so critical to keep the Web neutral, uncontrolled, and devoid of corporate or government interference.

In our convoluted world of constantly flowing disinformation, governments tell us the Web is a "privilege" to be paid for and lost if we misbehave, corporations tell us they invented it, and most of us use it without really thinking much about its intent. Very few people view the World Wide Web as the revolutionary creation it actually is.

Whether its "creators" or the vast numbers of techies who continue to develop the Web think about it politically or not, there is an underlying understanding that unifies their efforts: the human race is capable of constructive exchange of information which will bring us knowledge all humans want and benefit from, and in collaborating on that knowledge we can search for the truth. There is nothing more revolutionary than that because the discovered truth is the firing pin of all revolution.

Twenty years later, it's painfully ironic that, when they hear the word "Internet," most people probably think of Social Networking programs like Facebook and Twitter. As ubiquitous and popular as Social Networking is, it represents a contradiction to the Internet that created it and to the World Wide Web on which it lives. It is the cyber version of a "laboratory controlled" microbe: it can be and frequently is productive, but if used unchecked and unconsciously, it can unleash enormous destruction, reversing the

5

Alfredo Lopez writes for the TCBH! (This Can't Be Happening!) news collective. He is a political activist, radical journalist, and founding member of the progressive Web-hosting media service MayFirst/PeopleLink. This piece appeared on counterpunch.org on May 8, 2013.

gains we've made with technology and divorcing us from its control.

That's a harsh picture, so some explanation is called for.

You may think the World Wide Web and the Internet are the same thing. They're not. The Web is to the Internet what a city is to human existence. The first can't live without the second; the second is extended by the first. But they are not, and never can be, the same.

10   The Internet is a system of communications comprised of billions of computers that connect to each other through telecommunications lines. It allows people to interact in different ways like email, file upload, chat, and, of course, the good old Web.

The Web is a function of the Internet, a kind of subset through which data files stored on a computer (called a "server") can be accessed and viewed by people using a special piece of software called a "browser." You're reading this with a browser, and your browser is reading this as a file on a server and translating it into what you see. To do that, it uses a protocol called "Hyper Text Transfer Protocol" or "http." That is what makes the Web special because it produces "hot links" that you can click on to go to any site or page the link creator wants you to. . . . You can keep clicking and deepen your knowledge, broaden your understanding, investigate other connected ideas, and get other perspectives on those ideas.

The World Wide Web puts the knowledge and experience of the entire human race at your disposal. With the Web, the human race has finally experienced world-wide collaboration. That, essentially, is the power unleashed by the event that took place twenty years ago.

We can debate the Internet's contribution to social struggle, but there is no question that the era of the Web has seen, among other things, the democratization of the previously dictator-dominated Latin America, the democratic struggles in Northern Africa, the ascendancy of Asian countries as world powers and the resulting democratic struggles those developments feed, and, of course, the intense social struggles in the United States that have led to scores of movements, the massive Occupy movement, and a black President (probably impossible before the Web).

Compare that to the year 1968, when every continent in the world was awash with resistance and mass movements — fearing a revolutionary over-throw, the government of France actually moved its offices to Germany — and when the culture and social norms of the United States were radically shifted by left-wing activism. Because much going on in the rest of the world was hidden by our corporate-controlled media, most of us in this country didn't realize it was happening. And so we thought we were all alone, and in that perceived isolation, we were not able to envision the next steps in a struggle to create a just world.

That will never happen again because we   15 now have the Internet. We can envision the next step and we are taking it all the time. The difference is that forty-five years ago, "we" were the people of the United States (or some other individual society). In today's Web era, "we" are the entire world.

"At the heart of the original web is technology to decentralize control and make access to information freely available to all," writes the BBC's superb technology and science writer Pallab Ghosh. "It is this architecture that seems to imbue those that work with the web with a culture of free expression, a belief in universal access and a tendency toward decentralizing information. It is the early technology's innate ability to subvert that makes re-creation of the first website especially interesting."

How does "Social Networking" jibe with that original intent? To a large extent, it doesn't.

Social Networking is a marketing term. It isn't a protocol. It uses nothing new, has added no new technological concepts. It is entirely based on the very same programming the Web has functioned on for two decades. In fact, Social Networking is nothing more than lots of people using some very large Web sites. But technology's importance isn't how it's built; it's how people use and perceive it.

People use it . . . a lot. Last year, over a billion people had Facebook accounts. Twitter routinely logs similar numbers. In short, each of these "services" draws half of all estimated Internet users. There is no question that, in terms of numbers and speed of development, Social Networking is the most successful project in Internet history.

20   Ironically, the key to Social Networking's success is a central part of the danger it poses.

Facebook—a group of linked pages on a giant Web site—is constraining and not very powerful. In order to use it, you have to use it the way they want you to, and that's not a whole lot of "using." But there is a comfort in having one's options limited, being able to use something without learning anything about it or making many choices about how you use it. That alluring convenience is a poisoned apple, however. You may not have to learn much about Facebook to use it, but the people who own Facebook sure learn a lot about you when you do.

Social Networking is, by its nature, a capture environment. The companies that offer the services, particularly Facebook, host your site and control all the information on it. When you think about what that information says about you, the control is disturbing. CNN writer Julianne Pepitone called Facebook "one of the most valuable data sets in existence: the social graph. It's a map of the connections between you and everyone you interact with."

Not only is your personal data on Facebook but the personal data of all the people you designate as "friends." In many cases, their photos are displayed (as are yours) showing their faces, the faces of those they come into contact with, and the places where the contact took place. There are also long strings of thoughts, comments, reports on what you're planning to do or what you did and who you did it with. A single Web page offers a profile of your life, your activities, and your thinking. What's more, because others "comment" on your Facebook pages in an informal gathering of like minds (or social contacts), those connections are condensed.

This amalgamation of information isn't evil in and of itself. In fact, it could be remarkably empowering. But the problem is that all of it is in the hands of one large company and that company owns it. It will use it in marketing studies and advertising profiles, and it will turn that information over to any government agency that asks for it. You have no control over that. It's in the user agreement. It's published and it's no longer yours. It belongs to Facebook and anybody Facebook wants to share it with.

If you want to try to alter what's presented   25 and how, you can't. One of the charms and strengths of the Web is your ability to design and organize your presentations on a Web site that can easily be unique—showing what you want to show and hiding what you don't, protecting contact with others through easily created Web forms and discussion boards that let people "hide" their real identities, controlling what you share with the world. That can't happen with Facebook.

Social Networking displays information about you as an individual while restraining your ability to contribute information and thinking about the rest of the world. In fact, its structure often makes that contribution more difficult.

With Twitter, for example, you have 140 characters to make your statement. How much thinking can you communicate in 140 characters? Twitter feels like a room in which a large number of people are shouting single sentences—a lot of noise, even a few ideas, but mainly just individualized statements bereft of context, knowledge, or the need to exchange perspectives with anyone. Facebook carries so many one-sentence statements that writing anything longer seems strange and even rude.

The incremental "take-over" of the Internet by these programs has one other, even more serious, impact: it's oppressing people, particularly young people, by repressing their thinking and communication, the very benefits the Web has given us.

The World Wide Web is a classroom without walls, a library in which a library card isn't needed. Its power of access to so much information is expanded by the Web's inclusion of you, and every other human being, as a source of information. We not only learn what others think and know from the Web, we are free and even encouraged to add our own viewpoint, knowledge, and experiences to that massive mix of information. By adding the hyper-link to this system, its developers have erased national boundaries, combated cultural exclusivism, bat-tered racism and sexism, smashed into human isolation, gone a long way toward combating ignorance, and expanded our ability to effectively write and communicate.

The seed in the struggle for freedom is the belief that you, as an individual, have value and that your life, as you live it, is of interest and importance to others. That's a message that is repressed in this oppressive society, and keeping that truth hidden is the key to continued oppression. There is nothing more liberating than realizing that your thinking and your experience can be shared with others and that others actually can benefit from it. The Web is the intellectual champion of individual human worth.

But that's not Facebook and it's not Twitter. There is simply no way one can share the complexity of one's thinking or the analysis of one's life in a one-paragraph Facebook message or a 140-character Tweet. For many young people, the encouraged reliance on these tools of communication, often to the exclusion of the Web's more abundant capabilities, reverses the impact the Web has had. Used alone, it makes communications shallow, a series of "references" to what the writer hopes others will understand. It is to real discussion what a wink of the eye and poke in the ribs is to honest and revealing communication.

Does Social Networking have a purpose? Absolutely. Some use it to refer to Web pages; it's an effective means of announcement. Some use it to "stay in touch" or tell others about something happening—as Arab Spring activists used it. It is unquestionably useful.

But those who profit from it push the idea that rather than a support for the rest of Internet communications, Social Networking is a substitute for those communications. That is

30

proving very attractive to hundreds of millions of young people, and it is increasingly damaging the potential of the World Wide Web for, among other things, real social change.

The debate over its use and impact will continue and my own opinion is certainly not the last word, but I know one thing. The people who first developed this marvel we call the World Wide Web didn't have Social Networking in mind. In fact, what they envisioned (a vision that has come to fruition) is fundamentally different from Social Networking, and people who want to change this world need to actively and vigilantly protect and preserve that difference.

Social Media: The Rock Star of Online Marketing

ZEPHORIA

Before Reading: When you use social media sites such as Facebook, are the ads and suggested posts you see well targeted to you? How likely are you to try a new product or service you see on these sites?

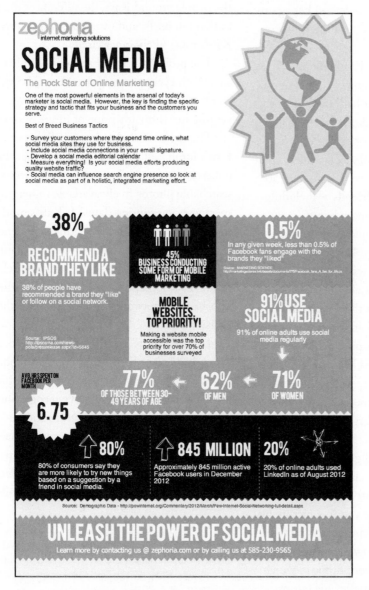

Dan Noyes/Zephoria, Inc.

Zephoria is an Internet marketing consulting company. This infographic appeared on its Web site, zephoria.com, in October 2013.

We Post Nothing about Our Daughter Online

AMY WEBB

Before Reading: What are the dangers, if any, of parents' posting pictures of and information about their children online?

Nothing. It's the only way to defend her against facial recognition, Facebook profiling, and corporate data mining.

I vividly remember the Facebook post. It was my friend's 5-year-old daughter "Kate" (a pseudonym) standing outside of her house in a bright yellow bikini, the street address clearly visible behind her on the front door. A caption read "Leaving for our annual Labor Day weekend at the beach," and beneath it were more than 50 likes and comments from friends — including many "friends" that Kate's mom barely knew.

The picture had been uploaded to a Facebook album, and there were 114 shots just of Kate: freshly cleaned and swaddled on the day of her birth . . . giving her Labradoodle a kiss . . . playing on a swing set. But there were also photos of her in a bathtub and an awkward moment posing in her mother's lacy pink bra.

I completely understood her parents' desire to capture Kate's everyday moments, because early childhood is so ephemeral. I also knew how those posts would affect Kate as an adult, and the broader impact of creating a generation of kids born into original digital sin.

5   Last week, Facebook updated its privacy policy again. It reads in part: "We are able to suggest that your friend tag you in a picture by scanning and comparing your friend's pictures to information we've put together from your profile pictures and the other photos in which you've been tagged." Essentially, this means that with each photo upload, Kate's parents are, unwittingly, helping Facebook to merge her digital and real worlds. Algorithms will analyze the people around Kate, the references made to them in posts, and over time will determine Kate's most likely inner circle.

The problem is that Facebook is only one site. With every status update, YouTube video, and birthday blog post, Kate's parents are preventing her from any hope of future anonymity.

That poses some obvious challenges for Kate's future self. It's hard enough to get through puberty. Why make hundreds of embarrassing, searchable photos freely available to her prospective homecoming dates? If Kate's mother writes about a negative parenting experience, could that affect her ability to get into a good college? We know that admissions counselors review Facebook profiles and a host of other websites and networks in order to make their decisions.

There's a more insidious problem, though, which will haunt Kate well into adulthood. Myriad applications, websites, and wearable technologies are relying on face recognition today, and ubiquitous bio-identification is only just getting started. In 2011, a group of hackers built an app that let you scan faces and immediately display their names and basic biographical details, right there on your mobile

Amy Webb is a columnist for *Slate*; the head of Webbmedia Group, a digital strategy agency; and the author of *Data, A Love Story* (2013). This article appeared on *Slate* on September 4, 2013.

phone. Already developers have made a working facial recognition API for Google Glass. While Google has forbidden official facial recognition apps, it can't prevent unofficial apps from launching. There's huge value in gaining real-time access to view detailed information about the people with whom we interact.

The easiest way to opt-out is to not create that digital content in the first place, especially for kids. Kate's parents haven't just uploaded one or two photos of her: They've created a trove of data that will enable algorithms to learn about her over time. Any hopes Kate may have had for true anonymity ended with that ballet class [her parents posted on] YouTube. . . .

10   Knowing what we do about how digital content and data are being cataloged, my husband and I made an important choice before our daughter was born. We decided that we would never post any photos or other personally identifying information about her online. Instead, we created a digital trust fund.

The process started in earnest as we were selecting her name. We'd narrowed the list down to a few alternatives and ran each (and their variants) through domain and keyword searches to see what was available. Next, we crawled through Google to see what content had been posted with those name combinations, and we also looked to see if a Gmail address was open.

We turned to KnowEm.com, a website I often rely on to search for usernames, even though the site is primarily intended as a brand registration service. We certainly had a front-runner for her name, but we would have chosen something different if the KnowEm results produced limited availability or if we found negative content associated with our selection.

With her name decided, we spent several hours registering her URL and a vast array of social media sites. All of that tied back to a single email account, which would act as a primary access key. We listed my permanent email address as a secondary—just as you'd fill out financial paperwork for a minor at a bank. We built a password management system for her to store all of her login information.

On the day of her birth, our daughter already had accounts at Facebook, Twitter, Instagram, and even Github. And to this day, we've never posted any content.

15   All accounts are kept active but private. We also regularly scour the networks of our friends and family and remove any tags. Those who know us well understand and respect our "no posts about the kid" rule.

When we think she's mature enough (an important distinction from her being technically old enough), we'll hand her an envelope with her master password inside. She'll have the opportunity to start cashing in parts of her digital identity, and we'll ensure that she's making informed decisions about what's appropriate to reveal about herself, and to whom.

It's inevitable that our daughter will become a public figure, because we're all public figures in this new digital age. I adore Kate's parents, and they're raising her to be an amazing young woman. But they're essentially robbing her of a digital adulthood that's free of bias and presupposition.

Facebook Makes Us Sadder and Less Satisfied, Study Finds
ELISE HU

Before Reading: If you have a Facebook account, what emotional effects does posting and reading posts have on you? If not, why do you choose not to?

Facebook's mission "to make the world more open and connected" is a familiar refrain among company leaders. But the latest research shows connecting 1.1 billion users around the world may come at a psychological cost.

A new University of Michigan study on college-aged adults finds that the more they used Facebook, the worse they felt. The study, published in the journal *PLOS One,* found Facebook use led to declines in moment-to-moment happiness and overall life satisfaction.

"There's a huge amount of interest . . . because Facebook is so widespread," says research co-author John Jonides, a University of Michigan cognitive neuroscientist. "With something like half a billion people who use Facebook every day, understanding the consequences of that use on our well being is of critical importance."

Researchers tested the variables of happiness and satisfaction in real time on 82 participants. The researchers text-messaged them five times a day for two weeks to examine how Facebook use influenced how they felt. Participants responded to questions about loneliness, anxiety, and general emotional well-being.

5   The study authors did not get at the reasons Facebook made their test subjects feel glum. But Jonides suspects it may have to do with social comparison.

"When you're on a site like Facebook, you get lots of posts about what people are doing. That sets up social comparison — you maybe feel your life is not as full and rich as those people you see on Facebook," he says.

Interestingly, Jonides notes, the study found the effects of Facebook are most pronounced for those who socialize the most "in real life." He says the folks who did the most direct, face-to-face socializing and used social media were the ones who reported the most Facebook-related mood decline.

"It suggests that when you are engaging in social interactions a lot, you're more aware of what others are doing and, consequently, you might be more sensitized about what's happening on Facebook and comparing that to your own life," Jonides says.

The researchers also tested and discounted other reasons for our unhappiness. The University of Michigan notes:

> "[Researchers] also found no evidence for two alternative possible explanations for the finding that Facebook undermines happiness. People were *not* more likely to use Facebook when they felt bad. In addition, although people were more likely to use Facebook when they were lonely, loneliness and Facebook use both independently predicted how happy participants subsequently felt. 'Thus, it was not the case that Facebook use served as a proxy for feeling bad or lonely,' says [lead author Ethan] Kross."

Elise Hu is an NPR reporter who covers technology and culture. Her article was posted to npr.org on August 20, 2013.

10   We reached out to Facebook for a response, but got an automatic reply. These findings, however, add data points in our quest to understand Facebook and other social media's effect on our emotional well-being, whether it's the behemoth social network's role after relationships end or our feelings of regret after pressing "share."

If you're feeling bummed, researchers did test for and find a solution. The prescription for Facebook despair is less Facebook. Researchers found that face-to-face or phone interaction—those outmoded, analog ways of communication—had the opposite effect. Direct interactions with other human beings led people to feel better.

Online Lives, Offline Consequences: Professionalism, Information Ethics, and Professional Students
ISAAC GILMAN

Before Reading: How could what college students post online now affect their ability to get into graduate school or professional school in the future or to get a job?

Introduction

The growth of the Internet over the past decade has made many tasks and personal interactions easier and faster. Students who have never experienced higher education without Google take for granted their ability to access information and entertainment at the click of a mouse and to live online lives unimpeded by anything except modem speed. For students enrolled in professional graduate programs (e.g. medicine, law, education), it is inevitable that their online experiences will shape their understanding of what is appropriate and what is ethical—which could have unanticipated professional consequences. To ensure that students' behaviors do not jeopardize their future careers, educators must understand the online activities that present ethical and professional issues and make every effort to educate students about appropriate behavior and interactions in an online environment (Gardner; Workman).

Academic Honesty and Information Ethics

For educators, perhaps the most familiar ethical issue facing students is that of academic honesty. For today's Internet-savvy students, who have become accustomed to cutting and pasting information on the fly with little attention to citations, the opportunity to use "free" online information is often too tempting to refuse. Studies over the past ten to fifteen years have confirmed that the ease of the Internet has exacerbated the misuse of others' intellectual property (Auer and Krupar; Szabo and Underwood 180). In an "open" online environment, there is no accountability for those who may inappropriately provide/use others' work. Thanks to the speed of cut-and-paste, there is also little time for students to even consider whether or not their use is ethical (Bodi 459). Even for students

Isaac Gilman is the Scholarly Communications and Research Services Librarian and Assistant Professor at Pacific University in Oregon, where he has helped graduate students and the university as a whole understand the ethics of copyright and intellectual property. This article appeared in the January–February 2009 issue of *Interface,* the electronic journal of the Berglund Center for Internet Studies at Pacific University.

who do stop to consider their actions, one study found that the majority of students "would give in to Internet plagiarism under the right combination of situational and personal factors" (Szabo and Underwood 196).

As familiar (and frustrated) as educators are with the unethical use of intellectual property, students are even more familiar with faculty lectures condemning the same. Honor codes, lectures on paper mills, and the evils of plagiarism—even the use of plagiarism detection services like Turnitin.com—have largely failed to make a lasting impression on students who do not recognize the seriousness of the issue (Harris 4). For many students, like 380 undergraduates surveyed about downloading copyrighted content, the use/misuse of others' intellectual property is still seen as a "victimless crime" (Siemens and Kopp 118). Indeed, for undergraduate students who believe that anything accessible is free, who do not anticipate publishing a journal article, and who may never depend on a scholarly or professional reputation, it can be difficult to convey the significance of academic honesty.

However, for graduate students who may one day contribute to the professional literature, creating ethical habits for the use of others' intellectual property is of the utmost significance. Whether these students go on to become academics or practitioners, their scholarly record and actions will likely contribute to their reputation and career prospects, for better or worse. Works created as students may also persist for years if posted online (as is the case with many theses, dissertations, and other culminating projects), and it is vital that students understand from the beginning of their programs not only how to avoid plagiarism but also how to ethically—and legally—use copyrighted materials.

Social Networking and Professionalism

Though both educators and students are largely familiar with the issues of plagiarism and academic honesty, it is an entirely new issue that poses the greatest threat to students' professionalism—and one that has, on its face, nothing to do with students' academic performance or professional aspirations.

Over the past decade, the social/communication possibilities on the World Wide Web have grown exponentially, with one of the most notable developments being the creation of social networking sites—MySpace, Facebook, et al. As with many technologies, students were early (and fervent) adopters, with Facebook the popular choice of nearly 80–90 percent of United States college students (Educause). Profiles on social networking sites like Facebook allow students to communicate with friends, share photos and videos, and connect with people with similar interests. For students, their online profiles and communities are as personal as their offline friendships and interactions—and, often, are an extension of their offline activities, with Facebook used as a collaborative event planner and photo album.

While social networking sites and the Web connect students to one another, another connection is created that students may not anticipate (or enjoy). With student photos, blogs, comments, and affiliations publicly available online (unless privacy settings are adjusted by the student), the digital world has removed the divide between "personal and professional identities" (Thompson et al. 954). Students'

5

(and employees') professionalism and fitness is no longer judged solely on their academic and on-the-job performance, but on their very public personal personas. Newspapers, blogs, and academic reports from the past five years are filled with stories of schools and employers who have begun accessing social networking profiles looking for any untoward information as a means of evaluation/investigation (Capriccioso; Epstein; Steinbach and Deavers; Vorster; Wilson; Read; Thomas; Bergstrom). New online services are dedicated to digging up digital dirt on prospective employees, with the promising of "automat[ing] candidate research across forty-one social networks" (Spokeo).

The blurring of the line between personal and professional identities is an important issue for any student or employee, but particularly so for those in professional fields wherein public perception of professional competence and appropriate separating from patients, clients, or students are vital. Though there is nothing inherently unethical about the use of social networking sites, publicly sharing unprofessional content (e.g., explicit or inappropriate comments/photos) or excessive personal information may be compromising for professionals. Educators and researchers from medical, law, education, and pharmacy schools have all expressed concern that professional students may not understand the consequences of their online activities, or the risk of their personal offline activities being made public online by others (Thompson et al.; Cain; Farnan et al.; Mangan).

Research and anecdotal evidence suggest that professional students either do not share educators' concerns or are not aware that their online lives could have any bearing on their pro-

fessionalism. In a recent study at the University of Florida, only 37.5 percent (n=362) of medical students and residents had private (viewable only by designated friends) Facebook profiles. The same study found that, in a small sample of students with public profiles (n=10), 70 percent of the students had photographs of themselves with alcohol and 30 percent had pictures or videos that showed "drunkenness, overt sexuality, foul language and patient privacy violations in non-U.S. locations" (Thompson et al. 955–56). Students in the study also belonged to Facebook groups with highly unprofessional names; e.g., "I don't need sex cause grad school f**ks me every day," "Party of Important Male Physicians (PIMP)," "Physicians look for trophy wives in training" (Ferdig et al.). There is also evidence to suggest that current undergraduates (and future professional students) share the same lack of concern and awareness. In a separate study by the same researchers at the University of Florida, researchers analyzed Facebook profiles of three hundred elementary education majors. Of the students with public profiles, 75 percent listed their sexual orientation and 73 percent had personal photo albums available (Univ. of Florida). A 2005 study by researchers at Carnegie Mellon University (CMU), determined that less than 1 percent of CMU Facebook users (n=4,450; a mix of students and faculty) had changed their default privacy settings to limit the visibility of their profiles (Gross and Acquisti). An informal online survey by the Pacific *Index*, the student newspaper at Pacific University (Oregon), found that 33 percent of respondents believed they would never get in trouble for photos posted on Facebook, while 17 percent were "not going to worry about what people think of my personal life" ("Do You Post"). Comments made in a thread started by a prospective pharmacy student on an online message board confirm all of these findings:

> mrsengle: "Pharmacists are in such high demand, employers put up with a LOT. As long as you have a license, don't have a DUI or possessions charge, have a degree and a pulse, you shouldn't worry about them checking an old myspace [sic] page" ("Grad schools/employers").

YouTube and Beyond

10   Unprofessional content posted on Facebook is not the only area of online concern for professional educators. Other venues for sharing personal (and/or unprofessional) material include blogs and video sharing sites such as YouTube. In one recent case, medical students posted a musical parody they had filmed on YouTube, which featured the students "dancing in the anatomy lab," "drinking 'blood' (actually chocolate) from plastic skulls," and "lying inside body bags" (Farnan et al. 518). The video was subsequently removed from YouTube at the request of the dean of the medical school (Farnan et al. 520).

The medical students' YouTube video illustrates an important reason for addressing online professionalism with professional students: There are notable differences between generations regarding what is/is not humorous, acceptable, and appropriate. As one educator has observed, "[w]hat looks like plagiarism, slander, copyright infringement, and embarrassing public behavior is for many students just creative and social entertainment" (Workman). While many students are beginning to understand that their personal behavior is reflective on their professional identities (Young), some still have

not made the connection, or even believe that what they are doing—and posting online—has the possibility of offending anyone.

Whether or not students believe that their online activities should have any relevance to their academic and professional lives, it is growing increasingly clear that students' online personalities will be at issue for schools, employers, and other professionals. There has been a call for lawyers' bar applications to include the "cyber equivalent" of a background check (Stellato), and in an unprecedented move, applicants who wished to work in President Barack Obama's administration were required to complete a background check that included the following requests:

- "Please list [. . .] any posts or comments on blogs or other websites you have authored, individually or with others. Please list all aliases or 'handles' you have used to communicate on the Internet."
- "If you have ever sent an electronic communication, including but not limited to an email, text message or instant message, that could suggest a conflict of interest or be a possible source of embarrassment to you, your family, or the President-Elect if it were made public, please describe."
- "Please provide the URL address of any websites that feature you in either a personal or professional capacity (e.g., Facebook, MySpace, etc.)." (Obama-Biden Transition)

Conclusion

Professional students must understand the implications of their online activities and the importance of extending professionalism to their online lives. To convey this understanding, there should be comprehensive instruction provided for all professional students that addresses the issues of intellectual property, plagiarism, social networking, blogging, personal Web sites, e-mail etiquette, etc. Individual workshops do already exist (Mangan), but to be the most effective, this instruction should be either integrated into program curriculum or made a required elective, and must be closely tied to the relevant professional association's code of ethics/conduct.

"E-literacy" (incorporating information ethics and online behavior standards) should be treated as a necessary competency for students to achieve, much like any other required knowledge/skills they receive in the course of their programs. Above all else, e-literacy instruction must help students realize that their online actions are not segregated from their professional lives, that their offline lives can easily end up online, and that anything posted on the Internet will persist long after it is removed. The guiding question for professional students should be, "Would it be appropriate for my mother/employer/patient/client to see what I am about to post?" (Keenan). Because if they have a computer and an Internet connection, they probably will.

WORKS CITED

Auer, Nicole J., and Ellen M. Krupar. "Mouse Click Plagiarism: The Role of Technology in Plagiarism and the Librarian's Role in Combating It." *Library Trends* 49.3 (2001). Print.

Bergstrom. Ida. "Facebook can ruin your life. And so can MySpace, Bebo . . ." *The Independent,* 10 February 2008. Web. 6 May 2008.

Bodi, Sonia. "Ethics and Information Technology: Some Principles to Guide Students." *The Journal of Academic Librarianship* 24.6 (1998): 459. Print.

Cain, Jeff. "Online Social Networking Issues within Academia and Pharmacy Education." *American Journal of Pharmaceutical Education* 72.1 (1998). Print.

Capriccioso, R. 2006. "Facebook Face Off." *Inside Higher Ed,* 14 February 2006. Web. 10 January 2009.

"Do you post photos on your Facebook that could possibly get you in trouble?" Poll. *The Pacific Index,* 2008. Web. 6 May 2008.

Educause. 7 things you should know about Facebook II. *Educause Learning Initiative,* 2007. Web. 10 January 2009.

Epstein, D. 2003. "Cleaning Up Their Online Acts." *Inside Higher Ed,* 3 October 2003. Web. 10 January 2009.

Farnan, Jeanne M., John A. M. Paro, Jennifer Higa, Jay Edelson, and Vineet M. Arora. "The YouTube Generation: Implications for Medical Professionalism." *Perspectives in Biology and Medicine* 51.4 (2008). Print.

Ferdig, Richard E., Kara Dawson, Erik W. Black, Nicole M. Paradise Black, and Lindsay A. Thompson. "Medical students' and residents' use of online social networking tools: Implications for teaching professionalism in medical education." *First Monday* 13.9 (2008). Web. 12 October 2008.

Gardner, Stephanie F. 2006. "Preparing for the Nexters." *American Journal of Pharmaceutical Education* 70(4): Article 87. Print.

"Grad schools/employers and Facebook/Myspace." Online bulletin board. *City-Data.com,* posted 26 July 2007. Web. 6 May 2008.

Gross, Ralph, and Alessandro Acquisti. "Information Revelation and Privacy in Online Social Networks (the Facebook case) [Pre-proceedings version]." *ACM Workshop on Privacy in the Electronic Society* (WPES), 2005. Print.

Harris, Benjamin R. "Credit Where Credit Is Due: Considering Ethics, Ethos, and Process in Library Instruction on Attribution." *Education Libraries* 28.1 (2005): 4. Print.

Keenan, T. P. "On the Internet, Things Never Go Away Completely," in *IFIP International Federation for Information Processing*, Vol. 262 (The Future of Identity in the Information Society). Eds. Simone Fischer-Hubner, Penny Duquenoy, Albin Zuccato, and Leonardo Marctucci. Boston: Springer, 2008. Print.

Mangan, Katherine. 2007. "Etiquette for the Bar." *The Chronicle of Higher Education,* 12 January 2007. Web. 5 December 2008.

Obama-Biden Transition Project. "Background Check Questionnaire." 2008. Web. 4 January 2009.

Read, Brock. "A MySpace Photo Costs a Student a Teaching Certificate." *The Chronicle of Higher Education,* 27 April 2007. Print.

Siemens, Jennifer C., and Steven W. Kopp. "Teaching Ethical Copyright Behavior: Assessing the Effects of a University-Sponsored Computing Ethics Program." *NASPA Journal* 43.4 (2006): 118. Print.

Spokeo Inc. Web. 2 November 2008. <http://www.spokeo.com/hr/>

Steinbach, Sheldon, and Lynn Deavers. "The Brave New World of MySpace and Facebook." *Inside Higher Ed,* 3 April 2007. Print.

Stellato, Jesse. "e-Ethics: Professional Responsibility of Law Students on the Internet." *Eagleionline,* 18 October 2007. Web. 5 January 2009.

Szabo, Attila, and Jean Underwood. "Cybercheats: Is Information and Communication Technology Fuelling Academic Dishonesty?" *Active Learning in Higher Education* 5.2 (2004): 180.

Thomas, Owen. "Bank Intern Busted by Facebook." *Your Privacy Is an Illusion* (blog), 12 November 2007. Web. 6 May 2008.

Thompson, Lindsay A., Kara Dawson, Richard Ferdig, Erik W. Black, J. Boyer, Jade Coutts, and Nicole Paradise Black. "The Intersection of Online Social Networking with Medical Professionalism." *Journal of General Internal Medicine* 23.7 (2008): 954. Web. 6 May 2008.

University of Florida College of Education. "UF Study Looks at Preservice Teachers' Facebook Entries." Web. 4 January 2009. <http://www.heinz.cmu.edu/~acquisti/papers/privacy-facebookgross-acquisti.pdf>

Vorster, Gareth. "Online social networking sites could have a negative impact on your career progression, new research has found." *Personnel Today,* 4 February 2008. Web. 6 May 2008.

Wilson, Erin. 2008. "Facebook Professionalism and Privacy." Blog. *UNI Journalism,* 6 May 2008. Web. 24 November 2008.

Workman, Thomas A. "The Real Impact of Virtual Worlds." *The Chronicle of Higher Education,* 19 September 2008. Web. 16 October 2008.

Young, Jeffrey R. "Educause Survey Shows Students Watch Their Privacy on Facebook." *The Chronicle of Higher Education,* 12 June 2008. Web. 13 June 2008.

Watch That Tweet! Monitoring of Student Athletes' Social Media

JOHN G. BROWNING

Before Reading: Why would college or professional sports organizations want to monitor athletes' social media use?

Facebook, Twitter, and other social media platforms have forever changed the landscape of communications and information sharing. Over 65 percent of all adult Americans have some kind of social media presence, with over a billion people on Facebook worldwide and over 340 million tweets every day. Modern sports have embraced social networking as well, providing athletes with a means of sharing with family, friends, and fans worldwide.

But as a plethora of incidents with athletes at every level has shown, exercising poor social media judgment can lead to lost scholarships, lost endorsement deals, and lost fans (witness U.S. Olympic hurdler Lolo Jones and her tweets about "shooting sports" after the Aurora, Colorado, massacre). To protect their brands, virtually every major sports league and governing body now imposes rules on the use of social media by its athletes.

Nowhere was this more evident than during the 2012 London Olympics, dubbed by some sportswriters as "the first social media Olympics." While the London Games marked the first time Olympic athletes and volunteers were given clearance to post, tweet, and blog during competition, both the International Olympic Committee and the U.S. Olympic Committee imposed sometimes draconian-sounding rules in an effort to protect valuable sponsors. The IOC issued a 4-page set of comprehensive guidelines aimed at protecting the Olympic brand and protecting official sponsors who had paid for the right to be associated with the Olympics.

Heightened regulation and monitoring of amateur athletes' social media activities has taken on new meaning at the collegiate level, where the NCAA already regulates the use of social media in recruiting. In an era in which big-time football or basketball programs can generate tens of millions of dollars in annual revenue through ticket sales, lucrative TV contracts, and licensing apparel, colleges and universities are protecting both a valuable brand and the school's reputation by policing the social media musings of student athletes. For some this may take the form of coach-imposed restrictions or a broad social media policy that applies to all students, but a growing number of universities are turning to third-party vendors to monitor the social media accounts of student athletes. The vendors use proprietary technology to scan and filter for key words that might point to discussion of drug or alcohol use, offensive comments, or references to potential NCAA violations. The student athletes are required to install the monitoring software, and the monitoring vendors report any flagged content to a coach or compliance official within the athletic department.

John G. Browning is a partner at the law firm Lewis Brisbois Bisgaard & Smith. This article appeared in January 2013 on dallasbar.org, a resource of the Dallas Bar Association.

5   Such monitoring raises a host of legal issues. First, putting the university in charge of what words warrant a red flag can be problematic. Two universities recently got in trouble when it was learned that, in addition to filtering for references to drugs, agents, and cheating, their 400 or so word list included words and phrases like "Arab," "Muslim," and "gay." Monitoring also violates most social networking sites' terms of service. Facebook, for example, explicitly forbids a user from sharing his password with a third party. In addition, the practice could lead to unanticipated civil liability. The family of Yeardley Love, the University of Virginia women's lacrosse player who was murdered by her ex-boyfriend (a member of the men's lacrosse team), is suing athletic department officials for $30 million in a negligence suit alleging that they ignored previous violent behavior of her attacker and other warning signs.

Besides such civil liability exposure, there are also constitutional issues. The landmark case *Tinker v. Des Moines Independent Community School District* made it clear that students do not leave their First Amendment rights at the schoolhouse door. Although courts have justified certain invasions of a student-athlete's Fourth Amendment rights in cases involving random drug testing, recent decisions in the digital age have protected a student's right to expression via social media. In addition to these constitutional concerns, a number of states have passed or are considering laws forbidding schools from requesting or requiring login information or from installing monitoring software. California and Delaware were the first states to adopt such laws, and they will not be the last.

The NCAA made it clear that a school would only have a duty to monitor social networking sites if it had some reasonable suspicion of rules violations, saying that the NCAA "declines to impose a blanket duty on institutions to monitor social networking sites."

While it is true that universities have both reputations and tangible investments at stake in their athletic programs, student-athletes are still students first and foremost and, as such, they have rights. Instead of undermining constitutional protections, risking civil liability, or potentially violating privacy laws, colleges concerned about social media fallout should focus on what they do best by educating student-athletes about the dangers of misusing social media.

Thinking and Writing about the Consequences of Social Networking

1. According to Alfredo Lopez, how is social networking at odds with the original intent of the World Wide Web?
2. In what sense is the take-over of the Internet by social networking sites oppressing people, especially young people?
3. Review the social media post "'Peaceful' Act of Compassion" in Chapter 3 (pp. 96–97). In what ways does this selection refute Lopez's claim?
4. After examining the infographic for Zephoria, what are some of the conclusions you can draw about social media as marketing sites?
5. In what ways does the Zephoria infographic support or contradict Lopez's argument?
6. Do you feel that Amy Webb and her husband are justified in going to the lengths they have to control their daughter's online identity? Why, or why not?
7. Is your experience with Facebook or another social networking site consistent with what Hu reports? Explain.
8. What should undergraduate students—and even younger students—do now to protect themselves from the type of future problems that Isaac Gilman predicts?
9. What is your response to Gilman's statements that admissions officers and potential employers use social networking sites to make decisions about applicants?
10. What are some of the other dangers associated with social networking?
11. What is your opinion about the monitoring of college athletes' social media use, sometimes by an outside vendor?
12. According to John G. Browning, what are some of the legal problems related to the monitoring of athletes' social media use?
13. What does Browning feel would be a better solution to athletes' misuse of social media?
14. What changes in social networking do you foresee in the next five years?
15. Choose one of the essays in this chapter, and explain to what extent your own experience with social networking either supports or contradicts its claim.

Violence on Campus

How Far Will We Go to Keep Our Schools Safe?

In the wake of the tragic school shootings in Newtown, Connecticut, in December 2012, some politicians argued that such a time was not the right time to make decisions about gun control. The assumption was that emotions were running too high and that it would be too easy to let what had just happened sway legislators' judgment. The suggestion was that advocates of gun control would be unfairly using emotional appeal to advance their cause. Opponents to this view hold that there is actually no better time to hear proposals for making our schools safer than when we have just seen how vulnerable students in our classrooms can be.

The shootings led to debates not only about gun control legislation but also about other ways to prevent similar disasters from happening in the future. Some people support arming teachers and administrators. Others advocate instituting the use of armed guards. Still others argue that the solution is to recognize those disturbed few who may become shooters before they ever pick up a gun.

Unfortunately, these rare instances of mass murder are not the only times when violence is a problem in our schools. On a daily basis, there are teachers who live in fear of violence from their students and students who live in fear of being bullied by other students.

How far will we go to keep our schools safe? All sides in the controversy agree that every student and every teacher should be safe at school and feel safe at school. The following viewpoints on the subject show just how much disagreement there is about how to achieve that goal.

What Should America Do about Gun Violence?

WAYNE LaPIERRE

Before Reading: What do you know or assume about the National Rifle Association's response to America's school shootings?

It's an honor to be here today on behalf of more than 4.5 million moms and dads and sons and daughters, in every state across our nation, who make up the National Rifle Association of America. Those 4.5 million active members are joined by tens of millions of NRA supporters.

And it's on behalf of those millions of decent, hardworking, law-abiding citizens . . . to give voice to their concerns . . . that I'm here today.

The title of today's hearing is "What should America do about gun violence?"

We believe the answer to that question is to be honest about what works — and what doesn't work.

5   Teaching safe and responsible gun ownership works — and the NRA has a long and proud history of teaching it.

Our "Eddie Eagle" children's safety program has taught over 25 million young children that if they see a gun, they should do four things: "Stop. Don't touch. Leave the area. Tell an adult." As a result of this and other private sector programs, fatal firearm accidents are at the lowest levels in more than 100 years.[1]

The NRA has over 80,000 certified instructors who teach our military personnel, law enforcement officers, and hundreds of thousands of other American men and women how to safely use firearms. We do more — and spend more — than anyone else on teaching safe and responsible gun ownership.

We joined the nation in sorrow over the tragedy that occurred in Newtown, Connecticut. There is nothing more precious than our children. We have no more sacred duty than to protect our children and keep them safe. That's why we asked former Congressman and Undersecretary of Homeland Security, Asa Hutchison, to bring in every expert available to develop a model School Shield Program — one that can be individually tailored to make our schools as safe as possible.

It's time to throw an immediate blanket of security around our children. About a third of our schools have armed security already — because it works.[2] And that number is growing. Right now, state officials, local authorities, and school districts in all 50 states are considering their own plans to protect children in their schools.

10   In addition, we need to enforce the thousands of gun laws that are currently on the books. Prosecuting criminals who misuse

Wayne LaPierre has served as the Executive Vice President and CEO of the National Rifle Association since 1991. His remarks were made before the Senate Judiciary Committee on January 30, 2013, following the Newtown, Connecticut, school shootings on December 14, 2012.

[1] Pre-1981 data from National Safety Council, Accident Facts (annual); 1981 foreword from Centers for Disease Control and Prevention, available at www.cdc.gov/injury /wisqars/fatal_injury_reports.html.

[2] Gary Fields et al., "NRA Calls for Arms in School," *Wall Street Journal*, Dec. 22, 2012, available at http://online.wsj .com/article/SB100014241278873244616045781933642 01364432.html.

firearms works. Unfortunately, we've seen a dramatic collapse in federal gun prosecutions in recent years. Overall in 2011, federal weapons prosecutions per capita were down 35 percent from their peak in the previous administration.[3] That means violent felons, gang members, and the mentally ill who possess firearms are not being prosecuted. And that's unacceptable.

And out of more than 76,000 firearms purchases denied by the federal instant check system, only 62 were referred for prosecution and only 44 were actually prosecuted.[4] Proposing more gun control laws—while failing to enforce the thousands we already have—is not a serious solution to reducing crime.

I think we can also agree that our mental health system is broken. We need to look at the full range of mental health issues, from early detection and treatment, to civil commitment laws, to privacy laws that needlessly prevent mental health records from being included in the National Instant Criminal Background Check System.

While we're ready to participate in a meaningful effort to solve these pressing problems, we must respectfully—but honestly and firmly—disagree with some members of this committee, many in the media, and all of the gun control groups on what will keep our kids and our streets safe.

Law-abiding gun owners will not accept blame for the acts of violent or deranged criminals. Nor do we believe the government should dictate what we can lawfully own and use to protect our families.

As I said earlier, we need to be honest about what works and what does not work. Proposals that would only serve to burden the law-abiding have failed in the past and will fail in the future.

Semi-automatic firearms have been around for over 100 years. They are among the most popular guns made for hunting, target shooting, and self-defense. Despite this fact, Congress banned the manufacture and sale of hundreds of semi-automatic firearms and magazines from 1994 to 2004. Independent studies, including a study from the Clinton Justice Department, proved that ban had no impact on lowering crime.[5]

And when it comes to the issue of background checks, let's be honest—background checks will never be "universal"—because criminals will never submit to them.

But there are things that can be done and we ask you to join with us. The NRA is made up of millions of Americans who support what works . . . the immediate protection for all—not just some—of our school children; swift, certain prosecution of criminals with guns; and fixing our broken mental health system.

We love our families and our country. We believe in our freedom. We're the millions of Americans from all walks of life who take responsibility for our own safety and protection as a God-given, fundamental right.

---

[3] Calculated from U.S. Department of Justice data available through Transactional Records Access Clearinghouse, http://tracfed.syr.edu.
[4] Ronald J. Frandsen, "Enforcement of the Brady Act, 2010: Federal and State Investigations and Prosecutions of Firearm Applicants Denied by a NICS Check in 2010," available at www.ncjrs.gov/pdffiles1/bjs/grants/239272.pdf.
[5] Jeffrey A. Roth & Christopher S. Koper, "Impact Evaluation of the Public Safety and Recreational Firearms Use Protection Act of 1994," (1997), available at www.sas.upenn.edu/jerrylee/research/aw_ban.htm.

Totally Safe Schools

PAT BAGLEY

Before Reading: How do you think schools have changed, if at all, in response to the threat of violence against students and faculty?

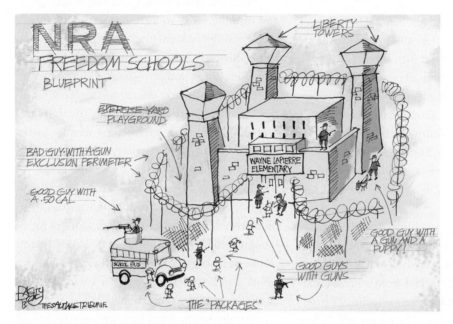

PoliticalCartoons.com/Pat Bagley

Pat Bagley is a cartoonist for the *Salt Lake Tribune*. This cartoon appeared on April 4, 2013.

Arming Teachers: A Terrible, Horrible, No Good, Very Bad Idea

M. D. ANDERSON

Before Reading: Do you believe that arming teachers is the way to protect students from violence? Why, or why not?

The unthinkable tragedy at Sandy Hook Elementary School left us all horrified with an uneasy feeling of vulnerability. Predictably, as we wrestle with questions about why and how something so gruesome and incomprehensible could happen, some reactions have been strong and swift: more gun control, better access to mental health services. Some have been feeble: curtailing violent movies and video games. And well, some can only be described as downright lunacy.

I readily admit, I hate guns. And the recent happening in Newtown has aggravated my feelings in this area. The tragedy also has me thinking a lot about teachers. Not from an academic point of view, but in the visceral feelings I have for teachers I have loved. There were only a few but they all had the same qualities in common: Patience. Compassion. Understanding. Passion.

Strangely enough, I don't recall any of them having the reflexes of a marksman able to shoot the spots off of a ladybug a mile away. Not exactly the most endearing quality a teacher can possess. But then, I graduated school before crazy became the new normal. Before the gun-rights cabal spied an opportunity to push its pro-gun agenda on schools, and gun manufacturers saw a chance to rake in fear-laden cash.

It kicked off with the benevolent NRA calling to arm teachers and other school officials. Of course, the nation's largest gun lobby is a true friend of public education—that's why it bankrolls a conservative group like ALEC aimed at defunding and dismantling public schools.

With the NRA edict, gun zealots were off and running, eager to turn the nation's teachers into gunslingers: launching a test program in tactical firearms training; offering free concealed weapons classes; and providing an "intensive three-day class" where educators can learn tactics "used by first responders." Silly me thinking law enforcement was a trained profession. Little did I know patrolling the playground was preparation for taking down a gun-wielding perp.

But what good is training if pistol-packing teachers are prohibited from bringing guns onto school property. Enter NRA acolytes in Congress, state legislatures, and governors' mansions—a smorgasbord of gun advocates who'd rather arm teachers than whisper a word about common-sense gun control.

Arming teachers is a knee-jerk reaction fueled by the absurd fantasy that armed civilians can stop a mass murderer. They can't. But they very well might get themselves killed or put bystanders in danger. In a classroom, that means someone's child!

With right-wing hysteria in full bloom, it's really easy to lose sight of who isn't crying out to turn schools into the OK Corral: local school districts, PTAs, and teachers themselves. I boldly deduce that the steely resolve to kill another human being may not be programmed

5

M. D. Anderson writes for borderlessnewsandviews.com, where this article appeared on January 9, 2013.

into someone who has just wiped a first-grader's snotty nose or asked a class of fidgety 8-year-olds to put on their listening ears.

The NRA and gun zealots push guns like a crack dealer, cloaking themselves in drivel about "freedom" in a country where there are more gun dealers than grocery stores. We can't allow their ridiculous arguments to go unchallenged any longer. They have shown themselves to be radical, tone-deaf, and, ultimately, more interested in gun sales than human lives.

Basically, they want to feel powerful. And 10 that is hardly sufficient justification for putting our kids at risk.

Teachers Packing Heat
BALTIMORE SUN

Before Reading: What does the National Rifle Association propose in response to recent incidents of school violence? Do you agree with their proposals? Why, or why not?

It is easy to dismiss the report released Tuesday by the National Rifle Association–financed school safety task force as nothing but an effort to change the topic from the broader issue of gun violence or especially gun control (even the watered-down stuff that's still alive in the U.S. Senate). But that would be a mistake, as it's really much worse than that.

Granted, much of the "National School Shield" report is pretty benign stuff about the need to make security assessments of schools and coordinate with local law enforcement agencies how best to respond to security threats. Most school systems are likely already engaged in such efforts—if they weren't long before the massacre in Newtown—and it's hard to argue with any of it. If the organization wants to help finance further studies of how best to evaluate school safety threats, closed circuit cameras, or buzz-in entry systems, or assess pre-incident "indicators" or judge a student body's mental health "climate," well, more power to them.

But what a good chunk of the report also does is pick up the line of reasoning voiced so outrageously by the NRA's Wayne LaPierre last year in the wake of the Connecticut shooting. What's needed, the report's authors argue, is sufficient training so that teachers and other school staff can carry firearms in school.

While that doesn't precisely echo Mr. LaPierre, who envisioned armed volunteers (a so-called "good guy with a gun") recruited off the streets to hang out in school buildings, it does embrace the central premise that the more guns, the better. And while 40-to-60 hours of training won't make the gym teacher a police officer, it should be helpful, the task force concludes.

It's difficult to know where to begin with 5 such an egregious line of thinking. Certainly, it reflects one of the core beliefs of the NRA and its ilk that the problem with America is not too many guns but too few chances to carry them around. But it also implies that the kind of crazed loner who would don body armor and shoot up a school might be deterred by the

This unsigned editorial from baltimoresun.com was posted on April 3, 2013.

potential presence of an armed assistant principal or social studies teacher. How do we know somebody bent on murder and suicide wouldn't, in fact, welcome the chance for a hallway shoot-out?

And that's just for starters. If schools might be made safer by having teachers packing heat, why stop there? What about day care centers? Are 4-year-olds not worthy of similar protection? Why not shopping mall sales clerks, movie theater ushers, or the guy taking orders at the fast-food drive-through? Kids hang out in all those places, too.

Surely, if there's any deterrent value to strapping a sidearm on the school librarian, it's bound to make the alternative venues more vulnerable. The only logical conclusion is to go one step beyond those small towns in Georgia where gun ownership is mandatory and require everyone to carry loaded weapons around wherever they go.

Might this boost accidental shootings and suicides? Might this cause more guns to fall into the hands of criminals, youngsters, or the mentally ill? Almost certainly, but that doesn't seem to enter into the task force's thought process in the slightest—although "thought process" may be a too-generous description of what's going on here.

What makes the task force report so outrageous is that it totally ignores the school security threat posed by the nation's lax attitude toward guns. What if you could take a gun out of the hands of a potential assailant? Wouldn't that be far better than an armed confrontation on school grounds? How could it not be?

Universal background checks for gun purchases (and improving the database on which such checks for criminal convictions or serious mental health issues are based) would seem like the least that could be offered. Polls still show strong public support for that idea. Yet that common sense measure is under assault in the U.S. Senate—abandoned not just by Republicans but some Democrats, too.

What a charade Washington's post-Newtown public conversation about gun violence is turning out to be. Republicans make hay with pro-gun constituents by resisting everything while Democrats talk big but may not even force a vote. In the end, the NRA wins, and the victims of Sandy Hook—and the tens of thousands of Americans shot to death each year—are gradually forgotten.

10

Mental Health Services a Defense against School Violence

ROBERT ROSS

Before Reading: Short of arming teachers, what might be done to prevent future school shootings?

These days, it seems like our leaders in Washington have trouble finding common ground. However, the State of the Union address and the Republican response offered a welcome moment of agreement. Both President Obama and Senator Marco Rubio called for urgent action to reduce violence in our schools and communities. It's certainly true that Republicans and Democrats may disagree on the steps we should take, but I was pleased nonetheless that both sides are considering the problem with the seriousness it deserves.

The debate is different this time. December's unspeakable tragedy at Sandy Hook Elementary School has focused the nation's attention on safety—and rightly so. Every morning, some 60 million American parents check homework, stuff backpacks, zip up jackets, and send their beloved children into the care of our nation's schools. Parents are demanding that our leaders do everything in their power to ensure that those kids return home, every day, safe and healthy.

There is no shortage of ideas on the subject, and the debate has been robust. But I'd argue that our national conversation has been missing one essential element: a physician's focus on prevention.

I have served as a practicing pediatrician in Philadelphia and in Camden, New Jersey, but you don't have to be a doctor to know that an ounce of prevention is worth a pound of cure. It's cheaper and more effective to stop violence before it starts.

The key to prevention is understanding the source: who are these disengaged, disconnected, and frequently mentally ill young people who are involved in so much violence in our schools and neighborhoods?   5

In bucolic communities like Columbine, Aurora, and Newtown, this crisis of disengaged youth may show up as a senseless, massive shooting. In neighborhoods like Compton, Richmond, Chicago, and North Philadelphia, it may be school dropout, gang involvement, and drive-by shootings. Either way, the problem will continue to haunt our civic life until we make prevention a priority.

Early detection and treatment is the key. We need to reach troubled children when problems first emerge, while there's still time to guide them back on the right track. And because young people spend so much time in school, that's where the first inklings of trouble are often detected—and it's why schools are essential places to focus prevention resources.

Every school should have the resources it needs to provide comprehensive health services, where nurses, counselors, and other experts can diagnose problems, whether mental or physical, and get kids the help they need. And whether at a school-based clinic or in another setting, every student should get a behavioral health check-up,

Robert K. Ross is the president and CEO of the California Endowment, a health foundation. Earlier he served as director of the Health and Human Services Agency for the County of San Diego and as Commissioner of Public Health for the City of Philadelphia. He is also an experienced clinician and public health administrator. His article appeared on February 20, 2013, on capitolweekly.net.

just like they get a physical check-up before starting the school year.

School counselors are an especially important part of the solution. In California, we have about one counselor per 1,000 students—the worst ratio in the nation and four times the recommended standard of 1 counselor per 250 students. The best counselor in the world can't keep tabs on 1,000 students, and we can't expect them to.

10   The research shows clearly that counseling delivers a wide range of benefits, including improved academic performance, reduced classroom disruptions, and fewer disciplinary problems, all of which lead to calmer school climates, emotionally healthy students, and reduced violence on campus. Access to school nurses is credited with decreasing absenteeism and improving graduation rates. And comprehensive approaches to providing health services that include counselors, nurses, and other experts have proven effective at preventing youth suicide and reducing violence in schools and communities.

Californians are enthusiastic about prevention-oriented approaches to reducing school violence. According to a survey of 1,200 California voters, 72 percent say we should emphasize strategies that focus on prevention generally, compared to just 22 percent who say the right approach is preparing to respond to violence with more metal detectors, fences, and armed security guards. Moreover, 84 percent of survey respondents favored increasing the number of trained counselors in schools (including 55 percent "strongly support"), and when asked whether placing counselors or armed police in schools was the more effective strategy for preventing violence, more than two-thirds picked counselors over police (67 percent to 26 percent).

If the social science research and public opinion isn't enough to convince you, consider the views of young people themselves—those most affected by the issue of school violence.

These young people gathered in Los Angeles shortly after the Newtown tragedy to deliver a strong message to policymakers: don't let Sandy Hook turn our schools into fortresses. Yes, take common-sense steps to ensure that schools are ready to respond to emergencies, but don't sacrifice education in the name of security. A different group of students subsequently released a video sharing their personal experiences with school counselors and urging California to improve our woefully inadequate student-to-counselor ratio.

The youth advocates in these videos wisely caution against a rush to place more armed guards in schools. After all, Columbine, Virginia Tech, and Ft. Hood all had armed guards, but they weren't able to prevent tragic acts of violence. In the years following the Columbine massacre, the federal government spent more than $900 million to pay the salaries of school police and offset other security costs, but all this new spending didn't fix the problem. Instead of continuing down the same path, we should refocus our energies and investments in prevention.

I'm pleased that prevention-oriented approaches to school violence seem to be getting   15
some traction. When I testified before Congress earlier this month, I was pleasantly surprised that members responded enthusiastically to my calls for a focus on mental health services. And more important, President Obama's plan to reduce school violence specifically highlights the role that school counselors can play.

These are positive developments, but it's just a start. To effectively prevent violence in schools, we need a complete approach. We need not only improved emergency response strategies but also better tools and resources to identify kids and adults who need help—so we can get them the care they need or get them off the streets if they pose a serious danger to themselves or others.

These are the strategies the California Endowment will be emphasizing over the coming weeks and months. What would you do to make schools safer? Join the conversation at www .CalEndow.org.

Overusing the Bully Label
SUSAN EVA PORTER

Before Reading: How do you define bullying?

A Florida mother was arrested this month for allegedly stabbing her two sons' bullies in the back with box cutters. News reports stated that after calming down an altercation between her sons and a group of boys, the mother reignited the situation and attacked the boys, sending two to the hospital.

Last year, a teenage boy posted something nasty and hurtful in response to a teenage girl's Facebook posting. The girl was distraught, contemplated hurting herself and complained to her mother that she had been bullied. This caused the mother to become distraught. A short time later, police say, the mother saw the boy in a mall and took matters into her own hands, literally. She allegedly choked him.

But the reaction among many to the news reports was that the story was about a heroic mother seeking vengeance against a terrible bully on behalf of her victimized daughter, not an adult choking a child.

Although these two examples are extreme reactions to alleged bullying, many of us are overreacting to childhood aggression in less-extreme, everyday circumstances. It is not uncommon for adults to define even minor difficulties between children, such as being left out of social situations, as bullying. This is fundamentally changing the way we understand childhood.

We hear a lot about bullying—on the playgrounds, in schools, in the media. As a culture, we are infuriated with the bullies and terrified for the victims, and rightly so when it is appropriate. But the idea that childhood today is full of bullies is misleading. We do have a problem, but it's not with our children. It's with us, the adults.

Today we see children as being either dangerous villains or helpless victims, but the truth is kids haven't changed that much in the past generation. I have worked as an educator and a clinician in schools for 25 years, and I can attest that children are not meaner, nastier, or more

5

Susan Eva Porter is a clinical social worker, school administrator, and author of *Bully Nation: Why America's Approach to Childhood Aggression Is Bad for Everyone* (2013). Her article appeared in the *Los Angeles Times* on March 15, 2013.

aggressive than they used to be. Nor are they more fragile. Admittedly, digital media amplifies some of their mistakes and pours salt into wounds, but the behavior and reactions aren't new. What's new is our reaction to childhood aggression—and our increasing impatience with children and readiness to label them when they make certain mistakes or experience pain.

What caused this shift? In a word, Columbine, but not for the reasons many believe.

Dave Cullen, in his book *Columbine*, wrote that after the 1999 Colorado school massacre, the media crafted the explanation that shooters Eric Harris and Dylan Klebold had been bullied. They apparently hadn't been, but the nation—fearing a repeat of the tragedy—adopted a zero-tolerance attitude toward many normal, albeit painful, aspects of childhood behavior and development, and defined them as bullying.

As a result, behaviors such as social exclusion, persistent unfriendliness, and a nasty remark on Facebook have become intolerable acts that cause grave victimization. We now react to the children who commit these acts with a degree of intolerance that we wouldn't consider in other areas of their lives, and we assume that when children feel pain as a result of such mistakes, they will be scarred for life.

10   Can you imagine if we called children stupid when they made mistakes in math? Or if we assumed they'd never recover when they fell off their bikes? This is how we're essentially reacting every time we label children bullies or victims for making typical childhood mistakes or when they feel any hurt in a relationship.

And we're doing this with an unprecedented degree of abandon.

Stanford professor and author Carol Dweck explains that labels create something called a "fixed mind-set," which limits how children learn and perceive themselves, and how we perceive them. Think about it: The mother in the box-cutter case allegedly initiated her assault after the situation had cooled off—fueled, no doubt, by the thought that the boys deserved it because they were bullies. And chances are the mother in the choking incident would have had a hard time justifying her behavior if the boy was someone who had simply made a mistake. But once he was labeled a bully, all bets were off. She and her daughter became victims and were therefore absolved of all responsibility for examining their own behavior.

This is not just a question of semantics. Our penchant for labeling children in situations such as these, and our increasingly fixed mind-set about their behavior, is a real threat to their welfare. As soon as children are labeled bullies, this seems to give us permission to unleash on them a degree of anger and scorn that is frightening. As for the ones we label victims, we keep them identified with their pain and deny them the opportunity to develop true resilience.

We must admit that our approach to childhood aggression is flawed. Our children are not worse than they used to be, nor are they less resilient. But we adults seem to be. Instead of being so quick to label them, we must teach them how to deal with their aggression and pain appropriately and to develop compassion, impulse control, and resilience in their relationships. And we must learn to do the same.

Thinking and Writing about School Violence

1. What appeals does Wayne LaPierre use in his argument? What part of his proposal (if any) do you find reasonable? What (if any) do you find unreasonable?

2. Read "In Gun Control Debate, Logic Goes out the Window" (pp. 11–13), by Richard J. Davis in Chapter 1. How might LaPierre respond to Davis's argument? How might Davis respond to LaPierre?

3. How does Pat Bagley make use of irony in his cartoon about protecting our schoolchildren?

4. What is the allusion in the title of M. D. Anderson's article?

5. What does Anderson believe is the motive of the NRA in wanting to arm teachers? In your opinion, is there justification for arming teachers? Why, or why not?

6. The *Baltimore Sun* editorial responds to a report from the National Rifle Association. What did the report recommend? Why does the writer of the editorial object?

7. Why is the whole conversation about school shootings so heated at times? Why is the issue so controversial? In his essay "Loaded Language Poisons Gun Debate" (pp. 152–56) in Chapter 5, where does Josh Levs claim the problem lies?

8. What claim does Robert Ross make in his essay? Return to Chapter 1 and read Liza Long's essay "I Am Adam Lanza's Mother" (pp. 15–17). How does Long's firsthand account support Ross's argument?

9. Violence at school does not always come from outside. What is bullying? Do you recall bullying being a problem when you were in elementary or secondary school? Explain your response.

10. According to Susan Eva Porter, why are adults guilty of overusing the bully label, and what are the dangers?

11. In her essay "Gun Debate: Where Is the Middle Ground?" (pp. 46–49) in Chapter 2, Mallory Simon searches for similar goals on all sides of the gun control debate. Do the readings in this chapter suggest any movement toward common ground? Explain your response.

Food Matters

How Do Politics and the Economy Affect What We Eat?

All of us at times think of food as a guilty pleasure. Mostly it is when we give in to the temptation to eat foods that we know are unhealthy or that will make it harder to fit into our favorite pair of jeans. A generation or two ago, parents or grandparents who remembered the Great Depression told children to clean their plates and to be grateful to have so much good food while children in some other countries had little or none. More recently, parents may feel a twinge of guilt as they buy their kids a Happy Meal for the third time in one week—but at least the kids like the toys.

Today there is increasing awareness that we have more to worry about than how many calories are in the French fries and how much sugar is in the soda. We have to worry about whole generations of children who because of obesity are confronting what used to be considered adult diseases such as coronary artery disease and adult-onset diabetes. We have to worry about where our food comes from and what life is like for the laborers who help move it from the fields to our tables. We have to worry about our society's impoverished people who live in "food deserts" far from supermarkets where healthy foods are available.

The economics of eating has a profound effect on who has enough to eat and who earns a living wage. We buy our favorite fast food at restaurants staffed by those who need a second job to make ends meet; we contribute to the poverty in other countries when we buy imported food instead of food grown locally. The way that food is grown, produced, distributed, and priced has global repercussions.

Food Fight
MICHAEL POLLAN

Before Reading: What do you think Pollan might mean by the term "food fight" in his title?

It might sound odd to say this about something people deal with at least three times a day, but food in America has been more or less invisible, politically speaking, until very recently. At least until the early 1970s, when a bout of food price inflation and the appearance of books critical of industrial agriculture threatened to propel the subject to the top of the national agenda, Americans have not had to think very hard about where their food comes from, or what it is doing to the planet, their bodies, and their society.

The dream that the age-old "food problem" had been largely solved for most Americans was sustained by the tremendous postwar increases in the productivity of American farmers, made possible by cheap fossil fuel (the key ingredient in both chemical fertilizers and pesticides) and changes in agricultural policies that emphasized boosting yields of commodity crops (corn and soy especially) at any cost.

But although cheap food is good politics, it turns out there are significant costs — to the environment, to public health, to the public purse, even to the culture — and as these became impossible to ignore in recent years, food has come back into view. Beginning in 2001 with the publication of Eric Schlosser's *Fast Food Nation* and, the following year, Marion Nestle's *Food Politics,* the food journalism of the past decade has succeeded in making clear connections between the methods of industrial food production, agricultural policy, foodborne illness, childhood obesity, the decline of the family meal, and, notably, the decline of family income beginning in the 1970s.

Falling wages made fast food both cheap to produce and a welcome, if not indispensable, option for pinched and harried families. The picture of the food economy Schlosser painted resembles an upside-down version of the social compact sometimes referred to as "Fordism": Instead of paying workers well enough to allow them to buy things like cars, as Henry Ford proposed to do, companies like Wal-Mart and McDonald's pay their workers so poorly that they can afford only the cheap, low-quality food these companies sell.

Cheap food has become an indispensable pillar of the modern economy. But it is no longer an invisible or uncontested one. One of the most interesting social movements to emerge in the past few years is the "food movement," or perhaps I should say "movements," since it is unified as yet by little more than the recognition that industrial food production is in need of reform because its social/environmental/public

5

Michael Pollan is an award-winning writer and journalist who focuses, according to his Web site, on "the places where nature and culture intersect: on our plates, in our farms and gardens, and in the built environment." He has written four *New York Times* bestsellers: *Food Rules: An Eater's Manual* (2010); *In Defense of Food: An Eater's Manifesto* (2008); *The Omnivore's Dilemma: A Natural History of Four Meals* (2006); and *The Botany of Desire: A Plant's-Eye View of the World* (2001). He has been a contributing writer to the *New York Times Magazine* since 1987 and in 2010 was named one of *Time*'s 100 most influential people. This article was published in the *New York Review of Books* on September 24, 2010.

health/animal welfare/gastronomic costs are too high.

It's a big, lumpy tent, and sometimes the various factions beneath it work at cross-purposes. For example, activists working to strengthen federal food safety regulations have recently run afoul of local-food advocates, who fear that the new regulation will cripple the revival of small-farm agriculture. But there are indications that these various voices may be coming together in something that looks more and more like a coherent movement. Many in the animal welfare movement have come to see that a smaller-scale, more humane animal agriculture is a goal worth fighting for. Stung by charges of elitism, activists for sustainable farming are starting to take seriously hunger and poverty.

Viewed from a middle distance, the food movement coalesces around the recognition that today's food and farming economy is "unsustainable"—that it can't go on in its current form much longer without courting a breakdown of some kind, whether it be environmental, economic, or both.

For some in the movement, the more urgent problem is environmental: The food system consumes more fossil fuel energy than we can count on in the future and emits more greenhouse gas than we can afford to emit. In the past few years, several major environmental groups have come to appreciate that a diversified, sustainable agriculture—which can sequester large amounts of carbon in the soil—holds the potential not just to mitigate but actually to help solve environmental problems.

But perhaps the food movement's strongest claim on public attention today is the fact that the American diet of highly processed food laced with added fats and sugars is responsible for the epidemic of chronic diseases that threatens to bankrupt the health care system. The health care crisis probably cannot be addressed without addressing the catastrophe of the American diet, and that diet is the direct (even if unintended) result of the way that our agriculture and food industries have been organized.

Michelle Obama's recent foray into food politics suggests that the administration has made these connections. Her new Let's Move campaign to combat childhood obesity might at first blush seem fairly anodyne, but in announcing the initiative in February, and in a surprisingly tough speech to the Grocery Manufacturers Association in March, the first lady has shifted the conversation about diet from the industry's preferred ground of "personal responsibility" to a frank discussion of the way food is produced and marketed. 10

"We need you not just to tweak around the edges," she told the assembled food makers, "but to entirely rethink the products that you're offering, the information that you provide about these products, and how you market those products to our children."

So far, at least, Michelle Obama is the food movement's most important ally in the administration, but there are signs of interest elsewhere. Under Commissioner Margaret Hamburg, the Food and Drug Administration has cracked down on deceptive food marketing. Attorney General Eric Holder recently avowed the Justice Department's intention to pursue antitrust enforcement in agribusiness. At his side was Secretary of Agriculture Tom Vilsack, who launched a new initiative aimed at promoting local food systems as a way to both rebuild rural economies and improve access to healthy food.

Though Vilsack has so far left mostly undisturbed his department's traditional deference to industrial agriculture, the new tone in Washington and the appointment of a handful of respected reformers has elicited a somewhat defensive, if not panicky, reaction from agribusiness. The American Farm Bureau recently urged its members to go on the offensive against "food activists," and a trade association representing pesticide makers called CropLife America wrote to Michelle Obama suggesting that her organic garden had unfairly maligned chemical agriculture and encouraging her to use "crop protection technologies"—i.e., pesticides.

The first lady's response is not known; however, the president subsequently rewarded CropLife by appointing one of its executives to a high-level trade post. This and other industry-friendly appointments suggest that while the administration may be sympathetic to elements of the food movement's agenda, it isn't about to take on agribusiness, at least not directly, at least until it senses at its back a much larger constituency for reform.

15   One way to interpret Michelle Obama's deepening involvement in food issues is as an effort to build such a constituency, and in this she may well succeed. It's a mistake to underestimate what a determined first lady can accomplish. Lady Bird Johnson's "highway beautification" campaign also seemed benign, but in the end it helped raise public consciousness about "the environment" (as it would soon come to be known). And while Michelle Obama has explicitly limited her efforts to exhortation ("We can't solve this problem by passing a bunch of laws in Washington," she told the Grocery Manufacturers, no doubt much to their relief), her work is already creating a climate in which just such a "bunch of laws" might flourish: a handful of state legislatures are considering levying new taxes on sugar in soft drinks, proposals considered hopelessly extreme less than a year ago.

The political ground is shifting, and the passage of health care reform may accelerate that movement. If health insurers can no longer keep people with chronic diseases out of their patient pools, it stands to reason that those companies will develop a keener interest in preventing those diseases. They will then discover that they have a large stake in things like soda taxes and in precisely which kinds of calories the farm bill is subsidizing.

It would be a mistake, however, to conclude that the food movement's agenda can be reduced to a set of laws, policies, and regulations, important as these may be. What is attracting so many people to the movement today is a much less conventional kind of politics, one that is about something more than food. The movement is also about community, identity, pleasure, and, most notably, about carving out a new social and economic space removed from the influence of big corporations and government.

One can get a taste of this social space simply by hanging around a farmers market. Farmers markets are thriving, and there is a lot more going on in them than the exchange of money for food. Someone is collecting signatures on a petition. Someone else is playing music. Children are everywhere, sampling fresh produce. Friends and acquaintances stop to chat. Someone buying food here may be acting not just as a consumer but also as a neighbor, a citizen, a parent, a cook.

Though seldom articulated as such, the attempt to redefine, or escape, the traditional role of consumer has become an important aspiration of the food movement. The modern marketplace would have us decide what to buy strictly on the basis of price and self-interest; the food movement proposes that we enlarge our understanding of both terms, suggesting that not just "good value" but also ethical and political values should inform buying decisions, and that we'll get more satisfaction from our eating when they do.

20   Put another way, the food movement has set out to foster new forms of civil society. But instead of proposing that space as a counterweight to an overbearing state, as is usually the case, the food movement poses it against the dominance of corporations and their tendency to insinuate themselves into any aspect of our lives from which they can profit. As Wendell Berry writes, corporations "will grow, deliver, and cook your food for you and (just like your mother) beg you to eat it. That they do not yet offer to insert it, prechewed, into your mouth is only because they have found no profitable way to do so."

The corporatization of something as basic and intimate as eating is, for many of us today, a good place to draw the line.

Food is invisible no longer and, in light of the mounting costs we've incurred by ignoring it, it is likely to demand much more of our attention in the future. It is only a matter of time before politicians seize on the power of the food issue, which besides being increasingly urgent is also almost primal, in some sense protopolitical.

For where do all politics begin if not in the high chair?—at that fateful moment when mother, or father, raises a spoonful of food to the lips of the baby who clamps shut her mouth, shakes her head no, and for the first time awakens to and asserts her sovereign power.

The Rich Get Richer, the Poor Go Hungry
SHARON ASTYK AND AARON NEWTON

Before Reading: When you were a child and you left food on your plate, you may have been told that children in other parts of the world were going hungry. Did you ever believe that? Do you believe it now? Why, or why not?

What is the most common cause of hunger in the world? Is it drought? Flood? Locusts? Crop diseases? Nope. Most hunger in the world has absolutely nothing to do with food shortages. Most people who go to bed hungry, both in rich and in poor countries, do so in places where markets are filled with food that they cannot have.

Despite this fact, much of the discourse about reforming our food system has focused on the necessity of raising yields. Though it is true that we might need more food in coming years, it is also true that the world produces more food calories than are needed to sustain its entire population. The problem is unequal access

Sharon Astyk is a former academic, a writer, and a farmer in upstate New York. She is the author of *Depletion and Abundance: Life on the New Home Front* (2008) and co-author, with Aaron Newton, of *A Nation of Farmers: Defeating the Food Crisis on American Soil* (2009). Newton is a sustainable systems land planner in North Carolina and director of environmental programs at Outdoor Living, a design firm. This excerpt is from *A Nation of Farmers*.

to food, land, and wealth, and any discussion must begin not from fantasies of massive yield increases, but from the truth that the hunger of the poor is in part a choice of the rich.

Inequity and politics, not food shortages, were at the root of almost all famines in the twentieth century. Brazil, for example, exported $20 billion worth of food in 2002, while millions of its people went hungry. During Ethiopian famines in the 1980s, the country also exported food. Many of even the poorest nations can feed themselves—or *could* in a society with fairer allocation of resources.

It can be hard to grasp the degree to which the Western lifestyle is implicated. We don't realize that when we buy imported shrimp or coffee we are often literally taking food from poor people. We don't realize that our economic system is doing harm; in fact, the system conspires to make it nearly impossible to figure out whether what we're doing is destructive or regenerative.

5   We have been assured that "a rising tide lifts all boats," that it is necessary for us to make rich people richer, because that will, in turn, enrich the poor. The consequences have been disastrous—for the planet and for the people whose food systems have been disrupted, who never had a chance to be lifted by any tide.

Journalist Jeremy Seabrook, in his book *The No-Nonsense Guide to World Poverty*, describes First World efforts to eliminate poverty and hunger this way:

It is now taken for granted that relief of poverty is the chief objective of all politicians, international institutions, donors, and charities. This dedication is revealed most clearly in a determination to preserve [the poor]. Like all great historical monuments, there should be a Society for the Preservation of the Poor; only, since it is written into the very structures of the global economy, no special arrangements are required. There is not the remotest chance that poverty will be abolished, but every chance that the poor themselves might perish.

It is hard for many of us to recognize that the society we live in helps create poverty and insecurity, but it is true. Our economy is based on endless growth. We're told that if the rich get richer, it makes other people less poor. Think about it for a moment—about how crazy that is. Wouldn't it make much more sense to enrich the poor directly, to help them get land and access to resources?

Historically, rural people have been quite poor, but often, despite their poverty, could grow enough food to feed themselves. Over recent decades, however, industrial agriculture and widespread industrialization have moved large chunks of the human population into cities, promising more wealth. But rising food and energy prices (rising because of this move and this urban population's new demands for energy and meat) have left people unable to feed their families.

Multinational food companies have also worked their way into the food budgets of the poor. Faith D'Aluisio and Peter Menzel are the authors of *Hungry Planet*. "Few of the families we met [in the developing world] could afford a week's worth of a processed food item at one time," they report in the *Washington Post*, "so the global food companies make their wares more affordable by offering them in single-serving packets."

10   Around the world, industrial agriculture has consolidated land ownership into the hands of smaller and smaller populations. Rich nations dumped cheap subsidized grain on poor nations. Local self-sufficiency was destroyed. Now, as the price of food has risen dramatically, those created dependencies on cheap grain, which doesn't exist anymore, mean that millions are in danger of starvation.

    Real alleviation of poverty and hunger means reallocating the resources of our world into the hands of people who need them most. This is not only ethically the right thing to do, it is necessary. There is no hope that newly industrializing nations will help us fight climate change if it means a great inequity between their people and those of the United States. Russia, India, and China have all said so explicitly. The only alternative to the death of millions in a game of global chicken is for everyone to accept that the world cannot afford rich people—in any nation.

    What is the best strategy of reallocation? One—that is, for those of us who live in nations where there is plenty of land and food so that we don't have to rely on the exports of poor nations—would be to enable the world's farmers to eat what they grow and to have sufficient land to feed themselves and their neighbors.

    Most of the world's poorest people are urban slum dwellers (often displaced farmers) or land-poor farmers, agroecologist Peter Rosset notes. Both groups are increasing, in large degree because of economic policies that favor food for export and allow large quantities of land to be held in the hands of the richest.

    "The expansion of agricultural production for export, controlled by wealthy elites who own the best lands, continually displaces the poor to ever more marginal areas for farming," Rosset writes in *Food Is Different*. "They are forced . . . to try to eke out a living on desert margins and in rainforests. As they fall deeper into poverty . . . they are often accused of contributing to environmental degradation."

    In this system, poor people who depend on 15 the land, and who best understand the urgency of preserving it, are forced by necessity to degrade and destroy it—and they, rather than we, are held responsible. But a large part of the responsibility rests on the way we eat. This is an important point, because it acknowledges that there are things that we in wealthy nations can do to enable poorer people to eat better—or even to eat at all.

One way to do this is simply to grow our own food, to rely not on foods grown thousands of miles away but on foods grown at local farms and gardens. We also can concentrate on creating food sovereignty in poor nations. We can cut back on global food trade, importing primarily high-value, fair-traded dry goods that take little energy to transport, and place limits on food speculation, which drives up prices so that multinational corporations can get richer at the expense of the poor.

    Most of all, we can recognize that self-sufficiency is as urgent in the rich world as in the poor. Globalization's demise is coming. The rising costs of transportation and the trade deficit in the United States make it inevitable that we will increasingly be looking to meet our basic needs locally.

    When we grow our own food, or buy it directly from local farmers, we take power away from multinationals. We make it harder for them to extract wealth and the best land of other nations—and if they don't need that land, local farmers may be able to use it for their own needs.

We also put power in the hands of our neighbors, many of whom are also victims of globalization. There are 49 million people in the United States who can't consistently afford a basic nutritious diet. It turns out that the things that make us poor—lack of education, lack of access to land and home, and the industrial economy—are precisely the things that make other people poor. By creating local food systems, we can enrich our immediate neighbors as we stop impoverishing our distant ones.

The Employer-Friendly Case for Pricier Big Macs
DIANE BRADY

Before Reading: Why do Americans continue to spend billions of dollars a year on fast foods when they know the health risks?

In all the debate about whether to raise fast-food wages—from Fox News (FOXA) anchor Neil Cavuto's fond memories of frying fish for $2 an hour at Arthur Treacher's to the specter of paying 25 percent more for a Big Mac—it's easy to forget the other costs associated with fast food.

Americans are expected to spend more than $188 billion at the country's 160,000 fast-food outlets this year, according to the National Restaurant Association. With 14,100 locations, McDonald's accounts for less than one-tenth of that spending. The nation will spend even more — about $190 billion a year—paying for the health consequences of obesity. For employers struggling to rein in health-care costs, that's a good reason to support the push to raise fast-food wages. Even if higher pay doesn't prompt those workers to spend more in other areas, higher menu prices could encourage them to make better food choices.

Of all the reasons why a third of U.S. adults are obese, the lure of cheap, unhealthy food ranks near the top. At least once a week, a new Gallup poll shows, half of Americans are likely to get just that when they eat at fast-food chains. Sure, customers could buy a salad or two, but the bulk of fast-food sales still comes from food that's high in sodium, sugar, and fat. Americans know that: More than three-quarters of those polled by Gallup think the food isn't good for them. The draw is that it's convenient, cheap, and tastes good. With numerous studies linking obesity rates to the proximity, price, and growth of fast-food restaurants, giving people a pocketbook-based reason to eat somewhere else isn't a bad thing.

Employers know firsthand the high cost of expanding waistlines, from heart disease and diabetes to reduced mobility and a greater risk of injury. It's why so many companies now offer weight-loss programs and discounts on gym memberships. It explains why heavier people often have a harder time getting hired. Remember that Wal-Mart Stores memo that looked at ways to attract a "healthier, more productive workforce" to curb health costs?

Diane Brady is a senior editor for *Bloomberg Businessweek* in New York. Her article appeared on businessweek.com on August 9, 2013.

5   As U.S. chains move beyond their saturated home market, they're also making other people fat. Our greatest export, says Gallup's Tom Rath, "is fast becoming diabesity," or diabetes caused by obesity. That should worry everyone. In his new book, *Eat Move Sleep*, Rath points out that what people eat every day doesn't just affect their weight but also has an immediate impact on productivity, mood, and judgment. Moreover, what their colleagues eat has a direct impact on their insurance premiums, taxes, health-care costs, and ability to make money. That's why Rath argues that "improving health is the biggest business challenge for employers today."

Higher prices on unhealthy food is just part of the puzzle. Creating a workplace that encourages people to make healthy choices for their families is another, as are efforts to boost health in local communities. The Centers for Disease Control and Prevention credits trends from higher breast-feeding rates to a greater variety of fresh produce in low-income neighborhoods for a drop in obesity rates among preschoolers.

Fast-food chains have raised their game with healthier menu offerings and support for programs that encourage physical activity, but they continue to thrive by selling high-calorie food. McDonald's salads, introduced in 1987, make up just 2 percent to 3 percent of U.S. sales. Its heavily promoted Dollar Menu, dominated by tasty treats such as double burgers and cookies, takes in about five times that amount. The industry creates so many jobs because Americans eat too much of those tempting foods. When a bag of fries costs less than a piece of fruit, it's hard to blame the consumer for buying it. And when a 40-hour week of flipping those fries still puts you below the federal poverty line, it's hard to blame the worker for wanting more, too.

With Americans still loading up on cheap tacos, burgers, and fried chicken, others are paying the price. A few years ago public outrage was directed at the products. Remember *Super Size Me*, the documentary about eating only McDonald's for a month? The threats of lawsuits? The eye-popping calorie counts suddenly showing up on menus? Several years later, we now have salads that are tough to sell, workers who can't support their families, and stories that say junk food can end obesity. Even those outside the industry can see that doesn't add up.

Can't Survive on $7.25

FAST FOOD FORWARD

Before Reading: How well are workers paid at America's fast-food restaurants?

CAN'T SURVIVE ON $7.25

Contrary to common belief, teens represent less than 12% of the low-wage work force.

25-64 years old

Teens

Over 60% of low-wage workers are 25-64 years old*, many with families to support.

*Source: Center for Economic and Policy Research "Low Wage Workers are Older and Better Educated Than Ever" April 2012

FAST FOOD FORWARD

Higher Pay for a Stronger New York

www.fastfoodforward.org

Fast Food Forward

Fast Food Forward is a labor organization in New York City.

Can the Food Industry Kick Its Cheap Labor Habit?

TWILIGHT GREENAWAY

Before Reading: How are farmers able to pay farm workers low wages and keep them in what are often deplorable working conditions?

As the nation inches closer to immigration reform—both the Obama administration and a bipartisan group of eight senators have expressed a commitment to working on a path toward citizenship for the 11 million people living in the U.S. without documentation—some big questions remain about how that reform will impact the food chain.

The fact is, many of those 11 million people are working to put food on our plates in one form or another. Around 1.2 million (nearly ten percent) of the nation's undocumented laborers are employed on farms. Add to that number the many people who work in feedlots, slaughterhouses, warehouses, factories, and restaurants and you get the idea; our cheap and plentiful food supply is really only possible because it is produced by undocumented workers.

They work long hours for pay that's often less than they've agreed to when hired. (According to the 2012 report *The Hands That Feed Us*, undocumented laborers are more than twice as likely to earn less than minimum wage and twice as likely to experience wage theft than their documented coworkers.) So it's probably not entirely surprising to learn that seven of the ten worst paying jobs in the nation are food-related. And because undocumented workers don't have the rights of citizens, they are often vulnerable to abuse, sexual assault, and inhumane working conditions.

Will immigration reform change the face of food work? Absolutely. But whether it will really mean improved working conditions for the people at the bottom of the food hierarchy is yet to be seen. While it's looking possible that some food workers could soon move along a path toward citizenship, big farms aren't likely to give up their claim to cheap labor. As a result, the year ahead could present labor groups, farmers, and immigration advocates with a complex dance to perform.

It's well known that American citizens simply refuse to do farm jobs (and other similar food system work). And the fact that the current Senate plan would allow undocumented residents to gain citizenship after paying a fine, paying back taxes, and undergoing background checks, is encouraging. But it raises the obvious question: When presented with more options for education, and living without the fear of deportation, will these men and women continue to fill the jobs that are exempt from minimum wage and overtime laws? Or are those jobs generally so grueling and underpaid that they will only ever be filled by people who have no other viable options?

This is where the idea of a revamping of the guest-worker program comes into the picture. Currently, guest workers in the U.S. are anything but our guests. The current program, called H-2A, is often characterized by broken contracts, lack of freedom on the part of the worker, and substandard housing.

5

Twilight Greenaway is an Oakland-based writer and editor. Her piece appeared on takepart.com on February 4, 2013.

Diana Tellefson Torres of United Farm Workers (UFW) is concerned about the vague language she's hearing from lawmakers about revamping the guest-worker program. For one, she knows it could undo the work her organization has done to keep workers from getting a raw deal under H-2A.

"We've worked for so many years to include protection from the abuse that farmworkers often endure in the guest-worker program," she says. "We saw it during the Bracero Program earlier this century, and we see it now. So we've fought hard for these changes."

Of course, in states such as California, where those labor protection laws are enforced, most farm owners simply avoid using the H-2A program altogether.

10 Eric Larson, head of the San Diego County Farm Bureau, told Public Radio International (PRI), "Sure, the H-2A program says go ahead and bring farm workers in, but the H-2A program doesn't work." The article continues:

> To participate, farmers have to prove to the U.S. Labor Department that they have tried to hire American workers but could not. They must transport guest workers from their home country, often Mexico, and provide housing and three meals a day. They must also show that their guest workers will not drag down local wages. All this means lots of money, paperwork and, often, attorneys.
>
> "Consequently, nobody uses it," said Larson. "I think we've got one farmer in San Diego County that uses the H-2A for about eight workers, where in reality we have 10,000 to 12,000 farm workers in San Diego County."

Subsequently, most farm owners simply hire undocumented workers who have already entered the country on their own steam.

And what about the farm labor shortages we keep hearing so much about? All over the country, farm owners talk about planting fewer rows and letting food go to waste in the fields because they can't find workers. And while it is true that other farm costs—like seeds, animal feed, and fertilizer—have all gone up in recent years, farm pay has stayed relatively constant.

But as John Carney over at CNBC pointed out, near the end of last year, "If there were a labor shortage, we'd see the price of farm labor rising rapidly. We just don't see that—indicating that there is no shortage at all." Instead, he continues, there is, "a consistent cry from the farm lobby for policy makers to adopt policies aimed at lowering labor costs."

UFW's Torres agrees. "When they say there's a labor shortage, I honestly feel that they would prefer to bring temporary workers using a program that doesn't have labor protection. The 'labor shortage' is a talking point to make that case. There is no real shortage of people."

15 A recent research paper from U.C. Davis, covered in the *Washington Post* last week, offers up another piece of the puzzle. The paper's authors argue that Mexico—the nation from where the bulk of our farm workers come—is gaining on the U.S. financially. "Not only are Mexican workers shifting into other sectors like construction, but Mexico's own farms are increasing wages. That means U.S. farms will have to pay higher and higher wages to attract a dwindling pool of available Mexican farm workers."

The answer, as the authors see it, is to increase mechanization and bring more high-tech harvesting systems to America's farms, which will mean fewer workers overall. This shift seems inevitable in today's technologically advancing world, but, in the meantime, it's possible that valuing our food more, wasting less of it, and spending just a little more on what we purchase could go a long way toward balancing the food-labor equation. In the case of produce, the math is clear.

Philip Martin, a labor economist at the University of California, Davis (and, not coincidentally, also one of the authors of the above paper) laid it out in the *New York Times*'s "Room for Debate" section in 2011. He wrote:

> For a typical household, a 40 percent increase in farm labor costs translates into a 3.6 percent increase in retail prices. If farm wages rose 40 percent, and this wage increase were passed on to consumers, average spending on fresh fruits and vegetables would rise about $15 a year, the cost of two movie tickets. However, for a typical seasonal farm worker, a 40 percent wage increase could raise earnings from $10,000 for 1,000 hours of work to $14,000 — lifting the wage above the federal poverty line.

Another option — and the one Torres and other advocates will be pushing for — is a guest-worker program more like the one they have in Canada. There, the workers aren't tied to a single farm, and if they complain, they can return home or move to a farm that treats them better. If these rights sound pretty basic, consider this: They're better than the ones workers who come to the U.S. through H-2A have now. And many farm owners are pushing for less.

The Fight over Food Deserts: Corporate America Smacks Its Way Down
ERIC HOLT-GIMÉNEZ

Before Reading: How can you explain the seeming paradox that lower-income individuals suffer from a higher rate of obesity than those of a higher economic level?

This June the City of Chicago approved Walmart's bid to open up dozens of new facilities, beginning with grocery stores in the city's chronically underserved South side. Just a month earlier the company committed $2 billion to fight hunger in the United States. But behind the high profile donations is a decidedly less charitable story repeating itself throughout corporate America.

In large part fueled by Michelle Obama's goal to eliminate food deserts in seven years, Walmart has set the PR machine in motion around its new battle cry: "The Great Grocery Smackdown:"

"If you've always lived near a grocery store or fresh market, here's something you've prob-

Eric Holt-Giménez, a food system researcher and agro-ecologist, is the executive director of FoodFirst/Institute for Food and Development Policy and the author of *Food Rebellions! Crisis and the Hunger for Justice* (2009). The article was posted on huffingtonpost.com on July 14, 2010.

ably never considered: There are neighborhoods across the United States where it's nearly impossible to find fresh produce. These places are called 'Food Deserts' and Walmart is committed to removing them from our communities." The Walmart proposal for Chicago has been framed as "the beginning of a major private-sector effort to address the food desert problem on the South side."

Walmart sees Chicago's South side as the key to the rest of the city—in fact as the key to all cities. According to the *Chicago Tribune,* in a recent meeting with Mayor Daley Walmart offered to open grocery stores in food deserts in exchange for access to the other, more desirable locations. "We have very small market share in the large cities within the United States, so we see a big opportunity for us to grow in those urban markets," said Hank Mullany, who runs Walmart stores in the Midwest, Northeast, and mid-Atlantic regions.

5   Not only will the company bring fresh produce in smaller grocery stores, the employer claims it will bring 12,000 jobs to Chicago.

A recent study out of Loyola University in Chicago focusing on the impact of a Walmart that opened on the west side of Chicago in 2006 indicates that the new facility cost the local economy as many jobs as it created. The Loyola University study also examined tax revenues for eighteen months before and after the retailer opened its doors and found no evidence of increased local economic activity.

In 2008, Walmart settled 63 cases of wage theft for a total of $352 million. Even when the company does pay the agreed upon wage, workers still come up short. According to Good Jobs First, taxpayers subsidize Walmart stores through numerous forms of public assistance—

Medicaid, Food Stamps, public housing—that often allow workers to subsist on the company's low wages. A report by the House Education and Workforce Committee conservatively places these costs deferred by the retail giant at $420,750 per store; the Walmart Foundation's per-store charitable giving is just 11 percent of that amount ($47,222). Now adding to the pot of public funds to be had, Michelle Obama and other well-intentioned groups concerned with food deserts may have made these areas much more profitable than they once were. As part of her Let's Move campaign the First Lady has pledged $400 million/year to ensure that all Americans have access to affordable food. In the words of Brahm Ahmadi, founder of People's Grocery in West Oakland,

> We're seeing a lot of funding being rolled out, but also what we're seeing is the corporate retail industry who literally two to three years ago wouldn't even talk to you about this [food deserts], now almost salivating over the opportunity for the windfalls that will come from free public money, essentially. Even though they could easily finance themselves to open stores in the inner city neighborhoods, why should they when the administration is perfectly happy to give them more money to do it?

Walmart is not the only major grocery chain salivating at the thought of public subsidies: Tesco, Target, Safeway, and Supervalu have all announced plans to open stores in urban centers.

But hunger and food security stem from poverty that in the United States comes from unemployment and poor wages. The solution to food security in America must come through a revitalized food economy—one that pays workers a living wage, that includes worker and minority owned businesses, and that keeps food dollars in local communities. Walmart does none of that.

10   Seventeen percent of American jobs are in the food system, and those jobs are among the lowest paid in the country. If food industry leaders are serious about improving food access, they need to start by tackling food insecurity where it starts—with sub-poverty wages. No amount of fresh produce will cure America's food and health gap unless it comes with a commitment to fight its root causes—poverty and inequality. To really fight food deserts, the Obamas should start by supporting living wages for workers and support the food businesses that create true economic development in the communities that need it most.

Thinking and Writing about the Political and Economic Costs of Food

1. Explain what Michael Pollan means when he writes, "Cheap food has become an indispensable pillar of the modern economy. But it is no longer an invisible or uncontested one" (para. 5).
2. Sharon Astyk and Aaron Newton argue that "the hunger of the poor is in part a choice of the rich" (para. 2). Explain what they mean by that.
3. If, as Astyk and Newton argue, the cause of hunger is unequal access to food, land, and wealth, how can any individual make a difference? How can any government?
4. According to Diane Brady, what is the connection between Americans' love of fast food and the minimum wage?
5. Brady quotes Tom Rath, who claims that "improving health is the biggest business challenge for employers today" (para. 5). Why must employers be concerned about health?
6. How does the infographic from Fast Food Forward use both imagery and text to make its point? Do you notice any discrepancy between the workers portrayed in the visual and those cited in the statistics?
7. Are the fast-food restaurants the villains, as the Fast Food Forward visual suggests, or is there a need for entry-level, low-paying jobs? Explain.
8. In what ways does Twilight Greenaway predict immigration reform will affect the food industry?
9. Why is Eric Holt-Giménez skeptical about Walmart's ability to solve the problem of food deserts on Chicago's South side?

10. From your reading, what conclusions can you draw about the food industry and the American economy?
11. In her essay "Food for Thought (and for Credit)" (pp. 288–90) in Chapter 9, how does Jennifer Grossman propose to combat some of the problems about food and economics raised in this chapter?

Competitive Sports

What Risks Should Athletes Be Allowed to Take?

It's not hard to understand why sports lovers are called "fans," from the original "fanatics." Sports are a deeply ingrained part of American culture. Our largest basketball arenas seat over 20,000 fans; our largest college football stadiums, over 100,000. Coaches at our colleges and universities are often paid far more than those schools' presidents. Professional athletes make exorbitant salaries, plus what they can add in endorsements.

We expect our athletes to be worth the money and the loyalty we invest in them. We expect their best. We hate to see a player injured, as long as it is our own, but the familiar "Hit 'em again, hit 'em again, harder, harder!" is mild compared to what we shout we want our players to do to the members of the other team. We applaud when an injured player gets up and returns to the sidelines, but our main concern with injuries is whether or not they will keep the player out of the next game.

The damage done to boxers over the years by hundreds of punches has been a concern for a long time. Now doctors and others are taking a closer look at the long-term effects of the hits suffered by football players at all levels of play. There is also concern over the effects on children and youth from overtraining or overuse of their muscles. It is relatively rare for a player to die on the field or during practice, but some of those tragic cases are getting a second look to see what can be learned for the good of future players. And researchers point out that cheerleaders on the sidelines may be subject to injuries as serious as the ones experienced by the team they cheer on.

In the pursuit of victory, some athletes have made use of performance-enhancing drugs. The fall from grace of some of the world's most respected athletes has cast a shadow on competitive sports as the desire to win has proved stronger than the desire to live by the rules. It has also proved stronger than physicians' Hippocratic oath and parents' concern for their children's health and well-being.

What price victory? How much danger should we tolerate in competitive sports? At what point do we agree that the win is not worth the risk?

For Children in Sports, a Breaking Point

JANE E. BRODY

Before Reading: Do you feel that children are sometimes pushed too far to excel at sports? Does the drive to excel come from within or from external sources? What are some of the consequences of the drive to excel?

I'd be the last person to discourage children from playing sports. Indeed, I wish many more would move away from their computers, put down their iPods and cellphones, and devote more time and energy to physical activities.

But for many children and adolescents, the problem is the opposite of being sedentary. Encouraged by parents and coaches, many with visions of glory and scholarships, too many young athletes are being pushed — or are pushing themselves — to the point of breaking down, physically and sometimes emotionally.

The statistics cited by Mark Hyman in his book *Until It Hurts: America's Obsession with Youth Sports and How It Harms Our Kids* (new in paperback from Beacon Press) are sobering indeed: "Every year more than 3.5 million children under 15 require medical treatment for sports injuries, nearly half of which are the result of simple overuse."

Injuries are only part of the problem, Mr. Hyman wrote. As adults become more and more involved, he noted, "with each passing season youth sports seems to stray further and further from its core mission of providing healthy, safe, and character-building recreation for children."

5   Mr. Hyman, a sports journalist, was prompted to tackle this subject in part by his own misguided behavior as the father of an athletically talented son. At 13, Ben Hyman was a prized pitcher for a local team when his shoulder began to hurt — and hurt enough for him to complain — just before the start of league playoffs.

Despite a professional assessment that Ben's problem was caused by throwing too many baseballs and a recommendation to rest his arm up to a month, his father put him in the game, and again three days later, urging him to "blaze a trail to the championship." When the injured boy began "lamely lobbing balls at home plate," Mr. Hyman realized his foolish shortsightedness in putting winning ahead of his son's well-being.

The Dangers of Overdoing It

The problem was put into focus three years ago by the American Academy of Pediatrics' Council on Sports Medicine and Fitness. In a report in the academy's journal, *Pediatrics,* Dr. Joel S. Brenner wrote, "Overuse injuries, overtraining, and burnout among child and adolescent athletes are a growing problem in the United States."

The goal of youth participation in sports, the council said, "should be to promote lifelong physical activity, recreation, and skills of healthy competition."

"Unfortunately," it went on, "too often the goal is skewed toward adult (parent/coach) goals either implicitly or explicitly. As more young

Jane E. Brody is the Personal Health columnist for the *New York Times*. This article was posted on May 24, 2010, on nytimes.com and appeared in a different version in the print edition on May 25, 2010.

athletes are becoming professionals at a younger age, there is more pressure to grab a piece of the 'professional pie,' to obtain a college scholarship, or to make the Olympic team."

10   (If you doubt the role of adults, I suggest you take in a Little League game between teams striving for a championship. But instead of watching the players, watch — and listen to — the parents and coaches screaming at them, and not just words of encouragement.)

But most young athletes and their parents fail to realize that depending on the sport, only a tiny few — 2 to 5 out of 1,000 high school athletes — ever achieve professional status.

Clearly we've gone too far when the emphasis on athletic participation and performance becomes all-consuming and causes injuries that can sometimes compromise a child's future.

The sports surgeon Dr. James R. Andrews said that he now sees four times as many overuse injuries in youth sports as he did just five years ago and that more children today are having to undergo surgery for chronic sports injuries.

Though far more common today, the problem is not new. In 1952, the National Education Association took aim at the "high-pressure elements" and "highly organized competition" in youth sports that gave youngsters "an exaggerated idea of the importance of sports and may even be harmful to them."

15   In 1988 in *The Archives of Disease in Childhood*, two London-based physicians, N. Maffulli and P. Helms, concluded, "Young athletes are not just smaller athletes, and they should not become sacrificial lambs to a coach's or parent's ego."

They cited an analysis of training regimens finding that "at least 60 percent of all injuries sustained were in direct relation to training and could be avoided by appropriate changes in training programs." They explained that young athletes are more prone to certain injuries, especially stress fractures; tendinitis; a degenerative condition called osteochondrosis; and damage to the growth plates of bones that can stunt them for life.

Whitney Phelps, the older sister of the Olympics wunderkind Michael Phelps, was the swimmer to watch in the 1990s, until she burned out her body. Motivated by her mother, her coach, and her own dreams of the Olympics, she recalls, she swam through pain in her back for years, pain sometimes so severe she could hardly stand up. At 14, Mr. Hyman recounts in his book, her arms would go numb when she turned her head, and she was found to have two bulging spinal discs, a herniated disc, and two stress fractures.

Playing It Safe

A major factor in the rising injury rate is the current emphasis on playing one sport all year long, which leaves no time for muscles and joints to recover from the inevitable microtrauma that occurs during practice and play. With increased specialization, there is also no cross-training that would enable other muscles to strengthen and lighten the load.

Even when a sport is done seasonally, daily practice can result in problems. The pediatrics council recommends that young athletes "have at least one to two days off per week from competitive athletics, sport-specific training, and competitive practice (scrimmage) to allow them to recover both physically and psychologically." The group also recommends that children and adolescents play on only one team a season and take a vacation of two or three months from a specific sport each year.

20   Whatever an athlete's age, playing through pain is a bad idea. Pain is the body's signal that something is awry. Ignore it and it is likely to get worse and worse, and the injury could become permanent. Get a professional diagnosis and follow the therapeutic advice. After a prescribed period of rest, return gradually to the sport, increasing training time, repetitions, or distance by no more than 10 percent each week.

The *Pediatrics* authors also suggest that it is a sign of possible burnout when an athlete "complains of nonspecific muscle or joint problems, fatigue, or poor academic performance." That's when a child's motivation to continue in the sport should be reassessed.

Why Parents Should Let Their Kids Play Dangerous Sports
JEB GOLINKIN

Before Reading: What lessons can children learn from participating in competitive sports? Is the knowledge they gain worth the risk of injury? Explain.

"Are you not entertained? Are you NOT entertained? Is this not why you are here?"

So shouts Russell Crowe's character Maximus in the most powerful scene of Ridley Scott's award-winning film *Gladiator*, after Maximus vanquishes his opponent with such aggressiveness that it leaves the crowd in stunned silence. Maximus's point—that the crowd was there for the violence and the danger—remains as true as ever. But today, our collective fascination with bigger, faster, stronger, higher, more aggressive, more dangerous, and more powerful athletic enterprises has very real costs for the participants who deliver the thrills.

The most recent and extreme example of the dangers of our sporting culture comes from the world of extreme snowmobiling. On Thursday, a 25-year-old Texan called Caleb Moore died from injuries sustained when his snowmobile came crashing down on his head after one of his tricks went horribly wrong during his run in the Snowmobile FreeStyle competition in the Winter X Games in Aspen, Colo. Moore suffered his injuries after he attempted to do a backflip on his snowmobile. He came up short and the skis on the front of his snowmobile caught the lip of the landing area, sending Moore flying over the handlebars. When Moore hit the snow, his 450-pound snowmobile came crashing down on his head, causing injuries that ultimately led to his death. The death was the first to occur in the X Games' 18-year history, which is something of a miracle given the activities involved. The injury that led to Moore's death was broadcast live on ESPN.

This is only the latest in a long list of recent episodes illustrating the undeniable fact that the sports we love are killing the athletes we worship for playing them. For example, San Diego

When this article was posted on theweek.com on February 2, 2013, Jeb Golinkin was a law student at the University of Texas School of Law. From 2008 to 2011, he served as an editor and reporter for Frum Forum/New Majority, and currently he writes about politics for theweek.com.

Chargers legend Junior Seau shot himself in the chest—allowing his brain to be preserved and studied. Researchers concluded that Seau suffered from chronic traumatic encephalopathy (CTE), a type of chronic brain damage that is increasingly becoming a side effect of being an NFL football player.

5   The list of dangerous sports goes on and on—hockey, soccer, rugby, skiing, snowboarding, baseball. And these realizations have given rise to a debate at dinner tables and in living rooms across the United States: Should children play sports, like football, that are demonstrably dangerous, and that have long-lasting health consequences?

Indeed, no less a figure than Barack Obama recently told *The New Republic,* "If I had a son, I'd have to think long and hard before I let him play football."

But children should absolutely be allowed to play such sports. Parental fear threatens to deprive many young people of the lessons of organized athletics—lessons they cannot learn anywhere else.

I respect the president's comments, and I think they reflect the views of many parents in the United States. But I also think it is a shame that people would not allow their children to play football or ski or play hockey because of the risk of concussions. Sports, even violent and dangerous sports, continue to represent something noble about the human spirit.

Many people watch the trick that Caleb Moore died trying and think, "what kind of lunatic would even think to do such a thing?" or "what kind of parent would allow their child to do such an obviously stupid thing?" But we nevertheless watch because the tricks are so audacious, so dangerous, so . . . crazy. Caleb Moore's death is a tragedy, but it should also be recognized that Moore died doing what all great humans do in one way or another: Pushing the limits of the possible. He literally died trying to fly.

Physical safety matters. But our collective   10 obsession with protecting our children from harm threatens to turn out a generation of children ill-equipped spiritually or emotionally to deal with the brave new world order in which only the tough and the persistent will thrive. Children in modern America are growing up in a country paralyzed by complacency and fear. Our political leaders are hardly great, and our economic power is sputtering. Life is not going to be easy, or safe, even for the competent. We would do well to remember that spiritual development is every bit as important as physical safety.

Between the lines, our children learn the importance of teamwork, sportsmanship, toughness, and competitiveness. Between the lines, our children learn to strive, to succeed, and most importantly, how to fail. When the time comes, let your kid play football, or hockey . . . or whatever, and let him decide for himself. He may break his leg or suffer a concussion, but he will be far better off for it over the course of his life than if he stays inside and plays video games.

It's Time to Quit Ignoring Sports Head Trauma's Very Real Dangers

KENT SEPKOWITZ

Before Reading: Who is responsible for the health and safety of professional athletes? Who makes the call when an athlete is out for the rest of the game, the rest of the season, or the rest of his or her life? What about cases that are less obvious, like when a football player suffers concussions but is still able to play?

During this week's Super Bowl, we all will get a chance to star in *Gladiator*—thankfully not as one of those Russell Crowe guys who gets ripped to shreds, but rather as an extra up in the bleachers: one of the wealthy, the drunk, the dudes with a hot date ready to watch the lions do their carnivorous stuff.

However [even more] than dismemberment and crushed bones, we Super Bowliators will witness a more subtle actuarial event—the early moments of chronic traumatic encephalopathy (also called CTE). It will be years till we know which players will be affected, but one or two (or three or four) eventually will appear as the sad story on page 20 of the sports section.

CTE is a progressive neurologic syndrome that causes an array of symptoms, from dementia to severe headaches to suicidal depression. Only five years have passed since its first descriptions by pathologists, and its *bona fides* in the most orthodox academic neurologic circles are not fully established. Yet the epidemiologic and neuroanatomic evidence is extremely compelling: it appears to be the direct product of frequent impact-related brain injury. To date, it has been found at autopsy in a variety of athletes, professional and amateur alike.

One and all seem stunned that repeated high impact trauma over years could actually cause a problem—though in boxing the association is so well established (and self-evident) that they have bequeathed a Latin-ish name, dementia pugilistica (a.k.a., being punch-drunk), on the syndrome. But even for football the news is not new. More than 100 years ago, the doctors for the Harvard football team described a player who "still complains of difficulty in studying and concentrating his mind and of almost constant headaches" one to two years after his concussion.

So here we are with a real problem: Behind curtain one, we have the greedy sports commissioners of various stripes who oversee the multi-billion-dollar sports industrial complex; behind curtain two, players who want to play, who are really talented, who want fame and fortune; behind curtain three, the drooling American public (including me) who loves it all—the violence, the danger, the incredible might of a great football game; and behind curtain four—*way* behind curtain four, the dithering doctors who meekly report these things, then run the other way to avoid the possibility of being yelled at.

The habits of this last group surely are not new: We doctors have been comparably pathetic through the decades, failing to stand up for the public health in issues such as cigarettes, firearms, automobile danger, obesity, nuclear

5

Kent Sepkowitz is an infectious disease specialist in New York City who has contributed to the *New York Times*, *Slate*, and *O* magazine. This article was posted on thedailybeast.com on February 2, 2012.

war, and on and on. To be fair, we often have other public-health catastrophes with more immediate bite and for the acute we're there: avian flu—count us in; SARS—where do I sign up? Katrina—next plane. *Semper paratus.*

But here's how leading CTE scientific investigators want to approach the problem: "Data from helmet concussion monitors that are used on soldiers and football players can aid in predicting the character and location of lesions from an impact of a given force at given coordinates while improving the accuracy of diaries of people at risk for traumatic brain injury. Accurate diaries, in turn, should help in determining more accurately the number and severity of head injuries, allowing estimation of athletes' cumulative risk."

In other words, citizens—we will study the problem! For a few years! OK then!

Given this confluence of remarkable greed, desperation, and dithering, I have a very immodest proposal—let's stop playing football till we can sort this out. That's right—no Super Bowl XLVI and maybe no XLVII either! Why the long face? After all, we live in a country where no one seemed too bent out of shape over stopping the U.S. government. Just last year, we allowed a few pissed-off congressmen to have a tantrum or two over—wait, I can't even remember the reason, and they drove the government to the brink before backing down. And football players themselves this very year decided their cut of the dough wasn't quite right and were locked out until it could be sorted out.

For physicians worried that the evidence on CTE just isn't there, I say this: our job is not to oversee the conduct of a giant clinical trial on the entire human population, then prepare PowerPoint slides for the next meeting. We have allowed our pursuit of solid evidence to serve as an alibi for our collective professional paralysis: can't intervene—no evidence. This stance conveniently provides us (and us alone) a double benefit: we both are ennobled by insisting upon clean data while being relieved of the pressures of decisionmaking or responsibility.

But please—it is not better, more-accurate helmet monitors we need or a new stain that can demonstrate tau protein more convincingly or a PET scan that can show CTE earlier or better or differently. It's us doctors, all 500,000 of us saying enough already, thumbs down on Russell Crowe and Eli Manning and the lot of them. We should not allow the gladiatorial slaughter to continue. And remind me—just what additional data are we waiting for?

10

Bring Truth into Play by Saying Yes to Drugs in Sport
CRAIG FRY

Before Reading: What are the arguments against the use of performance-enhancing drugs by athletes? Can you think of any arguments in favor of their use? Explain.

The 2012 Tour de France starts this weekend under yet another drugs cloud. The U.S. Anti-Doping Agency's recent announcement of "doping" charges against Lance Armstrong and others is no small matter.

If the case is proven, it will nullify Armstrong's record seven Tour de France wins between 1999 and 2005, and reverberate much more widely through international cycling. This being an Olympic year, it amplifies the relevance of this case for world sport generally.

It is a good time to reflect on our current thinking about performance enhancement in sport.

Most people are against performance enhancing drugs in elite sport based on the fairness and equity ideal of a level playing field, and a belief that "doping" is unnatural and poses a health risk.

5   But what is the truth of performance enhancement in elite competition? Let's take the level playing field idea first.

These days, elite-level sportspeople have an increasing array of performance enhancing options and technologies available — from lighter, smoother, stronger, and more aerodynamic competition clothing and equipment to scientifically advanced skills and fitness training regimes. The list goes on.

Access to these resources is far from equal. Major equity gaps exist across and within countries as a function of national wealth, develop-ment, and politics. Gaps also exist between certain sports due to differences in marketability and public profile, and related funding.

The genetic lottery of sporting ability is hardly fair either. The people who compete for Olympic medals, world championships, and Tour de France jerseys are the genetic exceptions, not the rule.

We might all agree in principle that striving for greater equity in sporting competition is important. But belief in that ideal doesn't commit us to judging all examples of advantage or disadvantage as unfair or morally wrong. Like it or not, in sport there is difference and this is determined by more than natural abilities alone.

10   What about the argument that performance enhancing drugs are problematic because they are unnatural, dangerous, and risky?

In elite sport no one gets to be the fastest, strongest, or most skilled through natural hard work alone. In addition to the performance technologies already highlighted above, a cornucopia of nutritional, medicinal, and other aids for energy, recovery, pain and stress relief, and emotional and mental health is now available to athletes.

Use of these consumable performance enhancers is widespread in the highest levels of all sports, with government-funded scientific programs and large teams of health and other professionals devoted to maximizing outcomes.

Craig Fry is a principal fellow at the Centre for Health & Society and Centre for Applied Philosophy and Public Ethics, Melbourne University (Australia), specializing in drugs in society, health ethics, and policy. His article appeared on theage.com on June 29, 2012.

Why make a distinction between these accepted examples and performance enhancement through use of corticosteroids, testosterone, erythropoietin, clenbuterol, and the like?

Many say such substances and other doping practices should be restricted because of risks to athlete health. There are indeed risks with the use of these banned substances.

15   But safe forms of most of these are in use in other areas of life. And legally obtained drugs and medicines have risks and side effects too if used inappropriately.

For many people, the fact that certain practices are defined as illegal or prohibited in the sporting context is reason enough to accept them as such. Regulations that aim to govern sporting conduct are necessary at all levels, but we should acknowledge there is no divine or universal truth to the rules of sporting competition. These are subjectively defined, and history confirms that these change over time as knowledge and attitudes evolve and societal expectations shift.

We may like to believe that our modern sporting rules and laws uphold the ideals of equity and natural risk-free achievement in elite sport. Yet current practices suggest that the true spirit of elite sporting competition is more consistent with the Athenian ideal of superhuman effort at any cost.

The truth is "health risk" occupies a central place in sporting competition. We applaud our sporting heroes when they take risks and triumph through injury. Putting your body on the line, pushing physical limits, and courageous play are as much a part of the allure of elite sporting competition as any interest in fairness and upholding the rules.

There will always be athletes at the highest levels willing to use banned drugs and other substances. The allure of fame, money, power, and position for the successful will see to that.

The inconvenient truth is that the current drugs and substances prohibited from elite sporting competition are not uniquely dangerous or risky, or inherently harmful. Nor are they the only or biggest sources of risk.   20

We have the knowledge to use such things safely in sport if we so choose. Instead, our approach encourages clandestine doping.

As we have seen with drugs and other substances regarded as dangerous, prohibition policies serve to create illicit markets of hidden, uninformed, and unregulated consumption. The evidence confirms such conditions exacerbate a range of health and other harms to both individual and community.

The level playing field and natural, risk-free achievement in elite sport are sentimental myths. Using these ideals to argue against performance enhancing drugs in sport makes little sense and does not reflect the truth of elite sporting competition as it occurs today.

An alternative would be an open and regulated approach to performance enhancing drugs in elite sport. This would be consistent with the range of other enhancement technologies and resources used now. It would also better enable us to prevent and or minimize the health risks to those athletes already using prohibited substances secretly.

Editor's note: In 2012, the U.S. Anti-Doping Agency banned Armstrong from cycling for life and stripped him of his seven Tour titles and other honors he had received between 1999 and 2005 after finding him guilty of using performance-enhancing drugs during those years.

Performance Enhancing Drugs

JIMMY MARGULIES

Before Reading: What do you know about PEZ candies?

PoliticalCartoons.com/Jimmy Margulies

Jimmy Margulies is the editorial cartoonist for *The Record* in the northern New Jersey suburbs of New York City. He is the past winner of both the National Headliner Award and the Fischetti Editorial Cartoon Competition. This cartoon appeared in January 2013.

No on Sickle Cell Trait Testing
MARK PELUSO AND PAUL BERKNER

Before Reading: We hear each year of those rare but tragic cases in which a high school or college athlete dies suddenly while participating in a sporting event or during practice. Do you feel that our schools do enough to protect the health of athletes? Could more be done to avoid these deaths? Explain.

This week, members of the National Collegiate Athletic Association's Division III will vote on a medically controversial and unsubstantiated policy regarding sickle cell trait (SCT) testing for Division III athletes. Based on the current medical literature, the delegates would be wise to vote against the proposal.

The policy stems from a 2009 settlement by the NCAA of a lawsuit involving the death of a Rice University football player. The death was attributed to SCT, and the NCAA began recommending that athletics departments confirm SCT status in all athletes, if it is not already known, during their required medical examinations. While individuals can opt out if they agree to education and sign liability waivers, mandatory SCT education and confirmation of SCT status of athletes began in Division I in 2010, and in Division II in 2011. The current NCAA proposal would extend the policy to Division III starting in 2013.

SCT is a genetic condition involving red blood cells. Unlike sickle cell disease, which can have serious health consequences, SCT individuals do not typically experience any symptoms and may not know that they have SCT. The red blood cells in individuals with sickle cell disease or SCT can become deformed and lead to health problems. This is known as sickling and

is far more common in individuals with sickle cell disease.

Recent reports in the medical literature have suggested that SCT may contribute to death in athletes. The topic remains highly controversial, with some authors suggesting that exertional sickling has killed or led to collapse of many athletes and military trainees. Other authors disagree and suggest that SCT screening is unnecessary and may be harmful, and that implementing education and universal safety measures would protect all athletes.

In January 2012 the American Society of Hematology (ASH) issued a statement opposing the NCAA SCT screening policy as a means to reduce exertion-related illness or death. Other expert groups and medical organizations, such as the American Medical Society for Sports Medicine and a Department of Health and Human Services advisory committee, have published papers or statements that recognize but do not endorse mandatory pre-participation SCT testing. The authors of these papers and statements advocate for further research, education of athletes and coaches, and implementation of safety measures rather than screening.

Hematology and sports medicine experts are correct in not endorsing mandatory testing because the pathophysiology of SCT-associated death remains unknown. The well-intentioned

5

Mark Peluso is medical director and head team physician at Middlebury College. Paul Berkner is medical director and team physician at Colby College. Their article was posted on insidehighered.com on January 18, 2013.

pro-SCT testing argument is based on limited information obtained from autopsies and case reports and may not have fully investigated other potential contributors to the athlete's demise. The presumption that SCT contributed to the athlete's death because deformed/sickled cells were found at autopsy may not be accurate. The problem is that the presence of sickled cells in postmortem tissue specimens from a person with SCT does not guarantee pre-mortem sickling. Red blood cells can become deformed in SCT patients when they are deprived of oxygen. Since this is exactly what happens when a person dies, we might expect to see sickled cells in an autopsy of a patient with SCT. As one author wrote: "Sickling seen in postmortem samples is most likely an artifact of death."

More importantly, good medical policy should rest on a foundation of evidence-based medicine. Unfortunately, well-controlled, hypothesis-driven prospective studies on SCT and exertional collapse are lacking. More research is needed to understand the pathophysiology of death in athletes with SCT and determine whether screening high-risk populations reduces mortality. It is particularly interesting that two recent papers on SCT, co-authored by the NCAA's director of health and safety, David Klossner, and published after the 2010 NCAA Division I SCT rule went into effect, have concluded that additional research is needed to understand the value of screening for SCT in athletes.

Epidemiologists have noted that an extremely small number of deaths in a highly prevalent carrier state implies that other genetic or environmental factors play a role. SCT is considered a fairly common condition, yet only a small number of athletes have presumably succumbed from SCT over the past 30–40 years. The reported deaths also have a high predilection for Division I football players. As one study noted, all but 2 of 19 deaths associated with SCT in NCAA athletes since 1973 have been in Division I football players. There were no deaths related to SCT in Division III athletes, including Division III football players.

The proposed testing method has also raised concerns. Due to cost, the NCAA is recommending that schools use a blood test that experts consider to be inferior and less accurate than more expensive methods. The NCAA-proposed test does not have the ability to identify other forms of blood disorders. False negative tests would provide false reassurance, potentially putting athletes at even greater risk. Finally, athlete and military recruit deaths have occurred despite knowledge of sickle cell trait in the individual.

While the NCAA should be praised for its interest in athlete safety, it has misrepresented medical data in its quest to mandate SCT testing for all athletes. For example, in the October 2012 NCAA DIII monthly update the NCAA stated that "Another study, published in 2012, concluded that student-athletes with sickle cell trait have a relative risk of exertion-related death that is 37 times higher than those without it." However, the original paper notes that "All deaths associated with SCT occurred in black Division I football athletes. The risk of exertional death in Division I football players with SCT was 37 times higher than in athletes without SCT."

That is an important distinction when considering a screening program that would annually affect thousands of athletes. The same NCAA Division III update also stated that

10

"13.6 percent of Division III schools that participated reported removing a student-athlete with sickle cell trait from a competition, practice, or workout because they were concerned they may be developing a dangerous condition secondary to their sickle cell trait status." However, supporting evidence that patient symptoms were due to complications from SCT is not provided, and their condition cannot be attributed to SCT. The NCAA's assertion that "the knowledge of a student-athlete's sickle cell trait status can lead to appropriate precautions and interventions" is not supported in the available medical literature and remains controversial.

The cost of an SCT screening program, while secondary to an institution's interest in protecting its students, must also be considered. The NCAA-published basic solubility test costs between $8.50 and $32.50 per test. The $8.50 test does not include phlebotomy costs, which would add $5 to $10 per test. Some schools do not have easy access to the lab associated with the NCAA pricing and are looking at costs as high as $75 per athlete tested. Administrative costs associated with tracking results and compliance have not been included in the NCAA

analysis and could place a significant burden on DIII sports medicine departments, which typically have fewer resources than other NCAA divisions. Most importantly, the cost of an unproven screening program may divert funding away from other important health issues.

Rather than succumb to fear or the NCAA's institutional momentum, the Division III delegates voting on the SCT screening measure should base their vote on sound scientific principles and recognize that many caring and responsible physicians and medical organizations have opposed screening for SCT. The NCAA has exaggerated existing medical data and is promoting use of an inferior screening test that may lead to false reassurances.

The delegates would be wise to pass a measure that promotes further research on the role of SCT in exertion-related collapse and death, emphasizes education of athletes around SCT and other issues that may cause harm, promotes a voluntary testing process that includes a personal discussion between athletes and their physicians, and most importantly, adopts universal safety precautions and measures to enhance the safety of all athletes.

The NFL Concussion Crisis & The Doctor-Patient Relationship
ANDREW M. BLECHER

Before Reading: What have you read or heard about the "concussion crisis" in professional football?

If you are reading this then you are already well aware of the current concussion crisis in the NFL. No matter where on the spectrum your opinions lie regarding this topic, there is one question that still remains: How did we get here? Surely if something has gone wrong then there must be someone to blame for it. Was it the league's fault? The coaches? The players? The doctors? Maybe it is the injury itself that's to blame? Perhaps it was just the perfect storm of a number of factors that put us in this situation? To truly get to the bottom of this, it is important to have a better understanding of the doctor-patient relationship. Not just in general, but specifically as it applies to concussed athletes in the NFL. Ultimately we may not find blame here, but we should at least shed some light on the realities of the situation.

As a sports medicine physician, I have taken care of thousands of concussed athletes at all levels. Eight-year-old hockey players, high school soccer players, collegiate football players, professional moto-cross racers, and skaters, you name it. For all of them, the doctor-patient dynamic is similar. However, for the NFL players, that dynamic is entirely different. Let's begin by looking at the usual non-NFL doctor-patient relationship. If I evaluate a concussed athlete either on the sideline of a college stadium or during clinic in my office, the roles are clearly defined. An injured athlete is being evaluated by an independent expert in the field of con-

cussions. Either the athlete has sought me out in the office or the school has asked me to be there because I am good at what I do. I am not employed by the athlete or by the team. I answer to nobody and base my decisions on my training and my instinct. When I diagnose a player with a concussion I educate them and their family that they should not be participating in activities that put them at risk of further head injury until they have fully recovered from the concussion, however long that will be. This education may not be easy. After all, the athlete wants to get back to play ASAP. The athlete considers the concussion to be minor and it doesn't inhibit their ability to play (so they think). That's the thing about concussions. It affects cognitive function and diminishes one's ability to make rational, thoughtful decisions. Therefore it can be extremely difficult to properly educate the athlete about why they must not be playing.

Why is this education so important? Because I cannot go home with them and hold their hand and prevent them from going skateboarding, or skiing, or playing pick-up basketball. I might be able to hold them out of their sanctioned sport by giving them a note that says they aren't cleared, but ultimately they must be convinced of what I am telling them in order to protect themselves. They aren't cleared to play

Andrew M. Blecher is a board certified sports medicine physician at the Southern California Orthopedic Institute who provides concussion management for both amateur and professional athletes. His article was posted on nflconcussionlitigation.com on April 29, 2012.

in a sanctioned event at their institution because of my note and because the institution doesn't want to assume the liability. But nobody is stopping them from doing what they do on their own time in their backyard or in their driveway. So ultimately the athlete and the family must trust that what I'm saying is in their own best interest. And why wouldn't it be? Because after all I am an independent expert who is a patient advocate who answers to nobody.

Now let's look at the doctor-patient relationship in the NFL. Many people may believe that the NFL team doctors are the very best of the best and are carefully sought out by NFL teams and are hired by the teams to provide the best medical care to their players so that their multi-million dollar investments are well protected. Makes sense right? Unfortunately this is not necessarily the case. NFL team doctors are not paid salaries by the teams. In fact, most team doctors pay the teams for the right to be the team doctors. Yes, you read that correctly. A medical group or hospital system will often pay the team for the right to be the team physicians. Why? Because they receive a marketing package to promote themselves as the team physicians. Is this valuable? Well, many physicians think so and are willing to pay hundreds of thousands of dollars a year (sometimes approaching $1 million/year) for the right to be NFL team physicians. This is not to say that some team physicians are not incredible doctors, because many times they are in fact the best of the best. However, that's usually not how they got the job. They got the job because of the marketing rights for the group or hospital. So now who is managing the concussions on an NFL sideline? Is it an independent expert in the field, or is it whomever is the best-trained representative of the medical team that paid for the rights to be there?

If you correctly understand this situation, then you would guess that historically the doctor on the sidelines to evaluate concussions would be either an orthopedic surgeon or an internist. Respectively they might be outstanding doctors in their field, but neither of them likely has had specific training in managing concussions. Even if they had, let's look at what that training might have entailed. For years there were many different guidelines for diagnosing and managing concussions. These were not based on any scientific evidence but instead on the opinions of various experts from the fields of neurology and neurosurgery. By and large these guidelines stated that it was OK to send an athlete back into the game if their concussion symptoms were minimal and temporary. So now let's look at a typical NFL concussion situation and see how this plays out.

It's the third quarter and the quarterback gets sacked. He is slow to get up and wobbles a little bit. He comes over to the sideline and says he has a headache but otherwise he feels fine. His team is down by a touchdown and he wants to get back into the game. Should he? And if not, who is going to stop him? Does the athletic trainer or the team doctor have an obligation to examine the athlete? Well, historically the answer is not really. If the athlete doesn't seek out medical assistance then he may not get it. If he is minimizing his symptoms and wants to be tough and get back out there (which of course is the culture of the game because continuing to play after getting your bell rung is a badge of honor) then he might not present to be evaluated or may even go so far as to refuse to be evaluated because he states that he is completely fine. Remember, the concussed athlete does not make good decisions due to the concussion itself. If the athlete happens to be lucky enough to be evaluated by the team physician, then hopefully he will have a thorough physical exam and cognitive evaluation and the diagnosis of concussion will be made. Was that always the case? We can't say for sure, but even if it was, then what? The physician must decide whether the athlete can return to play. With any return to play decision the physician takes two important things into consideration: 1) Is the player at risk of further injury by playing? 2) Is the player at risk of long term or permanent damage by playing? Historically there have not been solid answers to these questions. Guidelines have said that if symptoms are minimal and temporary (which of course they will be because the athlete is minimizing them) then return to play is OK. What's the real danger of returning to play anyway? Is it Second Impact Syndrome? Typically that is the correct answer, but no NFL player has ever suffered Second Impact Syndrome. In fact, Second Impact Syndrome is so rare that arguably there are less than 20 true occurrences that have ever been reported, and they all occurred in adolescents, not grown men. So we never really knew for sure that there was a risk of worsening the injury by returning an NFL player back into the game on the same day. There were also no good long-term studies that told us without a doubt that there was a risk of permanent long-term damage either. So the athlete wants to play, the team wants the athlete to play, and now the doctor must determine if it is OK to play. Well, there is no written evidence-based guideline for the physician to rely on to give a reason not to play. Even if the physician's instinct might be extremely conser-

vative and wants to hold the player out, does the physician really want to be the only doctor in the NFL who is doing this? As they say, NFL stands for "Not For Long" and the physician might find himself no longer on the sidelines if he is holding all of his team's players out against their will and the wishes of the team. After all, the doctor is easily replaceable with someone else who wants to be part of the marketing package. So with no real reason to hold the player out and many pressures to put them back in (including the athlete's own desire to go back in) . . . back in they go.

Maybe the athlete will take a few aspirin for the headache, but that's where the treatment ends. And what about the educational part where the player gets taught about his condition? No time for that because the clock is running and the game is going on. How about after the game? Well, the player finished the game just fine and just has a headache and does not want to be bothered by the medical staff with education about head injuries. The player might not even trust the medical staff's opinion anyway since the athlete believes that the medical staff works for the team. The athlete didn't seek out that specific physician for an opinion so how can he trust him to be an independent patient advocate looking out for his best interest? And is the athlete going to now go see his own personal doctor to be evaluated for the concussion? Of course not. Many of these players didn't even have personal doctors and even if they did they would be minimizing their symptoms and wouldn't feel the need to go. So unless they had family or friends who forced them to go get evaluated, it wasn't going to happen. So where should the educational part have come from? Should it have been mandated by the league? Who would have provided it and who would have really listened? With no educational part to the concussion management protocol, the athlete goes right back to practice and on to the next game.

This is how for years NFL players with mild concussions were able to keep playing and keep putting themselves at risk for the next head injury. It wasn't until all of these players got older and their permanent long-term effects became well documented that we were finally able to recognize the true seriousness of concussions. We now know that these injuries have cumulative effects. We now know that it is not OK for a concussed athlete to ever go back into the game. We now have league guidelines for head injuries and we have independent experts in the field of concussion who thoroughly evaluate all concussed players. We now have the tools to save the athletes from themselves. Younger players are learning from the older players and the culture is slowly changing. Should all of these revelations have occurred years ago? Absolutely. But they didn't. So whose fault was it? The player, the doctor, the league, the culture, the concussion, the perfect storm? . . . You decide.

Thinking and Writing about the Dangers of Competitive Sports

1. What is Jane Brody's claim in "For Children in Sports, a Breaking Point"? Is it a claim of fact, value, or policy? Explain.

2. What are some of the solutions that Brody offers?

3. Jeb Golinkin accepts that "the sports we love are killing the athletes we worship for playing them" (para. 4), yet he would not have parents keep their children from participating in these sports. What values are behind his claim?

4. What lessons do children learn from sports that they cannot learn anywhere else?

5. Which author builds a more convincing case, Brody or Golinkin? Why?

6. Is there any validity to Kent Sepkowitz's comparison between the Super Bowl and *Gladiator* (or Golinkin's between athletic events and *Gladiator*)? How do fans respond to injuries on the football field? Have you heard cheers that suggest fans encourage injuring the opposing team members?

7. What have "leading CTE scientific investigators" (para. 7) proposed? What does Sepkowitz suggest instead? How convincing do you find his argument?

8. How do you respond to Craig Fry's argument that risk is a central part of sports?

9. Do you agree with Fry that the spirit of current competitive sports is "more consistent with the Athenian ideal of superhuman effort at any

cost" than "the ideals of equity and natural risk-free achievement" (para. 17)? Explain.

10. What is Fry's solution to what he sees as the problem of regulating performance-enhancing drugs? Do you find that an acceptable solution? Why, or why not?

11. Explain how, in his cartoon, Jimmy Margulies is playing on the name of PEZ candies to make a point about drug use by athletes.

12. In "No on Sickle Cell Trait Testing," Mark Peluso and Paul Berkner downplay the fact that SCT affects almost exclusively members of some ethnic groups and not others. Is that fact relevant to the debate?

13. Do you find Peluso and Berkner's argument convincing? Why, or why not?

14. Explain how the doctor-patient relationship is different in the NFL than in other situations, according to Andrew Blecher.

15. Explain how the concussion crisis in the NFL is a result of the clash of values.

16. How does Sid Kirchheimer's essay, "Are Sports Fans Happier?" (pp. 188–91) in Chapter 6, contribute to the conversation about the role of sports in our culture?

Freedom of Speech

Are Limitations on Our Rights Ever Justified?

The First Amendment to the Constitution of the United States reads, "Congress shall make no laws respecting an establishment of religion, or prohibiting the free expression thereof; or abridging the freedom of speech, or of the press; or the right of the people peaceably to assemble, and to petition the Government for a redress of grievances." (The first ten amendments were ratified on December 15, 1791, and form what is known as the Bill of Rights.) The arguments in this section will consider primarily the issue of "abridging the freedom of speech."

The limits of free speech in the United States are constantly being adjusted as social values change and new cases testing those limits emerge. Several prominent areas of controversy are emphasized in the following selections.

The world of the Internet and all of the electronic communications devices that have come with it offer a whole new realm of means of "speaking." Words and images can reach the other side of the globe instantly, and the very speed and ease with which communication can take place have made people careless at times about sharing too much with too many. At the same time, there are more ways than ever of accessing the conversations of others, and some highly publicized cases have focused on the government's right to access private citizens' communications and to keep from private citizens any information about activities in which the government is involved.

Hate speech posted online is not illegal in the United States, as it is in some other countries. An exception are those cases in which online threats target the president of the United States, a fact that some have learned to their regret.

Are there times when limits should be placed on freedom of speech? And who decides? Those are two of the questions the selections in this chapter address.

Social Media Dark Side

MIKE KEEFE

Before Reading: What evidence of the dark side of social networking have you seen firsthand, or read or heard about through the media?

PoliticalCartoons.com/Mike Keefe

Mike Keefe is the winner of the 2011 Pulitzer Prize, and his cartoons are nationally syndicated by Cagle Cartoons. This cartoon appeared in May 2013.

The Case for Censoring Hate Speech on the Internet

SEAN McELWEE

Before Reading: Have you seen examples of hate speech on the social networking sites that you frequent? If so, what sort of response do they receive from other readers? If you have not seen any examples online, have you read or heard of cases in which hate speech led readers to exhibit violence against themselves or others? Explain.

For the past few years speech has moved online, leading to fierce debates about its regulation. Most recently, feminists have led the charge to purge Facebook of misogyny that clearly violates its hate-speech code. Facebook took a small step two weeks ago, creating a feature that will remove ads from pages deemed "controversial." But such a move is half-hearted. Facebook and other social networking websites should not tolerate hate speech and, in the absence of a government mandate, adopt a European model of expunging offensive material.

Stricter regulation of Internet speech will not be popular with the libertarian-minded citizens of the United States, but it's necessary. A typical view of the case against expunging hate speech comes from Jeffrey Rosen, who argues in *The New Republic* that:

> . . . given their tremendous size and importance as platforms for free speech, companies like Facebook, Google, Yahoo, and Twitter shouldn't try to be guardians of what Waldron calls a "well-ordered society"; instead, they should consider themselves the modern version of Oliver Wendell Holmes's fractious marketplace of ideas — democratic spaces where all values, including civility norms, are always open for debate.

This image is romantic and lovely but it's worth asking what this actually looks like. Rosen forwards one example:

> Last year, after the French government objected to the hashtag "#unbon juif" — intended to inspire hateful riffs on the theme "a good Jew . . ." — Twitter blocked a handful of the resulting tweets in France, but only because they violated French law. Within days, the bulk of the tweets carrying the hashtag had turned from anti-Semitic to denunciations of anti-Semitism, confirming that the Twittersphere is perfectly capable of dealing with hate speech on its own, without heavy-handed intervention.

It's interesting to note how closely this idea resembles free market fundamentalism: simply get rid of any coercive rules, and the "marketplace of ideas" will naturally produce the best result. Humboldt State University compiled a visual map that charts 150,000 hateful insults aggregated over the course of 11 months in the U.S. by pairing Google's Maps API with a series of the most homophobic, racist, and otherwise prejudiced tweets. The map's existence draws into question the notion that the "twittersphere" can organically combat hate speech. Hate speech is not going to disappear from Twitter on its own.

When Sean McElwee posted this piece to policymic.com in July 2013, he was a research assistant looking for a job in research, writing, and public policy.

5 The negative impacts of hate speech cannot be mitigated by the responses of third-party observers, as hate speech aims at two goals. First, it is an attempt to tell bigots that they are not alone. Frank Collins, the neo-Nazi prosecuted in *National Socialist Party of America v. Skokie* (1977), said, "We want to reach the good people, get the fierce anti-Semites who have to live among the Jews to come out of the woodwork and stand up for themselves."

The second purpose of hate speech is to intimidate the targeted minority, leading them to question whether their dignity and social status is secure. In many cases, such intimidation is successful. Consider the number of rapes that go unreported. Could this trend possibly be affected by Reddit threads like /r/raping women or /r/mensrights? Could it be due to the harassment women face when they even suggest the possibility they were raped? The rape culture that permeates Facebook, Twitter, and the public dialogue must be held at least partially responsible for our larger rape culture.

Reddit, for instance, has become a veritable potpourri of hate speech. Consider Reddit threads like /r/nazi, /r/killawoman, /r/misogyny, /r/killingwomen. My argument is not that these should be taken down because they are offensive, but rather because they amount to the degradation of a class that has been historically oppressed. Imagine a Reddit thread for /r/lynchingblacks or /r/assassinatingthe president. We would not argue that we should sit back and wait for this kind of speech to be "outspoken" by positive speech, but that it should be entirely banned.

American free-speech jurisprudence relies upon the assumption that speech is merely the extension of a thought, and not an action. If we consider it an action, then saying that we should combat hate speech with more positive speech is an absurd proposition; the speech has already done the harm, and no amount of support will defray the victims' impression that they are not truly secure in this society. We don't simply tell the victim of a robbery, "Hey, it's okay, there are lots of other people who aren't going to rob you." Similarly, it isn't incredibly useful to tell someone who has just had their race, gender, or sexuality defamed, "There are a lot of other nice people out there."

Those who claim to "defend free speech" when they defend the right to post hate speech online are in truth backwards. Free speech isn't an absolute right—no right is weighed in a vacuum. The Court has imposed numerous restrictions on speech. Fighting words, libel, and child pornography are all banned. Other countries merely go one step further by banning speech intended to intimidate vulnerable groups. The truth is that such speech does not democratize speech, it monopolizes speech. Women, LGBT individuals, and racial or religious minorities feel intimidated and are left out of the public sphere. On Reddit, for example, women have left or changed their usernames to be more male-sounding lest they face harassment and intimidation for speaking on Reddit about even the most gender-neutral topics. Even outside of the intentionally offensive sub-reddits (i.e. /r/imgoingtohellforthis) misogyny is pervasive. I encountered this when browsing /r/funny.

Those who try to remove this hate speech 10 have been criticized from left and right. At *Slate*, Jillian York writes, "While the campaigners on this issue are to be commended for raising awareness of such awful speech on Facebook's platform, their proposed solution is ultimately futile and sets a dangerous precedent for special interest groups looking to bring their pet issue to the attention of Facebook's censors."

It hardly seems right to qualify a group fighting hate speech as an "interest group" trying to bring their "pet issue" to the attention of Facebook censors. The "special interest" groups she fears might apply for protection must meet Facebook's strict community standards, which state:

> While we encourage you to challenge ideas, institutions, events, and practices, we do not permit individuals or groups to attack others based on their race, ethnicity, national origin, religion, sex, gender, sexual orientation, disability, or medical condition.

If anything, the groups to which York refers are nudging Facebook towards actually enforcing its own rules.

People who argue against such rules generally portray their opponents as standing on a slippery precipice, tugging at the question "What next?" We can answer that question: Canada, England, France, Germany, The Netherlands, South Africa, Australia, and India all ban hate speech. Yet, none of these countries have slipped into totalitarianism. In many ways, such countries are more free when you weigh the negative liberty to express harmful thoughts against the positive liberty that is suppressed when you allow for the intimidation of minorities.

As Arthur Schopenhauer said, "The freedom of the press should be governed by a very strict prohibition of all and every anonymity." However, with the Internet the public dialogue has moved online, where hate speech is easy and anonymous.

Jeffrey Rosen argues that norms of civility should be open to discussion, but in today's reality, this issue has already been decided. Impugning someone because of their race, gender, or sexual orientation is not acceptable in a civil society. Banning hate speech is not a mechanism to further this debate, because the debate is over.

As Jeremy Waldron argues, hate speech laws   15
prevent bigots from "trying to create the impression that the equal position of members of vulnerable minorities in a rights-respecting society is less secure than implied by the society's actual foundational commitments."

Some people argue that the purpose of laws that ban hate speech is merely to avoid offending prudes. No country, however, has mandated that anything be excised from the public square merely because it provokes offense, but rather because it attacks the dignity of a group—a practice the U.S. Supreme Court called in *Beauharnais v. Illinois* (1952) "group libel." Such a standard could easily be applied to Twitter, Reddit, and other social media websites. While Facebook's policy as written should be a model, its enforcement has been shoddy. Again, this isn't an argument for government intervention. The goal is for companies to adopt a European-model hate speech policy, one not aimed at expunging offense, but rather hate. Such a system would be subject to outside scrutiny by users.

If this is the standard, the Internet will surely remain controversial, but it can also be free of hate and allow everyone to participate. A true marketplace of ideas must co-exist with a multiracial society open to people of all genders, orientations, and religions, and it can.

Why Twitter Is Doing the Right Thing by Refusing to Identify Users Who Posted Anti-Semitic Comments
MATHEW INGRAM

Before Reading: Should freedom of speech mean that a person can say anything on a social networking site without fear of legal repercussions? Explain.

Whether it's being used as a communications tool for dissidents during the Arab Spring uprisings or a real-time newswire about events like the mass shooting at Sandy Hook elementary school, Twitter has become a crucial platform for speech of all kinds—and in many cases that speech is unpleasant and even offensive. That may be taken for granted in the United States, but it doesn't go over well in other countries with different views about speech, and that is making things increasingly difficult for Twitter. For now at least—to its credit—it seems determined to remain the "free-speech wing of the free-speech party."

Last fall, a Twitter hashtag—#UnBonJuif, or A Good Jew—resulted in a number of anti-Semitic posts. Although Twitter removed the offending tweets after a complaint by the Union of Jewish French Students (UEJF), the group was not satisfied and sued to force the service to reveal the identities of those who posted the messages. A French court eventually agreed to this demand, since anti-Semitic comments and other "hate speech" are illegal in that country.

So far, Twitter has not complied with the court order—it is appealing the judgement, arguing that since it is a U.S. company it only has to comply with such demands from U.S. courts and other authorities. Meanwhile, the UEJF said it plans to file a second lawsuit in criminal court, seeking damages of $50 million for Twitter's failure to provide the data.

A Private Company, but a Platform for Public Speech

Twitter has revealed user data in several cases after being forced to do so by U.S. courts, including personal data related to several users who were supporters of WikiLeaks, such as Icelandic MP Birgitta Jonsdottir and hacker Jacob Appelbaum. Twitter also handed over tweets by two members of the Occupy Wall Street movement, after being forced to do so by a court order, although it fought against both of these decisions—and also made the request for the Occupy supporters' data public even though it was asked not to do so.

What makes these kinds of cases so difficult is that Twitter is a private corporation with a proprietary platform, and yet it is being used as a public communications vehicle around the world, and one whose free-speech aspects are becoming increasingly important. And while we may all agree that certain types of speech are offensive, the idea that governments or courts can force Twitter to reveal the identities of those users is troubling in the extreme.

While Facebook and to some extent Google are also being used in this kind of context, Twitter is unique in the sense that it explicitly allows

5

Mathew Ingram is a writer, blogger, journalist, and social media fan. He formerly was a senior writer at the *Globe and Mail* newspaper in Toronto; was one of the founders of mesh, Canada's leading Web conference; and now is a senior writer at the GigaOm blog network. This article appeared on gigaom.com on March 27, 2013. In July 2013, the dispute between the UEJF and Twitter ended when Twitter agreed to turn the tweets in question over to the French prosecutors.

people to use pseudonyms. Facebook has a firm policy on the use of "real" or verified names, and while Google somewhat grudgingly allowed users to add pseudonyms to their Google+ accounts after what some called the "nym wars," the service is still designed primarily for "real" names. Twitter is one of the only communications platforms of its size and reach that freely allows users to be known by pseudonyms.

As sociologist Zeynep Tufekci and Jillian York of the Electronic Frontier Foundation (among others) have argued, anonymity or pseudonymity may allow for all kinds of offensive behavior—including the anti-Semitic comments in France and racist tweets posted by a number of users following the re-election of President Barack Obama—but protecting users' identities is also a crucial factor that allows Twitter to be used as a communications tool by all kinds of disadvantaged groups, including political dissidents.

The Free-Speech Wing of the Free-Speech Party

The pressure on Twitter to resist demands like the one from France stems in part from this, and also from repeated comments from the company's chief legal counsel, Alex Macgillivray, and CEO Dick Costolo that they are committed to being the "free-speech wing of the free-speech party." The company may get criticized by some

(including us) for the way it has shut down parts of its ecosystem, but its commitment to the rights of users remains.

The problem for Twitter is that as it becomes more global, it is running into country-specific demands like the one from France—or the one from Germany that led Twitter to block access to certain neo-Nazi tweets, since that kind of speech is also against the law. The risk here is that the network could easily fall victim to every government's demands for user identities or censorship in even the most ridiculous cases, such as Turkey's prohibition on comments that "insult Turkishness."

If Twitter backs down on the French order, what is to stop Syria from forcing it to reveal the identities of dissidents, or Iran from forcing it to reveal who is posting anti-Muslim comments—or Britain from forcing it to identify those who were involved in the London riots, or those who post about cases covered by the country's bizarre "super-injunctions"? Almost every country seems to have certain things that it prohibits people from saying publicly and is willing to go to court over.

But the bottom line is that freedom of speech—however offensive that speech might be—is a principle that needs all the help it can get, and Twitter deserves some credit for sticking to its guns, despite the obvious pressures it must be feeling.

Warning: College Students, This Editorial May Upset You
LOS ANGELES TIMES EDITORIAL BOARD

Before Reading: Are there subjects that should not be discussed in college classes because they could cause some students emotional or physical distress? Explain your opinion.

The latest attack on academic freedom comes not from government authorities or corporate pressure but from students. At UC Santa Barbara, the student Senate recently passed a resolution that calls for mandatory "trigger warnings"—cautions from professors, to be added to their course syllabi, specifying which days' lectures will include readings or films or discussions that might trigger feelings of emotional or physical distress.

The resolution calls for warnings if course materials will involve depictions and discussions of rape, sexual assault, suicide, pornography, or graphic violence, among other things. The professors would excuse students from those classes, with no points deducted, if the students felt the material would distress them; it is left unclear how students would complete assignments or answer test questions based on the work covered in those classes.

The student resolution is only advisory, a recommendation that campus authorities can turn into policy or reject. They should not only choose the latter course but should explain firmly to students why such a policy would be antithetical to all that college is supposed to provide: a rich and diverse body of study that often requires students to confront difficult or uncomfortable material, and encourages them to discuss such topics openly. Trigger warnings are part of a campus culture that is increasingly overprotective and hypersensitive in its efforts to ensure that no student is ever offended or made to feel uncomfortable.

Trigger warnings have been used on the Internet for a long time, first appearing on feminist websites visited by victims of sexual attacks; the goal was to protect assault victims from material that might trigger post-traumatic stress disorder. The warnings spread to a wide variety of websites and material that readers might find troubling.

That's fine for websites that voluntarily choose to caution their visitors, but it's exactly the wrong approach for colleges and universities. Oberlin College in Ohio already has gone further than UC Santa Barbara, issuing official trigger-warning guidelines for professors that sound almost like a parody of political correctness: "Triggers are not only relevant to sexual misconduct but also to anything that might cause trauma. Be aware of racism, classism, sexism, heterosexism, cissexism, ableism, and other issues of privilege and oppression. Realize that all forms of violence are traumatic."

Worse, the Oberlin guidelines go on to advise professors to remove "triggering material" from their courses entirely if it is not directly related to the course's learning goals. Such instructions come dangerously close to censorship.

Chinua Achebe's novel *Things Fall Apart* is listed by Oberlin as one possible "trigger" book because of its themes of colonialism, racism, religious prejudice, and more. At Rutgers, an op-ed in the student paper suggested that

5

This editorial was posted on latimes.com on March 31, 2014.

study of *The Great Gatsby* should require trigger warnings about violence and gore. And then what happens? Should students be excused from reading a work of great literature, or be allowed to read a sanitized version?

Professors, uncertain of what might be considered too sexual, too warlike, or so forth, might issue warnings so broad that they're meaningless, or feel pressured to bleach the syllabus to a pallid version of a real college course.

There are students who suffer from post-traumatic stress disorder, a serious psychological condition that calls for sensitive treatment. Students who have been diagnosed with it could explain their situation to individual professors, who almost certainly would be willing to work

out a sensible accommodation, preferably one that wouldn't involve missing multiple classes.

But the Santa Barbara resolution doesn't   10
cover only students who have been diagnosed with PTSD. Any student who is discomfited by the material would be excused from class if this were campus policy.

As psychologists point out, a post-traumatic response is just as likely to be triggered by something that has nothing to do with subject matter: a glimpse of the same blue-colored clothing that was visible during a traumatic event, or a certain scent that was in the air that day. Colleges cannot bubble-wrap students against everything that might be frightening or offensive to them.

140 Characters Spell Charges and Jail
ROBBIE BROWN

Before Reading: Where should the line be drawn between what is permissible free speech on Twitter and what is punishable by law?

One night last summer, Jarvis Britton of Birmingham, Ala., sent out a series of Twitter messages that he later described as "stupid" jokes. Prosecutors did not think they were funny.

"Let's Go Kill the President," wrote Mr. Britton, who is 26 and unemployed. "I think we could get the president with cyanide! #MakeItSlow."

When Secret Service agents showed up at his house to question him, Mr. Britton said he had been drunk and apologized. But in September, he posted another round of death threats against President Obama and was arrested. Last month, he was sentenced to a year in federal prison.

"Because of the repeated threats on Twitter, we took him seriously," said Joyce White Vance, the United States attorney for the Northern District of Alabama, who prosecuted the case.

Mr. Britton was the latest in a recent series   5
of social media users to overstep the boundary of legal free speech and face jail time for threatening the president's life. Last month, a Twitter user in Charlotte, N.C., Donte Jamar Sims, was sentenced to six months for posting "Ima assassinate president Obama this evening!" among other threats. And Daniel Temple of Columbus,

---

Robbie Brown is a news assistant for the *New York Times* in Atlanta. This article appeared on nytimes.com on July 2, 2013.

Ohio, is awaiting sentencing for saying on Twitter that he was "coming to kill" the president and "killing you soon."

A Secret Service spokesman, Brian Leary, said social media are increasingly useful for finding and tracking threats. In 2011, the agency created the @SecretService account, to let users report suspicious tweets. And a group of agents, called the Internet Threat Desk, focuses specifically on threats posted online.

"We get information from many sources. Social media is one of them," Mr. Leary said. "We have the right and certainly the obligation to determine a person's intent."

The Secret Service investigates an average of 10 threats against Mr. Obama each day, roughly the same number as during George W. Bush's administration, said Ronald Kessler, author of "In the President's Secret Service," a book about the agency. The agency would not confirm that number and does not say how many threats it receives and turns over to the Justice Department to prosecute.

But privacy advocates worry that remarks intended for friends and followers may be misinterpreted in a courtroom or that carelessly typed posts will be seen in the same light as letters mailed to the White House.

10   "Twitter makes it easier for people to say things they don't mean seriously and be broadcast far and wide," said Hanni Fakhoury, a staff lawyer for the Electronic Frontier Foundation, a privacy advocacy group. "If I say online that I want to kill Obama, it's far harder to assess how serious I am than if I'm standing across the street from the White House and I have a gun."

Federal law makes it punishable by up to five years in prison and a $250,000 fine to threaten the life of the president or anyone else under Secret Service protection. The law does not require proof that the suspect intended to carry out the plot.

Ms. Vance, the prosecutor, said the case against Mr. Britton was clear cut: He had posted two rounds of threatening messages and ignored the Secret Service's initial warning.

Mr. Britton, who is in prison, could not be reached. But his lawyer, Rick Burgess, said Mr. Britton had no actual plans to harm the president. Court records show that Mr. Britton has received medication for schizophrenia.

A spokeswoman for Twitter did not reply to requests for comment about whether the company removes death threats from the site or provides the Secret Service personal information about users accused of threatening the president. Court records show that in Mr. Britton's case, a woman saw his messages, alerted the Secret Service, and agents found his home address.

The Justice Department does not say how   15 many threats against the president have been prosecuted, according to a spokesman.

Last year, a college student in Florida said he was joking when he posted on Facebook about killing the president during a trip to the University of Miami. "Who wants to help me assassinate Obummer while hes at UM this week?" the student, Joaquin Serrapio, asked. He later was charged with threatening to harm the president, a felony. He pleaded guilty and received three years' probation.

In another case, Walter Bagdasarian of San Diego said he was drunk when he posted a rant on his blog saying the president "will have a 50 cal in the head soon," referring to a

.50-caliber rifle bullet. In federal court, he won an appeal by arguing that his comment stopped short of being a threat.

The cases based on such threats should be a reminder that there are limits on the First Amendment's protection of free speech, said Mr. Burgess, the defense lawyer. "Whether you meant it as a joke or not," he said, "a Twitter message takes on a whole new meaning when it's read in a courtroom."

In San Diego's BofA Case, Chalk One Up for the Jury System
PATT MORRISON

Before Reading: Are there limits to what graffiti is covered by the First Amendment? Should there be? Explain.

Well, that was a pretty pointless expenditure of tax money. Even some potential jurors said so.

The 12 people who did wind up on a San Diego jury deliberated for five hours before they acquitted a man who chalked anti-bank messages on sidewalks in front of the banks.

I hope deliberations lasted all of five hours because they were getting a free lunch.

Jeff Olson was on trial on 13 misdemeanor counts of vandalism, which could have brought, at the absurd and unlikely extreme, 13 separate one-year jail sentences for the 13 occasions Olson chalked the sidewalk with messages such as "No Thanks, Big Banks" and "Shame on Bank of America." Once or twice, he drew a tentacle octopus grabbing dollar bills.

5   By modern measures of protest and graffiti, these slogans could have been written by Emily Post.

Prosecutors sternly called it a "standard graffiti case," but this wasn't some gang menacingly marking its territory. And after all, it was, as San Diego Mayor Bob Filner said with asperity, *chalk*.

One BofA branch reportedly claimed that it spent $6,000 cleaning up the chalked messages. $6,000? Who was out there cleaning the sidewalk, the CEO? With a toothbrush?

(I just threw that out there, but looking around, it turns out that BofA CEO Brian Moynihan got paid $12 million last year. That's a million a month, $50,000 a day for a 20-day work month, and let's say a 10-hour workday, which works out to $5,000 an hour. So, a little over an hour's work cleaning chalk—sure, why not? I'll acknowledge the $6,000 cost—if it really was Moynihan out there mopping up.)

I'm sure that what galled BofA wasn't the mess but the message.

Olson hoped his chalked slogans would   10
prompt the public to consider switching accounts from BofA to local nonprofit credit unions.

His case was making headlines at the same time that former BofA employees were accusing BofA of rewarding employees with cash bonuses and gift cards if they lied and denied, delayed and obfuscated, and ultimately were able to boot out of their houses and foreclose on families who were paying their house payments and desperately trying to hold onto their homes.

Patt Morrison is a *Los Angeles Times* columnist and writer, having been part of two Pulitzer Prize–winning journalistic teams, and an Emmy-winning television host and commentator. This op-ed piece appeared on July 2, 2013, on latimes.com.

If BofA had my mortgage and I'd been chalking those messages, I wouldn't have been so !@#$@% polite.

Were these public sidewalks? And is free speech different when you're moving or walking—like carrying a sign or calling out protests—than if you're writing your message, even in a transitory medium like chalk?

The judge told Olson's lawyer that he couldn't use a 1st Amendment defense because free speech can't excuse vandalism. But in Florida last year, a federal judge found otherwise in the case of a man who had chalked messages on a public plaza, and he went free.

15   The necessary element in the San Diego vandalism law was "malice," and jurors evidently decided that Olson was not motivated by malice when he put out his anti-bank messages in Easter egg pastels.

Did either of the lawyers bring up that renowned legal precedent, *City of London vs. Bert*? Surely the city fathers of Edwardian London looked unkindly on the sidewalk chalk drawings made by that notorious chalk scofflaw Bert, the chimney sweep/screever in "Mary Poppins."

Bert chalked pictures of faraway and exotic places on public sidewalks, and then imagined himself—a scruffy sweep—sweeping a mere nanny away from their hidebound, class-ridden jobs and into a world where she was a lady and he was a toff.

Now that—that's seditious.

Thinking and Writing about the Limitations on Freedom of Speech

1. Explain how Mike Keefe's cartoon uses a combination of image and text to make a point about hate speech.
2. Sean McElwee states his claim clearly. What is that claim? Do you agree with him?
3. What is your own experience with hate speech on social networking sites?
4. Mathew Ingram's essay also deals with hate speech, but his is a different sort of claim from McElwee's. What claim is Ingram supporting? Do you agree? Why, or why not?
5. Do you agree with the editorial board of the *Los Angeles Times*, who oppose "trigger warnings" on college professors' syllabi? Why, or why not?
6. What do the *Los Angeles Times* editors suggest instead? Are there precedents for such accommodations? Explain.
7. In Chapter 3, read Alan Noble's piece "Valedictorian Prays but Should Christians Rejoice?" (pp. 98–102). Do you believe that the valedictorian's actions represent freedom of speech? Why, or why not? What about the comments following the post?
8. Did authorities go too far in the Jarvis Britton case? How can real threats be separated from "stupid jokes"?

9. Do you sympathize with Jarvis Britton, or not? Why? Have you ever texted or e-mailed anything that could have gotten you in trouble? Explain.

10. Patt Morrison's slanted language suggests that her article is about more than Olson's protests written in chalk. What is she saying about the Bank of America?

11. Read Carol Rose's "On Pins and Needles Defending Artistic Expression" (pp. 36–37) in Chapter 2. How do tattoos constitute a form of free speech? Based on your readings in this chapter, would all tattoos be protected by the First Amendment? Should they be? Explain.

Advancements in Medicine

CHAPTER

24

What Are the Ethical Costs of Modern Health?

With virtually every advance in medical science come new questions about medical ethics. "First, do no harm" sounds simple, but doctors are human beings too, with their own value systems. Does a doctor have the right to refuse to treat a patient because to do so would violate the doctor's moral code? What if the doctor neglects to inform the patient of all viable options for treatment because some violate the doctor's personal code of ethics?

Ethical issues also involve complex questions for parents. The ability to freeze and store embryos has been a godsend to many infertile couples. Now a decision must be made about what to do with leftover frozen embryos, and heated debate continues over what use should be made of embryonic stem cells. Is it ethical to use them at all, even if they show promise in treating conditions such as Parkinson's, diabetes, and spinal cord injuries? And now that testing is available for a host of genetically transmitted traits and conditions, from hair color to diabetes, to what extent should parents be allowed to manipulate the genetic heritage of their future children? Other questions have focused on children who are born with severe disabilities. Who makes decisions about the quality of life of individuals who are unable to make decisions for themselves?

Still other debates involve the role that money should play in medical research and treatment. When a patient's bodily tissue is used for medical research, how — if at all — should he or she be compensated? Finally, given the scarcity of donor organs and the thriving black market for healthy body parts, is it reasonable to consider the legalization of buying and selling human organs for transplant? Complex as the science is that makes possible brave new worlds of medicine, equally complex are the accompanying moral issues.

559

Pro-Life Health Professionals in Conflict between Conscience and Career

ERIC SCHULZKE

Before Reading: In what ways might a doctor's personal beliefs conflict with his or her professional responsibilities?

When Cathy DeCarlo arrived at New York's Mt. Sinai Hospital one Sunday morning in May 2009, she was ordered to assist in an abortion. A conscientious Catholic and a nurse, DeCarlo was on record as being unwilling to do abortions. She had first raised the matter when hired in 2004, and the hospital — in compliance with state and federal law — had agreed.

Because of this, DeCarlo assumed that she was there to help assist in a post-miscarriage treatment. But as she scanned the chart she realized she was actually being asked to assist in the abortion of a living 22-week-old pregnancy, just two weeks shy of full viability outside the womb. She asked her supervisor for a substitute. After checking with her own boss, the head nurse told DeCarlo she must assist with the abortion or face disciplinary action, according to court documents.

DeCarlo protested that the abortion was not an emergency. The patient was listed with pre-eclampsia, a serious but common high blood pressure condition occurring after the 20th week of pregnancy. Rarely requiring drastic measures, it is usually treated with bed rest. De-Carlo noted that the mother was not receiving magnesium sulfate, a key indicator of emergency pre-eclampsia. Her protests availed nothing. She was forbidden to seek a replacement. Mt. Sinai Hospital declined to comment for this article.

Fearing for her family's future should her career be compromised, DeCarlo assisted in the abortion. In an interview with the *New York Post,* she described the experience as "a horror film unfolding." In the aftermath, she began having nightmares and insomnia. "I couldn't believe that this could happen. I felt violated and betrayed," she said.

It was the specter of a DeCarlo case that 5
prompted Congress in 1973 to pass the Church amendments, named after then-Sen. Frank Church, D-Idaho. The legislation was meant to protect health care professionals from being forced to assist in abortions in the aftermath of *Roe v. Wade.* But the drafters of the law didn't include a path to follow when rights were violated. At the time, it was common for courts to assume that victims of conscience violations themselves could sue to enforce their rights, but legal doctrine later shifted, leaving the conscience protections without meaningful enforcement — unless the Department of Health and Human Services (HHS) chooses to act.

The incident at Mt. Sinai violated hospital policy, state law, and federal law, yet nearly three years later, DeCarlo remains without a remedy. The hospital shrugged her off. Her case in state courts is still pending. Federal courts held that she lacked a "private right of action" and must rely on HHS. Two years after acknowledging

Eric Schulzke is a political scientist who writes about national politics and policy for Salt Lake City's online *Deseret News,* where the article appeared on March 17, 2012.

her complaint, the Office of Civil Rights at HHS has still not responded.

DeCarlo stands at the front lines of a grinding war over abortion and professional norms in the health care industry. Many pro-life physicians, nurses, and now even pharmacists feel they are being asked to choose between conscience and career. Pro-choice advocates, meanwhile, believe that refusal to serve, inform, or refer patients stigmatizes the patient, undermines care, and dangerously isolates providers. In recent months, conflict has escalated in hospitals, medical schools, and professional organizations. Both sides feel that the other is upsetting a balance — either by shifting from objecting to a procedure to obstructing it, or by forcing objectors to choose between career and conscience.

Twelve New Jersey nurses faced this dilemma in October 2011 when their hospital announced they must undergo abortion training and begin assisting in abortions, threatening them with termination if they refused. Challenged in federal court by the Alliance Defense Fund, a legal nonprofit focused on religious liberty, the hospital responded that the nurses had no "private right of action." Unwilling to test its claims in court, the hospital settled on all key points, agreeing in December 2011 not to force the nurses to assist in abortions.

The Abortion Stigma Wars

The push to mainstream abortion in the health professions began in the early 1990s. Pro-choice advocates feared that abortion providers were being steadily driven from the field, isolating those who remained and leaving them vulnerable to threats and violence. They contended that what the Supreme Court had declared a

right in *Roe v. Wade* could become an illusion if women were unable to find providers or if they encountered stigma or hostility when they tried. A sense of solidarity under siege developed among abortion advocates and their allies in the professions.

In his 1991 book *The Hollow Hope*, University of Chicago Law Professor Gerald Rosenberg observed that many hospitals and OB/GYNs still refused to perform abortions, adding that "an increasing percentage of obstetrics and gynecology residency programs do not provide training for it." Abortion would be a genuine right, Rosenberg argued, only when it was mainstreamed. 10

These fears were not unfounded. In 1993, Randall Terry of the pro-life group Operation Rescue declared at a Florida rally that "the weak link is the doctor. We're going to expose them. We're going to humiliate them." A few days later, a Florida abortion doctor was murdered. Later that year, another was injured, and in 1994 four people were killed in two separate abortion clinic attacks. A doctor was injured in a third attempt. From 1995 to 1998, a number of doctors, nurses, and security guards were killed or injured in five separate incidents. After a ten-year lull, another doctor was murdered in 2009.

In 2010 Emily Bazelon wrote an article in the *New York Times* that outlined a determined effort to mainstream abortion within the health professions. The first moves were to require abortion training for OB/GYNs, shifting training and practice into teaching hospitals and encouraging mainstream doctors to become abortion providers. Bazelon called this a "deliberate and concerted counteroffensive" in which "abortion-rights advocates have quietly worked to reverse the marginalization."

Mainstreaming Abortion

As part of this agenda, Bazelon reported, the Accreditation Council for Graduate Medical Education (ACGME) ruled in 1995 that, with limited exceptions, OB/GYN residency programs must include abortion training or lose accreditation. Congress fired back by leveraging federal funding to block ACGME.

Some argue that little changed over the next decade. A 2009 American Congress of Obstetricians and Gynecologists (ACOG) opinion noted, "The number of abortion providers has decreased over the past two decades," falling eleven percent from 1996 to 2000 and another two percent in the next five years.

ACOG also observed that "highly charged emotional and political debate stigmatizes the women who undergo abortion and the providers who offer abortion," adding that this "negative atmosphere may be a deterrent to training providers and offering reproductive health services."

Dr. Donna Harrison, director of research and policy at the American Association of Pro-Life OB/GYNs, is well aware of ACOG's concern. "Physicians who have taken the Hippocratic oath have vowed never to perform abortion or euthanasia, which is a thorn in the side of the pro-abortion/pro-choice agenda," she said, "and thus a concerted effort is being made to eliminate the physician of conscience from the practice of obstetrics and gynecology."

Embattled Professional Norms

The national OB/GYN licensing board stoked these fears in 2007 when it announced it would take binding ethics guidelines from ACOG, which is a voluntary organization. ACOG had recently published an opinion that would require doctors to provide active referrals for abortion.

Then-HHS Secretary Michael Leavitt, who is now a member of the *Deseret News* editorial advisory board, began writing new HHS regulations to clarify abortion conscience protections. Among other things, the new rules made clear that threatening conscientious objectors through professional licensing would violate federal law. The rules also clarified the definition of "assist" in a manner that would have supported the New Jersey nurses in 2011.

The new HHS rules became intensely controversial. Critics contended they expanded protections beyond the statute. The result, they argued, could be professional chaos. In addition, critics viewed the compliance statements as onerous and overly vague legal traps.

In 2008, the Obama administration moved quickly to suspend the new HHS regulations, and in 2011 HHS Secretary Kathleen Sebelius officially reversed them, leaving only the complaint system in the HHS Office of Civil Rights — the system that has yet to respond to DeCarlo.

Vanderbilt Pushes the Limits

In the absence of HHS support, pushback on conscience defenses continues. In 2011 Vanderbilt University's nursing program began requiring program applicants to pledge that they would participate in abortions. "If you are chosen for the Nurse Residency Program in the Women's Health track," the application stated, "you will be expected to care for women undergoing termination of pregnancy.... If you feel you cannot provide care to women during this type of event, we encourage you to apply to a different track."

The Alliance Defense Fund filed a complaint with HHS, and Vanderbilt quickly backed down. "Christians and other pro-life members of the medical community shouldn't be forced to participate in abortions to pursue their profession. That's what federal law says, and that's why Vanderbilt is doing the right thing in changing its policy and application," said ADF Legal Counsel Matt Bowman.

Other medical school entrance practices are harder to monitor. A 1996 study by two doctors at the University of Texas–Houston Medical School, for example, contains piles of interview notes characterizing candidates' religiosity, rigidity, and presumed psychological disorders based on religious perspectives and attitudes toward abortion.

Sample comments from interviewer notes included: "He has found God but does not hear voices"; "Negative view of candidate who said she was Catholic and this influenced her view on abortion"; "Thoughts on euthanasia and abortion were downright naive"; "Applicant would dissuade and would not refer patient for abortion"; and "Do not recommend acceptance due to indecisiveness on abortion and pulling the plug."

Contraception Blurs Lines

25 Even as medical schools and nursing programs began filtering applicants, the professional norms conflict expanded beyond surgical abortion into pharmaceuticals, blurring the line between them. In the early 1980s, a drug called RU-486 emerged that induces abortion well into the first trimester.

Newer drugs pushed the line back to the first hours or days after intercourse. Two widely used emergency contraceptives (ECPs) are Plan B and Ella, though the term "contraception" itself is disputed by pro-life OB/GYNs. Much

hinges on whether one defines life as beginning at conception or implantation.

In 1998 Susan Cohen, now the director of governmental affairs at the pro-choice Guttmacher Institute, defended ECPs by distinguishing them from RU-486, which she called "clearly a method of abortion." Unlike RU-486, she wrote, "ECPs cannot disrupt an established pregnancy, and, therefore, cannot under any circumstances cause an abortion."

The newest ECP is Ella, approved by the FDA in 2010. "Ella is really just a second-generation RU-486," Dr. Harrison said, adding that it is more controversial than Plan B because while Ella can be used to prevent ovulation and implantation, it can also destroy an embryo after it implants — even months into a pregnancy when used in high doses.

Seattle Pharmacy under Fire

When the state of Washington began requiring pharmacies to carry ECPs in 2007, the owner of two local grocery stores objected. His alternative was a "facilitated referral," meaning he would "refer the customer to a nearby provider and, upon the patient's request, call the provider to make sure the product is in stock."

30 In February 2012 the U.S. District Court struck down the state regulation, noting that none of the "customers have ever been denied timely access to emergency contraception" and pointing to various secular reasons a pharmacy may not stock certain drugs. The court concluded that "literally all of the evidence demonstrates that the 2007 rulemaking was undertaken primarily (if not solely) to ensure that religious objectors would be required to stock and dispense Plan B." In short, the court held that the policy was crafted to sideline religious objectors.

Not about Access

The conscience vs. choice battle is at an uneasy stalemate at the moment. Congressional statutes hold professional organizations and medical schools at bay. Some states (like Kansas) push conscience protections to extremes, while others (like Washington) push them aside. The pressure on pro-life professionals is real, but voices of moderation are also in play.

"No one on the pro-choice side is saying they want to eliminate anyone with religious objections," said Luke Goodrich at the Becket Fund for Religious Liberty, which defended the Seattle pharmacist against the Washington emergency contraception rules. "They say they are trying to ensure access to health care, abortion, and emergency contraception. But when you scratch beneath the surface, you see an attempt to suppress conscientious objection even when it doesn't inhibit access."

Goodrich points to his client in Washington, noting that over thirty pharmacies within a five mile radius dispensed the disputed drug, and that his client would even call ahead to make sure they had it in stock.

"This isn't about access," Goodrich concludes. The goal, he said, is to "ensure that no one would ever encounter a health care professional who disagrees with the treatment they are seeking on religious or moral grounds."

But Adam Sonfield at the pro-choice Guttmacher Institute seems willing to compromise, supporting the right of conscientious objectors to not directly engage in abortion. "(But) there are some lines you can't cross," Sonfield added. "You can't deny information. You can't deny care in an emergency, and if you refuse care, you must make sure the patient isn't abandoned."

"We have seen a lot of laws that try to push these limits," Sonfield said. "For example, some would allow a doctor to refuse to tell a woman of a problem on a sonogram because she might turn around and have an abortion."

Striking a Balance

To the degree that abortion is legal, the pro-life side faces compromise on information and referrals — just as the pro-choice side is required to compromise on refusals.

Gallup's polling on abortion has been remarkably consistent for nearly thirty years. Current polls show 47 percent of Americans consider themselves "pro-life" and a matching 47 percent "pro-choice." Only 26 percent favor legalizing abortion under any circumstances, while just 20 percent oppose legalization in all circumstances. Half (51 percent) would legalize abortion only in certain circumstances.

Given such divisions, the search continues for a sustainable solution that somehow smooths the jarring chasm between the conscientious objector and the patient. An obvious answer is a facilitated referral like that offered by the Seattle pharmacy. But many pro-life health care providers balk at actively referring for abortion, and the controversial 2008 HHS rules were largely a response to calls for mandatory referrals. For many, running roughshod over this concern would undermine conscience protections.

Voices on both sides agree that the need for referrals could be reduced through broad prior notice about a provider's philosophy. In the case of pharmacies or OB/GYNs, this would allow most patients to align themselves philosophically in advance of need or to have backup plans in mind.

One ideal articulated by the American Pharmacists Association (APhA) is that the objector "step away, not in the way." At a minimum, this means scrupulously avoiding lecturing the patient. But some doubt whether any face-to-face refusal can be frictionless.

APhA also supports establishing systems that would protect a professional's right to conscientious refusal while ensuring the patient's right to obtain legally prescribed treatments. The best-case scenario, APhA holds, is "seamless to the patient, and the patient is not aware that the pharmacist is stepping away from the situation."

Such systems may be easier for nurses, who are embedded in institutions, than for pharmacists or doctors, who often stand at the front lines. Cathy DeCarlo thought she had struck such a seamless balance for five years at Mt. Sinai before she was blindsided on that still unexplained day in 2009.

So equilibrium remains elusive. If Goodrich is right that the real objective in some quarters is not to smooth access but to remove dissent altogether, then advocates for conscience may have a long way to go.

Embryo Selection May Help Prevent Some Inherited Disorders
STEVEN REINBERG

Before Reading: In in vitro fertilization, should embryos be tested for disease and implanted only if those tests are negative? Explain why this is a complex ethical issue.

When a 27-year-old woman wanted to have a baby using in vitro fertilization, there was one major problem — she was a carrier of Gerstmann-Straussler-Sheinker syndrome.

This rare, degenerative neurological condition is usually diagnosed in mid-life and is always fatal. Not wanting to risk having her child become a victim of the syndrome, she turned to a technique that tests embryos for certain mutated genes and only uses those embryos that don't carry the mutation for implantation.

"This disease was found in five generations in this family, and we stopped passing these bad genes to the next generation," said study co-author Svetlana Rechitsky, laboratory director at the Reproductive Genetics Institute in Chicago.

According to Dr. Ilan Tur-Kaspa, lead researcher and president and medical director of the Institute for Human Reproduction in Chicago, "These new cases can be prevented now by pre-implantation genetic diagnosis." Although this is the first report on using this method for a so-called prion disorder, it could also help prevent diseases like Huntington's and familial forms of Alzheimer's disease, he said.

Prion diseases involve abnormal foldings of the prion protein in the brain. The most commonly known one, which is not inherited, is bovine spongiform encephalopathy, or "mad cow" disease.

The report was published online February 3 in the journal *JAMA Neurology*.

The process started with a simple in vitro fertilization procedure. Eggs from the woman were removed and fertilized. Then came the tricky part.

5

Steven Reinberg is a senior staff reporter for healthday .com, where this article appeared on February 3, 2014.

Doctors removed single cells from the embryos, and because the syndrome is caused by a single gene mutation, they looked at DNA to find embryos that didn't have the mutated gene.

"We can identify which embryo is healthy, and which embryo has the bad gene," Rechitsky explained.

10   Two of the disease-free embryos were implanted, and the woman had twins delivered by cesarean section a little more than 33 weeks later. The remaining normal embryos were frozen for later use.

At 27 months, the twins had normal communication, social, and emotional skills, the researchers reported.

One expert noted the importance of the finding.

"Most of the genetic disorders identified by pre-implantation genetic diagnosis are caused by either single genes — such as cystic fibrosis, Huntington's disease, sickle cell anemia, Down syndrome, Trisomy 18 (Edwards syndrome) and chromosomal translocations — and most have no treatment or cure," said Christine Metz, director of Maternal-Fetal Medicine Research at the Feinstein Institute for Medical Research in Manhasset, New York. "Thus, it is important for young parents to know and understand their risks for inherited diseases prior to conception."

In addition, pre-implantation genetic diagnosis is beginning to be used to reduce the transmission of mutant cancer genes, such as the BRCA1/BRCA2 genes, which are tied to breast cancer, and the MLH1, MSH2, and APC genes that are linked to colon cancer, she said.

"Over several generations, we can hope to improve human health by reducing the transmission of several hereditary disorders," Metz said.   15

Rechitsky acknowledged that some people have ethical problems with the potential for this technology to be used to tailor babies to parents' desires. However, in the 25 years they have been doing the procedure it hasn't been a problem, she said.

"We had the first successful pregnancy in 1990," Rechitsky said. "Over the years, we have performed over 4,000 procedures for single-gene disorders. It has become a more widely accepted approach to prevent hereditary disease," she explained.

As to tailoring babies, "we have never ever had any requests like this," she said. Moreover, many of the things parents might want to select for like intelligence, involve many genes, not just one. "We don't know even how to approach this," she noted.

Dr. Avner Hershlag, chief of the Center for Human Reproduction at North Shore University Hospital in Manhasset, New York, said, "Like any sophisticated technique, reproductive technology can be abused. There are ethical issues."

Hershlag said that "the most ethical approach is that it should be used for identifying disease only, and for selecting embryos that are free of disease. I don't want it to ever head into that murky, questionable line between what is right and what is wrong. It is absolutely right to diagnose a disease in an embryo and to use embryos that don't have disease."   20

23andMe ■ Looking to Start a Family? You'll Pass on More Than Just Your Freckles

567

Looking to Start a Family? You'll Pass on More Than Just Your Freckles

23ANDME

Before Reading: What genetic conditions, if any, would you consider being tested for before having a child?

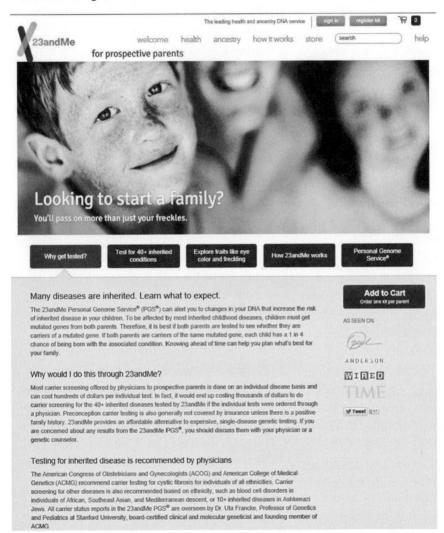

According to its Web site, "23andMe, Inc. is a privately held company dedicated to helping individuals understand their own genetic information using recent advances in DNA analysis technologies and web-based interactive tools."

Blurring the Line between Life and Death

LOS ANGELES TIMES EDITORIAL BOARD

Before Reading: What are your feelings about taking a patient off life support once he or she is brain dead?

Brain death needs a new name, some doctors and bioethicists say. Perhaps it should be called "death via cessation of brain function." Then, perhaps, the public might better understand that it's not just a serious coma or a severe brain injury or a persistent vegetative state. It's the end of life.

In fact, according to Arthur Caplan, a professor of bioethics at New York University, a determination of brain death is more certain than one of cardiac death. There are no absolute rules on how many times a doctor must apply the paddles of a defibrillator before declaring a patient dead, Caplan said; in extraordinarily rare cases, that has led to a patient regaining consciousness after that was thought to be beyond hope. In contrast, a long list of tests must be done by specialists, and various criteria must be met, to determine brain death.

The tragic case of Jahi McMath is testing the public's understanding — and the courts' mettle — when it comes to brain death. Both have been found lacking. Jahi is the 13-year-old girl who suffered bleeding and other rare complications after a tonsillectomy and surgery to treat her sleep apnea. Five doctors, the coroner, and a judge have declared her brain-dead, but Jahi's distraught mother, Nailah Winkfield, has not been willing to accept that this means true death. She took Children's Hospital Oakland to court, seeking to keep her daughter on a ventilator.

Jahi, she said, is still breathing. She is warm to the touch and her heart is beating.

But actually, Jahi is not breathing. A ventilator is pumping oxygenated air into her lungs, and her heart has responded to the oxygen by beating, Caplan said. That would end if the ventilator were removed. And the lack of any brain activity cannot be reversed. Jahi is sadly and irrevocably dead.

The problem is that even though the judge in the case agreed with that pronouncement, he ordered another delay, to Tuesday, while Winkfield worked on moving her daughter to a long-term care facility. The transfer out of Children's Hospital, to a destination that was not immediately divulged, took place Sunday evening. Meanwhile, support has come from people across the nation who think this is one of those cases in which doctors might have made an arrogant mistake.

But even if the family has found a competent facility willing to treat someone who is officially deceased, the process has blurred the lines between life and death. A death certificate was issued Friday, which made this a coroner's case, but the coroner released Jahi for treatment as though she were alive. Children's Hospital Oakland refused to perform a tracheotomy or to insert a feeding tube in preparation for the teenager's transfer; it said that it was inappropriate to perform medical procedures on a dead

This opinion piece by the editorial board of the *Los Angeles Times* appeared on January 6, 2014.

person, and three judges have backed its decision. Also unclear is who will pay for continued care. Whether the family is covered by insurance is not known, but neither insurance companies nor taxpayers should have to cover ongoing care for the deceased.

It's difficult not to sympathize with Winkfield, who must accept what seems so unacceptable to any parent. But the judge's decision to keep the ventilator in place for now has not helped the public understand the situation, nor has it helped Jahi.

The courts in this case have followed the predictable pattern, delaying and preventing change to the status quo, toward life or toward death; they have declined to order the ventilator removed or a feeding tube inserted. Unfortunately, that approach leads to more public confusion and a blurring of the lines about death. It sends a message that families might be better equipped than doctors to decide when a patient is dead, even though brain death has been considered true death for decades, encoded into law throughout the nation.

Nailah Winkfield sees her mission as keeping her daughter alive. But in truth, all the courts have allowed her to keep alive is the illusion of life.

10

Paying Patients for Their Tissue: The Legacy of Henrietta Lacks
ROBERT D. TRUOG, AARON S. KESSELHEIM, AND STEVEN JOFFE

Before Reading: Is it fair for medical research companies to profit from the donation of tissue from a patient? What if the tissue was used without the patient's knowledge?

In *The Immortal Life of Henrietta Lacks,* Rebecca Skloot tells the moving story of the woman who was the source of the first immortal cell line (HeLa).[1] The cells were obtained at Johns Hopkins University in 1951 from biopsies performed during her treatment for cervical cancer. Her physicians did not seek her consent before using her tissue for research, nor did they receive any personal financial gain from the cell line.

The cell line did become extremely lucrative, however. Although it is difficult to precisely quantify the total revenue generated from the HeLa line, it is not unreasonable to assume that the line has contributed to hundreds of millions of dollars in downstream revenue. Hundreds of patents contain the word "hela" in their claims,

and genetically modified versions of the line currently sell for as much as $10,000.

For many, it seems an injustice that the Lacks family never received any financial benefits from the HeLa line, especially given that they lived in poverty, unable to pay even for their own medical care. Christopher Lengauer, a cancer drug developer and former Hopkins faculty member, articulated this sense of inequity when he reportedly told Lacks's daughter that he thought Hopkins had "screwed up" by not sharing some of the proceeds from the HeLa cell line with the Lacks family.[1] Although this sentiment resonates with a sense of fairness

Robert D. Truog is a physician at Children's Hospital Boston, Aaron S. Kesselheim is a physician at Brigham & Women's Hospital, and Steven Joffe is a physician at Dana-Farber Cancer Institute. This article was published in the July 2012 issue of *Science*.

for many people, it requires critical examination before becoming accepted as precedent regarding payments to patients.

We recently had an opportunity to consider issues surrounding sharing revenues with patients who provide tissue for research when a young man (we will call him DF) was treated at Dana-Farber Cancer Institute for a rare metatastic malignancy. Shortly before he died, he was admitted to the hospital with increasing shortness of breath, requiring placement of a pleural drainage catheter. With his knowledge and permission, the physician-investigators obtained discarded fluid from the catheter to obtain and isolate tumor cells. The cells were processed into a cell line that holds promise for basic science research and the development of therapeutics. The line may result in a revenue stream for the medical center, as well as personal income for the physician-investigators.

5   After the patient died, the physician-investigators who cared for him were motivated to see that his family received some financial benefit from his contribution. They sought advice from the Research Ethics Consultation Service at the Harvard Clinical and Translational Science Center, on which we serve.

Property Rights in Human Tissue

If patients own their tissues, even after removal from their bodies, then it follows that they have the right to demand payment when a profitable discovery derives from them. One of the earliest cases addressing this question was *Moore v. Regents of the University of California*.[2] John Moore had his spleen removed as part of his treatment for hairy cell leukemia. Several years later, he initiated a lawsuit after learning that his physician at the University of California, Los Angeles, had developed a lucrative cell line (MO)

from this tissue; at the time Moore predicted a market value of around $3 billion. In 1990, the California Supreme Court decided that Moore did not have a property interest in his removed cells, worrying that giving property rights to patients would "hinder research by restricting access to the necessary raw materials" and might "destroy the economic incentive to conduct important medical research." Most other legal precedent supports the view that patients do not maintain a property interest in discarded tissue.[3]

Even if patients lack such property rights, there are many examples of individuals receiving financial compensation for donating tissue. A striking case was that of Ted Slavin, a man with hemophilia who developed extremely high antibody titers after contracting hepatitis B.[4] When his physician informed him that his blood might be valuable to medical researchers, he was able to sell his serum for as much as $10,000 per liter, providing himself with a source of income for the rest of his life.

Are the Moore or Slavin cases relevant to those of Lacks or DF? What are the salient features that determine whether patients should be paid for their tissue?

Investigators' Obligations to Individuals from Whom They Seek Tissue for Research

There are three distinct obligations that an investigator who seeks access to tissue might have toward an individual whose tissues, upon removal from the body, might hold value for biomedical research (see the table). In addressing each of these obligations, it is necessary to distinguish between situations in which the tissue constitutes excess material that remains after an indicated clinical procedure and those in which obtaining the tissue imposes incremental inconvenience, burden, or risk.

Investigators' Obligations to Individuals from Whom They Prospectively Seek Tissue for Research		
Investigators' obligations	Residual clinical tissues	Tissue collection requiring additional interventions
Consent to use tissue for research	+	+
Compensation for effort and burden of acquiring tissue	–	+
Rights to revenue streams derived from the tissue	–	–

10   *Consent:* Residual clinical tissues, such as those at issue in the case of DF, are obtained as a by-product of necessary care, involve no increased potential for harm or discomfort to the patient, and entail no extra effort or inconvenience beyond that inherent in the patient's medical treatment. Although consent is not always required for the use of residual clinical tissue (as with de-identified tissues obtained from pathology department archives), current U.S. regulatory standards require investigators to obtain the individual's consent whenever they prospectively intend to use residual clinical tissue for research. Of course, investigators must also obtain informed consent before undertaking additional procedures, beyond necessary clinical care, to procure tissues for research.

Compensation for effort and burden: By definition, the use of residual clinical tissue for biomedical research imposes no additional effort, burden, or risk on the patient. As a result, no compensation for such effort is owed. By contrast, when the procurement of the tissue imposes burdens over and above those required for indicated clinical care, it may be necessary to offer individuals, whether patients or healthy volunteers, compensation. Ample precedent

exists for offering payment when individuals are asked to cooperate with physicians or investigators for the benefit of others. For example, in research contexts beyond that of tissue acquisition, subjects are commonly compensated for the time, effort, and cooperation that participation requires.[5]

Similarly, payments are often made when renewable tissues are procured from volunteers, not for their medical benefit, but solely for the benefit of others. This is reflected in the markets that exist for blood and blood derivatives, oocytes, sperm, and breast milk. Although many individuals do not demand payment for these tissues (as reflected in the largely volunteer supply of banked blood), it is widely acknowledged that, as in the case of Ted Slavin, individuals may seek payment for these renewable tissues. In light of the *Moore* decision and other legal precedents holding that individuals do not retain property ownership over removed tissues, we suggest that a plausible rationale for justifying such payments is that they are made in exchange for the performance of a service, rather than for the transfer of property.

Rights to revenue streams: Cases such as Lacks and DF pose the question of whether investigators and institutions owe individuals payment for the potential value of the tissue, and in particular whether contributors should have rights to a portion of any revenue stream that derives from their tissue. As discussed, neither legal norms nor contemporary practice treat tissues that have been separated from the body as the ongoing property of the individual such that it would generate a revenue stream. Nevertheless, beyond legal duties, do ethics require that individuals whose tissues ultimately provide revenue for institutions and investigators be offered a share of the proceeds?

Several considerations mitigate against the claim that patients such as Lacks or DF should be offered financial compensation for use of their residual clinical tissue. First, although it is true that the patients have contributed "raw materials" necessary for development of the cell line, it is the investigators, not the patients, whose intellectual contributions lead to the creation of value.

15   Second, paying such individuals raises questions of fairness. Investigators may preferentially reward patients and families with whom they have become emotionally bonded, but not those who were equally generous but with whom personal relationships were absent.

Third, the implications of reconceptualizing tissue acquisition as an economic exchange rather than as a gift relationship must be carefully considered. Payment might paradoxically have a negative effect on patients' willingness to give their tissues for research. Providing upfront payments to all patients who donate tissue — independent of and without prior knowledge regarding the actual financial value of their contributions — suggests that the payments themselves would likely be quite modest. The enormous number of tissue samples collected, as compared with the relatively small number that acquire significant value, suggests that the prior estimated value of any given tissue sample is low. Such small payments might not merely fail to incentivize patients, but might actually be scorned as an unfair or token reward. In addition, there is a risk that invoking the extrinsic motivation of money would crowd out intrinsic motivations, such as the desire to contribute altruistically to improved knowledge and treatment.[6,7]

Finally, and perhaps most important, few individuals will contribute tissues that generate financial blockbusters. As a result, compensating such persons in effect rewards them for "winning the lottery," whereas the vast majority, despite their ex ante identical contributions, receive nothing. If financial rewards for the development of useful cell lines should be tied to material contributions rather than to luck, then compensating patients such as Lacks or DF, ostensibly in the service of justice, may lead to an outcome that is manifestly unjust.

Conclusion

Although Skloot's book is moving and compelling, we use caution in using the Lacks example as a model for thinking about compensating patients who provide tissue for research. Although one can point to the many injustices Lacks endured as a poor woman without access to needed medical care, the use of her residual clinical tissue, involving no additional risk or burden to her, does not demand any form of compensation. Furthermore, compensating such patients may have unintended consequences that could work to decrease the availability of tissue for research, and may paradoxically become a source of injustice. In the case of DF, we therefore advised the investigators not to offer his family any payments for use of the residual clinical tissue they obtained.

References and Notes

1. R. Skloot, *The Immortal Life of Henrietta Lacks* (Crown Publishers, New York, 2010).
2. *Moore v. Regents of the University of California,* 51 Cal. 3d 120, 793 P.2d 479; 271 Cal. Rptr. 146, 1990 Cal.
3. R. A. Charo, *New England Journal of Medicine.* 355, 1517 (2006).
4. R. Skloot, *New York Times Magazine,* 16 April 2006, p. 38.
5. C. Grady, *Journal of Clinical Investigation.* 115, 1681 (2005).
6. T. H. Murray, *Discover* 7, 90 (1986).
7. M. J. Sandel, in *What Money Can't Buy* (Farrar, Straus and Giroux, New York, 2012), pp. 93–130.

New York Man Pleads Guilty to Organ Trafficking

KIM CAROLLO

Before Reading: Given the long waiting list for organ transplants, should the sale of human organs be legalized? Why, or why not?

A Brooklyn, NY, man admitted in court Thursday that he purchased human kidneys from live Israeli donors that were ultimately transplanted into three New Jersey residents.

Levy Izhak Rosenbaum, 60, earned $410,000 from the three black-market sales and was conspiring to broker another deal when he was caught, federal prosecutors said in a statement. He received another $10,000 as down payment for that transaction.

Rosenbaum's attorneys, Ronald Kleinberg and Richard Finkel, issued a statement saying their client's motivation was to save the lives of people who would have died without the transplants because more than 90,000 Americans are on transplant waiting lists.

"The transplants were successful and the donors and recipients are now leading full and healthy lives," the attorneys said. "In fact, because of the transplants and for the first time in many years, the recipients are no longer burdened by the medical and substantial health dangers associated with dialysis and kidney failure."

But in a press release, New Jersey U.S. Attorney Paul Fishman called Rosenbaum's actions "an affront to human dignity" and said these black-market organ sales offer an unfair, life-saving advantage to people who can afford to buy organs. 5

Rosenbaum, an Israeli citizen, admitted the sales took place between 2006 and 2009. He was ultimately caught in a sting involving the FBI and a woman who told Rosenbaum her uncle needed a kidney transplant. According to prosecutors, Rosenbaum told the woman he knew the organ sales were illegal, but he had been in the business a long time. They agreed on a price of $150,000, part of which he said was to pay individuals for their part in finding a donor.

He faces three counts related to the kidney brokering and another count of conspiracy. He could spend up to 20 years in prison and have to pay a stiff fine. He will also pay back the

Kim Carollo is a health journalist. Her article appeared on abcnews.go.com on October 28, 2011.

$420,000 he earned and is under house arrest until he is sentenced in February.

Prosecutors did not name the hospitals where the transplants took place, but as for whether the institutions should hold any accountability, Dr. Linda Chen, surgical director of the Live Donor Kidney Program at the University of Miami's Miller School of Medicine, said it is difficult to determine whether individuals are being honest about where organs come from.

Chen also said that because waiting lists for kidneys across the country are so long—it is about two-and-a-half years in Florida and seven

to nine years in New York—it makes sense that there is such a profitable black market out there.

"But this is a big blow for the transplant community," she said. "We need to get the right message out there about the fact that it's a highly regulated process governed by the United Network for Organ Sharing and the Organ Procurement and Transplantation Network."   10

Chen also said there could be safety issues involved with internationally acquired organs.

"It's always a safety issue," she said. "How long can a kidney remain in a box while it's transported? There could be issues with prolonging preservation time."

Thinking and Writing about the Ethical Costs of Medicine

1. Review the speech by Kathleen Sebelius in Chapter 12 (pp. 396–99), especially paragraphs 12–31, in which she discusses the challenges facing those in public policy. How do her remarks relate to medical ethics and the moral dilemmas surrounding them?

2. After reading Eric Schulzke's "Pro-Life Health Professionals in Conflict between Conscience and Career," consider whether, if you were a doctor, there might be situations in which your personal beliefs would preclude your prescribing a certain medication or performing a certain procedure. How would you justify this to your patients?

3. Return to Chapter 5 and read "Morning-After Pill a Boon for Women" by Deborah Nucatola (pp. 160–61). How does this argument affect your reading of Schulzke's article?

4. What ethical issues are raised by the successes reported in "Embryo Selection May Help Prevent Some Inherited Disorders"?

5. Do you think that families with a history of inherited single-cell disease should be allowed to have their embryos tested for the disease before implementation? Why, or why not?

6. Write a defense of your position on human embryonic stem-cell research.

7. Read "Building Baby from the Genes Up," by Ronald M. Green, in Chapter 6 (pp. 205–08). Based on this article, why might some prenatal

genetic testing be a good idea even for those couples who would not consider abortion?

8. What appeals does the 23andMe Web site use to encourage parents to engage in genetic testing?

9. What prenatal genetic testing would you want your future children to have?

10. How convincing do you find the argument against Jahi McMath's mother in "Blurring the Line between Life and Death" by the *Los Angeles Times* editorial board?

11. Read "The 'Unnatural' Ashley Treatment Can Be Right for Profoundly Disabled Children," by Peter Singer in Chapter 1 (pp. 22–23). Which argument do you think is stronger: the *Los Angeles Times* editorial board's or Singer's? Why?

12. What is the claim of Robert D. Truog and others in "Paying Patients for Their Tissue: The Legacy of Henrietta Lacks"? Do you agree with this position? Why, or why not?

13. Read "I'm Sorry, Steve Jobs: We Could Have Saved You," by Siddhartha Mukherjee in Chapter 6 (pp. 196–99). What is the author's main concern about cancer research? Could this argument be used to strengthen or weaken Truog's position? How?

14. What arguments can be made on both sides of the issue of legalizing human organ sales? Which side do you support? Why?

15. Speculate as to some ethical dilemmas in the field of medicine that are likely to arise in the future.

CLASSIC
Arguments

AN EIGHTEENTH-CENTURY SATIRE

In 1729, Jonathan Swift was moved to write in protest against the terrible poverty in which the Irish were living under British rule. His resulting essay is acknowledged by almost all critics to be the most powerful example of irony in the English language. (Using *irony* means saying one thing but meaning another.) Notice that the essay is organized according to one of the patterns outlined in Part Four of this book (see Presenting the Stock Issues, Chapter 12, p. 378). First Swift establishes the need for a change, then he offers his proposal, and finally he lists its advantages.

A Modest Proposal

JONATHAN SWIFT

It is a melancholy object to those who walk through this great town[1] or travel in the country, when they see the streets, the roads, and cabin doors, crowded with beggars of the female sex, followed by three, four, or six children, all in rags and importuning every passenger for an alms. These mothers, instead of being able to work for their honest livelihood, are forced to employ all their time in strolling to beg sustenance for their helpless infants, who, as they grow up, either turn thieves for want of work, or leave their dear native country to fight for the Pretender in Spain, or sell themselves to the Barbados.[2]

I think it is agreed by all parties that this prodigious number of children in the arms, or on the backs, or at the heels of their mothers, and frequently of their fathers, is in the present deplorable state of the kingdom a very great additional grievance; and therefore whoever could find out a fair, cheap, and easy method of making these children sound, useful members of the commonwealth would deserve so well of the public as to have his statue set up for a preserver of the nation.

But my intention is very far from being confined to provide only for the children of professed beggars; it is of a much greater extent, and shall take in the whole number of infants at a certain age who are born of parents in effect as little able to support them as those who demand our charity in the streets.

As to my own part, having turned my thoughts for many years upon this important subject, and maturely weighed the several schemes of other projectors,[3] I have always found them grossly mistaken in their computation. It is true, a child just dropped from its dam may be supported by her milk for a solar year,

---

[1] Dublin. — EDS. [All notes are the editors'.]
[2] The Pretender was James Stuart, who was exiled to Spain. Many Irish men joined an army attempting to return him to the English throne in 1715. Others had become indentured servants, agreeing to work for a set number of years in Barbados or other British colonies in exchange for their transportation out of Ireland.

Jonathan Swift (1667–1745) was a prolific satirist and dean of St. Patrick's Cathedral in Dublin.

---

[3] Planners.

with little other nourishment; at most not above the value of two shillings, which the mother may certainly get, or the value in scraps, by her lawful occupation of begging; and it is exactly at one year that I propose to provide for them in such a manner as instead of being a charge upon their parents or the parish, or wanting food and raiment for the rest of their lives, they shall on the contrary contribute to the feeding, and partly to the clothing, of many thousands.

5   There is likewise another great advantage in my scheme, that it will prevent those voluntary abortions, and that horrid practice of women murdering their bastard children, alas, too frequent among us, sacrificing the poor innocent babes, I doubt, more to avoid the expense than the shame, which would move tears and pity in the most savage and inhuman breast.

The number of souls in this kingdom being usually reckoned one million and a half, of these I calculate there may be about two hundred thousand couples whose wives are breeders; from which number I subtract thirty thousand couples who are able to maintain their own children, although I apprehend there cannot be so many under the present distress of the kingdom; but this being granted, there will remain an hundred and seventy thousand breeders. I again subtract fifty thousand for those women who miscarry, or whose children die by accident or disease within the year. There only remain an hundred and twenty thousand children of poor parents annually born. The question therefore is, how this number shall be reared and provided for, which, as I have already said, under the present situation of affairs, is utterly impossible by all the methods hitherto proposed. For we can neither employ them in handicraft or agriculture; we neither build houses (I mean in the country) nor cultivate land. They can very seldom pick up a livelihood by stealing till they arrive at six years old, except where they are of towardly parts;[4] although I confess they learn the rudiments much earlier, during which time they can however be looked upon only as probationers, as I have been informed by a principal gentleman in the county of Cavan, who protested to me that he never knew above one or two instances under the age of six, even in a part of the kingdom so renowned for the quickest proficiency in that art.

I am assured by our merchants that a boy or a girl before twelve years old is no salable commodity; and even when they come to this age they will not yield above three pounds, or three pounds and a half a crown at most on the Exchange; which cannot turn to account either to the parents or the kingdom, the charge of nutriment and rags having been at least four times that value.

I shall now therefore humbly propose my own thoughts, which I hope will not be liable to the least objection.

I have been assured by a very knowing American of my acquaintance in London, that a young healthy child well nursed is at a year old a most delicious, nourishing, and wholesome food, whether stewed, roasted, baked, or boiled; and I make no doubt that it will equally serve in a fricassee or a ragout.[5]

10   I do therefore humbly offer it to public consideration that of the hundred and twenty thousand children, already computed, twenty thousand may be reserved for breed, whereof only one fourth part to be males, which is more

[4] Innate talents.
[5] Stew.

than we allow to sheep, black cattle, or swine; and my reason is that these children are seldom the fruits of marriage, a circumstance not much regarded by our savages, therefore one male will be sufficient to serve four females. That the remaining hundred thousand may at a year old be offered in sale to the persons of quality and fortune through the kingdom, always advising the mother to let them suck plentifully in the last month, so as to render them plump and fat for a good table. A child will make two dishes at an entertainment for friends; and when the family dines alone, the fore or hind quarter will make a reasonable dish, and seasoned with a little pepper or salt will be very good boiled on the fourth day, especially in winter.

I have reckoned upon a medium that a child just born will weigh twelve pounds, and in a solar year if tolerably nursed increaseth to twenty-eight pounds.

I grant this food will be somewhat dear, and therefore very proper for landlords, who, as they have already devoured most of the parents, seem to have the best title to the children.

Infant's flesh will be in season throughout the year, but more plentiful in March, and a little before and after. For we are told by a grave author, an eminent French physician,[6] that fish being a prolific diet, there are more children born in Roman Catholic countries about nine months after Lent than at any other season; therefore, reckoning a year after Lent, the markets will be more glutted than usual, because the number of popish infants is at least three to one in this kingdom; and therefore it will have one other collateral advantage, by lessening the number of Papists among us.

I have already computed the charge of nursing a beggar's child (in which list I reckon all cottagers, laborers, and four-fifths of the farmers) to be about two shillings per annum, rags included; and I believe no gentleman would repine to give ten shillings for the carcass of a good fat child, which, as I have said, will make four dishes of excellent nutritive meat, when he hath only some particular friend or his own family to dine with him. Thus the squire will learn to be a good landlord, and grow popular among the tenants; the mother will have eight shillings net profit, and be fit for work till she produces another child.

Those who are more thrifty (as I must confess the times require) may flay the carcass; the skin of which artificially[7] dressed will make admirable gloves for ladies, and summer boots for fine gentlemen.

As to our city of Dublin, shambles[8] may be appointed for this purpose in the most convenient parts of it, and butchers we may be assured will not be wanting; although I rather recommend buying the children alive, and dressing them hot from the knife as we do roasting pigs.

A very worthy person, a true lover of his country, and whose virtues I highly esteem, was lately pleased in discoursing on this matter to offer a refinement upon my scheme. He said that many gentlemen of his kingdom, having of late destroyed their deer, he conceived that the want of venison might be well supplied by the bodies of young lads and maidens, not exceeding fourteen years of age nor under twelve, so

15

---

[6] A reference to Swift's favorite French writer, François Rabelais (1494?–1553), who was actually a broad satirist known for his coarse humor.

[7] With art or craft.

[8] Butcher shops or slaughterhouses.

great a number of both sexes in every county being now ready to starve for want of work and service; and these to be disposed of by their parents, if alive, or otherwise by their nearest relations. But with due deference to so excellent a friend and so deserving a patriot, I cannot be altogether in his sentiments; for as to the males, my American acquaintance assured me from frequent experience that their flesh was generally tough and lean, like that of our schoolboys, by continual exercise, and their taste disagreeable; and to fatten them would not answer the charge. Then as to the females, it would, I think with humble submission, be a loss to the public, because they soon would become breeders themselves; and besides, it is not improbable that some scrupulous people might be apt to censure such a practice (although indeed very unjustly) as a little bordering upon cruelty; which, I confess, hath always been with me the strongest objection against any project, how well soever intended.

But in order to justify my friend, he confessed that this expedient was put into his head by the famous Psalmanazar,[9] a native of the island Formosa, who came from thence to London above twenty years ago, and in conversation told my friend that in his country when any young person happened to be put to death, the executioner sold the carcass to persons of quality as a prime dainty; and that in his time the body of a plump girl of fifteen, who was crucified for an attempt to poison the emperor, was sold to his Imperial Majesty's prime minister of state, and other great mandarins of the court, in joints from the gibbet, at four hundred crowns. Neither indeed can I deny that if the same use were made of several plump young girls in this town, who without one single groat to their fortunes cannot stir abroad without a chair, and appear at the playhouse and assemblies in foreign fineries which they never will pay for, the kingdom would not be the worse.

Some persons of a desponding spirit are in great concern about that vast number of poor people who are aged, diseased, or maimed, and I have been desired to employ my thoughts what course may be taken to ease the nation of so grievous an encumbrance. But I am not in the least pain upon that matter, because it is very well known that they are every day dying and rotting by cold and famine, and filth and vermin, as fast as can be reasonably expected. And as to the younger laborers, they are now in almost as hopeful a condition. They cannot get work, and consequently pine away for want of nourishment to a degree that if any time they are accidentally hired to common labor, they have not strength to perform it; and thus the country and themselves are happily delivered from the evils to come.

I have too long digressed, and therefore shall return to my subject. I think the advantages by the proposal which I have made are obvious and many, as well as of the highest importance.

For first, as I have already observed, it would greatly lessen the number of Papists, with whom we are yearly overrun, being the principal breeders of the nation as well as our most dangerous enemies; and who stay at home on purpose to deliver the kingdom to the Pretender, hoping to take their advantage by the absence of so many good Protestants, who have chosen rather to

20

---

[9] Georges Psalmanazar was a Frenchman who pretended to be Japanese and wrote an entirely imaginary *Description of the Isle Formosa*. He had become well known in gullible London society.

leave their country than to stay at home and pay tithes against their conscience to an Episcopal curate.

Secondly, the poorer tenants will have something valuable of their own, which by law may be made liable to distress,[10] and help to pay their landlord's rent, their corn and cattle being already seized and money a thing unknown.

Thirdly, whereas the maintenance of an hundred thousand children, from two years old and upwards, cannot be computed at less than ten shillings a piece per annum, the nation's stock will be thereby increased fifty thousand pounds per annum, besides the profit of a new dish introduced to the tables of all gentlemen of fortune in the kingdom who have any refinement in taste. And the money will circulate among ourselves, the goods being entirely of our own growth and manufacture.

Fourthly, the constant breeders, besides the gain of eight shillings sterling per annum by the sale of their children, will be rid of the charge of maintaining them after the first year.

25   Fifthly, this food would likewise bring great custom to taverns, where the vintners will certainly be so prudent as to procure the best receipts for dressing it to perfection, and consequently have their houses frequented by all the fine gentlemen, who justly value themselves upon their knowledge in good eating; and a skillful cook, who understands how to oblige his guests, will contrive to make it as expensive as they please.

Sixthly, this would be a great inducement to marriage, which all wise nations have either encouraged by rewards or enforced by laws and penalties. It would increase the care and tenderness of mothers toward their children, when

they were sure of a settlement for life to the poor babes, provided in some sort by the public, to their annual profit instead of expense. We should see an honest emulation among the married women, which of them could bring the fattest child to the market. Men would become as fond of their wives during the time of their pregnancy as they are now of their mares in foal, their cows in calf, or sows when they are ready to farrow; nor offer to beat or kick them (as is too frequent a practice) for fear of a miscarriage.

Many other advantages might be enumerated. For instance, the addition of some thousand carcasses in our exportation of barreled beef, the propagation of swine's flesh, and improvements in the art of making good bacon, so much wanted among us by the great destruction of pigs, too frequent at our tables, which are no way comparable in taste or magnificence to a well-grown, fat, yearling child, which roasted whole will make a considerable figure at a lord mayor's feast or any other public entertainment. But this and many others I omit, being studious of brevity.

Supposing that one thousand families in this city would be constant customers for infants' flesh, besides others who might have it at merry meetings, particularly weddings and christenings, I compute that Dublin would take off annually about twenty thousand carcasses, and the rest of the kingdom (where probably they will be sold somewhat cheaper) the remaining eighty thousand.

I can think of no one objection that will possibly be raised against this proposal, unless it should be urged that the number of people will be thereby much lessened in the kingdom. This I freely own, and it was indeed one principal design in offering it to the world. I desire the reader will observe, that I calculate my remedy

---

[10] Subject to possession by lenders.

for this one individual kingdom of Ireland and for no other that ever was, is, or I think ever can be upon earth. Therefore let no man talk to me of other expedients: of taxing our absentees at five shillings a pound: of using neither clothes nor household furniture except what is of our own growth and manufacture: of utterly rejecting the materials and instruments that promote foreign luxury: of curing the expensiveness of pride, vanity, idleness, and gaming in our women: of introducing a vein of parsimony, prudence, and temperance: of learning to love our country, in the want of which we differ even from Laplanders and the inhabitants of Topinamboo:[11] of quitting our animosities and factions, nor acting any longer like the Jews, who were murdering one another at the very moment their city was taken:[12] of being a little cautious not to sell our country and conscience for nothing: of teaching landlords to have at least one degree of mercy toward their tenants: lastly, of putting a spirit of honesty, industry, and skill into our shopkeepers; who, if a resolution could now be taken to buy only our native goods, would immediately unite to cheat and exact upon us in the price, the measure, and the goodness, nor could ever yet be brought to make one fair proposal of just dealing, though often and earnestly invited to it.

30   Therefore I repeat, let no man talk to me of these and the like expedients, till he hath at least some glimpse of hope that there will ever be some hearty and sincere attempt to put them in practice.

---

[11] District of Brazil.
[12] During the Roman siege of Jerusalem (70 B.C.E.), prominent Jews were charged with collaborating with the enemy and put to death.

But as to myself, having been wearied out for many years with offering vain, idle, visionary thoughts, and at length utterly despairing of success, I fortunately fell upon this proposal, which, as it is wholly new, so it hath something solid and real, of no expense and little trouble, full in our own power, and whereby we can incur no danger in disobliging England. For this kind of commodity will not bear exportation, the flesh being of too tender a consistence to admit a long continuance in salt, although perhaps I could name a country which would be glad to eat up our whole nation without it.

After all, I am not so violently bent upon my own opinion as to reject any offer proposed by wise men, which shall be found equally innocent, cheap, easy, and effectual. But before something of that kind shall be advanced in contradiction to my scheme, and offering a better, I desire the author or authors will be pleased maturely to consider two points. First, as things now stand, how they will be able to find food and raiment for an hundred thousand useless mouths and backs. And secondly, there being a round million of creatures in human figure throughout this kingdom, whose sole subsistence put into a common stock would leave them in debt two millions of pounds sterling, adding those who are beggars by profession to the bulk of farmers, cottagers, and laborers, with their wives and children who are beggars in effect; I desire those politicians who dislike my overture, and may perhaps be so bold to attempt an answer, that they will first ask the parents of these mortals whether they would not at this day think it a great happiness to have been sold for food at a year old in this manner I prescribe, and thereby have avoided such a perpetual scene of misfortunes as they have since gone through by the oppression of landlords, the impossibility of paying rent without money or trade, the want of common sustenance, with neither house nor clothes to cover them from the inclemencies of the weather, and the most inevitable prospect of entailing the like of greater miseries upon their breed forever.

I profess, in the sincerity of my heart, that I have not the least personal interest in endeavoring to promote this necessary work, having no other motive than the public good of my country, by advancing our trade, providing for infants, relieving the poor, and giving some pleasure to the rich. I have no children by which I can propose to get a single penny; the youngest being nine years old, and my wife past childbearing.

Discussion Questions

1. What implicit assumption about the treatment of the Irish underlies Swift's proposal? Do expressions such as "just dropped from its dam" (para. 4) and "whose wives are breeders" (para. 6) give the reader a clue?

2. In this essay Swift assumes a persona; that is, for the purposes of the proposal he makes, he pretends to be a different person. Describe the characteristics of that person. Point out the places in the essay that reveal them.

3. In several places, however, Swift reveals himself as the outraged witness of English cruelty and indifference. Note the language that seems to reflect his own feelings.

4. Throughout the essay Swift recites lists of facts, many of them in the form of statistics. How do these facts contribute to the persuasiveness of his argument? How do they affect the reader?

5. What social practices and attitudes of both the Irish and the English does Swift condemn?

6. Does Swift offer any solutions for the problems he attacks? How do you know?

7. When this essay first appeared in 1729, some readers took it seriously and accused Swift of monstrous cruelty. Can you think of reasons that these readers failed to recognize the ironic intent?

Writing Suggestions

1. Try writing an ironical essay of your own. Choose a subject that clearly lends itself to such treatment. As Swift did, use logic and restraint in your language.

2. Choose a problem for which you think you have a solution. Defend your solution by using the stock issues as your pattern of organization.

AN EIGHTEENTH-CENTURY DECLARATION

On June 10, 1776, the Continental Congress appointed a committee of five men to draft a statement of independence for the American colonies. Thomas Jefferson did the actual writing, and John Adams and Benjamin Franklin offered changes. The draft was revised in Congress over a two-day period and was adopted on July 4, 1776. The first printed copies that were circulated bore only the signatures of John Hancock, the president, and Charles Thomson, the secretary. Later that month, the declaration was engrossed (copied in a large hand) and signed by almost every member of Congress. The purpose of the document was to justify the colonies' break with England.

The Declaration of Independence
THOMAS JEFFERSON

When in the Course of human events, it becomes necessary for one people to dissolve the political bands which have connected them with another, and to assume among the powers of the earth, the separate and equal station to which the Laws of Nature and of Nature's God entitle them, a decent respect to the opinions of mankind requires that they should declare the causes which impel them to the separation.

We hold these truths to be self-evident, that all men are created equal, that they are endowed by their Creator with certain unalienable Rights, that among these are Life, Liberty, and the pursuit of Happiness.

— That to secure these rights, Governments are instituted among Men, deriving their just powers from the consent of the governed,

— That whenever any Form of Government becomes destructive of these ends, it is the Right of the People to alter or to abolish it, and to institute new Government, laying its foundation on such principles and organizing its powers in such form, as to them shall seem most likely to effect their Safety and Happiness. Prudence, indeed, will dictate that Governments long established should not be changed for light and transient causes; and accordingly all experience hath shewn, that mankind are more disposed to suffer, while evils are sufferable, than to right themselves by abolishing the forms to which they are accustomed. But when a long train of abuses and usurpations, pursuing invariably the same Object evinces a design to reduce them under absolute Despotism, it is their right, it is their duty, to throw off such Government, and to provide new Guards for their future security.

— Such has been the patient sufferance of these Colonies; and such is now the necessity which constrains them to alter their former Systems of Government. The history of the present King of Great Britain is a history of repeated injuries and usurpations, all having in direct object the establishment of an absolute Tyranny over these States. To prove this, let Facts be submitted to a candid world.

He has refused his Assent to Laws, the most wholesome and necessary for the public good.

5

Thomas Jefferson (1743–1826) served as governor of Virginia, minister to France, secretary of state, vice president under John Adams, and president from 1801 to 1809.

He has forbidden his Governors to pass Laws of immediate and pressing importance, unless suspended in their operation till his Assent should be obtained; and when so suspended, he has utterly neglected to attend to them.

He has refused to pass other Laws for the accommodation of large districts of people, unless those people would relinquish the right of Representation in the Legislature, a right inestimable to them and formidable to tyrants only.

He has called together legislative bodies at places unusual, uncomfortable, and distant from the depository of their public Records, for the sole purpose of fatiguing them into compliance with his measures.

10 He has dissolved Representative Houses repeatedly, for opposing with manly firmness his invasions on the rights of the people.

He has refused for a long time, after such dissolutions, to cause others to be elected; whereby the Legislative powers, incapable of Annihilation, have returned to the People at large for their exercise; the State remaining in the mean time exposed to all the dangers of invasion from without, and convulsions within.

He has endeavoured to prevent the population of these States; for that purpose obstructing the Laws for Naturalization of Foreigners; refusing to pass others to encourage their migrations hither, and raising the conditions of new Appropriations of Lands.

He has obstructed the Administration of Justice, by refusing his Assent to Laws for establishing Judiciary powers.

He has made Judges dependent on his Will alone, for the tenure of their offices, and the amount and payment of their salaries.

He has erected a multitude of New Offices, 15 and sent hither swarms of Officers to harass our people, and eat out their substance.

He has kept among us, in times of peace, Standing Armies without the Consent of our legislatures.

He has affected to render the Military independent of and superior to the Civil power.

He has combined with others to subject us to a jurisdiction foreign to our constitution, and unacknowledged by our laws; giving his Assent to their Acts of pretended Legislation:

For Quartering large bodies of armed troops among us:

For protecting them, by a mock Trial, from 20 punishment for any Murders which they should commit on the Inhabitants of these States:

For cutting off our Trade with all parts of the world:

For imposing Taxes on us without our Consent:

For depriving us in many cases, of the benefits of Trial by Jury:

For transporting us beyond Seas to be tried for pretended offences:

For abolishing the free System of English 25 Laws in a neighbouring Province, establishing therein an Arbitrary government, and enlarging its Boundaries so as to render it at once an example and fit instrument for introducing the same absolute rule into these Colonies:

For taking away our Charters, abolishing our most valuable Laws, and altering fundamentally the Forms of our Governments:

For suspending our own Legislatures, and declaring themselves invested with power to legislate for us in all cases whatsoever.

He has abdicated Government here, by declaring us out of his Protection and waging War against us.

He has plundered our seas, ravaged our Coasts, burnt our towns, and destroyed the lives of our people.

30 He is at this time transporting large Armies of foreign Mercenaries to compleat the works of death, desolation and tyranny, already begun with circumstances of Cruelty & perfidy scarcely paralleled in the most barbarous ages, and totally unworthy the Head of a civilized nation.

He has constrained our fellow Citizens taken Captive on the high Seas to bear Arms against their Country, to become the executioners of their friends and Brethren, or to fall themselves by their Hands.

He has excited domestic insurrections amongst us, and has endeavoured to bring on the inhabitants of our frontiers, the merciless Indian Savages, whose known rule of warfare, is an undistinguished destruction of all ages, sexes and conditions.

In every stage of these Oppressions We have Petitioned for Redress in the most humble terms: Our repeated Petitions have been answered only by repeated injury. A Prince whose character is thus marked by every act which may define a Tyrant, is unfit to be the ruler of a free people.

Nor have We been wanting in attentions to our British brethren. We have warned them from time to time of attempts by their legislature to extend an unwarrantable jurisdiction over us. We have reminded them of the circumstances of our emigration and settlement here. We have appealed to their native justice and magnanimity, and we have conjured them by the ties of our common kindred to disavow these usurpations, which, would inevitably interrupt our connections and correspondence. They too have been deaf to the voice of justice and of consanguinity. We must, therefore, acquiesce in the necessity, which denounces our Separation, and hold them, as we hold the rest of mankind, Enemies in War, in Peace Friends.

35 We, therefore, the Representatives of the united States of America, in General Congress, Assembled, appealing to the Supreme Judge of the world for the rectitude of our intentions, do, in the Name, and by Authority of the good People of these Colonies, solemnly publish and declare, That these United Colonies are, and of Right ought to be Free and Independent States; that they are Absolved from all Allegiance to the British Crown, and that all political connection between them and the State of Great Britain, is and ought to be totally dissolved; and that as Free and Independent States, they have full Power to levy War, conclude Peace, contract Alliances, establish Commerce, and to do all other Acts and Things which Independent States may of right do. And for the support of this Declaration, with a firm reliance on the protection of divine Providence, we mutually pledge to each other our Lives, our Fortunes and our sacred Honor.

Discussion Questions

1. Who was the audience for the Declaration? Was there more than one possible audience?
2. A large part of the document consists of a list. What is being listed, and who is the "he" that is referred to at the beginning of each item on the list?
3. What exactly are the colonists declaring?
4. Does history support the claim that the writers of this document truly believed that all men are created equal? Explain.

Writing Suggestions

1. How would you express the main idea of the Declaration of Independence in the form of a syllogism?
2. Why is it significant that the document states that men "are endowed by their Creator" (para. 2) with rights to life, liberty, and the pursuit of happiness? Where else in the document is God mentioned?
3. Why was it important for the ideas expressed here to be put into writing?

A NINETEENTH-CENTURY LECTURE

Henry David Thoreau delivered this lecture in 1848 to the Concord Lyceum in Concord, Massachusetts, and published it in 1849. "Civil Disobedience" was widely read, and it influenced both Mahatma Gandhi in the passive-resistance campaign he led against the British in India and Martin Luther King Jr. in the U.S. civil rights movement.

Civil Disobedience
HENRY DAVID THOREAU

I heartily accept the motto, — "That government is best which governs least"; and I should like to see it acted up to more rapidly and systematically. Carried out, it finally amounts to this, which also I believe, — "That government is best which governs not at all"; and when men are prepared for it, that will be the kind of government which they will have. Government is at best but an expedient; but most governments are usually, and all governments are sometimes, inexpedient. The objections which have been brought against a standing army, and they are many and weighty, and deserve to prevail, may also at last be brought against a standing

Henry David Thoreau (1817–1862), philosopher and writer, is best known for *Walden*, an account of his solitary retreat to Walden Pond, near Concord, Massachusetts. Here he remained for more than two years in an effort to "live deliberately, to front only the essential facts of life."

government. The standing army is only an arm of the standing government. The government itself, which is only the mode which the people have chosen to execute their will, is equally liable to be abused and perverted before the people can act through it. Witness the present Mexican war, the work of comparatively a few individuals using the standing government as their tool; for, in the outset, the people would not have consented to this measure.

This American government,—what is it but a tradition, though a recent one, endeavoring to transmit itself unimpaired to posterity, but each instant losing some of its integrity? It has not the vitality and force of a single living man; for a single man can bend it to his will. It is a sort of wooden gun to the people themselves. But it is not the less necessary for this; for the people must have some complicated machinery or other, and hear its din, to satisfy that idea of government which they have. Governments show thus how successfully men can be imposed on, even impose on themselves, for their own advantage. It is excellent, we must all allow. Yet this government never of itself furthered any enterprise, but by the alacrity with which it got out of its way. *It* does not keep the country free. *It* does not settle the West. *It* does not educate. The character inherent in the American people has done all that has been accomplished; and it would have done somewhat more, if the government had not sometimes got in its way. For government is an expedient by which men would fain succeed in letting one another alone; and, as has been said, when it is most expedient, the governed are most let alone by it. Trade and commerce, if they were not made of India-rubber, would never manage to bounce over the obstacles which legislators are continually putting in their way; and, if one were to judge these men wholly by the effects of their actions, and not partly by their intentions, they would deserve to be classed and punished with those mischievous persons who put obstructions on the railroads.

But, to speak practically and as a citizen, unlike those who call themselves no-government men, I ask for, not at once no government, but *at once* a better government. Let every man make known what kind of government would command his respect, and that will be one step toward obtaining it.

After all, the practical reason why, when the power is once in the hands of the people, a majority are permitted, and for a long period continue, to rule, is not because they are most likely to be in the right, nor because this seems fairest to the minority, but because they are physically the strongest. But a government in which the majority rule in all cases cannot be based on justice, even as far as men understand it. Can there not be a government in which majorities do not virtually decide right and wrong, but conscience?—in which majorities decide only those questions to which the rule of expediency is applicable? Must the citizen ever for a moment, or in the least degree, resign his conscience to the legislator? Why has every man a conscience, then? I think that we should be men first, and subjects afterward. It is not desirable to cultivate a respect for the law, so much as for the right. The only obligation which I have a right to assume, is to do at any time what I think right. It is truly enough said, that a corporation has no conscience; but a corporation of conscientious men is a corporation *with* a conscience. Law never made men a whit more just; and, by means of their respect for it, even the well-disposed are daily made the agents of injustice. A common and natural result of an undue respect for law is, that you may see a file of soldiers, colonel, captain, corporal, privates, powder-monkeys, and all, marching in admirable order over hill and dale to the wars, against their wills, aye, against their common sense and consciences, which makes it very steep marching indeed, and produces a palpitation of the heart. They have no doubt that it is a damnable business in which they are concerned; they are all peaceably inclined. Now, what are they? Men at all? or small moveable forts and magazines, at the service of some unscrupulous man in power? Visit the Navy-Yard, and behold a marine, such a man as an American government can make, or such as it can make a man with its black arts,—a mere shadow and reminiscence of humanity, a man laid out alive and standing, and already, as one may say, buried under arms with funeral accompaniments, though it may be,—

> Not a drum was heard, nor a funeral note,
> As his corse to the rampart we hurried;
> Not a soldier discharged his farewell shot
> O'er the grave where our hero we buried.

5   The mass of men serve the state thus, not as men mainly, but as machines, with their bodies. They are the standing army, and the militia, jailers, constables, posse comitatus, &c. In most cases there is no free exercise whatever of the judgment or of the moral sense; but they put themselves on a level with wood and earth and stones; and wooden men can perhaps be manufactured that will serve the purpose as well. Such command no more respect than men of straw, or a lump of dirt. They have the same sort of worth only as horses and dogs. Yet such as these even are commonly esteemed good citizens. Others,—as most legislators, politicians, lawyers, ministers, and office-holders,—serve the State chiefly with their heads; and, as they rarely make any moral distinctions, they are as likely to serve the Devil, without *intending* it, as God. A very few, as heroes, patriots, martyrs, reformers in the great sense, and *men,* serve the state with their consciences also, and so necessarily resist it for the most part, and they are commonly treated as enemies by it. A wise man will only be useful as a man, and will not submit to be "clay," and "stop a hole to keep the wind away," but leave that office to his dust at least:—

> I am too high-born to be propertied,
> To be a secondary at control,
> Or useful serving-man and instrument
> To any sovereign state throughout the
>   world.

He who gives himself entirely to his fellow-men appears to them useless and selfish; but he who gives himself partially to them is pronounced a benefactor and philanthropist.

How does it become a man to behave toward this American government today? I answer that he cannot without disgrace be associated with it. I cannot for an instant recognize that political organization as *my* government which is the *slave's* government also.

All men recognize the right of revolution; that is, the right to refuse allegiance to, and to resist, the government, when its tyranny or its inefficiency are great and unendurable. But almost all say that such is not the case now. But such was the case, they think, in the Revolution of '75. If one were to tell me that this was a bad government because it taxed certain foreign commodities brought to its ports, it is most probable that I should not make an ado about it, for I can do without them. All machines have their friction; and possibly this does enough good to counterbalance the evil. At any rate, it is a great evil to make a stir about it. But when the friction comes to have its machine, and oppression and robbery are organized, I say, let us not have such a machine any longer. In other words, when a sixth of the population of a nation which has undertaken to be the refuge of liberty are slaves, and a whole country is unjustly overrun and conquered by a foreign army, and subjected to military law, I think that it is not too soon for honest men to rebel and revolutionize. What makes this duty the more urgent is the fact, that the country so overrun is not our own, but ours is the invading army.

Paley,[1] a common authority with many on moral questions, in his chapter on the "Duty of Submission to Civil Government," resolves all civil obligation into expediency; and he proceeds to say, "that so long as the interest of the whole society requires it, that is, so long as the established government cannot be resisted or changed without public inconveniency, it is the will of God that the established government be obeyed, and no longer. . . . This principle being admitted, the justice of every particular case of resistance is reduced to a computation of the quantity of the danger and grievance on the one side, and of the probability and expense of redressing it on the other." Of this, he says, every man shall judge for himself. But Paley appears never to have contemplated those cases to which the rule of expediency does not apply, in which a people, as well as an individual, must do justice, cost what it may. If I have unjustly wrested a plank from a drowning man, I must restore it to him though I drown myself. This, according to Paley, would be inconvenient. But he that would save his life, in such a case, shall lose it. This people must cease to hold slaves, and to make war on Mexico, though it cost them their existence as a people.

In their practice, nations agree with Paley; but does any one think that Massachusetts does exactly what is right at the present crisis?

> A drab of state, a cloth-'o-silver slut,
> To have her train borne up, and her soul
>   trail in the dirt.

Practically speaking, the opponents to a reform in Massachusetts are not a hundred thousand politicians at the South, but a hundred thousand merchants and farmers here, who are more interested in commerce and agriculture than they are in humanity, and are not prepared to do justice to the slave and to Mexico, *cost what it may.* I quarrel not with far-off foes, but with those who, near at home, cooperate with, and do the bidding of, those far away, and without whom the latter would be harmless. We are accustomed to say, that the mass of men are unprepared; but improvement is slow, because the few are not materially wiser or better than the many. It is not so important that many should be as good as you, as that there be some absolute goodness somewhere; for that will leaven the whole lump. There are thousands who are *in opinion* opposed to slavery and to the war, who yet in effect do nothing to put an end to them; who, esteeming themselves children of Washington and Franklin, sit down with their hands in their pockets, and say that they know not

10

---

[1] William Paley (1743–1805), an English clergyman and Christian apologist, was known for his advocacy of the teleological argument for the existence of God — an argument based on a clear design in nature. —Eds.

what to do, and do nothing; who even postpone the question of freedom to the question of free-trade, and quietly read the prices-current along with the latest advice from Mexico, after dinner, and, it may be, fall asleep over them both. What is the price-current of an honest man and patriot today? They hesitate, and they regret, and sometimes they petition; but they do nothing in earnest and with effect. They will wait, well disposed, for others to remedy the evil, that they may no longer have it to regret. At most, they give only a cheap vote, and a feeble countenance and God-speed, to the right, as it goes by them. There are nine hundred and ninety-nine patrons of virtue to one virtuous man; but it is easier to deal with the real possessor of a thing than with the temporary guardian of it.

All voting is a sort of gaming, like checkers or backgammon, with a slight moral tinge to it, a playing with right and wrong, with moral questions; and betting naturally accompanies it. The character of the voters is not staked. I cast my vote, perchance, as I think right; but I am not vitally concerned that that right should prevail. I am willing to leave it to the majority. Its obligation, therefore, never exceeds that of expediency. Even voting *for the right* is *doing* nothing for it. It is only expressing to men feebly your desire that it should prevail. A wise man will not leave the right to the mercy of chance, nor wish it to prevail through the power of the majority. There is but little virtue in the action of masses of men. When the majority shall at length vote for the abolition of slavery, it will be because they are indifferent to slavery, or because there is but little slavery left to be abolished by their vote. *They* will then be the only slaves. Only *his* vote can hasten the abolition of slavery who asserts his own freedom by his vote.

I hear of a convention to be held at Baltimore, or elsewhere, for the selection of a candidate for the presidency, made up chiefly of editors, and men who are politicians by profession; but I think, what is it to any independent, intelligent, and respectable man what decision they may come to? Shall we not have the advantage of his wisdom and honesty, nevertheless? Can we not count upon some independent votes? Are there not many individuals in the country who do not attend conventions? But no: I find that the respectable man, so called, has immediately drifted from his position, and despairs of his country, when his country has more reason to despair of him. He forthwith adopts one of the candidates thus selected as the only *available* one, thus providing that he is himself *available* for any purposes of the demagogue. His vote is of no more worth than that of any unprincipled foreigner or hireling native, who may have been bought. O for a man who is *a man,* and, as my neighbor says, has a bone in his back which you cannot pass your hand through! Our statistics are at fault: The population has been returned too large. How many *men* are there to a square thousand miles in this country? Hardly one. Does not America offer any inducement for men to settle here? The American has dwindled into an Odd Fellow,—one who may be known by the development of his organ of gregariousness, and a manifest lack of intellect and cheerful self-reliance; whose first and chief concern, on coming into the world, is to see that the Almshouses are in good repair; and, before yet he has lawfully donned the virile garb, to collect a fund for the support of the widows and orphans that may be; who, in short, ventures to live only by the aid of the Mutual Insurance company, which has promised to bury him decently.

It is not a man's duty, as a matter of course, to devote himself to the eradication of any, even the most enormous wrong; he may still properly have other concerns to engage him; but it is his duty, at least, to wash his hands of it, and, if he gives it no thought longer, not to give it practically his support. If I devote myself to other pursuits and contemplations, I must first see, at least, that I do not pursue them sitting upon another man's shoulders. I must get off him first, that he may pursue his contemplations too. See what gross inconsistency is tolerated. I have heard some of my townsmen say, "I should like to have them order me out to help put down an insurrection of the slaves, or to march to Mexico;—see if I would go"; and yet these very men have each, directly by their allegiance, and so indirectly, at least, by their money, furnished a substitute. The soldier is applauded who refuses to serve in an unjust war by those who do not refuse to sustain the unjust government which makes the war; is applauded by those whose own act and authority he disregards and sets at nought; as if the State were penitent to that degree that it hired one to scourge it while it sinned, but not to that degree that it left off sinning for a moment. Thus, under the name of Order and Civil Government, we are all made at last to pay homage to and support our own meanness. After the first blush of sin, comes its indifference; and from immoral it becomes, as it were, *un*moral, and not quite unnecessary to that life which we have made.

The broadest and most prevalent error requires the most disinterested virtue to sustain it. The slight reproach to which the virtue of patriotism is commonly liable, the noble are most likely to incur. Those who, while they disapprove of the character and measures of a govern-ment, yield to it their allegiance and support, are undoubtedly its most conscientious supporters, and so frequently the most serious obstacles to reform. Some are petitioning the State to dissolve the Union, to disregard the requisitions of the President. Why do they not dissolve it themselves,—the union between themselves and the State,—and refuse to pay their quota into its treasury? Do not they stand in the same relation to the State, that the State does to the Union? And have not the same reasons prevented the State from resisting the Union which have prevented them from resisting the State?

How can a man be satisfied to entertain an opinion merely, and enjoy *it*? Is there any enjoyment in it, if his opinion is that he is aggrieved? If you are cheated out of a single dollar by your neighbor, you do not rest satisfied with knowing that you are cheated, or with saying that you are cheated, or even with petitioning him to pay you your due; but you take effectual steps at once to obtain the full amount, and see that you are never cheated again. Action from principle, the perception and the performance of right, changes things and relations; it is essentially revolutionary, and does not consist wholly with anything which was. It not only divides states and churches, it divides families; ay, it divides the *individual,* separating the diabolical in him from the divine.

Unjust laws exist: Shall we be content to obey them, or shall we endeavor to amend them, and obey them until we have succeeded, or shall we transgress them at once? Men generally, under such a government as this, think that they ought to wait until they have persuaded the majority to alter them. They think that, if they should resist, the remedy would be worse than the evil. But it is the fault of the government

15

itself that the remedy *is* worse than the evil. *It* makes it worse. Why is it not more apt to anticipate and provide for reform? Why does it not cherish its wise minority? Why does it cry and resist before it is hurt? Why does it not encourage its citizens to be on the alert to point out its faults, and *do* better than it would have them? Why does it always crucify Christ, and excommunicate Copernicus and Luther, and pronounce Washington and Franklin rebels?

One would think, that a deliberate and practical denial of its authority was the only offence never contemplated by government; else, why has it not assigned its definite, its suitable and proportionate penalty? If a man who has no property refuses but once to earn nine shillings for the State, he is put in prison for a period unlimited by any law that I know, and determined only by the discretion of those who placed him there; but if he should steal ninety times nine shillings from the State, he is soon permitted to go at large again.

If the injustice is part of the necessary friction of the machine of government, let it go, let it go: Perchance it will wear smooth,—certainly the machine will wear out. If the injustice has a spring, or a pulley, or a rope, or a crank, exclusively for itself, then perhaps you may consider whether the remedy will not be worse than the evil; but if it is of such a nature that it requires you to be the agent of injustice to another, then, I say, break the law. Let your life be a counter friction to stop the machine. What I have to do is to see, at any rate, that I do not lend myself to the wrong which I condemn.

As for adopting the ways which the State has provided for remedying the evil, I know not of such ways. They take too much time, and a man's life will be gone. I have other affairs to attend to. I came into this world, not chiefly to make this a good place to live in, but to live in it, be it good or bad. A man has not everything to do, but something; and because he cannot do *everything*, it is not necessary that he should do *something* wrong. It is not my business to be petitioning the Governor or the Legislature any more than it is theirs to petition me; and, if they should not hear my petition, what should I do then? But in this case the State has provided no way: Its very Constitution is the evil. This may seem to be harsh and stubborn and unconciliatory; but it is to treat with the utmost kindness and consideration the only spirit that can appreciate or deserves it. So is all change for the better, like birth and death, which convulse the body.

I do not hesitate to say, that those who call themselves Abolitionists should at once effectually withdraw their support, both in person and property, from the government of Massachusetts, and not wait till they constitute a majority of one, before they suffer the right to prevail through them. I think that it is enough if they have God on their side, without waiting for that other one. Moreover, any man more right than his neighbors, constitutes a majority of one already.

I meet this American government, or its representative, the State government, directly, and face to face, once a year—no more—in the person of its tax-gatherer; this is the only mode in which a man situated as I am necessarily meets it; and it then says distinctly, Recognize me; and the simplest, the most effectual, and, in the present posture of affairs, the indispensablest mode of treating with it on this head, of expressing your little satisfaction with and love for it, is to deny it then. My civil neighbor, the tax-gatherer, is the very man I have to deal with, — for it is, after all, with men and not with parchment that I quarrel, — and he has voluntarily chosen to be an agent of the government. How shall he ever know well what he is and does as an officer of the government, or as a man, until he is obliged to consider whether he shall treat me, his neighbor, for whom he has respect, as a neighbor and well-disposed man, or as a maniac and disturber of the peace, and see if he can get over this obstruction to his neighborliness without a ruder and more impetuous thought or speech corresponding with his action? I know this well, that if one thousand, if one hundred, if ten men whom I could name, — if ten *honest* men only, — aye, if *one* HONEST man, in this State of Massachusetts, *ceasing to hold slaves*, were actually to withdraw from this copartnership, and be locked up in the county jail therefor, it would be the abolition of slavery in America. For it matters not how small the beginning may seem to be: What is once well done is done forever. But we love better to talk about it: That we say is our mission. Reform keeps many scores of newspapers in its service, but not one man. If my esteemed neighbor, the State's ambassador, who will devote his days to the settlement of the question of human rights in the Council Chamber, instead of being threatened with the prisons of Carolina, were to sit down the prisoner of Massachusetts, that State which is so anxious to foist the sin of slavery upon her sister, — though at present she can discover only an act of inhospitality to be the ground of a quarrel with her, — the Legislature would not wholly waive the subject the following winter.

Under a government which imprisons any unjustly, the true place for a just man is also a prison. The proper place today, the only place which Massachusetts has provided for her freer and less desponding spirits, is in her prisons, to be put out and locked out of the State by her own act, as they have already put themselves out by their principles. It is there that the fugitive slave, and the Mexican prisoner on parole, and the Indian come to plead the wrongs of his race, should find them; on that separate, but more free and honorable ground, where the State places those who are not *with* her, but *against* her, — the only house in a slave State in which a free man can abide with honor. If any think that their influence would be lost there, and their voices no longer afflict the ear of the State, that they would not be as an enemy within its walls, they do not know by how much truth is stronger than error, nor how much more eloquently and effectively he can combat injustice who has experienced a little in his own person. Cast your whole vote, not a strip of paper merely, but your whole influence. A minority is powerless while it conforms to the majority; it is not even a minority then; but it is irresistible when it clogs by its whole weight. If the alternative is to keep all just men in prison, or give up war and slavery, the State will not hesitate which to choose. If a thousand men were not to pay their tax-bills this year, that would not be a violent and bloody measure, as it would be to pay them, and enable the State to commit violence and shed innocent blood. This is, in fact, the definition of a peaceable revolution, if any such is possible. If the tax-gatherer, or any other public officer, asks me, as one has done, "But what shall I do?" my answer is, "If you really wish to do any thing, resign your office." When the subject has refused allegiance, and the officer has resigned his office, then the revolution is accomplished. But even suppose blood should flow. Is there not a sort of blood shed when the conscience is wounded? Through this wound a man's real manhood and immortality flow out, and he bleeds to an ever-lasting death. I see this blood flowing now.

I have contemplated the imprisonment of the offender, rather than the seizure of his goods, — though both will serve the same purpose, — because they who assert the purest right, and consequently are most dangerous to a corrupt State, commonly have not spent much time in accumulating property. To such the State renders comparatively small service, and a slight tax is wont to appear exorbitant, particularly if they are obliged to earn it by special labor with their hands. If there were one who lived wholly without the use of money, the State itself would hesitate to demand it of him. But the rich man, — not to make any invidious comparison, — is always sold to the institution which makes him rich. Absolutely speaking, the more money, the less virtue; for money comes between a man and his objects, and obtains them for him; and it was certainly no great virtue to obtain it. It puts to rest many questions which he would otherwise be taxed to answer; while the only new question which it puts is the hard but superfluous one, how to spend it. Thus his moral ground is taken from under his feet. The opportunities of living are diminished in proportion as what are called the "means" are increased. The best thing a man can do for his culture when he is rich is to endeavor to carry out those schemes which he entertained when he was poor. Christ answered the Herodians according to their condition. "Show me the tribute-money," said he; — and one took a penny out of his pocket; — if you use money which has the image of Cæsar on it, and which he has made current and valuable, that is, *if you are men of the State*, and gladly enjoy the advantages of Cæsar's government, then pay him back some of his own when he demands it; "Render therefore to Cæsar that which is Cæsar's, and to God those things which are God's," — leaving them no wiser than before as to which was which; for they did not wish to know.

When I converse with the freest of my neighbors, I perceive that, whatever they may say about the magnitude and seriousness of the question, and their regard for the public tranquility, the long and the short of the matter is, that they cannot spare the protection of the existing government, and they dread the consequences to their property and families of disobedience to it. For my own part, I should not like to think that I ever rely on the protection of the State. But, if I deny the authority of the State when it presents its tax-bill, it will soon take and waste all my property, and so harass me and my children without end. This is hard. This makes it impossible for a man to live honestly, and at the same time comfortably, in outward respects. It will not be worth the while to accumulate property; that would be sure to go again. You must hire or squat somewhere, and raise but a small crop, and eat that soon. You must live within yourself, and depend upon yourself always tucked up and ready for a start, and not have many affairs. A man may grow rich in Turkey even, if he will be in all respects a good subject of the Turkish government. Confucius said: "If a state is governed by the principles of reason, poverty and misery are subjects of shame; if a state is not governed by the principles of reason, riches and honors are the subjects of shame." No: Until I want the protection of Massachusetts to be extended to me in some distant southern port, where my liberty is endangered, or until I am bent solely on building up an estate at home by peaceful enterprise, I can afford to refuse allegiance to Massachusetts, and her right to my property and life. It costs me less in every sense to incur the penalty of disobedience to the State, than it would to obey. I should feel as if I were worth less in that case.

25   Some years ago, the State met me in behalf of the Church, and commanded me to pay a certain sum toward the support of a clergyman whose preaching my father attended, but never I myself. "Pay," it said, "or be locked up in the jail." I declined to pay. But, unfortunately, another man saw fit to pay it. I did not see why the schoolmaster should be taxed to support the priest, and not the priest the schoolmaster; for I was not the State's schoolmaster, but I supported myself by voluntary subscription. I did not see why the lyceum should not present its tax-bill, and have the State to back its demand, as well as the Church. However, at the request of the selectmen, I condescended to make some such statement as this in writing: — "Know all men by these presents, that I, Henry Thoreau, do not wish to be regarded as a member of any incorporated society which I have not joined." This I gave to the town clerk; and he has it. The State, having thus learned that I did not wish to be regarded as a member of that church, has never made a like demand on me since; though it said that it must adhere to its original presumption that time. If I had known how to name them, I should then have signed off in detail from all the societies which I never signed on to; but I did not know where to find a complete list.

I have paid no poll-tax for six years. I was put into a jail once on this account, for one night; and, as I stood considering the walls of solid stone, two or three feet thick, the door of wood and iron, a foot thick, and the iron grating which strained the light, I could not help being struck with the foolishness of that institution which treated me as if I were mere flesh and blood and bones, to be locked up. I wondered that it should have concluded at length that this was the best use it could put me to, and had never thought to avail itself of my services in some way. I saw that, if there was a wall of stone between me and my townsmen, there was a still more difficult one to climb or break through, before they could get to be as free as I was. I did not for a moment feel confined, and the walls seemed a great waste of stone and mortar. I felt as if I alone of all my townsmen had paid my tax. They plainly did not know how to treat me, but behaved like persons who are underbred. In every threat and in every compliment there was a blunder; for they thought that my chief desire was to stand the other side of that stone wall. I could not but smile to see how industriously they locked the door on my meditations, which followed them out again without let or hindrance, and *they* were really all that was dangerous. As they could not reach me, they had resolved to punish my body; just as boys, if they cannot come at some person against whom they have a spite, will abuse his dog. I saw that the State was half-witted, and it was timid as a lone woman with her silver spoons, and that it did not know its friends from its foes, and I lost all my remaining respect for it, and pitied it.

Thus the State never intentionally confronts a man's sense, intellectual or moral, but only his body, his senses. It is not armed with superior wit or honesty, but with superior physical strength. I was not born to be forced. I will breathe after my own fashion. Let us see who is the strongest. What force has a multitude? They only can force me who obey a higher law than I. They force me to become like themselves. I do not hear of *men* being *forced* to live this way or that by masses of men. What sort of life were that to live? When I meet a government which says to me, "Your money or your life," why should I be in haste to give it my money? It may be in a great strait, and not know what to do: I cannot help that. It must help itself; do as I do. It is not worth the while to snivel about it. I am not responsible for the successful working of the machinery of society. I am not the son of the engineer. I perceive that, when an acorn and a chestnut fall side by side, the one does not remain inert to make way for the other, but both obey their own laws, and spring and grow and flourish as best they can, till one, perchance, overshadows and destroys the other. If a plant cannot live according to its nature, it dies; and so a man.

The night in prison was novel and interesting enough. The prisoners in their shirtsleeves were enjoying a chat and the evening air in the doorway, when I entered. But the jailer said, "Come, boys, it is time to lock up"; and so they dispersed, and I heard the sound of their steps returning into the hollow apartments. My roommate was introduced to me by the jailer, as "a first-rate fellow and a clever man." When the door was locked, he showed me where to hang my hat, and how he managed matters there. The rooms were white-washed once a month; and this one, at least, was the whitest, most simply furnished, and probably the neatest apartment in the town. He naturally wanted to know where I came from, and what brought me there; and, when I had told him, I asked him in my turn how he came there, presuming him to be an honest man, of course; and, as the world goes, I believe he was. "Why," said he, "they accuse me of burning a barn; but I never did it." As near as I could discover, he had probably gone to bed in a barn when drunk, and smoked his pipe there; and so a barn was burnt. He had the reputation of being a clever man, had been there some three months waiting for his trial to come on, and would have to wait as much longer; but he was quite domesticated and contented, since he got his board for nothing, and thought that he was well-treated.

He occupied one window, and I the other; and I saw, that if one stayed there long, his principal business would be to look out the window. I had soon read all the tracts that were left there, and examined where former prisoners had broken out, and where a grate had been sawed off, and heard the history of the various occupants of that room; for I found that even here there was a history and a gossip which never circulated beyond the walls of the jail. Probably this is the only house in the town where verses are composed, which are afterward printed in a circular form, but not published. I was shown quite a long list of verses which were composed by some young men who had been detected in an attempt to escape, who avenged themselves by singing them.

I pumped my fellow-prisoner as dry as I could, for fear I should never see him again; but at length he showed me which was my bed, and left me to blow out the lamp.

It was like travelling into a far country, such as I had never expected to behold, to lie there for one night. It seemed to me that I never had heard the town-clock strike before, nor the evening sounds of the village; for we slept with

30

the windows open, which were inside the grating. It was to see my native village in the light of the Middle Ages, and our Concord was turned into a Rhine stream, and visions of knights and castles passed before me. They were the voices of old burghers that I heard in the streets. I was an involuntary spectator and auditor of whatever was done and said in the kitchen of the adjacent village-inn, — a wholly new and rare experience to me. It was a closer view of my native town. I was fairly inside of it. I never had seen its institutions before. This is one of its peculiar institutions; for it is a shire town. I began to comprehend what its inhabitants were about.

In the morning, our breakfasts were put through the hole in the door, in small oblong-square tin pans, made to fit, and holding a pint of chocolate, with brown bread, and an iron spoon. When they called for the vessels again, I was green enough to return what bread I had left; but my comrade seized it, and said that I should lay that up for lunch or dinner. Soon after, he was let out to work at haying in a neighboring field, whither he went every day, and would not be back till noon; so he bade me good-day, saying that he doubted if he should see me again.

When I came out of prison, — for some one interfered, and paid that tax, — I did not perceive that great changes had taken place on the common, such as he observed who went in a youth, and emerged a tottering and gray-headed man; and yet a change had to my eyes come over the scene, — the town, and State, and country, — greater than any that mere time could effect. I saw yet more distinctly the State in which I lived. I saw to what extent the people among whom I lived could be trusted as good neighbors and friends; that their friendship

was for summer weather only; that they did not greatly propose to do right; that they were a distinct race from me by their prejudices and superstitions, as the Chinamen and Malays are; that, in their sacrifices to humanity, they ran no risks, not even to their property; that, after all, they were not so noble but they treated the thief as he had treated them, and hoped, by a certain outward observance and a few prayers, and by walking in a particular straight though useless path from time to time, to save their souls. This may be to judge my neighbors harshly; for I believe that many of them are not aware that they have such an institution as the jail in their village.

It was formerly the custom in our village, when a poor debtor came out of jail, for his acquaintances to salute him, looking through their fingers, which were crossed to represent the grating of a jail window, "How do ye do?" My neighbors did not thus salute me, but first looked at me, and then at one another, as if I had returned from a long journey. I was put into jail as I was going to the shoemaker's to get a shoe which was mended. When I was let out the next morning, I proceeded to finish my errand, and having put on my mended shoe, joined a huckleberry party, who were impatient to put themselves under my conduct; and in half an hour, — for the horse was soon tackled, — was in the midst of a huckleberry field, on one of our highest hills, two miles off, and then the State was nowhere to be seen.

This is the whole story of "My Prisons."   35

I have never declined paying the highway tax, because I am as desirous of being a good neighbor as I am of being a bad subject; and, as for supporting schools, I am doing my part to educate my fellow-countrymen now. It is for no particular item in the tax-bill that I refuse to pay it. I simply wish to refuse allegiance to the State, to withdraw and stand aloof from it effectually. I do not care to trace the course of my dollar, if I could, till it buys a man, or a musket to shoot one with, — the dollar is innocent, — but I am concerned to trace the effects of my allegiance. In fact, I quietly declare war with the State, after my fashion, though I will still make what use and get what advantage of her I can, as is usual in such cases.

If others pay the tax which is demanded of me, from a sympathy with the State, they do but what they have already done in their own case, or rather they abet injustice to a greater extent than the State requires. If they pay the tax from a mistaken interest in the individual taxed, to save his property or prevent his going to jail, it is because they have not considered wisely how far they let their private feelings interfere with the public good.

This, then, is my position at present. But one cannot be too much on his guard in such a case, lest his action be biased by obstinacy, or an undue regard for the opinions of men. Let him see that he does only what belongs to himself and to the hour.

I think sometimes, Why, this people mean well; they are only ignorant; they would do better if they knew how: why give your neighbors this pain to treat you as they are inclined to? But I think again, this is no reason why I should do as they do, or permit others to suffer much greater pain of a different kind. Again, I sometimes say to myself, When many millions of men, without heat, without ill will, without personal feelings of any kind, demand of you a few shillings only, without the possibility, such

is their constitution, of retracing or altering their present demand, and without the possibility, on your side, of appeal to any other millions, why expose yourself to this overwhelming brute force? You do not resist cold and hunger, the winds and the waves, thus obstinately; you quietly submit to a thousand similar necessities. You do not put your head into the fire. But just in proportion as I regard this as not wholly a brute force, partly a human force, and consider that I have relations to those millions as to so many millions of men, and not of mere brute or inanimate things, I see that appeal is possible, first and instantaneously, from them to the Maker of them, and, secondly, from them to themselves. But, if I put my head deliberately into the fire, there is no appeal to fire or to the Maker of fire, and I have only myself to blame. If I could convince myself that I have any right to be satisfied with men as they are, and to treat them according, and not according, in some respects, to my requisitions and expectations of what they and I ought to be, then, like a good Mussulman[2] and fatalist, I should endeavor to be satisfied with things as they are, and say it is the will of God. And, above all, there is this difference between resisting this and a purely brute or natural force, that I can resist this with some effect; but I cannot expect, like Orpheus, to change the nature of the rocks and trees and beasts.

I do not wish to quarrel with any man or 40
nation. I do not wish to split hairs, to make fine distinctions, or set myself up as better than my neighbors. I seek rather, I may say, even an excuse for conforming to the laws of the land. I am but too ready to conform to them. Indeed,

---

[2] Muslim. —EDS.

I have reason to suspect myself on this head; and each year, as the tax-gatherer comes round, I find myself disposed to review the acts and position of the general and State governments, and the spirit of the people, to discover a pretext for conformity.

> We must affect our country as our
>   parents;
> And if at any time we alienate
> Our love or industry from doing it honor,
> We must respect effects and teach the
>   soul
> Matter of conscience and religion,
> And not desire of rule or benefit.

I believe that the State will soon be able to take all my work of this sort out of my hands, and then I shall be no better a patriot than my fellow-countrymen. Seen from a lower point of view, the Constitution, with all its faults, is very good; the law and the courts are very respectable; even this State and this American government are, in many respects, very admirable and rare things, to be thankful for, such as a great many have described them; but seen from a point of view a little higher, they are what I have described them; seen from a higher still, and the highest, who shall say what they are, or that they are worth looking at or thinking of at all?

However, the government does not concern me much, and I shall bestow the fewest possible thoughts on it. It is not many moments that I live under a government, even in this world. If a man is thought-free, fancy-free, imagination-free, that which *is not* never for a long time appearing *to be* to him, unwise rulers or reformers cannot fatally interrupt him.

I know that most men think differently from myself; but those whose lives are by profession devoted to the study of these or kindred subjects, content me as little as any. Statesmen and legislators, standing so completely within the institution, never distinctly and nakedly behold it. They speak of moving society, but have no resting-place without it. They may be men of a certain experience and discrimination, and have no doubt invented ingenious and even useful systems, for which we sincerely thank them; but all their wit and usefulness lie within certain not very wide limits. They are wont to forget that the world is not governed by policy and expediency. Webster[3] never goes behind government, and so cannot speak with authority about it. His words are wisdom to those legislators who contemplate no essential reform in the existing government; but for thinkers, and those who legislate for all time, he never once glances at the subject. I know of those whose serene and wise speculations on this theme would soon reveal the limits of his mind's range and hospitality. Yet, compared with the cheap professions of most reformers, and the still cheaper wisdom and eloquence of politicians in general, his are almost the only sensible and valuable words, and we thank Heaven for him. Comparatively, he is always strong, original, and, above all, practical. Still his quality is not wisdom, but prudence. The lawyer's truth is not Truth, but consistency, or a consistent expediency. Truth is always in harmony with herself, and is not concerned chiefly to reveal the justice that may consist with wrong-doing. He well deserves to be called, as he has been called, the Defender of the Constitution. There are really no blows to

---

[3] Daniel Webster (1782–1852), a senator from Massachusetts and secretary of state, was a supporter of a strong federal government. —EDS.

be given by him but defensive ones. He is not a leader, but a follower. His leaders are the men of '87. "I have never made an effort," he says, "and never propose to make an effort; I have never countenanced an effort, and never mean to countenance an effort, to disturb the arrangement as originally made, by which the various States came into the Union." Still thinking of the sanction which the Constitution gives to slavery, he says, "Because it was a part of the original compact, — let it stand." Notwithstanding his special acuteness and ability, he is unable to take a fact out of its merely political relations, and behold it as it lies absolutely to be disposed of by the intellect, — what, for instance, it behooves a man to do here in America today with regard to slavery, but ventures, or is driven, to make some such desperate answer as the following, while professing to speak absolutely, and as a private man, — from which what new and singular code of social duties might be inferred? "The manner," says he, "in which the governments of those States where slavery exists are to regulate it, is for their own consideration, under their responsibility to their constituents, to the general laws of propriety, humanity, and justice, and to God. Associations formed elsewhere, springing from a feeling of humanity, or any other cause, have nothing whatever to do with it. They have never received any encouragement from me, and they never will."[4]

They who know of no purer sources of truth, who have traced up its stream no higher, stand, and wisely stand, by the Bible and the Constitution, and drink at it there with reverence and humility; but they who behold where it comes

trickling into this lake or that pool, gird up their loins once more, and continue their pilgrimage toward its fountainhead.

No man with a genius for legislation has appeared in America. They are rare in the history of the world. There are orators, politicians, and eloquent men, by the thousand; but the speaker has not yet opened his mouth to speak, who is capable of settling the much-vexed questions of the day. We love eloquence for its own sake, and not for any truth which it may utter, or any heroism it may inspire. Our legislators have not yet learned the comparative value of free-trade and of freedom, of union, and of rectitude, to a nation. They have no genius or talent for comparatively humble questions of taxation and finance, commerce and manufactures and agriculture. If we were left solely to the wordy wit of legislators in Congress for our guidance, uncorrected by the seasonable experience and the effectual complaints of the people, America would not long retain her rank among the nations. For eighteen hundred years, though perchance I have no right to say it, the New Testament has been written; yet where is the legislator who has wisdom and practical talent enough to avail himself of the light which it sheds on the science of legislation?

The authority of government, even such as I am willing to submit to, — for I will cheerfully obey those who know and can do better than I, and in many things even those who neither know nor can do so well, — is still an impure one: To be strictly just, it must have the sanction and consent of the governed. It can have no pure right over my person and property but what I concede to it. The progress from an absolute to a limited monarchy, from a limited monarchy to a democracy, is a progress toward a true respect for the individual. Even the Chinese

45

---

[4] These extracts have been inserted since the lecture was read. —Au.

philosopher was wise enough to regard the individual as the basis of the empire. Is a democracy, such as we know it, the last improvement possible in government? Is it not possible to take a step further towards recognizing and organizing the rights of man? There will never be a really free and enlightened State, until the State comes to recognize the individual as a higher and independent power, from which all its own power and authority are derived, and treats him accordingly. I please myself with imagining a State at last which can afford to be just to all men, and to treat the individual with respect as a neighbor; which even would not think it inconsistent with its own repose, if a few were to live aloof from it, not meddling with it, nor embraced by it, who fulfilled all the duties of neighbors and fellowmen. A State which bore this kind of fruit, and suffered it to drop off as fast as it ripened, would prepare the way for a still more perfect and glorious State, which also I have imagined, but not yet anywhere seen.

Discussion Questions

1. Summarize briefly Thoreau's reasons for arguing that civil disobedience is sometimes a *duty*.
2. Thoreau speaks of "unjust laws" (para. 16). What position does Thoreau feel that citizens should take in response to these laws?
3. What examples of government policy and action does Thoreau use to prove that civil disobedience is a duty? Explain why they are — or are not — effective.
4. Why do you think Thoreau provides such a detailed account of his one day in prison? What observation about the community struck Thoreau when he emerged from jail?

Writing Suggestions

1. Argue that civil disobedience to a school policy or action is justified. (Examples might include failure to establish an ethnic studies department, refusal to allow ROTC on campus, refusal to suspend a professor accused of sexual harassment.) Be specific about the injustice of the policy or action and the values that underlie the resistance.
2. Under what circumstances might civil disobedience prove to be dangerous and immoral? Can you think of cases of disobedience in which *conscience*, as Thoreau uses the term, did not appear to be the guiding principle? Try to identify what you think is the true motivation for the resistance.

A NINETEENTH-CENTURY SPEECH

Sojourner Truth's best-known speech was delivered extemporaneously (without preparation) in 1851 before the Ohio Women's Convention in Akron, Ohio. More than one version of the former slave's speech exists, and there is no consensus about which one is closer to the words Truth actually spoke. Some scholars argue that the speech did not even contain the words "ain't I a woman," but this version with the repetition of that key question is the one most often reprinted.

Ain't I a Woman?
SOJOURNER TRUTH

Well, children, where there is so much racket there must be something out of kilter. I think that 'twixt the negroes of the South and the women at the North, all talking about rights, the white men will be in a fix pretty soon. But what's all this here talking about?

That man over there says that women need to be helped into carriages, and lifted over ditches, and to have the best place everywhere. Nobody ever helps me into carriages, or over mud-puddles, or gives me any best place! And ain't I a woman? Look at me! Look at my arm! I have ploughed and planted, and gathered into barns, and no man could head me! And ain't I a woman? I could work as much and eat as much as a man — when I could get it — and bear the lash as well! And ain't I a woman? I have borne thirteen children, and seen most all sold off to slavery, and when I cried out with my mother's grief, none but Jesus heard me! And ain't I a woman?

Then they talk about this thing in the head; what's this they call it? [member of audience whispers, "intellect"] That's it, honey. What's that got to do with women's rights or negroes' rights? If my cup won't hold but a pint, and yours holds a quart, wouldn't you be mean not to let me have my little half measure full?

Then that little man in black there, he says women can't have as much rights as men, 'cause Christ wasn't a woman! Where did your Christ come from? Where did your Christ come from? From God and a woman! Man had nothing to do with Him.

If the first woman God ever made was strong enough to turn the world upside down all alone, these women together ought to be able to turn it back, and get it right side up again! And now they is asking to do it, the men better let them.

Obliged to you for hearing me, and now old Sojourner ain't got nothing more to say.

5

Sojourner Truth (1797–1883) was born a slave in New York and was named Isabella Baumfree until as an adult she took on the name she is now known by. She escaped with her infant daughter in 1826 and went on to become an activist for women's rights and for the rights of black men and women.

Discussion Questions

1. There are different versions of Truth's speech, which is not surprising considering the time and the circumstances. In this version, Truth's speech is reproduced as a southern dialect, but, in fact, Truth lived in the North. What effect does the dialect have on your reading of the speech?
2. What point is Truth trying to make about being a woman? What point is she trying to make about being a black woman?
3. What is your response to Truth's suggestion that intellect has nothing to do with women's rights or African Americans' rights?
4. How does Truth try to prove the power of women?

Writing Suggestions

1. Rewrite Truth's speech in standard English.
2. Explain how Truth was in a unique position to discuss the rights of both women and African Americans.
3. Describe Truth's tone in the speech. Is that tone surprising, given her position? Explain.

A TWENTIETH-CENTURY WARNING

The publication of Rachel Carson's *Silent Spring* in 1962 was critical to the history of environmentalism. She warned that the pesticide DDT, in spite of its perceived advantages, was poisoning the environment. In this second chapter of the book, she explains how a substance designed to kill agricultural pests could affect the whole web of life on earth. The book helped raise public awareness about the destructive effects of chemicals on the environment and was a major factor in the creation of what is now the Environmental Protection Agency.

The Obligation to Endure
RACHEL CARSON

The history of life on earth has been a history of interaction between living things and their surroundings. To a large extent, the physical form and the habits of the earth's vegetation and its animal life have been molded by the environment. Considering the whole span of earthly time, the opposite effect, in which life actually modifies its surroundings, has been relatively slight. Only within the moment of time represented by the present century has one species — man — acquired significant power to alter the nature of his world.

Rachel Carson (1907–1964) was a marine biologist and an influential writer. She began writing for the U.S. Bureau of Fisheries and eventually became editor-in-chief of all publications of the U.S. Fish and Wildlife Service. She wrote three books about the sea before turning her attention to the harm that humans were doing to their environment.

During the past quarter century this power has not only increased to one of disturbing magnitude but it has changed in character. The most alarming of all man's assaults upon the environment is the contamination of air, earth, rivers, and sea with dangerous and even lethal materials. This pollution is for the most part irrecoverable; the chain of evil it initiates not only in the world that must support life but in living tissues is for the most part irreversible. In this now universal contamination of the environment, chemicals are the sinister and little-recognized partners of radiation in changing the very nature of the world — the very nature of its life. Strontium 90, released through nuclear explosions into the air, comes to earth in rain or drifts down as fallout, lodges in soil, enters into the grass or corn or wheat grown there, and in time takes up its abode in the bones of a human being, there to remain until his death. Similarly, chemicals sprayed on croplands or forests or gardens lie long in soil, entering into living organisms, passing from one to another in a chain of poisoning and death. Or they pass mysteriously by underground streams until they emerge and, through the alchemy of air and sunlight, combine into new forms that kill vegetation, sicken cattle, and work unknown harm on those who drink from once pure wells. As Albert Schweitzer has said, "Man can hardly even recognize the devils of his own creation."

It took hundreds of millions of years to produce the life that now inhabits the earth — eons of time in which that developing and evolving and diversifying life reached a state of adjustment and balance with its surroundings. The environment, rigorously shaping and directing the life it supported, contained elements that were hostile as well as supporting. Certain rocks gave out dangerous radiation; even within the light of the sun, from which all life draws its energy, there were short-wave radiations with power to injure. Given time — time not in years but in millennia — life adjusts, and a balance has been reached. For time is the essential ingredient; but in the modern world there is no time.

The rapidity of change and the speed with which new situations are created follow the impetuous and heedless pace of man rather than the deliberate pace of nature. Radiation is no longer merely the background radiation of rocks, the bombardment of cosmic rays, the ultraviolet of the sun that have existed before there was any life on earth; radiation is now the unnatural creation of man's tampering with the atom. The chemicals to which life is asked to make its adjustment are no longer merely the calcium and silica and copper and all the rest of the minerals washed out of the rocks and carried in rivers to the sea; they are the synthetic creations of man's inventive mind, brewed in his laboratories, and having no counterparts in nature.

To adjust to these chemicals would require time on the scale that is nature's; it would require not merely the years of a man's life but the life of generations. And even this, were it by some miracle possible, would be futile, for the new chemicals come from our laboratories in an endless stream; almost five hundred annually find their way into actual use in the United States alone. The figure is staggering and its implications are not easily grasped — 500 new chemicals to which the bodies of men and animals are required somehow to adapt each year, chemicals totally outside the limits of biologic experience.

Among them are many that are used in man's war against nature. Since the mid-1940's over 200 basic chemicals have been created for use in killing insects, weeds, rodents, and other organisms described in the modern vernacular as "pests"; and they are sold under several thousand different brand names.

These sprays, dusts, and aerosols are now applied almost universally to farms, gardens, forests, and homes — nonselective chemicals that have the power to kill every insect, the "good" and the "bad," to still the song of birds and the leaping of fish in the streams, to coat the leaves with a deadly film, and to linger on in soil — all this though the intended target may be only a few weeds or insects. Can anyone believe it is possible to lay down such a barrage of poisons on the surface of the earth without making it unfit for all life? They should not be called "insecticides," but "biocides."

The whole process of spraying seems caught up in an endless spiral. Since DDT was released for civilian use, a process of escalation has been going on in which ever more toxic materials must be found. This has happened because insects, in a triumphant vindication of Darwin's principle of the survival of the fittest, have evolved super races immune to the particular insecticide used, hence a deadlier one has always to be developed — and then a deadlier one than that. It has happened also because, for reasons to be described later, destructive insects often undergo a "flareback," or resurgence, after spraying, in numbers greater than before. Thus the chemical war is never won, and all life is caught in its violent crossfire.

Along with the possibility of the extinction of mankind by nuclear war, the central problem of our age has therefore become the contamination of man's total environment with such substances of incredible potential for harm — substances that accumulate in the tissues of plants and animals and even penetrate the germ cells to shatter or alter the very material of heredity upon which the shape of the future depends.

Some would-be architects of our future look toward a time when it will be possible to alter the human germ plasm by design. But we may easily be doing so now by inadvertence, for many chemicals, like radiation, bring about gene mutations. It is ironic to think that man might determine his own future by something so seemingly trivial as the choice of an insect spray.

All this has been risked — for what? Future historians may well be amazed by our distorted sense of proportion. How could intelligent beings seek to control a few unwanted species by a method that contaminated the entire environment and brought the threat of disease and death even to their own kind? Yet this is precisely what we have done. We have done it, moreover, for reasons that collapse the moment we examine them. We are told that the enormous and expanding use of pesticides is necessary to maintain farm production. Yet is our real problem not one of *overproduction*? Our farms, despite measures to remove acreages from production and to pay farmers *not* to produce, have yielded such a staggering excess of crops that the American taxpayer in 1962 is paying out more than one billion dollars a year as the total carrying cost of the surplus-food storage program. And is the situation helped when one branch of the Agriculture Department tries to reduce production while another states, as it did in 1958, "It is believed generally that reduction of crop acreages under provisions of the Soil Bank will stimulate interest in use of chemicals to obtain maximum production on the land retained in crops."

All this is not to say there is no insect problem and no need of control. I am saying, rather, that control must be geared to realities, not to mythical situations, and that the methods employed must be such that they do not destroy us along with the insects.

The problem whose attempted solution has brought such a train of disaster in its wake is an accompaniment of our modern way of life. Long before the age of man, insects inhabited the earth — a group of extraordinarily varied and adaptable beings. Over the course of time since man's advent, a small percentage of the more than half a million species of insects have come into conflict with human welfare in two principal ways: as competitors for the food supply and as carriers of human disease.

Disease-carrying insects become important where human beings are crowded together, especially under conditions where sanitation is poor, as in time of natural disaster or war or in situations of extreme poverty and deprivation. Then control of some sort becomes necessary. It is a sobering fact, however, as we shall presently see, that the method of massive chemical control has had only limited success, and also threatens to worsen the very conditions it is intended to curb.

15   Under primitive agricultural conditions the farmer had few insect problems. These arose with the intensification of agriculture — the devotion of immense acreages to a single crop. Such a system set the stage for explosive increases in specific insect populations. Single-crop farming does not take advantage of the principles by which nature works; it is agriculture as an engineer might conceive it to be. Nature has introduced great variety into the landscape, but man has displayed a passion for simplifying it. Thus he undoes the built-in checks and balances by which nature holds the species within bounds. One important natural check is a limit on the amount of suitable habitat for each species. Obviously then, an insect that lives on wheat can build up its population to much higher levels on a farm devoted to wheat than on one in which wheat is intermingled with other crops to which the insect is not adapted.

The same thing happens in other situations. A generation or more ago, the towns of large areas of the United States lined their streets with the noble elm tree. Now the beauty they hopefully created is threatened with complete destruction as disease sweeps through the elms, carried by a beetle that would have only limited chance to build up large populations and to spread from tree to tree if the elms were only occasional trees in a richly diversified planting.

Another factor in the modern insect problem is one that must be viewed against a background of geologic and human history: the spreading of thousands of different kinds of organisms from their native homes to invade new territories. This worldwide migration has been studied and graphically described by the British ecologist Charles Elton in his recent book *The Ecology of Invasions.* During the Cretaceous Period, some hundred million years ago, flooding seas cut many land bridges between continents and living things found themselves confined in what Elton calls "colossal separate nature reserves." There, isolated from others of their kind, they developed many new species. When some of the land masses were joined again, about 15 million years ago, these species began to move out into new territories — a movement that is not only still in progress but is now receiving considerable assistance from man.

The importation of plants is the primary agent in the modern spread of species, for animals have almost invariably gone along with the plants, quarantine being a comparatively recent and not completely effective innovation. The United States Office of Plant Introduction alone has introduced almost 200,000 species and varieties of plants from all over the world. Nearly half of the 180 or so major insect enemies of plants in the United States are accidental imports from abroad, and most of them have come as hitchhikers on plants.

In new territory, out of reach of the restraining hand of the natural enemies that kept down its numbers in its native land, an invading plant or animal is able to become enormously abundant. Thus it is no accident that our most troublesome insects are introduced species.

20　These invasions, both the naturally occurring and those dependent on human assistance, are likely to continue indefinitely. Quarantine and massive chemical campaigns are only extremely expensive ways of buying time. We are faced, according to Dr. Elton, "with a life-and-death need not just to find new technological means of suppressing this plant or that animal"; instead we need the basic knowledge of animal populations and their relations to their surroundings that will "promote an even balance and damp down the explosive power of outbreaks and new invasions."

Much of the necessary knowledge is now available but we do not use it. We train ecologists in our universities and even employ them in our governmental agencies but we seldom take their advice. We allow the chemical death rain to fall as though there were no alternative, whereas in fact there are many, and our ingenuity could soon discover many more if given opportunity.

Have we fallen into a mesmerized state that makes us accept as inevitable that which is inferior or detrimental, as though having lost the will or the vision to demand that which is good? Such thinking, in the words of the ecologist Paul Shepard, "idealizes life with only its head out of water, inches above the limits of toleration of the corruption of its own environment. . . . Why should we tolerate a diet of weak poisons, a home in insipid surroundings, a circle of acquaintances who are not quite our enemies, the noise of motors with just enough relief to prevent insanity? Who would want to live in a world which is just not quite fatal?"

Yet such a world is pressed upon us. The crusade to create a chemically sterile, insect-free world seems to have engendered a fanatic zeal on the part of many specialists and most of the so-called control agencies. On every hand there is evidence that those engaged in spraying operations exercise a ruthless power. "The regulatory entomologists . . . function as prosecutor, judge and jury, tax assessor and collector, and sheriff to enforce their own orders," said Connecticut entomologist Neely Turner. The most flagrant abuses go unchecked in both state and federal agencies.

It is not my contention that chemical insecticides must never be used. I do contend that we have put poisonous and biologically potent chemicals indiscriminately into the hands of persons largely or wholly ignorant of their potentials for harm. We have subjected enormous numbers of people to contact with these poisons, without their consent and often without their knowledge. If the Bill of Rights contains no guarantee that a citizen shall be secure against lethal poisons distributed either by private individuals or by public officials, it is surely only because our forefathers, despite their considerable wisdom and foresight, could conceive of no such problem.

25   I contend, furthermore, that we have allowed these chemicals to be used with little or no advance investigation of their effect on soil, water, wildlife, and man himself. Future generations are unlikely to condone our lack of prudent concern for the integrity of the natural world that supports all life.

There is still very limited awareness of the nature of the threat. This is an era of specialists, each of whom sees his own problem and is unaware of or intolerant of the larger frame into which it fits. It is also an era dominated by industry, in which the right to make a dollar at whatever cost is seldom challenged. When the public protests, confronted with some obvious evidence of damaging results of pesticide applications, it is fed little tranquilizing pills of half truth. We urgently need an end to these false assurances, to the sugar coating of unpalatable facts. It is the public that is being asked to assume the risks that the insect controllers calculate. The public must decide whether it wishes to continue on the present road, and it can do so only when in full possession of the facts. In the words of Jean Rostand, "The obligation to endure gives us the right to know."

Discussion Questions

1. What was Carson's purpose in writing this chapter? How effective do you feel she was in achieving that purpose? Explain your response.
2. According to Carson, in what sense is time a factor in the harm that humans are doing to their world by using pesticides?
3. Just how much damage does Carson feel DDT has done? Why has it been allowed to happen?
4. How does Carson relate her subject to the Bill of Rights?
5. How do you explain the closing quote from Jean Rostand (1894–1977), a French experimental biologist and science writer, from which the chapter title is derived?

Writing Suggestions

1. Explain how Carson wrote about science for a lay audience in a way that they could understand.
2. Explain how Carson's chapter is based largely on an examination of cause-and-effect relationships.
3. Explain how relevant Carson's concerns are today, more than fifty years after the publication of *Silent Spring*.

A TWENTIETH-CENTURY SPEECH

The following speech, which Thurgood Marshall delivered at the Annual Seminar of the San Francisco Patent and Trademark Law Association in Maui, Hawaii, on May 6, 1987, was part of the celebration of the 200th anniversary of the United States Constitution. Marshall made headlines when instead of praising the Founding Fathers, as other speakers had, he pointed out that the document did not form "a more perfect Union," but rather was an imperfect document that had had to change with the times.

Reflections on the Bicentennial of the United States Constitution
THURGOOD MARSHALL

The year 1987 marks the 200th anniversary of the United States Constitution. A Commission has been established to coordinate the celebration. The official meetings, essay contests, and festivities have begun.

The planned commemoration will span three years, and I am told 1987 is "dedicated to the memory of the Founders and the document they drafted in Philadelphia." We are to "recall the achievements of our Founders and the knowledge and experience that inspired them, the nature of the government they established, its origins, its character, and its ends, and the rights and privileges of citizenship, as well as its attendant responsibilities."

Like many anniversary celebrations, the plan for 1987 takes particular events and holds them up as the source of all the very best that has followed. Patriotic feelings will surely swell, prompting proud proclamations of the wisdom, foresight, and sense of justice shared by the framers and reflected in a written document now yellowed with age. This is unfortunate — not the patriotism itself, but the tendency for the celebration to oversimplify, and overlook the many other events that have been instrumental to our achievements as a nation. The focus of this celebration invites a complacent belief that the vision of those who debated and compromised in Philadelphia yielded the "more perfect Union" it is said we now enjoy.

I cannot accept this invitation, for I do not believe that the meaning of the Constitution was forever "fixed" at the Philadelphia Convention. Nor do I find the wisdom, foresight, and sense of justice exhibited by the framers particularly profound. To the contrary, the government they devised was defective from the start, requiring several amendments, a civil war, and momentous social transformation to attain the system of constitutional government, and its respect for the individual freedoms and human rights, that we hold as fundamental today. When contemporary Americans cite "The Constitution," they invoke a concept that is vastly

Thurgood Marshall (1908–1993) was the first African American Associate Justice of the United States Supreme Court, serving from 1967 until 1991. Earlier he had gained fame as an attorney for his success in arguing cases before the Court, including a victory in the famous *Brown v. Board of Education* school desegregation case.

different from what the framers barely began to construct two centuries ago.

5   For a sense of the evolving nature of the Constitution we need look no further than the first three words of the document's preamble: "We the People." When the Founding Fathers used this phrase in 1787, they did not have in mind the majority of America's citizens. "We the People" included, in the words of the framers, "the whole Number of free Persons." On a matter so basic as the right to vote, for example, Negro slaves were excluded, although they were counted for representational purposes — at three-fifths each. Women did not gain the right to vote for over a hundred and thirty years.

These omissions were intentional. The record of the framers' debates on the slave question is especially clear: the Southern states acceded to the demands of the New England states for giving Congress broad power to regulate commerce, in exchange for the right to continue the slave trade. The economic interests of the regions coalesced: New Englanders engaged in the "carrying trade" would profit from transporting slaves from Africa as well as goods produced in America by slave labor. The perpetuation of slavery ensured the primary source of wealth in the Southern states.

Despite this clear understanding of the role slavery would play in the new republic, use of the words *slaves* and *slavery* was carefully avoided in the original document. Political representation in the lower House of Congress was to be based on the population of "free Persons" in each state, plus three-fifths of all "other Persons." Moral principles against slavery, for those who had them, were compromised, with no explanation of the conflicting principles for which the American Revolutionary War had ostensibly been fought: the self-evident truths "that all men are created equal, that they are endowed by their Creator with certain unalienable Rights, that among these are Life, Liberty and the pursuit of Happiness."

It was not the first such compromise. Even these ringing phrases from the Declaration of Independence are filled with irony, for an early draft of what became that declaration assailed the King of England for suppressing legislative attempts to end the slave trade and for encouraging slave rebellions. The final draft adopted in 1776 did not contain this criticism. And so again at the Constitutional Convention eloquent objections to the institution of slavery went unheeded, and its opponents eventually consented to a document which laid a foundation for the tragic events that were to follow.

Pennsylvania's Gouverneur Morris provides an example. He opposed slavery and the counting of slaves in determining the basis for representation in Congress. At the Convention he objected that the inhabitant of Georgia [or] South Carolina who goes to the coast of Africa, and in defiance of the most sacred laws of humanity tears away his fellow creatures from their dearest connections and damns them to the most cruel bondages, shall have more votes in a Government instituted for protection of the rights of mankind, than the Citizen of Pennsylvania or New Jersey who views with a laudable horror, so nefarious a practice.

10   And yet Gouverneur Morris eventually accepted the three-fifths accommodation. In fact, he wrote the final draft of the Constitution, the very document the bicentennial will commemorate.

As a result of compromise, the right of the Southern states to continue importing slaves was extended, officially, at least until 1808. We know that it actually lasted a good deal longer, as the framers possessed no monopoly on the ability to trade moral principles for self-interest. But they nevertheless set an unfortunate example. Slaves could be imported, if the commercial interests of the North were protected. To make the compromise even more palatable, customs duties would be imposed at up to ten dollars per slave as a means of raising public revenues.

No doubt it will be said, when the unpleasant truth of the history of slavery in America is mentioned during this bicentennial year, that the Constitution was a product of its times, and embodied a compromise which, under other circumstances, would not have been made. But the effects of the framers' compromise have remained for generations. They arose from the contradiction between guaranteeing liberty and justice to all, and denying both to Negroes.

The original intent of the phrase "We the People" was far too clear for any ameliorating construction. Writing for the Supreme Court in 1857, Chief Justice Taney penned the following passage in the Dred Scott case, on the issue of whether, in the eyes of the framers, slaves were "constituent members of the sovereignty," and were to be included among "We the People":

15

> We think they are not, and that they are not included, and were not intended to be included. . . . They had for more than a century before been regarded as beings of an inferior order, and altogether unfit to associate with the white race . . . and so far inferior, that they had no rights which the white man was bound to respect; and that the negro might justly and lawfully be reduced to slavery for his benefit. . . . [A]ccordingly, a negro of the African race was regarded . . . as an article of property, and held, and bought and sold as such. . . . [N]o one seems to have doubted the correctness of the prevailing opinion of the time.

And so, nearly seven decades after the Constitutional Convention, the Supreme Court reaffirmed the prevailing opinion of the framers regarding the rights of Negroes in America. It took a bloody civil war before the thirteenth amendment could be adopted to abolish slavery, though not the consequences slavery would have for future Americans.

While the Union survived the civil war, the Constitution did not. In its place arose a new, more promising basis for justice and equality, the fourteenth amendment, ensuring protection of the life, liberty, and property of all persons against deprivations without due process, and guaranteeing equal protection of the laws. And yet almost another century would pass before any significant recognition was obtained of the rights of black Americans to share equally even in such basic opportunities as education, housing, and employment, and to have their votes counted, and counted equally. In the meantime, blacks joined America's military to fight its wars and invested untold hours working in its factories and on its farms, contributing to the development of this country's magnificent wealth and waiting to share in its prosperity.

What is striking is the role legal principles have played throughout America's history in determining the condition of Negroes. They were enslaved by law, emancipated by law, disenfranchised and segregated by law; and, finally, they have begun to win equality by law. Along the way, new constitutional principles have emerged to meet the challenges of a changing society. The progress has been dramatic, and it will continue.

20   The men who gathered in Philadelphia in 1787 could not have envisioned these changes. They could not have imagined, nor would they have accepted, that the document they were drafting would one day be construed by a Supreme Court to which had been appointed a woman and the descendent of an African slave. "We the People" no longer enslave, but the credit does not belong to the framers. It belongs to those who refused to acquiesce in outdated notions of "liberty," "justice," and "equality," and who strived to better them.

And so we must be careful, when focusing on the events which took place in Philadelphia two centuries ago, that we not overlook the momentous events which followed, and thereby lose our proper sense of perspective. Otherwise, the odds are that for many Americans the bicentennial celebration will be little more than a blind pilgrimage to the shrine of the original document now stored in a vault in the National Archives. If we seek, instead, a sensitive understanding of the Constitution's inherent defects, and its promising evolution through 200 years of history, the celebration of the "Miracle at Philadelphia" will, in my view, be a far more meaningful and humbling experience. We will see that the true miracle was not the birth of the Constitution, but its life, a life nurtured through two turbulent centuries of our own making, and a life embodying much good fortune that was not.

Thus, in this bicentennial year, we may not all participate in the festivities with flag-waving fervor. Some may more quietly commemorate the suffering, struggle, and sacrifice that has triumphed over much of what was wrong with the original document, and observe the anniversary with hopes not realized and promises not fulfilled. I plan to celebrate the bicentennial of the Constitution as a living document, including the Bill of Rights and the other amendments protecting individual freedoms and human rights.

Discussion Questions

1. What is the invitation that Marshall refers to in paragraph 4 that he feels he cannot accept? Why can he not accept it?
2. How did the Constitution contradict the Declaration of Independence?
3. What role did compromise play in the drafting of the Constitution?
4. What does Marshall mean in the last paragraph when he says that the Constitution is a living document?
5. What does Marshall believe Americans should do to commemorate the bicentennial of the Constitution?

Writing Suggestions

1. Write an essay explaining Marshall's view of the Constitution.
2. Write an essay explaining how the Constitution, as it has evolved, has reflected America's view of African Americans.
3. Do the necessary research, and write an essay describing the reaction to Marshall's speech at the time it was given.

Acknowledgments

Amin Ahmad. "I Belong Here." From the *Sun*, January 2010. Reprinted by permission of the author.

M. D. Anderson. "Arming Teachers: A Terrible, Horrible, No Good, Very Bad Idea." From *Borderless News and Views*, January 9, 2013. Reprinted by permission.

Anonymous editorial. "Teachers Packing Heat." From the *Baltimore Sun*, April 3, 2013. Reprinted by permission.

Sharon Astyk and Aaron Newton. "The Rich Get Richer, the Poor Go Hungry." From *A Nation of Farmers* by Sharon Astyk and Aaron Newton. Reprinted by permission.

Monika Bartyzel. "Girls on Film: The Real Problem with the Disney Princess Brand." From the *Week*, May 17, 2013. Reprinted by permission.

Patricia E. Bauer. "A Movie, a Word, and My Family's Battle." From the *Washington Post*, August 17, 2008. Reprinted by permission of the author.

Julia Belluz and Steven J. Hoffman. "Katie Couric and the Celebrity Medicine Syndrome." From the *Los Angeles Times*, December 18, 2013. Reprinted by permission of the authors.

Steven Best. "Dispatches from a Police State: Animal Rights in the Crosshairs of State Repression." drstevebest.org.

Andrew M. Blecher, MD. "The NFL Concussion Crisis & The Doctor-Patient Relationship." From *NFL Concussion Litigation*, April 29, 2012. Reprinted by permission of the author.

Ishmeal Bradley, MD, MPH. "Conscientious Objection in Medicine: A Moral Dilemma." From *Clinical Correlations*, May 28, 2009. Reprinted by permission of the author.

Diane Brady. "The Employer-Friendly Case for Pricier Big Macs." From *Bloomberg Businessweek*, August 9, 2013. Copyright © 2014. All rights reserved. Used with permission of Bloomberg L.P.

Jane E. Brody. "For Children in Sports, a Breaking Point." From the *New York Times*, May 25, 2010. © 2010 the *New York Times*. All rights reserved. Used by permission and protected by the Copyright Laws of the United States. The printing, copying, redistribution, or retransmission of this Content without express written permission is prohibited.

Robbie Brown. "140 Characters Spell Charges and Jail." From the *New York Times*, July 3, 2013. © 2013 the *New York Times*. All rights reserved. Used by permission and protected by the Copyright Laws of the United States. The printing, copying, redistribution, or retransmission of this Content without express written permission is prohibited.

John G. Browning. "Watch That Tweet! Monitoring of Student Athletes' Social Media." From the *Dallas Bar Association Headnotes*, January 2013. Reprinted by permission of the publication and the author.

Christopher Caldwell. "Drivers Get Rolled." From the *Weekly Standard*, November 18, 2013. © The *Weekly Standard*. Reprinted by permission.

Kim Carollo. "New York Man Pleads Guilty to Organ Trafficking." From ABC News, October 28, 2011. http://abcnews.go.com/blogs/health/2011/10/28/n-y-man-pleads-guilty-to-organ-trafficking/. Reprinted by permission.

Rachel Carson. "The Obligation to Endure" from *Silent Spring*. Copyright © 1962 by Rachel L. Carson, renewed 1990 by Roger Christie. All rights reserved. Reprinted by permission of Houghton Mifflin Harcourt Publishing Company. Electronic rights by permission of Frances Collin, Trustee. All copying, including electronic, or redistribution of this text, is expressly forbidden.

Guy-Uriel Charles. "Stop Calling Quake Victims Looters." From CNN.com, January 21, 2010. Courtesy CNN. Reprinted by permission.

Anna Maria Chávez. "Address to the National Council Session/52nd Convention of the Girl Scouts of the USA." November 10, 2011. Reprinted with permission from Girl Scouts of the USA.

CNN Correspondents. "President Obama Announces Support for Gay Marriage; Inside the John Edwards Trial; Zuckerberg in Hot Water over Hoodie; Politics of Gay Marriage." From CNN.com transcript, aired May 9, 2012. Courtesy CNN. Reprinted by permission.

Richard J. Davis. "In Gun Control Debate, Logic Goes Out the Window." From CNN.com, January 26, 2013. Courtesy CNN. Reprinted by permission.

Frank Deford. "Why Keep Athletes Eligible but Uneducated?" From NPR.com, September 4, 2013. Reprinted by permission.

Jared Diamond. "Will Big Business Save the Earth?" From the *New York Times*, December 6, 2009. © 2009 the *New York Times*. All rights reserved. Used by permission and protected by the Copyright Laws of the United States. The printing, copying, redistribution, or retransmission of this Content without express written permission is prohibited.

Earth Open Source. "Why Genetically Engineered Food Is Dangerous: New Report by Genetic Engineers." From *Earth Open Source* Press Release, June 17, 2012. Reprinted by permission.

Terry Eastland. "Don't Stop Frisking." From the *Weekly Standard*, August 26, 2013. © 2014 the *Weekly Standard*. Reprinted by permission.

Christopher Elliott. "A Tale of Two Airlines." From *National Geographic Traveler*, December 2012/January 2013. Christopher Elliot/National Geographic Creative. Reprinted by permission.

Christopher M. Fairman. "The Case Against Banning the Word *Retard*." From the *Washington Post*, February 14, 2010. Reprinted by permission of the author.

Stephanie Fairyington. "The Gay Option." From *Dissent*, vol. 57, no. 1 (Winter 2010), pp. 7–10. Reprinted with permission of the University of Pennsylvania Press.

Marvin S. Fertel. "USEA Briefing, Marvin S. Fertel, Jan. 16, 2014." From *Nuclear Energy Institute*. Reprinted by permission.

Craig Fry. "Bring Truth into Play by Saying Yes to Drugs in Sport." From the *Sydney Morning Herald*, June 29, 2012. Reprinted by permission.

Michael Gerson. "GOP Fear of Common Core Education Standards Unfounded." From the *Washington Post*, May 20, 2013. © 2013 Washington Post Company. All rights reserved. Used by permission and protected by the Copyright Laws of the United States. The printing, copying, redistribution, or retransmission of this Content without express written permission is prohibited.

Isaac Gilman. "Online Lives, Offline Consequences: Professionalism, Information Ethics, and Professional Students." From *Interface*, 9 (1) (Jan/Feb 2009). http://bcis.pacificu.edu/interface/?p=3566. Reprinted by permission of the author.

Jeb Golinkin. "Why Parents Should Let Their Kids Play Dangerous Sports." From the *Week*, February 2, 2013. Reprinted by permission.

Ronald M. Green. "Building Baby from the Genes Up." From the *Washington Post*, April 13, 2008. Reprinted by permission of the author.

Twilight Greenaway. "Can the Food Industry Kick Its Cheap Labor Habit?" From *TakePart*, February 4, 2013. Reprinted with the permission of TakePart, LLC from www.takepart.com. © TakePart, LLC 2013.

Jennifer Grossman. "Food for Thought (and for Credit)." From the *New York Times*, September 2, 2003. Copyright © 2003 by Jennifer Grossman. Reprinted by permission of the author.

Elisha Dov Hack. "College Life versus My Moral Code." From the *New York Times*, September 9, 1997. Reprinted by permission of the author.

Warren Hartenstine. "College Athletes Should Not Be Paid." From the *Baltimore Sun*, November 2, 2013. Reprinted by permission of the author.

Adolf Hitler. "On Nation and Race." From *Mein Kampf* by Adolf Hitler, translated by Ralph Manheim. Copyright © 1943, renewed 1971 by Houghton Mifflin Company. Reprinted by permission of Houghton Mifflin Harcourt Publishing Company. All rights reserved.

Eric Holt-Giménez. "The Fight Over Food Deserts: Corporate America Smacks Its Way Down." From *Food First*, July 16, 2010. Published by the Institute for Food & Development Policy, 398 60th Street, Oakland, CA 94618. Reprinted by permission.

Elise Hu. "Facebook Makes Us Sadder and Less Satisfied, Study Finds." Originally published on NPR.org on August 20, 2013. © 2013 National Public Radio, Inc. Any unauthorized duplication is strictly prohibited. Used with the permission of NPR.

Roger D. McGrath. "A God-Given Natural Right." From *Chronicles*, October 2003. Copyright © 2003. Reprinted by permission of the author.

Patt Morrison. "In San Diego's BofA Case, Chalk One Up for the Jury System." From the *Los Angeles Times*, July 2, 2013. Copyright © 2013 *Los Angeles Times*. Reprinted with permission.

Siddhartha Mukherjee. "I'm Sorry, Steve Jobs: We Could Have Saved You." From *Newsweek*, September 24, 2012. Reprinted by permission of the author.

Alan Noble, PhD. "Valedictorian Prays but Should Christians Rejoice?" From *Christ and Pop Culture* at Patheos.com. Reprinted by permission.

Deborah Nucatola. "Morning-After Pill a Boon for Women." From CNN .com, April 10, 2013. Courtesy CNN. Reprinted by permission.

Mark Peluso and Paul Berkner. "No on Sickle Cell Trait Testing." From *Inside Higher Ed*, January 18, 2013. Reprinted by permission of the authors.

John Podhoretz. "Flood the Zone." From the *Weekly Standard*, April 14, 2014. © *The Weekly Standard*. Reprinted by permission.

Michael Pollan. "Food Fight." From the *New York Review of Books*. © 2010 by Michael Pollan. Used by permission. All rights reserved.

Susan Eva Porter. "Overusing the Bully Label." From the *Los Angeles Times*, March 15, 2013. Reprinted by permission of the author.

Ronald Reagan. Excerpt from "The 'Evil Empire' Speech." From "Remarks at the Annual Convention of the National Association of Evangelicals in Orlando, Florida," March 8, 1983. reaganfoundation.org.

Steven Reinberg. "Embryo Selection May Help Prevent Some Inherited Disorders." From *HealthDay*, February 3, 2014. Reprinted by permission.

The Robert Wood Johnson Foundation. "Childhood Obesity: The Challenge." From *Food, Inc.: A Participant Guide* by Participant Media and Karl Weber. Copyright © 2009. Reprinted by permission of PublicAffairs, a member of the Perseus Books Group.

T. J. Rodgers. "Put Profits First." From *Reason* magazine and Reason.com, October 2005. Reprinted by permission.

Carol Rose. "On Pins and Needles Defending Artistic Expression." From the *Boston Globe*, April 8, 2010. © 2010 *Boston Globe*. All rights reserved. Used by permission and protected by the copyright laws of the United States. The printing, copying, redistribution, or retransmission of this Content without express written permission is prohibited. Reprinted by permission of the author and the *Boston Globe*.

Robert Ross. "Mental Health Services a Defense against School Violence." From *Capitol Weekly*, February 20, 2013. Reprinted by permission.

Robert J. Samuelson. "In Health, We're Not No. 1." From the *Washington Post*, January 16, 2013. © 2013 Washington Post Company. All rights reserved. Used by permission and protected by the Copyright Laws of the United States. The printing, copying, redistribution, or retransmission of this Content without express written permission is prohibited.

Bruce Schneier. "The Internet Is a Surveillance State." From CNN.com, March 16, 2013. Courtesy CNN. Reprinted by permission.

Eric Schulzke. "Pro-Life Health Professionals in Conflict between Conscience and Career." From *Deseret News*, May 17, 2012. © Deseret News, Eric Schulzke. Reprinted by permission.

Kathleen Sebelius. "Remarks to Georgetown University's Public Policy Institute." May 18, 2012. washingtonpost.com.

Kent Sepkowitz. "It's Time to Quit Ignoring Sports Head Trauma's Very Real Dangers." From the *Daily Beast*, February 2, 2012. © 2012 The Daily Beast Company LLC. All rights reserved. Used by permission and protected by the copyright laws of the United States. The printing, copying, redistribution, or retransmission of this Content without express permission is prohibited.

Mallory Simon. "Gun Debate: Where Is the Middle Ground?" From CNN.com, January 31, 2013. Courtesy CNN. Reprinted by permission.

Scott Simon. "The Power of a Father's Love Overturns His Beliefs." From NPR.org. © 2013 National Public Radio, Inc. NPR news report titled "The Power of a Father's Love Overturns His Beliefs" by Scott Simon was originally published on NPR.org on March 15, 2013, and is used with the permission of NPR. Any unauthorized duplication is strictly prohibited.

Peter Singer. "The 'Unnatural' Ashley Treatment Can Be Right for Profoundly Disabled Children." From the *Guardian*, March 16, 2012. Copyright Guardian News & Media Ltd 2012. Reprinted by permission.

Robert A. Sirico. "An Unjust Sacrifice." From the *New York Times*, September 30, 2000. © 2000 the *New York Times*. All rights reserved. Used by permission and protected by the Copyright Laws of the United States. The printing, copying, redistribution, or retransmission of this Content without express written permission is prohibited.

Whitney Smith. "USC Course Evaluations Need New Strategy." From the *Daily Gamecock*, April 25, 2013. Reprinted by permission.

Robert D. Stuart. "Establishing Criteria for Law Enforcement Use." From fbi.gov, January 22, 2013.

Robert D. Truog, Aaron S. Kesselheim, and Steven Joffe. "Paying Patients for Their Tissue: The Legacy of Henrietta Lacks." From *Science*, 337:37–38 (July 6, 2012). Reprinted with permission from AAAS.

Kenneth Turan. "Spike Jonze's *Her* Shows Love's Perils — In Any Form." From the *Los Angeles Times*, December 17, 2013. © 2013 *Los Angeles Times*. Reprinted by permission.

Kiara Ventura. "Your Toxic Beauty Regime." From *YCteen*, Copyright 2011 by Youth Communication/New York Center, Inc. www.youthcomm.org. Reprinted by permission.

David Von Drehle. "It's All about Him." From *Time*, April 30, 2007. Copyright © 2007 Time Inc. All rights reserved. Reprinted from *Time* and published with permission of Time Inc. Reproduction in any manner in any language in whole or in part without written permission is prohibited.

Sadhbh Walshe. "Online Gambling Is Anything but Pretty." From the *Guardian*, November 20, 2013. Copyright Guardian News & Media Ltd 2013. Reprinted by permission.

Beau Watts. "Embryonic Stem Cell Research: A Moral Evil or Obligation?" From Drury University's Annual Undergraduate Interdisciplinary Research Conference, 2003. Reprinted by permission of the author.

Amy Webb. "We Post Nothing about Our Daughter Online." From *Slate*, September 4, 2013. © 2013 The Slate Group. All rights reserved. Used by permission and protected by the Copyright Laws of the United States. The printing, copying, redistribution, or retransmission of this Content without express written permission is prohibited.

Brian Whitaker. "The Definition of Terrorism." From the *Guardian Unlimited*, May 7, 2001. Copyright Guardian News & Media Ltd 2001. Reprinted by permission.

J. C. Willke, MD. "I'm Pro-Life and I Oppose Embryonic Stem Cell Research." From Lifeissues.org/Life Issues Institute, Inc. Reprinted by permission.

Jonathan Winchell. "Latest 3-D Films Add Dimension, Not Appeal; Recent Films Add Gimmick, Sacrifice Creative Vision." From the *Daily Gamecock*, September 17, 2013. Reprinted by permission.

Glossary

Abstract language: language expressing a quality apart from a specific object or event; opposite of *concrete language*

Ad hominem: "against the man"; attacking the arguer rather than the *argument* or issue

Ad populum: "to the people"; playing on the prejudices of the *audience*

Analogy: a complex comparison between two things similar in some ways but dissimilar in others, often used to explain the less familiar in terms of the more familiar

Anecdotal evidence: stories or examples used to illustrate a *claim* but that do not prove it with scientific certainty

Appeal to needs and values: an attempt to gain assent to a *claim* by showing that it will bring about what your *audience* wants and cares deeply about

Appeal to tradition: a proposal that something should continue because it has traditionally existed or been done that way

Argument: a process of reasoning and advancing proof about issues on which conflicting views may be held; also, a statement or statements providing *support* for a *claim*

Aristotelian rhetoric: the approach to oral persuasion espoused by Aristotle (384 BCE–322 BCE) and used to shape school curricula well into the nineteenth century; a rhetorical theory based on using a combination of *logos*, *ethos*, and *pathos* to move an audience to a change in thought or action

Audience: those who will hear an *argument*; more generally, those to whom a communication is addressed

Authoritative warrant: a *warrant* based on the credibility or trustworthiness of the source

Backing: the assurances on which a *warrant* or assumption is based

Begging the question: making a statement that assumes that the issue being argued has already been decided

Charged words: words that present a subject favorably or unfavorably

Claim: the conclusion of an argument; what the arguer is trying to prove

Claim of fact: a *claim* that asserts something exists, has existed, or will exist, based on facts or data that the *audience* will accept as objectively verifiable

Claim of policy: a *claim* asserting that specific courses of action should be instituted as solutions to problems

Claim of value: a *claim* that asserts some things are more or less desirable than others

Cliché: a worn-out expression or idea, no longer capable of producing a visual image or provoking thought about a subject

Common ground: used in Rogerian argument to refer to any concept that two opposing parties agree on and that can thus be used as a starting point for negotiation

Concrete language: language that describes specific, generally observable, persons, places, or things; in contrast to *abstract language*

Connotation: the overtones that adhere to a word through long usage

Credibility: the audience's belief in the arguer's trustworthiness; see also *ethos*

Data: facts or figures from which a conclusion may be inferred; see *evidence*

Deduction: reasoning by which we establish that a conclusion must be true because the statements on which it is based are true; see also *syllogism*

Definition: an explanation of the meaning of a term, concept, or experience; may be used for clarification, especially of a *claim*, or as a means of developing an *argument*

Definition by negation: defining a thing by saying what it is not

Emotive language: language that expresses and arouses emotions

Empirical evidence: *support* verifiable by experience or experiment

Enthymeme: a *syllogism* in which one of the premises is implied

Ethos: the qualities of character, intelligence, and goodwill in a writer or speaker that contribute to an *audience's* acceptance of the *claim*

Euphemism: a pleasant or flattering expression used in place of one that is less agreeable but possibly more accurate

Evaluation: a reader's reaction to an argument

Evidence: *facts* or opinions that support an issue or *claim*; may consist of statistics, reports of personal experience, or views of experts

Extended definition: a *definition* that uses several different methods of development

Fact: something that is believed to have objective reality; a piece of information regarded as verifiable

Factual evidence: *support* consisting of *data* that are considered objectively verifiable by the *audience*

Fallacy: an error of reasoning based on faulty use of *evidence* or incorrect *inference*

False analogy: assuming without sufficient proof that if objects or processes are similar in some ways, then they are similar in other ways as well

False dilemma: simplifying a complex problem into an either/or dichotomy

Faulty emotional appeals: basing an argument on feelings, especially pity or fear — often to draw attention away from the real issues or conceal another purpose

Faulty use of authority: failing to acknowledge disagreement among experts or otherwise misrepresenting the trustworthiness of sources

Figurative language: words that produce images in the mind of the reader

Hasty generalization: drawing conclusions from insufficient evidence

Induction: reasoning by which a general statement is reached on the basis of particular examples

Inference: an interpretation of the *facts*

Logos: an argument based on reason

Major premise: see *syllogism*

Metaphor: a comparison that does not make use of *like* or *as*

Minor premise: see *syllogism*

MLA: the Modern Language Association, a professional organization for college teachers of English and foreign languages

Motivational appeal: an attempt to reach an *audience* by recognizing their *needs* and *values* and how these contribute to their decision making

Motivational warrant: a type of *warrant* based on the *needs* and *values* of an *audience*

Multimodal argument: words in combination with another medium or an argument in a mode other than the printed word: photographs, illustrations, audio, video, or digital media, for example

Need: in the hierarchy of Abraham Maslow, whatever is required, whether psychological or physiological, for the survival and welfare of a human being

Negation: classification of a term by stipulating what it is not

Non sequitur: "it does not follow"; using irrelevant proof to buttress a *claim*

Paraphrase: a restatement of the content of an original source in your own words

Pathos: appeal to the emotions

Personification: giving human attributes to the nonhuman

Persuasion: the use of a combination of *logos, ethos,* and *pathos* to move an *audience*

Picturesque language: words that produce images in the minds of the *audience*

Plagiarism: the use of someone else's words or ideas without adequate acknowledgment

Policy: a course of action recommended or taken to solve a problem or guide decisions

Positional relationship: an audience's ideas about or position on an issue, represented by the audience-subject leg of the communications triangle

Post hoc: mistakenly inferring that because one event follows another they have a causal relation; from *post hoc ergo propter hoc* ("after this, therefore because of this"); also called "doubtful cause"

Proposition: see *claim*

Qualifier: a restriction placed on the *claim* to indicate that it may not always be true as stated

Quote: to repeat exactly words from a printed, electronic, or spoken source

Red herring: an attempt to divert attention away from the subject at hand

Referential relationship: the relationship between writer and subject

Referential summary: a summary that focuses on the author's ideas rather than on the author's actions and decisions

Refutation: an attack on an opposing view to weaken it, invalidate it, or make it less credible

Reservation: a restriction placed on the *warrant* to indicate that unless certain conditions are met, the warrant may not establish a connection between the *support* and the *claim*

Rhetorical relationship: the relationship between writer and audience

Rhetorical summary: a condensation of a passage in the writer's own words that stresses the author's decisions as a writer

Rogerian argument: a rhetorical theory based on the counseling techniques of Carl Rogers (1902–1987) that emphasizes a search for common ground that would allow two opposing parties to start negotiations

Simile: a comparison using *like* or *as*

Slanting: selecting *facts* or words with *connotations* that favor the arguer's bias and discredit alternatives

Slippery slope: predicting without justification that one step in a process will lead unavoidably to a second, generally undesirable step

Slogan: an attention-getting expression used largely in politics or advertising to promote support of a cause or product

Statistics: information expressed in numerical form

Stereotype: overgeneralized perception of an ethnic group, nationality, or any other group

Stipulative definition: a *definition* that makes clear that it will explore a particular area of meaning of a term or issue

Straw man: disputing a view similar to, but not the same as, that of the arguer's opponent

Style: choices in words and sentence structure that make a writer's language distinctive

Substantive warrant: a *warrant* based on beliefs about the reliability of *factual evidence*

Summary: a condensation of a passage into a shorter version in the writer's own words

Support: any material that serves to prove an issue or *claim*; in addition to *evidence*, it includes appeals to the *needs* and *values* of the *audience*

Syllogism: a formula of deductive *argument* consisting of three propositions: a major premise, a minor premise, and a logical conclusion

Thesis: the main idea of an essay

Toulmin model: a conceptual system of argument devised by the philosopher Stephen Toulmin; the terms *claim, support, warrant, backing, qualifier,* and *reservation* are adapted from this system

Two wrongs make a right: diverting attention from the issue by introducing a new point, e.g., by responding to an accusation with a counteraccusation that makes no attempt to refute the first accusation

Validity: logical consistency in a deductive conclusion that follows necessarily from the major and minor premises

Values: conceptions or ideas that act as standards for judging what is right or wrong, worthwhile or worthless, beautiful or ugly, good or bad

Warrant: a general principle or assumption that establishes a connection between the *support* and the *claim*

Index of Subjects

Index of Authors and Titles

Missing something? Instructors may assign the online materials that accompany this text. For access to them, visit **macmillanhighered.com/rottenberg**.

Inside LaunchPad Solo for *Elements of Argument*, Eleventh Edition

Tutorials

Critical Reading
> Active reading strategies
> Reading visuals: Purpose
> Reading visuals: Audience

Digital Writing
> Online research tools
> Presentations

Documentation
> Do I need to cite that?
> How to cite a book in MLA style
> How to cite an article in MLA style
> How to cite a Web site in MLA style
> How to cite a database in MLA style
> How to cite a website in APA style
> How to cite a database in APA style

LearningCurve Quizzes

Critical Reading

Topic Sentences and Supporting Details

Topics and Main Ideas

Working with Sources (MLA)

Working with Sources (APA)

Commas; Fragments; Run-Ons and Comma Splices; Active and Passive Voice; Appropriate Language; Subject-Verb Agreement

E-readings

Eric Allie, "Obama Shoots Hoops" [cartoon]

National Highway Traffic Safety Administration, "Neon Signs (Buzzed Driving)" [video]

Elizabeth Warren, "Democratic National Convention Speech" [video]

Jeff Masters, "Global Warming Continues with No Slowdown" [blog post]

Trevor Eissler, "Montessori Madness" [video]

Domtar Paper, "Paper Because" [Web site]

YCTeen, "Toxic Products" [slide show]

NASA, "Evidence of Active Water on Mars" [slide show]

Lego, "Lego Ship" [print advertisement]

Ronald Reagan, "'Evil Empire' Speech" [speech]

National Vaccine Information Center, "National Vaccine Information Center" [Web site]

Anna Maria Chávez, "Address to the National Council Session/52nd Convention of the Girl Scouts of the USA" [speech]